Supporting Users and Troubleshooting Desktop Applications on a Microsoft Windows® XP Operating System

Exam 70-272

Supporting Users and Troubleshooting Desktop Applications on a Microsoft® Windows® XP Operating System

Exam 70-272

First Edition

Kenneth C. Laudon, Series Designer
Brian Hill, MCSE, MCSA
Richard Watson, MCSE
David W. Tschanz, MCSE

The Azimuth Interactive MCSE/MCSA/MCDST Team

Carol G. Traver, Series Editor
Kenneth Rosenblatt
Russell Polo
David Langley
Robin Pickering
Megan Miller
Stacey McBrine, MCSE, MCSA
Brien Posey, MCSE
Russell Jones, MCSE
Tim Oliwiak, MCSE, MCT
Simon Sykes-Wright, MCSE
David Lundell, MCSE, MCT
L. Ward Ulmer, MCSE, MCT
Wale Soyinka, MCP
Frank Miller, MCSE, MCSA
Pete Grondin, MCSA
Lenny Bailes
Mark Maxwell

PEARSON
Prentice Hall

Upper Saddle River, New Jersey, 07458

Senior Vice President/Publisher: Natalie Anderson
Executive Acquisitions Editor: Stephanie Wall
Executive Editor Certification: Steven Elliot
Director of Marketing: Sarah Loomis
Marketing Manager: Sarah Davis
Marketing Assistant: Lisa Taylor
Project Manager, Editorial: Laura Burgess
Editorial Assistants: Alana Meyers, Bambi Dawn Marchigano, Brian Hoehl, Sandra Bernales
Managing Editor, Production: Lynda Castillo
Senior Project Manager, Production: Tim Tate
Manufacturing Buyer: Tim Tate
Art Director: Pat Smythe
Design Manager: Maria Lange
Interior Design: Kim Buckley
Cover Designer: Pat Smythe
Cover Photo: Joseph DeSciose/Aurora Photos
Manager, Multimedia: Christy Mahon
Copy Editor: Kim Lindros
Tech Editor: Will Willis
Full Service Composition: Azimuth Interactive, Inc.
Printer/Binder: Courier Companies, Inc., Kendallville
Cover Printer: Phoenix Color Corporation

Credits and acknowledgments borrowed from other sources and reproduced, with permission, in this textbook appear on appropriate page within text.

Microsoft® and Windows® are registered trademarks of the Microsoft Corporation in the U.S.A. and other countries. Screen shots and icons reprinted with permission from the Microsoft Corporation. This book is not sponsored or endorsed by or affiliated with the Microsoft Corporation.

10 9 8 7 6 5 4 3 2 1
0-13-149993-9

To our families,
for their love, patience,
and inspiration.

Brief Contents

Contents

Welcome to the Prentice Hall Certification Series!

You are about to begin an exciting journey of learning and career skills building that will provide you with access to careers such as network administrator, systems engineer, desktop support technician, network analyst, and technical consultant. What you learn in the Prentice Hall Certification Series will provide you with a strong set of networking skills and knowledge that you can use throughout your career as the Microsoft Windows operating system continues to evolve, as new information technology devices appear, and as business applications of computers continues to expand. The Prentice Hall Certification Series aims to provide you with the skills and knowledge that will endure, prepare you for your future career, and make the process of learning fun and enjoyable.

Microsoft Windows and the Networked World

We live in a computerized and networked world. Intel reports that more than one billion PCs are in use worldwide, with the United States alone accounting for about 500 million PCs. Over 95% of PCs worldwide use a Microsoft Windows operating system, and some version of Microsoft desktop applications. The Internet, the world's largest network, now has more than 800 million people who connect to it through more than 250 million Internet hosts. The number of local area networks associated with these 250 million Internet hosts is not known, but likely is in the tens of millions. About 60% of local area networks (LANs) in the United States are using a Windows network operating system. The other networks use Novell NetWare or some version of Unix (Internet Software Consortium, 2004). A growing number of handheld personal digital assistants (PDAs) also use versions of the Microsoft operating system called Microsoft CE. Most businesses, large and small, use some kind of client/server LAN to connect their employees to one another, and to the Internet. In the United States, the vast majority of these business networks use a Microsoft network operating system, either earlier versions such as Windows NT and Windows 2000, or the current version, Windows Server 2003.

The proliferation of Microsoft operating systems and applications means there is a significant demand for technical support, both within business firms and for private individuals. The Prentice Hall Certification Series prepares you to participate in this computer-intensive and networked world. This book will teach you how to support and troubleshoot the Microsoft Windows XP operating system and Microsoft desktop applications that run on a Windows XP operating system.

Prentice Hall Certification Series Objectives

The first objective of the Prentice Hall Certification Series is to help you build a set of skills and a knowledge base that will prepare you for a career in the networking field. There is no doubt that in the next five years, Microsoft will issue several new versions of its network operating system, client operating system, and desktop applications. In addition, a steady stream of new digital devices will require connecting to networks, existing clients, and client applications. Most of what you learn in the Prentice Hall Certification Series provides a strong foundation for understanding future versions of the operating system.

The second objective of the Prentice Hall Certification Series is to prepare you to become a certified desktop support technician and fill one of the thousands of such positions that will become available worldwide in the next five years. Specifically, this book prepares you to pass the two Microsoft Certified Desktop Support Technician (MCDST) certification exams, 70-271 and 70-272. Exam 70-271, Supporting Users and Troubleshooting the Microsoft Windows XP Operating System, focuses on providing support for users of the Windows XP operating systems. Exam 70-272, Supporting Users and Troubleshooting Desktop Applications on a Microsoft Windows XP Operating System, focuses on providing support for users of Microsoft applications such as Internet Explorer and Outlook Express, and desktop applications in the Office Suite, such as Word, Excel, and Access.

Why get certified? As businesses increasingly rely on Microsoft operating systems and applications to conduct business, employers want to make sure their desktop support staff has the skills needed to trouble shoot and support these applications for users. Although job experience is an important source of networking knowledge, employers increasingly rely on certification examinations to ensure that their staff has the necessary skills. The MCDST curriculum provides desktop support professionals with a well-balanced and comprehensive body of knowledge necessary to support and troubleshoot Microsoft operating systems and applications in a business setting.

There is clear evidence that having a Microsoft certification results in higher salaries and faster promotions for individual employees. Therefore, it is definitely in your interest to obtain certification, even if you have considerable job experience. If you are just starting out in the world of networking, certification can be very important for landing that first job.

Preparing you for a career involves more than satisfying the official MCDST exam objectives. You will also need a strong set of management skills. The Prentice Hall Certification Series emphasizes management and organizational skills along with technical knowledge and skills. As you advance in your career, you will be expected to participate in and lead teams of business professionals in their efforts to support the needs of your organization. You will be expected to work with customers and clients and help your firm diagnose and solve problems, and support employees using Microsoft systems. You will often be asked to develop written solutions and documentation to support desktop systems. We make a particular point in this Series of developing managerial skills such as analyzing business requirements, writing reports, and making presentations to other members of your business team.

Who Is the Audience for This Book?

The student body for the Prentice Hall Certification Series is very diverse, and the Series is written with that in mind. For all students, regardless of background, the series is designed to function as a *learning tool* first, and, second, as a compact reference book that can be readily accessed to refresh skills. Generally, there are two types of software books: books aimed at learning and understanding how a specific software tool works, and comprehensive reference books. This Series emphasizes learning and explanation and is student-centered.

The Prentice Hall Certification Series is well suited to beginning students. Many students will be just starting out in the desktop support field, most in colleges and training institutes. The series introduces these beginning students to the basic concepts of client operating systems and Microsoft desktop applications. We take special care in the introductory lessons of each book to provide the background skills and understanding necessary to proceed to more specific MCDST skills. We cover many more learning objectives and skills in these introductory lessons than are specifically listed as MCDST objectives. Throughout all lessons, we take care to *explain why things are done*, rather than just list the steps necessary to do them. There is a vast difference between understanding how Windows XP works and why, versus rote memorization of procedures.

A second group of students will already have some experience working with operating systems and Windows applications. This group already has an understanding of the basics, but needs more systematic and in-depth coverage of MCDST skills they lack. The Prentice Hall Certification Series is organized so that these more experienced students can quickly discover what they do not know, and can skip through introductory lessons quickly. Nevertheless, this group will also appreciate our emphasis on explanation and clear illustration throughout the series.

A third group of students will have considerable experience with previous Microsoft operating systems and applications. These students may be seeking to upgrade their skills, and they may be learning outside of formal training programs as self-paced learners, or in distance learning programs sponsored by their employers. The Prentice Hall Certification Series is designed to help these students quickly identify the new features of new versions of Windows operating systems and applications and to rapidly update their existing skills.

Prentice Hall Certification Series Skills and MCDST Objectives

In designing and writing the Prentice Hall Certification Series, we had a choice between organizing the book into lessons composed of MCDST domains and objectives, or organizing the book into lessons composed of skills needed to pass the MCDST certification examinations. (A complete listing of the domains and objectives for the relevant exam is found inside the front and back covers of the book.) We chose to organize the book around skills, beginning with introductory basic skills, and building to more advanced skills. We believe this is a more orderly and effective way to teach students the MCDST subject matter and the basic understanding of Windows operating systems.

We also wanted to make clear exactly how the skills related to the published MCDST objectives. In the Prentice Hall Certification Series, skills are organized into lessons. At the beginning of each lesson, there is an introduction to the set of skills covered in the lesson, followed by a table that shows how the skills taught in the lesson support specific MCDST objectives. All MCDST objectives for each of the examinations are covered; at the beginning of each skill discussion, the exact MCDST objective relating to that skill is identified.

What's Different About the Prentice Hall Certification Series—Main Features and Components

The Prentice Hall Certification Series has two distinguishing features that make it the most effective MCDST learning tool available today. These two features are a graphical, illustrated two-page spread approach and a skills-based systematic approach to learning MCDST objectives.

Graphical, illustrated approach. First, the Prentice Hall Certification Series uses a graphical, illustrated approach in a convenient *two-page spread format* (see illustration below). This makes learning easy, effective, and enjoyable.

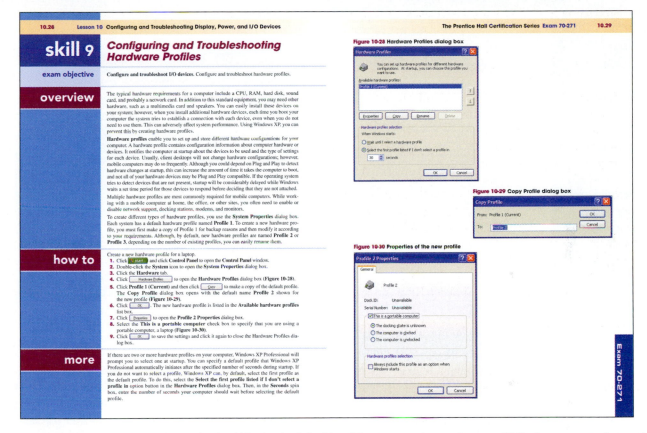

Each two-page spread is devoted to a single skill. On the left side of the two-page spread, you will find a conceptual overview explaining what the skill is, why it is important, and how it is used. On the right side of the two-page spread are graphics and screenshots that illustrate the concepts described in the skill. The pedagogy is easy to follow and understand.

In addition to these main features, each two-page spread contains several *learning aids*:

- *More:* A brief section that provides more information about the skill, alternative ways to perform the skill, and common business applications of the skill
- *Tips:* Hints and suggestions to follow when performing the skill, placed in the left margin opposite the text to which it relates
- *Caution:* Short notes about the pitfalls and problems you may encounter when performing the skill, also placed in the left margin opposite the text to which it relates

At the end of each lesson, students can test and practice their skills using the following end-of-lesson features:

- *Test Yourself:* An examination that tests your comprehension and retention of the material in the lesson
- *Projects: On Your Own:* Short projects that test your ability to perform tasks and skills in Windows without detailed, step-by-step instructions
- *Problem Solving Scenarios:* Real-world business scenarios that ask you to analyze or diagnose a networking situation, and then write a report or prepare a presentation that presents your solution to the problem

Skills-based systematic approach. A second distinguishing feature of the Prentice Hall Certification Series is a *skills-based* systematic approach to MCDST certification by using five integrated components:

- *Main Book:* Organized by skills.
- *Project Lab Manual:* Enables you to practice skills in realistic settings.
- *Examination Guide:* Organized by MCDST domains and objectives to practice answering questions representative of questions you are likely to encounter in the actual MCDST examination (available for selected books in the Series).
- *Interactive Solution multimedia CD-ROM:* Organized by MCDST domains and objectives—that allows students to practice performing MCDST objectives in a simulated Windows environment (available for selected books in the Series).
- *Powerful Web site:* Provides additional questions, projects, and interactive training.

Within each component, the learning is organized by skills, beginning with the relatively simple skills and progressing rapidly through the more complex skills. Each skill is carefully explained in a series of steps and conceptual overviews describing why the skill is important.

Supplements Available for This Series:

1. Test Bank

The Test Bank is a Word document distributed with the Instructor's Manual (usually on a CD). It is distributed on the Internet to instructors only. The purpose of the Test Bank is to provide instructors and students with a convenient way for testing comprehension of material presented in the book. The Test Bank contains 40 multiple-choice questions and 10 true/false questions per lesson. The questions are based on material presented in the book and are not generic MCDST questions.

2. Instructor's Manual

The Instructor's Manual (IM) is a Word document (distributed to instructors only) that provides instructional tips and answers to the Test Yourself questions and the Problem Solving Scenarios. The IM also includes an introduction to each lesson, teaching objectives, and teaching suggestions.

3. PowerPoint Slides

The PowerPoint slides contain images of all of the conceptual figures and screenshots in each book. The purpose of the slides is to provide the instructor with a convenient means of reviewing the content of the book in a classroom setting.

4. Companion Web Site

The Companion Web site is a Pearson learning tool that provides students and instructors with online support. On the Prentice Hall Certification Series Companion Web site, you will find the Interactive Study Guide, a Web-based interactive quiz composed of 15 questions per lesson. Written by the authors, there are more than 250 interactive questions on the Companion Web site, which are available free of charge. The purpose of the Interactive Study Guide is to provide students with a convenient online mechanism for self-testing their comprehension of the book material.

Exam 70-272 Supporting Users and Troubleshooting Desktop Applications on a Microsoft Windows XP Operating System

This book covers the subject matter of Microsoft's Exam 70-272, which focuses on troubleshooting and supporting desktop applications on Windows XP operating systems. You will learn how to develop a troubleshooting strategy; work with users in a professional manner; customize and troubleshoot operating system features; configure Internet Explorer; manage e-mail accounts, data storage, and application options in Outlook and Outlook Express; install Microsoft Office 20003; configure Office applications for usability and security; configure security settings and protect systems against viruses and other security incidents; and troubleshoot application connectivity problems due to network resource issues or permissions conflicts.

The following knowledge domains are discussed in this book:

- Configuring and Troubleshooting Applications
- Resolving Issues Related to Usability
- Resolving Issues Related to Application Customization
- Configuring and Troubleshooting Connectivity for Applications
- Configuring Application Security

How This Book Is Organized

This book is organized into a series of lessons. Each lesson focuses on a set of skills you will need to learn in order to master the knowledge domains required by the MCDST examinations. The skills are organized in a logical progression from basic knowledge skills to more specific skills.

At the beginning of each lesson, you will find a table that links the skills covered to specific exam objectives. For each skill presented on a two-page spread, the MCDST objective is listed.

MCDST Certification

MCDST certification is a recent but fast-growing credential in the information technology world. The skills learned in the MCDST program complement skills learned in other certification programs such as CompTIA's A+ certification in hardware and software. The MCDST certification is arguably less hardware-oriented but more troubleshooting-oriented than the A+ certification. By following a clear-cut strategy of preparation, you will be able to pass the MCDST certification exams. The first thing to remember is that there are no quick and easy routes to certification. No one can guarantee you will receive a certification-no matter what they promise. Real-world MCDST certified professionals get certified by following a strategy involving self-study, on-the-job experience, and classroom learning, either in colleges or training institutes. The following are answers to frequently asked questions that should help you prepare for the certification exams.

What Is the MCP Program?

The MCP program refers to the Microsoft Certified Professional program that certifies individuals who have passed Microsoft certification examinations. Certification is desirable for both individuals and organizations. For individuals, an MCP certification signifies to employers your expertise and skills in implementing Microsoft software in organizations. For employers, MCP certification makes it easy to identify potential employees with the requisite skills to develop and administer Microsoft tools. In a recent survey reported by Microsoft, 89% of hiring managers said they recommend a Microsoft MCP certification for candidates seeking IT positions.

What Are the MCP Certifications?

Today there are eight MCP certifications. Some certifications emphasize administrative as well as technical skills, whereas other certifications focus more on technical skills in developing software applications. The following is a listing of the current MCP certifications. The Prentice Hall Certification Series focuses on the first three certifications.

- *MCDST:* Microsoft Certified Desktop Support Technicians (MCDSTs) provide desktop support for the Microsoft Windows XP operating system and Microsoft desktop applications.
- *MCSA:* Microsoft Certified Systems Administrators (MCSAs) administer network and systems environments based on the Microsoft Windows platforms.
- *MCSE:* Microsoft Certified Systems Engineers (MCSEs) analyze business requirements to design and implement an infrastructure solution based on the Windows platform and Microsoft Server software.
- *MCDBA:* Microsoft Certified Database Administrators (MCDBAs) design, implement, and administer Microsoft SQL Server databases.
- *MCT:* Microsoft Certified Trainers (MCTs) are qualified instructors, certified by Microsoft, who deliver Microsoft training courses to IT professionals and developers.
- *MCAD:* Microsoft Certified Application Developers (MCADs) use Microsoft technologies to develop and maintain department-level applications, components, Web or desktop clients, or back-end data services.
- *MCSD:* Microsoft Certified Solution Developers (MCSDs) design and develop leading-edge enterprise-class applications with Microsoft development tools, technologies, platforms, and the Windows architecture.
- *Microsoft Office Specialist:* Microsoft Office Specialists (Office Specialists) are globally recognized for demonstrating advanced skills with Microsoft desktop software.

What Is the Difference Between MCDST, MCSA, and MCSE Certification?

There are three certifications that focus on the implementation, administration, and support of the Microsoft operating systems and networking tools: MCDST, MCSA, and MCSE.

MCDST certification is designed to train IT professionals for the task of supporting and troubleshooting the Windows XP operating system and desktop applications, such as Internet Explorer, and the Office suite of applications. The MCDST certification prepares you for jobs with titles such as desktop support technician, help desk technician, IT support technician, and help desk analyst.

MCSA certification is designed to train IT professionals who are concerned with the management, support, and troubleshooting of existing systems and networks. MCSA prepares you for jobs with titles such as systems administrator, network administrator, information systems administrator, network operations analyst, network technician, or technical support specialist. Microsoft recommends that you have six to twelve months of experience managing and supporting desktops, servers, and networks in an existing network infrastructure.

MCSE certification is designed to train IT professionals who are concerned with planning, designing, and implementing new systems or major upgrades of existing systems. MCSE prepares you for jobs with titles such as systems engineer, network engineer, systems analyst, network analyst, or technical consultant. Microsoft recommends that you have at least one year of experience planning, designing, and implementing Microsoft products.

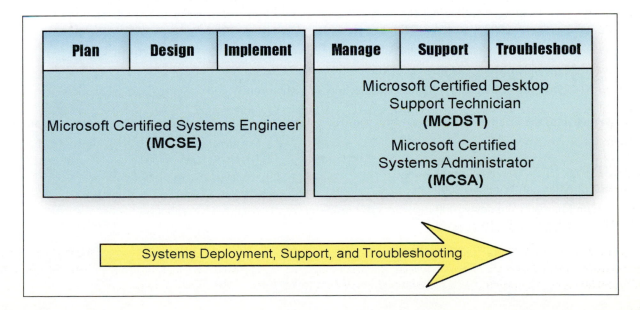

What Does the MCDST Certification Require?

MCDST candidates are required to pass two exams. The following list shows examinations that are included in the MCDST track.

Core Exams (2 Exams Required)

- *Exam 70-271:* Supporting Users and Troubleshooting a Microsoft Windows XP Operating System
- *Exam 70-272:* Supporting Users and Troubleshooting Desktop Applications on a Microsoft Windows XP Operating System

The MCDST certification counts as an elective for the MCSA certification described below. Other related certification programs are HDI's Customer Support Specialist (CSS) or Help Desk Analyst (HDA), and CompTIA's A+ certification for PC service and support. HDI is a professional association of help desk specialists, and CompTIA is an IT industry consortium both of which support industry efforts to develop training and certification for user support functions. Each of the three different support certifications are promoted as being complementary to one another.

What Does the MCSA on Windows Server 2003 Require?

MCSA candidates are required to pass a total of four exams: three core exams and one elective exam. The list below shows examinations that are included in the MCSA track.

Core Exams (3 exams required)

(A) Networking System (2 exams required)

- *Exam 70-290:* Managing and Maintaining a Microsoft Windows Server 2003 Environment

   and

- *Exam 70-291:* Implementing, Managing, and Maintaining a Microsoft Windows Server 2003 Network Infrastructure

(B) Client Operating System (1 exam required)

- *Exam 70-270:* Installing, Configuring, and Administering Microsoft Windows XP Professional

   or

- *Exam 70-210:* Installing, Configuring, and Administering Microsoft Windows 2000 Professional

Elective Exams (1 exam required)

- *Exam 70-086:* Implementing and Supporting Microsoft Systems Management Server 2.0
- *Exam 70-227:* Installing, Configuring, and Administering Microsoft Internet Security and Acceleration (ISA) Server 2000, Enterprise Edition
- *Exam 70-228:* Installing, Configuring, and Administering Microsoft SQL Server 2000 Enterprise Edition
- *Exam 70-284:* Implementing and Managing Microsoft Exchange Server 2003
- *Exam 70-299:* Implementing and Administering Security in a Microsoft Windows Server 2003 Network

As an alternative to the electives listed previously, you may substitute the following Microsoft certifications for an MCSA elective:

- MCDST
- MCSA on Microsoft Windows 2000
- MCSE on Microsoft Windows 2000
- MCSE on Microsoft Windows NT 4.0

You may also substitute the following third-party certification combinations for an MCSA elective:

CompTIA Exams: *CompTIA A+* and *CompTIA Network+*
                    CompTIA A+ and *CompTIA Server+*
                    CompTIA Security+

What Is the MCSE Curriculum for Windows Server 2003?

MCSE candidates are required to pass a total of seven exams: six core exams and one elective exam. The following list shows the examinations that are included in the MCSE for Microsoft Windows Server 2003 track.

Core Exams (6 exams required)

(A) Networking System (4 exams required)

- *Exam 70-290:* Managing and Maintaining a Microsoft Windows Server 2003 Environment
- *Exam 70-291:* Implementing, Managing, and Maintaining a Microsoft Windows Server 2003 Network Infrastructure
- *Exam 70-293:* Planning and Maintaining a Microsoft Windows Server 2003 Network Infrastructure
  and
- *Exam 70-294:* Planning, Implementing, and Maintaining a Microsoft Windows Server 2003 Active Directory Infrastructure

(B) Client Operating System (1 exam required)

- *Exam 70-270:* Installing, Configuring, and Administering Microsoft Windows XP Professional
  or
- *Exam 70-210:* Installing, Configuring, and Administering Microsoft Windows 2000 Professional

(C) Design (1 exam required)

- *Exam 70-297:* Designing a Microsoft Windows Server 2003 Active Directory and Network Infrastructure
  or
- *Exam 70-298:* Designing Security for a Microsoft Windows Server 2003 Network

Elective Exams (1 exam required)

- *Exam 70-086:* Implementing and Supporting Microsoft Systems Management Server 2.0
- *Exam 70-227:* Installing, Configuring, and Administering Microsoft Internet Security and Acceleration (ISA) Server 2000 Enterprise Edition
- *Exam 70-228:* Installing, Configuring, and Administering Microsoft SQL Server 2000 Enterprise Edition
- *Exam 70-229:* Designing and Implementing Databases with Microsoft SQL Server 2000 Enterprise Edition
- *Exam 70-232:* Implementing and Maintaining Highly Available Web Solutions with Microsoft Windows 2000 Server Technologies and Microsoft Application Center 2000
- *Exam 70-281:* Planning, Deploying, and Managing an Enterprise Project Management Solution
- *Exam 70-282:* Designing, Deploying, and Managing a Network Solution for a Small- and Medium-Sized Business
- *Exam 70-284:* Implementing and Managing Microsoft Exchange Server 2003
- *Exam 70-285:* Designing a Microsoft Exchange Server 2003 Organization
- *Exam 70-297:* Designing a Microsoft Windows Server 2003 Active Directory and Network Infrastructure
- *Exam 70-298:* Designing Security for a Microsoft Windows Server 2003 Network
- *Exam 70-299:* Implementing and Administering Security in a Microsoft Windows Server 2003 Network

As an alternative to the electives listed above, you may substitute the following Microsoft certifications for an MCSE elective:

- MCSA on Microsoft Windows 2000
- MCSE on Microsoft Windows 2000
- MCSE on Microsoft Windows NT 4.0

You may also substitute the following third-party certification combinations for an MCSE elective:

- *CompTIA Security+*
- Unisys UN0-101: Implementing and Supporting Microsoft Windows Server 2003 Solutions in the Data Center

What About Upgrading From a Previous Certification?

Microsoft provides upgrade paths for MCSAs and MCSEs on Windows 2000 so that they can acquire credentials on Windows Server 2003 efficiently and economically. For details on upgrade requirements, visit the following Microsoft Web pages:

http://www.microsoft.com/learning/mcp/mcsa/windows2003/
http://www.microsoft.com/learning/mcp/mcse/windows2003/

There currently is no upgrade path to the MCDST certification.

Do You Need to Pursue Certification to Benefit from This Book?

No. The Prentice Hall Certification Series is designed to prepare you for the workplace by providing you with networking knowledge and skills regardless of certification programs. Although it is desirable to obtain a certification, you can certainly benefit greatly by just reading these books, practicing your skills in the simulated Windows environment found on the MCSE/MCSA Interactive Solution CD-ROM, and using the online Interactive Study Guide.

What Kinds of Questions Are on the Exam?

The MCDST exams typically involve a variety of question formats. The most common question formats used on most Microsoft exams are described as follows:

(a) Select-and-Place Exam Items (Drag-and-Drop)

A select-and-place exam item asks candidates to understand a scenario and assemble a solution (graphically on screen) by picking up screen objects and moving them to their appropriate location to assemble the solution. For instance, you might be asked to place routers, clients, and servers on a network and illustrate how they would be connected to the Internet. This type of exam item can measure architectural, design, troubleshooting, and component recognition skills more accurately than traditional exam items can, because the solution—a graphical diagram—is presented in a form that is familiar to the computer professional.

(b) Case Study-Based Multiple-Choice Exam Items

The candidate is presented with a scenario based on typical Windows installations, and then is asked to answer several multiple-choice questions. To make the questions more challenging, several correct answers may be presented, and you will be asked to choose all that are correct. The Prentice Hall Certification Series Test Yourself questions at the end of each lesson give you experience with these kinds of questions.

(c) Simulations

Simulations test your ability to perform tasks in a simulated Windows environment. A simulation imitates the functionality and interface of Windows operating systems. The simulation usually involves a scenario in which you will be asked to perform several tasks in the simulated environment, including working with dialog boxes and entering information. The Prentice Hall Certification Series Interactive Solution CD-ROM gives you experience working in a simulated Windows environment.

(d) Computer Adaptive Testing

A computer adaptive test (CAT) attempts to adapt the level of question difficulty to the knowledge of each individual examinee. An adaptive exam starts with several easy questions. If you get these right, more difficult questions are pitched. If you fail a question, the next questions will be easier. Eventually the test will discover how much you know and what you can accomplish in a Windows environment.

You can find out more about the exam questions and take sample exams at the Microsoft Web site: **http://www.microsoft.com/learning/mcpexams/default.asp**.

How Long is the Exam?

Exams have 50 to 70 questions and last anywhere from 60 minutes to 240 minutes. The variation in exam length is due to variation in the requirements for specific exams (some exams have many more requirements than others), and because the adaptive exams take much less time than traditional exams. When you register for an exam, you will be told how much time you should expect to spend at the testing center. In some cases, the exams include timed sections that can help for apportioning your time.

What Is the Testing Experience Like?

You are required to bring two forms of identification that include your signature and one photo ID (such as a driver's license or company security ID). You will be required to sign a non-disclosure agreement that obligates you not to share the contents of the exam questions with others, and you will be asked to complete a survey. The rules and procedures of the exam will be explained to you by testing center administrators. You will be introduced to the testing equipment and you will be offered an exam tutorial intended to familiarize you with the testing equipment. This is a good idea. You will not be allowed to communicate with other examinees or with outsiders during the exam. You should definitely turn off your cell phone when taking the exam.

How Can You Best Prepare for the MCDST and Other Exams?

Prepare for the MCDST exam by reading this book, and then practicing your skills in a lab environment or at home on a personal computer that is not connected to a home network. It is best to practice on a spare computer, one that you do not need at home for e-mail or other pressing business. Certain changes you make to the operating system and to specific applications may require some time to reverse, or repair. Prior to taking the exam, you should have at least six months of practical experience support Windows XP operating systems and Microsoft applications.

An MCSA candidate should, at a minimum, have at least 6–12 months of experience implementing and administering desktop and network operating systems in environments with the following characteristics: a minimum of 200 users, 2 supported physical locations, typical network services and applications, including file and print, database, messaging, proxy server or firewall, dial-in server, desktop management, and Web hosting, and connectivity needs, including connecting individual offices and users at remote locations to the corporate network and connecting corporate networks to the Internet.

An MCSE candidate should have at least one year of experience in the above areas, but supporting a minimum of 5 physical locations, and at least one year of experience designing a network infrastructure.

Where Can You Take the Exams?

All MCP exams are administered by Pearson VUE and Thomson Prometric. There are three convenient ways to schedule your exams with Pearson VUE:
- Online: **www.pearsonvue.com/ms/**
- Toll free in the United States and Canada: Call (800) TEST-REG (800-837-8734), or find a call center in your part of the world at: **http://www.pearsonvue.com/contact/ms/**
- In person: Pearson VUE has over 3,000 test centers in 130 countries. To find a test center near you, visit: **www.pearsonvue.com**

To take exams at a Thomson Prometric testing center, call Prometric at (800) 755-EXAM (755-3926). Outside the United States and Canada, contact your local Thomson Prometric Registration Center. To register online with Thomson Prometric, visit the Thomson Prometric Web site at **www.prometric.com**.

How Much Does It Cost to Take the Exams?

In the United States, exams cost $125 USD per exam as of January, 2004. Certification exam prices are subject to change. In some countries/regions, additional taxes may apply. Contact your test registration center for exact pricing.

Are There Any Discounts Available to Students?

Yes. In the United States and Canada, as well as other select regions around the globe, full-time students can take a subset of the MCP exams for a significantly reduced fee at Authorized Academic Testing Centers (AATCs). For details on which countries and exams are included in the program, or to schedule your discounted exam, visit **www.pearsonvue.com/aatc**.

Can I Take the Exam More Than Once?

Yes. You may retake an exam at any time if you do not pass on the first attempt. However, if you do not pass the second time, you must wait 14 days. A 14-day waiting period will be imposed for all subsequent exam retakes. If you have passed an exam, you cannot take it again.

Where Can I Get More Information about the Exams?

Microsoft Web sites are a good place to start:

- MCP Program (general): **http://www.microsoft.com/learning/mcp/default.asp**
- MCDST Certification: **http://www.microsoft.com/learning/mcp/mcdst/default.asp**
- MCSE Certification: **http://www.microsoft.com/learning/mcp/mcse/default.asp**
- MCSA Certification: **http://www.microsoft.com/learning/mcp/mcsa/default.asp**

There are literally thousands of other Web sites with helpful information that you can identify using any Web search engine. Many commercial sites promise instant success, and some even guarantee that you will pass the exams. Be a discriminating consumer. If it were that easy to become an MCP professional, the certification would be meaningless.

Acknowledgments

A great many people have contributed to the Prentice Hall Certification Series. We want to thank Steven Elliot, our editor at Prentice Hall, for his enthusiastic appreciation of the project, his personal support for the Azimuth team, and his deep commitment to the goal of creating a powerful, accurate, and enjoyable learning tool for students. We also want to thank David Alexander of Prentice Hall for his interim leadership and advice as the project developed at Prentice Hall, and Jerome Grant for supporting the development of high-quality certification training books and CDs for colleges and universities worldwide. Finally, we want to thank Susan Hartman Sullivan of Addison-Wesley for believing in this project at an early stage and for encouraging us to fulfill our dreams.

The Azimuth Interactive MCSE/MCSA team is a dedicated group of technical experts, computer scientists, networking specialists, and writers with literally decades of experience in computer networking, information technology and systems, and computer technology. We want to thank the members of the team:

Kenneth C. Laudon is the Series Designer. He is Professor of Information Systems at New York University's Stern School of Business. He has written 12 books on information systems and technologies, e-commerce, and management information systems. He has designed, installed, and fixed computer operating systems and networks since 1982.

Carol G. Traver is the Senior Series Editor. She is General Counsel and Vice President of Business Development at Azimuth Interactive, Inc. A graduate of Yale Law School, she has co-authored several best-selling books on information technology and e-commerce.

Kenneth Rosenblatt is a Senior Author for the Series. He is an experienced technical writer and editor who has co-authored or contributed to over two dozen books on computer and software instruction. In addition, Ken has over five years of experience in designing, implementing, and managing Microsoft operating systems and networks. In addition to this book, Ken is a co-author of the Prentice Hall Certification Series Exam 70-216, Exam 70-270, Exam 70-271, and Exam 70-291 textbooks.

Robin L. Pickering is a Senior Author for the Series. She is an experienced technical writer and editor who has co-authored or contributed to over a dozen books on computers and software instruction. Robin has extensive experience as a Network Administrator and consultant for a number of small to medium-sized firms. In addition to this book, Robin is a co-author of the Prentice Hall Certification Series Exam 70-210, Exam 70-215, Exam 70-270, and Exam 70-290 textbooks.

Megan Miller is a Senior Editor and Project Manager with more than ten years of experience working for major New York publishers in editorial content development, Web development, and project management. Megan has worked on the Prentice Hall Certification Series A+ Hardware and Software textbooks, as well as assisted with other books and CDs in the Prentice Hall Certification Series.

Russell Polo is the Technical Advisor for the Series. He holds degrees in computer science and electrical engineering. He has designed, implemented, and managed Microsoft, Unix, and Novell networks in a number of business firms since 1995. He currently is the Network Administrator at Azimuth Interactive.

David Langley is an Editor for the Series. David is an experienced technical writer and editor who has co-authored or contributed to over 10 books on computers and software instruction. In addition, he has nearly 20 years of experience as a college professor, five of those in computer software training.

Brian Hill is a Technical Consultant and Editor for the Series. His industry certifications include MCSE 2000 and 2003, MCSA 2000 and 2003, MCSE+I (NT 4.0), CCNP, CCDP, MCT, MCP, Network+, and A+. Brian was formerly Lead Technology Architect and a Bootcamp instructor for Techtrain, Inc. His Windows 2000 experience spans back as far as the first beta releases. In addition to this book, Brian is also a co-author of the Prentice Hall Certification Series Exam 70-217, Exam 70-290, and Exam 70-294 textbooks.

L. Ward Ulmer is a former Information Technology Director with 11 years of experience. He began teaching Computer Science in 1996 and has held teaching positions at Patrick Henry Academy and Trident Technical College. He is the Department Chair of Computer Technology at Orangeburg-Calhoun Technical College. Ward's certifications include MCSE, MCSA, CCNA, MCP+I, MCT, and CCAI. Ward is a co-author of the Prentice Hall Certification Series Exam 70-217 and Exam 70-294 Project Lab Manuals.

Acknowledgments (cont'd)

Richard Watson has worked in the industry for 10 years, first as a Checkpoint Certified Security Engineer (CCSE), and then as a Lead Engineer for a local Microsoft Certified Solution Provider. Among his many other industry certifications are MCSE on Windows 2000 and Windows NT 4, CCNA, and IBM Professional Server Expert (PSE). Richard is currently the President of Client Server Technologies Inc., which provides network installation and support, Web site design, and training in Beaverton, Oregon. Richard is a co-author of the Prentice Hall Certification Series Exam 70-220, Exam 70-291, and Exam 70-298 textbooks.

Stacey McBrine has spent more than 18 years configuring and supporting DOS- and Windows-based PCs and LANs, along with several other operating systems. He is certified as an MCSE for Windows NT 4.0, and was one of the first 2000 individuals in the world to achieve MCSE certification for Windows 2000. He has brought his real world experience to the classroom for the last five years as a Microsoft Certified Trainer. He holds several other certifications for Cisco, Linux, Solaris, and Security. Stacey is a co-author of the Prentice Hall Certification Series Exam 70-293 textbook and Exam 70-270 Lab Manual.

Mark Maxwell is a Technical Consultant and Editor for the Series. He has over 15 years of industry experience in distributed network environments including TCP/IP, fault-tolerant NTFS file service, Kerberos, wide area networks, and virtual private networks. Mark is a co-author of the Prentice Hall Certification Series Exam 70-216 Lab Manual, and has also published articles on network design, upgrades, and security.

Dr. Russell Jones is an Associate Professor and Area Coordinator of Decision Sciences at Arkansas State University and currently holds the Kathy White Endowed Fellowship in MIS. Dr. Jones received his PhD from the University of Texas-Arlington and has been on the ASU faculty for 16 years. He holds certifications from Microsoft, Novell, CompTIA, and Cisco, and is a co-author of the Prentice Hall Certification Series Exam 70-290, 70-293, and 70-297 Project Lab Manuals.

David W. Tschanz, MCSE, MCP+I, A+, iNet+, CIW, is an American who has been living in Saudi Arabia for the past 15 years. There he has worked on a variety of projects related to Web-based information management, training, and applications, as well as computer security issues. He writes extensively on computer topics and is a regular contributor to *MCP Magazine*. In addition to this book, David is a co-author of the Prentice Hall Certification Series Exam 70-220 Lab Manual.

Brien M. Posey, MCSE, has been a freelance technical writer who has written for Microsoft, CNET, ZDNet, Tech Target, MSD2D, Relevant Technologies, and many other technology companies. Brien has also served as the CIO for a nationwide chain of hospitals and was once in charge of IT security for Fort Knox. Most recently, Brien has received Microsoft's MVP award for his work with Windows 2000 Server and IIS. Brien is a co-author of the Prentice Hall Certification Series Exam 70-218 textbook.

Tim Oliwiak, MCSE, MCT, is a network consultant for small- to medium-sized companies. He previously was an instructor at the Institute for Computer Studies, and a Network Engineer for the Success Network. Tim lives in Ontario, Canada. Tim is a co-author of the Prentice Hall Certification Series Exam 70-217 Lab Manual.

Simon Sykes-Wright, MCSE, has been a technical consultant to a number of leading firms, including NCR Canada Ltd. Simon is a co-author of the Prentice Hall Certification Series Exam 70-293 textbook.

David Lundell is a database administrator and Web developer for The Ryland Group in Scottsdale, AZ. He holds MCSE, MCDBA, MCSD, MCT, CAN, and CCNA certifications, as well as an MBA from the University of Arizona. David is a co-author of the Prentice Hall Certification Series Exam 70-291 Project Lab Manual.

Wale Soyinka is a systems and network engineering consultant. He holds MCP, CCNA, and CCNP certification. He is the author of a series of lab manuals on Linux, and is a co-author of the Prentice Hall Certification Series Exam 70-218 Lab Manual.

Frank Miller is an educational course developer and network support professional with many years of real-world industry experience. He holds MCP, MCSE, MCSA, MCDBA, and MCAD certifications. Frank is the author of the Prentice Hall Certification Series Exam 70-298 Project Lab Manual.

Pete Grondin is Adjunct Instructor at Valdosta Technical College and a professional educator and curriculum developer. He holds MCP, MCSA, and A+ certifications. Pete is the author of the Prentice Hall Certification Series A+ Hardware Project Lab Manual.

Lenny Bailes is an Instructor/Course Designer at San Francisco State University. He holds a Masters Degree in Instructional Technology and a B.A. in philosophy. Lenny holds an A+ certification. Lenny is the author of the Prentice Hall Certification Series A+ Hardware textbook and A+ Software Project Lab Manual.

Quality Assurance

The Prentice Hall Certification Series contains literally thousands of software instructions for working with Windows products. We have taken special steps to ensure the accuracy of the statements in this Series. The books and CDs are initially written by teams composed of Azimuth Interactive, Inc., MCDST/MCSE/MCSA professionals and writers working directly with the software as they write. Each team then collectively walks through the software instructions and screen shots to ensure accuracy. The resulting manuscripts are then thoroughly tested by an independent quality assurance team of MCDST/MCSE/MCSA professionals who also perform the software instructions and check to ensure the screen shots and conceptual graphics are correct. The result is a very accurate and comprehensive learning environment for understanding Windows products.

We would like to thank the primary members of the Quality Assurance team for their critical feedback and unstinting efforts to make sure we got it right. The primary technical editor for this book is Will Willis.

- Bold and/or italicized text enclosed within carets, such as *<Server_name>*, indicates a variable item. The carets and bold/italic formatting are solely to alert you to the variable nature of the enclosed text and will not be present in your file structure. If called on to enter the information referred to within the carets, type only the information itself, not the carets, and do not use bold or italics.

- Keys on the keyboard are enclosed within square brackets, such as **[Alt]**. A plus sign (**+**) between two key names indicates that you must press those keys at the same time; for example, press **[Ctrl]+[Alt]+[Del]**.

- Folder, file, and program names in the text are shown with initial capitals, although their on-screen appearance may differ. For example, in our text, you may see a reference to a Windows folder, but on your screen this folder may be shown as WINDOWS. Similarly, in our text, you may see a reference to the Iishelp folder, although on screen it may appear as iishelp. When typing folder and file names yourself, you may use uppercase and/or lowercase as you choose unless otherwise instructed.

- Commands to be entered at a command prompt are shown in lower case. Square brackets, carets, and/or bold/italic formatting used in command-line syntax statements indicate a variable item. As with material shown within carets, if called on to enter such an item, type only the information referred to within the brackets or carets, not the brackets or carets themselves, and do not use bold or italics.

- The term **%Systemroot%** is used to indicate the folder in the boot partition that contains the Windows system files.

Installing, Configuring, and Administering Microsoft® Windows® 2000 Professional Exam 70-210
ISBN 0-13-142209-X

Installing, Configuring, and Administering Microsoft® Windows® 2000 Server Exam 70-215
ISBN 0-13-142211-1

Implementing and Administering Microsoft® Windows® 2000 Network Infrastructure Exam 70-216
ISBN 0-13-142210-3

Implementing and Administering a Microsoft® Windows® 2000 Directory Services Infrastructure
Exam 70-217   ISBN 0-13-142208-1

Managing a Microsoft® Windows® 2000 Network Environment Exam 70-218   ISBN 0-13-144744-0

Designing Security for a Microsoft® Windows® 2000 Network Exam 70-220   ISBN 0-13-144906-0

Installing, Configuring, and Administering Microsoft® Windows® XP Professional Exam 70-270
ISBN 0-13-144132-9

Supporting Users and Troubleshooting a Microsoft® Windows® XP Operating System Exam 70-271
ISBN 0-13-149989-0

Managing and Maintaining a Microsoft® Windows® Server 2003 Environment Exam 70-290
ISBN 0-13-144743-2

Implementing, Managing, and Maintaining a Microsoft® Windows® Server 2003 Network
Infrastructure Exam 70-291   ISBN 0-13-145600-8

Planning and Maintaining a Microsoft® Windows® Server 2003 Network Infrastructure Exam 70-293
ISBN 0-13-189306-8

Planning, Implementing, and Maintaining a Microsoft® Windows® Server 2003 Active Directory
Infrastructure Exam 70-294   ISBN 0-13-189312-2

Designing a Microsoft® Windows® Server 2003 Active Directory and Network Infrastructure
Exam 70-297 ISBN 0-13-189316-5

Designing Security for a Microsoft® Windows® Server 2003 Network Exam 70-298
ISBN 0-13-117670-6

Introducing Desktop Support

The Microsoft Certified Desktop Support Technician certificate offers a road map to those who are seeking careers as support technicians for users of desktop applications and the Windows XP operating system. There are more than one billion personal computers (PCs) in the world today, and most of them run some version of the Microsoft Windows operating system and the Microsoft Office productivity suite. Using these programs effectively, and recovering from problems that can occur when using a PC, requires both user education and a support system of trained technicians. Increasingly, businesses realize that their employees need the support of skilled technicians for their employees to be productive. The Microsoft Certified Desktop Support Technician certificate provides you with an important set of skills that will allow you to become an effective support technician.

To be successful in passing the MCDST Exam 272, you must have a broad understanding of computers in general, how computers work in a networked environment, and the skills related to troubleshooting computer systems. In this text, you will have an opportunity to learn the skills required to pass the Microsoft Exam 70-272: Supporting and Troubleshooting Desktop Applications on a Microsoft Windows XP Operating System. More importantly, this book will take you beyond the basic skills needed to pass the exam and introduce you to higher-level human-relationship and problem-solving skills that will make you a more effective support technician. Remember, passing the examination is just the first step in your career toward becoming a valued support technician.

As a desktop support technician, you often will be the first person called when a user is having problems working with an operating system or running applications. You will be responsible for either solving the problem or ensuring that it is handed off to the proper person for resolution. You will also be the first person to deal with the frustration and embarrassment of a user who is unable to perform a task.

When providing desktop support customer service, there are many technical skills you need to be successful. There are also a number of human relationship skills that you need to provide professional customer service. Although we focus in this textbook primarily on concrete technical skills needed to support the Windows system environment, there are also many examples and suggestions on how to work with your users. The key to success will be to develop good troubleshooting skills, good technical knowledge, and the ability to serve customers in a way that relates to their needs.

Goals

In this lesson, you will learn about the role of the desktop support technician in different environments. You will learn about the types of users that you will be helping and the best ways to work with them. You will learn how to ask the right questions of the user and how to implement a troubleshooting methodology to enable you to find a working solution for your client. Finally, you will learn about helping the user to implement solutions and perform common maintenance tasks.

Lesson 1   Introducing Desktop Support

Skill	Exam 70-272 Objective
1. Understanding the Desktop Support Role	Basic knowledge
2. Exploring Desktop Support Environments and Positions	Basic knowledge
3. Working with Clients	Basic knowledge
4. Evaluating the User's Skill Level	Basic knowledge
5. Developing a Troubleshooting Strategy	Basic knowledge
6. Troubleshooting: Discovering the Problem	Basic knowledge
7. Evaluating System Configuration	Basic knowledge
8. Tracking Possible Solutions	Basic knowledge
9. Executing a Plan and Checking the Results	Basic knowledge
10. Taking a Proactive Approach	Basic knowledge

Requirements

To complete this lesson, you will need administrative rights on a Windows XP Professional computer with Service Pack 1 installed. The computer must also be able to access the Internet.

skill 1

Understanding the Desktop Support Role

exam objective

Basic knowledge

overview

Over the past two decades, the PC has become critical for business and professional workers in most industries. Today most business firms and professional organizations could not exist for even a few hours without PCs, local area networks (LANs), and access to the Internet. In 2004 there were more than 12 billion e-mail messages sent each day in the U.S., along with 2.4 billion instant messages. Soon, most business telephone service will be provided over Internet connections and LANs. Doing business and being at work today increasingly means working with PCs, handheld personal digital assistants (PDAs), cellular phones, and wireless computer networks. To assist business professionals in getting their jobs done, many companies either hire support technicians or outsource this function to other firms that provide this service. The role of the **desktop support technician** is to assist users when they require help with their computers, networks, and an ever-growing array of digital devices, from BlackBerry devices to cell phones with Internet connections.

Some desktop support technicians provide very specialized help on a single application or operating system. Other desktop support specialists offer broader, more general assistance to users. In most organizations, there is a **tiered support** structure in which the call from the user initially starts with a specialist with a broad knowledge base. The call is routed to a more specialized technician in the event that it cannot be solved by the first specialist.

The role of desktop support technician is typically seen as an entry-level position in an information technology (IT) infrastructure. Many employers believe that the experience working on a **help desk** is fundamental to understanding requirements for designing or managing IT infrastructures. It is important for you to understand that to be an effective desktop support technician, you need a broad skill set and you must be ready for continuous learning. You will work with many different types of users, from inexperienced to expert, in different fields and industries. You must understand the problem that the user is experiencing and find a resolution to that problem for them, which requires you to be part detective, part counselor, and part hero! With the right attitude, an interest in helping others, and interest in solving problems, being a desktop support technician can be interesting and exciting.

Of course, it can also be a challenge when a user is frustrated with his or her computer and decides it's your fault. This is where skills of a less technical nature are needed. When you begin looking for a job as a help desk support technician you can expect many job interview questions to center around how you will handle user interaction and conflict management.

Most computer environments today include several different networking components and operating systems with which a desktop support technician will work **(Table 1-1)**. In addition to being able to support the various systems in place in a company, the desktop support technician is usually required to learn applications which track, document, and manage the process of providing support and help to a firm's employees.

Although many desktop support technicians work in a call center where the majority of problems are solved over the telephone, there is also a growing need for desktop support technicians to provide support on site, in the place where the user works. Additionally, there is a growing use of **remote assistance software (Figure 1-1)** that enables a desktop support technician to take control of a user's computer to walk the user through a process or to resolve a problem. As a result, desktop support technicians can expect to work in a variety of different environments.

Table 1-1 Typical systems and associated support tasks

System	Typical Support Tasks
Computer hardware systems	Component replacement, device monitoring, capacity planning and maintenance, firmware updates
Computer operating systems	Configuration, repair, and maintenance
Client/server systems (file servers)	Network access, resource permissions
Database access	Database driver installation, network connectivity
E-mail and communications software	Configuration management
Office productivity applications	Maintenance, configuration, and repair
Accounting and financial management applications	Secondary authentication, resource location planning
Custom applications (of which there can be several hundred at a single site)	Varies from application to application

Figure 1-1 Remote assistance software

skill 2

Exploring Desktop Support Environments and Positions

exam objective

Basic knowledge

overview

There is considerable variety in help desk environments depending on the type of business, the type of network that the client systems are utilizing, industry-specific applications that may be used, and a variety of other factors. As such, it is difficult to describe a typical help desk environment. However, most help desks have many things in common.

As noted in Skill 1, most help desks follow a tiered structure **(Table 1-2)** in which calls are initially answered by a help desk support technician with more general troubleshooting skills and expertise. (Note that in some organizations the generalist may be referred to as Tier 1 support technician whereas in other organizations, Tier 1 would be a specialist.) Depending on the nature of the problem and whether or not it can be solved by the generalist, problems may be escalated to more specialized individuals.

Table 1-2 includes an estimate of how certifications might map to a tiered help desk environment. In addition to the Microsoft and CompTIA certifications, there are thousands of custom applications that require support and may have separate certifications or skill sets required.

In a smaller business environment, there may not be a formal help desk. Instead, the services that would normally be provided by a typical help desk may be provided by the network administrator. It is also possible that the desktop support technician may work in a retail repair shop or for an Internet service provider (ISP). In these environments, there may be a customized organizational structure based upon product areas, customer profiles, or some other category.

The role of desktop support technician can take on many different names, depending on the business firm. In large firms, the job title will be quite specific: Microsoft Office support technician, accounting software support technician, printing support technician, and so on. In smaller organizations, the job titles might be quite broad: systems manager, network administrator, information technology support (ITS).

In addition to being a job within a company, computer support is a growing component in a larger industry called computer services. The computer services industry includes maintenance, repair and installation of computers, consulting on business applications, and software development. You can find computer support being delivered by technicians at retail computer outlets, at software and hardware companies, and as independent professionals who own small computer repair and network support businesses.

Table 1-2 Desktop support technician job titles and roles

Tier	Typical Job Titles	Description	Typical Certification Levels
Tier 1:	Desktop support specialist Support technician	A desktop support technician/specialist with general skills related to operating systems, productivity applications, general hardware, and possibly a commonly used application within the industry-specific environment.	MCDST (Microsoft Certified Desktop Support Technician) A+ Hardware Support Specialist (CompTIA) Network+ (CompTIA)
Tier 2:	Application support specialist Senior support technician	A desktop support technician with both the general skills above as well as specialized skills in any, or all, of the areas mentioned. At Tier 2, the desktop support technician may also have specialized skills in a specific application. Some environments may refer to this tier as a senior support technician or help desk lead.	MCSA (Microsoft Certified Systems Administrator) MOS (Microsoft Office Specialist)
Tier 3:	Support engineer Systems engineer Applications engineer Application specialist	At this level, it is not uncommon for the position to change titles and become something along the lines of a support engineer, systems engineer, applications engineer, application specialist, or some other such title. The skill set at this level is very specific and may involve advanced skills related to networking, infrastructure, server applications, user management, and other skills of a more managerial nature.	MCSE (Microsoft Certified Systems Engineer)
Tier 4:	Security specialist Senior network analyst Systems manager	At this tier, the individual is often exceptionally specialized on a certain application and may even be part of the development team responsible for the application. Some help desk environments will use this level to refer to specialized vendor support. Again, at this level, there may be a title change to something along the lines of infrastructure engineer, systems architect, network engineer, or other titles which indicate a senior, design-based skill set.	MCDBA (Microsoft Certified Database Administrator), MCSD (Microsoft Certified Systems Developer) Various other certifications on specific applications

skill 3   *Working with Clients*

exam objective   Basic knowledge

overview

While technical skills are necessary to be a good support technician, by themselves they are not enough. In addition, you must also have good client service skills (**Figure 1-2**), which may be more difficult to learn than technical skills. The following are some important customer service skills:

Listening: This is the single most important skill you can acquire and apply. You must learn to let your client completely describe the problem to the best of his or her ability. You need to let the client finish describing the problem, then reflect back on what you were told to assure that you are both describing the same problem. The latter may require asking questions. You should avoid the use of technical jargon and if necessary, ask your question more than once or in different terms. You should also avoid trying to work out a solution to the problem until you have heard it completely described; otherwise, you are simply wasting your—and your client's time.

Empathy: Quite simply, empathy means putting yourself in someone else's shoes. It is important to understand that people can become quite frustrated when they are trying to do something on a computer for their job and are unable to complete the task.

Partnering: Partnering involves working with the customer to solve the problem. By creating a sense of teamwork in the face of a problem, the user is less likely to be frustrated and more likely to be able to contribute to the solution or its implementation.

Language skills: It is very easy, as you become more familiar with computer systems, to begin using specialized language, such as acronyms or terminology. It is important to use language that is appropriate for the listener and not the speaker.

Respect: You may often be helping an individual who is having difficulty performing a task that you would consider a basic computer skill, such as double-clicking an icon to start an application or process. It is important to remember that the individuals you are helping were hired for other critical skills and services for the company, not their computer experience. Fortunately, they have you!

Resilience: Especially in telephone support environments, a frustrated user may find it easier to blame you for the problem and treat you disrespectfully. You need to take the high road, be resilient to anything the user may say, and reach the point where you can help the user solve the problem as quickly as possible.

Follow-through: If the solution you are providing will take a period of time to resolve, then you need to inform the person you are helping about the progress you're making. It is also important to ensure that anything you say you will do gets done, is documented, and is communicated.

Positive attitude: Desktop support technicians are called into a situation when things don't work, and this can be very frustrating for users and technicians alike. If you reassure users having problems that you are serious about finding a solution, and if you maintain a positive, optimistic attitude that suggests you will indeed find a solution, you give the user confidence and you can perform your job more effectively.

Figure 1-2 Qualities for productive communication

skill 4 *Evaluating the User's Skill Level*

exam objective Basic knowledge

overview

By understanding the skills and role of users within your organization, you will be able to better assist them when they call you for help. One of the best places to start understanding users is with the company's organizational chart. By taking an overview of the various departments and functions within organization, you will understand how each group of users contributes to the organization as a whole. You can also roughly define users by their skill level with computer systems. To be an effective desktop support technician, the way you communicate and implement a solution to a user's problem should be appropriate to their skill level. User skill levels are generally categorized into three levels: novice, intermediate, and expert.

Novice: A **novice user** sees the computer at best as a tool for performing their job, and at worst, as a frustration which they must endure. They may have little interest in how a computer works and often they simply want to follow the routine they have always followed to complete their tasks. Some of these users may be interested in learning more, but many will be content if their computer simply does what it always has done and what they expect it to do. When assisting a novice user, it is important to explain each step that the user must perform in non-technical, straightforward language that is not condescending. As each step is performed, it is also important to solicit feedback as to what the user sees and exactly what has happened.

Intermediate: As more people use home computers, it is becoming more common to find **intermediate users** (users with an understanding of the basics). When assisting intermediate users, you may not need to explain each step in great detail. For example, you may be able to ask them to navigate to a specific location without having to explain each step involved in getting there. For these users, you may need to adopt more of a partnering role rather than a guiding role. Intermediate users often seek to learn something from their experience: Why the problem occurred, how to prevent it in the future, or specifically why you chose the path you chose when resolving the problem. They may also be more challenging if they feel that you are not following the same steps they would. However, they may be able to provide you with better ideas about how to solve the problem as well as better information about the problem.

Expert: There are several types **of expert users** which you may encounter: general expert users, who understand computer systems and applications very well, and specialist expert users, who may lack expertise on computer systems in general, but have very specialized knowledge of specific applications. You may often simply end up following an expert user's lead in resolving the problem. For example, such a user may know the solution to the problem, but lack the appropriate permissions to perform a network task or set up the appropriate environmental variables. Expert users may be able to provide you with new information about an application or solution—they may even end up being a resource for you for certain problems.

By taking a few moments to determine the skill level of the user you are serving, you will be in a far better position to assist them. This quick assessment can often make the user feel more involved in the process, more respected, and more committed to working with you. Try to avoid questions like: "Do you know much about computers?" Such questions may make them feel awkward answering in the negative. Ask more open-ended questions such as: "Have you ever experienced a similar problem in the past?" If the user answers this question by describing a detailed account of how he or she solved a complex problem, then chances are the user is intermediate or advanced (**Table 1-4**).

Table 1-4 **Comparison of user issues/solutions to e-mail account setup problems**

	Problem	Solution
Novice	My e-mail isn't working.	The novice will need to be guided through each step of the e-mail account set up.
Intermediate	My e-mail isn't working. I need to set up an account.	An intermediate user may need to be directed to the appropriate configuration screens, given the server information, but not require a step-by-step walk-through.
Expert	Can you tell me which mail server to connect to so that I can get my e-mail?	For the expert user, it is often sufficient simply to provide the server name required without further instructions.

skill 5 — *Developing a Troubleshooting Strategy*

exam objective   Basic knowledge

overview

Anytime a computer is disabled, someone has lost productivity, either in their private or professional lives. The job of desktop support personnel is to keep the downtime to a minimum and to get the system running again for the client. One of the best ways to get a computer system running quickly is to have a troubleshooting strategy to assess the situation and make the necessary adjustments or repairs. **Troubleshooting** is the process of isolating the source of a problem and then fixing it.

Microsoft's Troubleshooting Model: Microsoft has developed and encourages the use of a six-step troubleshooting model called the **Detect model**. Although this book specifically addresses problems related to the Windows XP operating system and Office applications, the same methodology can be applied to any system or application (**Figure 1-3**).

The six steps in the Detect model are:

1. **Document the problem**. This is the most important step. You must discover and record the symptoms and the conditions under which they occur.
2. **Assess the system configuration**. Is there anything in the way the system is set up that could be the source of the problem? Has new software or hardware been added? Are the drivers new and are they correct?
3. **Pursue possible solutions**. Conduct research to see if anyone else has addressed this issue. Review Microsoft Knowledge Base articles. Temporarily remove unnecessary hardware and software that is not needed to start the operating system. To assess your solutions, enable logging options.
4. **Implement a plan**. First, perform a complete backup of the system and data files. Then, implement your list of possible solutions. Have a backup plan if these solutions do not work or make things worse.
5. **Test the results**. Did the plan and solution work?
6. **Use a proactive method**. Make sure to prepare a post-action or "Lessons Learned" report. Record the changes you made and evaluate them. Was there a way to avoid the problem or a better way to address it? Do you have adequate documentation for someone else if the problem occurs elsewhere? Are there ways to prevent or diminish the effect of the problem in the future?

Figure 1-3 The Microsoft Detect model troubleshooting flowchart

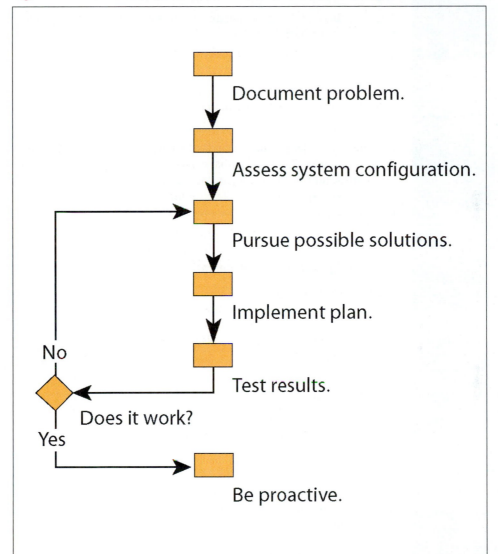

Document problem.

Assess system configuration.

Pursue possible solutions.

Implement plan.

No

Test results.

Does it work?

Yes

Be proactive.

skill 6

Troubleshooting: Discovering the Problem

exam objective

Basic knowledge

overview

tip

The best way to start troubleshooting is to gather information.

When you troubleshoot, the objective is to get your clients' computers back up and running as quickly as possible. You can take one of two approaches. The first is to treat the symptom, while the other is to locate the source of the problem and eliminate it. The latter approach is called **root-cause analysis**.

The only successful and meaningful way to solve a problem is to gather information, develop hypotheses, and then test them.

Typically, the user doesn't have the knowledge to adequately describe the problem or may only be telling you part of the problem. "It doesn't work" or "It's blinking at me" are typical responses you will receive from the end user. The client is principally concerned with lost data rather than with the root cause of the problem.

The first step is to develop a clear understanding of the symptoms and collect pertinent system information so that you understand the environment in which they occur. What was the user expecting to occur? Precisely what is not working correctly? Under what conditions does the problem occur? Is the problem specific to an application, or is it specific to a system (e.g., networks, video, etc.)? This is important, because you must fully understand the problem before you can begin the process of solving it.

After you have determined the scope of the problem, you are ready to begin troubleshooting. When you start troubleshooting a malfunctioning system, the first thing you should consider is **PHO (physical, hardware, operating system)**—the initial troubleshooting hierarchy.

PHO simply means that you should check all of the physical issues first, the hardware issues second and the operating system issues last. The main reason to use this strategy is that it follows the most generic to the most complex troubleshooting strategy, which is recommended by most professionals in the IT field.

As previously stated, all troubleshooting begins with observing and identifying the symptoms of a problem. You cannot begin to solve a problem until you have learned as much as you can about the circumstances in which problems occur and are familiar with the system behavior when issues arise.

You can use the following to help identify symptoms:

tip

The File Signature Verification utility can be used to confirm that only tested, certified, digitally signed files are installed on a computer **(Figure 1-5)**.

- ◆ **Error messages**: Record the error numbers, the precise message text, and a brief description of the events that occurred before the problem started and the events that follow the problem. It is also important to record the time and date of the error.
- ◆ **Event Viewer logs**: In the Event Viewer, you can view the Application, Security, and System logs. These logs may include entries that can help you to figure out what caused the problem **(Figure 1-4)**.
- ◆ **Other error log files**: A number of log files are created to record problems. Some error messages may tell you to look at the entries in these log files, which are typically text files that can be opened and read in Notepad or another text editor.
- ◆ **Random event or a pattern**: Does the problem happen randomly or when the user or the computer does something? Do all users have the problem or only some? Does the problem occur locally, over the network, or both? Pay special attention to recent changes, such as service packs applied, device drivers installed, and motherboard or peripheral firmware versions.
- ◆ **Baseline data**: System configuration and performance data can be taken by an administrator at various times to record hardware and software changes. If baseline

Figure 1-4 The System log in the Event Viewer

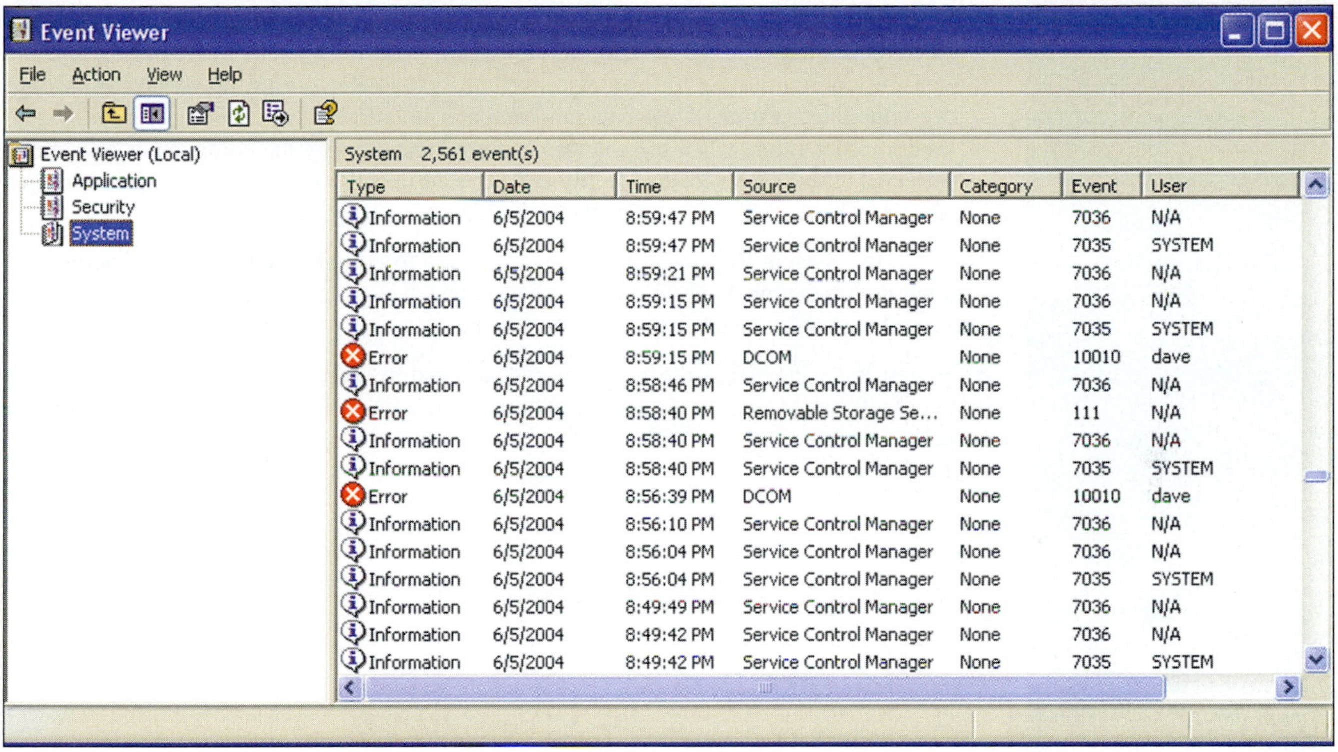

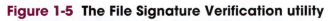

Event Viewer
File Action View Help
Event Viewer (Local)
Application
Security
System
System 2,561 event(s)
Type Date Time Source Category Event User
Information 6/5/2004 8:59:47 PM Service Control Manager None 7036 N/A
Information 6/5/2004 8:59:47 PM Service Control Manager None 7035 SYSTEM
Information 6/5/2004 8:59:21 PM Service Control Manager None 7036 N/A
Information 6/5/2004 8:59:15 PM Service Control Manager None 7036 N/A
Information 6/5/2004 8:59:15 PM Service Control Manager None 7035 SYSTEM
Error 6/5/2004 8:59:15 PM DCOM None 10010 dave
Information 6/5/2004 8:58:46 PM Service Control Manager None 7036 N/A
Error 6/5/2004 8:58:40 PM Removable Storage Se... None 111 N/A
Information 6/5/2004 8:58:40 PM Service Control Manager None 7036 N/A
Information 6/5/2004 8:58:40 PM Service Control Manager None 7035 SYSTEM
Error 6/5/2004 8:56:39 PM DCOM None 10010 dave
Information 6/5/2004 8:56:10 PM Service Control Manager None 7036 N/A
Information 6/5/2004 8:56:04 PM Service Control Manager None 7036 N/A
Information 6/5/2004 8:56:04 PM Service Control Manager None 7035 SYSTEM
Information 6/5/2004 8:49:49 PM Service Control Manager None 7036 N/A
Information 6/5/2004 8:49:42 PM Service Control Manager None 7036 N/A
Information 6/5/2004 8:49:42 PM Service Control Manager None 7035 SYSTEM

Figure 1-5 The File Signature Verification utility

File Signature Verification
To help maintain the integrity of your system, critical files have been digitally signed so that any changes to these files can be quickly detected.
Click Advanced to customize verification options.
Click Start to check for any system files that are not digitally signed.
Start
Close
Advanced

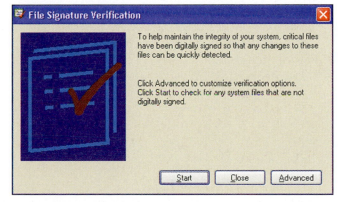

skill 6

Troubleshooting: Discovering the Problem *(cont'd)*

exam objective

Basic knowledge

overview

performance data exists, you can compare current performance parameters to your baseline data.

◆ **Examine previous backups:** Reviewing previous backups can help you isolate differences between the system configuration when the system was working and the current configuration. You can also use the System Restore utility to save or restore system states **(Figure 1-6)**. You can compare the current system state to past system states to determine when the changes occurred and identify the components or settings affected. The System Restore utility can be used to roll back operating system changes that may have made a system unstable, including Registry changes.

Although the System Restore utility cannot be used to completely rebuild a Windows XP installation, it is extremely useful for situations in which a new application or a system change has contributed to an unstable system state, but the system is still bootable.

After you have identified the problem and adequately described it, you should search technical information resources, such as Microsoft Knowledge Base articles, to determine if the problem is a known condition. A good starting point is the Windows XP Help and Support Center **(Figure 1-7)**.

Figure 1-6 **The System Restore tool**

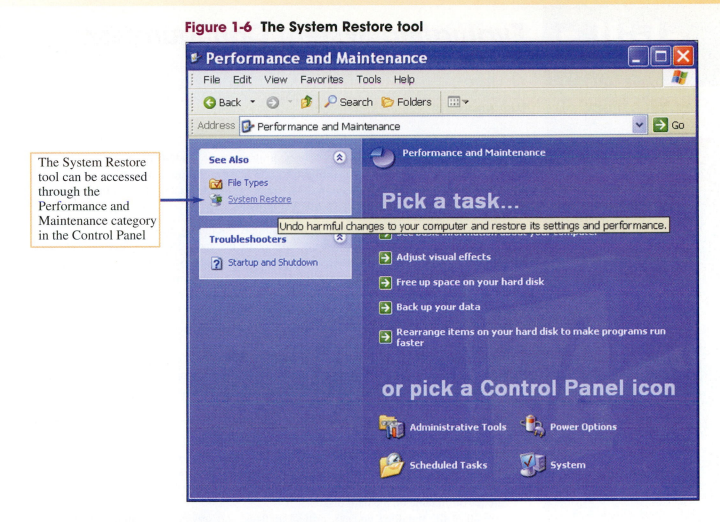

The System Restore tool can be accessed through the Performance and Maintenance category in the Control Panel

Figure 1-7 **The Windows XP Help & Support Center**

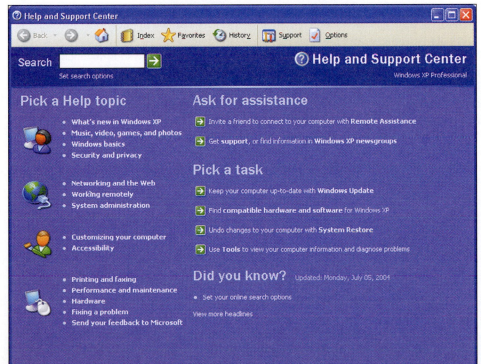

skill 7

Evaluating System Configuration

exam objective

Basic knowledge

overview

One of the underlying principles in troubleshooting and problem solving is that problems do not occur randomly but have a cause and effect. When you examine a problem, you should always examine the system configuration of the computer, especially if the problem can be isolated to a particular computer or group of computers.

You should examine and review any recent changes, including all hardware and software installed. Review existing baseline records. If there are no records, you may need to ask users, support technicians, or check the Device Manager and System Information console. The System Information console stores information about a computer, such as what devices are installed and loaded and the history of the drivers that have been installed on the computer. You can also access other troubleshooting tools from the System Information console.

Questions you should consider:

◆ Did problems occur shortly after the installation of an application or hardware device?
◆ Are any non–Plug and Play devices installed? Are they properly configured? Plug and Play is a standard that enables the operating system to automatically recognize a device when it is attached to a computer.
◆ Is there virus scanning software or a spyware scanner installed and does the virus scanning software include the latest updates? Before an upgrade to Windows XP you should update the virus definitions, run the virus scanning software, correct any problems, and then disable it if it is BIOS-based. BIOS-based virus scanning software can impede an installation because it will react badly when the Setup program accesses the partition table on the hard disk.
◆ Are all of the Windows updates, critical updates, and service packs up to date and configured appropriately for the system?
◆ If similarly configured computers in the organization are problem free when you are troubleshooting a problem compare the installed services and applications, software and hardware versions or revisions and system logs, if relevant.
◆ Which firmware version is being used? Firmware is operating system independent code that runs your computer and is executed before the operating system is loaded. Typically, if instability or Setup problems affect only a few Windows XP-based computers in your organization, you should check the motherboard and peripheral firmware. Peripheral firmware includes Small Computer System Interface (SCSI) adapters, CD and DVD-ROM drives, hard disks, video cards, and audio devices, which contain device-specific instructions that enable a device to perform specific functions, but are independent of the operating system. To check motherboard firmware, compare the Basic Input/Output System (BIOS) or Extensible Firmware Interface (EFI) version between working and non-working systems. If the versions differ, check the computer manufacturer's Web site for the latest firmware revisions. It might be, but rarely is, necessary to check peripheral firmware revisions for individual peripherals.

tip

Firmware is also known as the Basic Input/Output System (BIOS) on x86-based computers and internal adapters, and as Extensible Firmware Interface (EFI) on Itanium-based computers.

tip

EFI is an updated BIOS model, developed by Intel for Itanium based computers. The EFI interface is designed to be independent of any specific operating system platform so that it can concentrate on support for feature functionality rather than operating system compatibility. To read more about EFI, visit **http://developer.intel.com/technology/efi/**

how to

Check the firmware version on your computer.

1. Click **start** and then **Run** to open the Run dialog box.
2. Type **msinfo32** in the **Open** text box and press **[Enter]** to open the **System Information** console.
3. In the **Item** column, find **BIOS Version/Date (Figure 1-8)**.
4. Check the most recent version of firmware available on the computer manufacturer's Web site and compare it to the firmware you see here.

Figure 1-8 **Locating the firmware version on your computer**

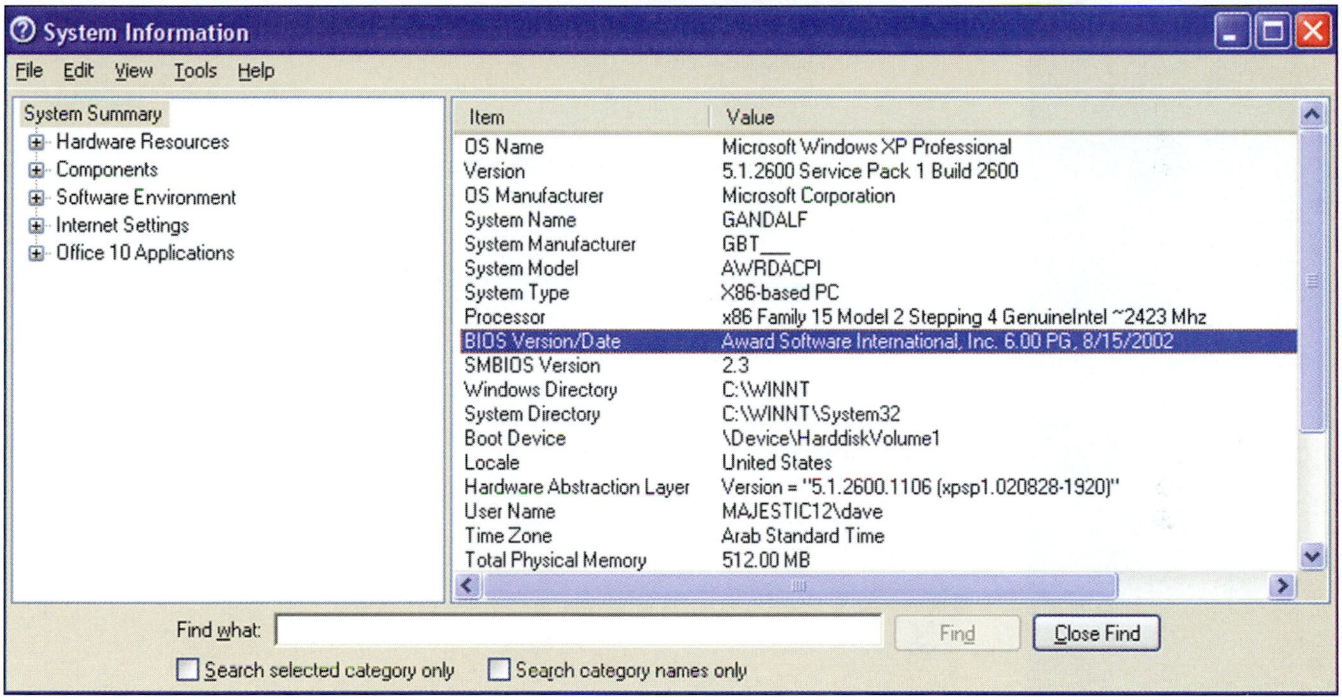

skill 7

Evaluating System Configuration
(cont'd)

exam objective

Basic knowledge

how to

Check the version of the operating system and the installed service packs.

1. Click **start** and then **Run** to open the **Run** dialog box.
2. In the **Open** box, type **winver**, and press **[Enter]** to open the **About Windows** dialog box (**Figure 1-9**).
3. Review and compare the operating system version and service pack number against the latest version available on the Microsoft Web site.

Figure 1-9 **The About Windows dialog box**

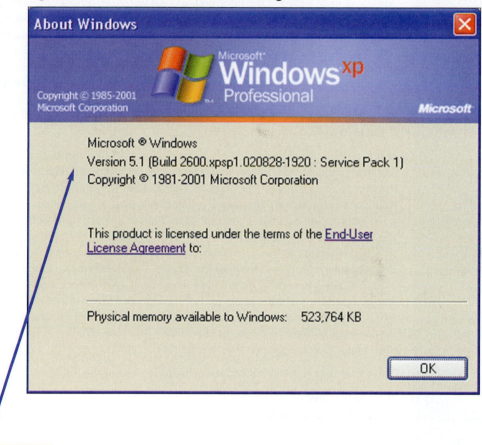

You can check the Windows version and the installed service packs here

skill 8   *Tracking Possible Solutions*

exam objective   **Basic knowledge**

overview

tip

Replacing defective hardware and diagnosing problems on a spare or test computer minimizes impact to the user due to the system being unavailable.

tip

You should always use the Device Manager to disable devices rather than physically removing a device. When you use the Device Manager, you do not risk damage to internal components.

tip

If you cannot use the Device Manager to disable a device, uninstall the device driver, turn off the computer, remove the part, and restart the computer.

After you have gathered the information necessary to describe a problem and determine any possible differences between a working system and a non-working system, you are ready to test some possible solutions. If you cannot locate information that applies to your problem or find more than one solution that may apply, try to further isolate your problem by grouping observations into different categories such as software-related symptoms (due to a service or application), hardware-related symptoms (by hardware types), and error messages. Prioritize your list by frequency of occurrence and eliminate symptoms that you can attribute to user error. This enables you to methodically plan the diagnostic steps to take, or to select the next solution to try.

When you troubleshoot hardware, the best approach is to start with a minimal configuration and then gradually add devices until you isolate the problem device. First, physically examine the components. A good approach to start with is to boot into Safe Mode, which loads a minimal configuration. Whether a problem persists in Safe Mode, or clears up, gives you good information on what to look for next. You can also try running diagnostic software from the manufacturer to verify a hardware failure. Another approach is to install the device on a different computer or use a device from a different computer to see if the problem is local to the computer configuration or to the device. Another thing to consider is driver changes. You may need to reverse them either using the Last Known Good Configuration (LKGC) startup option or you can use Driver Rollback in Safe Mode or normal mode. Booting into the LKGC is only helpful if the system will not boot at all after a driver change. After a computer is successfully booted into the graphical user interface (GUI), the LKGC is overwritten and you cannot return to the previous configuration.

You can isolate software related issues by trying one of the following:

◆ Close applications and processes one at a time, and observe the results. You can use Task Manager to end applications that have stopped responding.

◆ Temporarily disable services. A good tool, in addition to the Services Snap-in, is the System Configuration Utility (**Figure 1-10**). The System Configuration Utility can be used for a number of tasks, including stopping services. It is used to temporarily disable startup programs to alter how Windows XP Professional starts up. To use the System Configuration Utility, you must be logged on as an Administrator or a member of the Administrators group.

how to

caution

Do not initiate the rollback driver exercise unless told to do so by your instructor.

Rollback a driver.

1. Click **start** and then **Control Panel** to open the **Control Panel** window.
2. Double-click **System** to open the **System Properties** dialog box.
3. Click the **Hardware** tab (**Figure 1-11**).
4. Click Device Manager .
5. Select and expand the **Display Adapters** category.
6. Double-click your display adapter to open the **Properties** dialog box for the device.
7. Click the **Driver** tab. (**Figure 1-12**).
8. View the contents of the dialog box.
9. If you wanted to initiate the driver rollback process, you would click Roll Back Driver . **Do not** do so at this time.
10. Close all open windows.

Figure 1-10 The System Configuration Utility

The System Configuration Utility can be used for a number of tasks, including stopping services

System Configuration Utility

General | SYSTEM.INI | WIN.INI | BOOT.INI | Services | Startup

Startup Selection

○ Normal Startup - load all device drivers and services

○ Diagnostic Startup - load basic devices and services only

◉ Selective Startup

☑ Process SYSTEM.INI File

☑ Process WIN.INI File

☑ Load System Services

☐ Load Startup Items

◉ Use Original BOOT.INI   ○ Use Modified BOOT.INI

[Launch System Restore]   [Expand File...]

[OK]   [Cancel]   [Apply]   [Help]

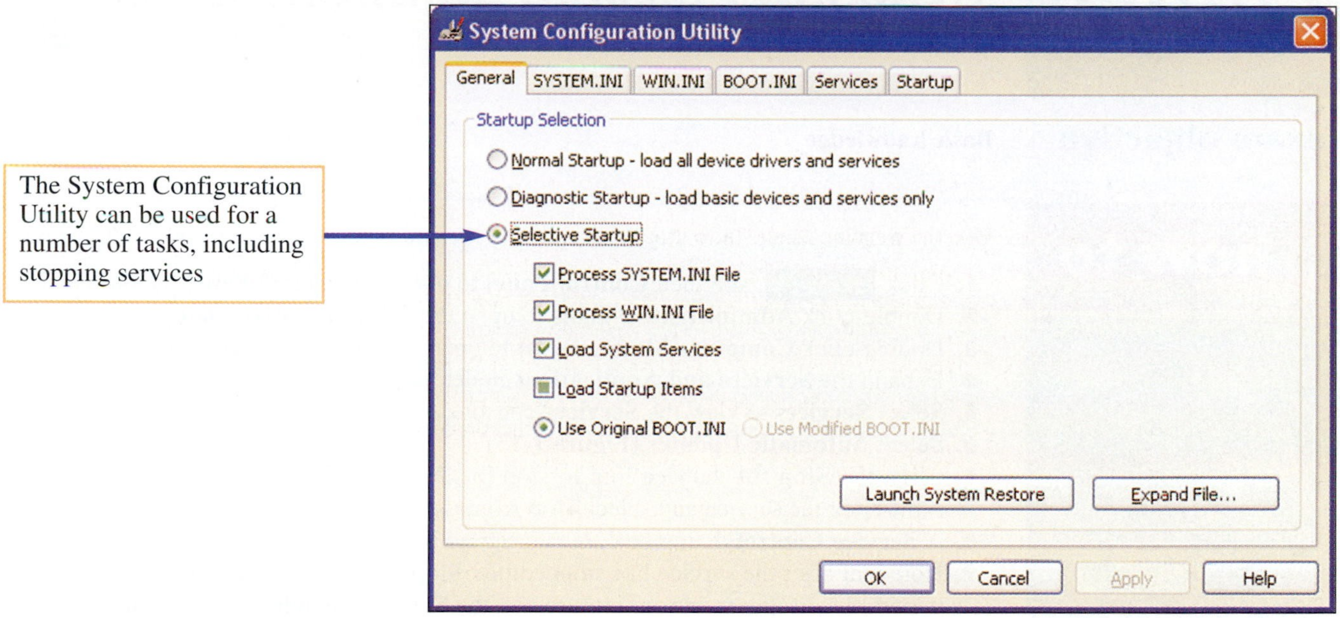

Figure 1-11 The Hardware tab in the Systems Properties dialog box

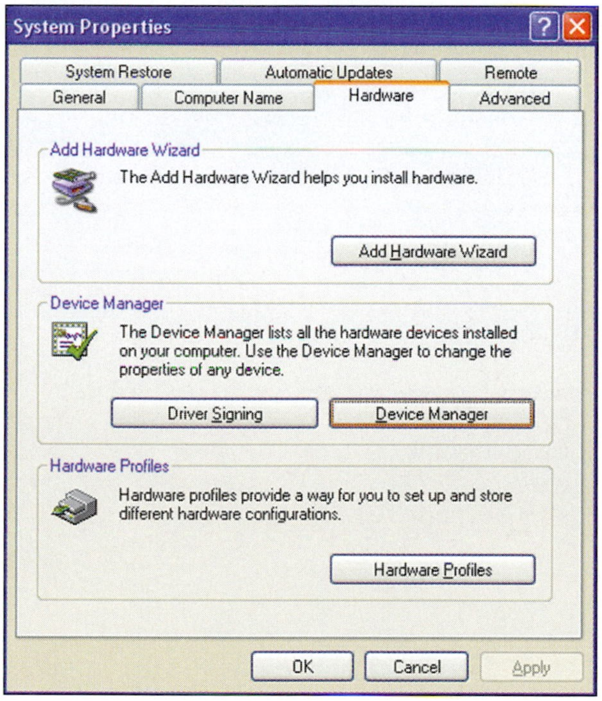

System Properties

| System Restore | Automatic Updates | Remote |
| General | Computer Name | Hardware | Advanced |

Add Hardware Wizard

The Add Hardware Wizard helps you install hardware.

[Add Hardware Wizard]

Device Manager

The Device Manager lists all the hardware devices installed on your computer. Use the Device Manager to change the properties of any device.

[Driver Signing]   [Device Manager]

Hardware Profiles

Hardware profiles provide a way for you to set up and store different hardware configurations.

[Hardware Profiles]

[OK]   [Cancel]   [Apply]

Figure 1-12 The Driver tab

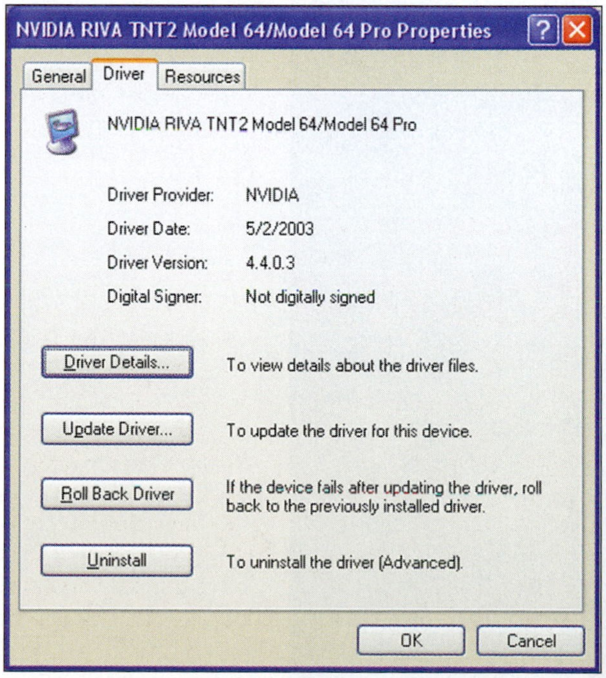

NVIDIA RIVA TNT2 Model 64/Model 64 Pro Properties

General | Driver | Resources

NVIDIA RIVA TNT2 Model 64/Model 64 Pro

Driver Provider: NVIDIA

Driver Date: 5/2/2003

Driver Version: 4.4.0.3

Digital Signer: Not digitally signed

[Driver Details...]   To view details about the driver files.

[Update Driver...]   To update the driver for this device.

[Roll Back Driver]   If the device fails after updating the driver, roll back to the previously installed driver.

[Uninstall]   To uninstall the driver (Advanced).

[OK]   [Cancel]

skill 8

Tracking Possible Solutions *(cont'd)*

exam objective

Basic knowledge

how to

Use the Services snap-in to stop a service.

1. Click **start**, and then **Control Panel** to open the **Control Panel** window.
2. Double-click **Administrative Tools** to open the **Administrative Tools** window.
3. Double-click **Computer Management** to open the **Computer Management** console.
4. Expand the **Services and Applications** node.
5. Select **Services** to view the **Services** console.
6. Select **Automatic Updates (Figure 1-13)**.
7. Click the **Stop the service** link to stop the Automatic Update service. You can also right-click the service and select **Stop** from the shortcut menu.
8. A **Service Control** dialog box and a progress bar open.
9. Note that after the service has stopped, the **Stop the service** and **Restart the service** hyperlinks disappear and are replaced by the **Start the service** link. Also note that the status of the service has changed to blank. **(Figure 1-14).**
10. To start the service, either click the **Start the service** link or right-click the service and select **Start**.
11. A **Service Control** dialog box and a progress bar open.
12. Make sure that the **Status** column now says **Started**.
13. Close the **Services** console.

Figure 1-13 Stopping a service

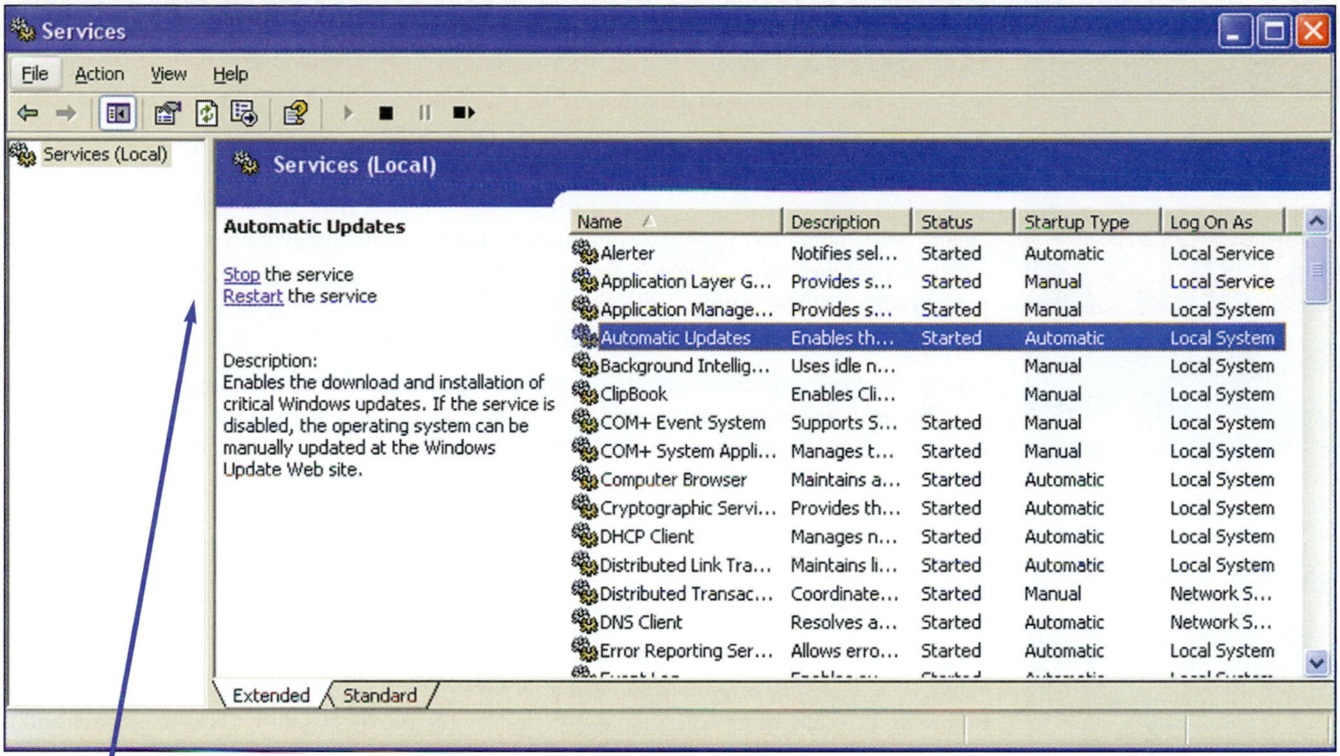

Click to stop the service

Figure 1-14 Changes to a service after it is disabled

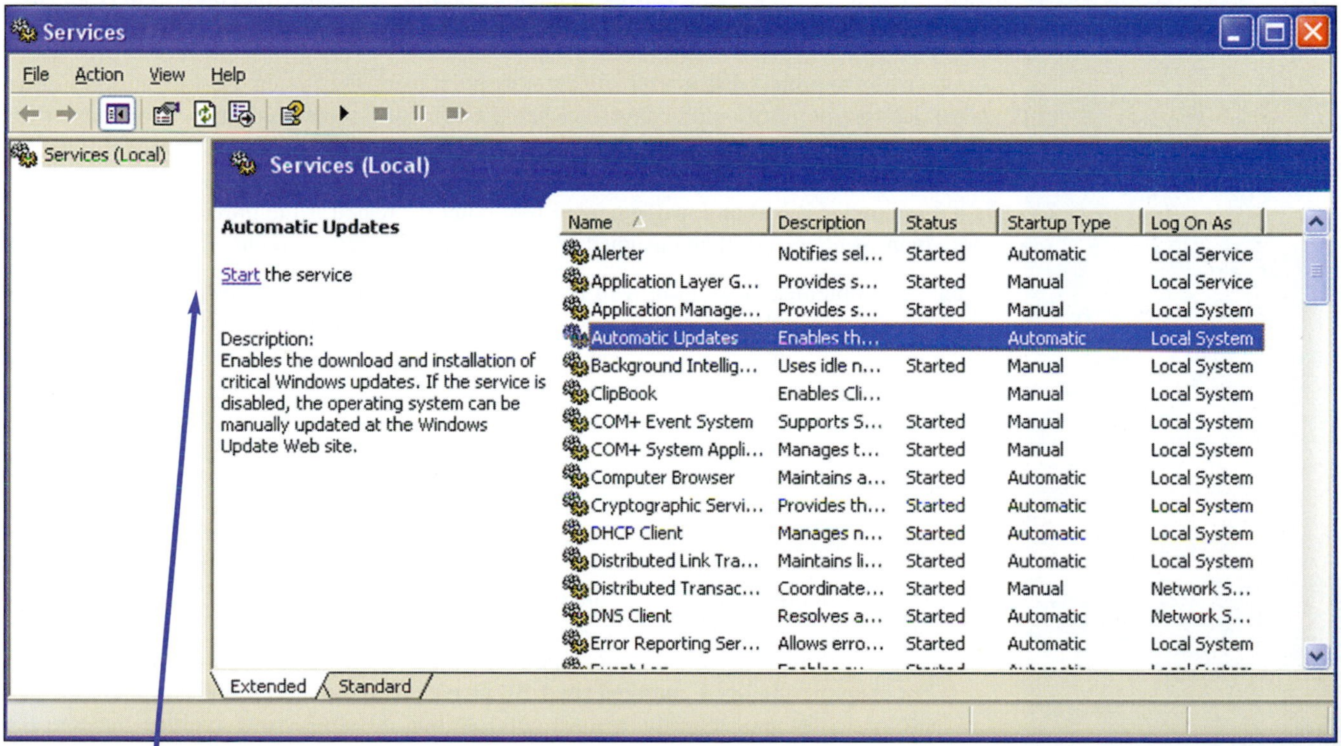

When a service is stopped, the Start the service link is displayed

skill 9

Executing a Plan and Checking the Results

exam objective   **Basic knowledge**

overview

Ideally, you should test potential solutions and have a contingency plan if these solutions do not work or if they have a negative impact on the computer. Before you implement a solution, you should carefully review your course of action. You can complicate a problem or the troubleshooting process by acting too quickly.

Potentially, the most devastating danger of all is not adequately identifying the problem. It is also the most common mistake made by troubleshooters. Simply stated, if you do not identify the problem adequately, you cannot solve it. If you do not make all essential observations before you respond, you can miss important information and spend considerable time pursuing the wrong course. To avoid such pitfalls, you must make sure that you record all data about the problem before you pursue a course of action. You must also make sure you that you check for other external causes, such as scheduled maintenance or known service outages. Never assume that past solutions will work again.

Always observe the effect of any changes you make to the system and record the changes you make. It is also very important to have a recovery strategy, such as a back-up return point. Before you try any other solution, always restore the previous settings. Do not troubleshoot several problems at once. Approach each problem separately. Never use incompatible or untested hardware and software and always thoroughly test new and replacement parts.

Even if you are completely confident that you know the cause of a problem you should take steps to safeguard both data and applications. If the system is bootable, before you try anything else that has the potential to harm the computer or the files on it, such as editing the Registry, you should back up system or application files using the Backup Utility (**Figure 1-15**). The Backup Utility also allows to you back up System State data.

Another way to protect data is to create a restore point using the System Restore utility (**Figure 1-16**). Restore points should be created when the computer starts and runs without any errors or problems. Restore points are snapshots of the data on a computer and the system state at a particular point in time. They are created by default every 24 hours if a Windows XP computer is left on, and if it is shut down, a new restore point is created if the previous restore point is more than 24 hours old. If an unsigned driver is installed, a restore point will also be created.

After you implement a solution, you must check the results. If everything works, you have successfully solved the problem your supported user encountered. If you could not solve the problem—or made things worse—don't despair. Implement your contingency plan, restore the system to its previous state if necessary, and reevaluate. If you have already formulated another plan to address unresolved issues, implement it.

tip

A System State backup is a collection of system-specific data maintained by the operating system that must be backed up as a unit. It is not a backup of the entire system. The System State data includes the Registry, COM+ Class Registration database, system files, boot files, and files under Windows File Protection.

how to

Create a new restore point in Windows XP.

1. Click ![start], point to **All Programs**, point to **Accessories**, point to **System Tools** and select **System Restore** to open the **System Restore Utility Wizard**.
2. On the **Welcome** screen, select the **Create a restore point** option button.
3. Click [Next >] to open the **Create a Restore Point** screen.
4. Type a description of the restore point in the **Restore point description** text box. (For example, **Before I changed the USB Driver**) (**Figure 1-17**). The date and time will automatically appear in the restore point so you do not have to include these in the description.
5. Click [Create]. After the new restore point is created, the **Restore Point Created** window opens.
6. Click [Close] to exit.

Figure 1-15 The Backup Utility Advanced Mode window

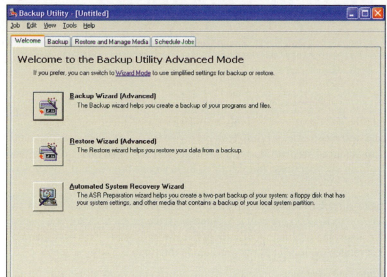

Figure 1-16 The System Restore utility

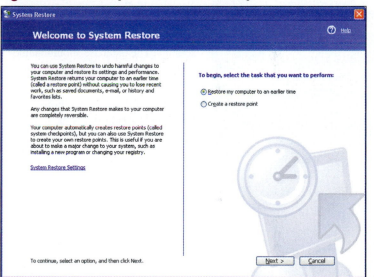

Figure 1-17 Naming the restore point

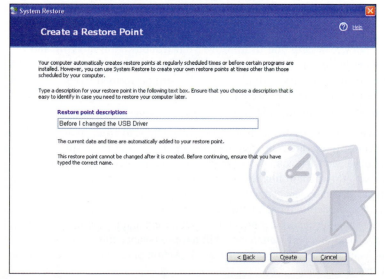

skill 10 *Taking a Proactive Approach*

exam objective Basic knowledge

overview

After you have expended time and effort to effectively troubleshoot a problem you will no doubt feel an understandable and deserved sense of pride. However, you must also make sure that all of that effort does not go to waste or have to be redone. After you have successfully finished troubleshooting a new problem, the first thing you should to do is write a brief description of what you did.

Furthermore, always make sure that you have documented the problem itself as well as the changes and the steps that you took along the way to troubleshoot the problem. After you resolve a problem, organize your notes and evaluate your experience. What lessons have you learned? Are there ways to avoid or reduce the impact of the problem in the future?

You should keep accurate and complete records of all steps and work done during the troubleshooting process. These records can be used to prevent redundant efforts, avoid fruitless procedures and highlight possible sources of preventative action.

You should also create a configuration management database. Microsoft and most professionals strongly encourage the establishment of a centralized database to record the history of changes, such as installed software and hardware, updated drivers, replaced hardware, and altered system settings. The database should include records that document the changes made, times and dates of changes, reasons for changes, who made the change, the effect of the change and any relevant additional information.

After you install new hardware or software, you should always update your baseline information. **Baseline information** is the documentation of the normal operating parameters for a computer. To detect atypical system behavior, you must first know what level of performance you have during normal usage and under typical workloads. In particular, you should establish baseline behavior when a computer first begins to run on the network and when the hardware or software configuration has been modified so that you can measure the effect made by the update. For example, to determine the baseline behavior for the processors, you can create a counter log in the Performance console (**Figure 1-18**), using the Processor-%Processing Time counter and the System-Processor Queue Length counter, which you should run for a few weeks to a month (**Figure 1-19**). However, you will want to set the log to record in samples, for example, at once per hour, if you are running the log for this long. Another good practice is to sample very frequently over specific key short periods of time, such as during morning logon, after lunch, etc. This way, at a later date when you make system modifications, you will have a benchmark range of values to evaluate against the new range of values you get after modification. These records can enable you to judge troubleshooting effectiveness. You can also use the data as the basis for troubleshooting procedure manuals and changes in policy for your organization.

A post-troubleshooting review can help you to improve your troubleshooting skills and the troubleshooting environment by identifying whether the changes improved (or worsened) the situation, what redundant or unnecessary activities, if any, were performed, what technical support resources were used and whether they were helpful, what other tools might have helped, and what lingering unresolved issues suggest the need for further root-cause analysis.

Another important component of your post-troubleshooting follow up is to write an **action plan**, which is a summary or report, to record your troubleshooting efforts and the results. Careful analysis of what you have done and what you have learned, either singly or collectively over time, will allow you to devise a set of relevant troubleshooting objectives and strategies that fits within your organization's configuration and management strategies. Does your troubleshooting suggest the need for an enterprise-wide deployment of the solution? What steps need to be taken? The corporate reality may be that a support technician will not have enough time to create these reports; however, this is the ideal. Support technicians will have to balance this ideal against the reality of having to close a certain number of cases per week. Action plans will reduce the time necessary to close future cases.

tip

When planning a configuration management database, keep in mind the need to balance scope and detail when deciding which items or attributes to track.

tip

If previous baseline information is not available, use System Information, Device Manager, the Performance tool, or industry standard benchmarks to generate data.

Figure 1-18 **The Performance console**

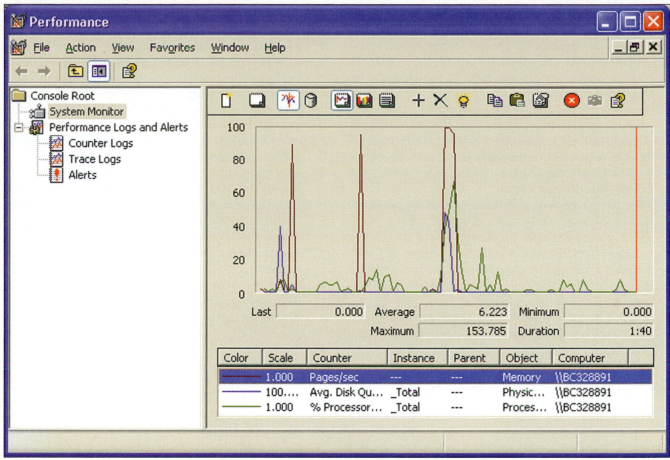

Figure 1-19 **Adding counters to create a baseline counter log**

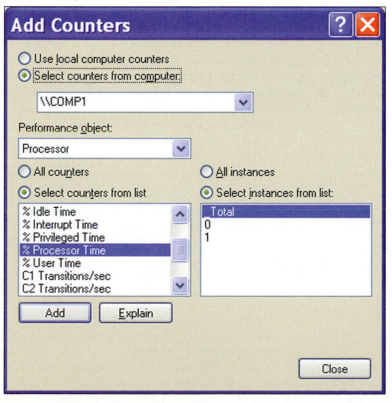

Summary

- Most organizations have a tiered support structure. It is important for the desktop support technician to determine when the problem needs to be escalated to the next level of support.
- Customer service skills are every bit as important as technical skills when it comes to solving user problems.
- Desktop support technicians may work in call centers or may be required to visit the desktops of users directly. In addition, understanding remote assistance software, will allow for better user support.
- The more advanced certifications that an individual holds, the more likely they are to perform at a higher level in a tiered support structure.
- Support technicians require the ability to work professionally and should have such skills as empathy, partnering, language skills, respect, resilience, follow-through, and a positive attitude.
- Users will fall into various categories depending upon their skill sets. It is important to determine whether a user is a novice, intermediate, or expert user in relation to the software with which they are having a problem.
- Beginning the troubleshooting process with a clear objective in mind will assist the desktop support technician in understanding when the problem has been successfully resolved.
- Error messages and system event logs provide significant information to the desktop support technician.
- Troubleshooting is the process of isolating the source of a problem and fixing it. Whether an issue stems from a physical, hardware, or a software problem, you must have a reliable troubleshooting plan. Guesswork and random solutions are unreliable and often unsuccessful.
- The Detect model is a troubleshooting model and strategy consisting of the following six steps: discover the problem, evaluate the system configuration, track possible solutions, execute a plan, check results, and take a proactive result.
- Typically, when you start troubleshooting a malfunctioning system the first thing you should consider is PHO: physical, hardware, operating system—the initial troubleshooting hierarchy. This means that you should check all of the physical issues first, the hardware issues second, and the operating system issues last.
- The main reason to use the PHO strategy is that it also follows the most generic to the most complex troubleshooting strategy recommended by most professionals in the IT field.
- Identifying (discovering) the problem is the first key step in troubleshooting. You cannot begin to solve the problem until you have learned as much as you can about the circumstances in which problems occur and become familiar with system behavior when issues arise.

- Some questions you should be asking include: Do error messages appear? Is there anything in the Event Viewer logs? Does the problem coincide with an application or activity? Do previous records exist for comparison? Is baseline information available? Does the problem seem related to user profiles? Does the problem seem network-related? Is incompatible or untested software or hardware installed? Are there backups to examine?
- After you have identified the problem and adequately described it, you should search technical information resources, such as Microsoft Knowledge Base articles, to determine if the problem is a known condition.
- Review the history of the computer to find out about recent changes, including all hardware and software installed.
- If baseline or change records exist, look for information about new devices, new applications, updated drivers, and change dates—as well as descriptions of the work done.
- If records are not available, you can query users and internal support personnel or use tools such as the Device Manager and the System Information console.
- You should also check firmware versions and compare current performance with baselines.
- After you observe the symptoms, check technical information sources, and review your system's history, you should be ready to test a possible solution based on the information that you have gathered.
- If you are unable to locate information that applies to your problem, or if you find more than one solution that applies, try to further isolate your problem by grouping observations into different categories such as software-related symptoms (due to a service or application), hardware-related symptoms (by hardware types), and error messages.
- Prioritize your list by frequency of occurrence and eliminate symptoms that you can attribute to user error. This enables you to methodically plan the diagnostic steps to take, or to select the next solution to try.
- Common pitfalls that you should avoid include:
  - Not identifying and documenting the problem adequately.
  - Not observing the effects of diagnostic changes.
  - Not documenting changes when troubleshooting.
  - Not adequately backing-up or preparing a restore point.
  - Not restoring a previous settings before trying something else.
  - Troubleshooting several problems at one time.
  - Using incompatible or untested hardware.
  - Failing to adequately test new and replacement parts.
  - Using incompatible software.
- Before you do anything that may potentially harm the computer or the files on it, such as editing the Registry,

you should back up critical system and application files and/or create a system restore point.

◆ You should also have a contingency plan in place in the event that your solution fails to resolve the problem.

◆ Always take a proactive approach to troubleshooting. This means that you must adequately document and routinely review the steps you take to troubleshoot problems. You can then combine information you gather while troubleshooting major and chronic problems to create a proactive plan to prevent or minimize problems for the long term.

Key Terms

Baseline information
Desktop support technician
Detect model
Expert user
Help desk

Intermediate user
Novice user
PHO (physical, hardware, operating system)
Remote assistance software

Root-cause analysis
Tiered support
Troubleshooting
Windows Backup
Windows Update

Test Yourself

1. Which of the following statements is true in reference to desktop support technicians? (Choose all that apply.)
   a. They are often senior management.
   b. They often work in a tiered environment.
   c. They are often the first line of connection between users and those that manage information technology.
   d. They require a broad base of knowledge relating to computer systems.

2. Which of the following will a desktop support technician not be required to work with?
   a. Operating systems
   b. Network hardware
   c. Database access
   d. Custom applications

3. Which of the terms below describe the practice of informing the persons you are helping about the progress being made and ensuring that anything you say you will do is documented, communicated, and completed?
   a. Follow-through
   b. Partnering
   c. Language skills
   d. Respect

4. Select the user category in which you would place a client if the client described his or her problem as follows: "Internet Explorer won't connect to the Internet, but I know I'm online because my e-mail works."
   a. Novice
   b. Intermediate
   c. Expert

5. In the troubleshooting acronym PHO, what does "P" stand for?
   a. Primary
   b. Protocol
   c. Physical
   d. Preliminary

6. The following types of logs can be found in the Event Viewer? (Choose all that apply.)
   a. System
   b. Driver
   c. Application
   d. Security

7. Which Windows XP feature enables you to recover from problems by reverting driver and Registry settings to those used during the last user session?
   a. Last Known Good Configuration
   b. Device driver rollback
   c. System Configuration Utility
   d. Baselining

8. To disable (stop) a service in Windows XP you can make use of which of the following methods? (Choose all that apply.)
a. System Configuration utility
b. Registry Editor
c. Services snap-in
d. Device Manager

9. Common pitfalls in troubleshooting include all of the following except:
a. Failing to record information before acting
b. Failing to disable the Alert service
c. Failing to check for scheduled maintenance events or known service outages
d. Assuming that past solutions will work again

10. Which tool allows you to review Windows XP to check for software not fully tested for compatibility with Windows XP or using unsigned drivers that can cause erratic behavior or instability?
a. System Configuration Utility
b. File Signature Verification utility
c. System Restore
d. Device Manager

11. Which of the following should be included in a configuration management database? (Choose all that apply.)
a. Changes made
b. Reasons for the changes
c. Users who made the changes
d. Positive and negative effects the changes had on system stability or performance

Projects: On Your Own

1. Research a recent computer problem you have had, or choose a common problem such as printing, at online help desks.
a. Open your Web browser.
b. Go to the Microsoft TechNet at **http://www.microsoft.com/technet**.
c. Type your problem, or "printing problem" in the TechNet search field. Explore the results.
d. Search for the same problem using the Google search engine at **http://www.google.com**.
e. Look for other online assistance. Search for computer help at Google or another search engine.

2. Research the different types of help desk software that are available, such as bug-tracking and customer service support software.
a. View online documentation for BugTrack at **http://www.ebugtrack.com**.
b. Type the search phrase "bug tracking software" into a search engine such as Google to find more examples.
c. View online documentation for CRMDesk at **http://www.crmdesk.com**.
d. Type the search phrase "help desk software" into a search engine such as Google.

Problem Solving Scenarios

You are working for Gideon Enterprises, a moderately large corporation that provided marketing support for several vineyards in the eastern New York state area. The company network is based on Windows Server 2003 and all workstations are standardized on a Windows XP Professional Service Pack 1 base. The company has installed a standard suite of applications on all computers in the company. The network uses TCP/IP exclusively. It is

8:00 AM on a Monday morning and you have just settled into your desk when your telephone rings. At the other end is a user named Helen who tells you, in a frantic tone of voice, "My computer isn't working and I have to make a presentation to the Board of Directors in one hour! I need my data. It was there Friday but now it's just disappeared on me." Explain the steps you would take to troubleshoot this problem. Which step would you take first?

Configuring and Troubleshooting the Operating System to Support Applications

As a Tier-1 desktop support technician, you will find yourself facing a multitude of problems. The problems can range from unlocking the taskbar so that a user can place it in a different place on the desktop, to configuring user's computers to support multiple languages. Each of these problems offers a unique opportunity for you to train, as well as assist, users in configuring their computers so they can perform at their optimum levels.

This lesson begins with a discussion on three common areas from which you are likely to receive support requests: the taskbar, the Start menu, and the notification area. Each will be discussed in detail and solutions to common questions will be provided.

Next, discussion turns to file associations. Every file created on a computer has an associated file extension. The file extension is used by the computer's operating system to determine which software program will be used to open the associated file. You will learn how to handle situations in which users need to re-establish file associations that have been changed by another program as well as how to add new file associations to support custom programs.

Skill 3 examines folder settings and provides you with insight into how you can configure the five different folder views (Thumbnails, Tiles, Icons, List, and Details), as well as set system-wide defaults for how all folders are viewed. You will also learn how to address user requests to view files that have been compressed/encrypted in a different color as well as how to make hidden files visible.

Skill 5 focuses on configuring regional options and multiple languages on Windows. The lesson also discusses common Windows XP troubleshooting tools. These include the System Configuration Utility (msconfig.exe), Chkdsk, Disk Defragmenter, System File Checker (sfc/scannow), and the System Information utility (msinfo32.exe).

The lesson concludes with a discussion on why it is important to keep Windows XP updated to protect against threats and vulnerabilities after its release.

Goals

In this lesson, you learn about how to customize the Start menu and taskbar, view and modify file associations, customize folders, configure regional and language settings, use Windows XP troubleshooting tools, and use Automatic Updates to protect against threats and vulnerabilities.

Lesson 2 Configuring and Troubleshooting the Operating System to Support Applications

Skill	Exam 70-272 Objective
1. Customizing the Start Menu, Taskbar, and Notification Area	**Resolve issues related to operating system features. Tasks include configuring operating system features and interpreting error messages.** **Resolve issues related to customizing the operating system to support applications.** Answer end-user questions related to customizing the operating system to support an application. Customize the Start menu and taskbar.
2. Working with File Associations	**Configure the operating system to support applications.** Answer end-user questions related to configuring the operating system to support an application. **Resolve issues related to operating system features. Tasks include configuring operating system features and interpreting error messages.** **Resolve issues related to customizing the operating system to support applications.** Answer end-user questions related to customizing the operating system to support an application.
3. Customizing Folder Settings and Fonts	**Resolve issues related to operating system features. Tasks include configuring operating system features and interpreting error messages.** Answer end-user questions related to customizing the operating system to support an application. **Resolve issues related to customizing the operating system to support applications.** Customize folder settings. Customize fonts.
4. Configuring Regional Options and Language Settings	**Resolve issues related to operating system features. Tasks include configuring operating system features and interpreting error messages.** **Resolve issues related to customizing the operating system to support applications.** Answer end-user questions related to customizing the operating system to support an application. Customize regional settings.
5. Using Windows XP Troubleshooting Tools	**Resolve issues related to operating system features. Tasks include configuring operating system features and interpreting error messages.** **Configure the operating system to support applications.** Answer end-user questions related to configuring the operating system to support an application.
6. Updating the Operating System	**Configure the operating system to support applications.**

Requirements

To complete this lesson, you will need administrative rights on a Windows XP Professional computer.

skill 1

Customizing the Start Menu, Taskbar, and Notification Area

exam objective

Resolve issues related to operating system features. Tasks include configuring operating system features and interpreting error messages.

Resolve issues related to customizing the operating system to support applications. Answer end-user questions related to customizing the operating system to support an application. Customize the Start menu and taskbar.

overview

tip

You cannot drag and drop icons into the notification area.

As a Tier 1 desktop support technician, you will have to address a variety of requests from users. Three very common requests have to do with areas of the operating system that users interact with the most: the taskbar, the Start menu, and the notification area (**Figure 2-1**).

The **taskbar** provides information regarding programs, files, and folders that are currently open or running on the computer. In Figure 2-1, the user has two programs (Microsoft Outlook and Microsoft PowerPoint) open. In addition to these programs, a file (salesfigures) and a folder (My Documents) are also open. To easily move between documents and programs on the taskbar, the user can either select the programs with a simple click of the mouse or use the [Alt]+[Tab] sequence. The **Start menu** provides access to other programs on the computer, documents that have been recently opened, and support tools, as well as many other items.

A third component shown in the bottom right of the figure is the **notification area**. The notification area was known as the system tray in previous versions of Windows. This area shows programs that are currently running in the background that are active but not seen by the user. This can include antivirus applications, messaging tools, third-party tools, or even icons for network connections. In many cases, the icon for the program is automatically added to the notification area when you install it. On other occasions, you may need to add or remove icons manually when requested by users. How this is accomplished depends upon the program you are using. For example, if you are running Norton AntiVirus 2005, the program automatically adds the Auto-Protect icon in the notification area during the installation process. The program also provides you with the ability to control whether or not the Auto-Protect icon shows up in the notification area through the **Show the Auto-Protect icon in the tray** option (**Figure 2-2**).

You can also add icons for network, dial-up, and wireless connections to the notification area. By adding icons for these types of connections, you can quickly gain access to information regarding connection status, connection speeds, and even access the connection's Properties dialog box. For example, the notification area in Figure 2-1 includes an icon for network connections that is shown as two computers. This does not appear by default but can be added by selecting the **Show icon in notification area when connected** option within the Properties dialog box of a local area connection. To do so, click Start, click Control Panel, and double-click **Network Connections**. Right-click the network connection you want to add to the notification area and select Properties on the menu. In the network connection's Properties dialog box, select the **Show icon in notification area when connected** check box (**Figure 2-3**).

By default, Windows XP displays icons for active programs in the notification area as well as urgent notifications and, in turn, hides inactive icons. Inactive icons can be viewed by selecting the program in the Customize Notifications dialog box, and changing its notification behavior to Always show, as discussed below (**Figure 2-4**). Although the notification area shown in Figure 2-1 takes up only a small amount of space on the taskbar, it can increase in size very quickly as more programs are added to the computer. If you want to minimize the area taken up by these icons, you can customize the notification behavior of programs within the notification area: First, right-click an empty area on the taskbar and select Properties. Make sure the **Hide inactive icons** check box is selected and then click the Customize button. In the **Customize Notifications** dialog box, you can reduce the number of icons in the notification area by modifying their behavior. Options include **Hide when inactive**, **Always hide**, and **Always show (Figure 2-5)**. For icons that you do not want to show in the notification area, select either **Hide when inactive** or **Always hide** and then click OK.

Figure 2-1 **Start menu, taskbar, and notification area**

Figure 2-2 **Selecting the Show the Auto-Protect icon in the tray option**

Start menu

Taskbar

Notification area

Show Auto-Protect icon option

Figure 2-3 **Adding an icon for a network connection in the notification area**

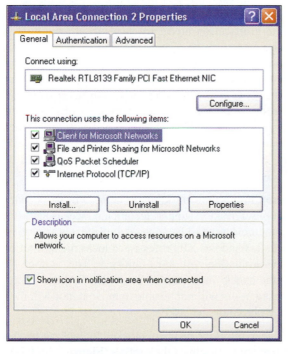

Figure 2-5 **Behavior options for icons in notification area**

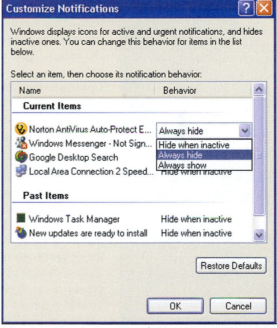

Figure 2-4 **Hidden icons in notification area**

Click to show hidden icons

skill 1

Customizing the Start Menu, Taskbar, and Notification Area (cont'd)

exam objective

Resolve issues related to operating system features. Tasks include configuring operating system features and interpreting error messages.

Resolve issues related to customizing the operating system to support applications. Answer end-user questions related to customizing the operating system to support an application. Customize the Start menu and taskbar.

overview

Although hiding inactive programs can assist you in controlling the space taken up by the program's icons in this area, it does not disable the program. In other words, the programs are still running in the background and consuming computer resources. There may be situations where you will need to temporarily disable a program. For instance, antivirus software is designed to keep unauthorized programs from reading and writing to certain Windows files. Some applications need the ability to read/write to these same files during the installation process to complete their installation successfully. If you install an application that must write to the Windows files, you may need to disable any Auto-Protect feature of the antivirus program temporarily. In the case of Norton AntiVirus 2005, you can do this by right-clicking the antivirus icon in the notification area and selecting **Disable Auto-Protect (Figure 2-6)**. You will then be presented with a dialog box to determine how long you want to disable the feature **(Figure 2-7)**. The options available for manipulating programs in the notification area vary from program to program, but generally include the ability to disable, open, and exit. Some programs, such as Microsoft's Windows Messenger, offer additional capabilities, such as sending instant messages and signing in and out.

As you read the information in the previous paragraph, you may have noticed the word *temporary* was used. By temporarily disabling a program, you can free computer resources, reduce the number of icons shown in the notification area and/or ensure a trouble-free program installation. Unfortunately, when you restart the computer or launch the program, the icon will be added to the notification area once again. If you want to make sure the program's icon is removed from this area and does not return, you can use the System Configuration Utility (msconfig.exe). This does not remove the program itself from the computer but instead removes its icon from the notification area, which ensures it is not running in the background and consuming resources. If the user launches the program from the Start menu, it will once again be added to the notification area. If the application is never used, consider removing it using the program's uninstall feature or via Add or Remove Programs applet in the Control Panel.

All users have their own special way of setting up their desktops to help them work more efficiently. One of the most common questions a desktop support technician faces is also one of the easiest to address and that is, "I cannot move my taskbar! I want to place it at the top of my desktop instead of the bottom." By default, Windows XP Professional locks the taskbar so that it cannot be moved. To get around this limitation, you must unlock it. This is done by right-clicking the taskbar and removing the check mark next to **Lock the Taskbar** in the pop-up menu. As long as the taskbar is locked, users will not be able to move it, nor will they be able to move any toolbars that have been placed on the taskbar.

Although it is not very obvious, it is possible to tell if the taskbar is locked by looking for the handles, a series of small vertical dots, in front of the toolbars themselves **(Figure 2-8)**. Users may complain about the taskbar getting in the way of an application or document they are using or voice frustration at it periodically appearing and reappearing when they place their mouse cursor over it. These issues can easily be addressed by making configuration changes in the **Taskbar and Start Menu Properties** dialog box. This is accessed by right-clicking a blank area of the taskbar and selecting **Properties**. If the user is complaining about a taskbar that is appearing and reappearing, remove the check mark from the **Auto-hide the taskbar** check box on the Taskbar tab. If the user is voicing a concern about the taskbar being in the

Figure 2-6 Disabling Auto-Protect for Norton AntiVirus

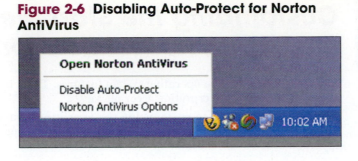

Figure 2-7 Selecting the duration for which Auto-Protect will be disabled

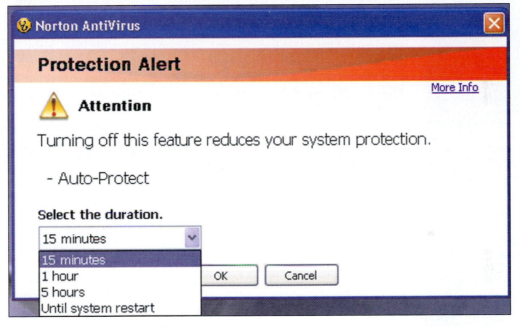

Figure 2-8 Toolbar handles indicate taskbar is not locked

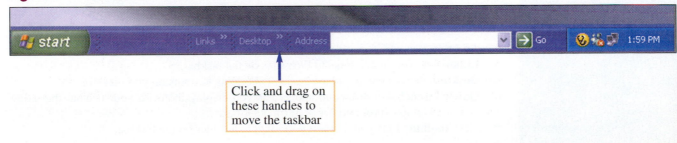

Click and drag on these handles to move the taskbar

skill 1

Customizing the Start Menu, Taskbar, and Notification Area *(cont'd)*

exam objective

Resolve issues related to operating system features. Tasks include configuring operating system features and interpreting error messages.

Resolve issues related to customizing the operating system to support applications. Answer end-user questions related to customizing the operating system to support an application. Customize the Start menu and taskbar.

overview

way when using their applications, remove the check mark from the **Keep the taskbar on top of other windows** check box.

As personal computers have become more powerful, users are able to take advantage of these powerful systems to run multiple programs simultaneously while keeping several files and folders open. There can be so many items open that the taskbar doesn't have enough space remaining to display them all. To compensate, the taskbar provides up and down arrows which allow the user to view the folders/files/programs that it cannot display (**Figure 2-9**). To minimize the space taken up, you can configure the taskbar to automatically group files opened by the same program into a single button. By clicking this button, the user can access the file he or she wants, or by right-clicking the button, close all the documents. The end result is a more organized taskbar that is less cluttered. To group program file icons, right-click a blank area on the taskbar and select Properties on the pop-up menu. On the Taskbar tab, in the Taskbar and Start Menu Properties dialog box, select the **Group similar taskbar buttons** check box (**Figure 2-10**) and click OK. The items on the taskbar are then grouped according to their relevant applications (**Figure 2-11**). If you want to close all files that are in the group, just right-click the Microsoft Word icon and select **Close Group** on the pop-up menu.

Another way to improve the end user's computing experience is to take advantage of Quick Launch. **Quick Launch** allows you to bypass the Start menu to find and launch your most frequently used programs. It can also be used to launch folders as well. To make Quick Launch show up, right-click a blank area of the taskbar, point to **Toolbars**, and then click **Quick Launch**. Quick Launch will be visible next to the Start button (**Figure 2-12**). In the figure, icons for Internet Explorer, Microsoft Outlook, Show Desktop, and Windows Media Player are present. These were added automatically by the programs when they were installed. You can remove icons from the Quick Launch by right-clicking the program's icon and selecting **Delete** on the pop-up menu. This removes only the program's icon and not the program itself. If you want to add icons to the menu, you first locate the program's executable, by using Windows Explorer, accessing it via the Start menu, or looking in All Programs on the Start menu. You can then drag the icon directly to the Quick Launch area and an icon for the program will be created in the Quick Launch. To add an icon for Help and Support (the Help and Support program provides access to help topics, tutorials, and other support service) using the All Programs option on the Start menu, click **Start** and then right-click the Help and Support link on the Start menu. While holding down the right mouse button, drag it to the Quick Launch area. Release the mouse button and select **Create Shortcuts Here** on the pop-up menu. The Quick Launch area should appear. To launch the Help and Support program, just click its icon.

There is also an assortment of toolbars that can be added to the taskbar that can make the user computing experience more efficient. These can be viewed by right-clicking a blank area of the taskbar and pointing to **Toolbars (Figure 2-13)**. The following provides a brief overview of each:

- ◆ **Address**: Lets you to enter a Web address to go to a Web page you specify.
- ◆ **Links**: Lets you to add links to Web sites on the taskbar.
- ◆ **Desktop**: Allows you to open a menu of shortcuts to items on your desktop.
- ◆ **Quick Launch**: As discussed above, lets you display icons on your taskbar that allow you quickly open programs or perform other tasks.
- ◆ **New Toolbar**: Lets you to place a shortcut to a folder on the taskbar.

tip

You can also drag an icon to the Quick Launch area and select Copy on the pop-up menu.

tip

You can also click the Help and Support link and drag it directly to the Quick Launch area.

Figure 2-9 Viewing hidden items on the taskbar

Click these arrows to view additional files or programs

Figure 2-10 Grouping similar taskbar buttons

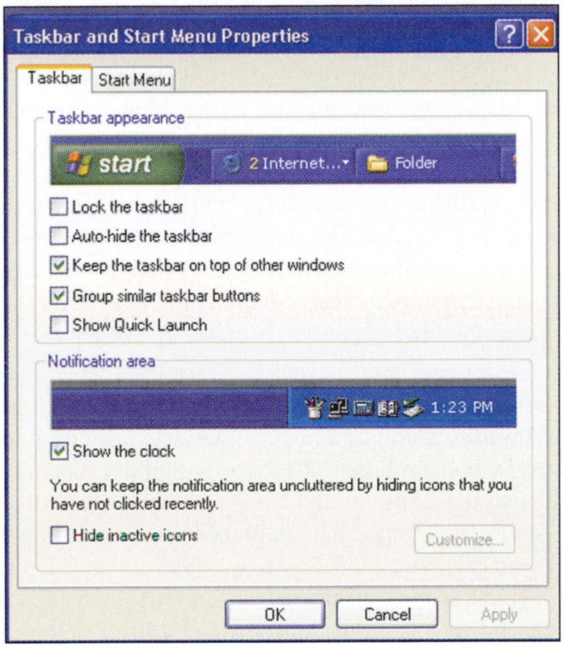

Figure 2-11 Taskbar redesigned by using grouping function

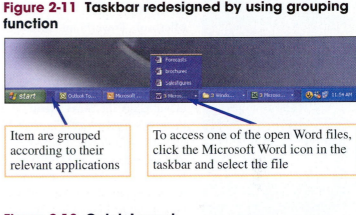

Item are grouped according to their relevant applications

To access one of the open Word files, click the Microsoft Word icon in the taskbar and select the file

Figure 2-12 Quick Launch

Quick Launch

Figure 2-13 Adding toolbars to taskbar

Frequently used programs

Pinned programs

Figure 2-14 Start menu

skill 1

Customizing the Start Menu, Taskbar, and Notification Area (cont'd)

exam objective

Resolve issues related to operating system features. Tasks include configuring operating system features and interpreting error messages.

Resolve issues related to customizing the operating system to support applications. Answer end-user questions related to customizing the operating system to support an application. Customize the Start menu and taskbar.

overview

Now that you have a better idea of how to work with and troubleshoot the taskbar and the notification areas, let's move to the Start menu.

The Start menu **(Figure 2-14)**, can be customized in several different ways. In the bottom left of the Start menu, six programs are displayed. (Microsoft Word, Command Prompt, Microsoft PowerPoint, Microsoft Excel, MSN Explorer, and Windows Media Player). This area of the Start menu is reserved for frequently used programs. The list will change as programs are opened and closed. It is possible for a program to disappear from the list if it has not been used in awhile. The default setting is to display six programs, but it can be increased or decreased as follows. First, right-click the taskbar and click Properties from the pop-up menu. Click the **Start Menu** tab in the Taskbar and Start Menu Properties dialog box, and then click **Customize (Figure 2-15)** to open the **Customize Start Menu** dialog box. Enter the number of programs you want to display, for example seven, in the **Number of programs on Start menu** spin box **(Figure 2-16)**.

In situations where users want to be able to launch their favorite programs from the Start menu, they can choose the Pinning option. **Pinning** a program involves creating a shortcut to it in the upper left of the Start menu. If you refer back to Figure 2-14, you will notice there are already two items pinned there by default: Internet Explorer and Microsoft Outlook. Unlike the frequently used programs area of the Start menu, items that are pinned remain until they are removed. For example, a Web designer who uses Microsoft FrontPage might choose to pin the program's icon to the Start menu for quick access. To do so, click Start, point to All Programs, right-click Microsoft FrontPage, and select Pin to Start menu **(Figure 2-17)**. An icon for Microsoft FrontPage should appear in the pinned area of the Start menu. To remove a pinned item, just right-click the item on the Start menu and select **Unpin from Start menu**.

The Start menu can also be further customized to control how programs are displayed, how it behaves when a program is installed, and what happens when a user moves the mouse over a menu item. To do so, right-click the taskbar and then click Properties. Select the Start Menu tab in the Taskbar and Start Menu Properties dialog box. Click Customize and then select the **Advanced** tab **(Figure 2-18)**. From here, you can decide whether to open menus when the user pauses on a menu item, highlight programs that have recently been installed, and control how items on the Start menu behave. For example, if you select the **Display as a link** option under **Control Panel**, when a user selects the Control Panel icon, a new window will open displaying the contents of the Control Panel **(Figure 2-19)**. If you choose the **Display as a menu** option. when a user selects the Control Panel icon, a pop-up list of its contents will appear **(Figure 2-20)**. If you do not want the Control Panel icon to appear on the Start menu, select **Don't display this item.**

You can also control whether or not documents that have been recently opened are visible on the Start menu. If you select the **List my most recently opened documents** check box on the Advanced tab, an icon for the **My Recent Documents** folder will be added to the All Programs submenu, as shown in **Figure 2-21**. To remove this listing, remove the check mark from the check box.

Windows XP also allows users to use the Classic Start menu. This menu has the same look as earlier releases of Microsoft Windows operating systems. It is typically used in situations where a company or user has recently upgraded to Windows XP and wants to minimize the learning curve by working with a familiar Start menu setup. In these types of situations, you will need to understand how to access and configure this menu type.

tip

You can reorder items in the All Programs submenu by right-clicking an item and selecting **Sort by Name.**

tip

You can remove items from the frequently used area of the Start menu by right-clicking and selecting **Remove from this list.**

tip

Items can also be pinned to the Start menu by dragging and dropping their shortcut to the pinning area.

Figure 2-15 **Customizing the Start menu**

Figure 2-16 **Selecting the number of programs to display on the Start menu**

Figure 2-17 **Pinning a program to the Start menu**

Figure 2-18 **Customize Start Menu dialog box**

Figure 2-19 **Control Panel configured to display as link**

Figure 2-20 **Control Panel displayed as a menu**

Figure 2-21 **Configuring display of recent documents**

skill 1

Customizing the Start Menu, Taskbar, and Notification Area *(cont'd)*

exam objective

Resolve issues related to operating system features. Tasks include configuring operating system features and interpreting error messages.

Resolve issues related to customizing the operating system to support applications. Answer end-user questions related to customizing the operating system to support an application. Customize the Start menu and taskbar.

overview

On the Start Menu tab of the Taskbar and Start Menu Properties dialog box, select the **Classic Start menu** option and then click **Customize** to open the Customize Classic Start Menu dialog box. Here, you can customize the Start menu using the buttons shown in **Figure 2-22**. **Add** allows you to create shortcuts by specifying the location of programs, files, and folders. **Remove** allows you to remove an item from the Start menu. **Advanced** allows you to search for an item to add or remove by using Windows Explorer. **Sort** allows you to rearrange items on the Programs menu and **Clear** removes the listing of recently accessed documents, programs, and Web sites. Items under the **Advanced Start menu options** section can be added or removed from the Start menu by either adding or removing the associated check mark.

how to

Remove a third party tool (in this case, Google Desktop Search) using the System Configuration Utility.

1. Click **start** and then click **Run**.
2. In the Run dialog box, type **msconfig** and click **OK**.
3. When the System Configuration Utility appears, select the **Startup** tab (**Figure 2-23**). In the figure, you can see there are five programs designed to automatically launch when the computer is started: ccApp and UsrPrmpt are associated with Norton AntiVirus; msmsgs is the executable for the Windows Messenger service; Google Desktop is the program you want to remove from the notification area; and Microsoft Office (osa.exe) is a program that launches common Microsoft Office components that help speed up the launching of Office programs.
4. Clear the check box next to the Google Desktop startup item to keep it from starting the next time you start the computer.
5. Click **OK** and then select **Restart** when prompted.
6. When the computer is restarted, you will be prompted to confirm the changes you made (**Figure 2-24**). Click **OK** to confirm your changes.
7. If you look in the notification area, you will notice that the icon for the Google Desktop Search program is no longer present (**Figure 2-25**).

Figure 2-22 Customize Classic Start Menu dialog box

Customize Classic Start Menu

Start menu

You can customize your Start menu by adding or removing items.

Add...
Remove...
Advanced
Sort

To remove records of recently accessed documents, programs, and Web sites, click Clear.

Clear

Advanced Start menu options:

- [ ] Display Administrative Tools
- [ ] Display Favorites
- [ ] Display Log Off
- [x] Display Run
- [x] Enable dragging and dropping
- [ ] Expand Control Panel
- [ ] Expand My Documents

OK   Cancel

Figure 2-23 Startup tab in the System Configuration Utility dialog box

System Configuration Utility

General | SYSTEM.INI | WIN.INI | BOOT.INI | Services | Startup

Startup Item	Command	Location
ccApp	"C:\Program Files\Com...	HKLM\SOFTWARE\Microsoft\Windows\CurrentVer...
UsrPrmpt	C:\Program Files\Com...	HKLM\SOFTWARE\Microsoft\Windows\CurrentVer...
msmsgs	"C:\Program Files\Mes...	HKCU\SOFTWARE\Microsoft\Windows\CurrentVer...
Microsoft Office	C:\PROGRA~1\MICR...	Common Startup
GoogleDesktop	"C:\Program Files\Goo...	SOFTWARE\Microsoft\Windows\CurrentVersion\Run

Enable All   Disable All

OK   Cancel   Apply   Help

Figure 2-24 Verifying Configuration Change

System Configuration Utility

You have used the System Configuration Utility to make changes to the way Windows starts.

The System Configuration Utility is currently in Diagnostic or Selective Startup mode, causing this message to be displayed and the utility to run every time Windows starts.

Choose the Normal Startup mode on the General tab to start Windows normally and undo the changes you made using the System Configuration Utility.

- [ ] Don't show this message or launch the System Configuration Utility when Windows start:

OK

Figure 2-25 Notification area

Google Desktop Search icon

After using the System Configuration Utility

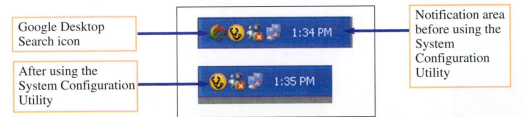

Notification area before using the System Configuration Utility

skill 2 *Working with File Associations*

exam objective

Configure the operating system to support applications. Answer end-user questions related to configuring the operating system to support an application.

Resolve issues related to operating system features. Tasks include configuring operating system features and interpreting error messages.

Resolve issues related to customizing the operating system to support applications. Answer end-user questions related to customizing the operating system to support an application.

overview

Every file created on a computer has an associated file extension. The file extension is used by the computer's operating system to determine which software program will be used to open the associated file. For example, when a user double-clicks a file with the .doc extension, Windows Explorer launches the program that uses the .doc extension (Microsoft Word in this case) and then tells it to open the file for you to view.

As more programs are installed on the computer, it is quite common to find that multiple programs can be used to open the same file. For example, Windows Media Player, installed by Windows XP during the initial installation, launches when you open .mpeg (Moving Picture Experts Group) files. If later you decide to download and install RealPlayer, another popular media player available on the Internet, you will be prompted to associate the .mpeg files with its program.

Another example would be a graphics file with the .jpeg (Joint Photographic Experts Group) file extension. For most users, having the file opened by the Windows Picture and Fax Viewer might be appropriate. Others may prefer to view the file within a Web browser window. A person working in a Graphics department may prefer the .jpg file be opened with a graphics editor, such as Adobe Photoshop. When these situations arise, you must map the file extension to the appropriate program. To modify files with the .jpeg extension to automatically open with the Microsoft Paint program instead of the Windows Picture and Fax Viewer, open the Control Panel window and double-click **Folder Options**. In the **Folder Options** dialog box, click the **File Types** tab (**Figure 2-26**). Under the **Registered file types** section, scroll down if necessary and select the JPEG extension. In the **Details for 'JPEG' extension** section, you will notice the file is configured by default to be opened by the Windows Picture and Fax Viewer. Now, click the Change button. The **Open With** dialog box opens. Select **Paint**, as shown in **Figure 2-27**, and click OK. If you look closely, you will notice the programs are categorized into **Recommended Programs** and **Other Programs** sections. Programs that have been identified by the operating system as capable of opening the particular file type are listed under the Recommended Programs section. Programs that are shown under the Other Programs section are those that are installed on the computer and may or may not be compatible with the file extension in question.

Figure 2-28 displays the results of the change made. Unless it is changed manually or a user allows a program installed to change the file associate, every time the user selects a file with the .jpeg extension, Paint will be launched to view it.

In situations where the file only needs to be opened with specific program every once in a while, you will need to take a different approach. Instead of mapping the file association to a specific program as just described, you will need to show the user how to use the **Open With** option. For example, if the user normally views files with the .bmp (bitmap) extension using the Windows Picture and Fax Viewer but would like to occasionally edit the files using Paint, this can be accomplished by locating the file using Windows Explorer, right-clicking the file and selecting **Open With** on the shortcut menu (**Figure 2-29**), and then selecting the Paint program.

tip

An excellent resource for identifying unknown file extensions can be found at http://www.filext.com.

Figure 2-26 File Types tab

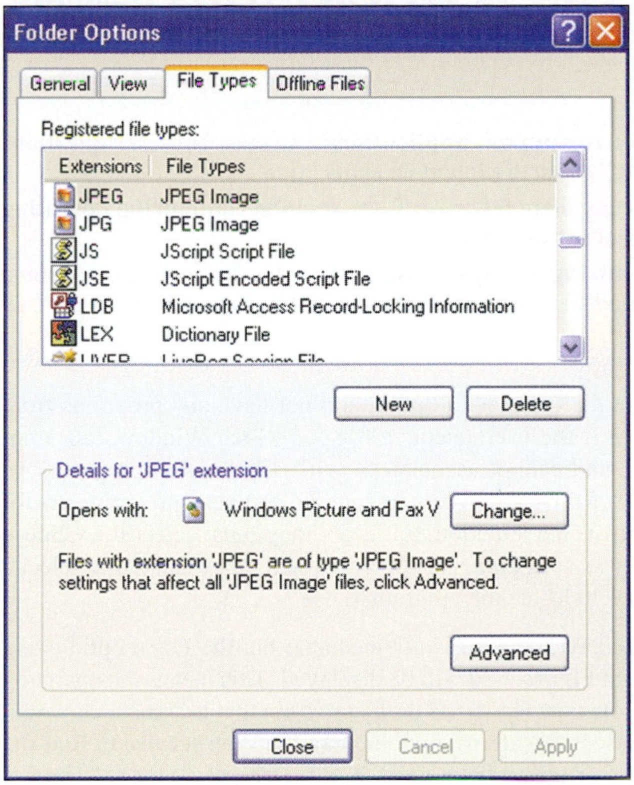

Folder Options

General | View | File Types | Offline Files

Registered file types:

Extensions	File Types
JPEG	JPEG Image
JPG	JPEG Image
JS	JScript Script File
JSE	JScript Encoded Script File
LDB	Microsoft Access Record-Locking Information
LEX	Dictionary File
LIVER	LiveReg Session File

New | Delete

Details for 'JPEG' extension

Opens with: Windows Picture and Fax V | Change...

Files with extension 'JPEG' are of type 'JPEG Image'. To change settings that affect all 'JPEG Image' files, click Advanced.

Advanced

Close | Cancel | Apply

Figure 2-27 Selecting Paint as the default program for an extension

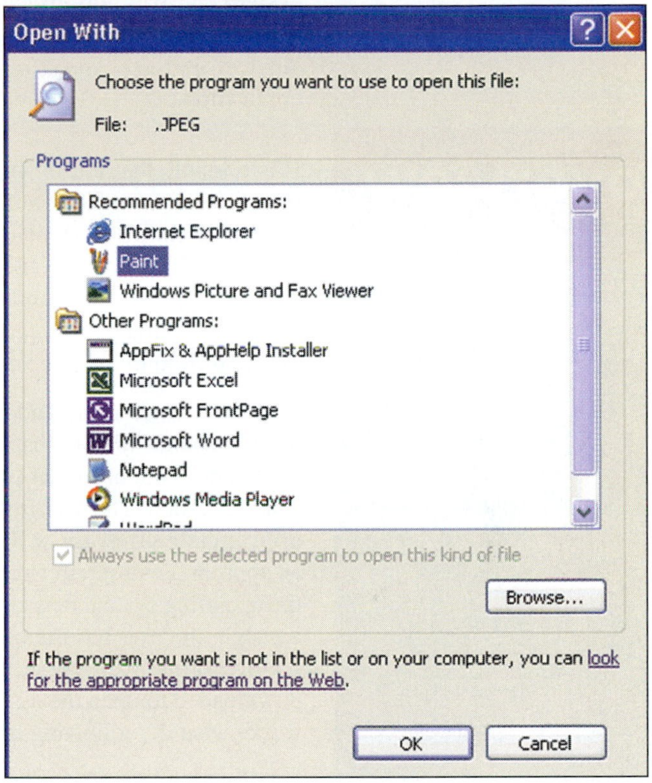

Figure 2-28 Paint program associated with JPEG file extension

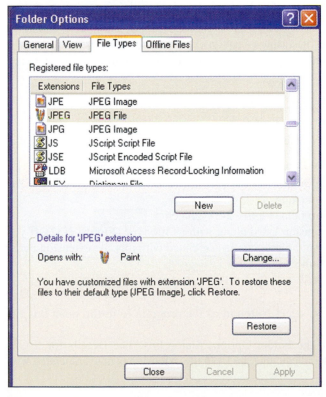

Figure 2-29 Using the Open With option

skill 2

Working with File Associations (cont'd)

exam objective

Configure the operating system to support applications. Answer end-user questions related to configuring the operating system to support an application.

Resolve issues related to operating system features. Tasks include configuring operating system features and interpreting error messages.

Resolve issues related to customizing the operating system to support applications. Answer end-user questions related to customizing the operating system to support an application.

overview

It is possible that a user might use the Open With option and not have any programs from which to choose. This can happen if the user selects a file for which Windows does not recognize the file extension type and cannot associate it with an installed program. An example might include a file used by a program written by internal company programmers for a custom application. To deal with such a situation, tell users they must select the **Choose Program** option, which can also be seen in **Figure 2-29**. From there, they can either select a program from those listed or browse to locate the program to use.

If a user selects a file and the Open With option is not available but the Open option is, a message box similar to that shown in **Figure 2-30** will be displayed. This means the operating system does not have that specific file type registered or the program that is associated with it is not installed. The user is then presented with two options: **Use the Web service to find the appropriate program** or **Select the program from a list**. The latter requires the selection of an appropriate program from a list of installed programs. If the Web service option is selected, the operating system first checks for the file association information locally. If it does not find a match, the user has the option to look for more information on Microsoft's **Windows File Associations** Web page. From there, the user can determine which program can be downloaded to open the associated file type. For more detailed discussion of how this service works, visit the following address:

http://www.microsoft.com/technet/prodtechnol/winxppro/maintain/xpmanaged/09_xpfil.mspx.

In situations where you have a file type with which Windows is not familiar, you can add the new file extension, as detailed in the following How To exercise. For example, you may be running a program that creates log files using a custom extension, such as .lgz. You know the log files can be viewed easily with Notepad, but Windows does not automatically associate the files with Notepad.

tip

Using the Windows file association Web service requires Internet connectivity.

how to

To associate the .lgz extension with Notepad.

1. Click [start], click **Control Panel**, and then select **Folder Options**.
2. In the **Folder Options** dialog box, select the **File Types** tab and click [New]. The **Create New Extension** dialog box opens.
3. Enter **.lgz** in the **File Extension** field (**Figure 2-31**) and click [OK].
4. You can now see the LGZ extension listed along with its file type (**Figure 2-32**). If you look closely, you will notice that no program is associated with this file extension under the **Details for 'LGZ' extension** section. Click [Change...].
5. When the Windows message box appears, choose **Select the program from a list** and click [OK].
6. In the **Open With** dialog box, select **Notepad** as the program to use to open this file (**Figure 2-33**.)
7. Click [OK] to return to the Folder Options dialog box. The Details for 'LGZ' extension section should now indicate that the LGZ file extension is now associated with Notepad (**Figure 2-34**).

Figure 2-31 Entering new file extension

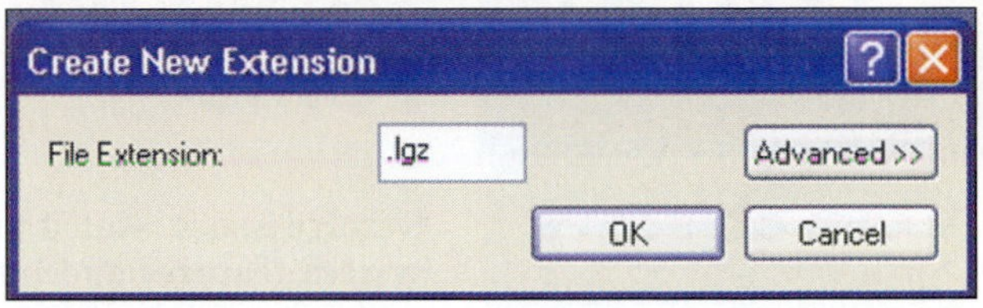

Figure 2-30 Windows message box

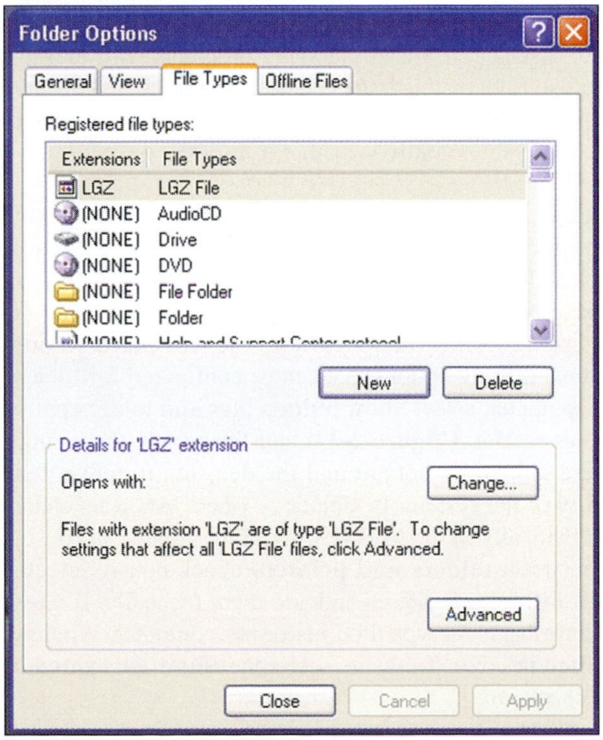

Figure 2-33 Selecting Notepad to open LGZ files

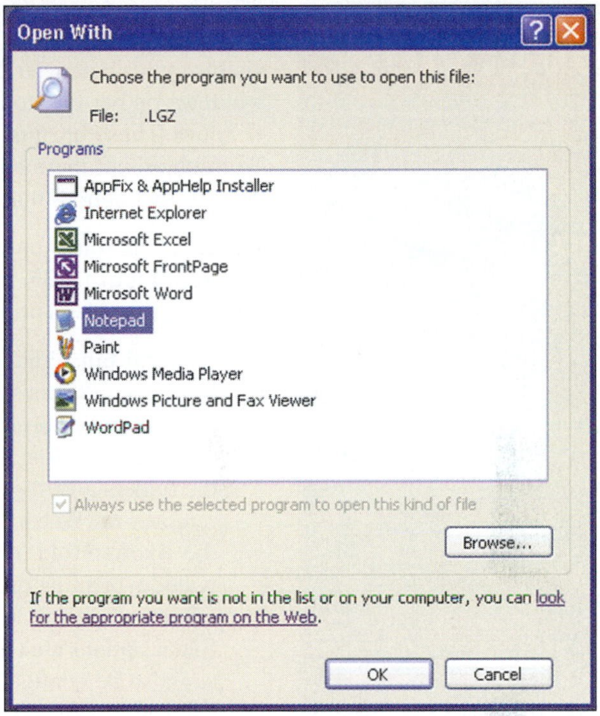

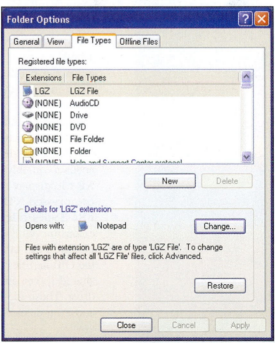

Figure 2-32 Results of adding new file extension (LGZ)

Figure 2-34 File extension (LGZ) associated with Notepad

skill 3 · *Customizing Folder Settings and Fonts*

exam objective

Resolve issues related to operating system features. Tasks include configuring operating system features and interpreting error messages. Answer end-user questions related to customizing the operating system to support an application.

Resolve issues related to customizing the operating system to support applications. Customize fonts. Customize folder settings.

overview

Jason, one of the more advanced users in your network, would like to make system files visible on his computer. Emma has come to you with a request to reduce the number of open windows on her desktop. It seems that every time she clicks on a folder, it opens in a new window. These are just a few of the issues facing users that you will need to address. To troubleshoot these and other folder-related problems, you need a basic understanding of the different options that can be configured for folders in Windows XP.

To access the folder options, double-click **Folder Options** in the Control Panel window. As shown in **Figure 2-35**, there are four tabs: General, View, File Types, and Offline Files. The following provides a brief discussion of the folder configuration options on each of these tabs:

tip

Before troubleshooting folder problems, consider restoring them to their default settings. This is accomplished in the Folder Options General tab.

◆ **General tab**: When the **Show common tasks in folders** option in the Tasks section of the General tab is selected, links appear in the left pane of the folder window that allow the user to perform maintenance tasks on files and folders. Such tasks include moving, copying, renaming, sharing, e-mailing, printing, and deleting files and folders. This gives the folders a Web page look and feel. Selecting the **Use Windows classic folders** option removes the Web look and replaces it with the classic Windows folder appearance. Under the **Browse folders** section, the folder can be configured to either open in the same window or in its own window. For instance, if a user is having problems with multiple windows opening when she clicked on folders, this issue can be resolved by making sure folder options are configured to **Open each folder in the same window**. Folder behavior can also be configured on the General tab to control whether a folder is opened with a single or double click.

◆ **View tab**: In the **Folder views** section, you can configure the default view for displaying folders. For example, if a user is working in Windows Explorer and prefers to use one of the five different folder views, such as Thumbnails, Tiles, Icons, List, and Details (**Figure 2-36**), he or she can apply the preferred view to all folders on the computer using the steps detailed in the How To exercise following this Overview. The **Advanced settings** section of this tab provides additional display options that can be configured for folders. To make system files visible on a computer, select **Show hidden files and folders** option under the **Hidden files and folders section (Figure 2-37)** and then apply the change. Keep in mind that system files are hidden by default and the decision to make them visible can compromise the stability of the system. In situations where you want shared folders and printers to appear automatically in the My Network Places folder, make sure the **Automatically search for network folders and printers** check box is selected (**Figure 2-37**). If it is not, the user will have to search and add them manually. If a user needs to quickly see which files have been encrypted on his or her computer, Windows XP can display these files in a different color. To do so, select the **Show encrypted or compressed NTFS files in color** check box.

◆ **File Types tab**: Configuration information in this tab allows you to associate file extensions with applications programs, as discussed in Skill 2.

◆ **Offline Files tab**: Configuration information in this tab allows you to take advantage of the Offline Files feature. By configuring Offline Files, a user is able to copy files from a shared folder on the network marked available for offline use to his or her local hard drive. These files are placed in a folder named Offline Files and can be read, modified, and even deleted while the user is offline. Once the user reconnects to the network, the

Figure 2-35 Folder Options dialog box

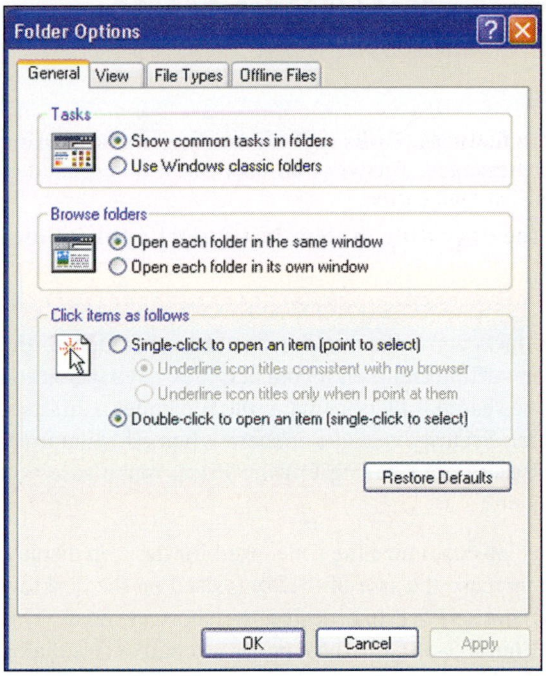

Figure 2-36 Folder view options

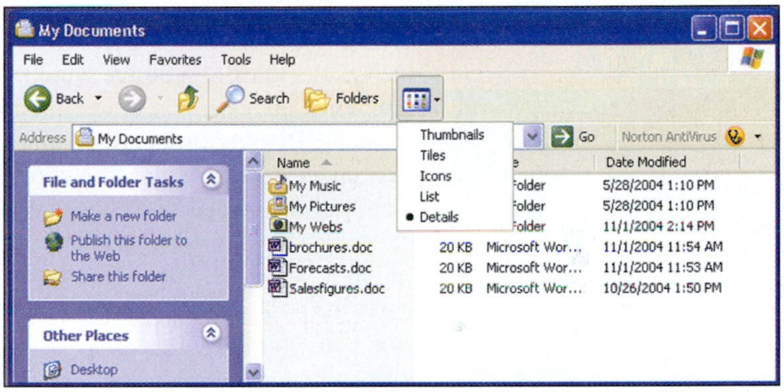

Figure 2-37 Show hidden files and folders

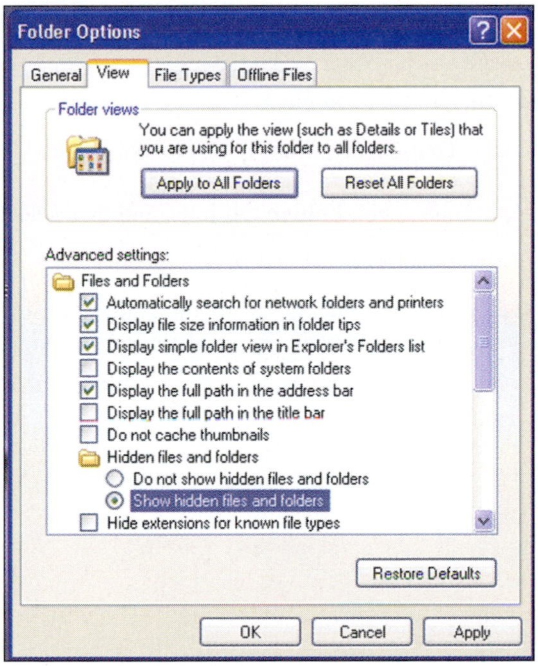

skill 3

Customizing Folder Settings and fonts (cont'd)

exam objective

Resolve issues related to operating system features. Tasks include configuring operating system features and interpreting error messages. Answer end-user questions related to customizing the operating system to support an application.

Resolve issues related to customizing the operating system to support applications. Customize fonts. Customize folder settings.

overview

files that have been changed are synchronized with those in the shared folder on the server. If two users modify the same file offline and then reconnect, they have the option of either replacing the existing file in the shared folder or saving the file under a different name while saving it to the shared folder. Security is also a concern when allowing users to take files off company premises. Before configuring Offline Files, make sure you understand the company's security policies.

In addition to customizing folders, you can also customize the fonts used for desktop display, such as the titles of message windows. To increase the size of the fonts used on the desktop, right-click anywhere on the desktop itself, and select Properties on the shortcut menu. This opens the **Display Properties** dialog box (**Figure 2-38**). On the Appearance tab of this dialog box, under **Font size**, you can choose to display normal, larger, or extra large fonts. Larger fonts can enable people with visual disabilities to view and navigate the desktop more easily. For some display items, you can specify additional font properties by clicking the Advanced button to open the **Advanced Appearance** dialog box (**Figure 2-39**). Under **Item**, you can select the desktop item you wish to modify and then apply various settings to that item. If you select an item that displays text, such as **Active Title Bar**, you will be given the option to select a font and its size, color, and style.

how to

Apply a folder view as the default view for all folders on a computer.

1. In **Windows Explorer**, set the desired view (Thumbnails, Tiles, Icons, List or Details) in a selected folder.
2. On the Windows Explorer menu bar, select **Tools**, click **Folder Options**, and then select the View tab.
3. On the View tab, click [Apply to All Folders].
4. A message box will appear, stating that you are about to set all the folders on the computer to match the current folder's view settings. To confirm the change, click [Yes].

caution

The Apply to All folders button is disabled if you access the Folder Options dialog box from the Control Panel.

Figure 2-38 **Appearance tab in the Display Properties dialog box**

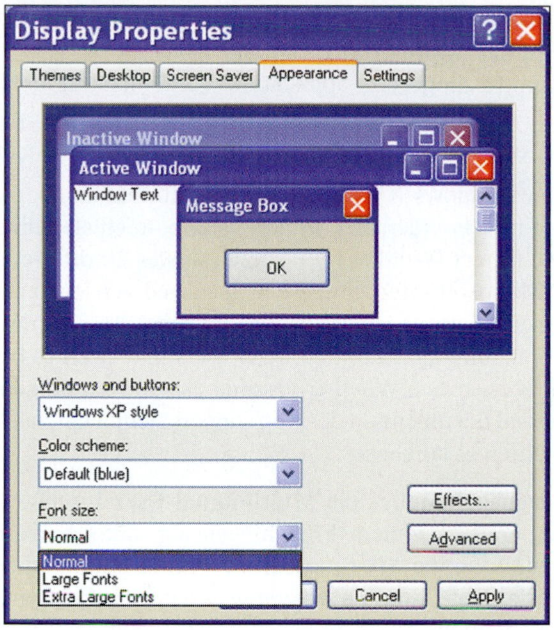

Figure 2-39 **Advanced Appearance dialog box**

skill 4

Configuring and Troubleshooting Regional Options and Language Settings

exam objective

Resolve issues related to operating system features. Tasks include configuring operating system features and interpreting error messages.

Configure the operating system to support applications. Answer end-user questions related to customizing the operating system to support an application. Customize regional settings.

overview

Configuring **regional options** controls how Windows XP and applications format numbers, currencies, dates, and times. Language settings provide users with the ability to create, edit, and print documents in several languages. In fact, Windows XP supports over 20 different language versions in addition to English. Microsoft refers to these as localized versions and includes options such as Japanese, French, German, and Spanish, to name just a few. In multilingual companies, it is possible that communication between users may need to be done across different languages to conduct business. Whether sending e-mail to a branch office in South America or exchanging internal documents, a desktop support technician must understand how to allow users to work in different languages.

The ability to switch the user interface language requires the **Multilingual User Interface (MUI) pack** which is available only to corporate customers through licensing contracts with Microsoft. In other words, you cannot purchase the MUI pack from a retail outlet. As a support technician, having the MUI pack is a tremendous advantage in situations where you have users who work in multiple languages. It allows the technician to go to a computer that has its system menus and dialogs displayed in Spanish, for example, and change it to English while troubleshooting. Once the problem is fixed, the user interface can be switched back to Spanish. It is very common for users who have changed their language settings to expect to see the menus and dialog boxes in the new language. This is not possible without first purchasing and installing the MUI pack.

Regional options can be changed by opening the Control Panel window, and double-clicking Regional and Language Options to open the Regional and Language Options dialog box, and then making sure that the Regional Options tab is selected (**Figure 2-40**). English is the default setting for most users' computers in the United States. Let's assume the user needs to be able to view numbers, currency, and date and time formats in Swedish. Select Swedish in the drop-down box and review the information under the Samples section to see how the information is changed. As you can see in **Figure 2-41**, the currency has now changed from United States dollars to the Sweden Kronor (kr). You can also see that both the long and short date format has also been changed. The United States short date format (11/4/2004) appears as 2004-11-04 and the Long date (Thursday, November 04, 2004) appear as den 4 november 2004.

It is possible to further customize the regional options by selecting the Customize button on the Regional Options tab. This may be necessary if the user wants to be able to make additional changes to the default settings in regard to numbers, currency, time and date settings. For example, the user may prefer to view the short date as 04-11-04 instead of 2004-11-04 or prefer to add the AM and/or PM symbols to the current time.

For users who need to read and type in another language, you will need to install the language(s) on their computer. For example, let's say that an English speaking supervisor needs to be able to both read and write documents in Italian in order to communicate with his Italian-speaking employees. To do so, open the **Regional and Language Options** dialog box, click the Languages tab, and then click **Details**. The **Text Services and Input Languages** dialog box opens. Click **Add** to open the **Add Input Language** dialog box. In the Input language text box, select the language the user wants to use, in this case Italian (Italy). For Keyboard layout/IME, select **US** and click OK. This identifies the keyboard type you are using to enter information with (**Figure 2-42**). Then click OK twice to close the two dialog boxes and apply the changes.

tip

To be able to check spelling and grammar of text, you must have the Microsoft Office XP Proofing Tools kit available from Microsoft. For more information, go to the following Web address: **http://www.microsoft.com/office/previous/xp/multilingual/prooftools.asp**

Figure 2-40 Regional Options tab

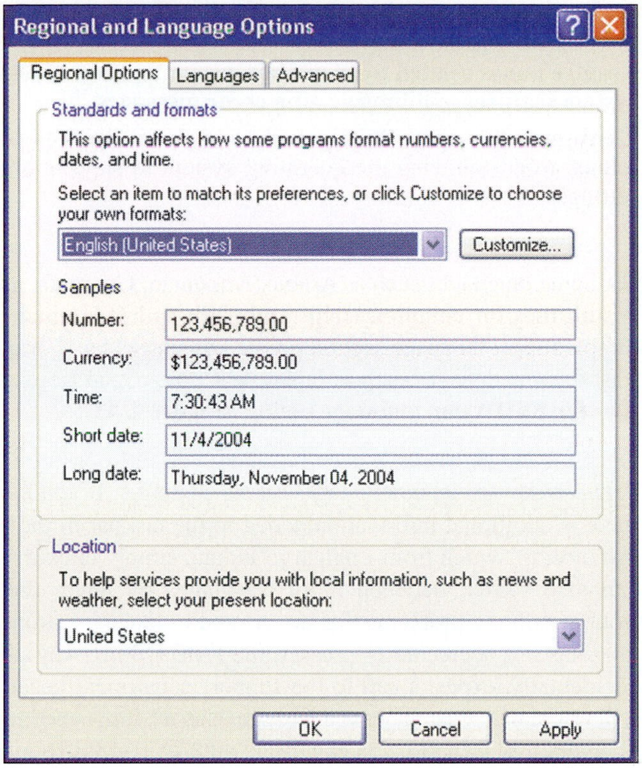

Figure 2-41 Selecting Swedish as the regional option

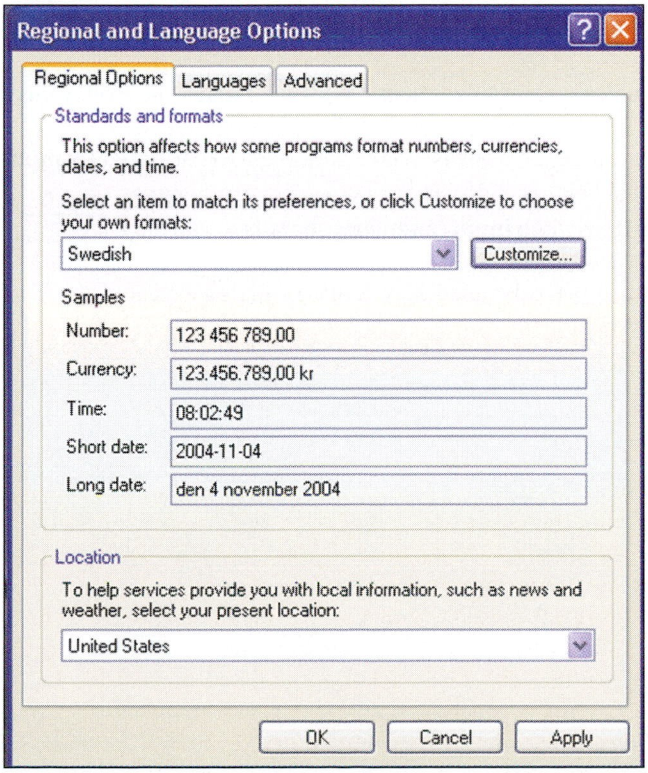

Figure 2-42 Input language/keyboard layout

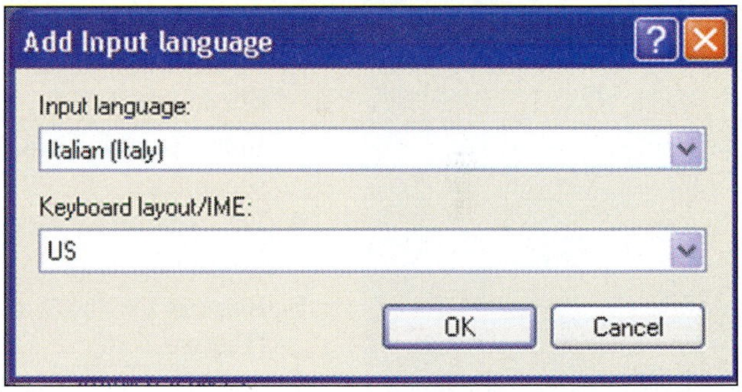

skill 4

Configuring and Troubleshooting Regional Options and Language Settings (cont'd)

exam objective

Resolve issues related to operating system features. Tasks include configuring operating system features and interpreting error messages.

Configure the operating system to support applications. Answer end-user questions related to customizing the operating system to support an application. Customize regional settings.

overview

For some languages such as Arabic, Armenian, Georgian, and Hebrew, you need to select the **Install files for complex script and right-to-left languages (including Thai)** option in the Supplemental language section on the Languages tab. For users who need to type and read in East Asian languages such as Japanese, Chinese, and Korean, make sure you select the **Install files for East Asian language** option. (**Figure 2-43**)

Once the languages have been installed, you must ensure that the user knows how to switch between the two input languages on his computer. If you look at **Figure 2-44**, you will notice there is additional information added to the taskbar in the form of a language indicator. For instance, to switch from English to Italian, simply click the indicator and select **Italian**. You can also switch between input languages by using the left [**Alt**]+[**Shift**] keys. When troubleshooting problems that are related to language issues, always check to make sure the user has not accidentally pressed the [Alt]+[Shift] key combination. If the user does this accidentally, expect a call to the support department because keys pressed on the keyboard will not match what they expect to see. Use the language indicator to reset the input language. To avoid this scenario, you can disable the [Alt]+[Shift] option by following the steps below.

tip

Installing East Asian files requires approximately 230 MB of hard disk space. Only use it if necessary to support the user.

how to

Disable the [Alt]+[Shift] command used for switching between languages.

1. Click **start**, point to **Control Panel,** and click **Regional and Language Options**.
2. In the **Regional and Language Options** dialog box, make sure the Languages tab is selected and click **Details...** .
3. In the **Text services and input languages** box, select **Key Settings...** under the **Preferences** section.
4. The **Advanced Key Settings** dialog box opens. Make sure the **Switch between input languages** action is highlighted (**Figure 2-45**) and select **Change Key Sequence...** .
5. Remove the check mark from the **Switch input languages** check box and click **OK** (**Figure 2-46**).
6. Click **OK** twice to close the Advanced Key Settings dialog box and the Text Services and Input Languages box.

Figure 2-43 Languages tab

Figure 2-44 Language Indicator on taskbar

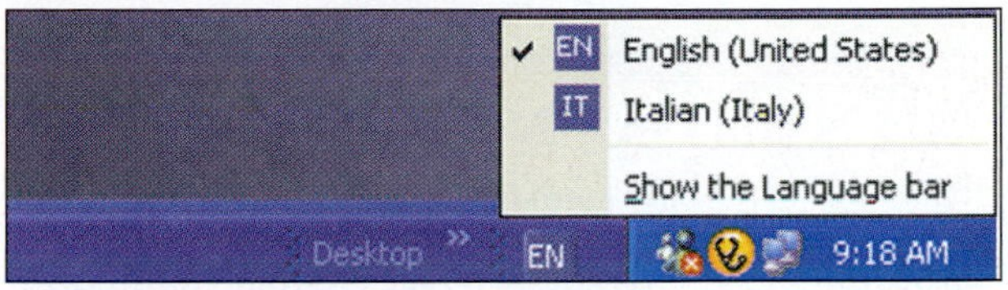

Figure 2-45 Switch between input languages

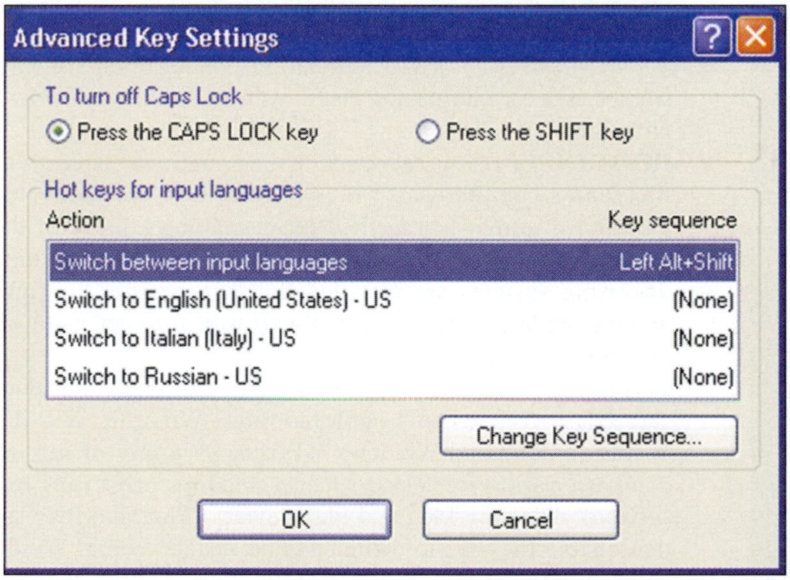

Figure 2-46 Disabling the (Alt)+(Shift) option

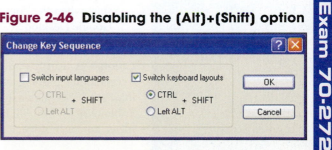

skill 5 *Using Windows XP Troubleshooting Tools*

exam objective

Resolve issues related to operating system features. Tasks include configuring operating system features and interpreting error messages.

Configure the operating system to support applications. Answer end-user questions related to configuring the operating system to support an application.

overview

Windows XP provides several basic tools that can be used to troubleshoot the operating system. These include the System Configuration Utility (msconfig.exe) introduced in Skill 1, Chkdsk, Disk Defragmenter, System File Checker (sfc /scannow), and msinfo32.exe.

The **System Configuration Utility (msconfig.exe)** (**Figure 2-47**) allows you to troubleshoot problems that occur during the startup process. As you learned in Skill 1, to run the utility, enter **msconfig.exe** in the **Open** text box in the Run dialog box and click OK. Once the utility is launched, you will see there are six tabs to choose from: General, SYSTEM.INI, WIN.INI, BOOT.INI, Services, and Startup.

◆ **General tab**: This tab provides the technician with the ability to choose among three startup options to isolate problems with the computer: Normal, Diagnostic, and Selective. Normal startup loads all services and devices. Diagnostic loads only basic devices and services and provides an excellent way to start with a clean boot. Starting with a clean boot means you are starting Windows with no applications running and only a very few drivers and services. Selective startup allows the technician to choose whether or not the system.ini, win.ini, system service, and startup items are processed.

◆ **SYSTEM.INI tab**: This tab provides information regarding the system.ini file, which serves as a storage area for system information that pertains to the hardware on the computer. It directs the operating system to components, such as device drivers.

◆ **WIN.INI tab**: This tab provides information regarding the win.ini file, which serves as a storage area for information that deals with specific system-wide information added by programs.

◆ **BOOT.INI tab**: This tab contains information related to a Microsoft initialization file named boot.ini. This file is located in the root directory of the active primary partition. It provides a method for displaying a menu of the operating systems that are installed on the computer and points to the location on the hard drive where the operating systems are installed. It also provides configuration information that determines how long the system will wait for user input until it selects the default operating system to boot.

◆ **Services tab**: This tab provides the technician with the ability to select which services to run when troubleshooting. Windows XP, just like its predecessors Windows 2000 and Windows NT, runs a variety of services in the background to handle a variety of tasks, such as sending print jobs to printers (Print Spooler service), detecting Plug and Play devices (Plug and Play service) and even services that enable the user to download and install critical Windows updates (Automatic Updates service). By selectively enabling services, a service that is causing problems on the computer can be isolated and fixed.

◆ **Startup tab**: This tab allows the technician to control which programs are allowed to start when the computer is booted. In Skill 1, you used the Startup tab to disable the Google Desktop Search program and remove it permanently from the notification area. It can also be used to keep other applications from loading as well.

Chkdsk is a utility that can be used to check for hard disk errors as well as provide information regarding the file system type that is in use (FAT or NTFS). Chkdsk goes through three stages, as shown in **Figure 2-48**. In stage 1, it scans each file's record in the **Master File Table (MFT)**. The MFT contains information regarding which cluster or clusters in which a file is stored. In stage 2, the drives directory structure is checked to ensure that each directory

Figure 2-47 System Configuration Utility

```
System Configuration Utility                                    X

General | SYSTEM.INI | WIN.INI | BOOT.INI | Services | Startup

  Startup Selection

    ○ Normal Startup - load all device drivers and services

    ○ Diagnostic Startup - load basic devices and services only

    ● Selective Startup

        ☑ Process SYSTEM.INI File

        ☑ Process WIN.INI File

        ☑ Load System Services

        ■ Load Startup Items

        ● Use Original BOOT.INI      ○ Use Modified BOOT.INI


                              [ Launch System Restore ]   [ Expand File... ]


                    [ OK ]      [ Cancel ]      [ Apply ]      [ Help ]
```

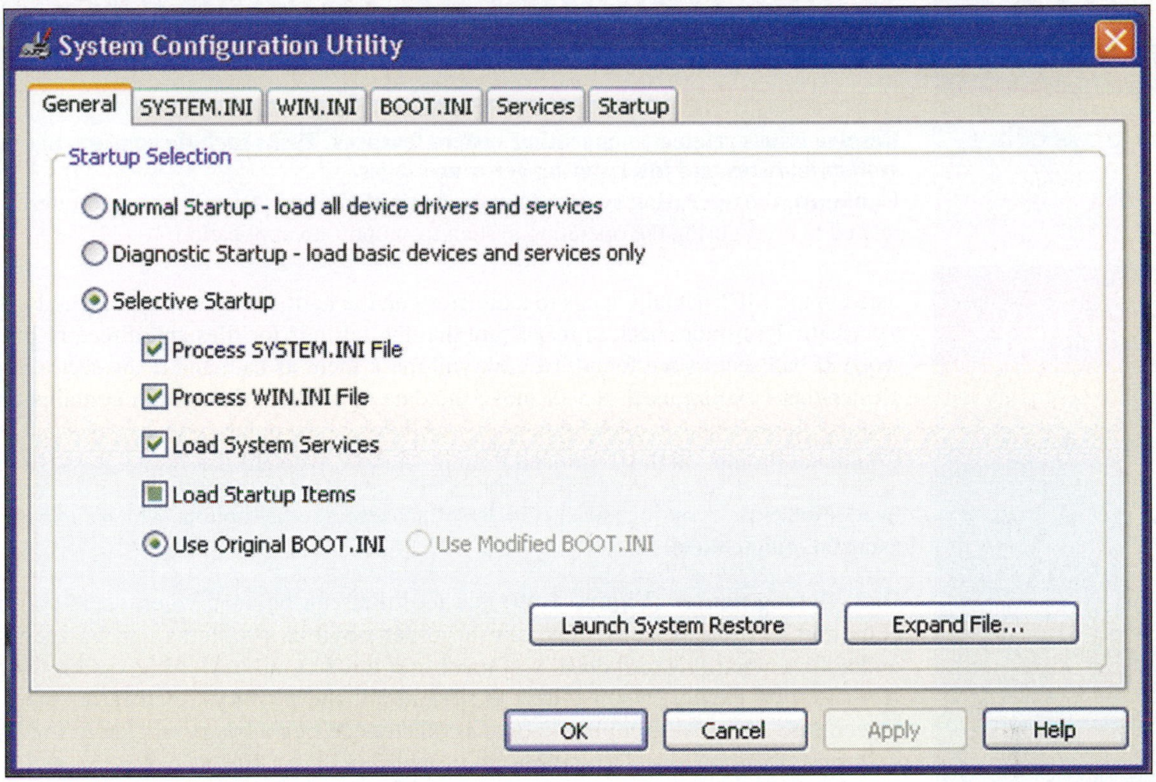

Figure 2-48 Chkdsk utility

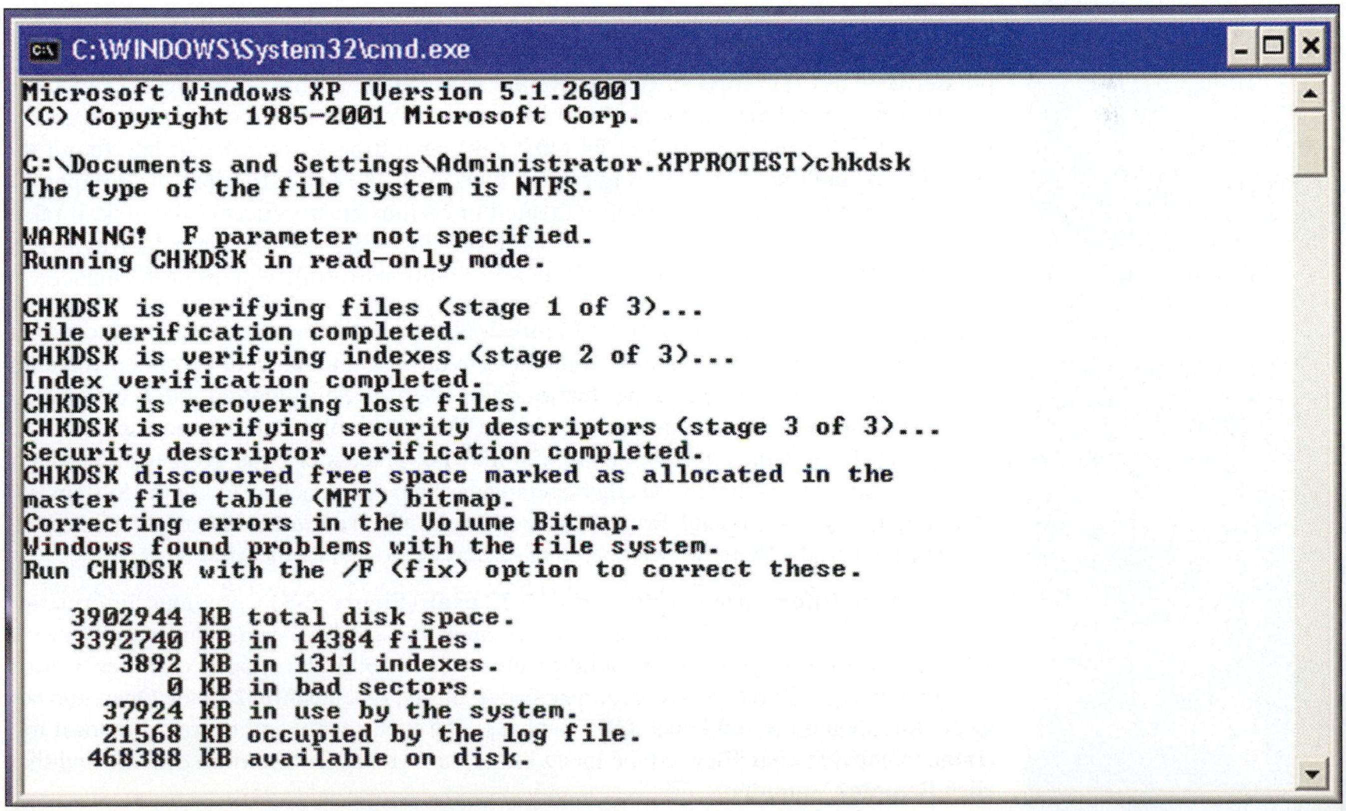

```
C:\WINDOWS\System32\cmd.exe                                    _ □ X

Microsoft Windows XP [Version 5.1.2600]
(C) Copyright 1985-2001 Microsoft Corp.

C:\Documents and Settings\Administrator.XPPROTEST>chkdsk
The type of the file system is NTFS.

WARNING!  F parameter not specified.
Running CHKDSK in read-only mode.

CHKDSK is verifying files (stage 1 of 3)...
File verification completed.
CHKDSK is verifying indexes (stage 2 of 3)...
Index verification completed.
CHKDSK is recovering lost files.
CHKDSK is verifying security descriptors (stage 3 of 3)...
Security descriptor verification completed.
CHKDSK discovered free space marked as allocated in the
master file table (MFT) bitmap.
Correcting errors in the Volume Bitmap.
Windows found problems with the file system.
Run CHKDSK with the /F (fix) option to correct these.

   3902944 KB total disk space.
   3392740 KB in 14384 files.
      3892 KB in 1311 indexes.
         0 KB in bad sectors.
     37924 KB in use by the system.
     21568 KB occupied by the log file.
    468388 KB available on disk.
```

skill 5

Using Windows XP Troubleshooting Tools (cont'd)

exam objective

Resolve issues related to operating system features. Tasks include configuring operating system features and interpreting error messages.
Configure the operating system to support applications. Answer end-user questions related to configuring the operating system to support an application.

overview

listed in the MFT actually maps to a directory on the hard drive. In stage 3, Chkdsk performs a security descriptor check to make sure that the settings for files and directory objects will work. If bad sectors are found, Chkdsk will mark them as bad, and if the sector is part of a cluster that is being used, it will move the data to another cluster that contains only good sectors. To run Chkdsk, click Start, point to All Programs, point to Accessories and then click Command Prompt. In the Command Prompt window, type **chkdsk /f** and press [Enter].

In addition to the /f option switch, chkdsk offers several other options which can be viewed by using entering **chkdsk /?**.

Disk Defragmenter (**Figure 2-49**) is a tool that can be used when users complain the computer is running very slow, and no other obvious problems can be identified. To understand what this tool does, you must first understand how a file system stores files. As indicated earlier, when a disk is formatted, the physical sectors on the drive are placed into a logical grouping known as clusters. When a file is written to the hard disk, it is stored in clusters. Depending upon the size of the file, it can be stored in one or more clusters. When the drive is first formatted, the chance of the file being stored in contiguous clusters (i.e., clusters that are next to each other on the hard drive) is highly possible. As files are deleted over time, clusters with free space will become available in various locations on the disk. Unfortunately, the operating system will not look for a group of clusters that are in contiguous order to store a particular file. In fact, it will store files in the first clusters it can find available, which might be clusters 4-6, 23, and 24. This is how files become fragmented. When the file needs to be retrieved, the operating system will check the MFT to determine the location of the first cluster where the file is stored. In our example, this would be cluster 4. Inside cluster 4, a pointer tells the operating system where the next cluster is that stores another piece of the file (cluster 5). Assuming the last piece of the file is stored in cluster 24, an end of file marker is included in cluster 24 telling the operating system that it has found the last piece of the file. The operating system then loads the entire file into the computer's memory. As a file becomes more fragmented in various clusters across the disk, it takes longer for the read/write heads on the hard disk to locate the file. Disk Defragmenter can be used to consolidate fragmented files to improve overall system performance.

System File Checker (sfc /scannow) (**Figure 2-50**), is a utility that was first introduced back in the days of Windows 98. It allows you to restore missing, modified, or corrupted operating system files. If the utility determines that a critical file has been compromised, it will prompt you to insert the Windows XP operating system CD to restore the file(s). Restoring these files will ensure the system avoids problems with the boot process or other problems that might show up when you attempt to use other operating system components. To use the System File Checker, open a Command Prompt window, type **sfc /scannow** and press [Enter]. If prompted, insert the Windows XP operating system CD to restore the files.

The System Information utility (msinfo32.exe) (**Figure 2-51**) provides information regarding the system's hardware resources, components, software environment, and Internet settings. This can be used to find out information about the local computer or, if necessary, a remote computer. To run the System Information utility, type **msinfo32** in the Open text box in the Run dialog box, and click OK. To change the focus of the utility from the local to a remote computer, click View on the menu bar in the **System Information** console and then click **Remote Computer**.

Figure 2-49 Disk Defragmenter

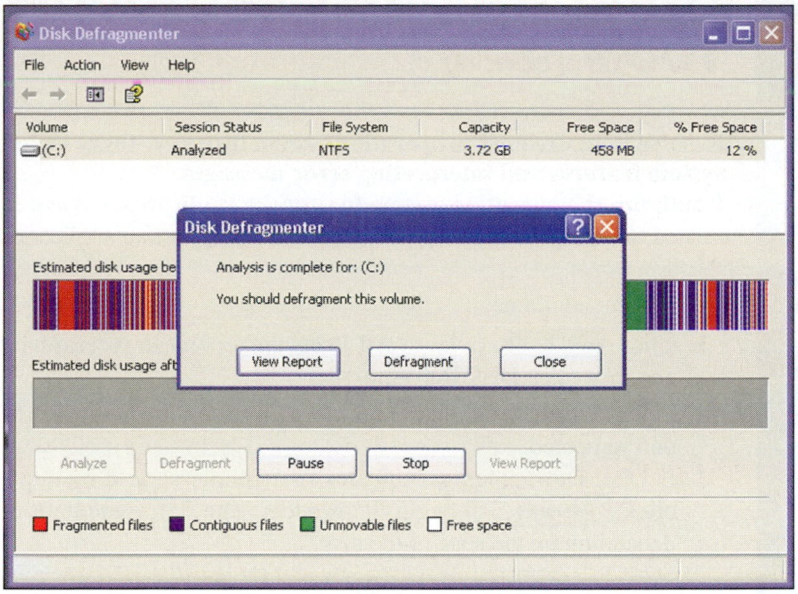

Figure 2-50 Using sfc /scannow

Figure 2-51 The System Information utility (msinfo32.exe)

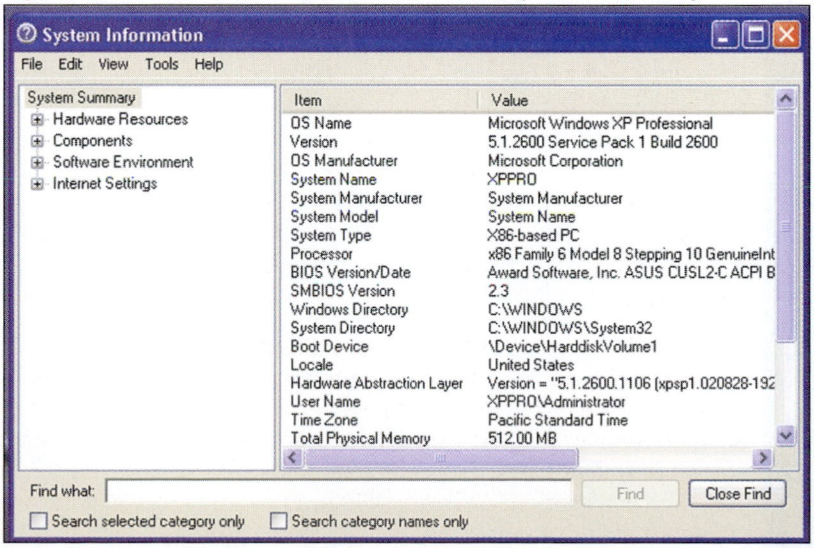

skill 5

Using Windows XP Troubleshooting Tools (cont'd)

exam objective

Resolve issues related to operating system features. Tasks include configuring operating system features and interpreting error messages.
Configure the operating system to support applications. Answer end-user questions related to configuring the operating system to support an application.

how to

Defragment a volume.

1. Click 🏁 **start** , point to **All Programs**, point to **Accessories**, point to **System Tools**, and then click **Disk Defragmenter**.
2. Select the disk volume and click [Analyze] to determine if the volume needs to be defragmented.
3. If Disk Defragmenter indicates the volume should be defragmented (**Figure 2-52**), click [Defragment] to begin the process. The defragmentation may take several hours, depending on the state of the disk.

caution

Before defragmenting a disk, make sure you disable antivirus applications and screen savers and close any running programs that might interfere with the defragmenting process.

more

Windows XP provides several **troubleshooting wizards**, each designed to troubleshoot a specific type of problem. These wizards are designed to help you diagnose and resolve problems that are occurring on your computer. When a wizard is started, you are asked a series of questions that deal with the problem you are currently experiencing. There are troubleshooters for hardware devices, system setup, Internet Explorer (**Figure 2-53**), Outlook Express, and more. To view the troubleshooting wizards that are available, access the Help and Support Center on your Windows XP computer. In the Search field, enter the following: **list of troubleshooters**.

Figure 2-52 Prompt to defragment the volume

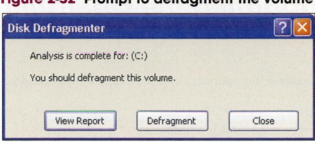

Figure 2-53 Internet Explorer Troubleshooter

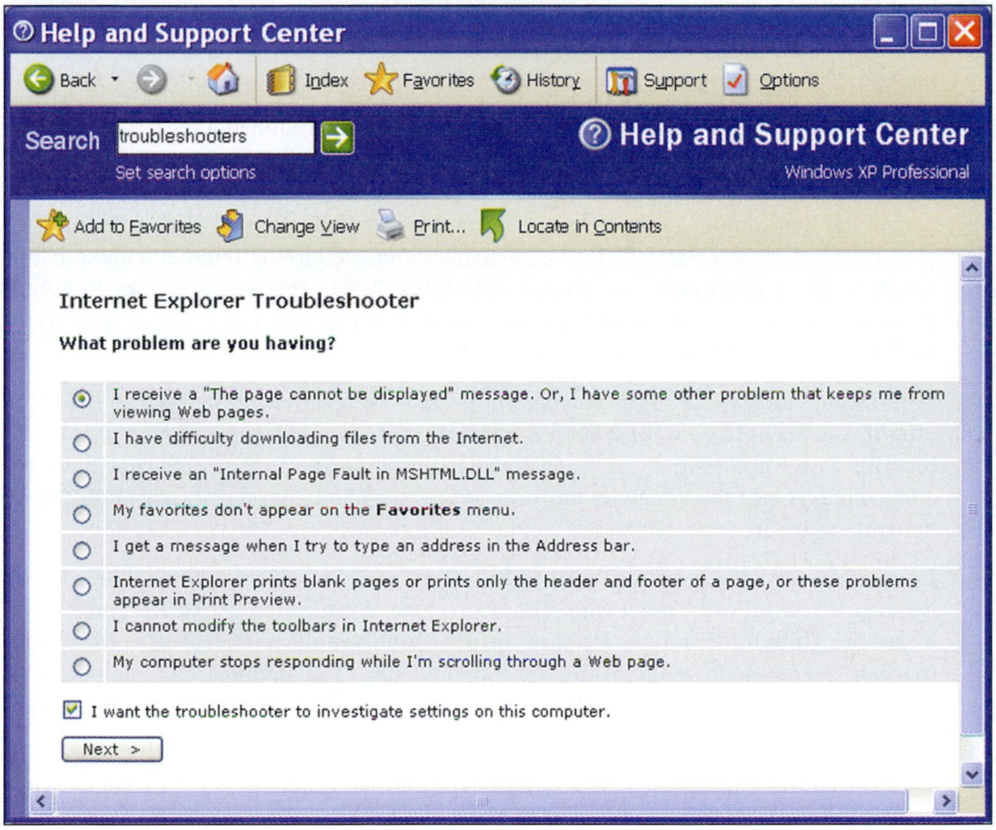

skill 6 | *Updating the Operating System*

exam objective | Configure the operating system to support applications.

overview

From the point that a computer is set up for an employee, decisions must be made to ensure the appropriate level of security is maintained. Although some of these are very obvious, such as using NTFS to secure files and folders, turning off any services that are not required, and using strong passwords for administrative and user accounts, others may be less evident. For example, by installing the client operating system or applications from media that has been compromised, you can introduce viruses. An administrator could install an application that included a Trojan horse (a type of virus) on a new system without realizing the virus was present. The new computers are then added to the company network already compromised.

To avoid this problem, you should always scan all installation media regardless of its source. Another concern is connecting computers to the Internet before they have been fully secured. Researchers at the Internet Storm Center, **http://isc.sans.org//survivalhistory.php**, which is part of the SysAdmin, Audit, Network, Security (SANS) Institute, indicate the survival time (i.e., time before being attacked) of a computer connected to the Internet without being fully patched was approximately 16 minutes in October, 2004. This is down from 49 minutes the previous year and introduces a major concern when it can take much longer than 16 minutes to download the patches that would protect the computer!

To protect Windows XP from vulnerabilities that are discovered or from threats that occur after it was released, you must keep it updated. If the computer is new, you should consider installing and updating it on an isolated network segment that does not have Internet connectivity. Once the computer has been securely updated, it can be moved off the isolated network segment.

From that point on, updating Windows XP can be accomplished by having the user visit the Microsoft's Windows Update site. To do so, select Start, point to All Programs, and click **Windows Update. Windows Update (http://windowsupdate.microsoft.com)** can be used to scan, recommend, and install security updates. The updates can include Windows components, security updates, and device drivers. To use the tool, you must have local administrator rights on the computer.

The **Automatic Updates** feature can be used to further automate this procedure. Automatic Updates recognizes when you are connected to the Internet and searches the Windows Update site in the background for critical and security-related updates. If updates are found, they are automatically downloaded and installed on the user's computer. Automatic Updates does not download previously released updates or non-critical updates. If users report problems related to their computer not receiving security updates regularly, check the following to ensure Automatic Updates is enabled. Open the Control Panel window and double-click **System** to open the **System Properties** dialog box. Click the **Automatic Updates** tab and select **Keep my computer up to date** (**Figure 2-54**).

In the Settings section of the tab, you have three options that can be used to determine how updates are installed. These are summarized below:

◆ Notifying the user when updates are downloaded and again before they are installed on the computer

◆ Automatically downloading the updates and notifying the user before they are ready to be installed.

◆ Automatically downloading and installing the updates without notification using scheduled installation.

Microsoft recommends configuring the user's computer to automatically download and install critical updates without notification using scheduled installation. In fact, critical and security-

tip

Enabling Automatic Updates downloads Windows XP critical updates. You must visit **http://office.microsoft.com** to obtain Microsoft Office updates.

tip

Before performing system updates using service packs/critical fixes, make sure you adhere to company policy. There may be other systems in place for deploying updates.

Figure 2-54 Enabling Automatic Updates

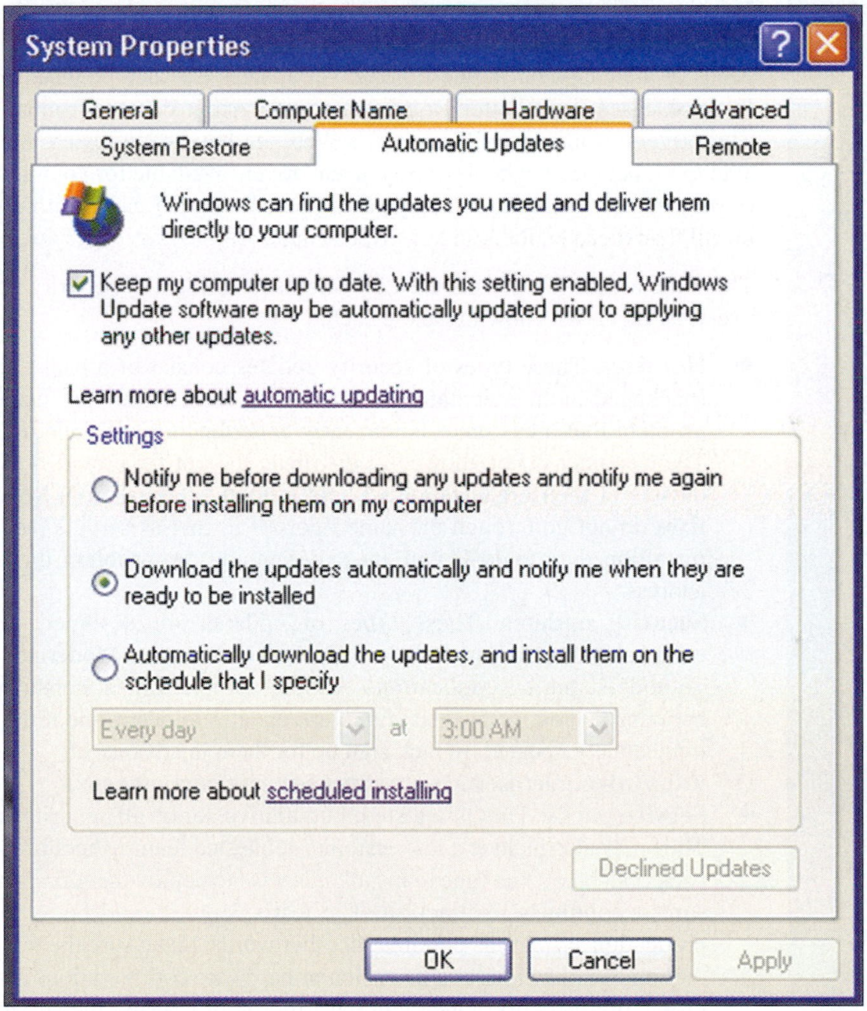

skill 6

Updating the Operating System
(cont'd)

exam objective

Configure the operating system to support applications.

overview

tip

You can also find more information on Service Pack 2 at Microsoft's web site at http://www.microsoft.com/ technet/prodtechnol/ winxppro/maintain/ winxpsp2.msp.

caution

Keep in mind that before any service packs, hot fixes, or security updates are installed, check with the administrator or the company involved. There may be a security policy in place the dictates how these types of updates are deployed. Always make sure a recent backup has been completed and the user's data is protected before performing any updates.

related updates are the only types handled by Automatic Updates unless your system has Windows XP Service Pack 2 (released in August, 2004) installed. With the introduction of this service pack, Automatic Updates can also download service packs, hot fixes (fixes released between service packs), and other security updates. Appendix A discusses Service Pack 2 in more detail.

For less critical updates, such as those that are released for applications or between service packs, you will need to visit the Windows Update site and select them based on the specific needs of the computer in question. Driver updates can also be installed in the same manner. In most cases, it is better to get the most current drivers from the vendor's Web site. The drivers available on Microsoft's Web site have been tested and certified to work on Windows, but may not be the most current drivers available for your network card, video card, or modem, for example. In many cases, the drivers that came with the device will be more recent than those on the Windows Update site.

There are a variety of terms used by Microsoft to identify security updates. Here is a brief overview along with how to handle each.

◆ **Hot fixes**: These types of security updates consist of a package of one or more files (packaged in an executable/self installing format) that are designed to fix a specific problem that a customer is currently experiencing with one of Microsoft's products. The customer is not allowed to distribute the hot fix provided by Microsoft to anyone outside of their organization without written approval from Microsoft. In general, hot fixes do not go through the same rigorous testing as service packs; therefore, consider installing them only if you are experiencing the problem the hot fix is designed to address.

◆ **Security updates**: These types of updates are designed to fix security-related vulnerabilities and are rated as Critical, Important, Moderate, or Low (**Table 2-1**). To understand the implications of these vulnerabilities, consider reading the security bulletins that are associated with these updates to determine if the computer needs to be immediately updated. In fact, sign up for them in advance at: **http://www.microsoft.com/technet/security/current.aspx.**

◆ **Service packs**: This is a tested, cumulative set of all security updates and hot fixes. They may also include a few customer-requested features/modifications. Because service packs can take some time to install, it is wise to deploy them first on a test system to make sure it continues to function. The test system should be as close a match to your production systems as possible. In other words, make sure the test system(s) are running the same applications and have similar hardware configurations as those running on your production network. Once you have thoroughly tested the service pack, you can then schedule deployment at a time that it will least affect users.

When Microsoft released Windows XP Service Pack 2 in August 2004 through Automatic Updates, several software compatibility issues were discovered. To allow companies time to address the issues that were discovered, Microsoft has provided a temporary mechanism to disable the automatic download of Service Pack 2 while still providing access to critical updates. On April 16, 2005, Microsoft will start to deliver Service Pack 2 to all computers running Windows XP or Windows XP Service Pack 1 using Automatic Updates.

For more details on this mechanism and how to block Service Pack 2, visit the following link: **http://www.microsoft.com/technet/prodtechnol/winxppro/maintain/sp2aumng.mspx.**

Table 2-1   Security Ratings

Rating Classification	Explanation
Critical	Vulnerabilities that can compromise the system and allow the spread of Internet worms without the user's knowledge. The worm is a program that uses bugs in programs and security loopholes to distribute itself to computers across the Internet. Once on a computer, it uses up all available processor time.
Important	Vulnerabilities that can compromise the availability, confidentiality, integrity of a user's data. The vulnerability, if not addressed, can also impact the integrity and availability of processing resources.
Moderate	Vulnerabilities that are not very easy to take advantage of. In many cases, the vulnerability can be diminished by addressing default configurations and auditing.
Low	Vulnerabilities that are very hard to take advantage of. The vulnerability, if exploited, has minimal impact.

Summary

- The taskbar provides information regarding programs, files, and folders that are currently open or running on the computer.
- The Start menu provides access to other programs on the computer, documents that have been recently opened, support tools, and many other items.
- The notification area shows programs that are currently running in the background that are active but not seen by the user.
- By default, Windows XP Professional locks the taskbar so that it cannot be moved.
- You can tell if the taskbar is locked or not by looking for the handles in front of the toolbars themselves.
- The taskbar can be configured to automatically group files opened by the same program into a single button.
- Quick Launch allows you to bypass using the Start menu to find and launch your most frequently used programs. It can also be used to launch folders as well.
- A program can be pinned to the Start menu by selecting the program's executable and selecting Pin to Start Menu. This creates a shortcut to the program in the upper left area of the Start menu.

- To minimize the learning curve of Windows XP, it is possible to use the Classic Start menu option. This menu has the same look as earlier releases of Microsoft Windows operating systems.
- Every file created on a computer has an associated file extension. The file extension is used by the computer's operating system to determine which software program will be used to open the associated file.
- There are five folder views that can be used to customize how folders appear to users. These include Thumbnails, Tiles, Icons, List, and Details.
- Regional options control how Windows XP and applications format numbers, currencies, dates, and times. Language settings provide users with the ability to create, edit, and print documents in several languages.
- Windows XP provides several basic tools that can be used to troubleshoot the operating system. These include the System Configuration Utility (msconfig.exe), Chkdsk, Disk Defragmenter, System File Checker (sfc /scannow), and the System Information utility (msinfo32.exe).
- To keep a Windows XP computer updated after it has been released, use the Windows Update site. Automatic Updates can be used to further automate this procedure.

Key Terms

Automatic Updates
Chkdsk
Disk Defragmenter
File association
Hot fix
Master File Table (MFT)
Msinfo32.exe
Multilingual User Interface (MUI)
    Pack

Notification area
Pinning
Quick Launch
Regional options
Security updates
Service pack
Start menu
System Configuration Utility
System File Checker (sfc /scannow)

Taskbar
Troubleshooting wizards
Windows File Association
Windows Update

Test Yourself

1. Samantha, a user in the HR Department, has contacted the help desk. She has been trying to relocate the taskbar to the top of her screen but it will not move. How would you tell her to address the problem? (Choose all that apply.)
   a. Access the Taskbar and Start Menu Properties dialog box and select the Auto-hide taskbar option under the Taskbar tab.
   b. Right-click the Taskbar and remove the check mark next to Lock the Taskbar.
   c. Access the Taskbar and Start Menu Properties dialog box and remove the check mark from the Lock the taskbar check box.
   d. Double-clicking the taskbar will automatically unlock it.

2. Matthew has been asked to add a shortcut to a program for Alexis. She wants to be able to quickly launch the program without having to use the Start menu. She does not want the program shortcut added to her desktop which she claims is already too cluttered. Which toolbar would you add to the taskbar to accomplish this goal?
   a. Address toolbar
   b. Links toolbar
   c. Desktop
   d. Quick Launch

3. A user in the Graphics department calls the help desk and wants to know why a graphics program (FrontPage) he uses infrequently keeps disappearing from his Start menu. After asking the user a few more questions, you discover he is referring to the area just above the All Programs submenu, which stores information regarding frequently used programs. The user would like the program to be placed in the upper left corner of the Start menu with Internet Explorer and Microsoft Outlook and remain there regardless of how often he uses it. How would you address this user's need? (Choose all that apply.)
   a. Click on the Customize button in the Taskbar and Start Menu Properties dialog box and change the number of programs on Start menu option to a higher number on the General tab.
   b. Drag a shortcut to FrontPage to the pinned area of the Start menu.
   c. Locate the FrontPage shortcut by clicking Start, pointing to All Programs, and right-clicking it. Select Pin to Start menu.
   d. None of the above options will provide this capability.

4. Olivia and Andrew work in the same department cubicle. Andrew has noticed that Olivia has the ability to access her My Documents folder directly from her Start menu. He would like you to set up his computer's Start menu to behave the same way. How can this be done? (Choose all that apply.)
   a. On the Advanced tab of the Customize Start menu, locate My Documents under the Start menu items and select Display as a link.
   b. On the Advanced tab of the Customize Start menu, locate My Documents under the Start menu items and select Display as a menu.
   c. On the Advanced tab of the Customize Start menu, locate My Documents under the Start menu items and select Don't display this item.
   d. On the Advanced tab of the Customize Start menu, make sure the Open submenus when I pause on them with my mouse option button is selected.

5. A user has contacted the help desk and would like to remove two icons that are in the notification area of the taskbar. The icons in question represent programs that are no longer used and that should not be running in the background at all. How can the user keep the icons from appearing in the notification area after startup?
   a. Double-click the program icons in the notification area and select Disable Notification Startup.
   b. Select Hide inactive icons via the Taskbar in the Taskbar and Start Menu Properties dialog box.
   c. Use msconfig.exe to disable the two programs via the Startup tab.
   d. Use msinfo32.exe to disable the two programs via the Startup tab.

6. You suspect that a critical system file has either been corrupted or deleted and needs to be replaced. Which tool could be used to fix the problem?
   a. Disk Defragmenter
   b. msinfo32.exe
   c. System File Checker
   d. Chkdsk

7. Which of the following represent valid options for determining how updates are installed when using Automatic Updates? (Choose all that apply.)
   a. Notify me before downloading any updates and notify me again before installing them on my computer.
   b. Download the updates automatically and notify me when they are ready to be installed.
   c. Automatically download the updates, and install them on the schedule that I specify.
   d. Download the updates manually and install them on the schedule that I specify.

8. You suspect there is a problem with a user's network adapter. Which troubleshooting tool can provide you with more information regarding the network adapter's product type?
   a. Chkdsk
   b. msinfo32.exe
   c. msconfig.exe
   d. System File Checker

9. Elizabeth, a user in the Sales department, has called the help desk to solve a problem she encountered after installing RealPlayer. She was using Windows Media Player to play mp3 files, but now when she attempts to play an mp3 file, RealPlayer opens instead. She would like to change her settings back so that Windows Media Player will open automatically when she selects a file with the mp3 extension. How can this be accomplished?
   a. Reinstall Windows Media Player and answer Yes when prompted to associate all media files with the application.
   b. Select the Files Types tab in the Folder options dialog box, locate the mp3 extension, and change the files with the extension to open with Windows Media Player.
   c. Tell her to right-click the mp3 file and select Open With to select Windows Media Player.
   d. Tell her she must uninstall RealPlayer for Windows Media to become the default player for mp3 files.

10. A user named Michael has contacted you with a problem he has recently experienced. It appears that when he types characters into his word processing program, strange looking characters start appearing. Which of the following are true statements? (Choose all that apply.)
   a. Michael has additional languages configured for his computer and has most likely pressed the left [Alt]+[Shift] keys by accident.
   b. Michael needs to install the Multilingual User Interface (MUI) pack to address the problem.
   c. Michael can use the Language Indicator located on the taskbar to switch back to English.
   d. None of the above.

Projects: On Your Own

1. Analyze the fragmentation on your hard disk.
   a. Log onto Windows XP.
   b. Click **Start**, point to **All Programs**, point to **Accessories**, point to **System Tools**, and then click **Disk Defragmenter**.
   c. Select a volume on your hard drive and click **Analyze**.
   d. To see the results of the analysis, click **View Report**. You can print this report out if you want.
   e. Look for information in the report regarding the average fragments per file. This is a good indicator on how fragmented the files really are. If the average fragments per file is 1.00, then most files are contiguous. If the number is 1.20, then about 20% of the files are fragments of two or more pieces. 1.30 indicates 30% of the files are fragments of two or more pieces, and 2.00 indicates most, if not all, files are in fragments of two or more pieces. So for example, if your analysis reports average fragments per file = 1.38, you can assume that at least 30% of your files are fragmented.
   f. Defragment the volume and then compare this information again.

2. Use msinfo32.exe to learn more about your operating environment.
   a. Log onto Windows XP.
   b. Click **Start** and then click **Run**.
   c. In the Open text box of the Run dialog box, enter **msinfo32**, and click OK.
   d. Click **Internet Settings**. Identify the version and build number of Internet Explorer your computer is running.
   e. Click **Software Environment**. Identify what programs are configured to run when the computer starts. Can you configure these programs via this utility to not start up? If not, what tool would you use?
   f. Click **Components**. Identify the make and model of your graphics card.
   g. To maintain a record of the information, print a report by clicking File on the menu bar and then clicking Print.

Problem Solving Scenarios

1. A user wants to make sure there is enough room on her taskbar to show all her open program and files. She has heard from other users in her department that there is a way to automatically group files opened by the same program into a single button. This sounds like a great idea to the user and she has asked you to explain how she can accomplish this.

2. You have just been hired to work as a Tier 1 desktop support technician for a help desk firm. Your first call of the day comes from a user who asks a simple question. "How can I reorder the items listed in the All Programs section of the Start menu?" Describe the actions you will take to help the user solve this problem.

Supporting Internet Explorer

This lesson provides an introduction to Internet Explorer, which is the Web browser that is installed with Windows XP. Web browsers (software that fetches Web pages and displays them to you) send requests over the Internet to Web servers (specialized computer systems located around the globe that host Web pages and Web sites).

Internet Explorer allows you to roam the World Wide Web in search of information regarding every conceivable topic. You can use it to watch the news, download pictures and documents, and shop. It is, without much exaggeration, a tool that opens a broad world of information to you.

The aim of this lesson is to assure that you have the essential background to address and troubleshoot many of the requests and issues that come from users regarding Internet Explorer—from changing the language that Web pages appear in to setting specific security and content handling options.

Internet Explorer is very configurable and allows you to change the appearance of the toolbar and customize a number of general features, such as text size, fonts, and background colors. Users can put shortcuts to their most frequently visited pages on the Links bar. They can export all or part of their Favorites list or alternatively import another user's list or a Favorites list from another browser, such as Netscape Navigator.

Security, content, and privacy features allow users to protect their privacy and make their computers and personal information more secure. Security zones can be to set different levels for different areas of the Web based on a user's needs. A special feature, the Content Advisor, allows the user to screen out objectionable content using industry-standard ratings that have been defined independently by the Platform for Internet Content Selection (PICS) committee.

If a user has a particular program he or she prefers to use as an e-mail client, HTML editor, or newsgroup reader, you can configure Internet Explorer to open these specific programs when needed. For people with disabilities, you can customize Internet Explorer in conjunction with or separately from general Windows accessibility features.

Goals

In this lesson, you will learn how to customize the Internet Explorer toolbar and customize the look and behavior of Internet Explorer itself. You will learn how to display Web pages in specified languages and how to use Internet Explorer's accessibility features. You will learn about the various security and privacy features and settings in Internet Explorer and how to use and modify them. You will also learn about the Content Advisor tool, certificates, and the Personal Information Assistant. Additionally, you will learn how to use Internet Explorer to configure your Internet connection, and how to configure Internet Explorer to work with other Internet applications. Finally, you will learn about the most common issues that users have with Internet Explorer and how to troubleshoot them.

Lesson 3   Supporting Internet Explorer

Skill	Exam 70-272 Objective
1. Customizing Internet Explorer Toolbars	Resolve issues related to customizing Internet Explorer. Resolve issues related to Internet Explorer support features. Tasks include configuring Internet Explorer and interpreting error messages. Configure and troubleshoot Internet Explorer.
2. Configuring Internet Explorer General Settings	Same as above
3. Implementing Internet Explorer Language and Accessibility Options	Same as above
4. Setting Internet Explorer Security Levels	Same as above
5. Examining Privacy Options in Internet Explorer	Same as above
6. Personalizing Content in Internet Explorer	Same as above
7. Configuring Internet Explorer Connectivity Options	Same as above
8. Working with Internet Explorer Program Options	Same as above
9. Troubleshooting Internet Explorer: Common User Issues	Same as above

Requirements

To complete this lesson, you will need administrative rights on a Windows XP Professional computer with Service Pack 1 installed. The computer must also be able to access the Internet in order for you to be able to complete some of exercises.

skill 1 *Customizing Internet Explorer Toolbars*

exam objective

Resolve issues related to customizing Internet Explorer.

Resolve issues related to Internet Explorer support features. Tasks include configuring Internet Explorer and interpreting error messages.

Configure and troubleshoot Internet Explorer.

overview

Although the default Internet Explorer (IE) toolbars and settings are normally adequate for most purposes, your users may want to change the configuration and customize them for their own use. Similarly, large enterprises and corporations may want to use a standard configuration they will deploy company-wide that varies from the default settings.

There are three principal toolbars: Standard Buttons, Address bar, and Links (**Figure 3-1**). You can hide or display any of these toolbars by right-clicking a blank space on the toolbar or on the menu bar and selecting that toolbar in the pop-up menu (**Figure 3-2**). Displayed toolbars have a check mark next to them. Select a checked toolbar in the pop-up list to remove the check mark and hide the toolbar. Similarly, select an unchecked toolbar in the list to place a check mark and display the toolbar.

Standard Buttons toolbar: The **Standard Buttons toolbar** includes the Search, Media, History, Favorites, Media, and Folder buttons. Clicking on any of these buttons opens the Explorer bar, a left-hand pane in the browser window, for that function. You can also open the Explorer bar for any of these functions through the **Explorer Bar** command on the View menu.

- ◆ **Search**: The Search button provides access to different categories of searches.
- ◆ **Media**: The Media button opens a Media window that contains the control and links that make it simple to play music, video, or multimedia files. Users can tune in and listen to a favorite Internet radio station through the Media button.
- ◆ **History**: The History button opens a window containing links to a list of Web pages visited recently.
- ◆ **Favorites**: The Favorites button presents you with a list of saved links to Web pages.
- ◆ **Folders**: The Folders button opens a Windows Explorer window that shows the files on your computer.

You can add, remove, and reorder the standard buttons or resize them to the size used in Microsoft Office or as large icons. You can also configure the text labels accompanying the buttons.

There are several buttons that by default are not present on the Standard Buttons toolbar but that you can add through the Customize command available on the Toolbars submenu, such as the Related button. The Related button is standard toolbar button that can aid users who need to access related information quickly. Clicking on the Related button opens the Explorer bar and presents a list of other Internet sites that contain information similar to what the user is currently viewing.

Address bar: The Address bar contains a text box in which you can type a Web address to visit. You can move the Address bar (and the other toolbars, including the menu bar) by dragging it to a new location. You can also combine a toolbar with another by dragging it over the other.

Links toolbar: The Links toolbar contains predefined links to Web pages. You can add your own items to the Links toolbar by dragging the Web page icon from the Address bar, or by dragging a link from a Web page. You can rearrange items on the Links bar by dragging them up, down, left, or right. You can also edit the text accompanying the link by right clicking it and selecting Rename from the Properties dialog box. You can even move them into the menu bar.

tip

You can also check or uncheck toolbars through the Toolbars command on the View menu.

Figure 3-1 Internet Explorer toolbars

Menu bar

Standard
Buttons toolbar

Links toolbar

Address bar

The Explorer bar
is opened by
clicking the
Search, Favorites,
History, Folders,
or Media button

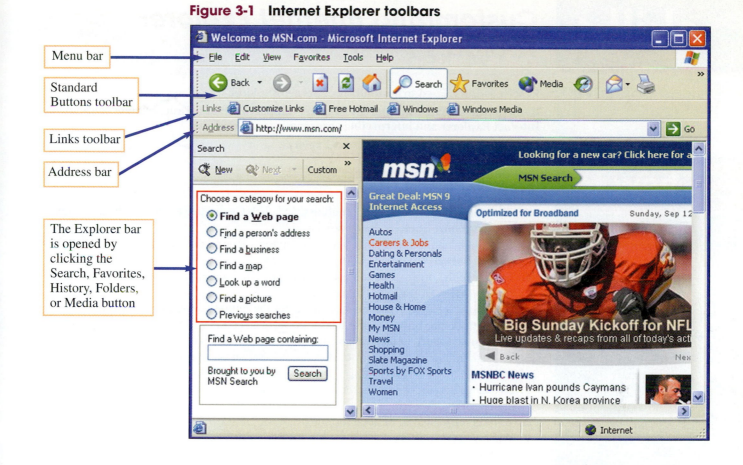

Figure 3-2 Selecting toolbars to display

You can select which
toolbars to display
by right-clicking on
an empty space on
the toolbar or menu
bar and selecting the
toolbar from the
drop-down list

Some Internet-
related applications
can add their own
toolbars to Internet
Explorer

skill 1

Customizing Internet Explorer Toolbars (cont'd)

exam objective

Resolve issues related to customizing Internet Explorer.

Resolve issues related to Internet Explorer support features. Tasks include configuring Internet Explorer and interpreting error messages.

Configure and troubleshoot Internet Explorer.

how to

Customize Internet Explorer toolbars.

1. Open **Internet Explorer**.
2. Click the **View** menu, point to **Toolbars,** and click **Customize** on the Toolbars submenu. The **Customize Toolbox** dialog box opens.
3. To add a button to the toolbar, select the button's icon in the left pane under **Available toolbar buttons (Figure 3-3),** and click [Add ->].
4. To change the order of buttons on the toolbar, select the button you want to move and click [Move Down] or [Move Up] to reposition.
5. To remove a button from the toolbar, select the button's icon in the right pane under **Current toolbar buttons** and click [<- Remove]. The button will be removed from the right pane list and added to the available buttons list in the left pane.
6. To change how text appears on the toolbar, select an option from the Text options pull-down menu **(Figure 3-4)**.
7. To change the size of icon buttons on the toolbar, select Small or Large icons on the Icon options drop-down list.
8. To reset the toolbar to its default settings, click [Reset].
9. When you are finished customizing the toolbar, click [Close].

tip

To open the Customize Toolbar dialog box, you can also right-click anywhere on the toolbar and select **Customize** from the pop-up menu.

Figure 3-3 Customize Toolbar dialog box

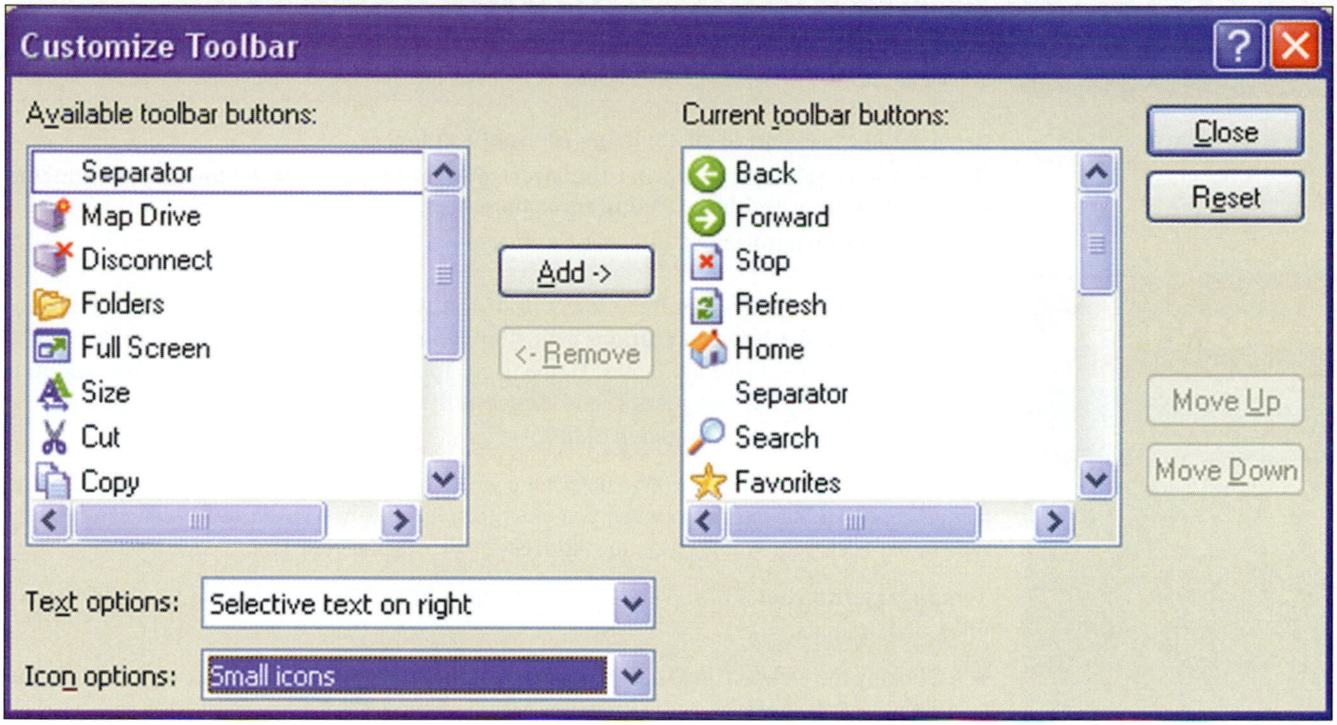

Customize Toolbar

A̲vailable toolbar buttons:

- Separator
- Map Drive
- Disconnect
- Folders
- Full Screen
- Size
- Cut
- Copy

Curre̲nt toolbar buttons:

- Back
- Forward
- Stop
- Refresh
- Home
- Separator
- Search
- Favorites

A̲dd ->

<- R̲emove

C̲lose

R̲eset

Move U̲p

Move D̲own

Te̲xt options: Selective text on right

Ico̲n options: Small icons

Figure 3-4 Text options

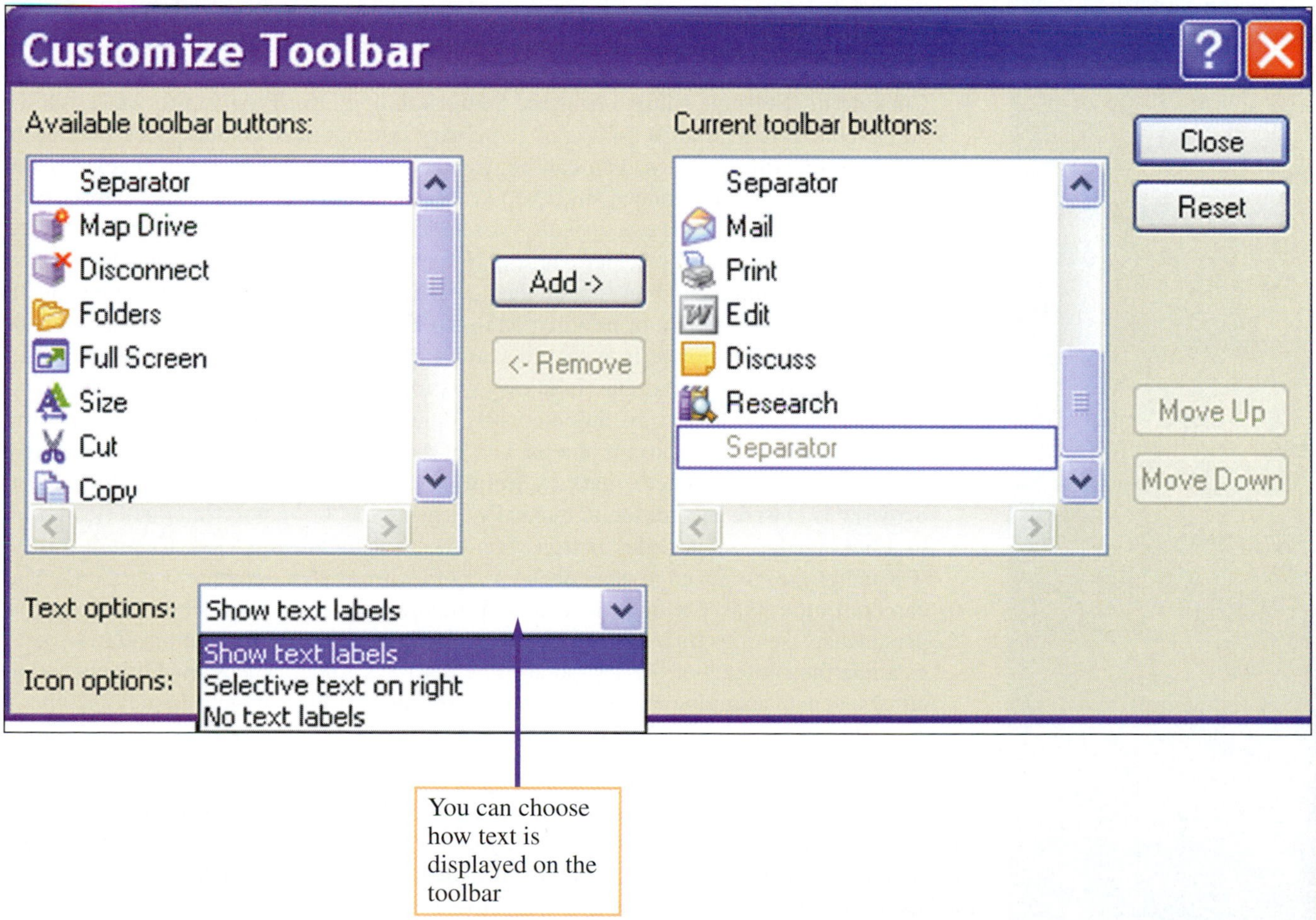

Customize Toolbar

Available toolbar buttons:

- Separator
- Map Drive
- Disconnect
- Folders
- Full Screen
- Size
- Cut
- Copy

Current toolbar buttons:

- Separator
- Mail
- Print
- Edit
- Discuss
- Research
- Separator

Add ->

<- Remove

Close

Reset

Move Up

Move Down

Text options: Show text labels

Show text labels
Selective text on right
No text labels

Icon options:

You can choose
how text is
displayed on the
toolbar

skill 2
Configuring Internet Explorer General Settings

exam objective

Resolve issues related to customizing Internet Explorer.

Resolve issues related to Internet Explorer support features. Tasks include configuring Internet Explorer and interpreting error messages.

Configure and troubleshoot Internet Explorer.

overview

To configure IE's general settings, select **Tools** on the menu bar, and then select **Internet Options** to open the **Internet Options** dialog box. Make sure the General tab is selected. The General tab is divided into four areas: Home page, Temporary Internet files, History, and four buttons: Color, Fonts, Languages, and Accessibility (**Figure 3-5**). (The Languages and Accessibility buttons are covered in Skill 3.)

Home Page: You use this section to determine which page, if any, will be the **Home page** (the page IE opens to, or returns to when you click the Home button) used in IE. You can directly type in the URL of a Web page in the **Address** box to use as your Home page.

Temporary Internet Files: This section contains three buttons—Delete Cookies, Delete Files, and Settings.

◆ Clicking the **Delete Cookies** button removes all the cookies from your computer. Deleting them is often useful as both a troubleshooting methodology and as a security measure.

◆ Clicking the **Delete Files** button empties the contents of the Temporary Internet Files folder (or folders). **Temporary Internet files** are the Web pages, files, graphics, and cookies that are stored as you browse using IE. This local storage increases the speed of reloading these items if you return to the same Web page. Microsoft recommends using the Delete Files option when disk space is low and you no longer need quick access to recently viewed pages. In addition, deleting temporary files is often a valuable troubleshooting technique as occasionally corrupted files can be cached in this area.

◆ Clicking the **Settings** button opens the Settings dialog box (**Figure 3-6**) which allows you to configure additional aspects of Temporary Internet files. Under **Check for newer versions of stored pages,** you can configure how often the browser checks to see whether the page has changed since you last viewed it (**Table 3-1**). Under **Temporary Internet files folder,** you can view the current location of the stored files and select the amount of disk space the folder can use. You can relocate the folder by selecting the **Move Folder** button and browsing to the new location. Your computer should be able to hold a fairly large amount of information in the Temporary Internet Files folder without any noticeable slowdown. However, if you do have limited disk space available, then deleting Temporary Internet files is an easy way to free up some space on your hard drive. You can set these files to be automatically deleted through the **Advanced** tab of the Internet Options dialog box. In the list box of Advanced settings, scroll to the Security **category** and place a check mark by **Empty Temporary Internet Files folder when browser is closed**. In addition to manually clearing the Temporary Internet Files folder by clicking the Delete Files button, Windows XP includes a Disk Cleanup utility, (Cleanmgr.exe) designed to clear unnecessary files from your computer's hard disk. You can configure Disk Cleanup to remove Temporary Internet files while leaving your personalized settings for Web pages intact. Selecting the **View Files** button allows you to examine the contents of the Temporary Internet Files folder. The **View Objects** button allows you to examine the Downloaded Programs folder, which displays ActiveX controls and Java controls that have been downloaded to your computer.

History: The **History folder** contains links to the Web pages you've visited for quick access to recently viewed pages. You can specify the number of days to keep pages in the History folder. The length of the history can be shortened or lengthened depending on your needs and the amount of available disk space. Clicking the **Clear History** button deletes the contents of the History folder.

tip

If you want to see the most current version of a specific page, regardless of setting, click the Refresh button on the Standard Buttons toolbar. Occasionally, however, manually refreshing a page may not be enough to update it. Clearing the cache and closing the browser may be required in these cases.

tip

Signs that your Temporary Internet Files folder is taking up too much space on your hard drive include the inability or reduced ability to browse a site, inability to save graphics files, play videos, or open files online (such as PDF documents).

Figure 3-5 The General tab in the Internet Options dialog box

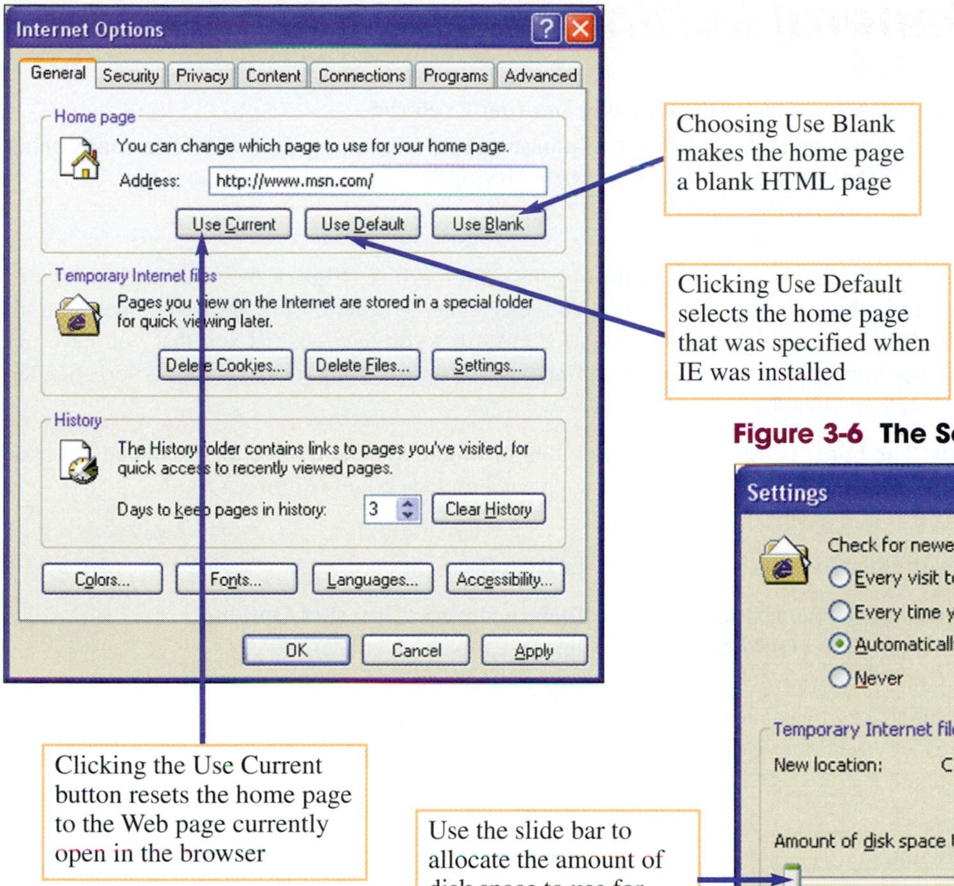

Choosing Use Blank makes the home page a blank HTML page

Clicking Use Default selects the home page that was specified when IE was installed

Clicking the Use Current button resets the home page to the Web page currently open in the browser

Figure 3-6 The Settings dialog box

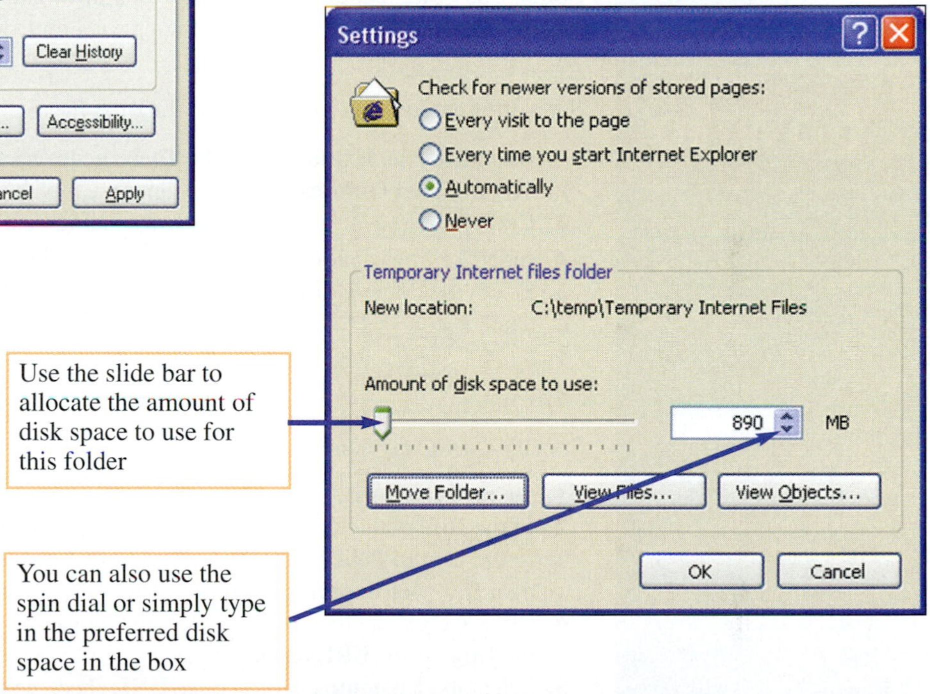

Use the slide bar to allocate the amount of disk space to use for this folder

You can also use the spin dial or simply type in the preferred disk space in the box

Table 3-1   Settings for checking for newer versions of stored Web pages

Setting	Description
Every visit to the page	This setting means that when you return to a Web page you viewed previously, IE will determine if the page changed since you last viewed it. If this is the case, IE stores the newer page in the Temporary Internet Files folder. Note that opting for this method can negatively impact the speed that you browse Web pages you have already viewed.
Every time you start IE	When you return to a Web page you viewed previously, Internet Explorer will not check to see whether the page has changed since you last viewed it. IE checks for new content only when you return to a page that was viewed in an earlier session or on a previous day. Note that if you opt for this modality, you will enhance the rapidity with which the page is displayed.
Automatically	This is the default setting, which means that IE checks only when you return to a Web page that was viewed in an earlier session of IE or on a previous date. This provides the best speed when browsing pages already seen.
Never	With this setting, IE will not automatically check for new Web pages.

skill 2

Configuring Internet Explorer General Settings (cont'd)

exam objective

Resolve issues related to customizing Internet Explorer.

Resolve issues related to Internet Explorer support features. Tasks include configuring Internet Explorer and interpreting error messages.

Configure and troubleshoot Internet Explorer.

overview

Colors: Selecting the **Colors** button opens a dialog box **(Figure 3-7)** that allows you to customize the colors used by IE. You can specify font colors and the background. Additionally, you can designate colors for links that you have visited and that you have not visited, as well as the color to use for a link that you are pointing to. To select a color, click the box, and then click the color you want.

Fonts: The **Fonts** button opens a dialog box in which you can choose the fonts that are used on Web pages and documents that do not have a font specified **(Figure 3-8)**.

how to

Set a different location for Temporary Internet files.

1. Open **Internet Explorer**. On the **Tools** menu, click **Internet Options**.
2. The **Internet Options** dialog box opens. Click the **General** tab.
3. Click ⌊ Settings... ⌋ to open the **Settings** dialog box.
4. In the Settings dialog box, click ⌊ Move Folder... ⌋ to open the **Browse for Folder** window.
5. Select the folder you want to hold the Temporary Internet files.
6. Click ⌊ OK ⌋ to close the **Browse for Folder** window.
7. Click ⌊ OK ⌋ to close the Settings dialog box.
8. Click ⌊ OK ⌋ to close Internet Options dialog box.

Specify a company home page for a local computer by using Group Policy.

1. On the **Start** menu, click **Run**.
2. In the **Run** dialog box, type **gpedit.msc** in the **Open** text box.
3. In the **Group Policy** console, expand **User Configuration**, then **Windows Settings**, and then **Internet Explorer Maintenance**.
4. Click **URLs** and then in the right window pane, double-click **Important URLs** to open the **Important URLs** dialog box.
5. Select the **Customize Home page URL** check box and in the **Home page URL** text box, specify the URL of the page you want to be the default for all users of this computer **(Figure 3-9)**. A domain administrator can specify a policy for the entire domain from a domain controller. Note that the domain Group Policy will override the local Group Policy.
6. Click ⌊ OK ⌋ to close the **Important URLs** dialog box.
7. Close the Group Policy console.

tip

Some companies may want to specify which home page their employees see when opening Internet Explorer. This can be done though the use of Group Policies.

more

Group Policy allows administrators to define what actions a user is and isn't allowed to perform on the network and on their own computer. It is the mechanism by which an administrator can configure certain options for a domain, site, or organizational unit (OU). In addition, policies (essentially configurations that are required) can also be employed on the local computer. You should be aware that many features of IE can be customized through the use of Group Policies, including not only the home page, but also the search page, help page, appearance of the browser (title, logos, etc.), connection and proxy settings, security zone and content rating configurations, and what programs are specified on the Programs tab in the Internet Options dialog box.. However, many companies limit or curtail the ability of a desktop technician to modify Group Policies. When you realize an issue is due to Group Policy, you may need to bump the user request up to the next tier of support.

Figure 3-7 The Colors dialog box

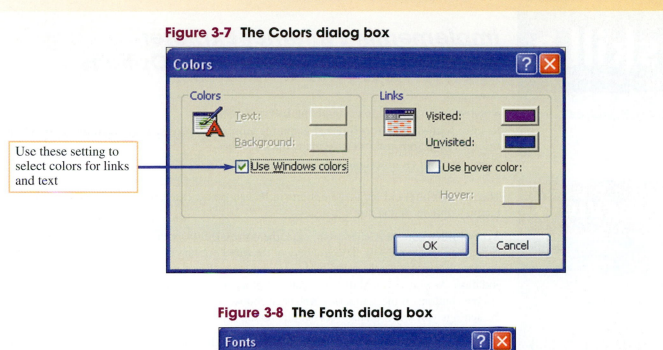

Use these setting to select colors for links and text

Figure 3-8 The Fonts dialog box

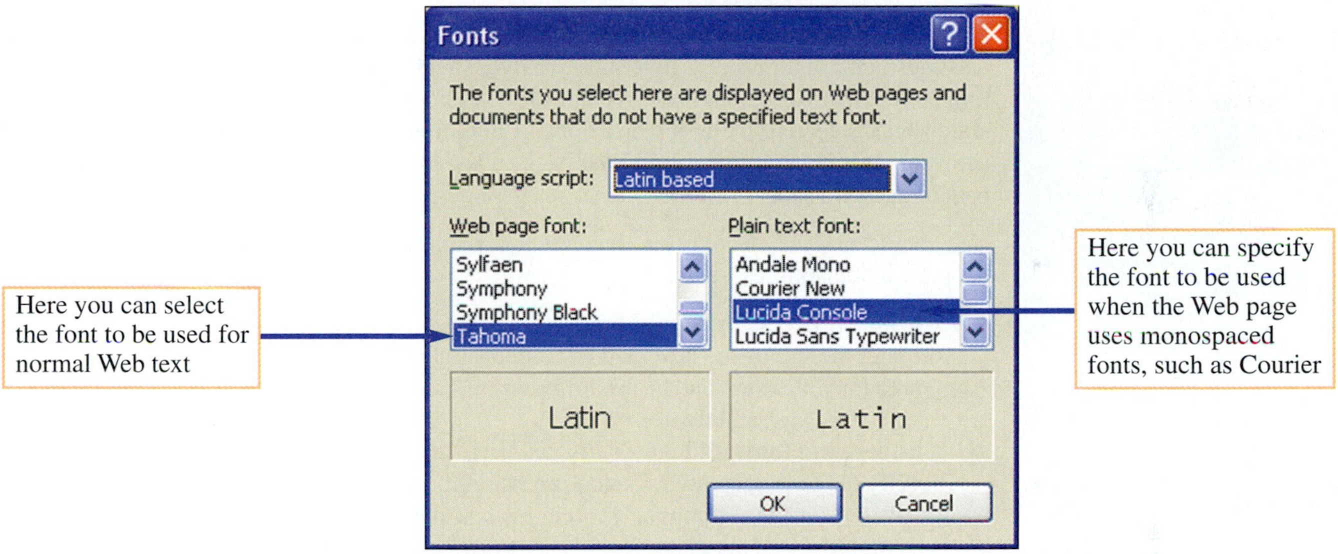

Here you can select the font to be used for normal Web text

Here you can specify the font to be used when the Web page uses monospaced fonts, such as Courier

Figure 3-9   Specifying a default home page through Group Policy

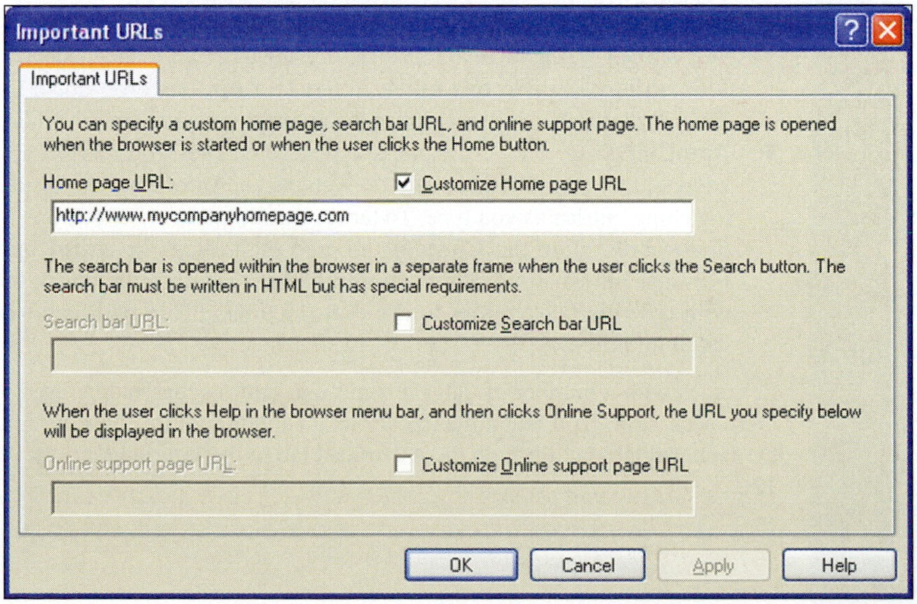

Important URLs

You can specify a custom home page, search bar URL, and online support page. The home page is opened when the browser is started or when the user clicks the Home button.

Home page URL: ☑ Customize Home page URL
http://www.mycompanyhomepage.com

The search bar is opened within the browser in a separate frame when the user clicks the Search button. The search bar must be written in HTML but has special requirements.

Search bar URL: ☐ Customize Search bar URL

When the user clicks Help in the browser menu bar, and then clicks Online Support, the URL you specify below will be displayed in the browser.

Online support page URL   ☐ Customize Online support page URL

OK   Cancel   Apply   Help

skill 3

Implementing Internet Explorer Accessibility and Language Options

exam objective

Resolve issues related to customizing Internet Explorer.

Resolve issues related to Internet Explorer support features. Tasks include configuring Internet Explorer and interpreting error messages.

Configure and troubleshoot Internet Explorer.

overview

The accessibility and language options in IE can be accessed from the General tab in the Internet Options dialog box.

Accessibility: On the General tab, click the **Accessibility** button to open the Accessibility dialog box (**Figure 3-10**). Selecting any of the three options in the Formatting area specifies that IE will always use the color, font style, and font settings you choose for text, background, and links. As you saw in Skill 1, you can set colors and fonts on the General tab via the Colors or Fonts buttons. If the author of a Web page chooses different colors for text and background, the settings you select on the Accessibility dialog box will override them.

Another means of specifying the default font size, style, colors, and background for text and headings is through use of a style sheet. A **style sheet** is a template that specifies the default font style, size, colors, and background for text and headings. Under the subheading **User style sheet,** selecting the check box **Format documents using my style sheet** causes IE to use your style sheet to format all Web pages when they are displayed. You must specify the path to the style sheet.

You should also be aware of the features that make Internet Explorer more accessible for people with disabilities, such as:

◆ **Keyboard access**. Like all Microsoft products, all of the features in IE are accessible through the use of the keyboard or the mouse. Pressing **[Tab]** and **[Shift]+[Tab]** allows you to move forward and backward between screen elements such as links, hot spots, the various toolbars, and frames.

◆ **Customizing fonts and colors**. As you have already seen in the previous skill, you can specify the font sizes, styles, colors, and foreground and background colors of Web pages displayed on your computer screen, even if the author of the Web page has already specified these. This is particularly useful for people who are color-blind, need larger fonts, or need high-contrast colors.

◆ **Customizing the toolbars**. As discussed in Skill 1, there are a variety of customizations you can make to IE's toolbars that are useful for people with disabilities. For those with poor vision, you may wish to add the Size button to the Standard Buttons toolbar for quick access to the relative font size. If using a screen reader, selecting **Small Icons** in the **Icon options** and **No text labels** in the **Text options** drop-down lists in the Customize Toolbar dialog box will maximize the amount of screen space available for Web material.

◆ **AutoComplete.** The AutoComplete feature enables you to save time when typing Web addresses or completing entries on Web pages. AutoComplete displays a list of previous matching entries as you type. To turn AutoComplete on or off, open the Internet Options dialog box, click the **Content** tab, and then click the **AutoComplete** button in the Personal information section (**Figure 3-11**). Clearing the check boxes may help users with cognitive disabilities to avoid distractions. (This will be covered again in greater detail in Skill 5.)

IE comes with a number of other features and options that can be used to make the program more accessible. You reach them, curiously enough, not through the Accessibility button on the **General** tab, but through the **Advanced** tab in the Internet Options dialog box (**Figure 3-12**).

tip

To access advanced settings in IE, select the Tools menu, click Internet Options, and then click the Advanced tab.

Figure 3-10   The Accessibility dialog box

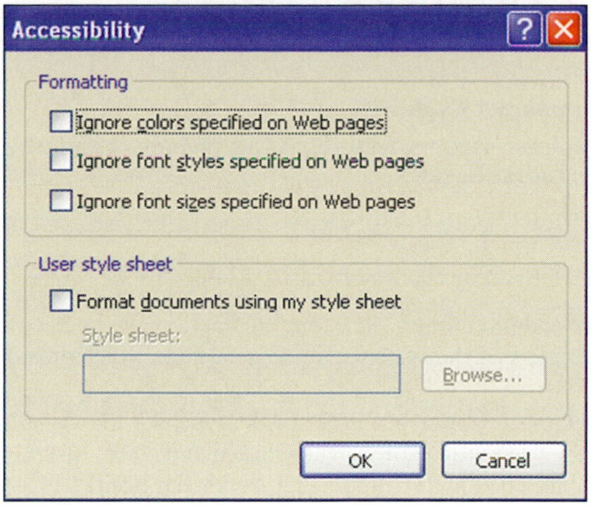

Accessibility

Formatting

☐ Ignore colors specified on Web pages
☐ Ignore font styles specified on Web pages
☐ Ignore font sizes specified on Web pages

User style sheet

☐ Format documents using my style sheet

Style sheet:

[   ]   Browse...

OK   Cancel

Figure 3-11   The AutoComplete Settings dialog box

AutoComplete Settings

AutoComplete lists possible matches from entries you've typed before.

Use AutoComplete for

☑ Web addresses
☐ Forms
☑ User names and passwords on forms
   ☐ Prompt me to save passwords

Clear AutoComplete history

[Clear Forms]   [Clear Passwords]

To clear Web address entries, on the General tab in Internet Options, click Clear History.

OK   Cancel

Figure 3-12   Options available on the Advanced tab

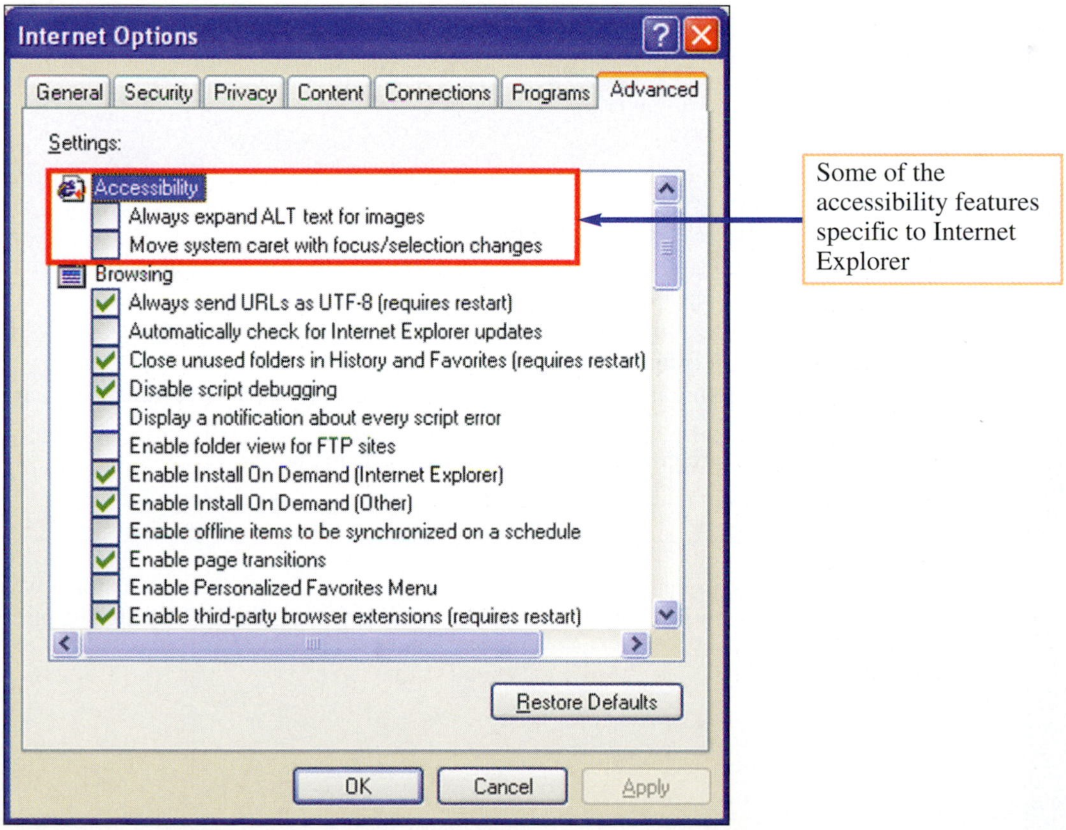

Internet Options

General | Security | Privacy | Content | Connections | Programs | **Advanced**

Settings:

🔲 Accessibility
   ☐ Always expand ALT text for images
   ☐ Move system caret with focus/selection changes
🔲 Browsing
   ☑ Always send URLs as UTF-8 (requires restart)
   ☐ Automatically check for Internet Explorer updates
   ☑ Close unused folders in History and Favorites (requires restart)
   ☑ Disable script debugging
   ☐ Display a notification about every script error
   ☐ Enable folder view for FTP sites
   ☑ Enable Install On Demand (Internet Explorer)
   ☑ Enable Install On Demand (Other)
   ☐ Enable offline items to be synchronized on a schedule
   ☑ Enable page transitions
   ☐ Enable Personalized Favorites Menu
   ☑ Enable third-party browser extensions (requires restart)

[Restore Defaults]

OK   Cancel   Apply

Some of the accessibility features specific to Internet Explorer

skill 3

Implementing Internet Explorer Accessibility and Language Options (cont'd)

exam objective

Resolve issues related to customizing Internet Explorer.

Resolve issues related to Internet Explorer support features. Tasks include configuring Internet Explorer and interpreting error messages.

Configure and troubleshoot Internet Explorer.

overview

The following settings on the Advanced tab can be changed to assist disabled users:

◆ **Move system caret with focus/selection changes**. Selecting this option assists people using a screen reader or magnifier that uses the system caret to determine which area of the screen to read or magnify.

◆ **Always expand ALT text for images**. Recommended for people, typically the visually impaired, who rely on alternate (ALT) text instead of viewing the actual pictures (usually, in those cases, the **Show pictures** check box in the Multimedia section has been cleared). This ensures that the text is not cut off if the amount of text is larger than the image area.

◆ **Use smooth scrolling** and **Enable page transitions**. Clearing these check boxes in the Browsing section reduces interference and problems for users employing screen magnification or screen reader programs and also aids those using voice recognition programs that encounter errors during smooth scrolling and transitions.

◆ **Show pictures**, **Play animations**, and **Play videos**. Clearing these check boxes in the Multimedia section can be of value to people with impaired vision. Similarly, users with sensitivity to screen flashing can benefit from turning some of these options off.

◆ **Play sounds**. Clear this option in the Multimedia section to prevent distractions for the cognitively impaired and to reduce interference with screen readers for the visually disabled.

◆ **Print background colors and images**. Clearing this check box in the Printing section can help improve print readability for those with reduced vision.

Languages: A growing number of Web sites provide their content in several languages. If you have a preferred language, you can use this feature to add languages to your list in Internet Explorer.

how to

Add a language.

1. Open **Internet Explorer**.
2. On the **Tools** menu, click **Internet Options**.
3. In the Internet Options dialog box, click the **General** tab if it is not already selected. Click [Languages...] to open the **Language Preference** dialog box (**Figure 3-13**).
4. Click [Add...] to open the **Add Language** dialog box. Choose the language you want to include on your list (**Figure 3-14**).
5. Click [OK] to return to the Language Preference dialog box and the added language appears (**Figure 3-15**).
6. Close the Language Preference and Internet Options dialog boxes.

more

If you select several languages you can arrange them in order of preference so that if a Web site offers multiple languages, content will appear in the language that has the highest place on the list.

Figure 3-13   The Language Preference dialog box

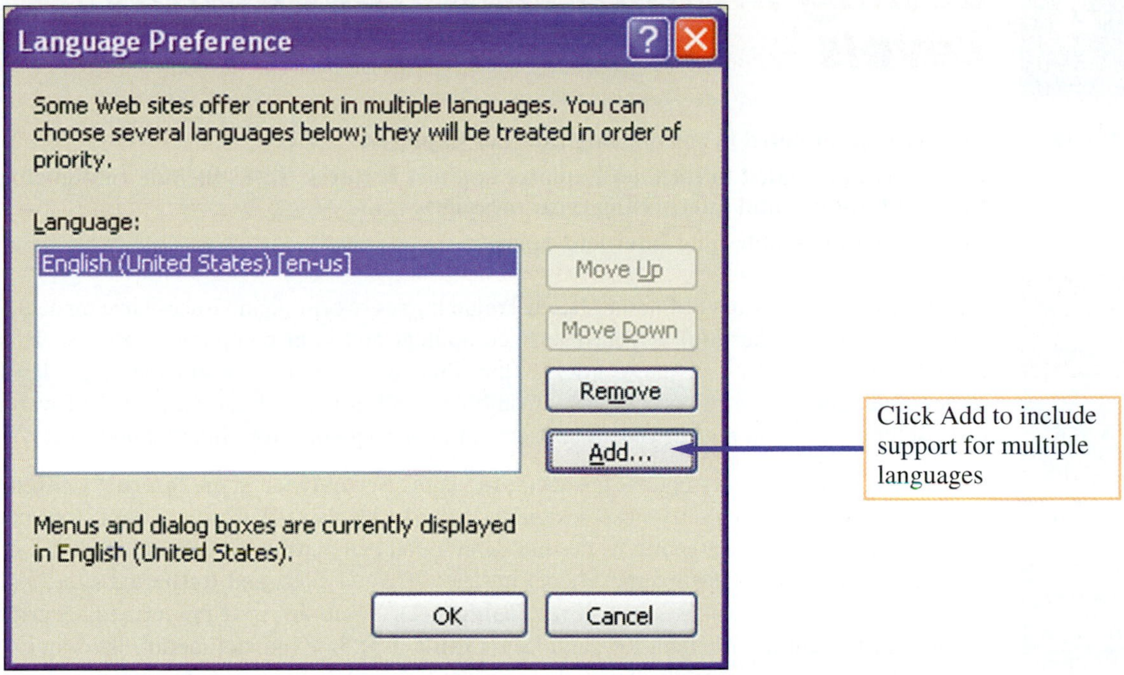

Language Preference

Some Web sites offer content in multiple languages. You can choose several languages below; they will be treated in order of priority.

Language:

English (United States) [en-us]

Move Up
Move Down

Remove

Add...

Menus and dialog boxes are currently displayed in English (United States).

OK   Cancel

Click Add to include support for multiple languages

Figure 3-14   Adding a language

Add Language

Language:

Gaelic [gd]
Galician [gl]
Georgian [ka]
German (Austria) [de-at]
German (Germany) [de]
German (Liechtenstein) [de-li]
German (Luxembourg) [de-lu]
German (Switzerland) [de-ch]
Greek [el]
Gujarati [gu]
Hebrew [he]
Hindi [hi]
Hungarian [hu]
Icelandic [is]

User defined:

OK   Cancel

Figure 3-15   Prioritizing languages

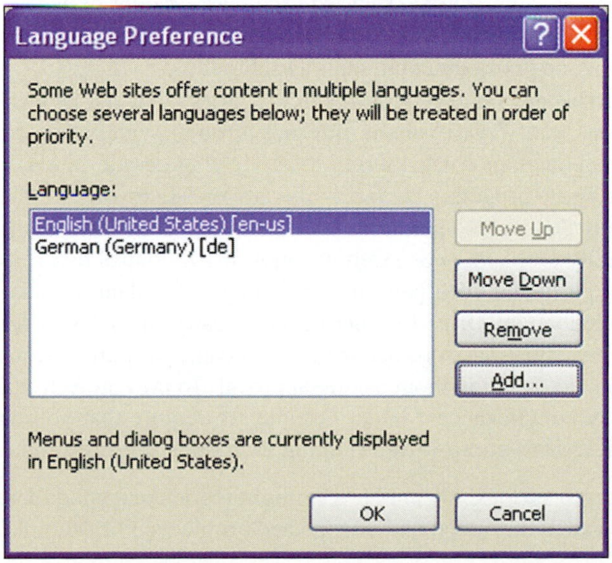

Language Preference

Some Web sites offer content in multiple languages. You can choose several languages below; they will be treated in order of priority.

Language:

English (United States) [en-us]
German (Germany) [de]

Move Up
Move Down
Remove
Add...

Menus and dialog boxes are currently displayed in English (United States).

OK   Cancel

skill 4

Setting Internet Explorer Security Levels

exam objective

Resolve issues related to customizing Internet Explorer.

Resolve issues related to Internet Explorer support features. Tasks include configuring Internet Explorer and interpreting error messages.

Configure and troubleshoot Internet Explorer.

overview

The burgeoning explosion of Internet-based Trojan horses, worms, and viruses have made the Internet potentially harmful to your users' computers and your company's network. It is essential that you understand the security settings that come with IE to assure the proper level of computer security at the proper time. Combined with a firewall and antivirus software, these settings will help protect you, your users, and your network from Internet malware.

Internet Explorer's security options are accessed via the **Security** tab in the **Internet Options** dialog box (**Figure 3-16**). To make assigning security levels to Web sites easier, Internet Explorer has defined four security zones into which you can place Web sites or categories of Web sites. These zones are Internet, Local intranet, Trusted sites, and Restricted sites, and each comes with a default security level (**Table 3-2**). There are four predefined security levels: High, Medium, Medium-low, and Low (**Table 3-3**), but you can modify the security settings for each zone as needed by clicking on the **Custom Level** button to change specific settings within the framework of the current security level.

Some key security settings available at the Custom Level are those that govern how Java applets and ActiveX controls are handled.

◆ **Java Security Settings**: The custom security settings allow you to explicitly define Java permissions for signed and unsigned **Java applets**, which are mini-programs written in the cross-platform Java language, often used for multimedia and games. Java applets typically request a specific level of access to files, folders, and network connections on your computer. If a Java applet requests greater access than you have specified, you will be prompted whether to allow more access permissions for that applet. The Microsoft Java Virtual Machine must be installed to configure the custom Java permissions. Use caution when you adjust Java permissions. Some Java-based programs may not work properly after you change permissions. Some changes to Java permissions can also make your computer vulnerable to security breaches by hackers. Microsoft recommends that you do not change the default permissions unless you have a specific purpose for doing so. There are five levels of access: Low safety, Medium safety, High safety, Disable Java, and Custom. To allow the greatest amount of access, click Low safety. To permit a moderate amount of access, click Medium safety. To assure the least amount of access, click High safety. To customize your Java permissions even further, click Custom. To prohibit Java applets from running on your computer, click Disable Java.

◆ **ActiveX settings**: **ActiveX controls** are small program building blocks that can be used to create distributed applications that work over the Internet through Web browsers. Examples include customized applications for gathering data, viewing certain kinds of files, and displaying animation. These programs are available only on Microsoft Internet Explorer browsers. Although most ActiveX content contained in Web pages is safe, some ActiveX content can cause security problems. For example, an ActiveX control that runs automatically when you load a particular Web page might damage your data or cause your computer to become infected with a virus. Internet Explorer uses safety levels for active content to help prevent this situation from occurring. You can configure various ActiveX control settings to Enable, i.e., run without asking approval. To prevent ActiveX controls from running under any circumstances, select Disable. To require that you be asked to approve/disapprove an ActiveX control from running each time, select Prompt.

Although adjusting zones and settings to various "secure" levels might seem like a good idea, setting them at the wrong level can lead to unwanted and unexpected problems. For example,

tip

IE's security zones are really predefined categories to help you in assigning security levels. Microsoft has left these zones fully customizable. This can create some confusion because you can place a site in the Restricted zone, for example, but set the actual zone level to Low.

Figure 3-16 The Security tab in the Internet Options dialog box

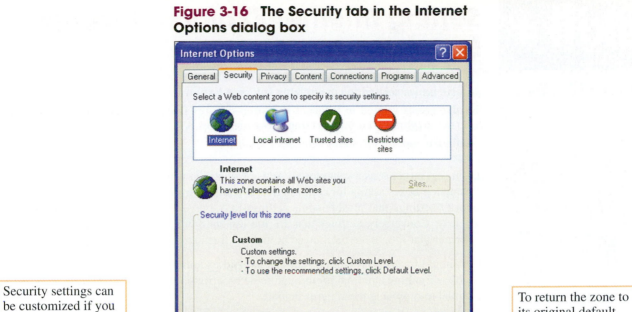

Security settings can be customized if you prefer not to use the default settings for the various zones

To return the zone to its original default security level, click Default Level

Table 3-2 Security zones

Zone	Default Web Sites	Default Security Level
Internet	Any Web site visited that has not been placed into another zone is treated with the security level assigned to the Internet zone.	Medium
Local intranet	By default, this zone includes all sites on your intranet, sites that bypass any proxy server, and any network directories.	Medium-low
Trusted sites	Empty by default; you can use this zone to your place sites that you trust will not damage computer.	Low
Restricted sites	Empty by default, you can use this zone to place sites deemed potentially harmful or that you don't want users to be able to access.	High

Table 3-3 Security levels

Level	Description
High	This is the default security level for Restricted sites. It prevents most potentially harmful items from being downloaded and allows lower levels of functionality from Web sites.
Medium	This is the most functional security level while still preventing serious potential security risks, such as unsigned ActiveX controls, from being downloaded.
Medium-low	This level is the same as Medium but with less frequent prompts. It is appropriate for your local intranet sites or sites you completely trust.
Low	This security level has the minimum safeguards and prompts. Most content is run or downloaded without any prompts. Active content, such as scripting, runs without prompting you to allow it. This setting should almost never be used and only then on sites which are completely trusted.
Custom	A security level that you have modified so that it is not an exact match to any of the above levels.

skill 4

Setting Internet Explorer Security Levels *(cont'd)*

exam objective

Resolve issues related to customizing Internet Explorer.

Resolve issues related to Internet Explorer support features. Tasks include configuring Internet Explorer and interpreting error messages.

Configure and troubleshoot Internet Explorer.

overview

if you set "prompt" as a value for all ActiveX controls, you or your users may be confronted with dialog boxes asking for confirmation to continue every few moments. Similarly, setting security settings that disable some settings may prevent certain Web pages from loading properly. Conversely, settings that are too lenient can allow things to happen on a client computer that should not be allowed or that can threaten the computer.

You should browse through the settings list and examine the functionality you can enable, disable, or require a prompt for through these security settings. Being familiar with this list is essential to providing meaningful support.

how to

Assign a Web site to a Restricted sites security zone.

1. Open **Internet Explorer**.
2. Select **Internet Options** on the **Tools** menu.
3. Click the **Security** tab to bring it forward.
4. On the Security tab, click the **Restricted** zone.
5. Click [Sites...] to open the **Restricted sites** dialog box (**Figure 3-17**).
6. Type the URL of the Web site in the **Add this Web site to the zone** text box, and then click [Add] .
7. Click [OK] to close the Restricted sites dialog box.
8. Click [OK] to close the Internet Options dialog box.

Modify the security level for the Internet zone to prevent downloads.

1. Open **Internet Explorer**.
2. Select **Internet Options** on the **Tools** menu.
3. In the Internet Options dialog box, click the **Security** tab.
4. On the Security tab, click the **Internet** zone.
5. Click [Custom Level...] . The **Security Settings** dialog box opens (**Figure 3-18**).
6. Scroll down through the **Settings** list and under the **Downloads** category, select the **Disable** option button.
7. Click [OK] to close the Restricted sites dialog box.
8. Click [OK] to close the Internet Options dialog box.

tip

You cannot assign a Web site to the Internet zone.

Figure 3-17 The Restricted Sites dialog box

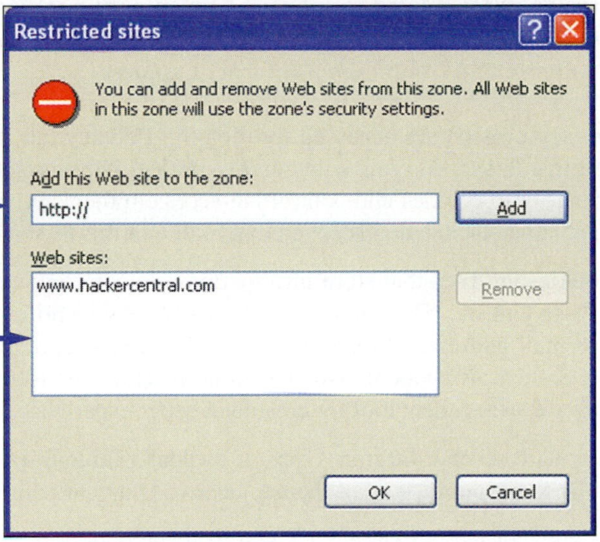

Enter a Web site address to add the Web site to the Restricted sites zone

List of defined sites for the Restricted sites zone

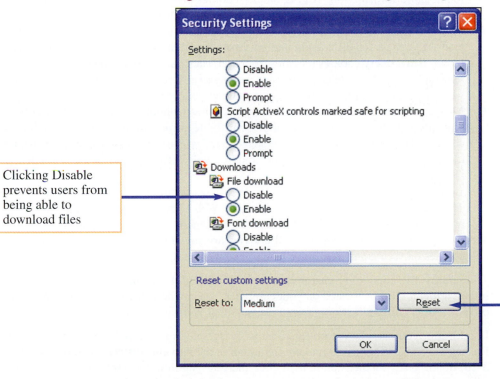

Figure 3-18 The Security Settings dialog box

Clicking Disable prevents users from being able to download files

If you want to reassign the zone to one of the other predefined security levels, select the level from the drop-down list and click Reset

skill 5 — *Examining Privacy Options in Internet Explorer*

exam objective

Resolve issues related to customizing Internet Explorer.

Resolve issues related to Internet Explorer support features. Tasks include configuring Internet Explorer and interpreting error messages.

Configure and troubleshoot Internet Explorer.

overview

caution

Some Web sites require cookies. If you choose a setting that does not allow cookies, you might not be able to view certain Web sites.

tip

Privacy settings affect only Web sites in the Internet zone.

Privacy options are accessed through the **Privacy** tab in the Internet Options dialog box (**Figure 3-19**). As you will quickly notice, privacy settings in Internet Explorer relate primarily to cookies and controlling access to them. Privacy related matters with respect to content personalization is covered in Skill 6 of this lesson.

Cookies are files that store information on your computer, such as your preferences when visiting that site. They may also store personally identifiable information, such as your name or e-mail address. Years ago, cookies got a bad reputation because some Web sites were perceived as using them to track their users. However, from a Web site producer's perspective, they are an excellent tool for creating a better experience for users.

There are several different types of cookies (**Table 3-4**). In IE, you can choose whether to allow some, none, or all of them to be saved on your computer.

As you can see in Figure 3-19, you have the option to move the slide bar to select from six different levels (represented by the small hash marks along each side of the slide bar) of cookie handling:

- **Block All Cookies** prevents cookies from all Web sites from being placed on a local computer and at the same prevents the reading of existing cookies on the local computer.
- **High** blocks cookies unless the Web site has explicit consent to use your personally identifiable information. It also blocks cookies from Web sites that do not have a **compact privacy policy** (a condensed computer-readable privacy statement).
- **Medium High** blocks **first-party cookies** (from the Web site you are currently viewing) that use your personally identifiable information without your implicit consent and also blocks **third party cookies** (cookies from Web sites other than the one you are currently viewing) if the Web site does not have a compact privacy policy or it it attempts to use your personally identifiable information without your explicit consent.
- **Medium** blocks cookies from third-party Web sites without a compact privacy policy or that attempt to use your personally identifiable information without your implicit consent. This setting also deletes cookies from first-party Web sites that use personally identifiable information without your implicit consent from your computer when you close IE.
- **Low** blocks cookies from third-party Web sites without a compact privacy policy. This setting deletes cookies from third-party Web sites that use personally identifiable information without your implicit consent from your computer when you close IE.
- **Accept all cookies** means that all cookies are saved on your computer and existing cookies on your computer can be read by the Web sites that created them.

To import a file containing custom privacy settings, click **Import** on the Privacy tab. To import a file, it must be located on your computer. You can download files containing custom privacy settings from privacy organizations and other Web sites on the Internet.

In addition, you can change options manually by selecting the **Advanced** button on the Privacy tab and setting the desired configuration in the **Advanced Privacy Settings (Figure 3-20)** dialog box. Another option is to click the Edit button in the **Web Sites** section of the Privacy tab. This opens the **Per Site Privacy Actions** dialog box (**Figure 3-21**), where you can edit settings to allow or block cookies from individual sites regardless of the privacy settings.

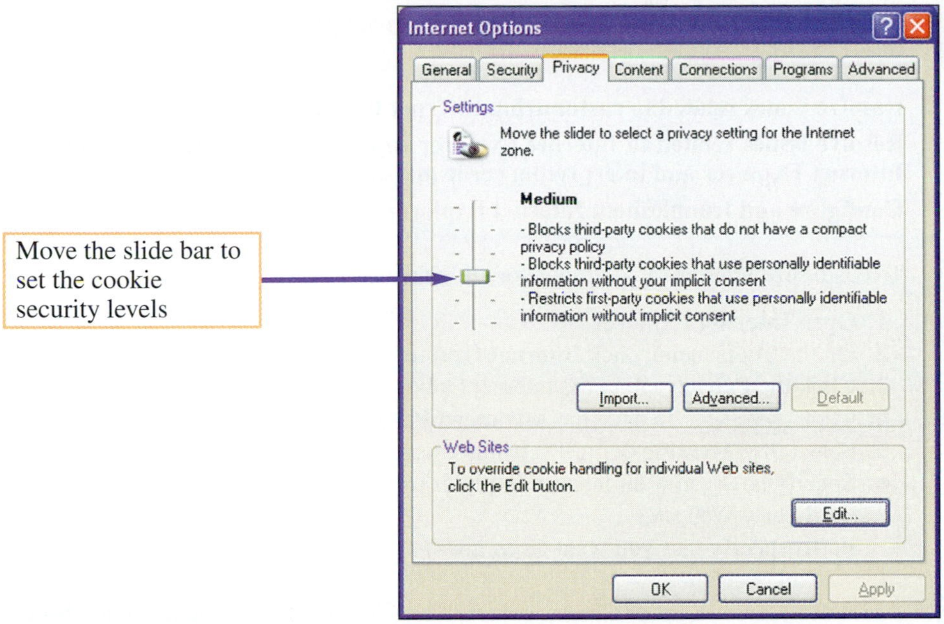

Figure 3-19 The Privacy tab in the Internet Options dialog box

Move the slide bar to set the cookie security levels

Table 3-4 Types of cookies

Type	Description
Persistent cookie	A persistent cookie is stored as a file on your computer, remaining there after you close Internet Explorer. This type of cookie is typically created by a Web site to use to customize the site on later visits.
Temporary or session cookie	A temporary or session cookie is stored for the current browser session only. It is deleted when you close Internet Explorer. Temporary cookies enable a site to determine the client browser, language, and screen resolution that the user is using. When a user clicks the Back and Forward buttons, he or she will not lose the information previously entered.
First-party cookie	A first-party cookie is created by the Web site you are currently viewing. These cookies are usually used to store a user's preferences and other user-specific information, preferences when visiting that site. First-party cookies can be persistent or temporary.
Third-party cookie	A third-party cookie is sent to your computer from a Web site different from the one you are currently viewing. Third-party cookies can either be persistent or temporary. The most common use is by advertisers tracking page use for targeted marketing.
Unsatisfactory cookie	Unsatisfactory cookies are those that might be used to gain access to personal identifiable information without your consent.

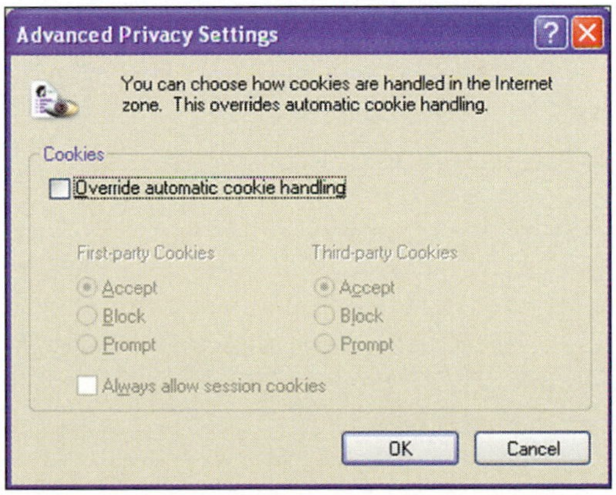

Figure 3-20 The Advanced Privacy Settings dialog box

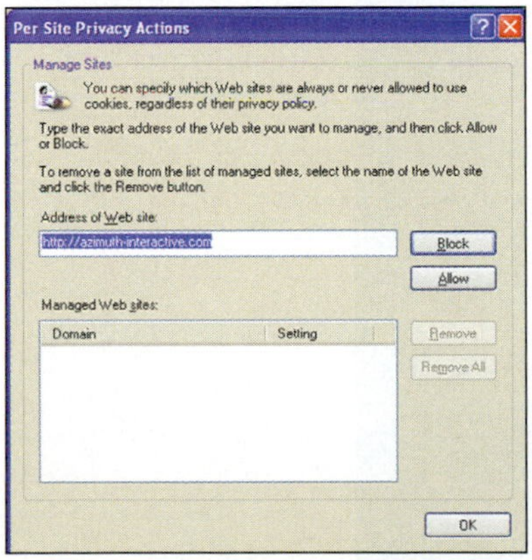

Figure 3-21 The Per Site Privacy Actions dialog box

skill 5

Examining Privacy Options in Internet Explorer *(cont'd)*

exam objective

Resolve issues related to customizing Internet Explorer.

Resolve issues related to Internet Explorer support features. Tasks include configuring Internet Explorer and interpreting error messages.

Configure and troubleshoot Internet Explorer.

how to

To customize your privacy settings for all Web sites.

1. Open **Internet Explorer**.
2. On the **Tools** menu, click **Internet Options**.
3. Click the **Privacy** tab in the Internet Options dialog box.
4. Click Advanced... to open the **Advanced Privacy Settings** dialog box.
5. Select the **Override default settings** check box (**Figure 3-22**).
6. Specify how you want Internet Explorer to handle cookies from first-party Web sites and third-party Web sites.
   - To specify that you want IE to always allow cookies to be saved on your computer, click **Accept**.
   - To assure IE never allows cookies to be saved on your computer, click **Block**.
   - To require IE to ask whether or not you want to allow a cookie to be saved on your computer, click **Prompt**.
7. To force IE to always allow session cookies (cookies that are deleted from your computer when you close IE) to be saved on your computer, click the **Always allow session cookies** check box.
8. When you are finished selecting settings, click OK .

more

When you change privacy settings, they might not affect cookies already on your computer. To be certain that all of the cookies on your computer are consistent with the new privacy settings, you should delete all of the existing cookies on your computer. Upon returning to sites that previously had saved cookies on your computer, those sites that match the new privacy settings will be able to save cookies on your computer again, whereas those that do not will not be allowed to save cookies on your computer.

Figure 3-22 **The Advanced Privacy Settings dialog box with the Override automatic cookie handling check box selected**

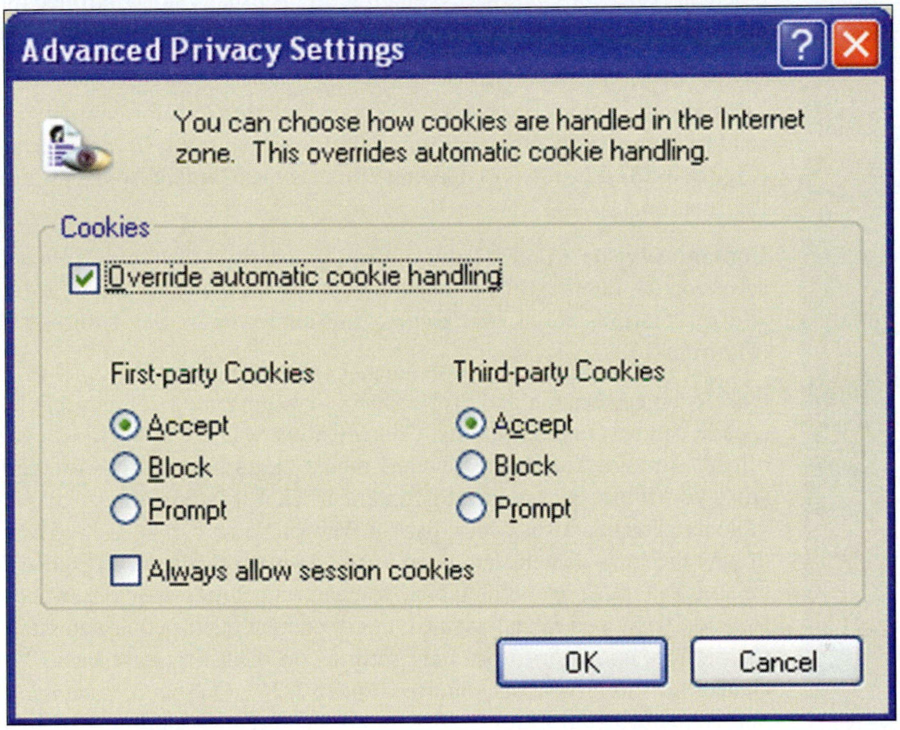

skill 6

Personalizing Content in Internet Explorer

exam objective

Resolve issues related to customizing Internet Explorer.

Resolve issues related to Internet Explorer support features. Tasks include configuring Internet Explorer and interpreting error messages.

Configure and troubleshoot Internet Explorer.

overview

tip

Not all Internet content is rated. If you choose to allow other people to view unrated sites on your computer, some of those sites could contain inappropriate material.

tip

When downloading software from a Web site, use certificates to verify that it is coming from a known, reliable source.

tip

Viewing information almost never presents a security risk, but sending information, such as your credit card number, often does. Therefore, you might want to disable the warnings for viewing Web pages but retain them for sending information.

Some information on the Internet may not be suitable for every viewer. You might want to prevent your children from seeing Web sites that contain violent or sexual content or control the sort of content that can be viewed by users using a corporate Internet connection. As a practical issue, corporate access and filtering is usually not controlled through IE, but through third-party software. Software that is more robust than IE's Content Advisor is also available for parental control.

The types of content, as well as other items relating to information types you receive from or send to Web sites can be configured on the Content tab in the Internet Options dialog box (**Figure 3-23**). The tab is divided into three areas: Content Advisor, Certificates, and Personal Information.

Content Advisor: Content Advisor helps you control the types of content that a computer can access on the Internet. It is disabled by default. To activate Content Advisor and configure the various features, click the Enable button to open the **Content Advisor** dialog box (**Figure 3-24**).

Once enabled, Content Advisor ensures that only rated content that meets or exceeds your criteria can be viewed. Initially, Content Advisor is set to the most restrictive (least likely to offend) settings. You can review and adjust the ratings settings on the Ratings tab to reflect what you think is appropriate content in each of four areas: language, nudity, sex, and violence. You can also specify lists of Web sites that can be viewed or not viewed regardless of how the site's contents are rated on the **Approved Sites** tab (**Figure 3-25**). On the General tab in Content Advisor dialog box, you can set a **supervisor password** that controls Content Advisor. Here, you can adjust the types of content other people can view, with or without your permission, and override content settings on a case-by-case basis. You can also view and change the rating systems you use (**Figure 3-26**). On the Advanced tab, you can add ratings bureaus and install Platform for Internet Content Selection (PICS) Rules files which are effective on Web sites that include PICS labels (**Figure 3-27**).

Certificates: The Certificates section on the Content tab in the Internet Options dialog box allows you to use digital certificates to positively identify yourself, certification authorities, and publishers. It also allows you to manage them and configure as necessary.

IE uses two types of certificates:

- ◆ **Personal certificates** verify that you are who you say you are and are used when you send personal information over the Internet to a Web site that requires a certificate verifying your identity.
- ◆ **Web site certificates** confirm that the specified Web site is secure and genuine; that is, it prevents another Web site from assuming the identity of the original secure site and getting away with it. When sending personal information via the Internet, always check the Web site certificate to be certain it protects your personal information.

You can click **Clear SSL State** to remove all client authentication certificates from the Secure Sockets Layer (SSL) cache. Clicking the **Certificates** button opens the **Certificates** dialog box (**Figure 3-28**). From here, you can require a secure Web site to send you its security certificates before you send any information. Secure Web sites send IE a digital certificate containing information about security for that site. IE verifies the Internet address stored in the certificate and that the current date precedes the expiration date. If there is a problem, Internet Explorer will display a warning. Selecting the **Publishers** button displays the list of certificate publishers.

Figure 3-23 The Content tab in the Internet Options properties dialog box

Figure 3-24 Content Advisor dialog box

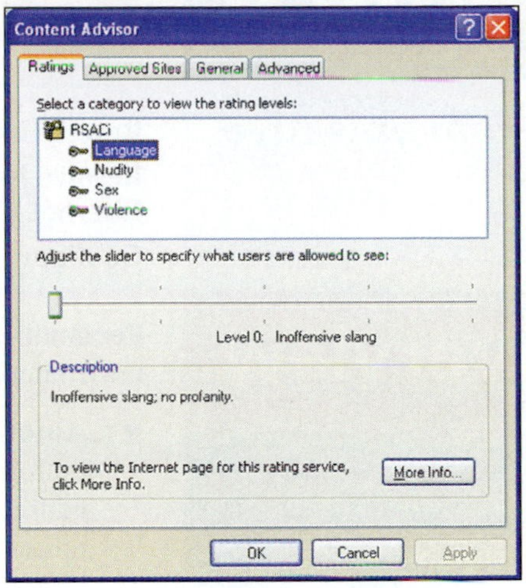

Figure 3-25 Approved Sites tab allows you to designate approved and forbidden sites

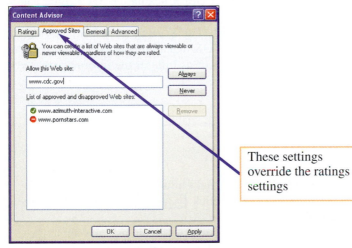

These settings override the ratings settings

Figure 3-26 The General tab in the Content Advisor dialog box

Figure 3-27 The Advanced tab

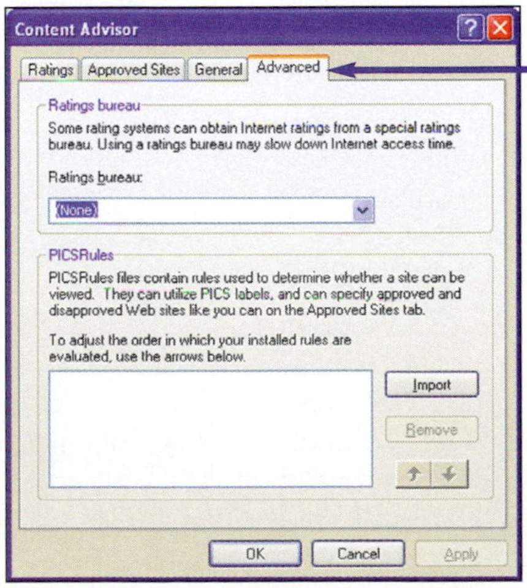

The Advanced tab allows you to designate third-party rating bureaus to assess content as well as which PICS rules to enforce

Figure 3-28 List of Intermediate Certificate Authorities recognized by IE on your computer

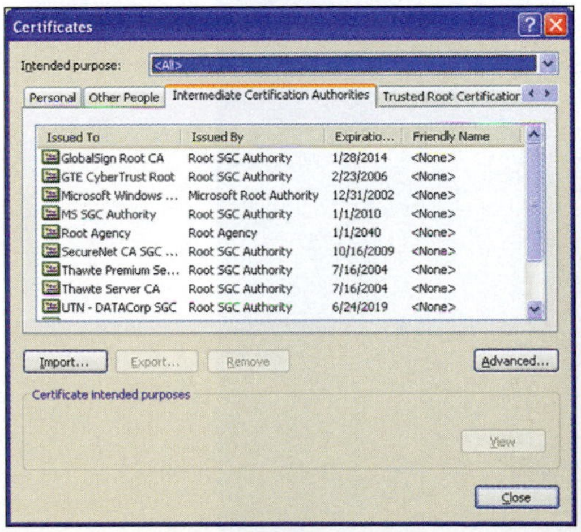

skill 6

Personalizing Content in Internet Explorer (cont'd)

exam objective

Resolve issues related to customizing Internet Explorer.

Resolve issues related to Internet Explorer support features. Tasks include configuring Internet Explorer and interpreting error messages.

Configure and troubleshoot Internet Explorer.

overview

tip

You can encrypt your personal information when it is transmitted and as it is stored on your computer.

Personal Information: There are two buttons related to the Personal information section on the Contents tab.

◆ **AutoComplete**: Clicking the AutoComplete button opens the AutoComplete Settings dialog box **(Figure 3-29)**, which enables auto-completion of forms and Web site addresses based on material you've entered in the past. You can configure which options to use AutoComplete for and clear histories.

◆ **My Profile**: The Profile Assistant can save you from having to enter basic information, such as your address or e-mail name, every time you visit a new Web site that requests it. Profile Assistant stores your personal information on your computer, while assuring that no one can access it without your permission. Typically, when a Web site asks for information from Profile Assistant, the request will include the URL of the requesting site, the type of information being sought, how it will be used, and whether the site has SSL (which allows you to verify the site's certificate). Clicking the **My Profile** button opens the **Address Book-Choose Profile** dialog box. Here you can create a new entry in the Address Book to represent your profile or select an existing entry from the Address Book. After you choose one of the options, click OK and a Properties dialog box opens **(Figure 3-30)** where you can complete as much or as little of the information as you wish.

how to

tip

You can also open Internet Options via the Control Panel.

Turn on Content Advisor and set the content limits.

1. Open **Internet Explorer**.
2. Click **Tools** on the menu bar, and then click **Internet Options**
3. On the **Content** tab, under **Content Advisor,** click [Enable...] to open the Content Advisor dialog box **(Figure 3-31).**
4. Click a category in the list, and then move the slider to set the limits you want to use.
5. Repeat this process for each category you want to limit, and then click [OK] .
6. If a supervisor password has not already been set up for your computer, you are prompted to create one. Enter your password in the boxes provided and click [OK] .
7. A message box informs you that the Content Advisor has been enabled. Click [OK] .
8. Close the Internet Options dialog box.

Figure 3-29 AutoComplete Settings dialog box

Figure 3-30 Properties dialog box for a personal profile

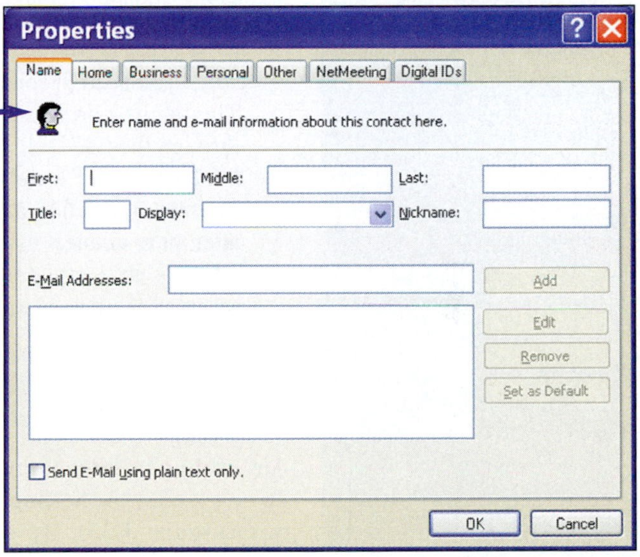

You can supply as much or as little information that you want to make automatically available when a site requests it

Figure 3-31 The Content Advisor dialog box

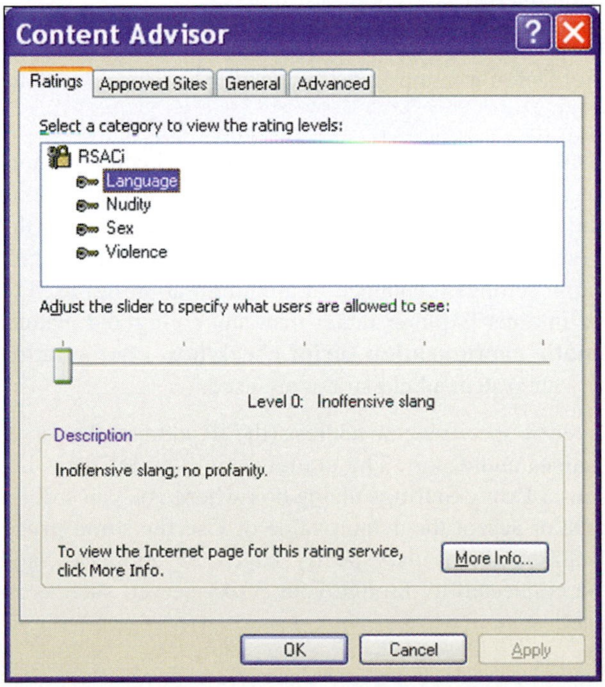

skill 7 Configuring Internet Explorer Connectivity Options

exam objective

Resolve issues related to customizing Internet Explorer.

Resolve issues related to Internet Explorer support features. Tasks include configuring Internet Explorer and interpreting error messages.

Configure and troubleshoot Internet Explorer.

overview

You can create and configure connections in on the **Connections** tab in the Internet Options dialog box (**Figure 3-32**). If you do not already have an Internet connection configured, you can click the **Setup** button to launch the **New Connection Wizard**. The remainder of the tab is divided into two areas reflecting the two primary ways users connect to the Internet: Dial-up and Virtual Private Network settings and Local Area Network (LAN) settings. Dial-up and Virtual Private Network settings deals with connections typically made through telephone lines and modem. Local Area Network (LAN) settings are where you configure proxy settings for your LAN connection.

Dial-up and Virtual Private Network settings: The list box directly underneath the Dial-up and Virtual Private Network settings heading on the Connections tab shows the list of all dial-up and virtual private network setting you currently have enabled for your use. If no connections are set up, clicking the **Add** button will launch the New Connection Wizard (bypassing the Welcome screen displayed when you click the Setup button). You can use the **Remove** button to remove a connection from the list.

Below the list box, there are three options that enable you to control how IE handles dial-up connections when first launched:

◆ **Never dial a connection** means that IE will not automatically dial a connection for you when you need to connect to the Internet, but requires that you manually start the dialing. This is the normal selection for enterprises and corporations that have users connect through the LAN to the Internet.

◆ **Dial whenever a network connection is not present** tells IE that when you need an Internet connection and a network connection is not available, IE should automatically attempt to connect using the default Dial-Up Networking connection.

◆ **Always dial my default connection** requires IE to dial the specified connection whenever you need to connect to the Internet.

Selecting either **Dial whenever a network connection is not present** or **Always dial my default connection** will activate the **Set Default** button and allow you to designate a specific connection as your default.

Any dial-up or virtual private network connection will likely need additional configuration. To do so, click the **Settings** button and open the selected dial-up connection's Settings dialog box (**Figure 3-33**). By selecting the **Automatically detect settings** check box in the **Automatic Configuration** section, you require IE to automatically detect the proxy server settings or other automatic configuration settings (contained in a configurable file) used to connect to the Internet and customize Internet Explorer rather than any configured manual settings. If you mark the **Use automatic configuration script** check box, configuration settings provided in a file prepared by your system administrator are used.

You can manually specify a proxy server by specifying an address (the IP address, the server name, or a fully qualified domain name) and a port. The default value for HTTP is 80. Clicking on the **Advanced** button opens a **Proxy Settings** dialog box where you can specify different servers for different protocols, or accept the default value of **Use the same proxy server for all protocols (Figure 3-34)**. You can also specify URLs, IP addresses, and computers that you do not want to be connected to through your proxy server, such as an address accessible through your intranet.

tip

A **proxy server** acts as an intermediary between your internal network (intranet) and the Internet, retrieving files from remote Web servers.

tip

You can use wild cards to match domain and host names or addresses—for example, *.vanguard.com; 10.*.*.*, www.gideonenterprises. com, and so on.

Figure 3-32 The Connections tab of the Internet Options dialog box

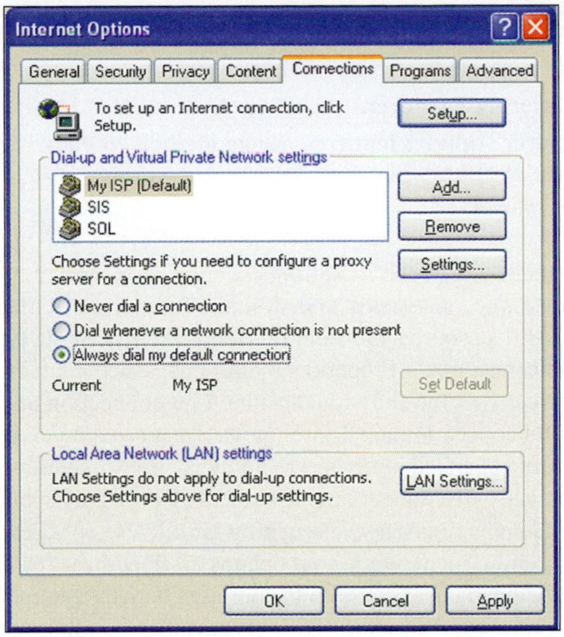

Figure 3-33 The My ISP Settings dialog box

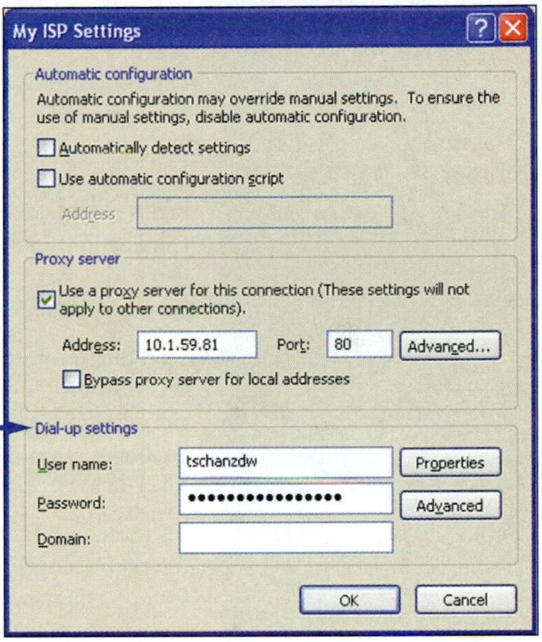

Settings for each dial-up connection are individualized to that connection

Figure 3-34 The Proxy Settings dialog box

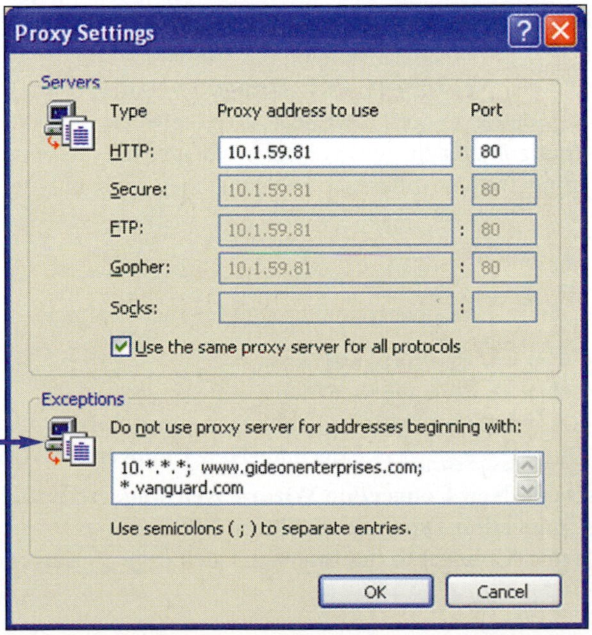

Note that wild cards are allowed

skill 7

Configuring Internet Explorer Connectivity Options *(cont'd)*

exam objective

Resolve issues related to customizing Internet Explorer.

Resolve issues related to Internet Explorer support features. Tasks include configuring Internet Explorer and interpreting error messages.

Configure and troubleshoot Internet Explorer.

overview

In the **Dial-up settings** section of the connection's Settings dialog box (refer to Figure 3-30), you can specify the user name, password and domain for the particular connection depending on the settings provided you by the Internet Service Provider (ISP). Clicking the **Properties** button opens the connection's Properties dialog box which contains five tabs. The **General** tab relates specifically to the individual phone line connection and configuration matters related to the physical connection itself through the designated modem. On the **Options** tab (**Figure 3-35**), you can specify dialing and redialing options, including how often to redial and when to automatically disconnect, among others. The **Security** tab contains configurable settings related to authentication. The **Networking** tab allows you access a Settings dialog box for the dial-up connection, including how it obtains an IP address (or if one is already manually assigned). The **Advanced** tab allows you to configure both the Internet Connection Firewall (ICF) and Internet Connection Sharing (ICS) (**Figure 3-36**). Although these topics are outside the scope of the current lesson and the exam objectives, you should become familiar with them and the fact that they can be configured from within IE.

Enabling the **Internet Connection Firewall (ICF)** activates a software firewall that prevents sets restrictions on what information computers outside your network can view and how they can access resources on your computer and on your home or small office network. You should enable ICF on the Internet connection of any computer that is connected directly to the Internet, especially if Internet Connection Sharing (ICS) is enabled.

As the name implies, **Internet Connection Sharing (ICS)** allows you to share a single Internet connection among multiple computers. This method is typically used in homes and small businesses. Larger enterprises tend to use dedicated proxy servers behind third-party hardware and software firewalls. One ripple effect of using ICS is that any existing TCP/IP connections on the home or small office network for the ICS computer are lost and need to be reestablished.

In the Dial-up settings section of the specific connection's Settings dialog box (refer to Figure 3-30), you can also set dialing, redialing and disconnect options for the connection by clicking the Advanced button. (**Figure 3-37**).

Local Area Network (LAN) settings:To configure LAN settings, simply click the **LAN Settings** button to open the **Local Area Network (LAN) Settings** dialog box (**Figure 3-38**). The configuration changes you can make here are the same as those you can make for a dial-up setting, the sole difference being that they apply only to the LAN connection.

how to

Set up an Internet connection through Internet Explorer.

1. Open **Internet Explorer**.
2. Select **Tools** on the Menu bar.
3. Select **Internet Options** to open the Internet Options dialog box. Click the **Connections** tab.
4. Click [Setup...] to launch the **New Connection Wizard**.
5. On the **New Connection Wizard Welcome** screen, click [Next >] to open the **Network Connection Type** screen (**Figure 3-39**).
6. Select **Connect to the Internet**. Click [Next >] to open the **Getting Ready** screen.

Figure 3-35 The Options tab in the My ISP Properties Settings dialog box

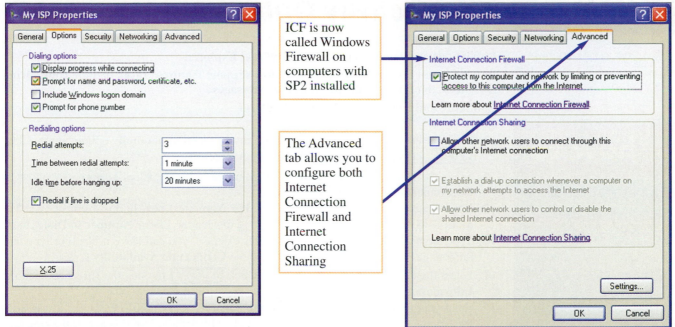

Figure 3-36 The Advanced tab in the My ISP dialog box

ICF is now called Windows Firewall on computers with SP2 installed

The Advanced tab allows you to configure both Internet Connection Firewall and Internet Connection Sharing

Figure 3-37 The Advanced button allows you to configure dialing, redialing, and idle options

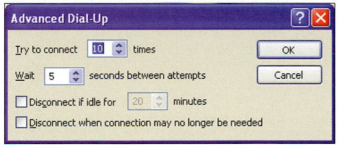

Figure 3-38 The Local Area Network (LAN) Settings dialog box

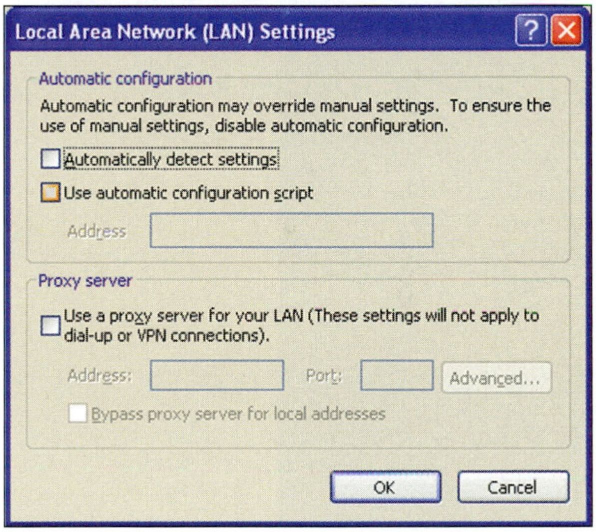

Figure 3-39 The Network Connection Type screen in the New Connection Wizard

| skill 7 | *Configuring Internet Explorer Connectivity Options (cont'd)* |

exam objective

Resolve issues related to customizing Internet Explorer.

Resolve issues related to Internet Explorer support features. Tasks include configuring Internet Explorer and interpreting error messages.

Configure and troubleshoot Internet Explorer.

how to

7. From the list of choices, select the **Set up my connection manually** option button. Click `Next >` to open the **Internet Connection** screen.

8. Select the **Connect using a dial-up modem** option button. Click `Next >` to move to the **Connection Name** screen.

9. Provide a name for the connection in the **ISP Name** text box. In this exercise, type **My Sample ISP (Figure 3-40)**. Click `Next >` to open the **Phone Number to Dial** screen.

10. Type the phone number of the ISP. (In this exercise, you can leave it blank or type in a random number.) Click `Next >` to open the **Connection Availability** screen.

11. Select the **Anyone's Use** option button. Click `Next >` to open the **Internet Account Information** screen.

12. Enter your user name, and password in the Password and Confirm Password text boxes.. Review the three check boxes which are marked by default: **Use this account name and password when anyone connects to the Internet from this computer**; **Make this the default Internet connection**; and **Turn on Internet Connection Firewall for this connection (Figure 3-41)**. Clear those features you do not want to enable. Click `Next >` to open the **Completing New Connection Wizard** screen.

13. Review the content. Click `Next >` to create the connection and close the wizard.

Figure 3-40 The Connection Name screen in the New Connection Wizard

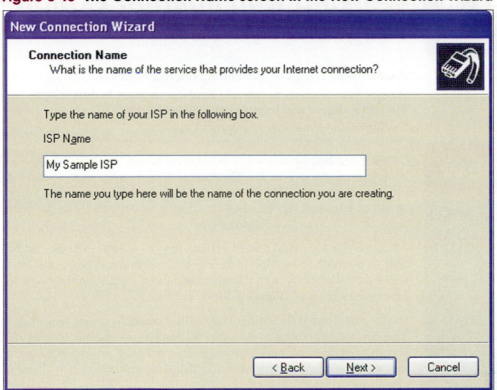

Figure 3-41 The Internet Account Information screen in the New Connection Wizard

skill 8

Working with Internet Explorer Program Options

exam objective

Resolve issues related to customizing Internet Explorer.

Resolve issues related to Internet Explorer support features. Tasks include configuring Internet Explorer and interpreting error messages.

Configure and troubleshoot Internet Explorer.

overview

On the **Programs** tab in the Internet Options dialog box, you can specify the use of certain default programs as your HTML Editor, e-mail, Newsgroups, Internet call, Calendar, and Contact list programs **(Figure 3-42)**. Clicking the drop-down arrow will present you with a choice of programs that IE has detected on your computer that can be used as the default program for that function **(Figure 3-43)**.

An interesting and useful feature of IE allows you to send messages, add contacts, and place calls from within IE by clicking the File menu, pointing to New, and then choosing from the submenu either the type of communication you want to initiate or to open your contact management program **(Figure 3-44)**.

Clicking the **Reset Web Settings** button will return to the default IE settings for your Home and Search pages, and prompt to make Internet Explorer your default browser if it is not already the default browser. You should remember that this will only reset these settings if you have installed another browser after installing IE and the new browser has altered the default settings.

Marking the **Internet Explorer should check to see whether it is the default browser** check box means that each time Internet Explorer starts, it checks to make sure it is still registered as the default Internet browser. If another program has become the default browser, IE will prompt you about whether or not you want to restore IE as the default browser.

how to

Configure Internet Explorer to use Microsoft Outlook at the default e-mail client.

1. Open **Internet Explorer**.
2. On the **Tools** menu, click **Internet Options**.
3. Click the **Programs** tab in the Internet Options dialog box.
4. Click the **E-mail** drop-down arrow.
5. Select **Microsoft Outlook**.
6. Click [OK].
7. Close the Internet Options dialog box.

Figure 3-42 The Programs tab in the Internet Options dialog box

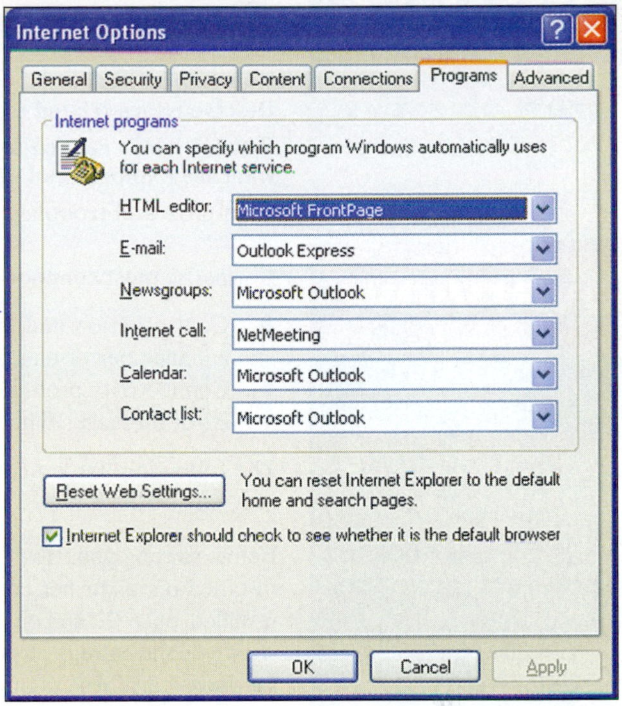

Your particular options may differ

Figure 3-43 Specifying a program

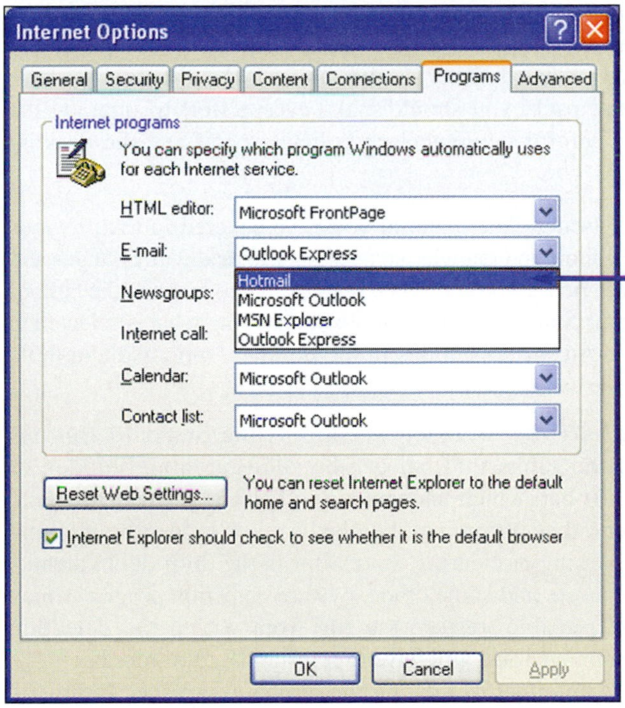

Drop-down boxes, such as those shown here for e-mail, allow you to select from options IE has detected on your computer

Figure 3-44 Sending a message from the Internet Explorer File menu

skill 9

Troubleshooting Internet Explorer: Common User Issues

exam objective

Resolve issues related to customizing Internet Explorer.

Resolve issues related to Internet Explorer support features. Tasks include configuring Internet Explorer and interpreting error messages.

Configure and troubleshoot Internet Explorer.

overview

Normally, most common user issues with IE fall into one of the following categories:

◆ Configuration and customization issues to meet enterprise mandated changes or to enhance performance and security
◆ Connectivity problems or issues in accessing Web sites
◆ Error messages when browsing Web pages on the Internet

The following list is far from exhaustive but touches on common issues not addressed in previous skills.

Before starting your troubleshooting, check which version of IE and Windows XP the user has installed on his or her computer. To check the version number and which service packs are installed, open IE, and on the **Help** menu, select **About Internet Explorer**. The dialog box will show you the current version installed on the computer (**Figure 3-45**). If the user does not have the most current version and service pack, you should make every effort to upgrade the application. Most large enterprises enforce computer-use policies specifying the desktop standards.

Configuration and Customization Issues: The material you have covered in the previous eight skills has equipped you with the tools and knowledge necessary to deal with changes and configuration to the basic IE interface. Hence you should be readily able to manage the bulk of common user issues by customizing the Standard Buttons toolbar, changing what is selected in the View menu, or personalizing the Advanced settings in the Internet Options dialog box. Some typical problems arising in these areas include:

◆ **Missing toolbars or Status bar**: As discussed in Skill 1, the Standard Buttons toolbar, the Address bar, and the Links tool bar can be configured and hidden or displayed by the user. The Status bar, which appears at the bottom of the screen and shows users which security zone they are in, can be displayed or hidden by clicking View from the menu bar and marking or clearing Status Bar in the drop-down menu.
◆ **Related button is missing**: Ad-aware and some other spyware detection programs may remove the Related button. If possible, restore the file from within the detection application. If the file has been removed you will have to reinstall IE to restore it.
◆ **Toolbars cannot move**: This is an effect of locking the toolbars in place. To unlock them, therefore allowing them to be moved, go to the View menu, select Toolbars and clear the check mark next to Lock the Toolbars.
◆ **Problems with Favorites Menu**: Reports from users that they cannot find their Favorites listed is usually the result of having Personalized Favorites Menu enabled on the Advanced tab in the Internet Options dialog box (**Figure 3-46**). This option causes the menu to display only links that are frequently accessed as a means of reducing the size and clutter of a lengthy Favorites list. Users can access the missing links by clicking the down arrow at the end of the Favorites list. You can turn on or disable personalized menus by checking or clearing the check box on the Advanced tab.
◆ **Issues with Download Complete Notification**: By default, IE informs you when a download is complete through opening a dialog box and/or playing a sound. This option can be turned on and off on the Advanced tab by selecting or clearing the **Notify when downloads complete** check box (refer to Figure 3-46).

Figure 3-45 About Internet Explorer

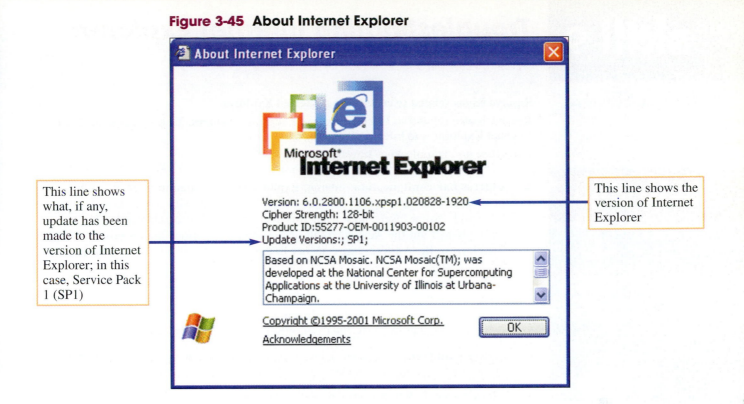

This line shows what, if any, update has been made to the version of Internet Explorer; in this case, Service Pack 1 (SP1)

This line shows the version of Internet Explorer

Figure 3-46 Enabling Personalized Favorites and notifying when downloads complete

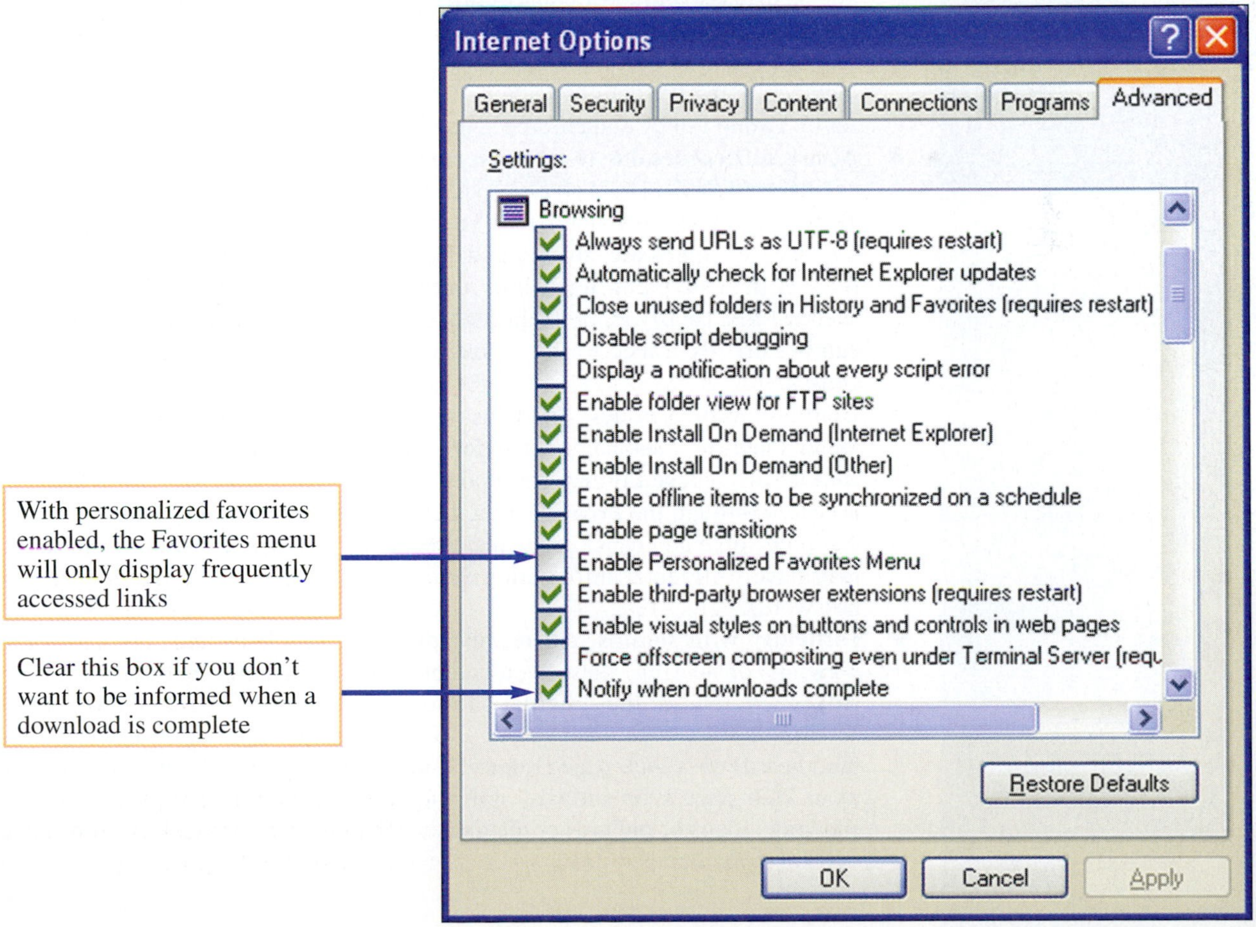

With personalized favorites enabled, the Favorites menu will only display frequently accessed links

Clear this box if you don't want to be informed when a download is complete

skill 9

Troubleshooting Internet Explorer: Common User Issues *(cont'd)*

exam objective

Resolve issues related to customizing Internet Explorer.

Resolve issues related to Internet Explorer support features. Tasks include configuring Internet Explorer and interpreting error messages.

Configure and troubleshoot Internet Explorer.

overview

◆ **Address bar configuration**: Internet Explorer is configured to allow the user to use the Address bar as a search tool, and then to open the site most likely to answer the search. Some users may want this feature disabled or changed. This can be accomplished via the Advanced tab of the Internet Options dialog box. Under the **Search from the Address bar** category in the Advanced tab's list box (**Figure 3-47**), the options are:
- Display results and go to the most likely site
- Do not search from the Address bar
- Just display the results in the main window
- Just go to the most likely site.Connectivity and Access Issues:

Connectivity and Access Issues: These issues include problems in connecting to the Internet, as well as being able to view and find expected content.

◆ **Internet connection**: A user may report that although she can connect to the Internet through a modem or LAN connection, she is unable to browse and the connection times out. This is often due to having either an incorrect proxy server set on the connection or not having a proxy server set at all. To troubleshoot this problem, examine the address specified in the **Use proxy server** section of the Settings dialog box as discussed in Skill 6 and confirm that it is correct. If not, reset it to the correct proxy server. Users may also complain that when they type in a local intranet address they are taken to an Internet address instead. Confirm that the correct addresses are included in the Exceptions section of Proxy Settings dialog box. These values can be set by Group Policy and enforced enterprise-wide.

◆ **Access difficulties due to security, content and privacy issues**: Many problems with accessing Web sites or Web pages are related to security, content and privacy settings. These may be settings required by your company, or they may have been inadvertently set. Security zones are covered in detail in Skill 3. It is important to be familiar with the settings and configurations outlined there in order to troubleshoot them successfully. Nearly all problems with security, privacy (Skill 4), and content (Skill 5) can be directly traced to the individual settings for these areas, and how they are configured.

◆ **Cookie handling issues**: Problems with accessing or using Web sites may be due to the enabled (or disabled) settings for cookies as discussed in Skill 4. For example, if cookies are blocked it may be impossible to access a Web page. Cookie settings are accessed through the Privacy tab in the Internet Options dialog box. Deleting cookies can both solve and cause problems. Frequently deleting cookies will mean that users may have to re-enter information that was automatically inputted (such as a saved password).

◆ **Difficulty with sounds, videos, and pictures**: Problems and complaints relating to viewing (or hearing) these Web components can usually be addressed through the Advanced tab in the Internet Options dialog box. Scroll to the Multimedia section and there you can select or disable options that control what can be seen (and heard) on a Web page (**Figure 3-48**). These setting may be configured to speed up a Web page's opening by not allowing bandwidth-intensive actions such as showing videos or pictures or playing sounds. Resetting these to the user's preference will solve the issues.

Figure 3-47 Search from the Address bar options

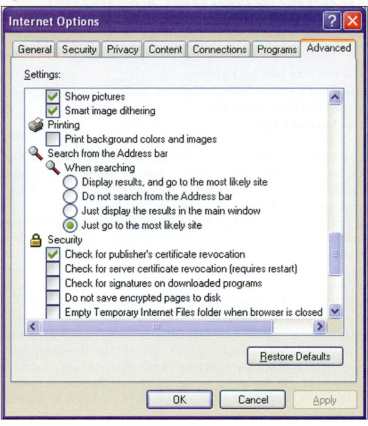

Figure 3-48 The Multimedia section on the Advanced tab

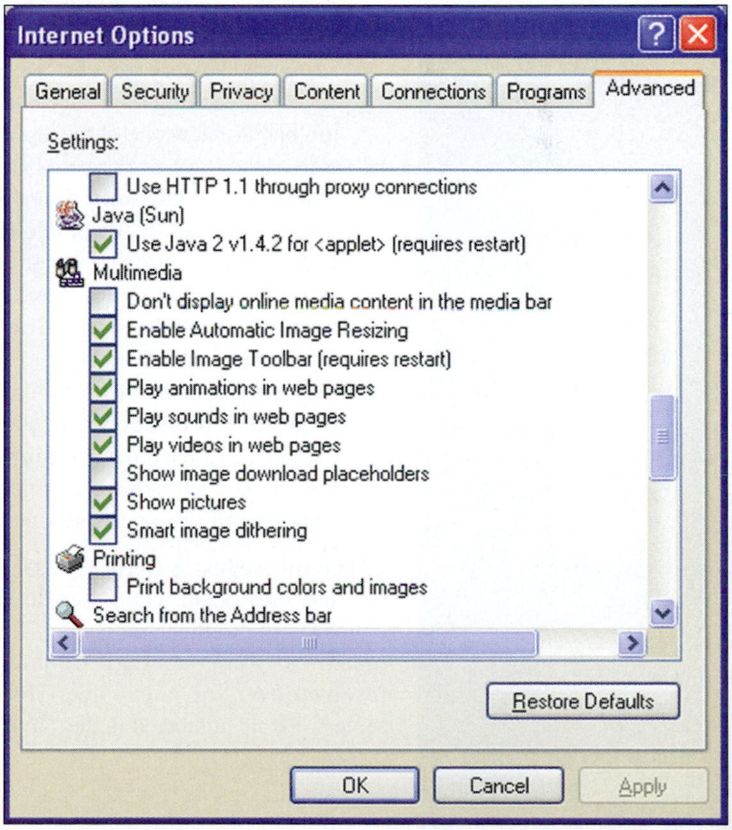

skill 9

Troubleshooting Internet Explorer: Common User Issues *(cont'd)*

exam objective

Resolve issues related to customizing Internet Explorer.

Resolve issues related to Internet Explorer support features. Tasks include configuring Internet Explorer and interpreting error messages.

Configure and troubleshoot Internet Explorer.

overview

◆ **Difficulties reading Web pages**: This is likely due to user configured settings. Depending on the exact nature of the problem, you can instruct the user to either turn or turn off settings in the Accessibility section of the General tab in the Internet Options dialog box, as described in Skill 1.

◆ **Missing or changed Home page**: Users may report that their Home page has been changed to a different Web site than the one selected and that they cannot change their Home page selection to the Web site desired. Or they may complain that when trying to change the Home page on the General tab in the Internet Options dialog box, they are not able to type an address in the Address text box, and the buttons are unavailable or grayed out. Finally, they may report they are able to change the Home page but when they restart the computer, it changes to a different site than the one they selected. Assuming the cause is not a virus or malicious code (these should be checked for) another possibility is that the Home page is being changed by third-party software. In a large enterprise, however, the likelihood is that the Home page has been configured by a network administrator using the Microsoft Internet Explorer Administration Kit (IEAK), Group Policy (as explained in Skill 1), or manual Registry settings, for example, through a logon script.

◆ **Difficulty finding previously viewed pages**: There are several ways that a user can find the pages viewed in the last few days or weeks. To find a page you've seen in the last few days, click the History button on the Standard Buttons toolbar to open the History bar, which contains links for Web sites and pages visited in previous days and weeks, depending on the setting. In the History bar, click a week or day, click a Web site folder to display individual pages, and then click the page icon to display the Web page. To sort or search the History bar, click the arrow next to the View button at the top of the History bar. If you are looking for a page you just visited, click the Back button on the Standard Buttons toolbar. To view one of the last nine pages you visited in this session, click the arrow to the side of the Back or Forward button, and then click the page you want from the list.

◆ **Third-party add-ons**: User problems may be due to the interaction of third-party add-ons placed in IE. In addition you may find it necessary to disable these features when troubleshooting other problems. You do so by opening the Advanced tab in Internet Options dialog box. In the Browsing section, clear the **Enable third-party browser extensions (requires restart)** check box. You must restart IE for the setting to be come effective.

◆ **Missing Favorites**: Corruption in the Favorites folder can cause all or some of the files in the folder to disappear or not display correctly. To repair, restore the folder from a backup. If a user is switching to a new computer or Web browser, you can save and transfer their Favorites by exporting the Favorites list and then importing it in another browser or in IE on the new computer.

Error messages: Strictly speaking, most error messages are not a problem with IE, but because they occur when users are browsing the Internet, you are almost certain to receive calls relating to these messages. **Table 3-5** summarizes common error messages, what they mean and some standard troubleshooting methods for resolving them, if they can be resolved from the client side. These errors are usually due to errors on Web pages or on Web servers. Errors numbered in the "400s" are client side errors that you may be able to help the user

Table 3-5   Common Error Messages Appearing While Browsing the Internet

Type	Description
52 Runtime Error	This occurs when a script in the Web page's code cannot find a file or Web page component it is looking for and is most likely a connectivity problem. Clearing the Temporary Internet Files folder may resolve the problem, but if it does not, then contact the site administrator.
400 Bad File Request	This indicates that the URL for the site being visited was entered incorrectly. An uppercase letter may have been entered for a lowercase, or vice versa, or there may be a misspelling. Make sure users double-check the address they want to enter as well as the address they entered.
401 Unauthorized	This occurs when the Web site server expected and was not given some authentication or encryption key, or when a user enters the wrong password. It is also possible that a user changed his or her password, but the local cache of temporary files is using the old logon credentials. This may occur especially with enterprises that have strict password change policies.
403 Forbidden/ Access Denied	A password and/or user name may not be correctly recorded in the site's database or proper permission may not be set up on the Web server's folders.
404 File Not Found	This means the page cannot be found. If refreshing the page (press [F5] or click the Refresh icon) doesn't resolve this error, there may be an error in the URL because a user typed it incorrectly or if the Web designer made an error when setting up the hyperlink. It may also mean that the page is no longer available (moved, deleted, etc.). It may also indicate Internet congestion.
408 Request Timeout	The client computer stopped the request before the server finished retrieving it. This may be due to a connectivity problem or a slow server.
500 Internal Error	The Web server is unable to retrieve the HTML document because of server-configuration problems.
501 Not Implemented	The contacted Web server doesn't support a requested feature.
502 Service Temporarily Overloaded	The server is congested due to heavy traffic. Alternatively, it can indicate a denial of service underway against the site.
503 Service Unavailable	This error can occur when the server is busy, or if the site has moved. It also may occur when a dial-up Internet connection is dropped.
Bad File Request	Internet Explorer may not be configured to support the type of page requested
Connection Refused by Host	You do not have proper credentials to access the site.
Errors on Page	This is a catch-all message triggered when there is something on the Web page that the IE either hasn't read properly (likely due to a connectivity problem) or there are missing items in the Web page itself. This error normally affects the graphics on a Web page. In many cases the error can result from the user not allowing sufficient time to download the page they are requesting. Remind users to wait until the bottom left-hand corner of the page reads 'done' before selecting any other links on the page. . On the server side, this can be a temporary problem (e.g., insufficient bandwidth) or due to more complex and longer term problems.
Failed DNS Lookup	The Domain Name System (DNS) server can't translate your domain request into a valid Internet address. The Web server may be busy or down, or an incorrect URL was entered.
File Contains No Data	This is a server-side error resulting from bad table formatting, or stripped header information.
Host Unavailable	Host server down. Click Reload or go to the site later.
Network Connection Refused by the Server	The Web server is busy. To resolve this problem, refresh the page.
Runtime Error	When you attempt to browse to various Web sites or use an online form, you may receive an error message similar to the following: "A runtime error has occurred. Do you wish to debug? Line number Error: Permission Denied." This means that there is a problem at the Web server and the way the page or application is configured. Inform the Web administrator.
Script Error	Script errors are caused by code on the Web page that is not working correctly. This may be due to connectivity problems or by browser incompatibilities.
Unable to Locate Host	There are a number of possible causes: The Web server is no longer connected to the Internet or is malfunctioning; the user's Internet connection is dropped; the Web address is not valid, etc. If refreshing the page doesn't work, try clearing the Temporary Internet Files and History and refreshing again.

skill 9
Troubleshooting Internet Explorer: Common User Issues (cont'd)

exam objective

Resolve issues related to customizing Internet Explorer.

Resolve issues related to Internet Explorer support features. Tasks include configuring Internet Explorer and interpreting error messages.

Configure and troubleshoot Internet Explorer.

overview

with. Errors in the "500s" are server side problems that should be handled by the server administrator responsible for the Web site in question. Other error message-related problems include:

◆ **Issues with script error**: Some users might complain that they are constantly receiving script error messages and are being prompted to debug them. In the Browsing section **(Figure 3-49)** of the Advanced tab in the Internet Options dialog box, you can select Disable script debugging and disable Display a notification about every script error.

◆ **Page faults and other unrecoverable errors**: In Internet Explorer, you may receive an error message that says **Iexplore.exe has generated errors and must be shut down.** This type of message indicates that an unrecoverable error, also known as a fault or exception, has occurred. The causes of unrecoverable errors could consume several volumes. Typically, in IE, they occur if a process tries to read or write to a memory location that has not been allocated to it. ActiveX controls, Browser Helper Objects, tool bands, and other components that let you customize IE components run in the same memory space as the browser, and may generate faults or exceptions on IE or one of its components (including Outlook Express). IE also interacts with other parts of your computer. For example, you use your display driver, display hardware, and installed fonts to display Web pages, and printer drivers and hardware to output the pages. Other programs may also interact with IE, and they can cause unrecoverable errors. There are two types of unrecoverable errors. The first is transient and occurs only once, due to a unique combination of circumstances. The other is persistent and occurs regularly. There are a number of troubleshooting techniques that might work, but frequently these are a matter of trial and error. Microsoft has included a tool in IE that can help address these problems The **Internet Explorer Error Reporting** tool is automatically installed with Windows XP and is used to report serious errors in IE, such as unrecoverable errors, general protection faults, or invalid page faults, to Microsoft for analysis. If the report indicates the error is due to a known problem, a link is provided to the appropriate service pack, hot fix, or to a Microsoft Knowledge Base article. If the problem is a new one, it is stored in a Microsoft problem database for investigation and helps Microsoft develop new hot fixes and service packs.

how to

Export Internet Favorites to an .htm file.

1. Open **Internet Explorer**.
2. Click **File** on the menu bar, and then click **Import and Export** to initiate the **Import/Export Wizard**.
3. On the **Welcome** screen of the wizard click [Next >].
4. On the **Import/Export Selection** screen, select **Export Favorites (Figure 3-50)**. Click [Next >]
5. On the **Export Favorites Source** page you can select the main Favorites folder or a specific subfolder for your export. All sub-folders are automatically included from every folder you select. Select the folder you want to export, and click [Next >] to open the **Export Favorites Destination** screen.
6. Select the location to which you want to export the file **(Figure 3-51)**. Click [Next >].
7. The wizard informs you that you are about to export your Favorites. Click [Finish].
8. After a moment or two, a dialog box appears, informing you that the export is successful. Click [OK] to close the wizard.

tip

Favorites can be exported for sharing, backing up, distribution to others and to create a Web page with links.

Figure 3-49 The Advanced tab of Internet Options dialog box

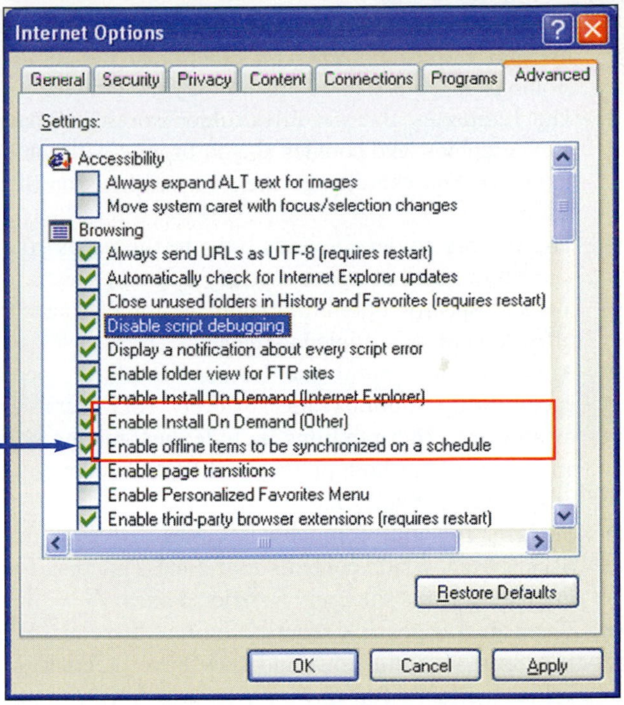

Clearing these check boxes prevents prompts and error messages about scripts written into the Web page

Figure 3-50 The Import/Export Wizard

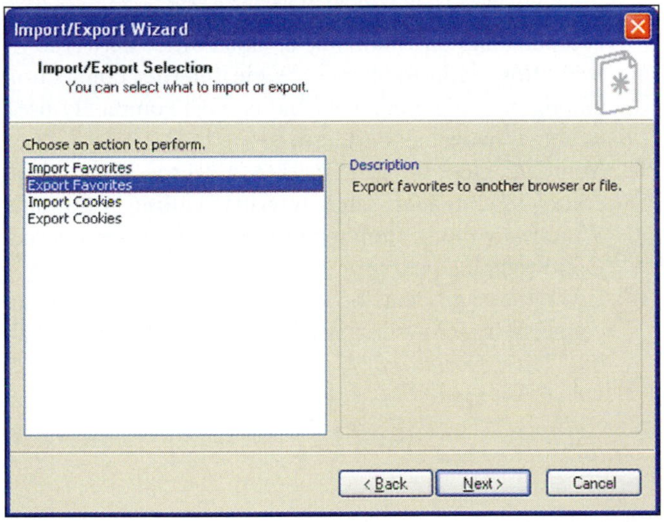

Figure 3-51 Selecting the Export Favorites destination

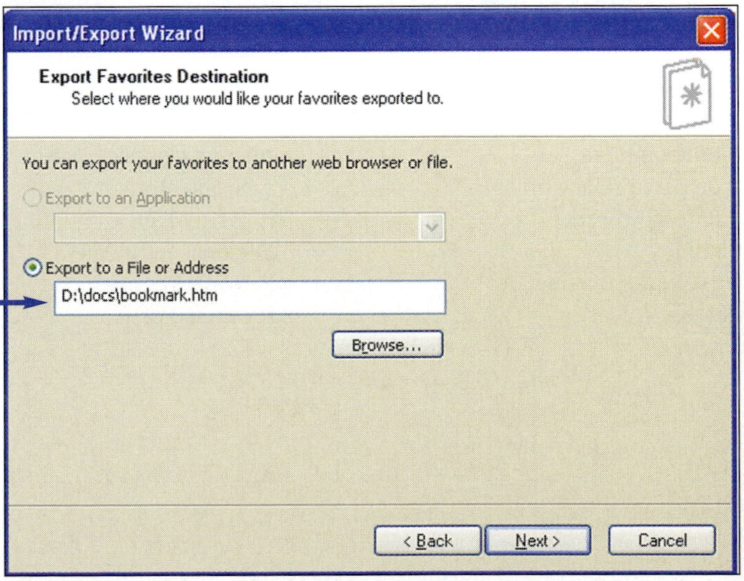

You need to designate a location for the exported Favorites file, called bookmark.htm by default

Summary

◆ Internet Explorer users can customize the toolbars, Home page, colors, and fonts used by the browser.

◆ The Temporary Internet Files folder stores Web pages, files, graphics, and cookies as you browse with Internet Explorer. You can change the size and location of the folder.

◆ The History folder provides links to the pages you've visited for quick access to recently viewed pages.

◆ You can specify a preferred language for Web sites that offer content in multiple languages.

◆ A variety of general and Internet Explorer specific accessibility options are offered for users with disabilities. These options include customizing colors and configuring how pictures, videos, and sounds are displayed and loaded in pages.

◆ Security for your computer is controlled through the Security tab, which contains four zones: Internet, Local intranet, Trusted sites, and Restricted sites.

◆ There are five possible security settings: these four High, Medium, Medium-Low, and Low have preconfigured values suitable for most purposes. A fifth setting, Custom, can be set with the values you choose.

◆ Privacy options primarily deal with how to handle cookies.

◆ Cookies are files placed on your computer by a Web site that contain information such as your preferences when visiting that site. They are used primarily for easing use of a site as well as marketing and advertising.

◆ Types of cookies include persistent, temporary (session), first-party, third-party, and unsatisfactory cookies.

◆ You can configure your privacy settings to handle cookies as strictly or as leniently as you need.

◆ Content Advisor can be enabled to assure that only rated content that meets or exceeds your criteria can be viewed.

◆ The Certificates section allows you to use digital certificates to identify yourself, certification authorities, and publishers. It also allows you to manage certificates and configure as necessary.

◆ AutoComplete can be used to complete forms and Web site addresses based on material you've entered in the past.

◆ You can use a dial-up, VPN, or a local area network connection to connect to the Internet. You can also specify a proxy server to connect through.

◆ You can configure and enable both Internet Connection Firewall (ICF) and Internet Connection Sharing (ICS) through Internet Explorer.

◆ Enabling the ICF activates a software firewall that prevents sets restriction on what information computers outside your network can view and access on your computer and on your home or small office network.

◆ ICS allows you to share a single Internet connection among multiple computers and is most commonly used in homes and small businesses.

◆ You can select the e-mail, HTML editor, newsgroup, contacts, calendar, and Internet calling programs Windows will use from the Programs tab of the Internet Options dialog box.

◆ Error messages can be due to problems relating to connectivity, browser configuration, or difficulties with the Web server.

Key Terms

ActiveX controls
Address bar
AutoComplete
Compact privacy policy
Content Advisor
Cookie
First-party cookie
History folder

Home page
Internet Connection Firewall (ICF)
Internet Connection Sharing (ICS)
Java applet
Links toolbar
Personal certificate
Persistent cookie
Proxy server

Security zone
Standard Buttons toolbar
Style sheet
Temporary (or session) cookie
Temporary Internet files
Third-party cookie

Test Yourself

1. Which of the following toolbar items allows you to reach selected Web sites with a single click?
   a. Links toolbar
   b. Address bar
   c. Status bar
   d. Home page

2. Which of the following is true about Temporary Internet files? (Choose all that apply.)
   a. They speed page loading.
   b. Deleting them can eliminate problems.
   c. This is where Web pages, files, graphics, and cookies are stored as you browse them with IE.
   d. They must be stored on the same partition as Internet Explorer.

3. Which folder contains links to the pages you've visited for quick access to recently viewed pages?
   a. Temporary Internet Files folder
   b. History folder
   c. Links folder
   d. Search folder

4. Which Advanced option would you select to assist people using a screen reader or magnifier?
   a. Move system caret with focus/selection changes.
   b. Enable magnifier
   c. Play videos
   d. Print background colors and images

5. What is the default security setting for the Internet zone?
   a. High
   b. Medium High
   c. Medium
   d. Medium Low

6. Which of the following is not a security zone in Internet Explorer?
   a. Local intranet
   b. Trusted sites
   c. Limited sites
   d. Restricted sites

7. Which type of cookie is stored on your computer only for the current browsing session, and is deleted when you close Internet Explorer?
   a. First-party cookie
   b. Persistent cookie
   c. Session cookie
   d. Security cookie

8. Medium privacy settings will:
   a. Cause cookies from first-party Web sites that use personally identifiable information without your implicit consent to be deleted from your computer when you close the browser.
   b. Block first-party cookies that use your personally identifiable information without your implicit consent.
   c. Block only cookies from third-party Web sites without a compact privacy policy.
   d. Block cookies from any Web site that does not have a compact privacy policy.

9. You can adjust Content to reflect what you think is appropriate content which of the following areas? (Choose all that apply.)
   a. Cookies
   b. Temporary files
   c. Language
   d. Active-X

10. Which feature can save you from having to enter basic information, such as your address or e-mail name, every time you visit a new Web site that requests it? (Choose all that apply.)
    a. Personal Assistant
    b. Personal Profile
    c. Profile Assistant
    d. AutoComplete

11. For which of the following program types can you specify that Internet Explorer open a specific application? (Choose all that apply.)
    a. Newsgroups
    b. Contacts
    c. Internet call
    d. Tasks

12. If a user complains that he or she cannot move a toolbar, what should you do?
    a. Empty the Temporary Internet Files folder.
    b. Click the Refresh button.
    c. Unlock the toolbar.
    d. Hide and then unhide the toolbar to release it.

Projects: On Your Own

1. Change the way colors and fonts are displayed.
   a. Start **Internet Explorer**.
   b. On the **Tools** menu, click **Internet Options**.
   c. On the **General** tab, click **Colors**.
   d. Clear the **Use Windows Colors** check box if it is checked.
   e. Change the color settings to the settings that you want for text, background, and links.
   f. Click **OK** to return to the General tab.
   g. Click **Fonts**.
   h. In the **Web page font** and **Plain text font** boxes, click the fonts that you want.
   i. Click **OK** twice to exit **Internet Options.**
   j. Visit a few Web sites. Note that changes will not always happen if a default font or color was specified by the Web site developer (e.g., **www.yahoo.com**), whereas others that use the client's font (e.g., **us.imdb.com**) will use the one you specified.
   k. On the General tab, click **Colors**.
   l. Check the **Use Windows Colors** check box.
   m. Restore the links' colors if you changed them.
   n. Click **OK** to return to the General tab.
   o. Click **Fonts**.
   p. In the **Web page font** and **Plain text font** boxes, restore the fonts to their previous settings.
   q. Click **OK** twice to exit the Internet Options dialog box.

2. There may be some cases in which you want to manually delete all Temporary Internet files to ensure that these are off the system. Temporary Internet Files are stored in a subfolder under the user's name in the Documents and Settings folder. You will need to make sure first that you will be able to view these files and folders. To do so, click **Tools** on the menu bar of the **Explorer** window and select **Folder Options**. In the **Folder Options** dialog box, select **View**. Scroll down the **Advanced Settings** list box to the **Hidden files and folders** category. Make sure that the **Show hidden files and folders** option button is selected.
   a. Click **Start** and select **My Computer**.
   b. Double-click the **C:** drive in the right pane of the My Computer window.
   c. Open the **Documents and Settings** folder.
   d. Open the folder with the user name for whom you want to delete the Temporary Internet files.
   e. Open the **Local Settings** folder.
   f. Open the **Temporary Internet Files** folder.
   g. Select all the files in the Temporary Internet files folder.
   h. Select **Delete** on the **File** menu, and confirm in the message box that appears that you wish to delete the files.

Problem Solving Scenarios

1. You are working for Gideon Enterprises, a small corporation that provides marketing support for several vineyards in the eastern New York state area as as a desktop support technician. Gideon Enterprises wants to know in what ways the look and feel of Internet Explorer can be configured for their employees' needs. Gideon's management wants to discourage browsing on the Internet and have Internet Explorer link to the company's own intranet and to company Web sites. Prepare a PowerPoint presentation recommending an Internet Explorer configuration for Gideon Enterprises.

2. The children's museum you are providing technical support for is setting up a bank of computers for public Internet use. The Director of the museum wants to know what measures can be taken to ensure the safety of the children's browsing, and of the computers themselves. Prepare a memo that answers her questions.

Supporting E-Mail: Outlook Express

This lesson provides an introduction to both the concept of e-mail and newsgroups and to Outlook Express, the free e-mail client that comes bundled as a component of Internet Explorer.

If e-mail is among the greatest inventions of the last century, it is because of the way it has revolutionized communications. For example, this book is the result of a collaborative effort among a number of people, some of whom are separated by thousands of miles, have never met face to face, or even spoken over the phone because of the time zone differences. E-mail technology allowed the transfer of files, graphics, and information in a matter of seconds. Without e-mail, none of this global collaboration would have been possible without long delays and complex logistics.

Outlook Express was originally called Internet Mail & News in early versions of Internet Explorer. In Internet Explorer 4.0, Microsoft changed its name to Outlook Express. Outlook Express is designed to work with any standard mail system, including Simple Mail Transfer Protocol (SMTP), Post Office Protocol 3 (POP3), and Internet Message Access Protocol 4 (IMAP4). Support is also available for Lightweight Directory Access Protocol (LDAP), Multipurpose Internet Mail Extension Hypertext Markup Language (MHTML), Hypertext Markup Language (HTML), Secure/Multipurpose Internet Mail Extensions (S/MIME), and Network News Transfer Protocol (NNTP). Outlook Express can be configured to receive e-mail from multiple accounts and deliver them to a single inbox. It is easy to set up and use and provides secure, personalized, and complete messaging and newsgroup features.

The aim of this lesson is to ensure that you have the essential background necessary to address requests that come from users regarding the look and feel of Outlook Express, such as layout, message appearance, and some specific security and content handling options. The primary focus of the lesson, however, will be on providing the necessary information to troubleshoot user problems. The majority of these problems have to do with the inability to communicate with mail and news servers and maintaining and securing message and address databases.

Goals

In this lesson, you will learn how to configure and troubleshoot common issues with Outlook Express.

Lesson 4   Supporting E-Mail: Outlook Express

Skill	Exam 70-272 Objective
1. Understanding How E-mail Works	Basic knowledge
2. Introducing Outlook Express	**Configure and troubleshoot Outlook Express.** Answer end-user questions related to configuring Outlook Express. Configure and troubleshoot e-mail account settings. **Resolve issues related to Outlook Express features. Tasks include configuring Outlook Express and interpreting error messages.**
3. Configuring E-mail Accounts in Outlook Express	**Configure and troubleshoot Outlook Express.** Answer end-user questions related to configuring Outlook Express. Configure and troubleshoot e-mail account settings. **Resolve issues related to Outlook Express features. Tasks include configuring Outlook Express and interpreting error messages.**
4. Accessing Newsgroups using Outlook Express	**Configure and troubleshoot Outlook Express.** Answer end-user questions related to configuring Outlook Express. Configure and troubleshoot newsreader account settings. **Resolve issues related to Outlook Express features. Tasks include configuring Outlook Express and interpreting error messages.**
5. Personalizing the View in Outlook Express	**Configure and troubleshoot Outlook Express.** Answer end-user questions related to configuring Outlook Express. **Resolve issues related to Outlook Express features. Tasks include configuring Outlook Express and interpreting error messages.** **Resolve issues related to customizing Outlook Express.**
6. Customizing Outlook Express Options	**Configure and troubleshoot Outlook Express.** Answer end-user questions related to configuring Outlook Express. **Resolve issues related to Outlook Express features. Tasks include configuring Outlook Express and interpreting error messages.** **Resolve issues related to customizing Outlook Express.**
7. Working with Other Features of Outlook Express	**Configure and troubleshoot Outlook Express.** Answer end-user questions related to configuring Outlook Express. Configure and troubleshoot newsreader account settings. Configure and troubleshoot e-mail account settings. **Resolve issues related to Outlook Express features. Tasks include configuring Outlook Express and interpreting error messages.** **Resolve issues related to customizing Outlook Express.**
8. Managing Data in Outlook Express	**Configure and troubleshoot Outlook Express.** Answer end-user questions related to configuring Outlook Express.
9. Backing Up and Recovering Data in Outlook Express	**Configure and troubleshoot Outlook Express.** Answer end-user questions related to configuring Outlook Express. **Resolve issues related to Outlook Express features. Tasks include configuring Outlook Express and interpreting error messages.**
10. Troubleshooting Outlook Express: Common User Issues	**Configure and troubleshoot Outlook Express.** Answer end-user questions related to configuring Outlook Express. Configure and troubleshoot newsreader account settings. Configure and troubleshoot e-mail account settings. **Resolve issues related to Outlook Express features. Tasks include configuring Outlook Express and interpreting error messages.** **Resolve issues related to customizing Outlook Express**

Requirements

To complete this lesson, you will need administrative rights on a Windows XP Professional computer with Internet Explorer 6.0 Service Pack 1 installed. The computer must also be able to connect to the Internet.

skill 1   *Understanding How E-mail Works*

exam objective   Basic knowledge

overview

E-mail has quickly established itself as one of the key developments of the last century and a critical communications tool. Yet although nearly everyone recognizes the value and importance of e-mail, very few users know how it works beyond composing the message, picking an recipient, and clicking the Send button. To effectively answer user questions on this topic, you must understand the underpinnings that hold the whole e-mail system together.

E-mail messages are created and sent from individual computers using e-mail programs or **mail-user agents (MUAs)**. These programs typically have a text editor of some sort to allow you to compose the message and a means of addressing the message. Most e-mail programs these days include an **Address Book** function that stores previously entered addresses.

E-mail addresses include a user name followed by the symbol @, the domain name, the root domain designation, and finally the country name when appropriate. An example of an e-mail address is *myname@mycompany.com*. The elements of the address break down as follows:

◆ *myname* is the user name (or the network ID or the mailbox name—terms that are used interchangeably to mean the same thing in this context)
◆ *mycompany* is the domain or network name, typically the company or provider supplying the e-mail account, such as Yahoo or Hotmail.
◆ *com* is the root domain designation.

Common **root domain** designations include *com* for commercial, *org* for organization and *edu* for educational institutions (**Table 4-1**). E-mail addresses from service providers outside the United States typically have a two letter country code appended after the root domain designation. These are not always obvious. For example, the country code for South Africa is "za" (sa is used for Saudi Arabia); for Switzerland, the country code is "ch," not "sw," which is the country code for Swaziland. **Table 4-2** lists a few common country codes.

When you click the Send button, the message starts on a journey from the sender system to a **message transfer agent (MTA)**. The MTA evaluates the message and either delivers it within the local network or sends it to another MTA for distribution over the Internet. This may require several iterations, but the message eventually arrives at the recipient's mailbox. The recipient can then access the message using e-mail software, such as Outlook Express, Outlook, Netscape, or Eudora.

E-mail software displays each message's recipient and sender addresses, the subject field, and the message body. E-mail messages also include technical information called **headers**. E-mail headers, which are typically hidden by e-mail software, include the sender and recipient addresses, the routing and timing of the message through various servers, and the subject heading.

Nearly all e-mail programs allow you to send attachments with the message. **Attachments** can include any sort of file, including text documents, digital pictures, sound files, and other multimedia.

Table 4-1   Top-level domain names

Domain name	Description
.aero	Aviation corporations
.biz	Business organizations
.com	Commercial
.coop	Co-operative organizations
.edu	Educational institutions
.gov	U.S. Government institutions
.info	Unrestricted
.int	International organizations
.mil	U.S. Department of Defense
.museum	Museums
.name	Personal
.net	Networks
.org	Organizations

Table 4-2   Sample country codes

Code	Country	Code	Country
.ar	Argentina	.at	Austria
.be	Belgium	.br	Brazil
.ca	Canada	.ch	Switzerland
.cl	Chile	.cn	China
.cr	Costa Rica	.cu	Cuba
.de	German	.dk	Denmark
.do	Dominican Republic	.eg	Egypt
es	Spain	.fr	France
.ie	Ireland	.in	India
.it	Italy	.jm	Jamaica
.mx	Mexico	.nl	The Netherlands
.no	Normay	.nz	New Zealand
pk	Pakistan	.pr	Puerto Rico
.ru	Russia	.sa	Saudi Arabia
.th	Thailand	.tw	Taiwan
.uk	United Kingdom	.us	United States
.ve	Venezuela	.za	South Africa

skill 1

Understanding How E-mail Works
(cont'd)

exam objective   Basic knowledge

overview

tip

If the SMTP server is unable to determine the location of the recipient's mailbox, the message will bounce and the sender will receive an error message, typically saying the message is undeliverable.

When sent, the message is delivered to an e-mail server that determines the most efficient way to route the message and then sends it out using the **Simple Mail Transfer Protocol (SMTP)**. SMTP, part of the Transmission Control Protocol/Internet Protocol (TCP/IP) suite, is the most commonly used network protocol to send e-mail between servers **(Figure 4-1)**.

The SMTP server establishes that the e-mail address is valid, determines the best path for the e-mail to reach the recipient, and sends the message. Before reaching the recipient, an e-mail message may make any number of stops at other mail servers. Each of these will route the message based on its assessment of the best way for it to arrive at its final destination. Once it has reached its last stop, it is placed in the recipient mailbox for retrieval. Accessing received mail requires using another protocol from the TCP/IP suite, either **Post Office Protocol 3 (POP3)** or **Internet Message Access Protocol (IMAP)**. POP3 is by far the most commonly used.

With a POP3 e-mail account, messages are received and held on a mail server (either on a local network or at an ISP). Your e-mail software accesses the server to download the messages and deletes them from the server once they are downloaded. IMAP is similar except that the messages are not downloaded to your computer. Instead, they are stored on the server and you work with them there.

When an e-mail account is acquired through a Web-based mail service (such as Yahoo!) the e-mail program is accessed through a Web browser rather than as a separate application on your computer. One logs on to the site through a user name/network ID and password specific to the Web-based account.

Most free Web-based e-mail providers offer limited storage space and/or may restrict the size of attachments. This means you must perform regular maintenance to stay below the storage limit. Whereas you must be connected to the Internet to use Web-based e-mail, non-Web based e-mail programs, such as Outlook Express, can be used offline for reading, composing, or deleting messages.

Figure 4-1   Sending and receiving e-mail

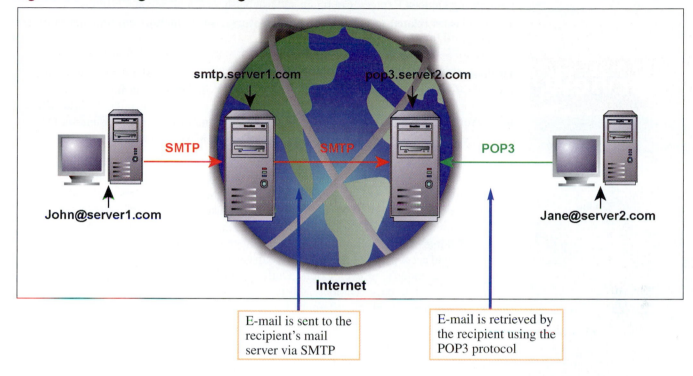

E-mail is sent to the recipient's mail server via SMTP

E-mail is retrieved by the recipient using the POP3 protocol

skill 2

Introducing Outlook Express

exam objective

Configure and troubleshoot Outlook Express. Answer end-user questions related to configuring Outlook Express. Configure and troubleshoot e-mail account settings.

Resolve issues related to Outlook Express features. Tasks include configuring Outlook Express and interpreting error messages.

overview

Outlook Express is a free e-mail and newsgroup client that is installed along with Internet Explorer. Although not actually a part of the browser, it integrates with Internet Explorer to extend its capabilities. Macintosh users are able to obtain a stand-alone client for Mac OS 8.1 to 9x. You can configure Outlook Express to retrieve e-mail from your account via POP or configure it as an IMAP client to access your mail on an IMAP mail server.

Outlook Express was designed to serve as a basic e-mail client with limited functionality. By contrast, Microsoft Outlook is a full-featured, high-end, sophisticated messaging and collaborative e-mail program that comes bundled with the Microsoft Office suite (Lesson 6). Although it can be used as a standalone product, it is usually integrated into both Microsoft Office and used with Exchange Server. In addition to messaging, Outlook includes a calendar, a robust Address Book, and it allows you to integrate and manage not only e-mail from multiple e-mail accounts, but personal and group calendars, contacts, and tasks. Programmers can customize, modify, or even extend Outlook functions through add-ins, a feature not present in Outlook Express. Outlook is discussed in further detail in Lesson 5. For now it is important you understand the difference between the two products and what each can and cannot do as outlined in **Table 4-3**.

Microsoft intended Outlook Express for home users looking for easy and reliable Internet, e-mail, and newsgroup functionality. Outlook, on the other hand, is targeted at corporate or enterprise users who require additional e-mail functionality and tight integration between e-mail and other productivity and business tools, such as the Microsoft Office Suite, to handle information management and digital collaboration.

Outlook Express comes with migration tools to enable you to easily import existing mail settings, Address Book entries, and e-mail messages from Eudora, Netscape, Microsoft Exchange Server, Outlook, and other mail client programs. The program also includes full support for **HTML mail**, which allows you to send messages with custom backgrounds and colors.

tip

Outlook Express for Mac OS and Mac OS X is called Entourage. Entourage is an IMAP client with added functionality to more closely resemble Outlook.

caution

Outlook 2003 requires Exchange 2003 for group functionality.

how to

Create an e-mail account in Outlook Express.

1. Click **start**, point to **All Programs**, and select **Outlook Express**.
2. Click **Tools** on the menu bar, and then click **Accounts,** which will open the **Internet Accounts** dialog box.
3. Select the **Mail** tab, click [Add ▶], and then click **Mail** on the pop-up menu. The **Internet Connection Wizard** starts.
4. Type a name into the **Display name** text box (**Figure 4-2**). This name will appear on any outgoing messages (**Figure 4-3**). Click [Next >].
5. Type your **e-mail address**. The network administrator or your ISP provides this information when you sign up for an account. Click [Next >].
6. Select the type of incoming mail server: **POP3**, **IMAP, or HTTP**. Provide the names of the incoming and outgoing mail servers. Click [Next >].
7. Provide the **user name** and **password** for the account provided by your network administrator or ISP. Click [Next >].
8. Click [Finish] to close the Internet Connection Wizard.

Table 4-3   Comparison of Microsoft Outlook Express and Outlook

Features	Outlook Express	Outlook 2003 and 2002
Send and receive e-mail	Yes	Yes
Works with IMAP, HTTP, and POP Internet e-mail servers	Yes	Yes
Integrates with Microsoft Exchange Server	No	Yes
Address book and/or Contacts folder for addresses	Yes	Yes
Supports multiple Address Books	No	Yes
Can use as calendar for event scheduling, appointments, etc.	No	Yes
Can record tasks and maintain a "to do" list	No	Yes
Has a dedicated, automatic junk mail filter	No	Yes
Can write and retain "notes" outside of the Address Book	No	Yes
Support for newsgroups	Yes	No*
E-mail signatures and stationery	Yes	Yes
Secure e-mail messaging through digital certificates	Yes	Yes
Automatic archiving	No	Yes
Allows integration and collaboration within a workgroup	No	Yes
Can send a fax	No	Yes
Can dial phone number from Address Book	Yes	Yes

Note: Although it may appear that Outlook 2003 does have newsgroup support, when you launch the newsreader, it actually opens in an Outlook Express window.

Figure 4-2 Adding a display name

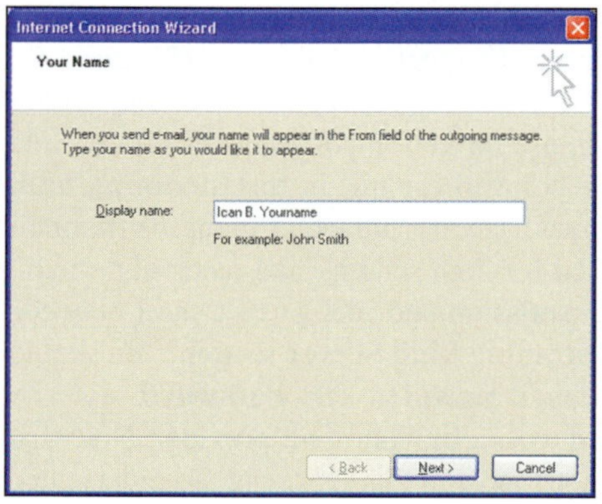

Figure 4-3 Display name shown in Outlook Express Today panel

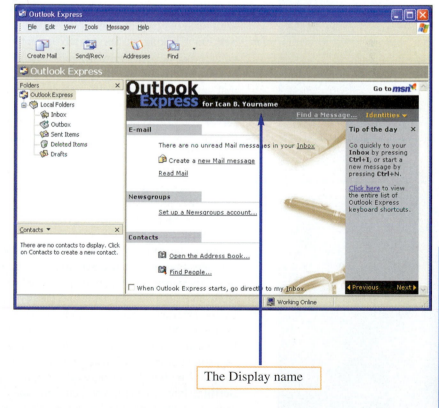

The Display name

skill 3

Configuring E-mail Accounts in Outlook Express

exam objective

Configure and troubleshoot Outlook Express. Answer end-user questions related to configuring Outlook Express. Configure and troubleshoot e-mail account settings.

Resolve issues related to Outlook Express features. Tasks include configuring Outlook Express and interpreting error messages.

overview

To configure the account you created in Skill 2, first open Outlook Express, click **Tools** on the menu bar and then select **Accounts** to open the Internet Accounts dialog box. Click the **Mail** tab. Highlight the e-mail account you want to configure and click the Properties button to open that e-mail account's **Properties** dialog box. Note that each account can have a separate configuration.

You will see that there are five tabs: General, Servers, Connection, Security, and Advanced. Understanding the contents of these tabs is necessary to configure and troubleshoot an e-mal account.

◆ **General tab**: The General tab **(Figure 4-4)** has two sections. The first, **Mail Account**, contains a text box in which you can specify the name used to refer to this account in the accounts list. This name does not have to be the one you used in identifying the server during the setup phase and you can change it to something more user friendly, like "My Personal Account" or "Office Server." In the **User Information** section, you can add or change the name you want displayed in the "From " line of an e-mail message and the organization you want to have displayed, as well as the sending e-mail address. The latter identifies the e-mail address that people should use when sending e-mail to you at this account. The e-mail address must be in the format username@network.com, as shown in **Figure 4-4**. The Reply address box can be used if you want to have recipients reply to an e-mail address other than one from which you sent the e-mail. If you do not select this option, replies to your e-mail messages are sent to the e-mail account from which you send them. If you want Outlook Express to check for new messages for the e-mail account when sending and receiving, select the **Include this account when receiving mail or synchronizing** check box at the bottom of the dialog box.

◆ **Servers**: Clicking the Servers tab opens the **Servers Properties** dialog box **(Figure 4-5),** where you can configure settings specific to the mail server for this account. Under **Server Information,** you specify the protocol to use for your incoming mail server. Note that setting this incorrectly will prevent the receipt of e-mail. In the **Incoming mail (POP3)** and **Outgoing mail (SMTP)** text boxes, specify the exact name of the mail server you use. Typically the same server is used for both sending and receiving e-mail. Entering the wrong name will prevent the transmission and receipt of e-mail between Outlook Express and your mail server. In the **Incoming Mail Server** section, you should enter your account name as provided by the mail provider. The **Password** text box provides a space to enter the password assigned to you by your mail provider. Note that for security purposes, the actual characters do not appear in this space but are represented by an asterisk or other symbol. This box becomes active only if you select the **Remember password** check box, although if you enter a password and clear the check box, it will be retained. Selecting the **Log on using Secure Password Authentication** check box indicates that you can use Secure Password Authentication to log on to this server. If this option is selected, you may be prompted to log on when connecting to this server. If you are prompted for a user name and password, this account information is usually supplied by the Internet service or content provider when you sign up for their service. **In the Outgoing Mail Server** section, selecting the **My server requires authentication** check box means that you must log on to your outgoing e-mail server. Here, as above, you might be prompted to log on when you connect to this server using the account information supplied by the ISP or network administrator. Selecting this check box activates the **Settings** button which, when clicked, opens a dialog box allowing you to either use the same credentials as your incoming server, or to specify different ones.

Figure 4-4 General tab

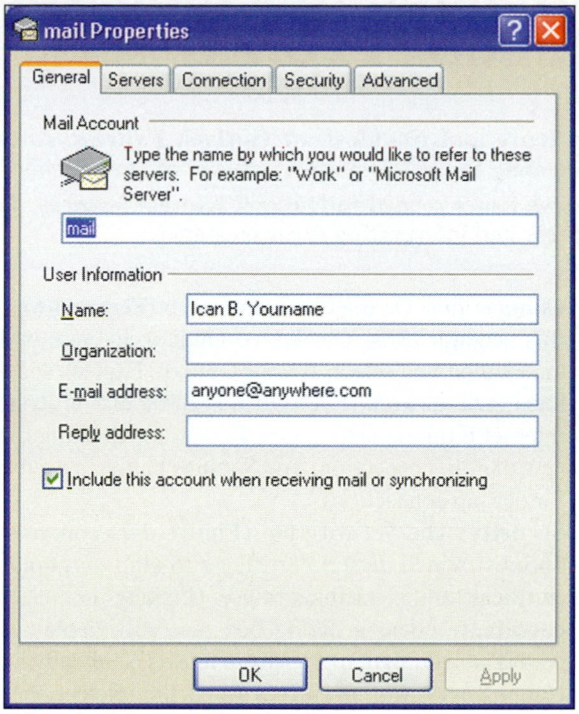

Figure 4-5 Servers tab

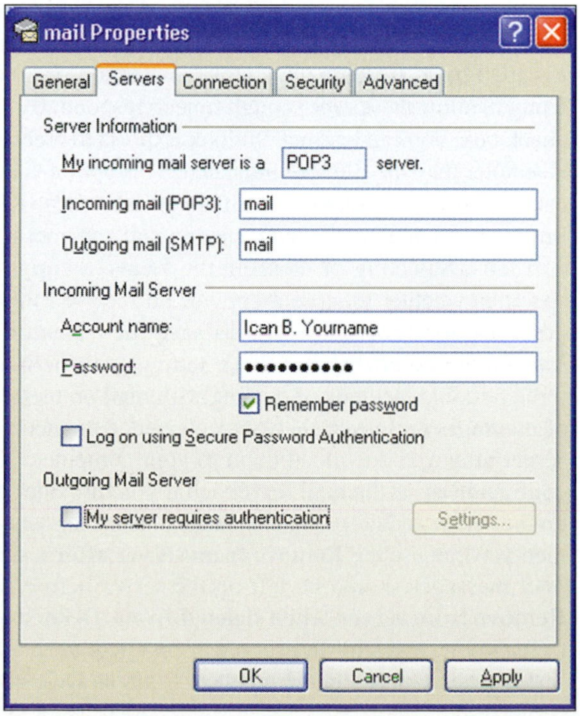

skill 3

Configuring E-mail Accounts in Outlook Express *(cont'd)*

exam objective

Configure and troubleshoot Outlook Express. Answer end-user questions related to configuring Outlook Express. Configure and troubleshoot e-mail account settings.

Resolve issues related to Outlook Express features. Tasks include configuring Outlook Express and interpreting error messages.

overview

◆ **Connections**: On the Connections tab **(Figure 4-6)**, if you select the **Always connect to this account using** check box, Outlook Express will always connect to the Internet by the method you select. If your Outlook Express account requires you to connect using a local area network (LAN) or a specific dial-up connection, this setting overrides your Internet Explorer setting (see Lesson 3). Clicking the Add button allows you to create a new dial-up connection. The Settings button is used to display and configure the settings for dial-up connections.

◆ **Security**: The Security tab **(Figure 4-7)** contains the configuration menus for two options: which digital certificate to sign outgoing mails with and which encryption certificate and algorithms to use. Clicking the Select button under the heading **Signing certificate** opens a dialog box that will display and allow you to select the digital certificate you want to use (from those you already have) when sending signed messages. Under **Encrypting preferences,** clicking **Select** opens a new dialog box that allows you to choose the encryption certificate other people will use to encrypt messages to you. You can also select the encryption algorithm that other people should use to encrypt messages to you. This setting is transmitted with each piece of digitally signed e-mail you send. Normally this setting should not be changed unless you frequently move between machines that support different algorithms.

◆ **Advanced**: The Advanced tab **(Figure 4-8)** allows you to configure several options. In the **the Server Port Numbers** section, you can specify the port the outgoing mail server will connect to in the Outgoing mail (SMTP) text box (the default value is 25). Similarly, you can set the port for the Incoming mail (POP3) server (the default value is 110). Both mail server settings allow you to specify if the Secure Sockets Layer (SSL) protocol is used in the **This server requires a secure connection** check box. The administrator or ISP for the server will indicate if SSL is required. **The Server Timeouts** slider specifies how long to wait for a response from the server before stopping an attempt to send or receive e-mail messages. If you have a fast connection to your server, move the slider toward **Short**. If you have a slow connection or a busy server, move the slider toward **Long** to allow the server enough time to respond. By selecting the **Break messages apart** check box, you can instruct Outlook Express to break up large messages, so that each part is smaller than the file size indicated. This option is available because some older servers cannot handle messages larger than 64 kilobytes (KB) and by breaking large messages into smaller messages, you ensure that the messages are transmitted and received correctly. Selecting or clearing the **Leave a copy of messages on server** check box specifies whether to store a copy of all received messages on your server. If your mail provider does not allow you to save messages on the server, a dialog box appears informing you of that and these settings will be moot. The **Delivery** section provides three possible methods of dealing with mail on the server. If you leave the **Leave a copy of messages on server** check box cleared, then incoming messages are deleted from your server after you download them to your computer. This option can be ignored based on configurations at the mail server and if your provider does not allow you to save messages on the server, a dialog box will appear informing you of that. If the check box is selected, then you can use the **Remove from server after x days** spin box to indicate how long e-mail messages should be left on the server before being deleted. The final check box, **Remove from server when deleted from 'Deleted Items'**, is active only when you opt to leave messages on the server. It instructs the server to a delete a message from the server when you delete the message from the Deleted Items folder on your computer.

Figure 4-6 Connection tab

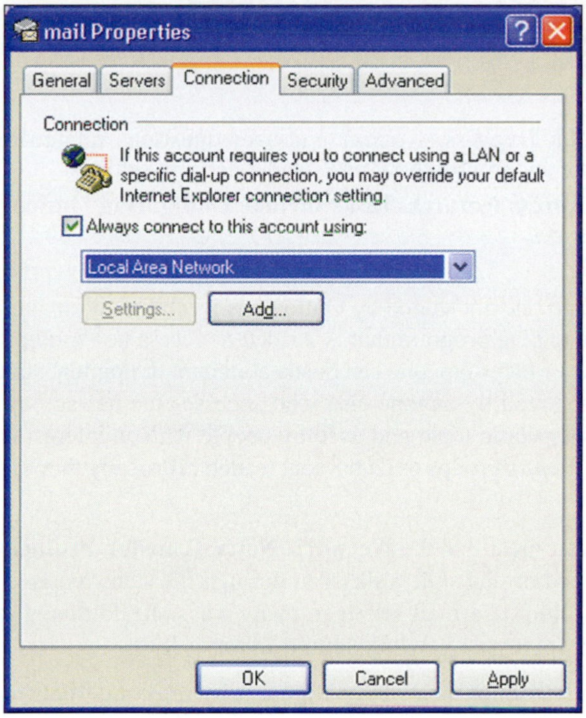

Figure 4-7 Security tab

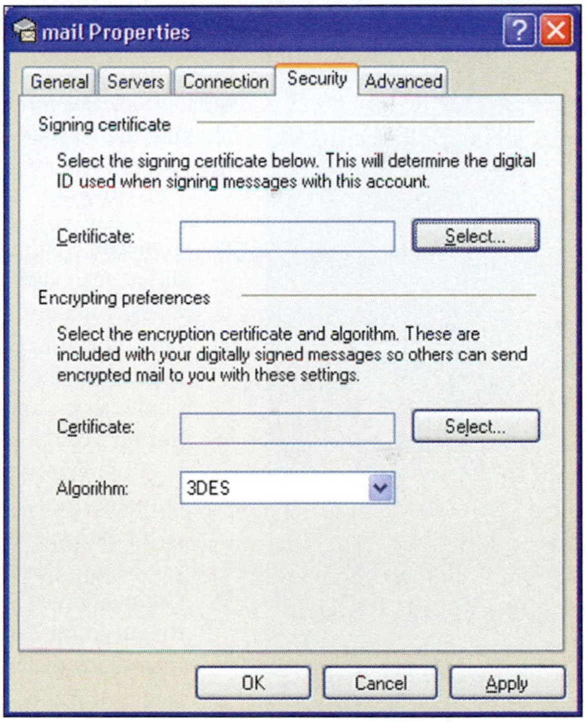

Figure 4-8 Advanced tab

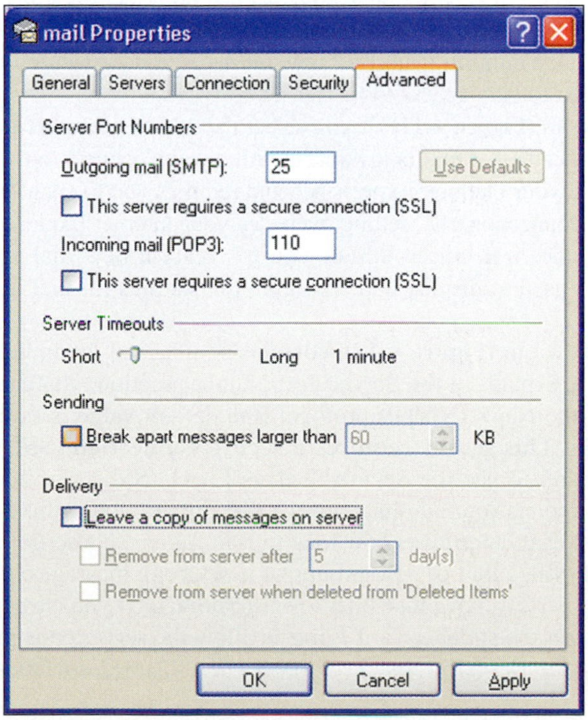

skill 4

Accessing Newsgroups Using Outlook Express

exam objective

Configure and troubleshoot Outlook Express. Answer end-user questions related to configuring Outlook Express. Configure and troubleshoot newsreader account settings.

Resolve issues related to Outlook Express features. Tasks include configuring Outlook Express and interpreting error messages.

overview

A key capability of Outlook Express, and one not shared by Outlook, is its ability to function as a newsreader. A newsreader is a messaging program that is needed to access newsgroups. A **newsgroup** is a shared message board where someone can post a comment or opinion, start a discussion or ask for help that can be read by anyone else who accesses the newsgroup. Typically, newsgroups are devoted to a specific topic and used by people with an interest in that topic—examples include Microsoft users groups or Cub Scout leaders. Basically they are used by people with common interests.

To connect to a newsgroup server, you must use the **Network News Transfer Protocol (NNTP)**. The How to exercise at the end of this skill walks you through the steps required, which aren't that different from connecting to a mail server in many ways. To do this, you need the name of the newsgroup server from your network administrator or ISP.

After you have created your newsgroup account, you can configure it by selecting **Tools** on the Outlook Express menu bar, clicking **Accounts** to open the Accounts dialog box, and then clicking the **News** tab. On the News tab, select the account you want to configure, and click the Properties button. The news server's Properties dialog box opens and presents you with four tabs: General, Server, Connections, and Advanced **(Figure 4-9)**.

◆ **General**: Configuring general settings is very much like that for an e-mail account. The key difference, other than the fact that you are supplying information for display in a newsgroup, is that you only have the option to **Include this account when checking for new messages** rather than receive and synchronize. Selecting this option assures that Outlook Express will look in the newsgroups you subscribe to whenever it checks for new messages. The number of unread messages in those newsgroups will be displayed next to the newsgroup name.

◆ **Server**: The Server tab **(Figure 4-10)** is also similar to that for an e-mail account. There is only one server name setting because a newsgroup server handles both incoming and outgoing message traffic. Checking or clearing the **This server requires me to log on** check box specifies whether you must either transmit an account name and password or use Secure Password Authentication to gain access to the server.

◆ **Connections**: On the Connections tab **(Figure 4-11)**, if you select the **Always connect to this account using** check box, it means that Outlook Express will always connect to the Internet by the method you select. If your Outlook Express account requires you to connect using a LAN or a specific dial-up connection, this setting overrides your Internet Explorer setting (see Lesson 3). Clicking the Add button allows you to create a new dial-up connection. The Settings button is used to display and configure the settings for dial-up connections.

◆ **Advanced**: The Advanced tab, shown in **(Figure 4-12)**, contains similar and dissimilar configuration options from that for e-mail. In the Server Port Number section, you can configure the port to be used by the News (NNTP) protocol (the default value is Port 119). By clearing or selecting the **This server requires a secure connection (SSL)** check box, you can specify whether to use the Secure Sockets Layer (SSL) security protocol when connecting to this server. Your administrator or ISP can tell you if this is required. The Server Timeouts slide bar determines how long to wait for a response from this server before canceling the downloading of newsgroups or newsgroup messages. If you have a fast connection to your server, move the slider toward **Short**, or if you have a slow connection or a busy server, set the slider toward **Long** to allow the server enough time to respond. The **Use newsgroup descriptions** check box, when selected, includes

Figure 4-9   The General tab of the news server's Properties dialog box

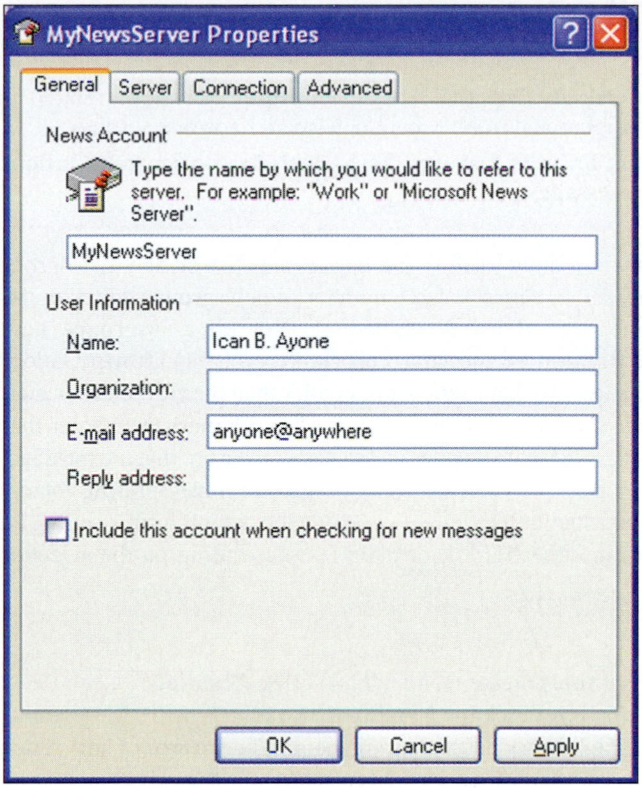

MyNewsServer Properties

General | Server | Connection | Advanced

News Account

Type the name by which you would like to refer to this server. For example: "Work" or "Microsoft News Server".

MyNewsServer

User Information

Name: Ican B. Ayone

Organization:

E-mail address: anyone@anywhere

Reply address:

☐ Include this account when checking for new messages

OK | Cancel | Apply

Figure 4-10   Server tab

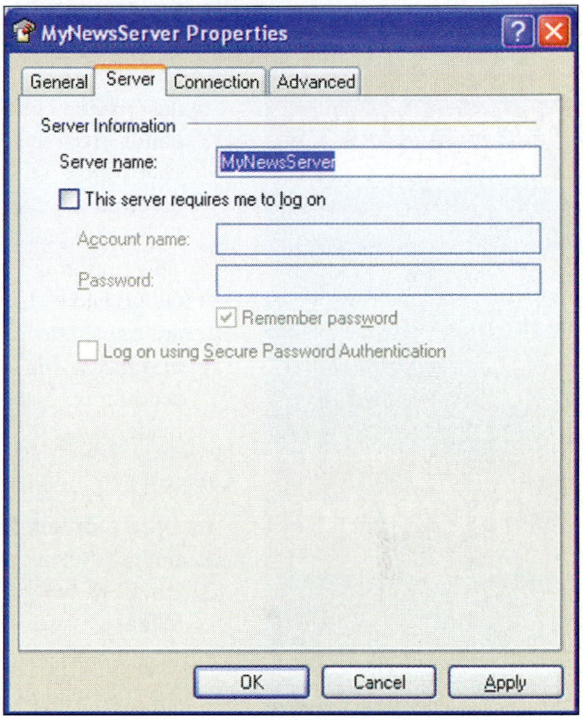

MyNewsServer Properties

General | Server | Connection | Advanced

Server Information

Server name: MyNewsServer

☐ This server requires me to log on

Account name:

Password:

☑ Remember password

☐ Log on using Secure Password Authentication

OK | Cancel | Apply

Figure 4-11   Connection tab

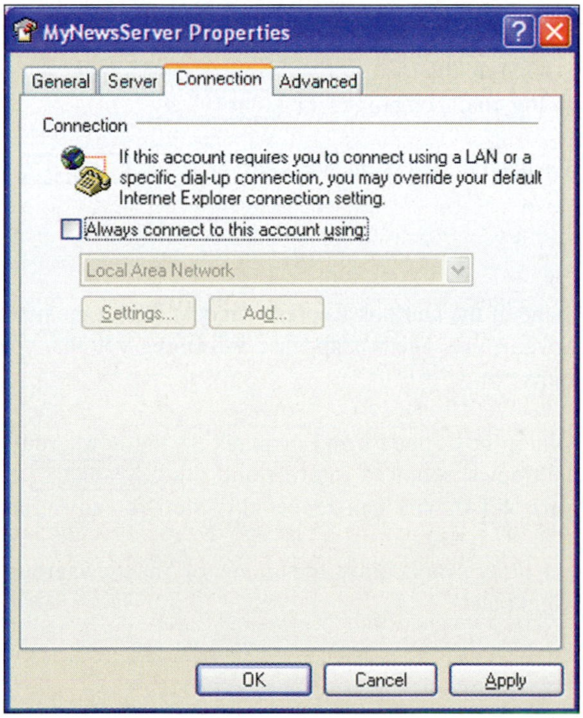

MyNewsServer Properties

General | Server | Connection | Advanced

Connection

If this account requires you to connect using a LAN or a specific dial-up connection, you may override your default Internet Explorer connection setting.

☐ Always connect to this account using:

Local Area Network

Settings... | Add...

OK | Cancel | Apply

Figure 4-12   Advanced tab

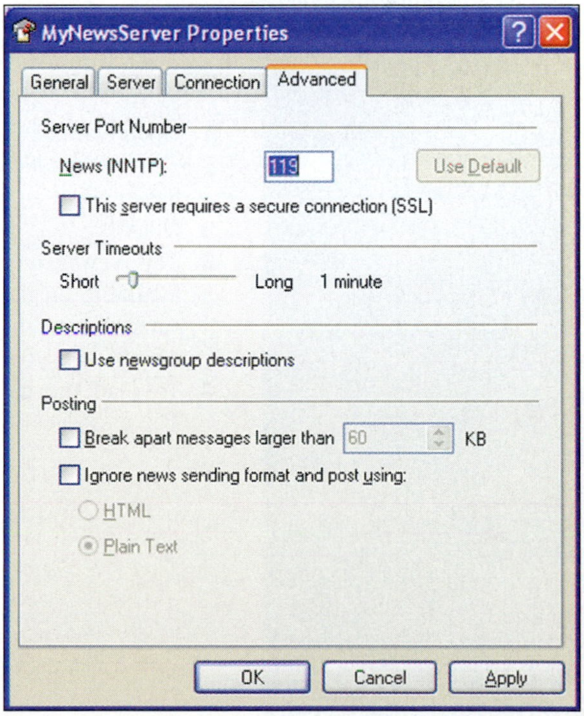

MyNewsServer Properties

General | Server | Connection | Advanced

Server Port Number

News (NNTP):   119   Use Default

☐ This server requires a secure connection (SSL)

Server Timeouts

Short ──○─────── Long   1 minute

Descriptions

☐ Use newsgroup descriptions

Posting

☐ Break apart messages larger than   60 ⇕ KB

☐ Ignore news sending format and post using:

○ HTML

◉ Plain Text

OK | Cancel | Apply

skill 4

Accessing Newsgroups Using Outlook Express (cont'd)

exam objective

Configure and troubleshoot Outlook Express. Answer end-user questions related to configuring Outlook Express. Configure and troubleshoot newsreader account settings.

Resolve issues related to Outlook Express features. Tasks include configuring Outlook Express and interpreting error messages.

overview

descriptions of newsgroups when downloading the newsgroup list or new newsgroup names from this server. If this server carries a large number of newsgroups, clearing this check box reduces the time needed for downloading. Not all newsgroups have descriptions. By selecting the **Break messages apart** check box, you can instruct Outlook Express to break up large messages, so that each part is smaller than the file size indicated. This option is available because some older servers cannot handle messages larger than 64 KB and by breaking large messages into smaller messages, you ensure that the messages are transmitted and received correctly. When selected, the **Ignore news sending format and post using** check box causes Outlook Express to override the default format setting for sending newsgroup messages in either HTML or plain text depending on the selection made.

how to

Create a newsgroup account.

1. Open **Outlook Express**. Select **Tools** on the menu bar and click **Accounts**.
2. In the **Internet Accounts** dialog box, click the **News** tab.
3. Click [Add ▸] and then click **News** on the pop-up menu. The **Internet Connection Wizard** starts.
4. Type your name in the **Display name** text box and click [Next >] to open the Internet News E-mail Address screen.
5. Type your **e-mail address** and click [Next >] to open the Internet News Server screen.
6. Enter the name of the news server supplied by your administrator or ISP in the **News (NNTP) server** text box. (**Figure 4-13**). If the news server requires credentials, select the **My news server requires me to log on** check box. Click [Next >].
7. Type the **user name** and **password** needed to access the news server. Click [Next >].
8. Click [Finish].

View and select newsgroup accounts.

1. Open Outlook Express. In the left pane of the Outlook Express window, select the news server you added in the exercise above. A message box appears, informing you that you have not subscribed to any newsgroups .
2. Click [Yes] to subscribe now.
3. The **Newsgroups Subscriptions** dialog box appears and displays all the newsgroups available on the news server. Select newsgroups of interest and click [Subscribe] to subscribe to the newsgroup (**Figure 4-14**). You can repeat this step for any other newsgroups you want to add.
4. To read the messages posted to a newsgroup, click the name of the newsgroup. The messages are displayed in the right pane.

Figure 4-13 Internet News Server Name screen

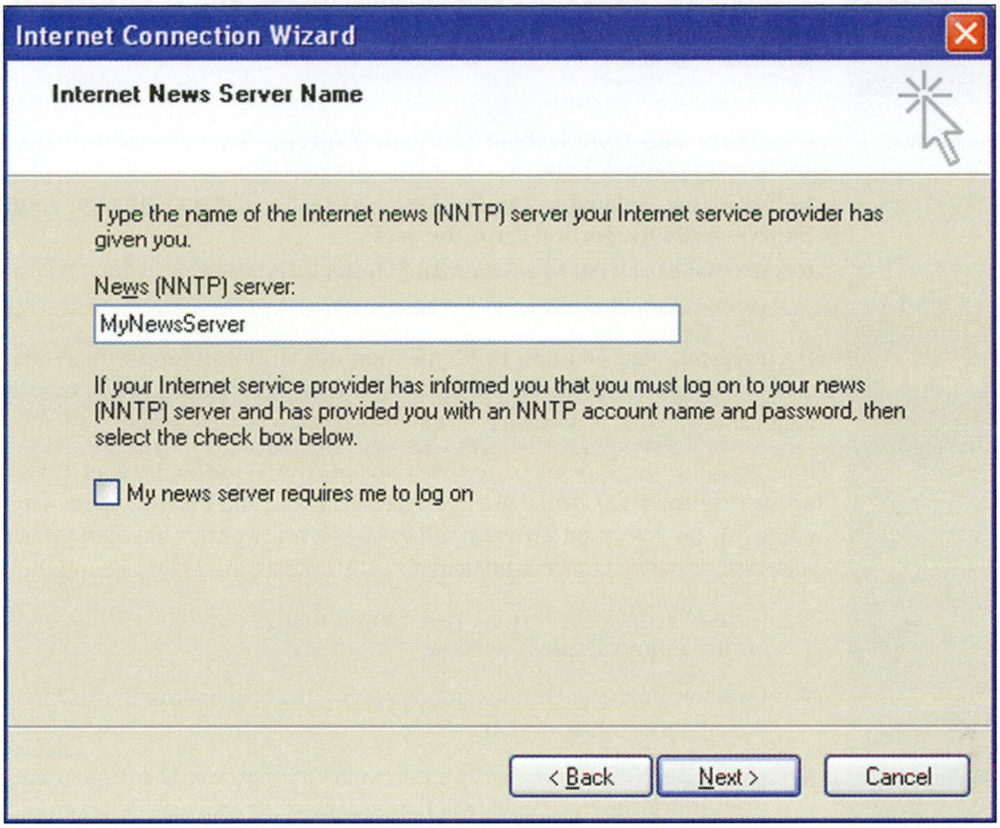

Internet Connection Wizard

Internet News Server Name

Type the name of the Internet news (NNTP) server your Internet service provider has given you.

Ne_w_s (NNTP) server:

MyNewsServer

If your Internet service provider has informed you that you must log on to your news (NNTP) server and has provided you with an NNTP account name and password, then select the check box below.

☐ My news server requires me to _l_og on

[< _B_ack] [_N_ext >] [Cancel]

Figure 4-14 Subscribing to newsgroups

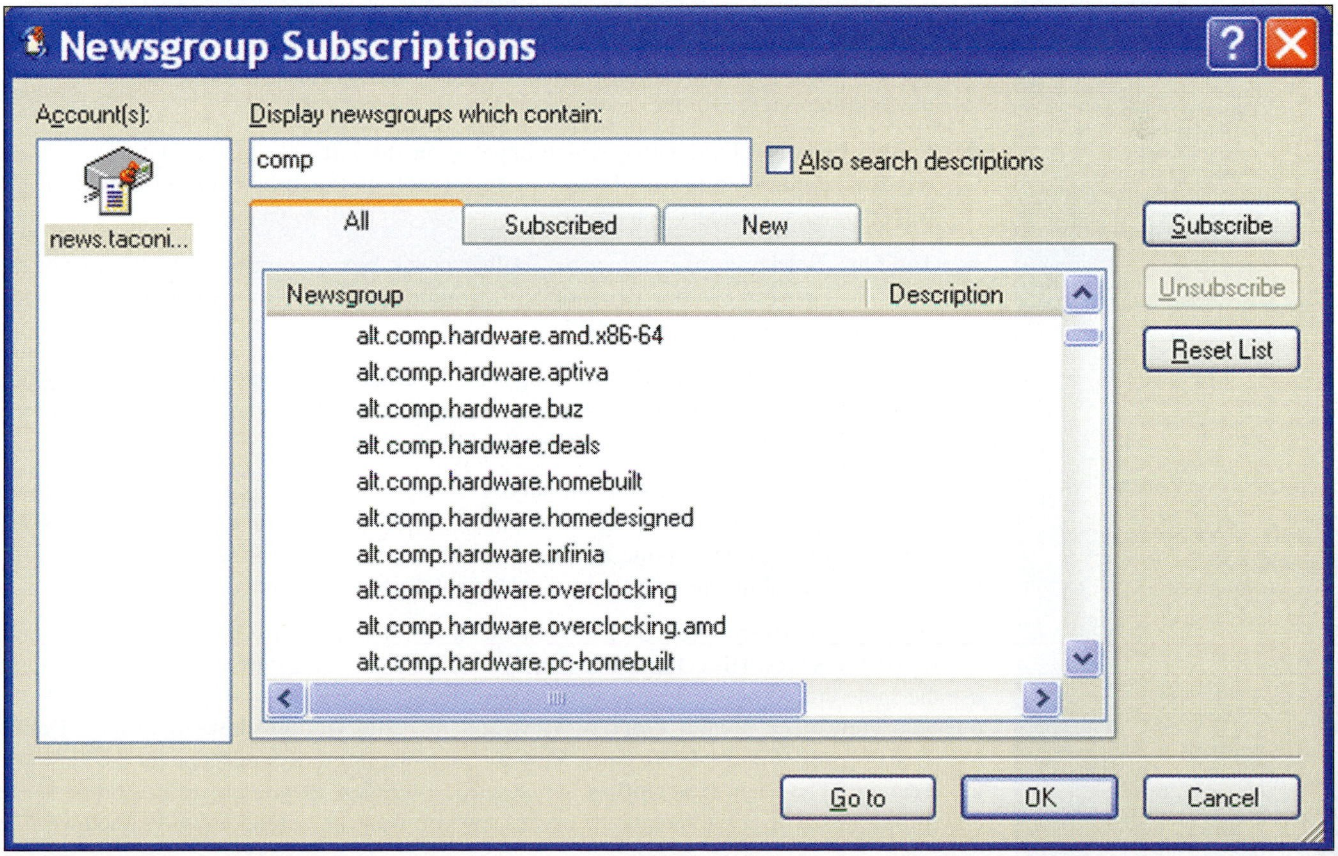

Newsgroup Subscriptions

A_c_count(s):

news.taconi...

Display newsgroups which contain:

comp

☐ _A_lso search descriptions

| All | Subscribed | New |

Newsgroup	Description
alt.comp.hardware.amd.x86-64	
alt.comp.hardware.aptiva	
alt.comp.hardware.buz	
alt.comp.hardware.deals	
alt.comp.hardware.homebuilt	
alt.comp.hardware.homedesigned	
alt.comp.hardware.infinia	
alt.comp.hardware.overclocking	
alt.comp.hardware.overclocking.amd	
alt.comp.hardware.pc-homebuilt	

[_S_ubscribe]
[_U_nsubscribe]
[_R_eset List]

[_G_o to] [OK] [Cancel]

skill 5

Personalizing the View in Outlook Express

exam objective

Configure and troubleshoot Outlook Express. Answer end-user questions related to configuring Outlook Express.

Resolve issues related to Outlook Express features. Tasks include configuring Outlook Express and interpreting error messages.

Resolve issues related to customizing Outlook Express.

overview

If you decide that you don't like the look of Outlook Express, there are several ways to customize or personalize the interface. The tools and commands you use to personalize the application's look are accessed via Outlook Express's View menu.

Start by selecting **Layout** on the View menu. The **Window Layout Properties** dialog box opens (**Figure 4-15**). There are two sections: Basic and Preview Pane. Options under **Basic** allow you to select the different components you want to have on your Outlook Express interface. Possible components include:

◆ **Contacts**: This displays a list of names from your Address Book on the lower left side of the Outlook Express window.

◆ **Outlook Bar**: The Outlook bar displays a list of icons similar to Microsoft Outlook on the left side of the window.

◆ **Views Bar**: The Views bar is a horizontal bar between the toolbar and the message list that allows you to change which messages are displayed. For example, you can choose to hide all messages you have already read. If you create custom views, you can select one from this list also.

◆ **Folder Bar**: The Folder bar (**Figure 4-16**) is a horizontal bar between the toolbar and the message list that shows the name of the currently displayed folder.

◆ **Status Bar**: This is a horizontal bar along the lower edge of the Outlook Express window that shows the current status of the selected folder; for example, how many messages are in the folder.

◆ **Folder List**: The Folder list, which appears on the left side of the Outlook Express window, contains a list of default folders (such as the Inbox, Outbox, and Drafts folders) and any folders you create.

◆ **Toolbar**: Selecting or clearing the Toolbar check box determines whether or not the Outlook Express toolbar (intended to provide quick access to the most common options) is displayed (**Figure 4-17**).

Clicking the **Customize toolbar** button opens a separate dialog box (**Figure 4-18**), which allows you to specify what buttons appear, the size of the icons, whether or not text labels are used to identify them and the order in which they appear.

In the **Preview Pane** section, you can choose to show the contents of a message without actually opening it as well as whether to display it above or below the message (**Figure 4-19**) Selecting the **Show preview pane header** check box causes the information in the To, From, and Subject boxes of the message to be displayed at the top of the preview pane.

You can select **Current View** on the **View** menu and determine if Outlook Express should **Show All Messages**, **Hide Read Messages**, or **Hide Read or Ignored Messages**. You can use the same drop-down menu to create additional customized views of messages. To do so, open the **View** menu, point to **Current View**, and then click **Define Views** to open the **Define Views** dialog box (**Figure 4-20**). Click **New** and then one or more conditions for the view you are creating. (The **View Description** box describes the view as you create it. Add or delete conditions, as necessary, to create the exact view you want.) Clicking an underlined word in

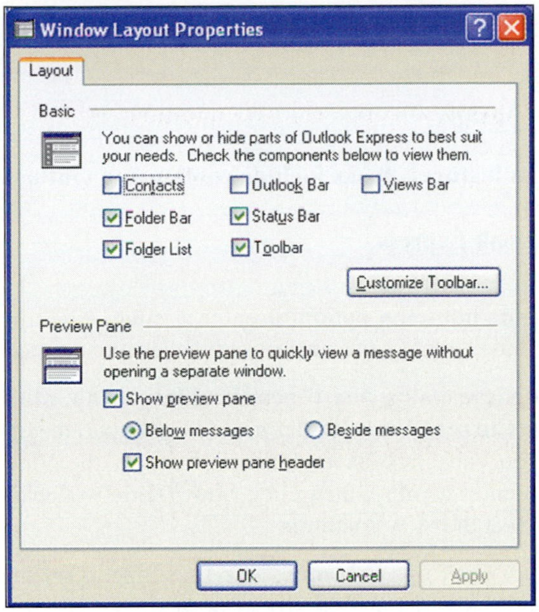

Figure 4-15 Window Layout Properties dialog box

Figure 4-16 The Folder bar

Figure 4-17 The toolbar

Figure 4-18 Customize Toolbar dialog box

Figure 4-19 Preview pane allows you to see contents of a message without opening it

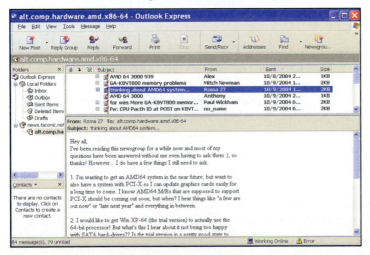

Figure 4-20 Define Views dialog box

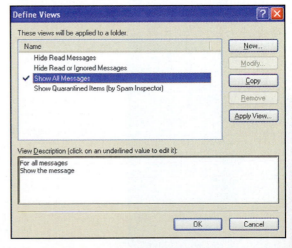

skill 5 | *Personalizing the View in Outlook Express (cont'd)*

exam objective

Configure and troubleshoot Outlook Express. Answer end-user questions related to configuring Outlook Express.

Resolve issues related to Outlook Express features. Tasks include configuring Outlook Express and interpreting error messages.

Resolve issues related to customizing Outlook Express.

overview

the **View Description** box to allows you to choose an option or enter a value. Clicking **Show/Hide** determines whether to show or hide the messages that meet the view conditions.

You can utilize the **Customize Current View** dialog box (open the **View** menu, click **Current View**, and then click **Customize Current View**) to define additional parameters (**Figure 4-21**). As with Define Views, you can click an underlined word in the View Description box to choose an option or to enter a value, then click **Show/Hide** to decide whether to show or hide the messages that meet the view conditions.

You can also use the **View** menu commands **Sort by**, **Columns**, and **Text Size** to set the method for sorting messages, which columns to display, and the size of the text.

how to

Customize the toolbar.

1. Open Outlook Express. Click **View** on the menu bar and then click **Layout** to open the **Window Layout Properties** dialog box. Click **Customize Toolbar** to open the **Customize Toolbar** (refer to Figure 4-18) dialog box.
2. To modify the toolbar text, select an item from the **Text Options** list box.
3. To modify the icon size, select an item from the **Icon Options** list box.
4. To add or remove buttons, click the button name in the **Available toolbar buttons** list box, and then click [Add ->] or [<- Remove]. You can also change the order in which buttons appear by clicking the button in the **Current toolbar buttons** list box, and then clicking [Move Up] or [Move Down].
5. Upon completion of your customization, click [Close] to close the Customize Toolbar window.
6. Click [OK] to close the Window Layout Properties dialog box and return to Outlook Express.

Figure 4-21 **Customize Current View dialog box**

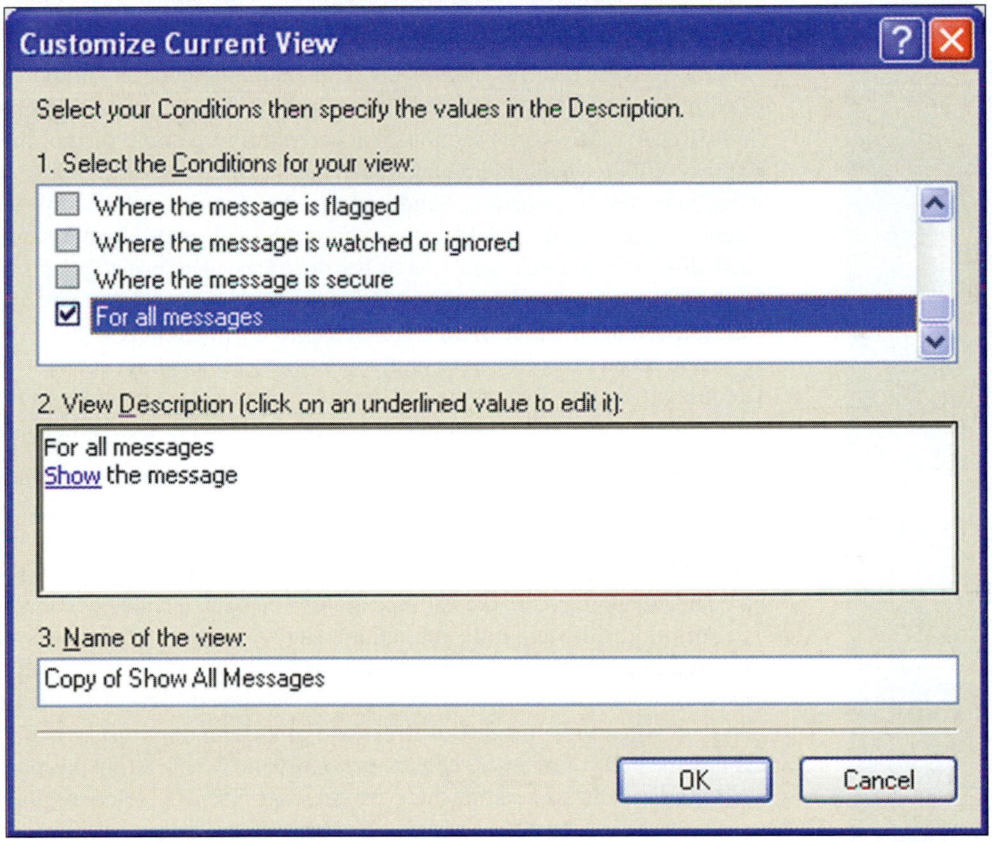

skill 6

Customizing Outlook Express Options

exam objective

Configure and troubleshoot Outlook Express. Answer end-user questions related to configuring Outlook Express.

Resolve issues related to Outlook Express features. Tasks include configuring Outlook Express and interpreting error messages.

Resolve issues related to customizing Outlook Express.

overview

Outlook Express offers dozens of options that allow you to customize a number of aspects of the program. To access Outlook Express options, click **Tools** on the Outlook Express menu bar and select **Options**. This will open the **Options** dialog box, as shown in **Figure 4-22**. There are nine tabs, each with a number of subsections and options that allow you to fully customize Outlook Express and provide you access to a number of troubleshooting methods.

◆ **General**: In the General section of this tab, you can specify a number of options for how Outlook Express behaves upon opening, including whether it should start in your Inbox (the default view is to open in the Outlook Today splash screen/portal). In the **Send/Receive Messages** section, you can configure some of the things that Outlook Express will do when sending and receiving messages. Settings allow you to Play sound when new messages arrive, Send and receive messages at startup (Meaning Outlook Express automatically checks for new messages and sends any messages in your Outbox each time it is started), and Check for new messages every [x] minutes (which tells Outlook Express to check for new messages at the interval you specify). If you are not connected to the Internet when Outlook Express will attempt to check for new messages, you can remain offline or have Outlook Express establish an Internet connection. In the **Default Messaging Programs** section, you can specify whether or not Outlook Express should be your default mail or news program by clicking the **Make Default** button.

◆ **Read**: This tab allows you to configure how messages and news are read and displayed as shown in **Figure 4-23**. The **Reading Messages** section allows you to specify whether a message should be marked as read after you have previewed it for the number of seconds indicated. If you clear the **Mark message read after displaying for [x] second(s)** check box, messages are not marked as read unless you open the message in a message window. The **Automatically expand grouped messages** check box determines whether to display threads and all replies in the message list when you open a newsgroup. If you clear this check box, only the original message is displayed. The **Automatically download message when viewing in the Preview Pane** check box instructs Outlook Express to display the body of a message in the preview pane whenever the header is selected in the message list. You can also display the message body by selecting the header and then pressing the spacebar. If you select the **Read all messages in plain text** check box, all messages will be opened and displayed in plain text regardless of the original formatting. If you select the **Show ToolTips in the message list for clipped items** check box, it shows ToolTips when an item is cut off by another column. You can specify the color to use in the **Highlight watched messages** check box as well (watched messages are parts of conversation that you are interested in. A conversation is the original message and all its replies). The **News** section contains settings that allow you to specify whether to download the chosen number of messages when viewing a newsgroup or to download all messages in the newsgroup, as well as whether or not to mark all the messages in the newsgroup as read when you exit the group. In the **Fonts** section, you can set the font and text size of incoming messages by clicking the **Fonts** button. Click the **International Settings** button to review the list of character-set substitutions that you have previously used for incoming messages.

◆ **Receipts**: In the **Requesting Read Receipts** section of this tab, you can select the **Request a read receipt for all sent messages** check box (**Figure 4-24**). However, you

Figure 4-22 General tab

Figure 4-23 Read tab

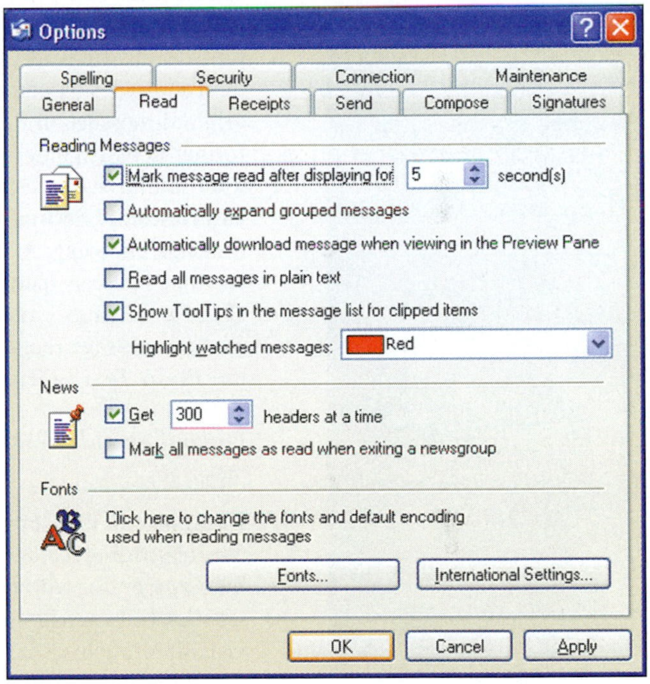

Figure 4-24 Receipts tab

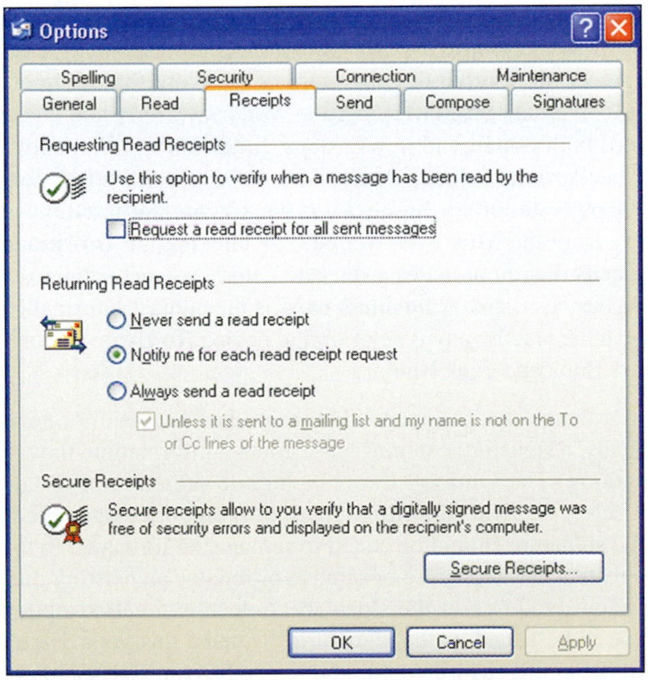

skill 6

Customizing Outlook Express Options (cont'd)

exam objective

Configure and troubleshoot Outlook Express. Answer end-user questions related to configuring Outlook Express.

Resolve issues related to Outlook Express features. Tasks include configuring Outlook Express and interpreting error messages.

Resolve issues related to customizing Outlook Express.

overview

should remember that a read receipt will be sent only if the message recipients agree. The **Returning Read Receipts** section allows you to determine when you will send receipts—always, never, or to be prompted by notification. The Secure Receipts button opens a dialog box where you can specify options for requesting and sending secure receipts. Only digitally signed messages can contain requests for secure receipts.

◆ **Send**: The **Sending** section **(Figure 4-25)** of this tab allows you to customize a variety of actions that take place when a message is sent. Options include specifying whether to save a copy in the Sent Items folder, when to send messages, whether to put people you reply to in your Address Book, whether to use an Auto-complete function to complete e-mail addresses based on the content of your Address Book; including or not including the original message in the reply and finally whether or not to reply to messages using the format in which they were sent. Format in this context means either plain text or HTML. This setting overrides other text formatting settings, such as bold or italics. Clicking the **International Settings** button opens a dialog box where you can make set the format for message encoding, message line length, and reply format. In the **Mail Sending Format** section, you can specify whether to send e-mail as HTML or Plain Text. Clicking the **HTML Settings** button opens a dialog box where you can set the message encoding format, message reply format, and whether to send pictures with the message. Clicking the **Plain Text Settings** button opens a dialog box where you can configure format settings for message encoding, message line length, and reply format. The **News Sending Format** section contains identical settings, except that these apply to Newsgroup messages.

◆ **Compose**: In the **Compose Font** section of this tab, you can configure the fonts you can use for sending mail and news messages **(Figure 4-26)**. Clicking the corresponding **Font Settings** button allows you select the font, style, size, and color. Note that recipient settings will override your settings. In the **Stationery** section, you can specify and create visually attractive messages for both e-mail and newsgroups. **Stationery** is basically a template that can include a background image, unique text font colors, and custom margins. You can create your own stationery by clicking the **Create New** button or download additional stationery from the Microsoft Web site by clicking the **Download More** button. The **Business Cards** section provides a space to enter a contact name from your Address Book to use as a business card. A **business card** is the contact information stored in a **vCard file**, which can be read by any type of digital device. To create an entry for yourself, open your Address Book and click New.

◆ **Signatures**: A signature is information that is appended at the end of an e-mail or news message. **(Figure 4-27)**. Typically, a signature contains basic contact information, though in reality, it can contain anything. The Outlook Express default value is not to add signatures. To add a signature, select the **Add signatures to all outgoing messages** check box. You can also specify if the signature should be added to replies and forwards. In the **Signatures** section, you can create a new signature or remove or rename an existing one. The **Edit Signature** section allows you to edit the signature. Selecting the **Text** option button causes the text you type to be added as the signature. To make this your default signature, click **Set as Default**. Selecting the **File** option button adds a file you specify to

Figure 4-25 Send tab

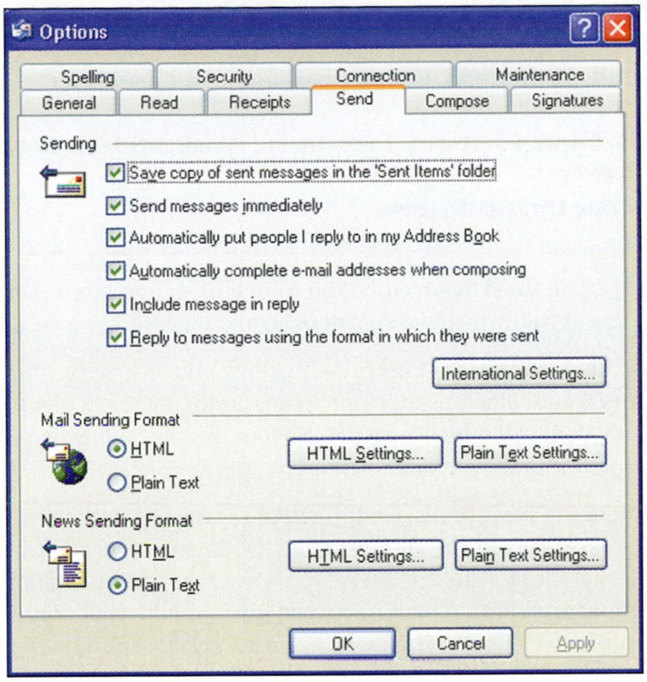

Figure 4-26 Compose tab

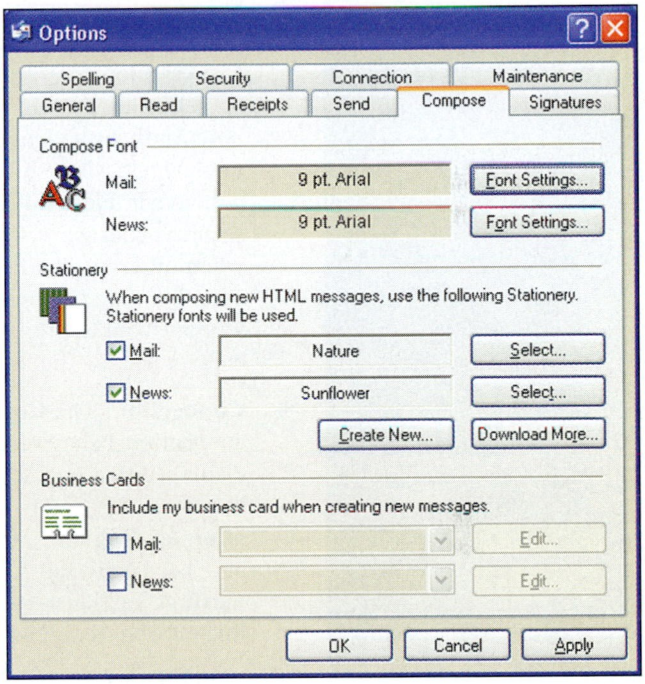

Figure 4-27 Signatures tab

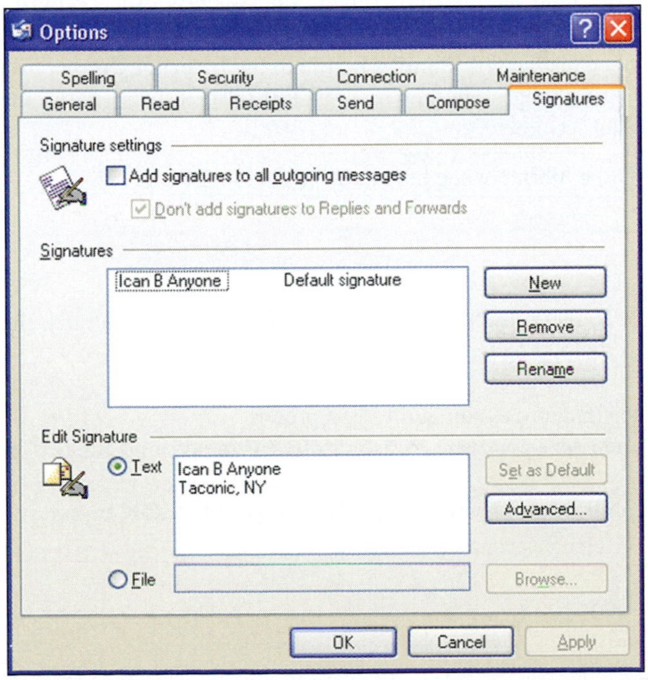

skill 6

Customizing Outlook Express Options (cont'd)

exam objective

Configure and troubleshoot Outlook Express. Answer end-user questions related to configuring Outlook Express.

Resolve issues related to Outlook Express features. Tasks include configuring Outlook Express and interpreting error messages.

Resolve issues related to customizing Outlook Express.

overview

the end of outgoing messages. Click the **Advanced** button to open a dialog box where you can specify the mail account(s) with which the signature should be used.

◆ **Spelling**: Options available on the **Spelling** tab (**Figure 4-28**) allow you to specify when spell check should be performed and which portions or words in the message can be skipped. You can also select a dictionary to use and customize your own by adding words or alternate spellings that may not be in the standard dictionary.

◆ **Security**: The Security tab (**Figure 4-29**) is primarily devoted to file attachment security issues. Most viruses are currently spread through e-mail attachments and Outlook Express allows you to control what file attachments users are allowed to open by clearing or selecting the **Do not allow attachments to be saved or opened that could potentially be a virus** check box. Note that this feature is not an acceptable substitute for running anti-virus software and should be viewed as a minor tool in the arsenal. As you will note in **Figure 4-29**, several other security settings can be configured. For increased security, consider setting the Internet security zone to Restricted. Select the **Warn me when other applications try to send mail as me** check box to help prevent viruses and other malware from sending a message to contacts in your Address Book or Contacts list without your approval. The **Secure Mail** section provides settings that allow you to encrypt and use digital certificates when sending messages.

◆ **Connection**: The Connection tab (**Figure 4-30**) allows you to configure some basic connection behaviors. In the **Dial-up** section, you can choose to have a message displayed that enables you to cancel a connection that isn't working. This setting is available only if you have more than one dial-up connection. Selecting the **Hang up after sending and receiving** check box closes the dial-up connection once messages have been delivered. Lastly, you can click the **Change** button in the **Internet Connection Settings** section if you wish to change whether or not Outlook Express shares the Internet connection with Internet Explorer.

◆ **Maintenance**: The settings on the Maintenance tab are discussed in Skill 9.

how to

To create a new signature.

1. Open Outlook Express. Click **Tools** on the menu bar, click **Options**, and then click the **Signatures** tab in the **Options** dialog box (refer to Figure 4-27).
2. Click the **New** button.
3. Rename the default title of the signature to something you prefer.
4. In the **Edit Signature** box, enter text you want to use or click **File** and find the text or HTML file you'd like to use.
5. Select the **Add signatures to all outgoing messages** check box. Click **OK** to exit the Options dialog box.

Figure 4-28 Spelling tab

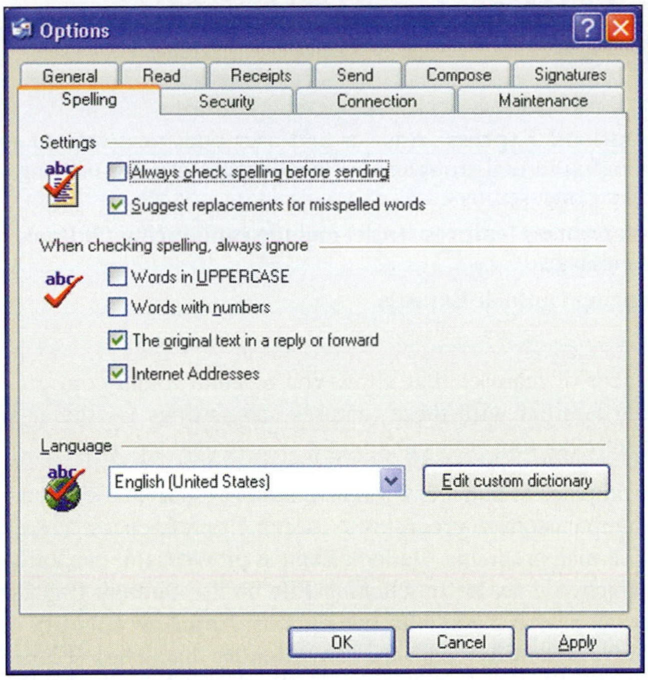

Figure 4-29 Security tab

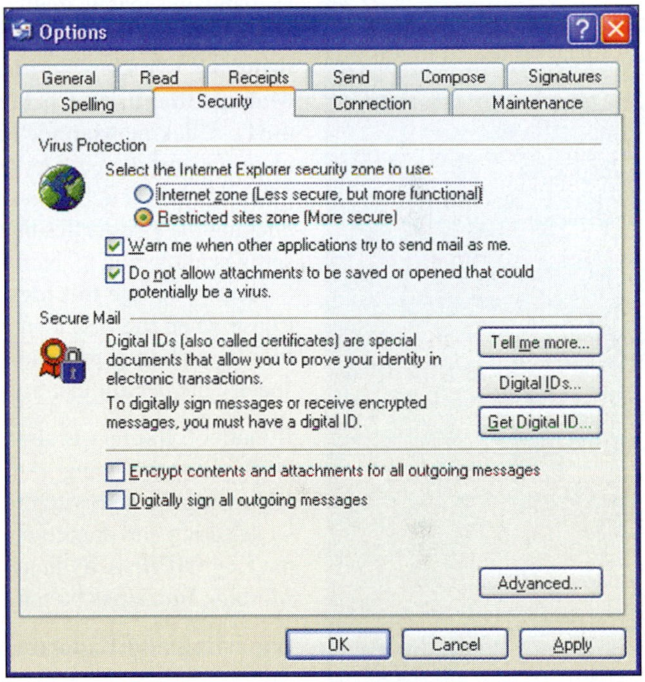

Figure 4-30 Connection tab

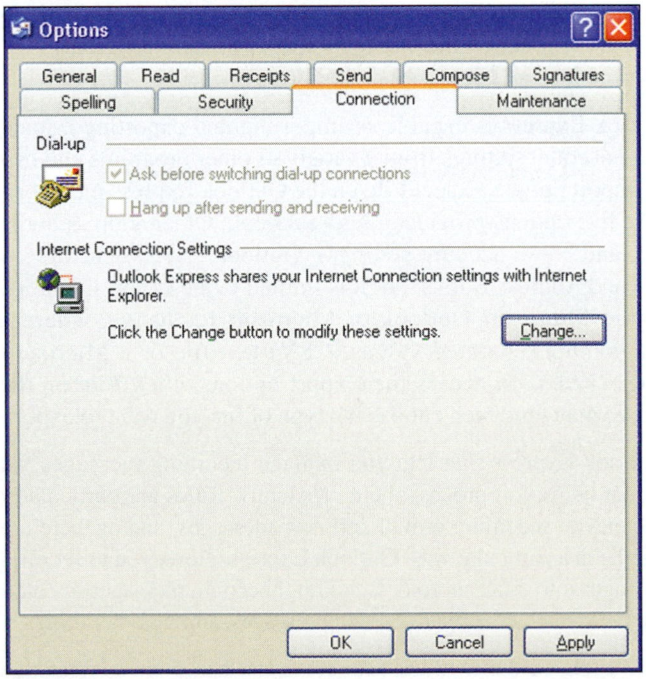

skill 7
Working with Other Features of Outlook Express

exam objective

Configure and troubleshoot Outlook Express. Answer end-user questions related to configuring Outlook Express. Configure and troubleshoot newsreader account settings. Configure and troubleshoot e-mail account settings.

Resolve issues related to Outlook Express features. Tasks include configuring Outlook Express and interpreting error messages.

Resolve issues related to customizing Outlook Express.

overview

Outlook Express includes a number of features that allow you to control and configure various important settings. Being familiar with these features and settings is crucial to providing desktop support and troubleshooting issues that might arise related to them.

Identities: It is not unusual in a workplace or home environment to have multiple users share a single computer. Most users want to customize programs to meet their preferences, as well as maintain separate mailboxes for e-mail programs. Outlook Express provides this capability through the Identities features, which you access by clicking **File** on the Outlook Express menu bar. Clicking the **Identities** tab provides you with two options: **Add New Identity** or **Manage Identities**. Clicking **Add New Identity** opens the **New Identity** dialog box **(Figure 4-31)**. Clicking **Manage Identities** opens a separate dialog box **(Figure 4-32)** displaying the identities installed in Outlook Express. You can select your preferred identity from this page. Clicking the **New** button opens the **New Identity** dialog box. Highlighting an identity and clicking the **Properties** button allows you to edit the name and set a password, if the identity settings allow you to. Normally it is good practice to configure your identity with a password. Selecting the **Use this identity when starting a program** check box specifies which identity to use when the first identity-aware program (such as Outlook Express) starts. The **Use this identity when a program cannot ask you to choose an identity** list box enables you to specify the default identity that should be used.

If Outlook Express is already using one identity and you need to switch to another, you can easily do so by going to the Outlook Express menu bar, clicking **File**, and selecting **Switch Identities**. In the Switch Identities dialog box **(Figure 4-33)**, you can select the new identity by selecting and double-clicking it, Outlook Express will reopen in the new identity. Clicking the **Log Off Identity** button logs out the identity and closes all identity-aware programs. The **Manage Identities** button opens the **Manage Identities** dialog box.

Importing and Exporting: Outlook Express is capable of importing and exporting e-mail, Address Books, and news and mail account settings from a variety of other programs and in a variety of formats. To access the Import options, select **File** on the Outlook Express menu bar, click **Import** and select one of the five options provided (Address book, Other address book, messages, Mail account settings, and News account settings). Outlook Express includes a feature to export e-mail messages and Address Books, but it is limited to the export modality. Messages can be exported only to Microsoft Outlook or Microsoft Exchange, whereas addresses can be sent only to a comma separated values (CSV) text file or a Microsoft Exchange Personal Address Book (PAB). To access the Export options, click **File** on the Outlook Express menu bar, select **Export**, and then choose the type of file you want to export.

Rules: Rules are a feature of Outlook Express that lets you manage incoming messages via e-mail and newsgroups in a way that helps you process them efficiently. Rules are particularly valuable when you have large volumes of incoming e-mail and new messages, and/or there are certain messages you wanted to handle in a particular way. Outlook Express allows you to set rules to automatically sort incoming messages into different folders, highlight certain messages in color, flag them, automatically reply to some e-mail, or forward certain messages, among other things.

To access the **Rules** settings, click **Tools** on the Outlook Express menu bar, point to **Message Rules**, and select one of the three options available on the submenu: **Mail**, **News**, or **Blocked Senders List**. Selecting any of these options opens the Message Rules dialog box. The Message

tip

When there are multiple identities on a computer, Outlook Express displays the name of the current one in the main title bar and the top of the window.

Figure 4-31 New Identity dialog box

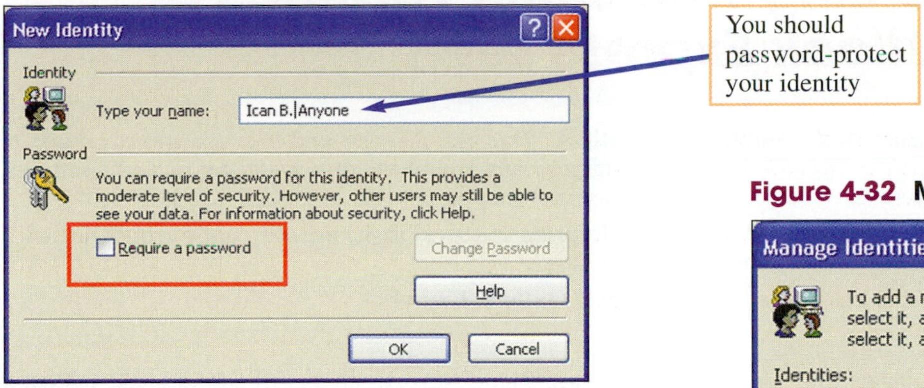

You should password-protect your identity

Figure 4-32 Manage Identities dialog box

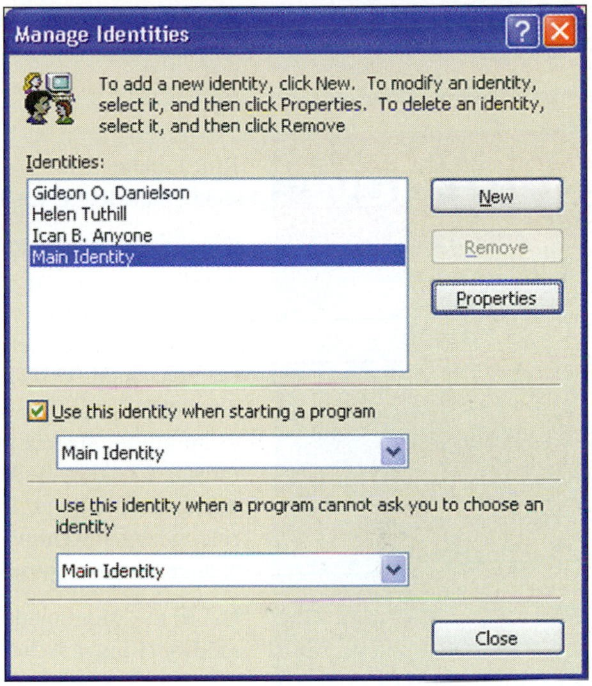

Figure 4-33 Switch Identities dialog box

Figure 4-34 Message Rules dialog box displaying a rule

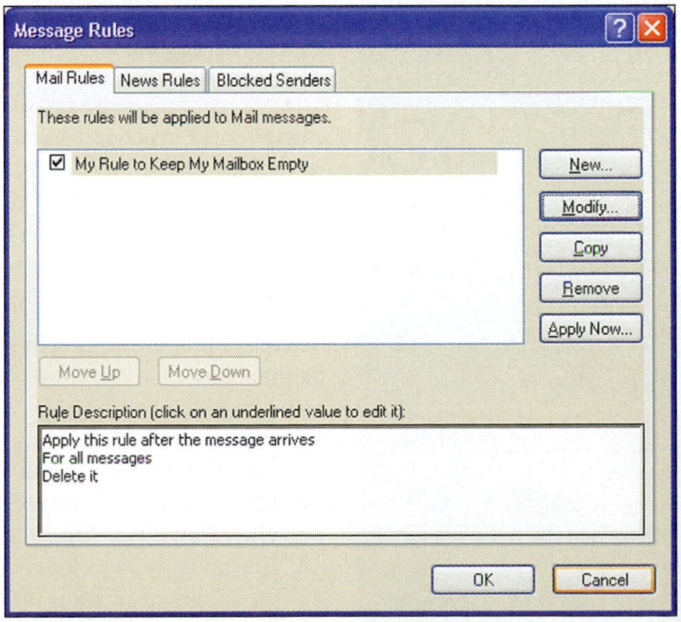

skill 7 *Working with Other Features of Outlook Express (cont'd)*

exam objective

Configure and troubleshoot Outlook Express. Answer end-user questions related to configuring Outlook Express. Configure and troubleshoot newsreader account settings. Configure and troubleshoot e-mail account settings.

Resolve issues related to Outlook Express features. Tasks include configuring Outlook Express and interpreting error messages.

Resolve issues related to customizing Outlook Express.

overview

Rules dialog box has three tabs: Message Rules, News Rules, and Blocked Senders (**Figure 4-34**). Note that if you have no rules, you are taken to the **New Rules** dialog box to create one.

Clicking the **New** button on the Mail Rules tab opens the **New Mail Rule** dialog box (**Figure 4-35**) where you can set conditions and actions for incoming new messages. The settings here are self-explanatory (e.g., if e-mail is sent from a particular person, then copy the message to this folder, etc.). It is important to remember that rules are processed in the order in which they are listed. This can have an impact if, for example, you have a rule that moves a file with the word "school" to the folder Student. If there is a subsequent rule that states the message is to be highlighted in green, it will not be executed on that message because it was already moved. Clicking the **Modify** button displays the **Edit Mail Rule** dialog box and allows you to change an existing rule. **Copy** allows you to use the settings in one rule as a template for a new rule, whereas **Remove** deletes the rule. The **Move Up** and **Move Down** buttons allow you to change the rule's position in the sequence and the order in which it is executed.

Using the same methods described for creating new mail rules, you can both specify and modify (**Figure 4-36**) rules and conditions for newsgroup messages on the **News Rules** tab. The **Block Senders** tab in the Message Rules dialog box contains a list of e-mail addresses and/or domain names. Accounts in this list will have their messages automatically sent to the Deleted items folder (if a mail message) and/or not displayed if it is a newsgroup message.

Another way to create a rule to highlight the message, then click Message on the Outlook Express menu bar and select **Create Rule From Message (Figure 4-37)**.

Synchronizing: You can set up Outlook Express to make newsgroup messages or headers available offline through the synchronization option. This enables you to read them offline and at your leisure without being connected to the Internet. Synchronization configuration settings are accessed by selecting **Tools** on the Outlook Express menu bar and one of the following four items: **Synchronize All**, **Synchronize Newsgroup**, **Mark for Offline**, and **Get Next 300 Message Headers**.

You can make all messages, only headers, or only new messages available for offline viewing by changing the synchronization settings for individual folders. To do so, right-click a folder or newsgroup on the **Folders** list in the main Outlook Express window, point to **Synchronization Settings**, and then click to change the setting to one of the following: **All Messages**, **New Messages Only** (i.e., new to the server since you last synchronized), or **Headers Only** (subject, author, date, and size of message). If you do not want messages from a particular folder or newsgroup to be downloaded, click **Don't Synchronize**.

Select certain messages within a newsgroup to be downloaded the next time you connect to the Internet.

how to

1. While offline, select the previously downloaded message headers that you want to specify for downloading the next time you connect.
2. Open Outlook Express. Click **Tools** on the menu bar, point to **Mark for Offline**, and then click **Download Message Later**.
3. Repeat these steps for each newsgroup whose messages you want to read later. When you go online, click **Tools** on the menu bar, then click **Synchronize All**.
4. Go offline to read the selected messages after they are downloaded.

Figure 4-35 New Mail Rule dialog box

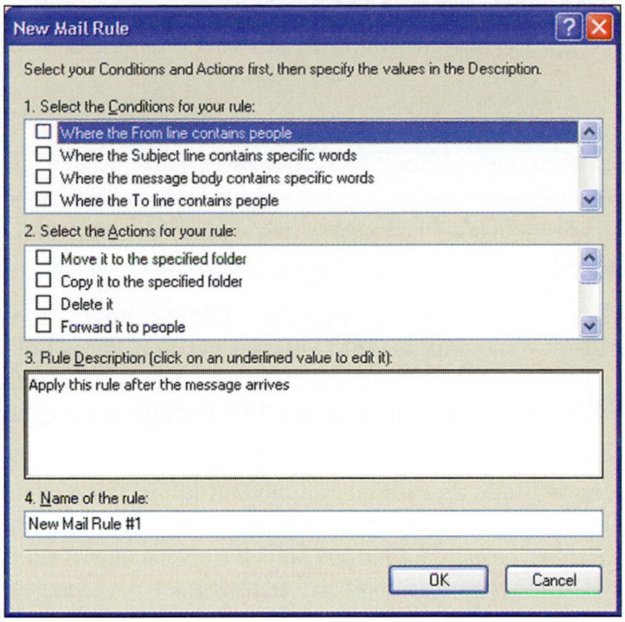

```
New Mail Rule                                          [?][X]

Select your Conditions and Actions first, then specify the values in the Description.

1. Select the Conditions for your rule:
   [ ] Where the From line contains people
   [ ] Where the Subject line contains specific words
   [ ] Where the message body contains specific words
   [ ] Where the To line contains people

2. Select the Actions for your rule:
   [ ] Move it to the specified folder
   [ ] Copy it to the specified folder
   [ ] Delete it
   [ ] Forward it to people

3. Rule Description (click on an underlined value to edit it):
   Apply this rule after the message arrives

4. Name of the rule:
   New Mail Rule #1

                              [ OK ]   [ Cancel ]
```

Figure 4-36 Edit News Rule dialog box

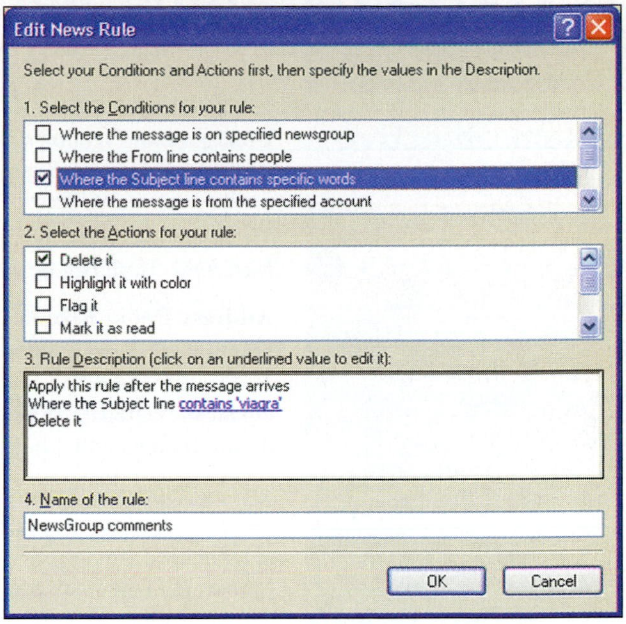

```
Edit News Rule                                         [?][X]

Select your Conditions and Actions first, then specify the values in the Description.

1. Select the Conditions for your rule:
   [ ] Where the message is on specified newsgroup
   [ ] Where the From line contains people
   [x] Where the Subject line contains specific words
   [ ] Where the message is from the specified account

2. Select the Actions for your rule:
   [x] Delete it
   [ ] Highlight it with color
   [ ] Flag it
   [ ] Mark it as read

3. Rule Description (click on an underlined value to edit it):
   Apply this rule after the message arrives
   Where the Subject line contains 'viagra'
   Delete it

4. Name of the rule:
   NewsGroup comments

                              [ OK ]   [ Cancel ]
```

Figure 4-37 Create Rule From Message command

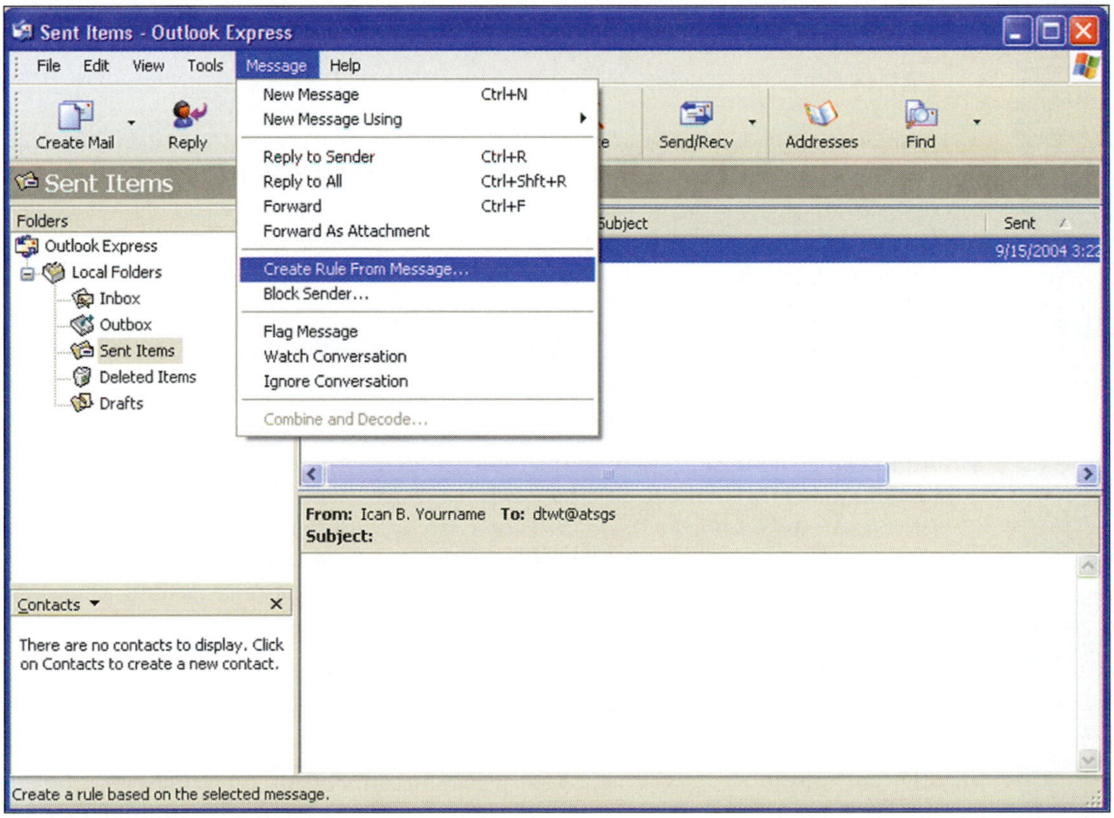

```
Sent Items - Outlook Express                          [_][□][X]

File   Edit   View   Tools   Message   Help

                        New Message              Ctrl+N
  [Create Mail]  [Reply] New Message Using        ▶     [Send/Recv]  [Addresses]  [Find]

                        Reply to Sender          Ctrl+R
  Sent Items            Reply to All         Ctrl+Shft+R
                        Forward                  Ctrl+F
Folders                 Forward As Attachment          Subject              Sent
  Outlook Express                                                   9/15/2004 3:22
  Local Folders         Create Rule From Message...
    Inbox               Block Sender...
    Outbox
    Sent Items          Flag Message
    Deleted Items       Watch Conversation
    Drafts              Ignore Conversation

                        Combine and Decode...

                        From: Ican B. Yourname   To: dtwt@atsgs
                        Subject:

Contacts ▼                        X

There are no contacts to display. Click
on Contacts to create a new contact.

Create a rule based on the selected message.
```

skill 8 *Managing Data in Outlook Express*

exam objective

Configure and troubleshoot Outlook Express. Answer end-user questions related to configuring Outlook Express.

overview

There are two basic types of data stores maintained by Outlook Express: Address Book and Messages. Both can be configured for ease of use and maintenance.

Address Book: Like nearly all e-mail programs, Outlook Express's **Address Book** allows you to record and store information about your contacts. The Outlook Express Address Book allow users to store the following information: name, e-mail address, mailing address, business-related information **(Figure 4-38)**, personal information, NetMeeting details, and digital ID data and other notes.

The contents of their electronic Address Book are extremely important to most users. The Address Book is also one of the most important datasets moved during migration from one computer or e-mail program to another. As you saw in Skill 7, Outlook Express allows you to import and export Address Book contacts. Therefore, if you have Address Book contacts from another e-mail program (or a database program, such as Microsoft Access), you can import the contacts into Outlook Express instead of re-creating all the entries **(Figure 4-39)**. Conversely, you can also export an Address Book from Outlook Express for use within another e-mail program by rendering it as a CSV file or directly into a Microsoft Exchange PAB.

In addition to importing an Address Book, there are several ways to add new e-mail addresses and contact information to an Address Book. You can add names directly from e-mail messages, enter the names and addresses manually, add people and business you find on the Internet, or import a business card (vCard).

◆ **Adding names directly from e-mail messages**: You can set up Outlook Express so that when you reply to a message, the recipients are automatically added to your Address Book. In addition, any time you send or receive a message in Outlook Express, you can add the recipient's or sender's name to your Address Book by opening the **Tools** menu, selecting **Options**, then clicking the **Send** tab and selecting the **Automatically put people I reply to in my Address Book** check box. Alternatively, when you are in an open message, right-click the person's name, and then click **Add to Address Book**. Similarly, you can highlight a message in your Inbox or other mail folder, right-click a message, and then click **Add Sender to Address Book**.

◆ **Enter names and addresses manually**: Select Tools on the Outlook Express menu bar, click Address Book, and then select New. On the Address Book menu bar, click New Contact and then enter the desired information.

◆ **Add people and businesses from the Internet**: In the Address Book, click **Find People** on the toolbar. In the **Look in** drop-down list, select the directory you want to search (if you have one configured). On the **People** tab, type the name or e-mail address of the person you want to look for and click **Find Now**. You can use the **Advanced** tab to define the search criteria you want by filling in the top three boxes and then clicking **Add**. Specify all the search criteria you want and click **Find Now**.

◆ **Import a business card (vCard)**: In the Address Book, click **File** on the menu bar, select **Import**, and then click **Business Card (vCard)**. Locate the business card file on your computer or a network drive, select it, and then click **Open**.

Messages: Outlook Express comes with a handful of default folders used to handle messaging: Inbox, Sent Items, Outbox, Deleted Items, and Drafts. In addition, Outlook Express allows you to create new folders and subfolders to suit your needs. To create a new folder, simply right-click the folder under which you would like to place a subfolder and select **New Folder**. Alternatively, you can select **File** on the menu bar. click **New** and then

tip

The Outlook Express Address Book is stored in a database file with a *.**wab** extension.

tip

Each mail folder is a separate database with the extension *.dbx.

Figure 4-38 Business data for a contact in the Address Book

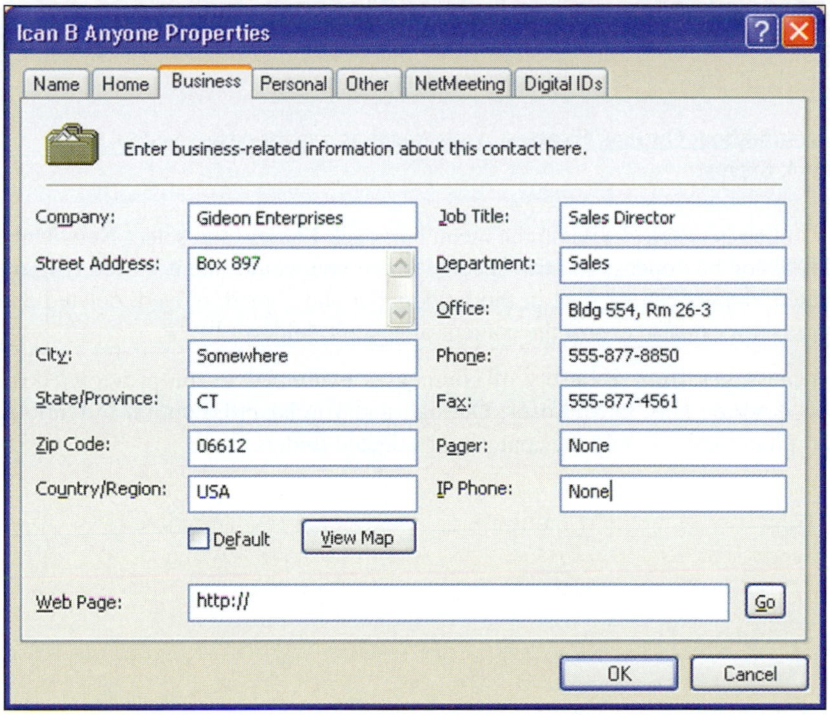

Figure 4-39 Address Book Import Tool dialog box

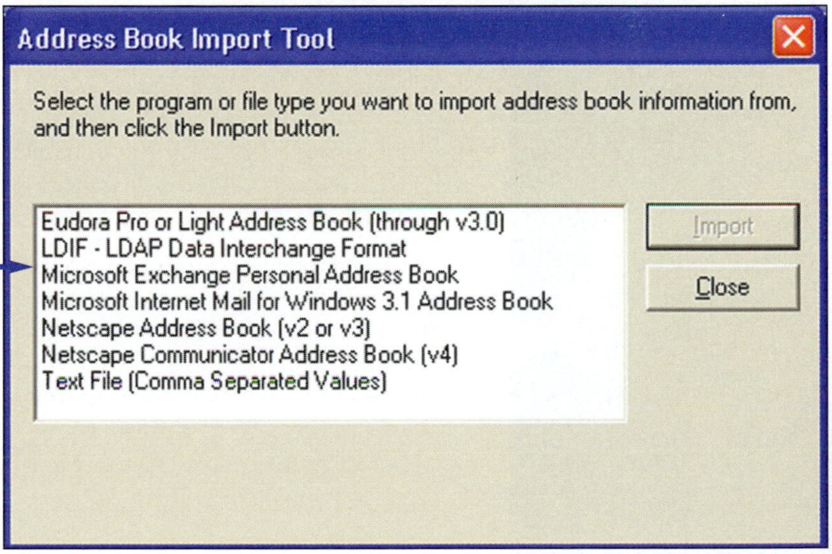

Outlook Express can import mailboxes from a variety of mail programs

skill 8

Managing Data in Outlook Express
(cont'd)

exam objective

Configure and troubleshoot Outlook Express. Answer end-user questions related to configuring Outlook Express.

overview

Folder. Another option is to select **File** on the menu bar, click **Folder**, and select **New**. Once the Create Folder dialog box opens, you can specify where you would like it placed **(Figure 4-40)**. Once created, folders can be seen in the Folders bar and copied, moved, deleted and renamed as desired. You can also export the content of specific folders.

You can import messages from a variety of sources as explained in the previous skill. Messages can be exported only to Microsoft Outlook and you have the option in Outlook Express to export all message or only the contents of selected folders.

Figure 4-40   **Create Folder dialog box**

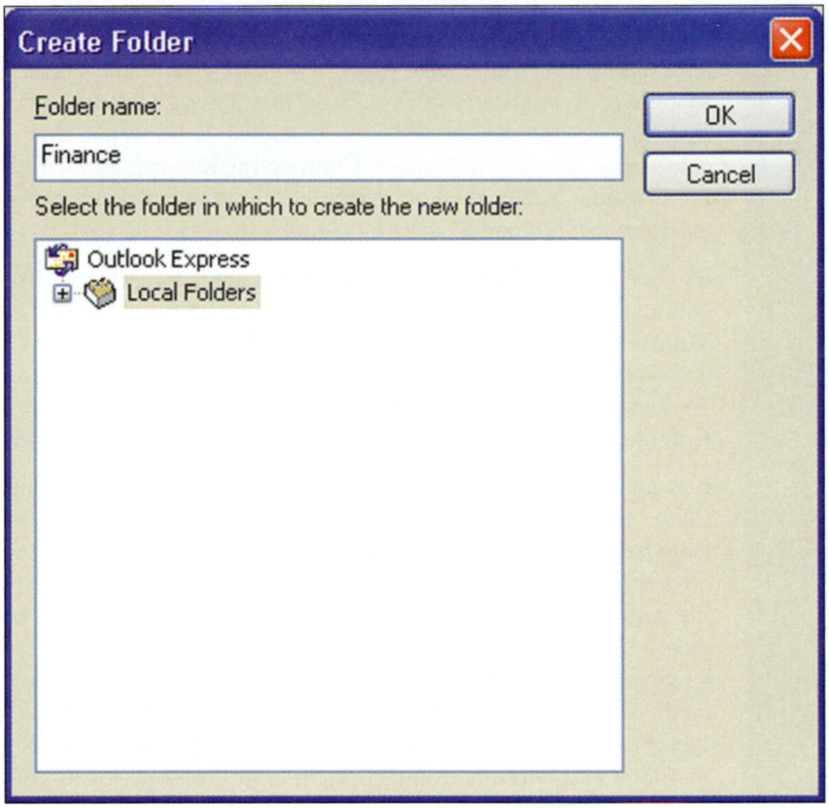

skill 9

Backing Up and Recovering Data in Outlook Express

exam objective

Configure and troubleshoot Outlook Express. Answer end-user questions related to configuring Outlook Express.

Resolve issues related to Outlook Express features. Tasks include configuring Outlook Express and interpreting error messages.

overview

It is very important to back up messages that are stored as entries within a database. Usually each folder is its own database, both for disaster recovery purposes (i.e., to preserve a copy of the material) or when you no longer need to keep the messages active, but would like to preserve them in an offline (i.e., out of Outlook Express) archive. As you learned in Skill 2, Outlook Express does not have auto-archive functions, but it can be backed up manually.

In addition to backing up, you should also compact your mail folders as part of routine maintenance. As already mentioned, Outlook Express stores messages as entries within a database that can grow in size and, if not properly managed, the burgeoning behemoth of mail databases will consume disk space in prodigious amounts and degrade system performance. Matters are complicated because a deleted message, even if deleted and then deleted again from the deleted folder, really isn't deleted in the sense that the erased record will still continue to consume disk space. **Compacting** removes all the records that have been marked for deletion from your computer, thus freeing up disk space by finally clearing those messages out of your database and improving performance.

By default, Outlook Express is configured to compact folders in the background automatically during periods of inactivity. You can turn off this feature using the **Maintenance** tab in the **Options** dialog box **(Figure 4-41)**. This is not a recommended procedure, but should you do so you should manually compact your folders at least monthly. To do that, simply click the **Clean Up Now** button located on the **Maintenance** tab and click **Compact** from the **Local File Clean Up** dialog box **(Figure 4-42)**.

It is not advisable to back up a mail folder until you have compacted it first. Backing up folders requires nothing more than selecting the file or files you want to back up and copying them to a floppy disk, CD, DVD, or network share. Outlook Express e-mail folders have a **.dbx** extension (for example, "Sent Items.dbx"—the mail folder name is always used as the file name). There are two simple ways to locate .dbx files. The first is to use Windows XP's search function to find *.dbx files or a specific .dbx file if you know the mail folder you are looking for. **Figure 4-43** shows the results of a Windows XP search for *.dbx files. The other method is to click the **Store Folder** button on the Maintenance tab and navigate to the specified location. To complete the back up, copy the file to the properly sized media. You should always store backups offsite (not at the same location as the computer) whenever possible for safety's sake.

To restore the file, simply access the backup media and copy the file(s) to the folder holding the .dbx files.

tip

If you receive the **Cannot compact, folder is in use** error message, close down Outlook Express. Then reopen the application and try running the Compact feature again.

how to

Compact and back up e-mail folders.

1. Open Outlook Express. Select an e-mail folder.
2. Click **File** on the menu bar, select **Folder**, and then click **Compact**. The file is compacted.
3. To back up the folder, find the folder file as descried above, and then copy it to a backup folder, floppy disk, CD, DVD, network drive, or other media.

Figure 4-41 **Maintenance tab**

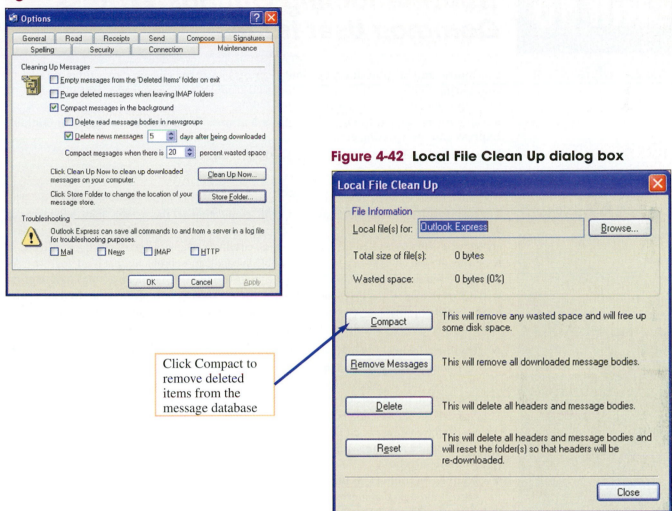

Figure 4-42 **Local File Clean Up dialog box**

Click Compact to remove deleted items from the message database

Figure 4-43 **Highlighted search results**

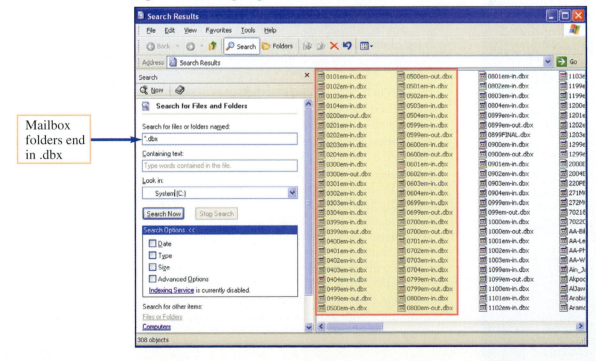

Mailbox folders end in .dbx

skill 10

Troubleshooting Outlook Express: Common User Issues

exam objective

Configure and troubleshoot Outlook Express. Answer end-user questions related to configuring Outlook Express. Configure and troubleshoot newsreader account settings. Configure and troubleshoot e-mail account settings.

Resolve issues related to Outlook Express features. Tasks include configuring Outlook Express and interpreting error messages.

Resolve issues related to customizing Outlook Express.

overview

tip

Windows XP SP1 automatically selects the **Do not allow attachments to be saved or opened that could potentially be a virus** check box.

Normally, most common user issues with Outlook Express fall into a few broad categories. The category involves problems associated with connecting to the server, mail accounts, or newsgroups. The second category involves problems with e-mail attachments. Messages may appear or disappear and entire message stores are inaccessible. If you have been diligent in reviewing the last nine skills, you should be able to handle most problems that head your way. As always, your greatest allies in troubleshooting are listening to the problem; asking clarifying and relevant questions of the user; and last but not least, staying informed and up to date on the products and applications you are supporting. The following list of common issues is far from exhaustive, but are issues you are most likely to face.

◆ **Unable to connect to mail server**: First confirm that there is connectivity with the LAN or Internet. If Internet connectivity is not the problem, then try to identify the error message. This message usually gives you a good indication as to what the problem is. If you are still unable to determine the problem, review the following:
- Is all the information in the e-mail account Properties dialog box correct?
- Do the settings match those of the ISP or local mail servers? (They should.)
- Are there any misspellings in the server name, user name, or password? (Check for trailing spaces.)

◆ **Unable to connect to news server**: See above to confirm connectivity settings are correct but note that most news server use port 119.

◆ **Able to connect to news server but not able to view newsgroup**: Check to see if the user is required to log on to the news server, and if so, confirm that the correct user name and password is specified. If the connection times out, increase the server timeout value on the Advanced tab for the news account (**Figure 4-44**).

◆ **Users want to block participants or posts contained in newsgroups**: To solve this issue, use the Block Senders option as described in Skill 7. Open the newsreader. From the list of messages in a newsgroup, open a message from the sender you want to block. Click **Message** and click **Block Sender**. Click OK to block all messages from that sender.

◆ **Messages in folder are corrupted or unavailable**: Restore from backup as described in Skill 9. If no backup exists, use this opportunity to explain the importance of regularly backing up files, including e-mail.

◆ **Attachments are not available in the message**: This is typically due to a setting in the **Security** tab of the **Options** dialog box as discussed in Skill 6. To address the problem, click **Tools** on the menu bar, select **Options**, click the **Security** tab in the Options dialog box, and clear the **Do not allow attachments to be saved or opened that could potentially be a virus** check box. You will need to close and reopen Outlook Express for the new setting to take effect (**Figure 4-45**).

◆ **Attachments are present but will not open**: In a corporate environment, consult with a system administrator if you think there may be a Group Policy in effect deleting or preventing the opening of certain files (e.g., those with a .zip or .exe extension, though typically these policies delete the files). Additionally, a user will not be able to open a file attachment if there is no program associated with it. For example, a user may receive a file with a .ram extension (Real Audio) but the file's program is not on the

Figure 4-44 Server timeouts slide bar

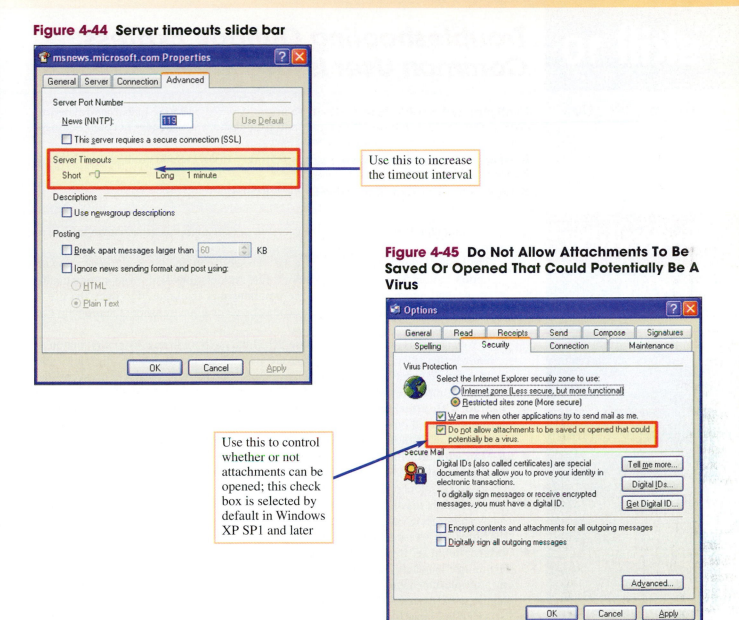

Figure 4-45 Do Not Allow Attachments To Be Saved Or Opened That Could Potentially Be A Virus

Use this to increase the timeout interval

Use this to control whether or not attachments can be opened; this check box is selected by default in Windows XP SP1 and later

skill 10 *Troubleshooting Outlook Express: Common User Issues (cont'd)*

exam objective

Configure and troubleshoot Outlook Express. Answer end-user questions related to configuring Outlook Express. Configure and troubleshoot newsreader account settings. Configure and troubleshoot e-mail account settings.

Resolve issues related to Outlook Express features. Tasks include configuring Outlook Express and interpreting error messages.

Resolve issues related to customizing Outlook Express.

overview

user's computer. If this is the case the user will get a warning like that shown in **Figure 4-46**.

- The best solution is to select the Use the web service to find the appropriate program option button. The Microsoft Windows File Associations Web page automatically opens, and information regarding the programs that can be used to open the file is listed. Depending on the findings, you may be given a link to where the program can be downloaded.
- If Web access is not available, choose Select the program from a list option button to see whether any compatible programs are available on the computer. This allows you look for a compatible program that may be installed but Windows does not recognize it as a compatible file type.

◆ **E-Mail with attachments remains in Outbox**: This is usually due to third-party software installed on the computer. Check for Internet filtering programs on the system and either uninstall the program or reconfigure it to allow attachments to be sent.

◆ **E-Mail with attachments causes errors when sending**: Typically this is the result of hardware configuration or compatibility problems with modems or firewalls or other devices. The solution is device-dependent.

◆ **"My e-mail is deleted after I read it."** This is a surprisingly common complaint. The mail can be "restored" by opening the **View** menu, clicking **Custom View** and selecting the **Show All Messages** check box, thus un-hiding read messages.

◆ **International settings and encoding**: Multilingual users sending and receiving e-mails in multiple languages can run into problems in these areas. Sending and receiving e-mail in multiple languages using Outlook Express requires that regional options for the language have been set via the Control Panel (see Lesson 2). Next make sure that Text Services and Input Languages have been configured to include the language to be used, as explained in Lesson 2. You should also confirm that the user knows how to switch between languages and that any necessary keyboard is installed when applicable. Finally, make sure that the encoding option has been selected by looking in the International Settings dialog box. (To access the International Settings dialog box, click Tools on the Outlook Express menu bar, select Options, click the Send tab in the Options dialog box, and then click the International Settings button.)

Figure 4-46 Error message advising you that a program cannot be found

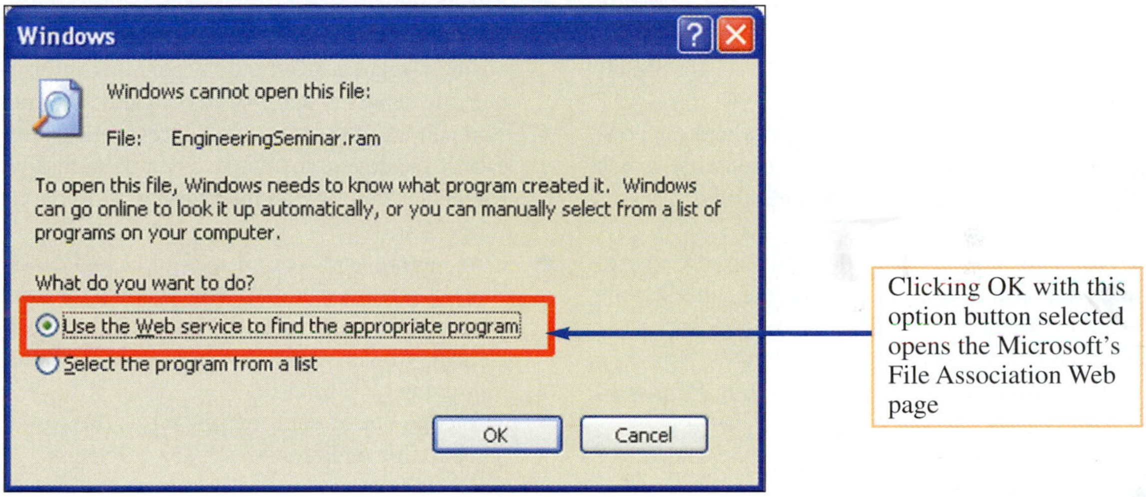

Clicking OK with this option button selected opens the Microsoft's File Association Web page

Summary

- E-mail is one of the greatest inventions in the history of communications.
- SMTP is used to send e-mail, whereas POP3 or IMAP is used to receive e-mail.
- Outlook Express is a free e-mail client bundled with Internet Explorer that can send e-mail and connect to newsgroups.
- Unlike Outlook, Outlook Express does not have a Calendar, Tasks, or Notes function and does not have automated archiving.
- You can specify a preferred language for Web sites that offer content in multiple languages.
- You can import and export messages and Address Books as a method for backing up and restoring Outlook Express. You can use this also as method for migrating from other e-mail software.
- Default port numbers are 119 for NNTP, 25 for SMTP, and 110 for POP3.
- A newsgroup is a shared message board where someone can post a comment or opinion, start a discussion, or ask for help that can be read by anyone else who accesses the newsgroup.
- The Server Timeouts slide bar determines how long to wait for a response from this server before canceling the downloading of newsgroups or newsgroup messages.
- You can customize and personalize Outlook Express's appearance through the Window Layout Properties dialog box.
- The Preview pane, when enabled, shows the contents of a message without actually opening it.
- You can request a receipt from mail recipients to determine if the message has been received. Recipients can decide whether or not to send a receipt.
- You can use plain text or HTML formatting to control how messages are composed or displayed.

- Stationery is a template of background fonts and colors that can be used to enhance the appearance of your messages.
- You can configure signatures to place at the end of your message that can be used to provide additional information about you.
- Identities provide a way of letting many people share the same computer but still create and retain their own settings and folders in Outlook Express.
- Rules are a feature of Outlook Express that lets you manage incoming messages from e-mail and newsgroups.
- You can make newsgroup messages or headers available offline through the synchronization option.
- The Address Book is used to store the following information: name, e-mail address, mailing address, business-related information, personal information, net meeting details and digital id data and other notes.
- You can add names to the Address Book directly from e-mail messages, manually enter then, add people and businesses you find on the Internet, or import a business card (vCard).
- Compacting removes all messages and other Outlook Express records that have been marked for deletion from your computer, thus freeing up disk space by finally clearing those messages out of your database and improving performance.
- The contents of each mailbox is stored in a separate database file ending with a *.dbx extension.

Key Terms

Address Book	Internet Mail Application Protocol	Outlook Express
Attachment	(IMAP)	Post Office Protocol 3 (POP3)
Business card (vCard)	Mail-user agent (MUA).	Root domain
Compacting	Message transfer agent (MTA)	Signature
E-mail	Network News Transfer Protocol	Simple Mail Transfer Protocol
.dbx	(NNTP)	(SMTP)
HTML mail	Newsgroup	Stationery

Test Yourself

1. Which of the following protocols is used to send messages from a mail client to a mail server? (Choose all that apply.)
   a. POP3
   b. IMAP
   c. SMTP
   d. HTML

2. Which of the following Outlook features are available in Outlook Express? (Choose all that apply.)
   a. Message sending
   b. Newsgroups
   c. Tasks list
   d. Address Books

3. Which of the following is the default port used by POP3 to receive messages?
   a. 25
   b. 119
   c. 80
   d. 110

4. Which feature, when used, allows you to place a disclaimer on every e-mail you send? (Choose all that apply.)
   a. Identities
   b. Digital signing
   c. Signatures
   d. Stationery

5. A user complains that he receives an error message stating that the connection to the news server has timed out. What should he do?
   a. Open Internet Explorer and use the Server Timeouts slider on the Advanced tab of the Internet Options dialog box.
   b. This is a hardware problem; he should buy a faster modem or obtain a faster connection.
   c. In Outlook Express, use the Server Timeouts slider on the Advanced tab of the news account's Properties dialog box.
   d. Reset the clock in Control Panel.

6. Which method(s) allow you to insert pictures in the body of a message? (Choose all that apply.)
   a. None, this is not possible.
   b. Set the message format to Rich Text (HTML).
   c. Set the message format to Rich Text (RTF).
   d. Set the message format to Plain Text.

7. What is the most likely cause of a user complaint that other recipients using Outlook Express cannot see the pictures and graphics included in the message body?
   a. The recipient has chosen to receive all incoming messages as plain text.
   b. The recipient is using Windows 98.
   c. The sender is not using Windows XP SP1.
   d. The recipient is using Windows XP Home, which cannot receive graphics.

8. A new user complains that Outlook Express always prompts for a password when checking for new messages. How can he change this so logon proceeds automatically?
   a. Select the My server requires authentication option.
   b. Change the security zone in Internet Explorer to Low.
   c. Reset the password.
   d. Select the Remember Password option on the Servers tab of the account properties.

9. You want all the messages you receive from a particular client or sender placed in a specific folder as soon as they are received. What is the best way to do this?
   a. Import all the sender's e-mail messages into the folder.
   b. Manually move message into the folder after you read them.
   c. Outlook Express does not have a way to do this.
   d. Create a rule that moves all e-mail messages from your boss into a specific folder.

10. What feature allows you to view the contents of a message without opening it?
    a. Preview pane
    b. Review pane
    c. Mark as Read option
    d. Inbox Viewer

Projects: On Your Own

1. Configure Outlook Express to check for new messages every 30 minutes.

   a. Start Outlook Express.
   b. Click **Tools** on the menu bar and then click **Options**.
   c. Make sure the **General** tab is selected.
   d. Select the **Check for new messages every** check box if it is not already selected.
   e. Highlight the value in the "minutes" text box and type **30**. Alternatively, you can use the up/down arrows to set the value to 30.
      Note: In the drop-down box, the If my computer is not connected at this time check box specifies how you want to send and receive e-mail if you are not connected to the Internet. You can work offline, remain disconnected, or try to establish a new connection.
   f. Click **OK** to apply the new settings and return to Outlook Express.

2. Configure Outlook Express to leave copies of incoming messages on a server.

   a. Start Outlook Express.
   b. On the **Tools** menu, click **Accounts**.
   c. Highlight an account to use and click the **Properties** button.
   d. Click the **Advanced** tab.
   e. In the **Delivery** section, select the **Leave a copy of messages on server** check box.
      Note: If your Internet service provider (ISP) does not allow you to save messages on the server, a dialog box will appear informing you of that when you log on to the server.
   f. You can use the additional check boxes in the section to choose whether messages should be removed from the server after a specified number of days or when you employ the Deleted Items for the account on your computer.

Problem Solving Scenarios

1. You are working for Germane Inc, a small corporation that provides technical support for several local companies. Your company is recommending that several of the smaller companies use Outlook Express. Your job is to create a PowerPoint presentation that outlines the advanced features of Outlook Express.

2. You have just installed Outlook Express as the new e-mail program on the computers at Bonapart Company. The employees previously used Eudora. You must now create a short user guide for the employees showing how they should configure their accounts. Their e-mail addresses follow the rule **firstname_lastname@bonapart.com** and the mail server names are smtp.bonapart.com and pop3.bonapart.com. Additionally, every company e-mail should end with the line "Bonapart Company".

Supporting E-mail: Microsoft Outlook

Microsoft Outlook is an application designed to support and improve interoffice and external communications. Outlook includes all of the following features to meet these goals:

- ◆ Support for e-mail from a wide variety of servers
- ◆ Support for contact management and schedule management using both an internal database and Microsoft Exchange
- ◆ Support for private folders stored locally or on a Microsoft Exchange server
- ◆ Support for public folders stored on a Microsoft Exchange server
- ◆ Support for tracking of communications through a built-in Journal feature
- ◆ Support for custom forms and macros

Although most users are aware of only a small portion of these features, as a technician, you will be required to understand and support nearly all of them. For this reason, you need to become intimately familiar with all of the advanced features and configuration options available in Outlook 2003.

Goals

In this lesson, you will learn how to configure and troubleshoot Outlook 2003.

Lesson 5   Supporting E-mail: Microsoft Outlook

Skill	Exam 70-272 Objective
1. Creating and Configuring E-mail troubleshoot **Accounts in Outlook**	**Configure and troubleshoot Office applications.** Configure and e-mail account settings.
2. Implementing Multiple E-mail troubleshoot **Accounts in Outlook**	**Configure and troubleshoot Office applications.** Configure and e-mail account settings.
3. Customizing Outlook	**Resolve issues related to customizing an Office application.** Answer end-user questions related to customizing an Office application. Customize toolbars. Personalize Office features.
4. Managing Contacts in Outlook	**Configure and troubleshoot Office applications.** Answer end-user questions related to configuring Office applications.
5. Working with Data Storage in Outlook	**Resolve issues related to customizing an Office application.** Manage data, including configuring, importing, and exporting data, and repairing corrupted data.
6. Troubleshooting Outlook: Common User Issues	**Configure and troubleshoot Office applications.** Answer end-user questions related to configuring Office applications.
	Resolve issues related to Office application support features. Tasks include configuring Office applications and interpreting error messages.
	Resolve issues related to customizing an Office application. Answer end-user questions related to customizing Office applications.

Requirements

To complete this lesson, you will need administrative rights on a Windows XP Professional computer with Microsoft Outlook 2003 installed. The computer must also be able to access the Internet in order for you to be able to complete some of the exercises.

skill 1
Creating and Configuring E-mail Accounts in Outlook

exam objective

Configure and troubleshoot Office applications. Configure and troubleshoot e-mail account settings.

overview

Microsoft Outlook is used primarily as an e-mail application by most users, and for this reason, understanding how to configure and troubleshoot e-mail access is perhaps your highest priority in relation to the software. First, let's examine the wide variety of servers that Outlook is capable of retrieving e-mail from:

◆ **Post Office Protocol version 3 (POP3)**: This is perhaps the most widely used e-mail protocol. POP3 is widely used on the Internet and is the protocol responsible for logging you on to your e-mail server to retrieve e-mail. When using POP3 mail servers, e-mail is sent using Simple Mail Transfer Protocol (SMTP).

◆ **Internet Message Access Protocol version 4 (IMAP4)**: This is a more advanced e-mail retrieval protocol that is beginning to gain wide acceptance. IMAP4 supports considerable additional functionality including increased security and a wide variety of mail retrieval options. Similar to POP3, IMAP4 uses SMTP to send e-mail messages.

◆ **Microsoft Exchange Server**: This is a very popular groupware server capable of supporting public and private data storage, advanced e-mail functionality, integration of other groupware systems, and integration with external data stores. Correctly implemented, Microsoft Exchange provides a highly scalable and redundant messaging platform that can also integrate data from many different sources. Outlook utilizes **Mail Application Program Interface (MAPI)** to communicate with Exchange servers.

◆ **HyperText Transfer Protocol (HTTP)**: This is most commonly associated with Web site access. However, due to the plethora of available Web-based e-mail options, Outlook 2002 and Outlook 2003 both support e-mail access using Web-based e-mail accounts, such as Microsoft Hotmail.

◆ **Fax servers**: Many third-party solutions exist that allow you to receive faxes as e-mail messages from within Outlook. Outlook connects to these services using MAPI.

Additionally, most e-mail servers (including Microsoft Exchange Server) are capable of supporting multiple e-mail protocols, although functionality may be reduced if you are not using the server's native protocol.

To configure an e-mail account, you need to know which type of server you are connecting to. Because the most common configuration you will likely perform is for POP3 or IMAP4 e-mail access, let's examine configuration of these types of accounts first.

To begin, open Outlook, click **Tools** on the menu bar, and select **E-mail Accounts**. (Or in the Control Panel, double-click the **Mail** applet (**Figure 5-1**) and click the **E-mail Accounts** button.) The E-mail Accounts Wizard opens (**Figure 5-2**). Select the **Add a new e-mail account** option button and click **Next**. On the **Server Type** screen (**Figure 5-3**), choose the type of server from which you wish to retrieve e-mail. Selecting **POP3** presents you with the **Internet E-Mail Settings (POP3)** screen (**Figure 5-4**). Similarly, selecting **IMAP** presents you with the **Internet E-Mail Settings (IMAP)** screen (**Figure 5-5**). As you can see, settings for both types of servers are similar. To continue, you need several pieces of information from your e-mail provider (typically, your Internet service provider [ISP]). These include the following:

◆ The e-mail address for your account
◆ The incoming mail server DNS name (for example, mail.corp.com)
◆ The outgoing mail server DNS name (it may not be the same as the incoming mail server)
◆ The user name and password associated with your account
◆ Whether or not Secure Password Authentication (SPA) is supported on the server (if so, enable that option to enhance security)

caution

Outlook 2003 does not support Usenet newsgroups. Although older versions included a command to open newsgroups, it simply activated Outlook Express in newsreader mode. To read Usenet newsgroup messages, use Outlook Express or a dedicated newsreader.

caution

Although Outlook dials a defined entry upon demand, it does not disconnect this entry when finished. You need to configure your dialer to do this, based on activity.

Figure 5-1 **Mail Setup-Outlook dialog box**

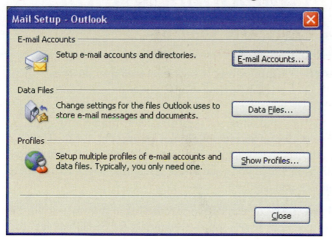

Figure 5-2 **E-mail Accounts Wizard**

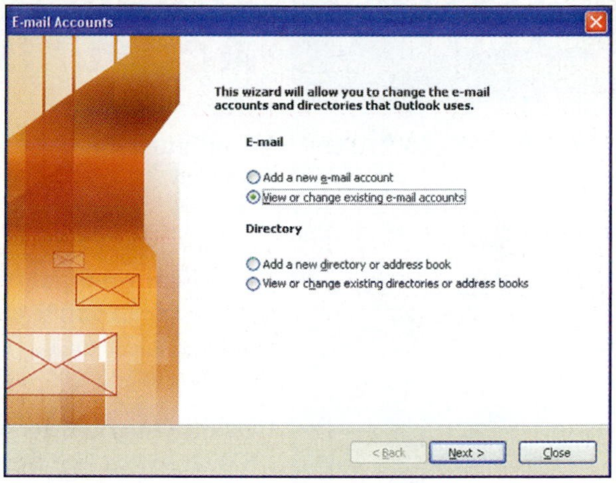

Figure 5-3 **Server Type screen**

Figure 5-4 **Internet E-mail Settings (POP3) screen**

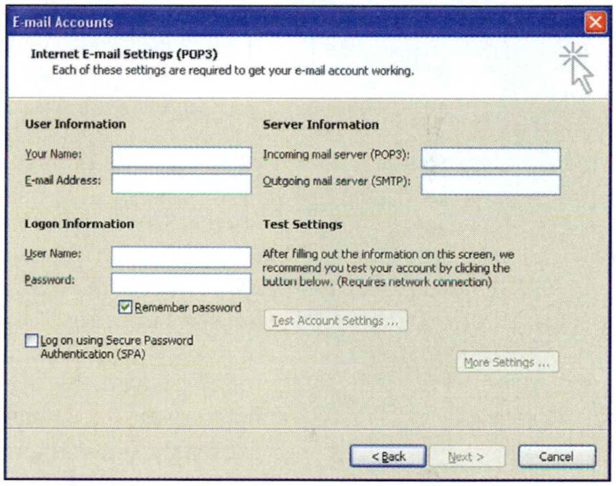

Figure 5-5 **Internet E-mail Settings (IMAP) screen**

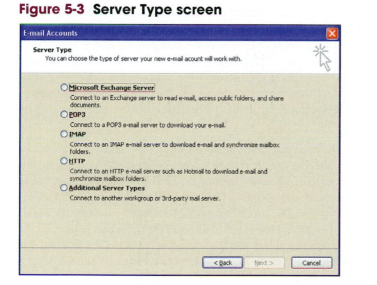

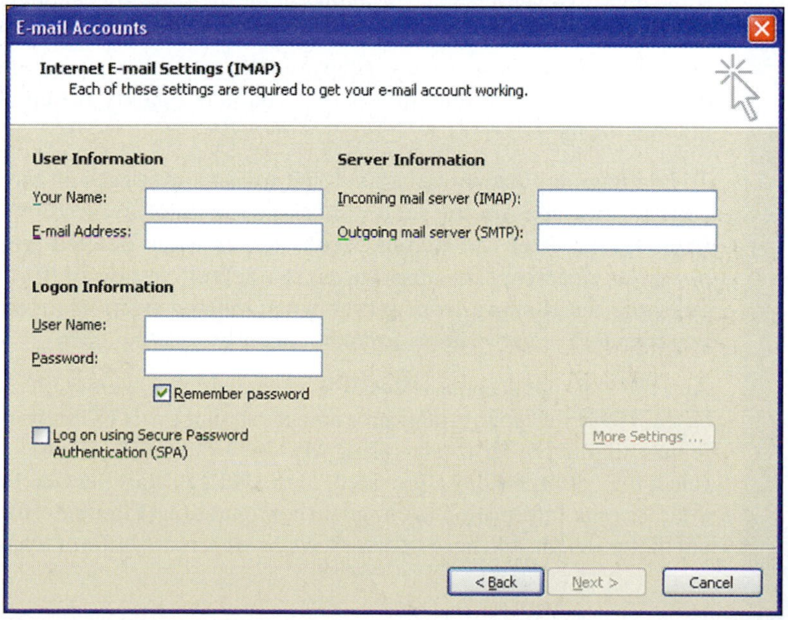

skill 1 — *Creating and Configuring E-mail Accounts in Outlook (cont'd)*

exam objective

Configure and troubleshoot Office applications. Configure and troubleshoot e-mail account settings.

overview

Additionally, clicking the **More Settings** button opens the **Internet E-mail Settings** dialog box (**Figure 5-6**), where you can configure advanced options for the account. On the **General** tab, you can define a different address to use as the Reply to address in all sent e-mail messages. This is useful in situations in which you want return e-mail messages to be sent to a different account, such as an auto-responder.

On the **Outgoing Server** tab (**Figure 5-7**), you can define specific logon information for the SMTP server. The default settings use your POP3 server credentials for SMTP servers that require authentication. However, in some situations, you may need to define a separate account. Your provider should inform you if this is necessary.

On the **Connection** tab (**Figure 5-8**), you can define how Outlook connects to the mail server, either via LAN or dial-up modem. You should select the **Connect using my local area network (LAN)** option if you use some form of high-speed connectivity (such as broadband Internet access) to connect. If you select the LAN option, you can specify that Outlook should connect using a modem if the LAN connection is unresponsive. If you use a dial-up modem, you can choose to use a phone line, or Internet Explorer's or a third-party dialer to establish the connection. In either case, Outlook will initiate a dial-up connection when checking or retrieving e-mail.

On the **Advanced** tab (**Figure 5-9**), you can specify the ports Outlook will use to connect to the mail server, the server timeout interval, and, if you are working with an IMAP account, the root folder path on the server. In general, the only option you need to modify on this tab is **Server Timeouts**. The server timeouts setting defines how long Outlook waits for the server to respond before Outlook aborts an e-mail transfer and displays an error message. If a mail transfer fails in this manner, it will be attempted again at the next e-mail retrieval interval. In most cases, the default setting is adequate, but you may need to increase the interval for extremely slow servers. You should not modify the default port settings or enable Secure Sockets Layer (SSL) encryption unless advised to do so by your mail provider. Similarly, you should not modify the default root path setting unless advised to do so by your provider.

One feature many users will want to make use of when working with Internet e-mail accounts is the ability to leave messages on the server for a specific amount of time after the messages are downloaded to the system. This configuration allows you to retrieve your e-mail messages on multiple systems by leaving a copy of all e-mail messages on the mail server. However, the downside to this configuration is that you may quickly fill up all available space in your mailbox on the server.

To configure an Internet e-mail account to leave messages on the server, select the **Leave a copy of messages on the server** check box on the Advanced tab. Then, select the **Remove from server after** and **Remove from server when deleted from 'Deleted Items'** check boxes, as necessary. In most cases, the default setting of 10 days should be sufficient. Selecting the **Remove from server when deleted from 'Deleted Items'** check box allows you to quickly remove items from the server by deleting them.

An HTTP e-mail account is even easier to configure than POP3 or IMAP accounts, in most cases. However, your e-mail provider must support HTTP retrieval using Outlook for this feature to function. If you are using MSN or Hotmail HTTP e-mail accounts, you can simply select the option for those providers in the **HTTP Mail Service Provider list**, and then type your account information to complete configuration (**Figure 5-10**). However, if you are using another provider, you need to enter the correct server Uniform Resource Locator (URL) in the

tip

Outlook supports only HTTP access to premium Hotmail accounts.

Figure 5-6 Internet E-mail Settings dialog box

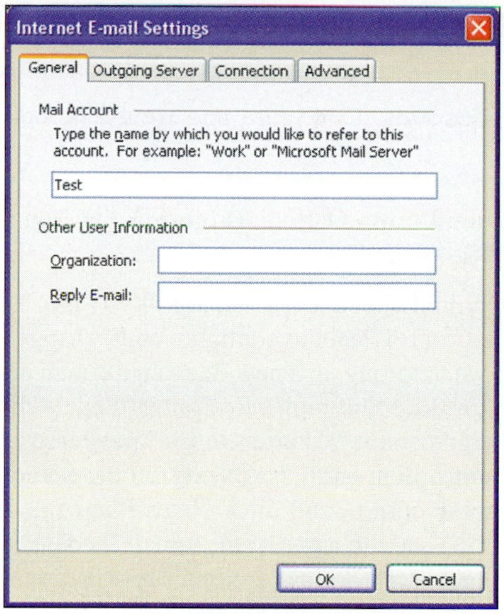

Figure 5-7 Outgoing Server tab

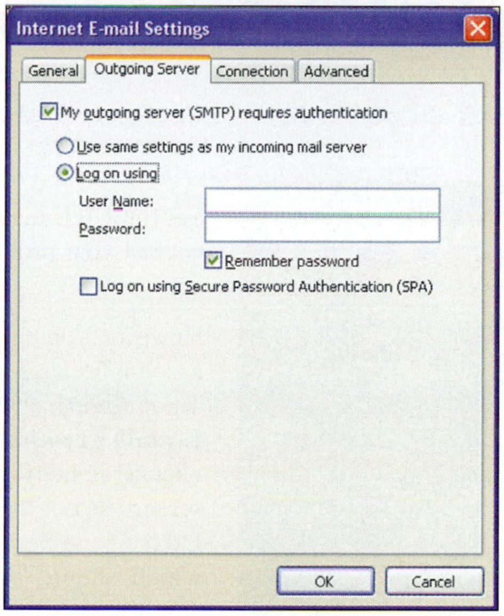

Figure 5-8 Connection tab

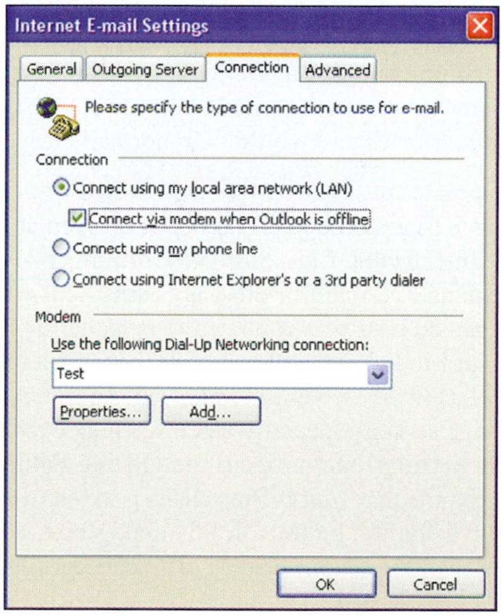

Figure 5-9 Advanced tab

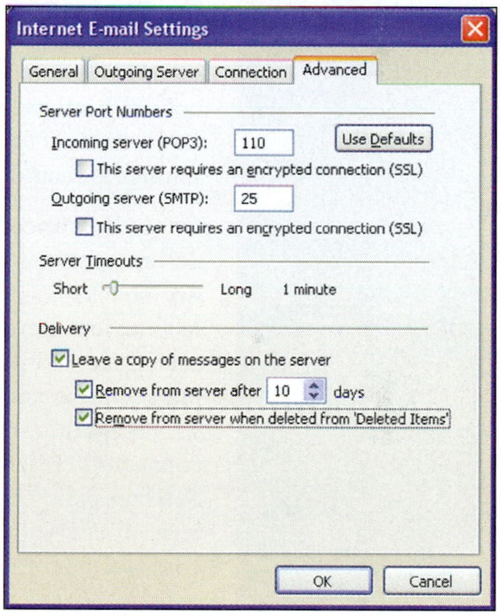

Figure 5-10 Adding an HTTP account

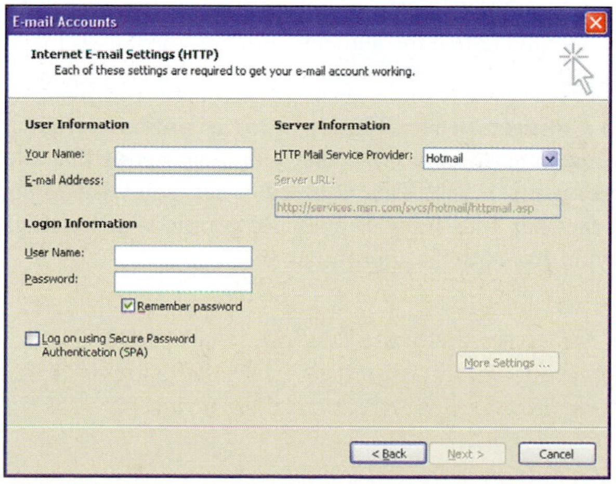

skill 1

Creating and Configuring E-mail Accounts in Outlook *(cont'd)*

exam objective

Configure and troubleshoot Office applications. Configure and troubleshoot e-mail account settings.

overview

Server URL text box to support e-mail retrieval using Outlook (**Figure 5-11**). You should contact your provider for this information.

Configuring a Microsoft Exchange Server e-mail account is even simpler (**Figure 5-12**). However, you must use the Mail applet in the Control Panel to configure an Exchange e-mail account because Outlook must be shut down when setting up a new Exchange e-mail account. To configure an Exchange e-mail account, in the Mail applet in Control Panel, click the **E-mail Accounts** button to open the E-mail Account Wizard. On the first screen of the wizard, select the **Add a new e-mail account** option and click **Next**. On the Server Type screen, select the **Microsoft Exchange Server** option, and click **Next**. Enter the correct Exchange server name (either NetBIOS or DNS) and the name of the e-mail account, both of which should be given to you by your provider (typically your organization's mail administrator). You can click the **More Settings** button to open the Microsoft Exchange Server dialog box, which enables you to set advanced configuration options for Exchange (**Figure 5-13**).

On the **General** tab, you can choose to have Outlook automatically detect the connection state or to manually configure it. This distinction determines how Outlook accesses the Exchange server. For instance, when connected via a dial-up connection, Outlook, by default, uses the options configured on the **Remote Connections** tab to retrieve e-mail. You can also define the server timeout here, but as when configuring Internet e-mail, you should normally leave these settings at their defaults.

On the **Advanced** tab (**Figure 5-14**), you can define additional mailboxes to open at logon, define caching settings, and configure offline folder file settings. Defining additional mailboxes to open allows you to read and respond to e-mail for other accounts. This is useful in situations in which you have a generic e-mail address that you need to respond to (such as sales@corp.com). Enabling Cached Exchange Mode keeps a local copy of your Exchange mail store on your local system and uses the local copy when possible. This configuration is very helpful for reducing traffic to the Exchange server, especially when working over a slow connection. Clicking the **Offline Folder File Settings** button opens the **Offline Folder File Settings** dialog box, in which you can define the file that your offline cache is saved to and the level of encryption for that file. Additionally, using the buttons in this dialog box, you can compact the offline folder file (reducing the size of the file) or disable offline folder file usage entirely.

On the **Security** tab (**Figure 5-15**), you can choose to encrypt all data transmitted between Outlook and the Exchange server, require the user to log on when opening the Exchange account, and define the authentication protocol used by Outlook. Again, these options should generally not be modified unless you are directed to do so.

The **Connection** tab (**Figure 5-16**) is similar to the Connection tab available for POP3 account configuration, with one additional setting that allows you to connect to the Exchange server using HTTP. This is useful when you wish to access the Exchange server over the Internet but your firewall does not permit MAPI traffic. Your e-mail administrator should provide you with the appropriate settings.

Figure 5-11 Entering an alternate provider address

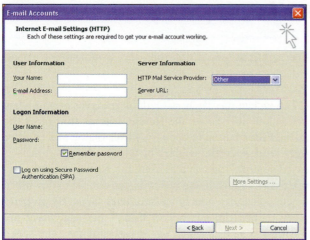

Figure 5-12 Configuring an Exchange account

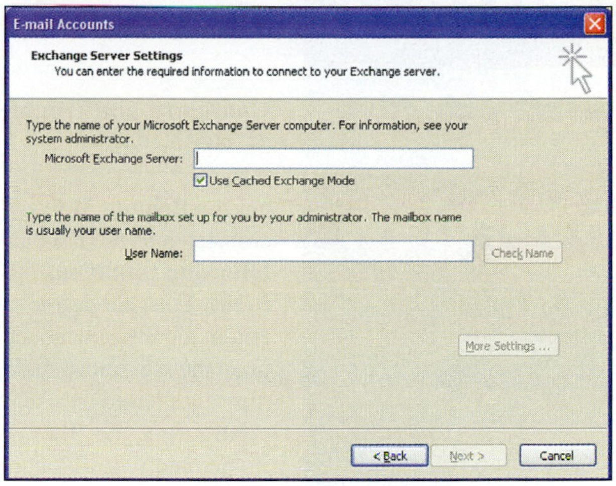

Figure 5-13 Microsoft Exchange Server dialog box

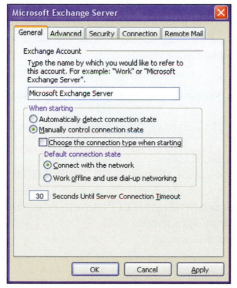

Figure 5-14 Advanced tab

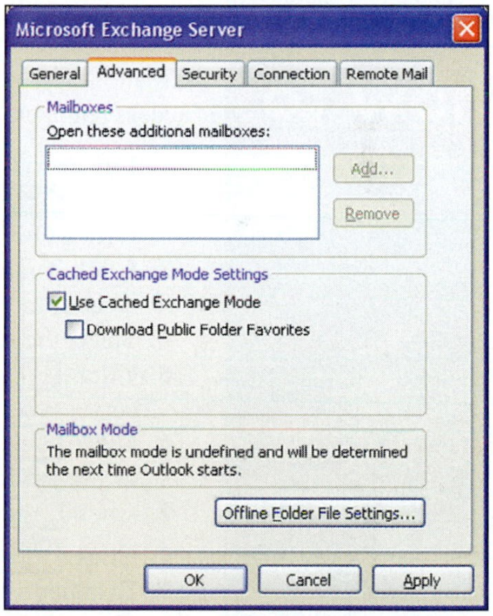

Figure 5-15 Security tab

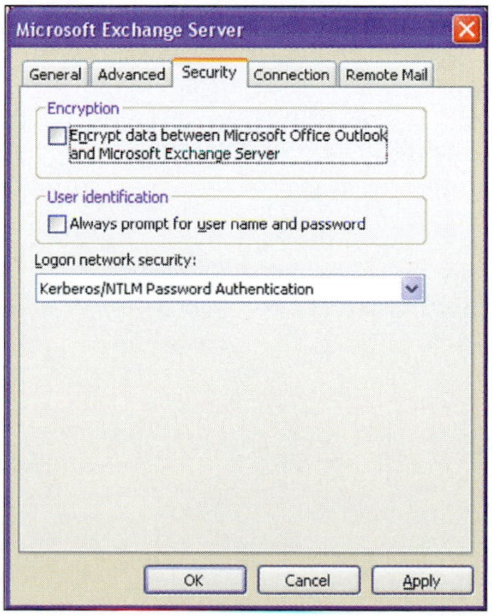

Figure 5-16 Connection tab

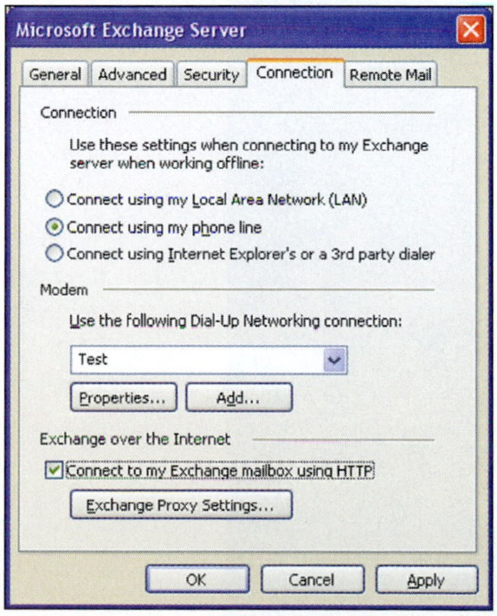

skill 1 *Creating and Configuring E-mail Accounts in Outlook (cont'd)*

exam objective

Configure and troubleshoot Office applications. Configure and troubleshoot e-mail account settings.

overview

On the **Remote Mail** tab **(Figure 5-17)**, you can modify how Outlook retrieves e-mail when connected to the Exchange server over a slow link. Select the **Retrieve items that meet the following conditions** option and click the **Filter** button to open the **Filter** dialog box **(Figure 5-18)**. You can define that e-mail only from specific senders or with specific subjects is automatically downloaded. For increased control, you can also click the **Advanced** button to open the **Advanced** dialog box **(Figure 5-19)**. In this dialog box, you can choose to download messages based on size, date, importance, sensitivity, attachments, or read status. By properly configuring the filter, you can greatly reduce the number of e-mail messages that are immediately downloaded when accessing Exchange, which can greatly improve the speed with which you are able to access your e-mail messages over a slow link. Remember, however, that for the settings on this tab to function, the connection state (on the General tab) must be correctly defined.

how to

Create a new e-mail account to retrieve Hotmail e-mail messages. You will need Internet access and a premium Hotmail account to complete this exercise.

1. Log on to the computer as an administrator.
2. Click **start**, point to **All Programs,** point to **Microsoft Office**, and click **Microsoft Office Outlook 2003**.
3. Click **Tools** on the menu bar and then click **E-mail Accounts** to open the **E-mail Accounts Wizard** (refer to Figure 5-2).
4. Select the **Add a new e-mail account** option button.
5. Click **Next >** to open the **Server Type** screen **(Figure 5-20)**. Select **HTTP** as the server type.
6. Click **Next >** to open the **Internet E-mail Settings (HTTP)** screen. Select **Hotmail** as the service provider and enter your account information.
7. Click **Next >** to open the **Congratulations!** screen.
8. Click **Finish**.
9. Examine your e-mail from Hotmail.
10. Close all applications and log off of the system.

Figure 5-17 Remote Mail tab

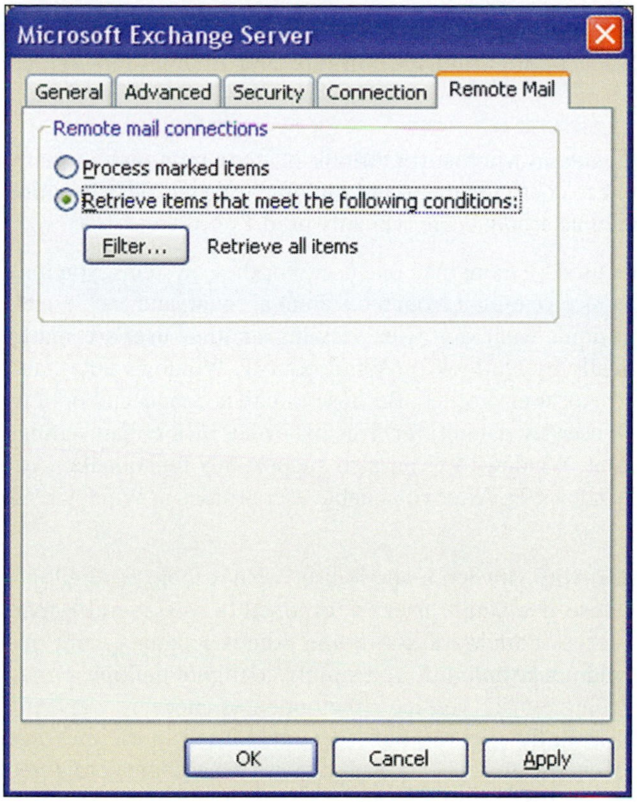

Microsoft Exchange Server

General | Advanced | Security | Connection | Remote Mail

Remote mail connections

○ Process marked items

◉ Retrieve items that meet the following conditions:

[Filter...]   Retrieve all items

[OK]   [Cancel]   [Apply]

Figure 5-18 Filter dialog box

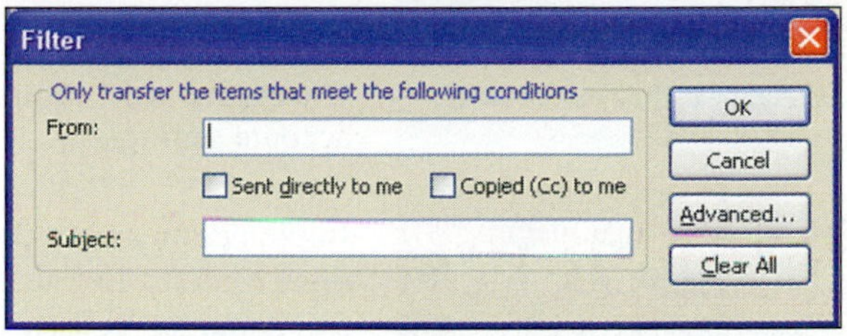

Filter

Only transfer the items that meet the following conditions

From: [   ]

☐ Sent directly to me   ☐ Copied (Cc) to me

Subject: [   ]

[OK]
[Cancel]
[Advanced...]
[Clear All]

Figure 5-19 Advanced dialog box

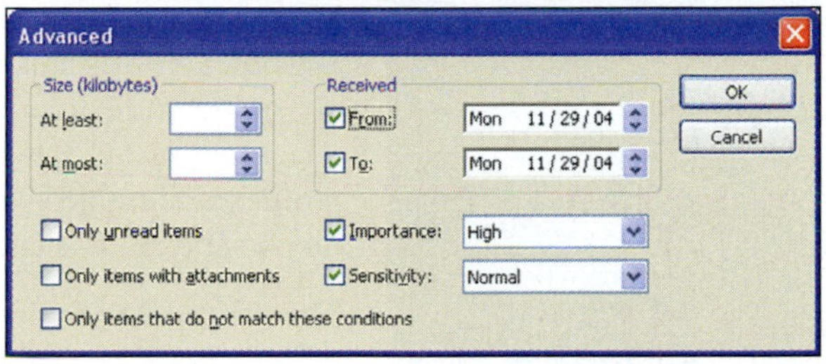

Advanced

Size (kilobytes)
At least: [   ]
At most: [   ]

Received
☑ From: Mon 11 / 29 / 04
☑ To: Mon 11 / 29 / 04

☐ Only unread items
☐ Only items with attachments
☐ Only items that do not match these conditions

☑ Importance: High
☑ Sensitivity: Normal

[OK]
[Cancel]

Figure 5-20 Server Type screen

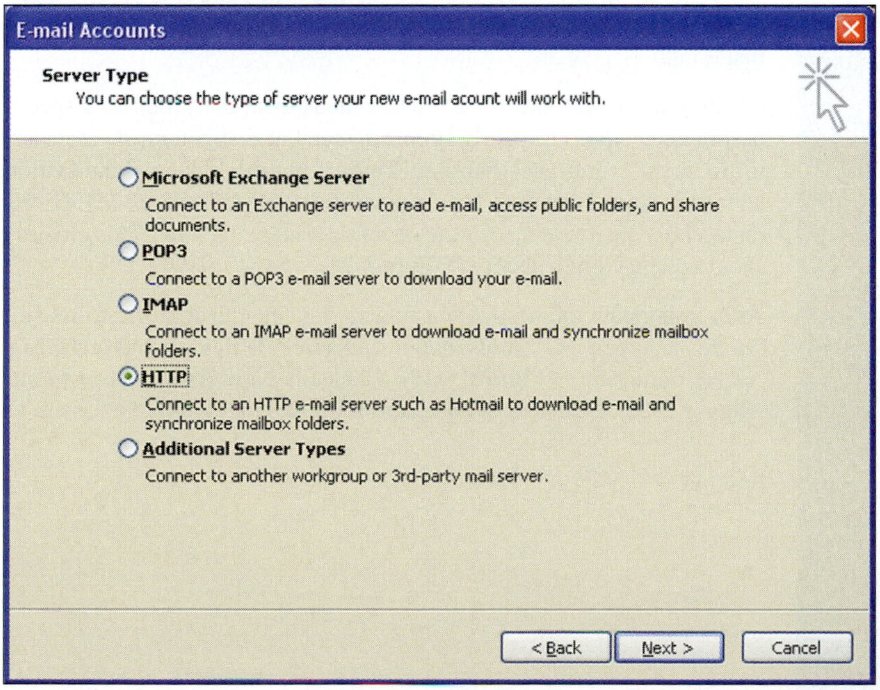

E-mail Accounts

Server Type
You can choose the type of server your new e-mail account will work with.

○ **Microsoft Exchange Server**
Connect to an Exchange server to read e-mail, access public folders, and share documents.

○ **POP3**
Connect to a POP3 e-mail server to download your e-mail.

○ **IMAP**
Connect to an IMAP e-mail server to download e-mail and synchronize mailbox folders.

◉ **HTTP**
Connect to an HTTP e-mail server such as Hotmail to download e-mail and synchronize mailbox folders.

○ **Additional Server Types**
Connect to another workgroup or 3rd-party mail server.

[< Back]   [Next >]   [Cancel]

skill 2

Implementing Multiple E-mail Accounts in Outlook

exam objective

Configure and troubleshoot Office applications. Configure and troubleshoot e-mail account settings.

overview

Implementing multiple e-mail accounts in Microsoft Outlook is a common task in many organizations. Before examining how to configure the use of multiple accounts, let's examine two common scenarios in which multiple accounts are typically used.

First, you may have systems that are used by more than one user. For these systems, you may have several users who each need to receive e-mail from a different account, and each e-mail inbox needs to be separate. (You don't want one user viewing another user's e-mail.) This scenario is handled automatically by Outlook on Windows NT, Windows 2000, and Windows XP systems through the use of user profiles. Because e-mail accounts and options are stored in the user's profile, each user, by default, receives his or her own e-mail settings when logged on to his or her account. Windows 9x can also support this functionality, but profiles are disabled by default in Windows 9x. After you enable user profiles in Windows 9x, this functionality is enabled.

The other case you may need to deal with is when a single user wishes to access multiple e-mail accounts. This can be the case if a single user is responsible for several e-mail addresses, or if a user wishes to access both work and home e-mail accounts from one location. Again, ordinarily, this should not be an issue. You simply configure multiple e-mail accounts within Outlook. When sending e-mail, you have the option of choosing a specific e-mail account to send the e-mail from by clicking the Accounts button in the message window (**Figure 5-21**). If you do not choose an account, Outlook uses the account configured as the default e-mail account. To modify the default account, open the **Tools** menu and click **E-mail Accounts**. When the E-mail Account Wizard opens, select **View or Change an existing e-mail account**. The E-mail Accounts screen appears, with a list of the accounts available on the computer (**Figure 5-22**). Select the e-mail account you wish to set as the default account and click the **Set as Default** button.

The default functionality of Outlook places all e-mail from all accounts into the Inbox folder, which may not be desirable. For instance, some users may want their home e-mail and work e-mail in separate folders within Outlook. To accomplish this, you can use an Outlook rule. **Rules** are specific matching agents that perform an action on e-mail based on the contents of that e-mail.

Creating a rule in Outlook to move e-mails from the Inbox to a specific folder based on the destination address is a fairly simple matter, but first you must create a folder to move the mail to. To do this, right-click **Personal Folders** in the left pane of the Outlook application window and click **New Folder** in the drop -down menu (**Figure 5-23**). In the **Create New Folder** dialog box, enter a name for the new folder and click OK. This creates the new folder, which should display immediately (**Figure 5-24**).

After you create the destination folder, you can create a rule to move e-mail into the folder. To do so, open the **Tools** menu and click **Rules and Alerts** to open the **Rules and Alerts** dialog box (**Figure 5-25**). Click the **New Rule** button to start the **Rules Wizard** (**Figure 5-26**). Select the **Start from a blank rule** option, select the **Check messages when**

Figure 5-21 Selecting the e-mail account to send messages from

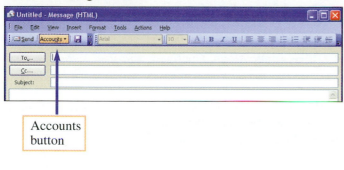

Accounts button

Figure 5-22 Modifying the default account

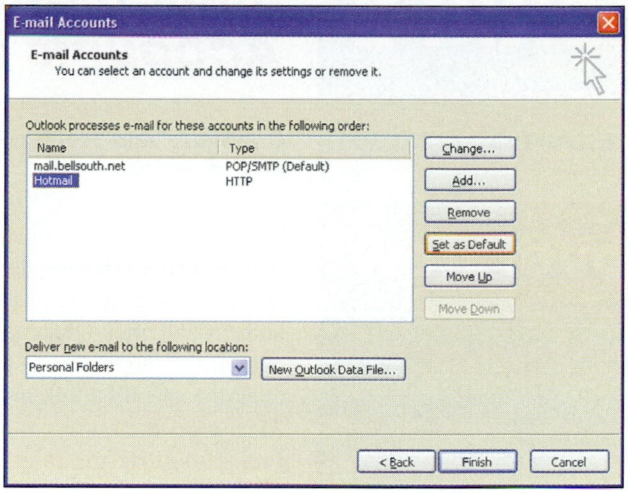

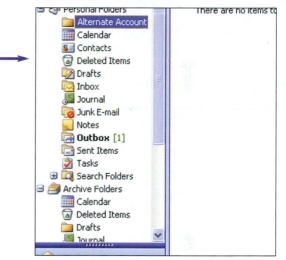

Figure 5-23 Create New Folder command

Figure 5-24 Viewing the new folder

The new folder will display in the Folders list

Figure 5-25 Rules and Alerts dialog box

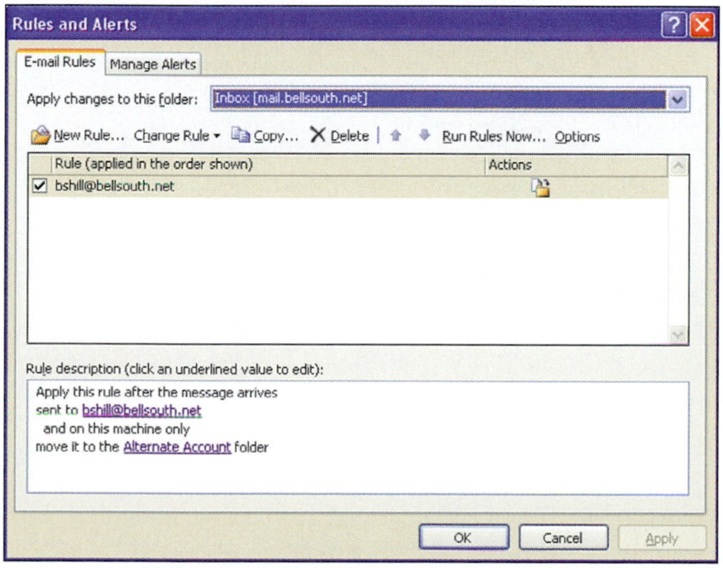

Figure 5-26 Rules Wizard

skill 2

Implementing Multiple E-mail Accounts in Outlook (cont'd)

exam objective

Configure and troubleshoot Office applications. Configure and troubleshoot e-mail account settings.

overview

they arrive task, and click Next **(Figure 5-27)**. In the **Conditions** screen, select the **Sent to people or distribution list** option **(Figure 5-28)** and click the **people or distribution list** link in the lower pane to open the **Rule Address** dialog box **(Figure 5-29)**. Enter the destination address and click OK to close the Rule Address dialog box. In the Rules Wizard, click **Next**, and on the next screen, select the **Move it to a specified folder** option **(Figure 5-30)**, and click the specified link in the lower pane. The Rules and Alerts dialog box opens **(Figure 5-31)**. Select the correct folder, click OK to close the Rules and Alerts dialog box, and click Finish to close the rules filter. The rule will automatically activate and move e-mail as necessary.

how to

Create a new e-mail account to retrieve POP3 e-mail. You need Internet access, a valid POP3 e-mail account, and account setup information to complete this exercise.

1. Log on to the computer as an administrator.
2. Click **start**, point to **All Programs**, point to **Microsoft Office**, and select **Microsoft Office Outlook 2003** to open Outlook.
3. On the **Tools** menu, select **E-mail Accounts** to open the **E-mail Accounts Wizard**.
4. Select **Add a new e-mail account**.
5. Click **Next >** to open the **E-mail Accounts** screen (refer to Figure 5-20). Select **POP3** as the server type.
6. Click **Next >** to open the **Internet E-mail Settings (POP3)** screen. Enter your account information.
7. Click **Next >** to open the **Congratulations!** screen.
8. Click **Finish**.
9. Examine your e-mail from your ISP.
10. Close all applications and log off of the system.

Figure 5-27 Selecting the Check messages when they arrive option

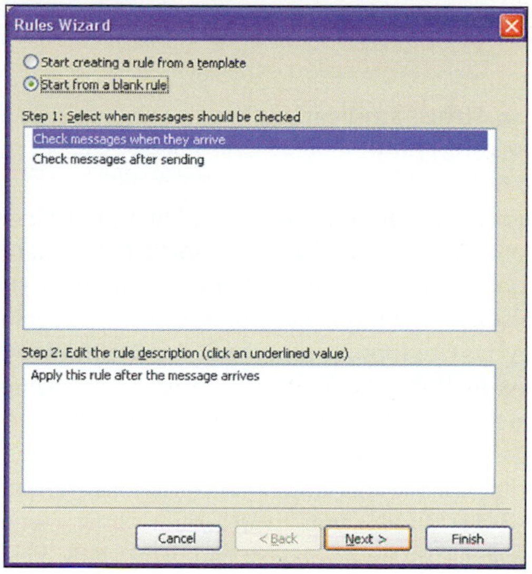

Figure 5-28 Selecting the Sent to people or distribution list option

Figure 5-29 Rule Address dialog box

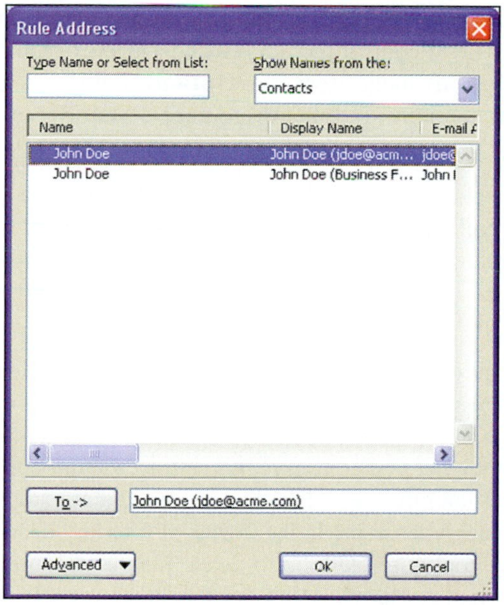

Figure 5-30 Choosing the Move it to the specified folder option

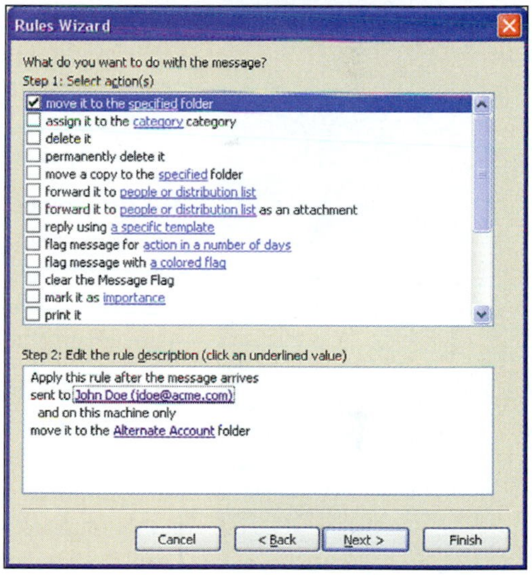

Figure 5-31 Rules and Alerts dialog box

skill 3

Customizing Outlook

exam objective

Resolve issues related to customizing an Office application. Answer end-user questions related to customizing an Office application. Customize toolbars. Personalize Office features.

overview

Like most Office applications, many customization options are available in Outlook that allow you to tailor your working environment. Although most of these options are self-explanatory, a few deserve special mention. First, to begin customizing Outlook, you can make use of both the Options and Customize commands on the Tools menu. Let's examine the Customize command first. After clicking the **Customize** command, the **Customize** dialog box opens (**Figure 5-32**). This dialog box includes three tabs—Toolbars, Commands, and Options. The **Toolbars** tab allows you to define which toolbars are shown in Outlook, as well as create new toolbars. The **Commands** tab (**Figure 5-33**) allows you to define which commands are included on each toolbar and menu, and allows you to reorganize the listed commands. The **Options** tab (**Figure 5-34**) allows you to determine how menus are displayed; define how icons, fonts, and ScreenTips are displayed; and define how menus are animated. Additionally, you can click the **Reset menu and toolbar usage data** button to reconfigure all menus and toolbars to their default settings. This button is very useful when a user has accidentally removed critical menu items.

Whereas the **Customize** dialog box allows you to control the appearance of menus and toolbars, the **Options** dialog box allows you to control more advanced aspects of Outlook's general operation. After clicking the **Options** menu item, the **Options** dialog box opens (**Figure 5-35**). The **Options** dialog box contains six tabs: Preferences, Mail Setup, Mail Format, Spelling, Security, and Other. Let's examine each tab individually.

The **Preferences** tab has five sections: E-mail, Calendar, Tasks, Contacts, and Notes. The E-mail section contains two buttons—**Junk E-mail** and **E-mail Options**. Pressing the Junk E-mail button opens the **Junk E-mail Options** dialog box (**Figure 5-36**). This dialog box controls how aggressively Outlook filters e-mail and how it deals with junk e-mail. Junk e-mail consists of spam, chain letters, viruses, and other e-mail that you do not necessarily want to see.

The Options tab in the Junk E-mail Options dialog box allows you to set the level of aggressiveness Outlook will use to filter e-mail. The higher you configure this setting, the more junk e-mail Outlook will remove before it reaches your inbox. However, false positives are common with e-mail filtering, and the higher you configure this setting, the more likely it is that Outlook will remove a legitimate e-mail message. For this reason, you are advised to keep close watch over the Junk E-mail folder when using higher levels of filtering. In addition to setting the filtering level, you can also configure Outlook to delete junk e-mail messages instead of moving them to the Junk E-mail folder by selecting the **Permanently delete suspected junk e-mail** check box. This option is generally not recommended, as even with the lowest filter setting, false positives are still possible. The only exception to this is when you are using the **No Automatic Filtering** setting. In this case, the only e-mail messages that will be deleted are those that are from senders that you have told Outlook to block.

The **Safe Senders**, **Safe Recipients**, and **Blocked Senders** tabs allow you to define e-mail addresses or entire domain names that are either trusted or untrusted. The Safe Senders list on the Safe Senders tab (**Figure 5-37**) defines which senders are trusted and will never be filtered. By default, the **Also trust e-mail from my Contacts** check box is selected, which means that all contacts listed in Outlook will be considered safe. Although this feature can save considerable time, when configuring the safe senders list, you must be certain that only trusted parties are listed in your contacts. The Safe Recipient lists on the Safe Recipients tab (**Figure 5-38**) tells Outlook that all mail sent to a particular destination e-mail address is considered safe. This is useful if you receive e-mail from a distribution list or other mailing list where the destination e-mail address does not match your own and you want to ensure that mail sent to this list is never filtered. The Blocked Senders list on the Blocked Senders tab

Figure 5-32 Toolbars tab   **Figure 5-33 Commands tab**   **Figure 5-34 Options tab**

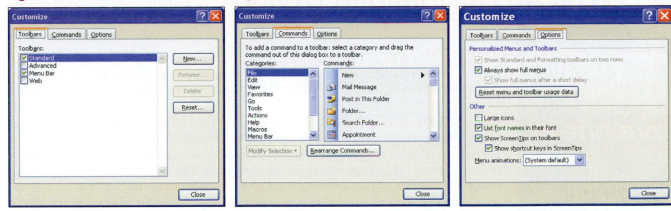

Figure 5-35 Options dialog box

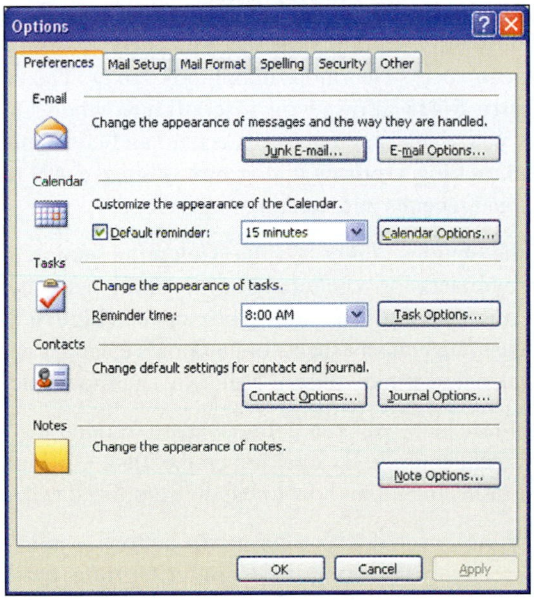

Figure 5-36 Junk E-mail Options dialog box

Figure 5-37 Safe Senders tab   **Figure 5-38 Safe Recipients tab**   **Figure 5-39 Blocked Senders tab**

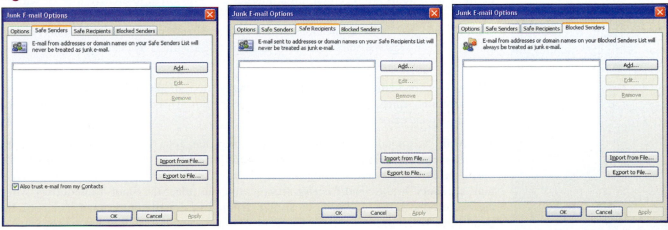

skill 3

Customizing Outlook (cont'd)

exam objective

Resolve issues related to customizing an Office application. Answer end-user questions related to customizing an Office application. Customize toolbars. Personalize Office features.

overview

(Figure 5-39) allows Outlook to specifically filter e-mail from certain senders. E-mail received from anyone on this list will be immediately removed. As you may have noticed, on all three tabs there are buttons to import and export these lists. These buttons import or export the entire contents to or from a text file. So, for instance, if you have configured Outlook on one system to block a large number of senders and wish to replicate this list to other systems, you can simply export the list as a text file and then import the list on the other systems.

The other button in the E-mail section of the Preferences tab in the Options dialog box is **E-mail Options**. Clicking this button opens the **E-mail Options** dialog box **(Figure 5-40)**. In this dialog box, you can choose how to handle replies and forwarding, as well as set general message handling options. Additionally, by clicking the **Advanced E-mail Options** or **Tracking Options** buttons, you can access two more dialog box boxes. The **Advanced E-mail Options** dialog box **(Figure 5-41)** allows you to configure when Outlook saves messages, how Outlook notifies you when new messages arrive, and configure the default settings for new messages. The **Tracking Options** dialog box **(Figure 5-42)** allows you to define how Outlook responds to read receipts and meeting requests.

Back on the Preferences tab of the Options dialog box, the **Calendar** section allows you to configure and enable or disable reminders for scheduled events. Additionally, by clicking the Calendar Options button, the **Calendar Options** dialog box opens **(Figure 5-43)**. In this dialog box, you can modify and customize most aspects of Outlook's calendar and scheduling features, including work week, calendar format, defined holidays, and time zone.

In the **Tasks** section of the Preferences tab, you can define when to remind the user of tasks each day, as well as disable reminders entirely. By clicking on the **Task Options** button, you can modify advanced options for tasks, including how to handle completed tasks.

In the **Contacts** section of the Preferences tab, you have two buttons available to control contacts and journal entries, respectively. Clicking the **Contact Options** button opens the **Contact Options** dialog box, in which you can define the naming patterns used and choose to show a duplicate contact list in a secondary language. Alternately, clicking the **Journal Options** button opens the **Journal Options** dialog box **(Figure 5-44)**, in which you can define which items are recorded in the journal and how often to archive journal entries. Configuring items in the journal allows you to keep track of how and when you are using Outlook and other Office applications, which can be very useful in some professions (such as sales). You can view the entries recorded based on these settings by clicking the journal item in the folder view within Outlook.

The final section of the Preferences tab, the **Notes** section, simply contains one button labeled **Note Options**, which opens the **Note Options** dialog box. This dialog box simply allows you to configure the color and font for notes.

The **Mail Setup** tab in the Options dialog box has four sections: E-mail Accounts, Send/Receive, Data Files, and Dial-up **(Figure 5-45)**. Clicking the **E-mail Accounts** button opens the **E-mail Accounts** dialog box, in which you can add or modify your configured e-mail accounts. In the **Send/Receive** section, you can select the **Send immediately when connected** check box to enable or disable sending of e-mails immediately, or click the **Send/Receive** button, which opens the **Send/Receive** dialog box. In this dialog box, you can create or modify groups of e-mail accounts, and then apply the options at the bottom to define when this particular group of accounts will send and receive e-mail.

Figure 5-40 E-mail Options dialog box

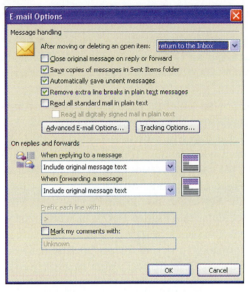

Figure 5-41 Advanced E-mail Options dialog box

Figure 5-42 Tracking Options dialog box

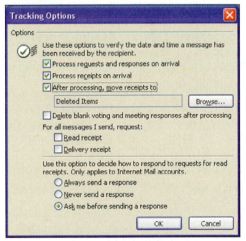

Figure 5-43 Calendar Options dialog box

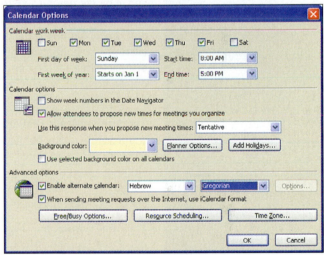

Figure 5-44 Journal Options dialog box

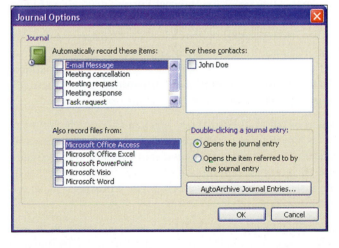

Figure 5-45 Mail Setup tab

skill 3

Customizing Outlook (cont'd)

exam objective   **Resolve issues related to customizing an Office application.** Answer end-user questions related to customizing an Office application. Customize toolbars. Personalize Office features.

overview

The **Data Files** section in the Mail Setup tab of the Options dialog box consists of the **Data Files** button, which opens the **Outlook Data Files** dialog box (**Figure 5-46**). In this dialog box, you can view or modify the personal data file, stored in a .pst file, that Outlook is using. Outlook uses .pst files only when it is connecting to non-Exchange e-mail accounts. For Exchange-based e-mail accounts, the core data resides on the Exchange server, although a cached copy of this data can be stored locally in an offline storage file (.ost extension). For personal data files, you can click the **Settings** button in the Outlook Data Files dialog box to open a dialog box for the selected data file (**Figure 5-47**), in which you can modify the password used on the file and compact the file to reduce its size. Compacting is recommended after deleting large quantities of information from your folders (such as many e-mail messages), because the data file does not reduce its size automatically after data has been deleted.

The last section of the Mail Setup tab, **Dial-up,** determines how Outlook utilizes dial-up connections. The first two options—**Warn before switching an existing dial-up connection** and **Always use an existing dial-up connection**—control how Outlook utilizes multiple dial-up connections. The first option, which is the default, allows Outlook to use a different dial-up connection if it cannot communicate (due to line errors or other problems) using the currently established dial-up connection. However, Outlook will warn you before disconnecting the first connection and attempting to use the second connection. The second option forces Outlook to use the existing connection only and prevents Outlook from disconnecting the first connection and utilizing a second connection.

The **Automatically dial during a background Send/Receive** option allows Outlook to skip the confirmation dialog box that normally appears when it attempts to connect a dial-up connection when using a background send/receive. The **Hang up after manual Send/Receive** option allows Outlook to automatically disconnect the dial-up connection after each manually initiated send/receive operation. This option can be useful when you are charged connect time for being connected to the remote system (such as when you are dialing long-distance).

The **Mail Format** tab (**Figure 5-48**) defines how outgoing e-mails are formatted, and is broken into three sections: Message Format, Stationary and Fonts, and Signatures. In the **Message Format** section, you can choose which format e-mail messages are composed in (plain text, rich text, or HTML), and whether or not to use Office Word 2003 to view and/or edit e-mail messages. Clicking the **Internet Format** button opens the **Internet Format** dialog box (**Figure 5-49**), in which you can define how to format messages sent to Internet recipients. In the **Plain text options** section of this dialog box, two advanced options allow you to determine the text-wrap limit and encoding format for attachments for e-mail messages sent as plain text. E-mail messages sent as HTML or rich text are not affected by these options. Clicking the **International Options** button on the Mail Format tab opens the **International Options** dialog box (**Figure 5-50**), in which you can define language options if you are using more than one language.

In the **Stationary and Fonts** section of the Mail Format tab, you can choose which type of stationary and font style to use as the default for outgoing messages. Note that using stationary will add a small graphics file to each outgoing message, increasing the message's size. Additionally, not all e-mail applications support the use of stationary, and those that do not will not display the stationary. Instead, the stationary graphics file will simply appear as an attachment along with each e-mail.

In the **Signatures** section, you can define which signature is used with each account, as well as which signature is used in new messages as well as replies and forwards. To import a signature from a raw text file or manually create one, click the **Signature** button to open the **Create Signature** dialog box (**Figure 5-51**).

Figure 5-46 Outlook Data Files dialog box

Outlook Data Files

Data Files
Select a data file in the list, then click Settings for more details or click Open Folder to display the folder that contains the data file. To move or copy these files, you must first shut down Outlook.

Name	Filename	Comment
Archive Folders	D:\Documents and Settin...	
Hotmail	D:\Documents and Settin...	
Personal Folders	D:\Documents and Settin...	Mail delivery l...

Tell Me More...
Settings...
Open Folder...
Add...
Remove
Close

Figure 5-47 Personal Folders dialog box

Personal Folders

General

Name: Personal Folders
Filename: ings\Application Data\Microsoft\Outlook\Outlook.pst
Encryption: Compressible Encryption
Format: Personal Folders File

Change Password...   Changes the password used to access the personal folder file
Compact Now   Reduces the size of your personal folder file

Comment

OK   Cancel   Apply

Figure 5-48 Mail Format tab

Options

Preferences | Mail Setup | Mail Format | Spelling | Security | Other

Message format
Choose a format for outgoing mail and change advanced settings.
Compose in this message format: HTML
☐ Use Microsoft Office Word 2003 to edit e-mail messages
☐ Use Microsoft Office Word 2003 to read Rich Text e-mail messages
Internet Format...   International Options...

Stationery and Fonts
Use stationery to change your default font and style, change colors, and add backgrounds to your messages.
Use this stationery by default: <None>
Fonts...   Stationery Picker...

Signatures
Select signatures for account: mail.bellsouth.net
Signature for new messages: <None>
Signature for replies and forwards: <None>
Signatures...

OK   Cancel   Apply

Figure 5-49 Internet Format dialog box

Internet Format

HTML options
☑ When an HTML message contains pictures located on the Internet, send a copy of the pictures instead of the reference to their location

Outlook Rich Text options
When sending Outlook Rich Text messages to Internet recipients, use this format:
Convert to HTML format

Plain text options
Automatically wrap text at   76   characters
☐ Encode attachments in UUENCODE format when sending a plain text message

Restore Defaults   OK   Cancel

Figure 5-50 International Options dialog box

International Options

General Settings
☐ Use English for message flags
☐ Use English for message headers on replies and forwards

Encoding Options
☑ Auto select encoding for outgoing messages
Preferred encoding for outgoing messages:
Western European (ISO)

OK   Cancel

Figure 5-51 Create Signature dialog box

Create Signature

Signature:

Edit...
Remove
New...

Preview:

Unable to preview selected signature, or no signature selected.

OK   Cancel

skill 3

Customizing Outlook (cont'd)

exam objective

Resolve issues related to customizing an Office application. Answer end-user questions related to customizing an Office application. Customize toolbars. Personalize Office features.

overview

On the **Spelling** tab of the Options dialog box **(Figure 5-52)**, you can enable, disable, or modify the functionality of AutoCorrect, Microsoft's real-time spelling and grammar checking and editing engine. Additionally, you can define the dictionary that AutoCorrect uses, as well as edit your custom entries to the dictionary.

On the **Security** tab **(Figure 5-53)**, you can define a number of security options to enhance or reduce Outlook's default levels of security. This tab is divided into four sections: Encrypted e-mail, Security Zones, Download Pictures, and Digital IDs (certificates). The first section, **Encrypted e-mail**, defines the encryption and signing options for outgoing e-mail. For the settings in this section to function, you need to obtain a digital certificate for use with e-mail. The **Encrypt contents and attachments for outgoing messages** option enables encryption on both outgoing message bodies and attachments. By configuring encryption, you prevent third parties from viewing the content of your e-mail. However, for this to function properly, a public key infrastructure (PKI) must be properly configured so that you can retrieve public keys for all intended recipients. A public key infrastructure is a framework for issuing, validating, and revoking certificates. It will include one or more certificate authorities (CAs), servers which are responsible for issuing and revoking certificates.

A **digital certificate** is a digitally signed document that functions as a component of PKI. Digital certificates verify the identity of a user, computer, or service. A Certificate Authority (CA) signs the certificate to confirm that the private key that is linked to the public key in the certificate is owned by the subject named in the certificate. The CA is responsible for authenticating the public keys and certificate information. Public key cryptography uses a pair of mathematically related keys: one public and one private. When one of these keys is used to encrypt a message, the other key can be used to decrypt it. The public key is widely disseminated, while the private key is only issued to an authorized user and must be kept secure. Both keys, however, are associated with a certificate, allowing the user to encrypt and/or digitally sign data with the certificate.

Most CAs are private, meaning they are only reachable from clients in the internal network. While there are public CAs, retrieving a certificate from a public CA can cost anywhere from $20 per year to several thousand dollars per year, depending upon the certificate's intended usage. To properly configure encryption or digital signing in Outlook, you need to be given a certificate from a CA, which is generally the responsibility of your security department. In order for you to encrypt a message to be sent to a recipient, you must be able to contact the recipient's CA and retrieve his or her public key. Similarly, for clients to send an encrypted message to you, they must be able to contact your CA. As you can see, it is important that the PKI be configured properly outside of Outlook in order for these settings within Outlook to function properly.

Certificates are normally installed through the Microsoft Management Console (MMC) Certificates snap-in. The process of installing a certificate is normally handled by the security or network administrative team, however. After installation of the certificate, you use the Digital IDs (certificates) section of the Security tab within Outlook to associate the certificate with e-mail and use it to encrypt and/or digitally sign the e-mail. Associating an existing certificate is done using the Import/Export button under the Digital IDs section. Retrieving a new certificate from a public CA can be done by clicking the **Get a Digital ID** button, which will take you to a Microsoft Web site containing a short list of providers. Be aware, however, that obtaining a certificate from these providers will incur a fee, and that you should really follow the guidelines issued by your security or network administration departments regarding digital IDs.

When sending a digitally signed e-mail message, your certificate and public key are automatically sent with the message. To send an encrypted message, you must already possess a certificate that is associated with the recipient's contact object within Outlook. One

tip

Digital IDs and certificates are synonymous in Outlook.

tip

You must already possess a digital certificate for each user you wish to send an encrypted message to.

Figure 5-52 Spelling tab

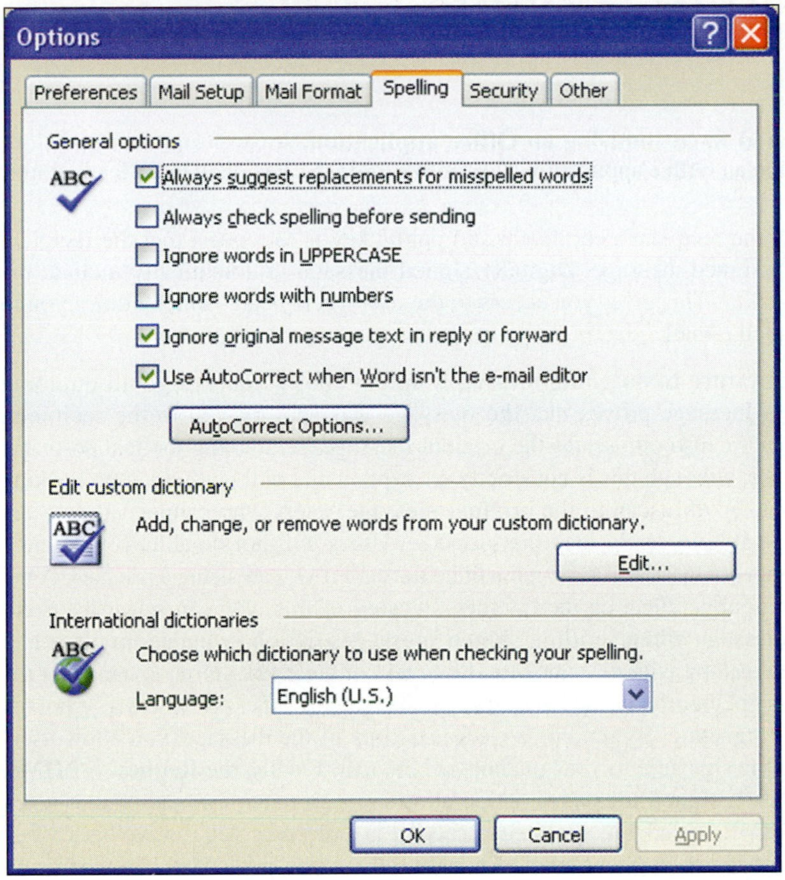

Figure 5-53 Security tab

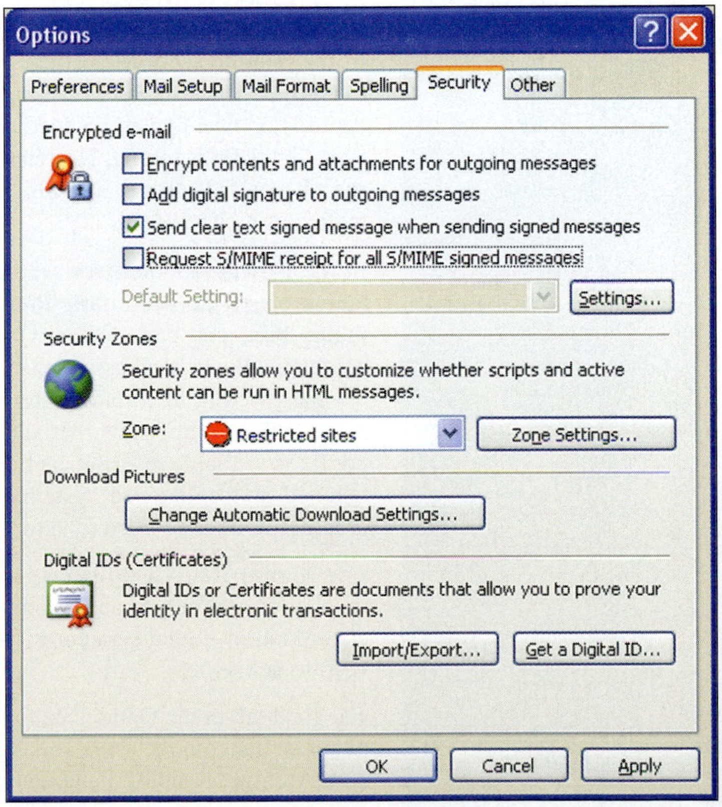

skill 3

Customizing Outlook (cont'd)

exam objective

Resolve issues related to customizing an Office application. Answer end-user questions related to customizing an Office application. Customize toolbars. Personalize Office features.

overview

easy way to retrieve the recipient's certificate and public key is to request that the recipient send you a digitally signed message. Digitally signed messages automatically include the certificate and public key. This gives you access to the user's certificate, which allows you to send the user encrypted e-mail.

The **Add digital signature to outgoing messages** option allows you to sign all outgoing messages. Signing a message proves that the message was sent by you to the recipient. By default, this signature also obfuscates the original message, scrambling the text so that it makes no logical sense, although this is not strictly encryption and will not hold up to hacking techniques. However, by obfuscating the original message, users who cannot validate the signature will not be able to easily read the message. Users will not be able to validate a signature if they cannot contact the CA, which will be the case if you are using a private CA but are sending mail to a public client on the Internet. Because of this, you can select the **Send clear text signed message when sending signed messages** option to include a plain text version of the message along with the signature. Plain text or clear text simply means that the text of the message is not modified in any way, and can be read regardless of whether or not the user can validate the signature. By sending a clear text copy of the message, you allow users who cannot validate the signature to view the body of the text. Finally, the **Request S/MIME receipt for all S/MIME signed messages** option allows you to request a read receipt when users open your S/MIME signed e-mails. A **read receipt** is a message you receive back when the remote party opens and reads your e-mail. While this allows you to keep track of when your e-mail is read, it is also considered rude by some users. **S/MIME** stands for Secure Multipurpose Internet Mail Extensions and is an open standard for e-mail encryption and digital signatures. All encryption and digital signatures used by Outlook conform to the S/MIME standards, which means they are compatible with any product that also supports S/MIME.

In the **Security Zones** section, you can modify the default zone that HTML e-mails are treated as. Because HTML e-mails can contain links to active content (such as ActiveX controls or Java applets), which can potentially cause great harm to the system, you should leave the default setting, **Restricted sites**. This setting disables both ActiveX and Java from running on HTML e-mail, which will go a long way toward protecting the system from malicious active content.

In the **Download Pictures** section, clicking the **Change Automatic Download Settings** button opens the **Automatic Picture Download Settings** dialog box (**Figure 5-54**). In this dialog box, you can choose whether or not to download picture links in HTML e-mail automatically, as well as whether or not you are notified of content downloads. This setting has increased in importance lately due to a security vulnerability in the released versions of some Office components that allows execution of code within .jpg attachments. Although a hot fix is available to eliminate this vulnerability, this setting is still highly important on both patched and unpatched systems, as it can reduce the number of offensive or malicious graphics users are forced to view.

The **Digital IDs (Certificates)** section (discussed previously) simply allows you to add or modify digital certificates used with encrypted or signed e-mail. If you are using e-mail encryption or digital signatures, your security team will inform you of the settings you will need to define here.

The final tab in the Options dialog box, **Other (Figure 5-55)**, allows you to define a number of miscellaneous settings for Outlook. This tab is divided into four sections: General, AutoArchive, Reading Pane, and Person Names. The **General** section contains options to

Figure 5-54 Automatic Picture Download Settings dialog box

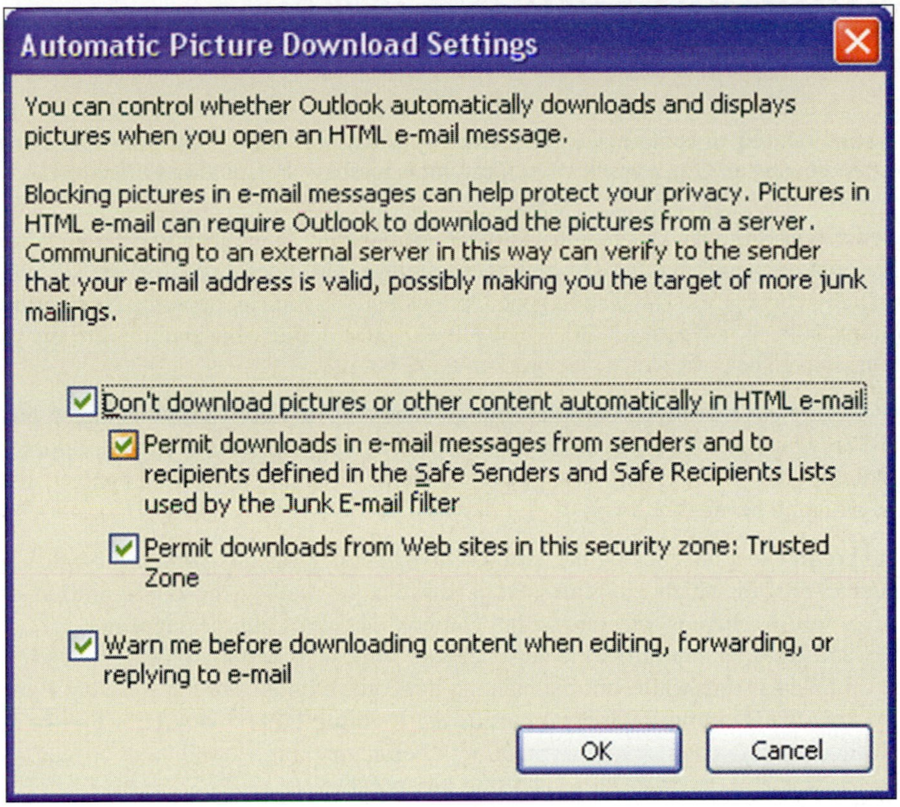

Automatic Picture Download Settings ☒

You can control whether Outlook automatically downloads and displays pictures when you open an HTML e-mail message.

Blocking pictures in e-mail messages can help protect your privacy. Pictures in HTML e-mail can require Outlook to download the pictures from a server. Communicating to an external server in this way can verify to the sender that your e-mail address is valid, possibly making you the target of more junk mailings.

☑ Don't download pictures or other content automatically in HTML e-mail

   ☑ Permit downloads in e-mail messages from senders and to recipients defined in the Safe Senders and Safe Recipients Lists used by the Junk E-mail filter

   ☑ Permit downloads from Web sites in this security zone: Trusted Zone

☑ Warn me before downloading content when editing, forwarding, or replying to e-mail

OK   Cancel

Figure 5-55 Other tab

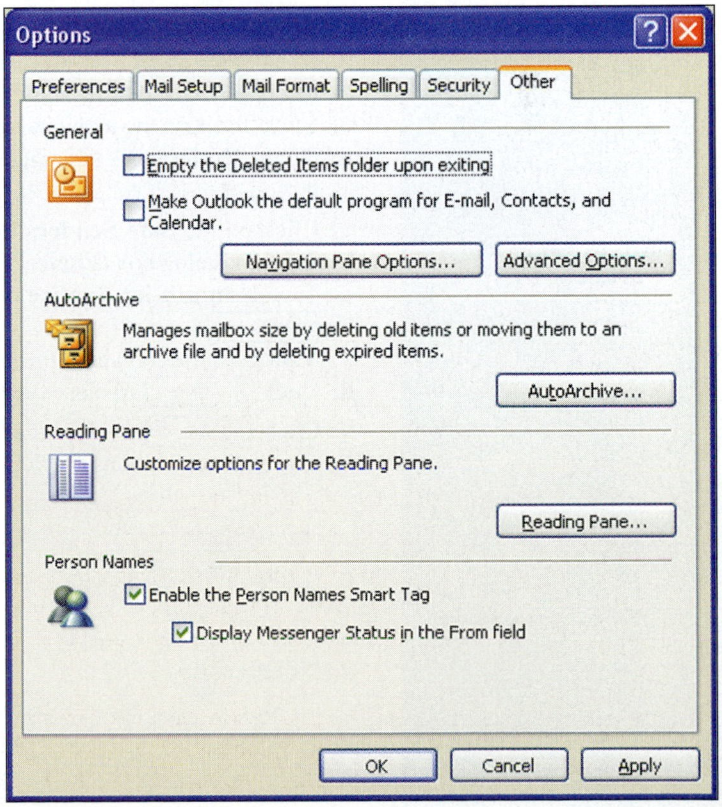

Options ? ☒

Preferences | Mail Setup | Mail Format | Spelling | Security | Other

General

☐ Empty the Deleted Items folder upon exiting

☐ Make Outlook the default program for E-mail, Contacts, and Calendar.

Navigation Pane Options...   Advanced Options...

AutoArchive

Manages mailbox size by deleting old items or moving them to an archive file and by deleting expired items.

AutoArchive...

Reading Pane

Customize options for the Reading Pane.

Reading Pane...

Person Names

☑ Enable the Person Names Smart Tag

   ☑ Display Messenger Status in the From field

OK   Cancel   Apply

skill 3   *Customizing Outlook* (cont'd)

exam objective

Resolve issues related to customizing an Office application. Answer end-user questions related to customizing an Office application. Customize toolbars. Personalize Office features.

overview

empty deleted items from the Deleted Items Folder when exiting (permanently deleting those items when you exit) and making Outlook the default e-mail application on the system. Additionally, by clicking the Navigation Pane Options button, you can open the **Navigation Pane Options** dialog box (**Figure 5-56**), which allows you to define which buttons are shown in the left navigation pane, as well as the order of those buttons.

Similarly, clicking the **Advanced Options** button opens the **Advanced Options** dialog box (**Figure 5-57**), which is where you can set a number of highly advanced Outlook options. Most of these options are used only when troubleshooting or to support special content, and should not generally be modified.

In the **AutoArchive** section, clicking the **AutoArchive** button opens the **AutoArchive** dialog box (**Figure 5-58**), in which you can enable, disable, or modify the configuration of AutoArchive. **AutoArchive** is a feature within Outlook that saves old messages in a special archive file, and removes them from the personal data store. This feature allows space to be conserved in the data store while still maintaining a record of e-mail. In the **Reading Pane** section, clicking the **Reading Pane** button opens the **Reading Pane** dialog box (**Figure 5-59**), which allows you to configure how long to wait before marking viewed items as read, as well as disable or enable single-key reading using the spacebar.

Finally, the **Person Names** section enables or disables the display of person names and MSN messenger status in all e-mail messages.

how to

Add an entire DNS domain to the Safe Senders list.

1. Log on to the computer as an Administrator.
2. Click ![start], point to **All Programs**, point to **Microsoft Office**, and select **Microsoft Outlook** from the drop-down menu to open Outlook.
3. Click **Tools** on the menu bar and then select **Options** to open the **Options** dialog box.
4. On the **Preferences** tab, click [Junk E-mail...] to open the **Junk E-Mail Options** dialog box.
5. Click on the **Safe Senders** tab and click [Add...] to open the **Add address or domain** dialog box (**Figure 5-60**).
6. Type **azimuth-interactive.com** to add this domain to the safe senders list and click [OK].
7. View the new domain in the safe senders list (**Figure 5-61**).
8. Click [OK] to close the Junk E-Mail Options dialog box.
9. Click [OK] to close the Options dialog box.
10. Close all applications and log off of the system.

Figure 5-56 Navigation Pane Options dialog box

Figure 5-57 Advanced Options dialog box

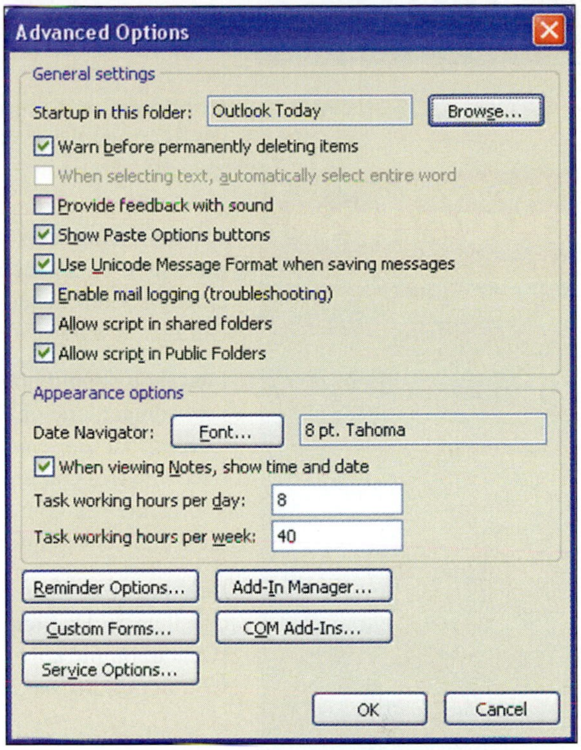

Figure 5-58 AutoArchive dialog box

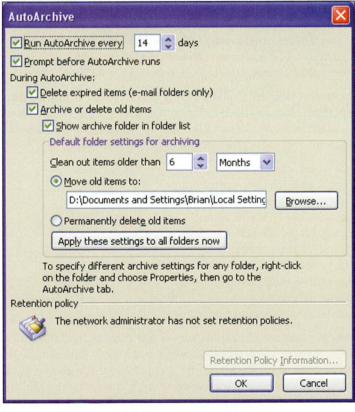

Figure 5-59 Reading Pane dialog box

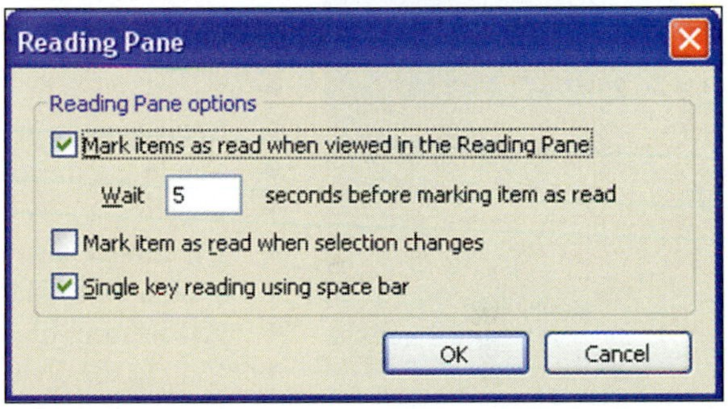

Figure 5-60 Add address or Domain dialog box

Figure 5-61 Safe Senders list

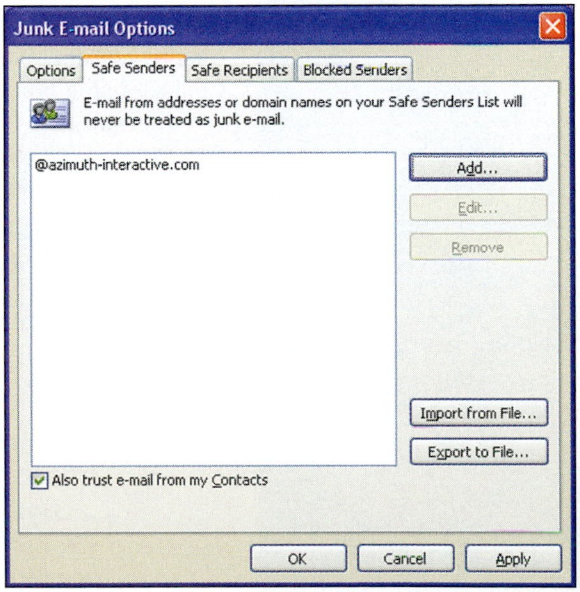

skill 4

Managing Contacts in Outlook

exam objective

Configure and troubleshoot Office applications. Answer end-user questions related to configuring Office applications.

overview

As you have seen in your exploration of Outlook, it can store many types of data, including contacts. **Contacts** are objects that contain information on various ways of reaching an individual or organization, along with other information (such as birth date or position). By creating contacts and populating these contacts with notes and other information, you can use Outlook as a powerful contact management application.

First, you should understand how to create a contact. Although there are many ways to add a new contact, one of the simplest is by opening the Contact view and then right-clicking in the Contact list and choosing new contact. Regardless of the method used to create the contact, once you do, you are presented with an **Untitled - Contact** dialog box **(Figure 5-62)**. Here, you create the contact by filling out any fields you may require. When finished, select the Save and Close button at the top of the dialog box to add the contact to the database.

Deleting or modifying a contact is just as simple. To delete a contact, simply select the contact and then right-click and choose Delete. Alternately, you can select the contact and press [Delete] on the keyboard. To modify a contact, simply double-click on the contact to open the **Contact** dialog box, make your modifications, and then click the Save and Close button.

You will most likely need to support business requirements beyond simple editing, creation, and deletion of contacts. To perform more advanced tasks, such as setting a follow-up task for a contact, right-click the contact. A menu opens **(Figure 5-63)** containing a number of different tasks that can be performed for the contact, including :

◆ Creating a new e-mail message to the contact
◆ Setting up an appointment in your schedule for the contact
◆ Sending a meeting request to the contact
◆ Creating a new task to be associated with the contact
◆ Creating a new journal entry for the contact
◆ Linking e-mail or other Outlook items to the contact
◆ Associating files with the contact
◆ Calling the contact using a phone or NetMeeting
◆ Scheduling a follow-up with the contact
◆ Placing the contact into a category to organize the contact

Although most of these advanced tasks are self explanatory, a few deserve special mention. Linking e-mail or other Outlook items to a Contact lists those items on the Activities tab in the Contact dialog box. This allows you to keep track of the correspondence to and from the contact. Similarly, linking a file to a contact creates a Journal entry containing the file, and then shows a link to that Journal entry on the contact's Activities tab. This allows you to keep up with files and other information specific to the contact.

As you can see, there are a number of advanced options available in Outlook that make it a powerful contact management application. Understanding how to use and access these features will make supporting the users that use these features that much easier.

tip

You can undo deleting a contact.

Figure 5-62 Untitled - Contact dialog box

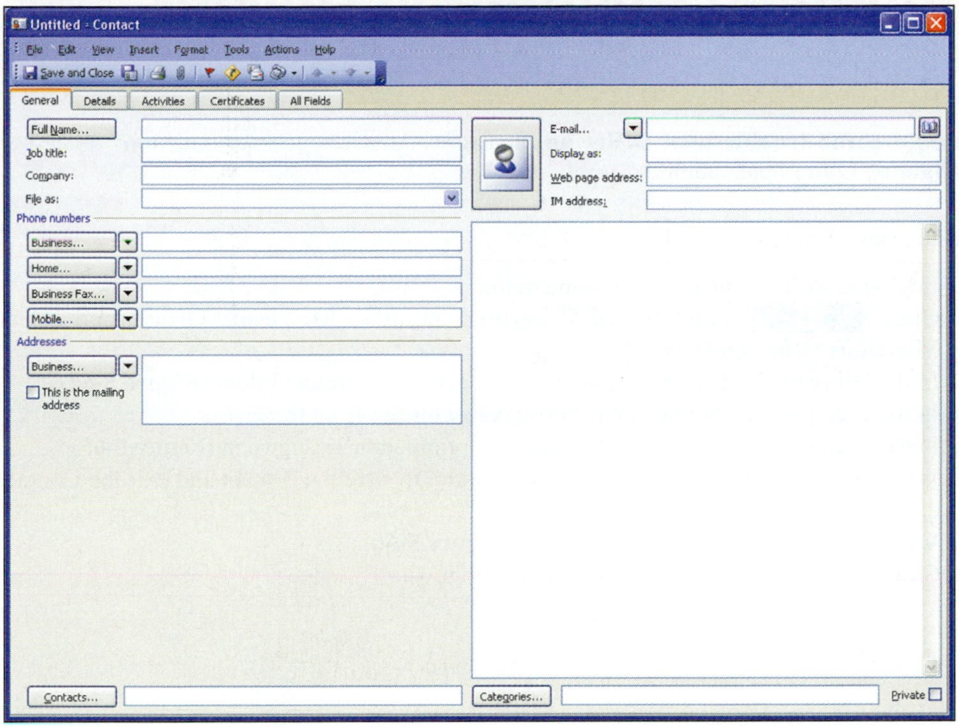

Figure 5-63 Advanced tasks

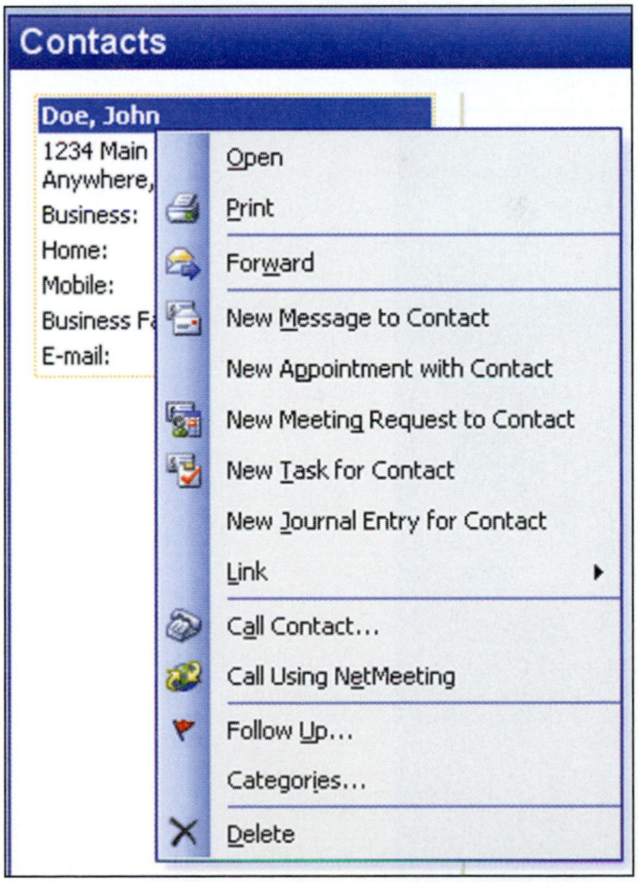

skill 4

Managing Contacts in Outlook (cont'd)

exam objective

Configure and troubleshoot Office applications. Answer end-user questions related to configuring Office applications.

how to

Create a new contact.

1. Log on to the computer as an administrator.
2. Click **start**, point to **All Programs**, point to **Microsoft Office**, and select **Microsoft Office Outlook 2003** to open Outlook.
3. In the left pane, click the **Contacts** icon to open the **Contacts** folder (**Figure 5-64**).
4. In the right pane, right-click and choose **New contact** from the menu.
5. In the **Contact** dialog box, type the contact's information, as shown in (**Figure 5-65**).
6. When finished, click the **Save and Close** button to save the contact and exit the Contact dialog box.
7. View the new contact in the Contact list (**Figure 5-66**).
8. Close all applications and log off of the system.

Figure 5-64 Contacts folder

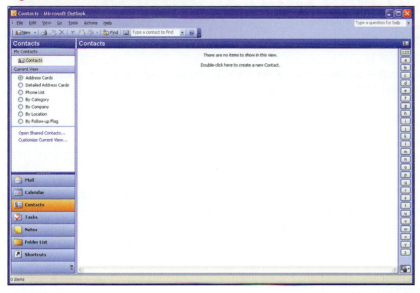

Figure 5-65 John Doe - Contact dialog box

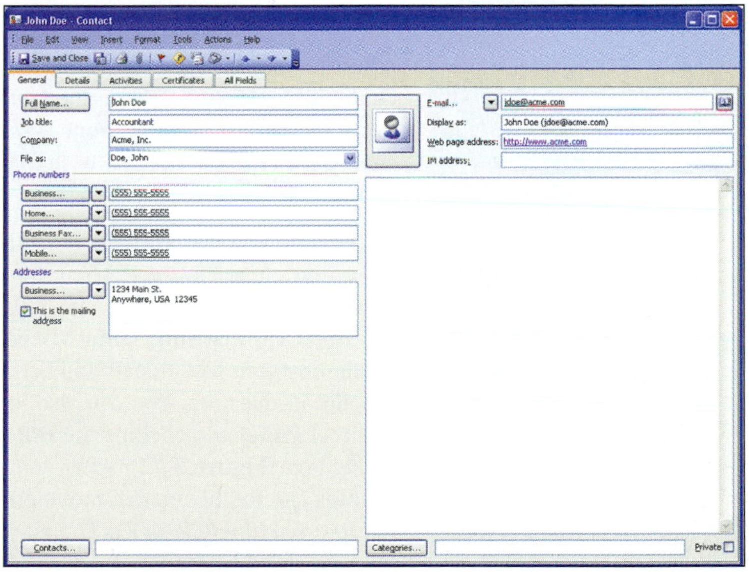

Figure 5-66 The new contact

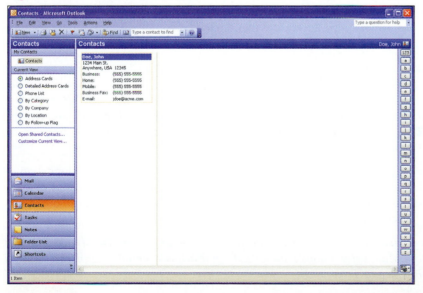

skill 5

Working with Data Storage in Outlook

exam objective

Resolve issues related to customizing an Office application. Manage Outlook data, including configuring, importing, and exporting data, and repairing corrupted data.

overview

tip

When choosing a format, be sure you examine the descriptive text at the bottom of the wizard. This text will tell you which types of data are associated with your chosen format.

Eventually, you will need to perform different maintenance tasks on the personal storage **.pst** file for Outlook. These tasks may include importing or exporting data, backing up data, restoring data, or even repairing corrupted .pst files. The first of these tasks can be done from within Outlook itself and is very simple to perform.

To import or export data, first you need to ensure that the import and export tools are installed. To do this, insert your Office 2003 CD into your CD-ROM drive, run **setup.exe** from the CD, choose **Add or Remove Features (Figure 5-67)**, and on the Custom Setup screen, select the **Choose advanced customization of applications** check box **(Figure 5-68)**. This option allows you to specify the components available for each Office application **(Figure 5-69)**. To ensure that the import and export tools are available, on the Advanced Customer screen, either expand Microsoft Office Outlook and choose **Run from My Computer** under **Importers and Exporters (Figure 5-70)**, or simply select **Microsoft Office Outlook** and choose **Run from My Computer** for the entire application (which will install all options).

After the import and export tools have been installed, you can import and export data from Outlook by clicking File on the Outlook menu bar and selecting **Import and Export**. This starts the **Import and Export Wizard (Figure 5-71)**. In this wizard, you simply need to choose the type of data you wish to import or export, the location of that data, and the folder you wish to import the data to or export the data from.

Backing up and restoring data is a slightly more complicated process. To back up a file, you must first close Outlook. Then, locate the folder which contains the .pst file. The default location of the pst file is **C:\Documents and Settings\%USERNAME%\Local Settings\Application Data\Microsoft\Outlook\Outlook.pst**, where C: is the drive containing your Documents and Settings folder, and %USERNAME% is the name of the user account in question. You can also locate the correct path by opening the **Mail** applet in the **Control Panel** and clicking the **Data Files** button to display the Outlook Data Files-Outlook dialog box **(Figure 5-72)**. After you have located the .pst file, simply copy the file to another location (preferably on a different physical disk) to make a backup of it. You can also copy the file to a writable CD or DVD, and store the CD or DVD in an off-site location to protect it from natural disaster.

Unfortunately, repairing a corrupted .pst file is not as simple as importing or exporting data. Typically, your best bet for a simple and painless recovery is to restore a recent backup of the .pst file. To do this, simply copy the backup file into the correct directory and overwrite the original .pst file.

If a recent backup is not available, before using recovery tools, make sure that you have a backup of the current data file. Most recovery tools will corrupt a file further if they fail during the process, so this step should not be skipped under any circumstances. There are two Microsoft approved tools for repairing .pst files, the **Inbox repair** tool **(Scanpst.exe)** and the **Oversized PST Crop** tool **(2GB152.exe)**. Before using either tool, you need to determine if the cause of the problem is due to the size of the .pst file.

Personal folder files used in Outlook 2002 and earlier have a hard-coded size limitation of 2 GB. Although this size may sound large, if users regularly receive large e-mail attachments, they may quickly use up this space. When a .pst or .ost file exceeds the 2 GB limit, you will receive an error when starting Outlook that is similar to the following:

Errors have been detected in the file C:\Documents and Settings\John Doe\Local Settings\ Application Data\Microsoft\Outlook\Outlook.pst. Quit all mail-enabled applications, and then use the Inbox Repair Tool.

Figure 5-67 Microsoft Office 2003 Setup

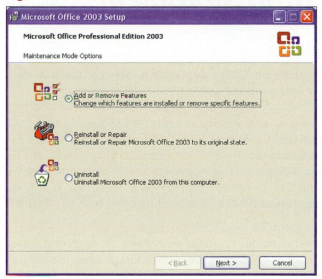

Figure 5-68 Choosing to customize the installation

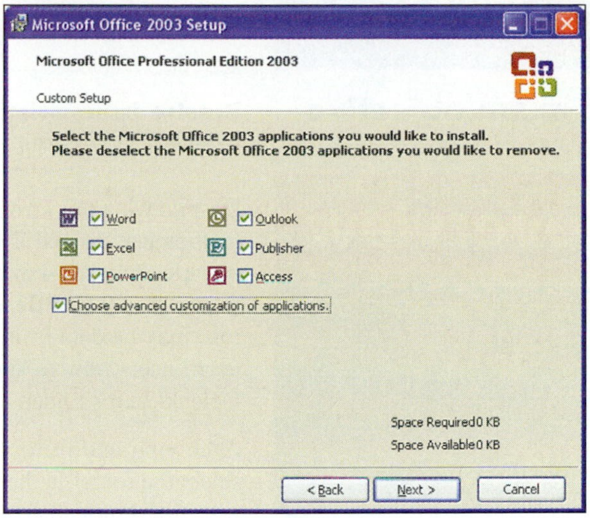

Figure 5-69 Specifying components

Figure 5-70 Installing importers and exporters

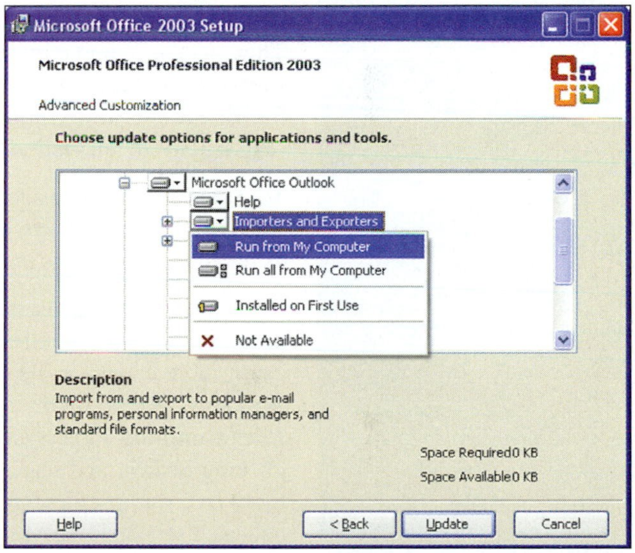

Figure 5-71 Import and Export Wizard

Figure 5-72 Examining the data files location

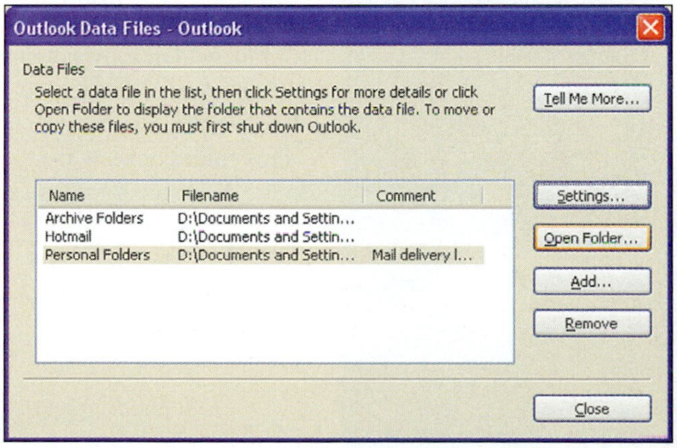

skill 5

Working with Data Storage in Outlook (cont'd)

exam objective

Resolve issues related to customizing an Office application. Manage Outlook data, including configuring, importing, and exporting data, and repairing corrupted data.

overview

tip

The Archive option will not appear for empty folders.

Despite what this error message advises, you should first examine the file size and ensure that it does not exceed 2 GB in size. If the file does exceed 2 GB in size, you will need to download the Oversize PST and OST Crop tool from Microsoft and use it to truncate the file to less than 2 GB. Be aware that you will lose data when using this tool and that the data you lose may be data from any part of the file. To prevent this problem in the future, you should teach users how to save needed attachment files on their hard disk and how to clear their Deleted Items folder.

Archiving and restoring archived items are fairly simple procedures. To archive a folder, select the folder in the Folder List (reached by clicking **Go** on the Outlook menu bar and then selecting **Folder List**), then open the File menu and select **Archive**. The **Archive** dialog box opens (**Figure 5-73**), in which you choose the folder you wish to archive and the location you wish to archive it to.

To restore an archive, first select **Import and Export** on the **File** menu, When the Import and Export File Wizard opens. Select **Import from another program or file (Figure 5-74)**. Then, on the Import a File screen, select **Personal Folder File (.pst) (Figure 5-75)**. When the Import Personal Folders screen appears, select the archive file from which to import (**Figure 5-76**). Choose how Outlook should handle duplicates. Click Next, and on the next screen (**Figure 5-77**), tell Outlook where to import the messages.

To download the Oversize PST and OST Crop tool, visit **support.microsoft.com**, and search for Knowledge Base article 296088. This article contains a link to the file download, as well as detailed instructions in the use of the utility.

If the .pst file is smaller than 2 GB in size, you may use the Inbox Repair Tool to resolve the problem. Be aware that the Inbox Repair Tool cannot solve all problems and that it can actually cause more extensive file corruption in some cases. The Inbox Repair Tool is available on all Windows XP systems in the following directory on your boot partition: **\Program Files\Common Files\System\Mapi\1033\NT**. You can also locate the file by clicking Start, clicking Search, and searching for the file **Scanpst.exe**. For detailed information on using the tool to recover .pst files, see Knowledge Base article 287497. One additional feature you need to educate users on is the **Mailbox Cleanup** command on the **Tools** menu. The **Mailbox Cleanup** dialog box (**Figure 5-78**) includes several options that users can use to selectively reduce the size of their mailbox. The first button in this dialog box, **View Mailbox Size,** shows you how large the total mailbox is, as well as how large each folder within the mailbox is. Below the **View Mailbox Size** button are two option buttons allowing you to search for items older than a certain date or larger than a certain size. This tool is very useful for helping users find unneeded e-mail, which may potentially be using large amounts of space. Clicking the **AutoArchive** button runs AutoArchive on the mailbox, moving items that meet the AutoArchive criteria defined under options to the AutoArchive location. Next, you can delete files in the Deleted Items folder or view the total size of items in this folder. Finally, you can use the Delete button in the Alternate Versions section to delete all duplicates of an item in your mailbox.

Figure 5-73 Archive dialog box

Figure 5-74 Import and Export Wizard

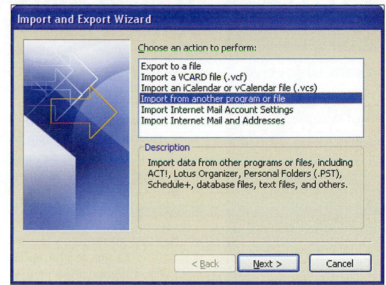

Figure 5-75 Choosing to import a .pst file

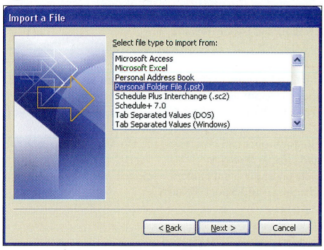

Figure 5-76 Selecting the archive file

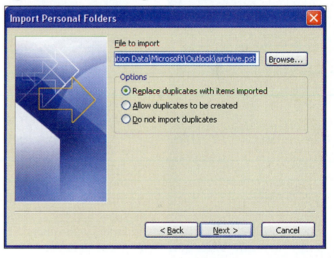

Figure 5-77 Telling Outlook where to import the messages

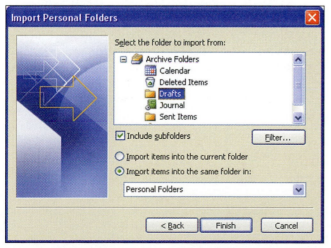

Figure 5-78 Mailbox Cleanup dialog box

skill 5

Working with Data Storage in Outlook *(cont'd)*

exam objective

Resolve issues related to customizing an Office application. Manage Outlook data, including configuring, importing, and exporting data, and repairing corrupted data.

how to

Export your contacts to a .csv file. Then, delete the contacts from your Contacts folder. Finally, import your contacts from the .csv file.

1. Log on to the system as an administrator.
2. Click ![start], point to **All Programs**, point to **Microsoft Office**, and click **Microsoft Office Outlook 2003** to open Outlook.
3. Select the **Contacts** folder by clicking **Contacts** on the left menu bar. Make sure that at least one contact is defined.
4. Click **File** and then click **Import and Export** to start the **Import and Export Wizard**.
5. Select the **Export to a file option** and click [Next >].
6. Choose **Comma Separated Values (Windows)** in the **Create a file of type** list on the Export to a File screen (**Figure 5-79**) and click [Next >].
7. Ensure that the **Contacts** folder under **Personal Folders** is selected (**Figure 5-80**) and click [Next >].
8. Type **c:\contacts.csv** in the **Save exported file as** text box (**Figure 5-81**), and click [Next >].
9. Click [Finish] to close the Import and Export Wizard.

Delete all contacts.

1. Click **File** and then click **Import and Export** to start the **Import and Export Wizard**.
2. Select the **Import from another program or file** option and click [Next >].
3. Choose **Comma Separated Values (Windows)** in the **Create a file of type** list (**Figure 5-82**) and click [Next >].
4. Type **c:\contacts.csv** in the **File to import** text box, select the **Do not import duplicate items** option (**Figure 5-83**), and click [Next >].
5. Make sure that the **Contacts** folder under **Personal Folders** is selected, and click [Next >].
6. Click [Finish] to close the **Import and Export Wizard**.
7. Examine the imported contacts.
8. Close all programs and log off the system.

Figure 5-79 Choosing comma separated values as the file type

Figure 5-80 Ensuring the correct folder is selected

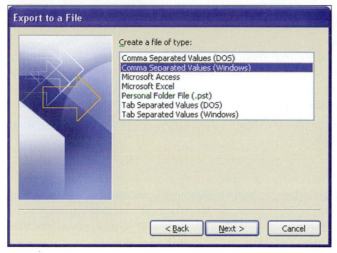

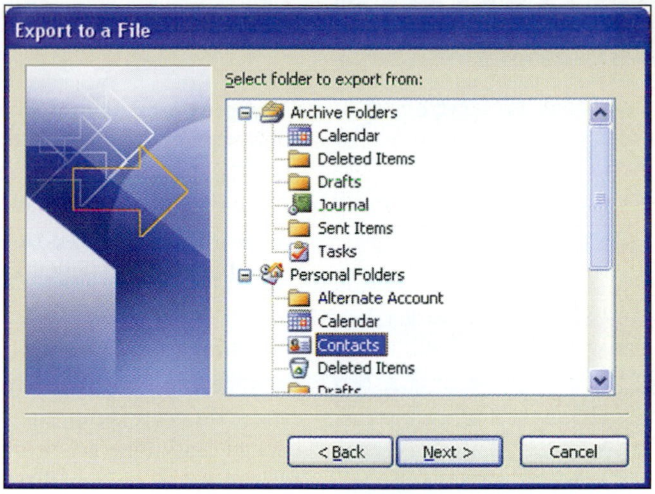

Figure 5-81 Naming the file

Figure 5-82 Choosing the file type to import

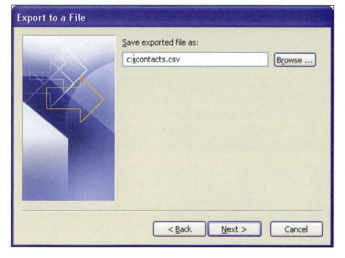

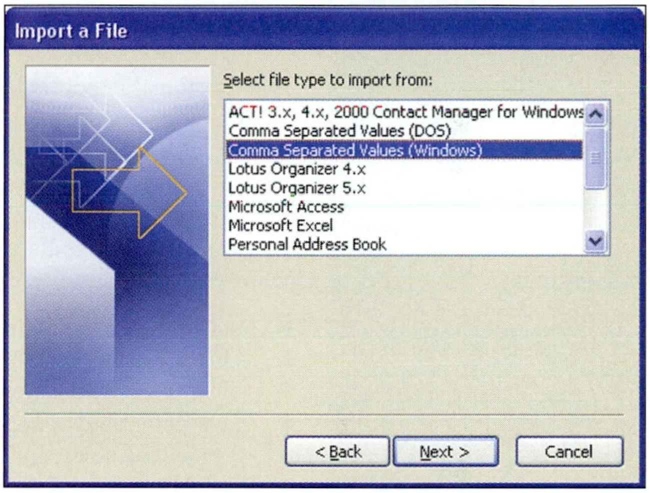

Figure 5-83 Choosing what to import and how to handle duplicates

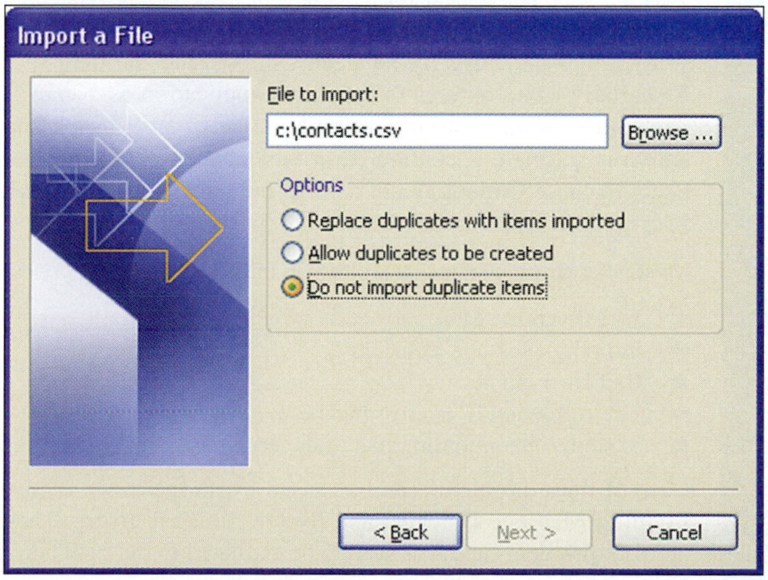

skill 6 *Troubleshooting Outlook: Common User Issues*

exam objective

Configure and troubleshoot Office applications. Answer end-user questions related to configuring Office applications.

Resolve issues related to Office application support features. Tasks include configuring Office applications and interpreting error messages.

Resolve issues related to customizing an Office application. Answer end-user questions related to customizing Office applications.

overview

Even in the best of situations, errors will eventually occur when using Outlook. The most common Outlook errors, by far, are related to e-mail. Although other errors (such as data file errors) do occur from time to time, most of them can be repaired by restoring from a recent backup, and none are nearly as common as e-mail-related errors. For this reason, this skill focuses solely on e-mail-related errors.

There are a number of common errors that users report quite regularly in Outlook (**Table 5-1**). One of the most common errors is the inability to open an attachment. The specific error usually generated by Outlook in this case is similar to the following: *Outlook blocked access to the following potentially unsafe attachments: Virus.exe*

This functionality occurs because the default Outlook security settings prohibit the user from opening attachments that could potentially contain a virus. In this case, the best advice is usually to leave the settings as they are and explain to the user why the attachment has been blocked. However, if the user simply must receive executables or other questionable files via e-mail, modify the attachment security settings in Outlook by following the steps outlined in Microsoft Knowledge Base article 829982 and then educate the user about precautions to take before opening these files. These precautions should include, at a minimum:

♦ Never open any attachments from people you do not know.
♦ Always ensure that e-mail virus scanning and on-access virus scanning are enabled.
♦ Always ensure that your virus definitions are up to date.
♦ Save potentially damaging files to disk and scan the files individually with your virus scanner before executing them.
♦ Always have a recent full system backup.

Another common error message is the following message: *Outlook was unable to send your email message because the connection to your email server was interrupted.*

This message can appear for a number of reasons, but one common reason is that your virus scanning software has become unresponsive. Many antivirus programs that monitor e-mail do so by placing themselves between Outlook and the mail server as a kind of mail proxy. Essentially, Outlook sees the antivirus application as a mail server, although the antivirus application is only passing information between Outlook and the real mail server. If the antivirus software is configured in this manner, any errors in the antivirus application are likely to cause Outlook to fail to send and receive mail. To resolve this problem, ensure that your antivirus application's executable files are up to date.

Most other common errors are related to mistyped addresses or network problems. These include:

♦ Undeliverable Mail
♦ Looping Message Detected
♦ Bad Host Name
♦ The following IP address had permanent fatal errors
♦ System timeout during mail transfer

Each of these problems can be caused by an incorrect address, with the exception of the Looping Message Detected and System timeout errors. These errors are both related to network problems and will need to be escalated to the mail administrator.

Table 5-1 Common Outlook errors

Error	Common Causes	Solution
Outlook blocked access to the following potentially unsafe attachments.	The default Outlook security settings prohibit the user from opening attachments that could potentially contain a virus.	Modify the attachment security settings in Outlook by following the steps outlined in Microsoft Knowledge Base article 829982.
Outlook was unable to send your e-mail message because the connection to your e-mail server was interrupted.	Antivirus errors, connection problems.	Update your antivirus software; troubleshoot your network connectivity.
Undeliverable Mail Looping Message Detected Bad Host Name The following IP address had permanent fatal errors System timeout during mail transfer	Incorrect address in e-mail, server problems.	Ensure that the correct e-mail address is entered; report the problem to your mail administration team.

Summary

- Outlook can retrieve e-mail from servers using POP3, IMAP4, Exchange (MAPI), and HTTP.

- Outlook 2003 does not support Usenet Newsgroups.

- One feature many users will want to make use of when working with Internet e-mail accounts is the ability to leave messages on the server for a specific amount of time after they are downloaded to the system. This configuration allows you to retrieve your e-mail on multiple systems by leaving a copy of all e-mail on the main server. However, the downside to this configuration is that you may fill up all available space on the server's mailbox quickly.

- Your HTTP e-mail provider must support e-mail retrieval using Outlook for the HTTP e-mail feature of Outlook to function.

- For Hotmail accounts, Outlook only supports HTTP access to premium Hotmail accounts.

- Defining additional Exchange mailboxes to open allows you to read and respond to e-mail for other accounts.

- For systems that are utilized by more than one user, you may have several users who each need to receive e-mail from a different account, and each inbox will need to be separate.

- When sending e-mail, you have the option of choosing a specific e-mail account to send the e-mail with.

- Rules are specific matching agents that perform an action on e-mail based on the contents of that e-mail.

- The Customize dialog box allows you to control the appearance of menus and toolbars and the Options dialog box allows you to control more advanced aspects of Outlook's general operation.

- The higher you configure the junk mail agressiveness setting, the more junk e-mail Outlook will remove before it reaches your inbox. However, false positives are common with e-mail filtering, and the higher you configure this setting, the more likely it is that Outlook will remove a legitimate e-mail.

- The Safe Senders, Safe Recipients, and Blocked Senders tabs allow you to define e-mail addresses or entire domain names that are either trusted or untrusted.

- By default, the Also trust e-mail from my contacts option is selected. This means that all contacts listed in Outlook will be considered safe. While this feature can save considerable time when configuring the safe senders list, you must be certain that only trusted parties are listed in your contacts.

- Configuring items in the Journal allows you to keep track of how and when you are using Outlook and other Office applications, which can be very useful in some professions (such as sales).

- Outlook uses .pst files only when it is connecting to non-Exchange e-mail accounts. For Exchange-based e-mail accounts, the core data resides on the Exchange server, though a cached copy of this data can be stored locally in an offline storage file (.ost extension).

- By configuring encryption, you prevent third parties from viewing the content of your e-mail. However, for this to function properly, a Public Key Infrastructure (PKI) must be properly configured so that you can retrieve public keys for all intended recipients.

- Digitally signing a message proves that the message was sent by you to the recipient.

- AutoArchive is a feature within Outlook that saves messages marked as old in a special archive file and removes them from the personal data store. This feature allows space to be conserved in the data store while still maintaining a record of e-mail.

- Linking e-mail or other Outlook items to a Contact lists those items under the Activities tab within the contact. This allows you to keep track of the correspondence to and from the contact. Similarly, linking a file to a contact creates a Journal entry containing the file, and then shows a link to that journal entry under the contact's Activities tab. This allows you to keep up with files and other information specific to the contact.

- To import or export data, first you need to ensure that the import and export tools are installed.

- Typically, your best bet for a simple and painless recovery is to restore a recent backup of the .pst file.

- If a recent backup is not available, before using recovery tools, make sure that you have a backup of the current data file. Most recovery tools will corrupt a file further if they fail during the process, so this step should not be skipped under any circumstances.

- Personal folder files have a hard-coded size limitation of 2 GB.

- If a .pst or .ost file exceeds 2 GB in size, you will need to download the Oversize PST and OST Crop tool from Microsoft and use it to truncate the file to less than 2 GB.

- The Mailbox Cleanup dialog box includes several options that users can use to selectively reduce the size of their mailbox.

- One of the most common errors reported by users is the inability to open an attachment. This typically occurs because the default Outlook security setting prohibits the user from opening attachments that could potentially contain a virus.

Key Terms

AutoArchive
Clear text (plain text)
Contacts
Digital certificate

Mail Application Program Interface
    (MAPI)
Microsoft Exchange
Offline storage file (.ost)
Rule

Personal storage file (.pst)
Public Key Infrastructure (PKI)
Read receipt
S/MIME

Test Yourself

1. You have a user who wishes to receive e-mail from both his home and work e-mail accounts. Both e-mail accounts are POP3 accounts. Additionally, the user does not wish to receive the e-mails in the same folder. How would you configure Outlook to meet these requirements with the least amount of administrative effort? (Choose all that apply.)
   a. Create an account for his work e-mail
   b. Create a folder called alternate e-mail
   c. Create an account for his home e-mail
   d. Add an additional mailbox for Outlook to open at start-up
   e. Create a rule to move mail sent by his home e-mail address to the alternate e-mail folder
   f. Create a rule to move mail destined to his home e-mail address to the alternate e-mail folder

2. You have a user who is receiving the error below when she receives certain business-critical attachments:

   Outlook blocked access to the following potentially unsafe attachments: Corporate App.exe

   The user wants to know why this error occurs. What should you tell the user?
   a. The error occurs because Outlook cannot open .exe files.
   b. The error occurs because Outlook is improperly installed.
   c. The error occurs because the latest service pack has not been installed.
   d. The error occurs because, by default, Outlook blocks attachments that could potentially contain a virus.

3. A user is receiving the error stating that Outlook cannot open her .pst file each time she tries to start Outlook. Given the following options, what should you do first to attempt to resolve her problem?
   a. Check to see if the .pst file is in excess of 2 GB
   b. Download and run 2GB152.exe on their file
   c. Attempt to restore the .pst file from a recent backup
   d. Run scanpst.exe on the .pst file

4. Which of the following protocols does Outlook support? (Choose all that apply.)
   a. HTTP
   b. NNTP
   c. SMTP
   d. SNTP
   e. SNMP
   f. POP3
   g. IMAP
   h. MAPI

5. You have a client who is complaining of problems downloading pictures linked in HTML e-mail. Since all e-mail company-wide is HTML formatted, this problem is causing the user significant difficulty. Where would you go in Outlook to resolve this user's problem?
   a. Tools>Customize
   b. Go>Customize
   c. Tools>HTML
   d. Tools>Options
   e. File>Preferences

6. In which of the following locations could you find the location of the .pst file used by a client? (Choose all that apply.)
   a. Control Panel>Mail
   b. Outlook>Tools>Customize
   c. Outlook>File>Preferences
   d. Outlook>Tools>Options

7. You have a client who has configured the junk e-mail setting in Outlook to the high setting. The user wants to know if there are any disadvantages to this setting. What should you tell the user?
   a. The high setting will likely filter many legitimate e-mails as well as junk e-mails.
   b. The high setting will likely filter less junk e-mails than the low setting.
   c. The high setting will move all e-mail into the junk e-mail folder, and the user will have to restore legitimate e-mail manually.
   d. The high setting will filter all e-mail except those listed under the safe senders list.
   e. The high setting will automatically delete all suspected junk e-mail by default.

8. You have a user who wishes to receive e-mail from multiple IMAP accounts in the Inbox. Which of the following must you do to configure Outlook to meet the user's requirements? (Choose all that apply.)
   a. Create an IMAP e-mail account within Outlook for each e-mail account
   b. Create a custom folder for e-mail from the second account
   c. Create a custom rule to move e-mail from the second account into the custom folder.
   d. Configure the primary e-mail account to open additional mailboxes

9. You have a user who regularly receives large attachments in his e-mail. The user needs to have a copy of all e-mail received for the last two years as per company policy. However, the user does not regularly view e-mail more than two months old. The user does not want to constantly perform any type of manual process in order to keep the size of the .pst file manageable. What should you tell the user to do in order to reduce the size of the .pst file?
   a. Enable AutoArchive and modify the settings to archive anything older than two months.
   b. Tell the user to archive e-mail once every two months.
   c. Tell the user to manually move items more than two months old into a separate folder.
   d. Create a rule to move e-mail older than two months into its own folder.

10. What type of file is the offline storage for Exchange accounts stored in?
    a. .pst files
    b. .mdb files
    c. .eml files
    d. .ost files

Projects: On Your Own

1. Create a rule to move e-mail destined for an alternate e-mail address to an alternate folder. You will need Internet access and two configured e-mail accounts to complete this exercise.
   a. Log on to the system as a local **Administrator**.
   b. Open **Outlook**.
   c. Open the folder view on the left-hand pane.
   d. Create a new folder and name it **Alternate Folder**.
   e. Open the **Rules and Alerts** dialog box from the tools menu.
   f. Create a new rule that checks all e-mail upon receipt and moves any e-mail to your alternate e-mail address to the Alternate Folder location.
   g. Close the **Rules and Alerts** dialog box.
   h. Send a test e-mail to the account specified in the rule to test the rule.
   i. Close all open applications and log off of the system.

2. Attach a text file to a contact.
   a. Log on to the system as a local **Administrator**.
   b. Create a text file using Notepad.
   c. Open **Outlook**.
   d. Open the **Contacts** folder.
   e. Right-click on a contact and choose **Link** and then **File**.
   f. Locate and select the text file you created in Step b, and click the insert button.
   g. Close the journal entry that opens. Choose **Yes** when asked if you wish to save changes.
   h. Open the folder view in the left pane and select **Journal**.
   i. View the new entry.
   j. Close all open applications and log off of the system.

Problem Solving Scenarios

1. You are a desktop support technician for Hyperbole Corp., a major PC accessory manufacturer. Sales employees of Hyperbole are required to answer all e-mail sent to the general sales e-mail address, as well as their own personal e-mail. Hyperbole utilizes Exchange Server for all e-mail. Describe how you would configure the sales accounts.

2. You have recently been promoted to senior desktop support technician at Agua Caliente, Inc., a small waste-water equipment supplier. As part of your promotion, you must define a standard set of archival options for all e-mail. As part of Agua Caliente's business, large images are regularly sent in e-mail as attachments. Additionally, all e-mail must be retained for a period of no less than five years, due to government regulations, though users will likely have no need to refer back to e-mail older than four months old. Define the AutoArchive settings you would configure.

Supporting Microsoft Office Applications

Microsoft Office is one of the most popular software suites currently on the market. Whether creating documents, spreadsheets, managing e-mail, or multimedia presentations, it offers tools to make users more productive. With the release of Microsoft Office 2003, there are now six editions. A recent change at Microsoft has made these six editions a core component of the Microsoft Office System. As you will discover in this lesson, Microsoft Office has evolved from a suite of personal tools designed to make the user more productive to a set of products designed to help groups of users work more efficiently.

This lesson begins with a discussion of some of the new changes to the core applications in Microsoft Office 2003 Professional Edition. These include the new Reading Layout view in Microsoft Word 2003, the List feature in Excel 2003, and the new interface provided with Outlook 2003. You will also learn which applications are included in each of the six Office editions.

Next, you will learn how to prepare for an installation of Office 2003, including information regarding system requirements, software/hardware compatibility issues, licensing features, and activation procedures. You will also learn how to create restore points to ensure you can return a system to a previous state if a problem occurs. Once you have a good understanding of what needs to be done before you start the installation, you will move on to the actual steps involved and learn about some of the prompts you will encounter during the installation process itself. You will also learn how to troubleshoot the installation should something go wrong.

As a support technician, you must be able to assist users when they need to customize their applications. This involves a solid understanding of how to add, remove, and customize toolbars and menus used in the programs. The lesson provides step-by-step instructions on how to add commands to menu bars, rearrange commands, and reset toolbars to their default settings when a computer needs to be assigned to a new user. The lesson also discusses how to use some of the most common proofing tools to edit documents. These include the AutoSummarize, AutoCorrect, AutoFormat, and AutoType options.

The lesson concludes by examining various methods of addressing common user issues in Word 2003, PowerPoint 2003, and Excel 2003.

Goals

In this lesson, you will learn about the programs included in Microsoft Office 2003, how to perform and troubleshoot an installation of the product, customize programs in the application suite and troubleshoot common user issues with Word 2003, PowerPoint 2003, and Excel 2003.

Lesson 6 Supporting Microsoft Office Applications

Skill	Exam 70-272 Objective
1. Introducing the Microsoft Office Application Suite	**Basic knowledge**
2. Preparing to Install Microsoft Office	**Configure and troubleshoot Office applications.** Set application compatibility settings. Answer end-user questions related to configuring Office applications. Troubleshoot application installation problems.
3. Installing Microsoft Office	**Configure and troubleshoot Office applications.** Answer end-user questions related to configuring Office applications. Troubleshoot application installation problems.
4. Updating Microsoft Office	**Configure and troubleshoot Office applications.** Answer end-user questions related to configuring Office applications.
5. Troubleshooting Microsoft Office Installations	**Configure and troubleshoot Office applications.** Troubleshoot application installation problems. Answer end-user questions related to configuring Office applications.
6. Customizing Office Applications	**Resolve issues related to customizing an Office application.** Personalize Office features. Answer end-user questions related to customizing Office applications. Customize toolbars.
7. Working with Proofing Tools	**Resolve issues related to customizing an Office application.** Configure proofing tools. Answer end-user questions related to customizing Office applications.
8. Troubleshooting Word: Common User Issues	**Configure and troubleshoot Office applications.** Answer end-user questions related to configuring Office applications. **Resolve issues related to Office application support features. Tasks include configuring Office applications and interpreting error messages.**
9. Troubleshooting Excel: Common User Issues	**Configure and troubleshoot Office applications.** Answer end-user questions related to configuring Office applications. **Resolve issues related to Office application support features. Tasks include configuring Office applications and interpreting error messages.**
10. Troubleshooting PowerPoint: Common User Issues	**Configure and troubleshoot Office applications.** Answer end-user questions related to configuring Microsoft applications. **Resolve issues related to Office application support features. Tasks include configuring Office applications and interpreting error messages.**

Requirements

To complete this lesson, you will need administrative rights on a Windows XP Professional computer with Service Pack 1 installed and Microsoft Office 2003 Professional Edition installed.

skill 1

Introducing the Microsoft Office Application Suite

exam objective

Basic knowledge

overview

Microsoft Office 2003 is a software suite that consists of a collection of applications designed to help improve productivity for users in enterprise environments, as well as those who work at home. There are currently six Office 2003 Editions to choose from. These are shown in **Table 6-1**.

The six suites listed in the table are a portion of the overall **Microsoft Office System** (version 11), which also includes Microsoft Office Share Point Server 2003, Microsoft Office Project, and Project Server 2003, Microsoft Exchange Server 2003, Microsoft Office Live Communications Server 2003, Microsoft Office Live Meeting, Microsoft Office FrontPage 2003, Microsoft Office OneNote 2003, Microsoft Office Visio 2003, and the Microsoft Office Solution Accelerators.

As you can see, Microsoft Office has evolved from a suite of personal tools (Excel, Word, PowerPoint, and Outlook) designed to increase the productivity of individual users to a set of products designed to help groups of users work together to solve business problems.

This lesson uses Microsoft Office 2003 Professional Edition as the basis for discussions. The Office 2003 edition includes the following applications: Access, Excel, Outlook with Business Contact Manager (BCM), PowerPoint, Publisher, and Word. The following provides a brief overview of the applications included in this edition and some of their new features:

Microsoft Word 2003 and **Microsoft Excel 2003** are two of the most well-known programs in use today for creating documents and spreadsheets. As a desktop support technician, you should be aware of some of the new features introduced with these two programs. With the release of Microsoft Word 2003, you will encounter a feature known as document workspaces. **Document workspaces** allow users to save documents to a shared workspace (a Microsoft Windows SharePoint Services site) to support cowriting, editing, and document review among a group of users. The shared workspace allows users to keep each other current on the status of a project by providing documents and other relevant information. Word also introduces document protection features that allow a user to restrict others from formatting and changing styles in their document. It is also flexible enough to let them control which users can edit certain areas of the document.

As a desktop support technician, you will likely find yourself spending a considerable amount of time in front of a monitor reading technical white papers and other relevant troubleshooting articles. Microsoft has introduced the Reading Layout view, which you will find very useful. This view displays pages side by side (**Figure 6-1**), removes toolbars to reduce clutter, allows you to increase/decrease text size, and utilizes Microsoft's ClearType technology, which makes the document much easier to read.

Microsoft Excel 2003 introduces the **Smart Documents** feature, which allows you to reuse content. Some companies use an Excel workbook template to record and report employee weekly expense information. By using the Smart Document feature, you can link the document to a database that automatically completes information entered. When you enter a name into the document, information in the database is automatically entered. For example, information such as the title, employee number, and manager's name can be added to the spreadsheet. When the information has been completed, click the Submit button and the weekly expense report will be automatically routed to the manager listed in the Smart Document for approval. Excel 2003 also provides the List feature **(Figure 6-2),** which allows Excel to identify data that is related and automatically carry over the same calculations and formatting. For example, you can maintain an Excel spreadsheet to keep track of the weekly expense data reported by employees. By specifying a range of cells as a list in Excel, Excel

tip

To take advantage of group capabilities, you must use the Professional or Enterprise editions of Office and may need access to additional servers/services.

tip

Opening a Microsoft Word document that is included as an e-mail attachment causes Word to switch to Reading Layout view.

Table 6-1   Microsoft Office 2003 editions

Edition	Access	Excel	Outlook	Outlook with Business Contact Manager	PowerPoint	Publisher	Word	InfoPath
Professional Enterprise Edition	●	●	●	●	●	●	●	●
Professional Edition	●	●	●	●	●	●	●	
Small Business Edition		●	●	●	●	●	●	
Standard Edition		●	●		●		●	
Student/Teacher Edition		●	●		●		●	
*Basic Edition		●	●				●	

*Basic Edition is only available on pre-installed systems that are available from selected computer manufacturers.

Figure 6-1   Reading Layout view in Word 2003

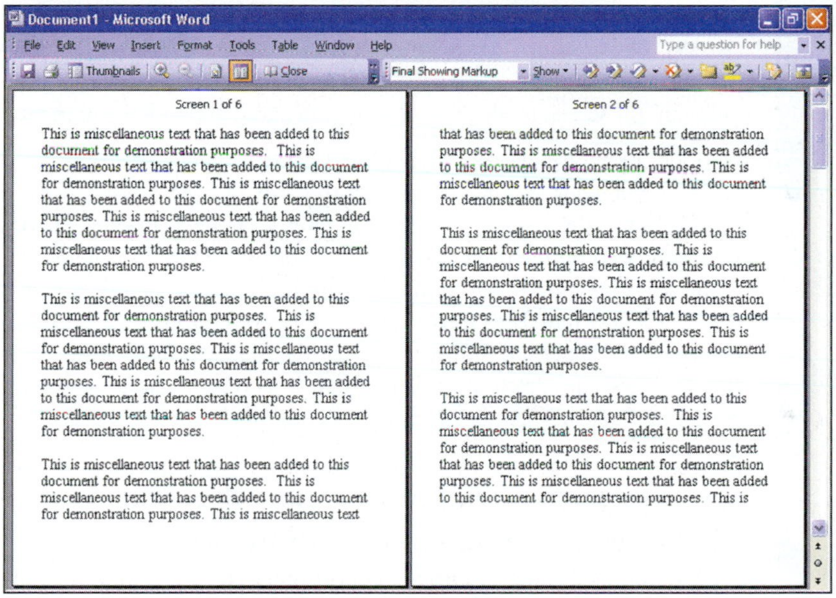

Figure 6-2   List function in Excel 2003

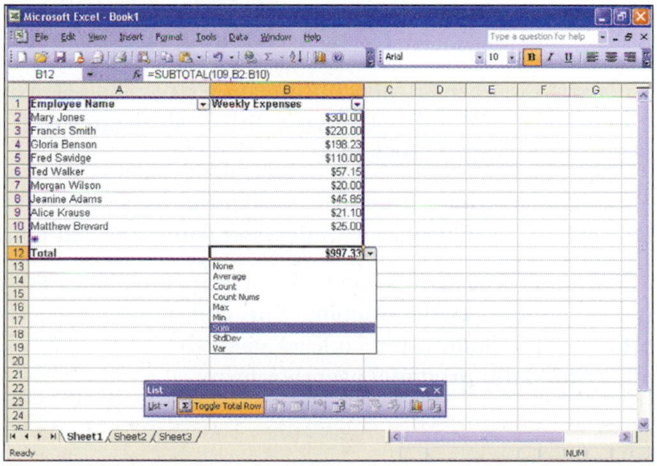

skill 1

Introducing the Microsoft Office Application Suite (cont'd)

exam objective

Basic knowledge

overview

will see the information is related and automatically apply the same calculations and formatting to new information added. In addition, Excel now adds drop-down boxes to be used to auto-filter the data the user wants to view.

Access 2003, a powerful database program, has become more dependable in its latest release. It now adds error checking features that flag common errors made in forms and reports. The user is then provided options for correcting the errors found, which results in a more accurate approach to creating forms and reports. Because Access 2003 uses Access 2000 as the default file format for new databases, it is backwardly compatible with Access 2000 and Access 2002.

PowerPoint 2003, which allows you to create multimedia presentations, also has a few new features. For instance, you can now control distribution of the presentations created in the Professional Editions of Office 2003 by using information rights management to specify an expiration date. Once the expiration date is reached, the presentation cannot be viewed or changed. This requires the use of Windows Server 2003 running **Rights Management Services (RMS)**. PowerPoint 2003 also includes an improved PowerPoint viewer, which allows users who do not have PowerPoint 2003 to view presentations. It also provides the ability to view video in full screen mode as well as stream audio and video within a presentation.

Outlook 2003 provides both e-mail and calendar functions. With the addition of the Business Contact Manager feature, you can automatically link notes, appointments, and even e-mail messages to sales contacts, which can later be tracked in preformatted reports. Microsoft has also improved on the user interface by displaying more information on the screen at one time while still making it easier to find **(Figure 6-3)**. Outlook 2003 can also be configured to inform you when new messages arrive. This is done in the form of a desktop alert that shows you the name of the sender, the subject line, and the first two lines of the message. This allows you to flag the message, delete it, or even mark it as read without opening the Inbox. It can also be configured to send desktop alerts for meetings and scheduled tasks.

Publisher 2003 provides the ability to design, create, and publish marketing materials such as newsletters, brochures, and postcards for the Web, print, and e-mail distribution.

Microsoft Word 2003, Microsoft Excel 2003, and Microsoft Access 2003 included in the Professional Editions of Office support the Extensible Markup Language (XML). XML is a data description language that allows different programs and operating systems to share information without worrying about incompatibility issues between programs. This allows the user to analyze and manipulate XML data with any program that can process standard XML.

more

To learn more about how information is managed using XML in Microsoft Office Professional Edition 2003, visit **http://www.microsoft.com/office/editions/prodinfo/ technologies/xml.mspx#EFAA**.

To learn more about what products and technologies are included in each version of Microsoft Office 2003, visit **http://www.microsoft.com/office/editions/ howtobuy/compare.mspx.**

Microsoft provides Microsoft Office System Product Evaluation kits that can be obtained for free—you just pay the shipping. For more information, visit **http://www.microsoft.com/ office/trial/default.mspx**. To learn more about Infopath, visit **http://www.microsoft.com/ office/infopath/ prodinfo/ overview.mspx**

Figure 6-3 **New user interface for Outlook 2003**

skill 2 *Preparing to Install Microsoft Office*

exam objective

Configure and troubleshoot Office applications. Set application compatibility settings. Answer end-user questions related to configuring Office applications. Troubleshoot application installation problems.

overview

tip

To view system information, click Start, select Run, and type msinfo32 in the Run dialog box.

tip

The products listed in the Windows Catalog are not the only ones that work with Windows XP. Others may also work but have not been submitted to Microsoft for inclusion into the Windows Catalog.

tip

Product keys are used for both Office 2003 and Windows XP. Keep track of which key is used for each unique computer.

As a desktop support technician, it is your responsibility to ensure the computer on which you are installing Microsoft Office meets the minimum system requirements (**Table 6-2**). Many manufacturers list the minimum system requirements in their product literature as a marketing ploy to make it appear as though their product is compatible with a wide range of computers. Technically, if the computer meets the minimum system requirements for the product, it will run the program. Unfortunately, in many cases, the user will experience a system that runs slower and their productivity will suffer. The best approach is to identify the recommended system requirements instead, which are usually included in the product's documentation or packaging.

You must also consider the impact of using additional features available with the product. For instance, Internet connectivity is required to use Online Help functions that are available in all of the programs included in the Office suite. Of course, to use e-mail and many other features available within Outlook 2003, you need a connection to the Internet. Some features, such as speech recognition, require the purchase of an additional close-talk microphone and compatible audio card. Others features may require that a Windows Server 2003 computer be available on the network to process and manage requests in group environments. For example, to take advantage of the information rights management, you need a Windows Server 2003 running the RMS. Information rights management allows you to prevent e-mails from being copied, forwarded, or printed when using Outlook 2003. When used in Word 2003, Excel 2003, and PowerPoint 2003, it can prevent documents from being printed or used to set expiration dates on a file so that after a predetermined time, it can no longer be opened. For a more detailed look at these requirements, visit **http://www.microsoft.com/office/ork/ 2003/one/ch1/PlaB02.htm**.

Another important task to perform before installing any program onto a system running Windows XP is to make sure the program is compatible with Windows XP. Microsoft provides the Windows Catalog (**http://www.microsoft.com/windows/catalog/**) as a gateway for identifying applications and devices that have been verified by Microsoft to be compatible with Windows XP. Products that are shown in the catalog may be designated as Designed for Windows XP or Compatible with Windows XP. Microsoft indicates on the Windows Catalog Web site that the difference between the two is as follows: "Products carrying the Designed for Windows XP logo, will not only be compatible with Windows XP but also improve your experience, reduce your frustration, and encourage good Windows XP product development fundamentals among software and hardware manufacturers."

Before you install Microsoft Office, it is important that you confirm that the user or company has the appropriate licenses to run and use the program. Microsoft offers three ways to obtain licenses for its products. The full packaged **product license** comes with the product that is purchased through retail outlets. Users who only need a few copies will find this to be the most appropriate option. An **original equipment manufacturer (OEM)** or **system builder license** is obtained when you purchase a new computer with the operating system and applications already installed. A third option for licensing, **volume licensing**, can be obtained when multiple computers (5-5000) will use the same software. Several benefits can be obtained by purchasing a volume license agreement. These include spreading payments out annually and the ability to purchase newer software at today's current pricing.

After confirming licensing issues, your next step is to make sure you have a product key for the program being installed. **Product keys** are a 25-character alphanumeric string that is broken into groups of five characters, separated by dashes (**Figure 6-4**). Microsoft Office 2003 requires you enter this number before installation can be completed. The product key is located on the Microsoft Office 2003 CD or inside the packaging box. If the copy of software

Table 6-2   Microsoft Office 2003 edition system minimum requirements

Edition	Processor	Memory	Hard Disk	Drive	Display	Operating System
Professional	Intel Pentium 233 Mhz or greater; BCM requires 450 MHz or greater	128 MB; BCM—256 MB	400 MB; BCM—590 MB	CD-ROM or DVD drive	SuperVGA (800 x 600) or greater	Windows 2000 with Service Pack 3 or later; Windows XP or later
Standard	Intel Pentium 233 MHz or greater	128 MB	260 MB	CD-ROM or DVD drive	SuperVGA (800 x 600) or greater	Windows 2000 with Service Pack 3 or later; Windows XP or later
Small Business	Intel Pentium 233 MHz or greater; BCM requires 450 MHz or greater	128 MB; BCM— 256 MB	380 MB; BCM— 570 MB	CD-ROM or DVD drive	SuperVGA (800 x 600) or greater	Windows 2000 with Service Pack 3 or later; Windows XP or later
Student/Teacher	Intel Pentium 233 MHz or greater	128 MB	260 MB	CD-ROM or DVD drive	SuperVGA (800 x 600) or greater	Windows 2000 with Service Pack 3 or later; Windows XP or later

Although the information in the table specifies minimum requirements, Microsoft recommends a Pentium III processor but a Pentium 4 offers the best level of performance. You should also consider adding an additional 200 to 300 MB of hard disk space to handle additional options and the installation files cache. When installing Microsoft Office 2003 from a CD or compressed image, the setup program caches the entire installation source by default if there is sufficient disk space. This local source (in the form of compressed cabinet (CAB) files, is then used to repair, reinstall, and update Office later. For a more detailed look at these requirements, visit: **http://www.microsoft.com/office/editions/prodinfo/sysreq.mspx**.

For frequently asked questions about Microsoft Office 2003, visit the following link: **http://www.microsoft.com/office/editions/ prodinfo/faq.mspx**.

Figure 6-4 Product Key screen

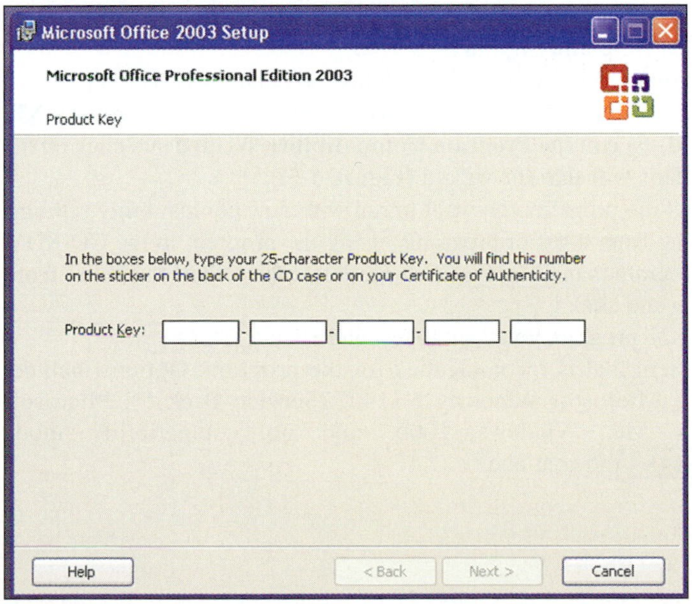

skill 2

Preparing to Install Microsoft Office
(cont'd)

exam objective

Configure and troubleshoot Office applications. Set application compatibility settings. Answer end-user questions related to configuring Office applications. Troubleshoot application installation problems.

overview

was purchased from an OEM, the product key may have already been entered. Each product key can be used to install the product on a selected number of computers depending upon the licensing agreement purchased.

Prior to performing the installation of any program or modifying system configuration information, you should create a **restore point** using the **System Restore** wizard provided by Windows XP. By using System Restore to create a restore point, users have the option of returning their system to a previous state. This restores all system and application settings to where they were when the restore point was created. This includes applications, driver, and operating system files changed. Any data files created by the application will not be affected. There are a few situations in which System Restore automatically creates restore points for the user. These trigger points include: installation of a System Restore compliant application (for example, Office 2003), when the Auto-Update feature is used to download and install critical updates from the Windows Update site, and when a system restore is selected. The last trigger point can occur when a user selects the wrong restore point and needs to undo the last restore operation. System Restore also creates a restore point every 24 hours. See the More exercise following this Overview for details on creating and reverting to restore points manually.

Although Windows XP can run many programs without any problems, some programs that were originally designed to run on earlier versions of Microsoft operating systems may introduce compatibility problems. If you find yourself in a situation where a program that originally ran without any problems under Windows NT 4.0 no longer functions correctly under Windows XP, it's time to use the Program Compatibility Wizard.

The Program Compatibility Wizard allows you to test the program in different environments, also referred to as compatibility modes. The modes available include: Microsoft Windows 95, Microsoft Windows NT 4.0 (Service Pack 5), Microsoft Windows 98/Windows Me, and Windows 2000.

tip

Restore points, also known as system checkpoints, are compressed to preserve disk space.

how to

Use the Program Compatibility Wizard.

1. Click **start** and open **Help and Support**.
2. Type **Program Compatibility Wizard** in the **Search** text box and press **[Enter]**.
3. In the **Search Results** box, select **Getting older programs to run on Windows XP**. Locate the section entitled, **To run the Program Compatibility Wizard** and click on the link under the first step. This will start the wizard (**Figure 6-5**).
3. Click Next > to select the program you want to run with new compatibility settings. Options include: Choosing from a list of programs, using the program in the CD-ROM drive, and locating the program manually (**Figure 6-6**). Select the **I want to choose from a list of programs** option and click Next >.
4. In the next screen, select the program you want to test and click Next >.
5. Select the operating system that is recommended for the program. Options include: Microsoft Windows 95, Microsoft Windows NT 4.0 (Service Pack 5), Microsoft Windows 98/Windows Me, Windows 2000, and no compatibility mode (**Figure 6-7**). Click Next > to continue.

tip

An alternative method of starting the Wizard is to click Start, select Run, and enter hcp://system/compatctr/compatmode.htm in the Run dialog box.

Figure 6-5 Starting the Program Compatibility Wizard

Figure 6-6 Selecting the program to test

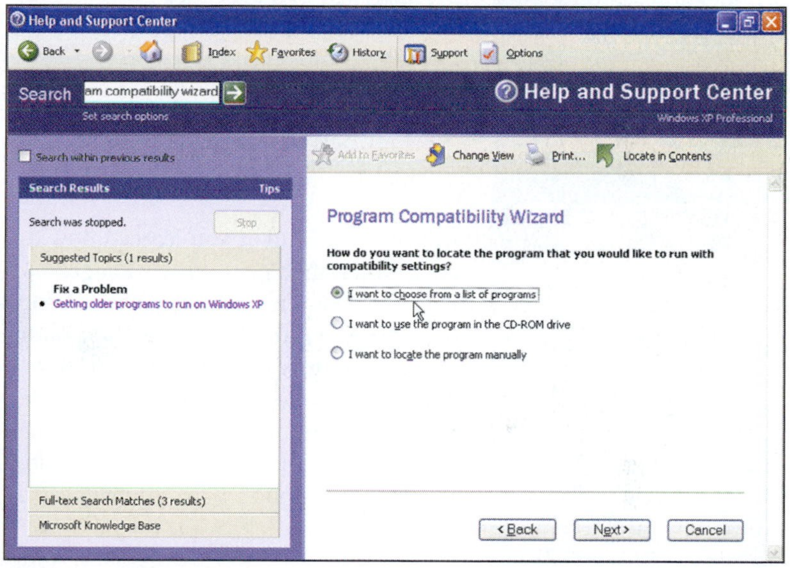

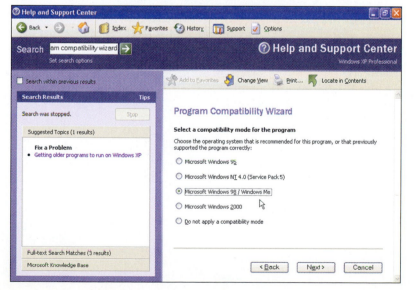

Figure 6-7 Selecting the compatibility mode

skill 2

Preparing to Install Microsoft Office
(cont'd)

exam objective

Configure and troubleshoot Office applications. Set application compatibility settings. Answer end user questions related to configuring Office applications. Troubleshoot application installation problems.

how to

tip

You can also configure a program's compatibility settings by locating it using Windows Explorer, right-clicking its executable file and selecting Properties. Access the Compatibility tab and configure the compatibility mode and display settings directly (Figure 6-9).

6. In the next screen, select the display setting you want to use for the program. The options are used for games or other educational programs. If the program does not fall into either of those categories, continue without making a selection. Options include: 256 colors, 640x480 screen resolution, and disable visual themes used by Windows XP. Click Next >.

7. The next screen lists the settings with which you have chosen to test the program. Click Next > to test the program with the new settings. Once your testing is completed, return to the wizard and determine whether you want to set the program to the new compatibility settings, try different ones, or discontinue trying compatibility settings (**Figure 6-8**).

more

In Lesson 1, Skill 9, you learned how to create a restore point. To revert to a restore point, click **Start**, then point to **All Programs**, point to **Accessories**, point to **System Tools**, and then click **System Restore**. On the **Welcome to System Restore** screen, select the **Restore my computer to an earlier time** option (**Figure 6-10**) and click **Next**. In the **Select a Restore Point** screen, choose the restore point you created earlier and click **Next** (**Figure 6-11**). In the **Confirm Restore Point Selection** screen, click **Next** to restore your computer. System Restore will then collect information about the selected restore point before it shuts down and restarts the computer, returning it to the state it was in at the time you created the restore point. Upon reboot, you will see the Restoration Complete screen (**Figure 6-12**).

Figure 6-8 **Configure final settings**

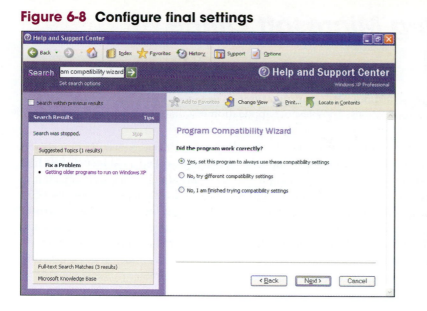

Figure 6-9 **Configuring compatibility settings manually**

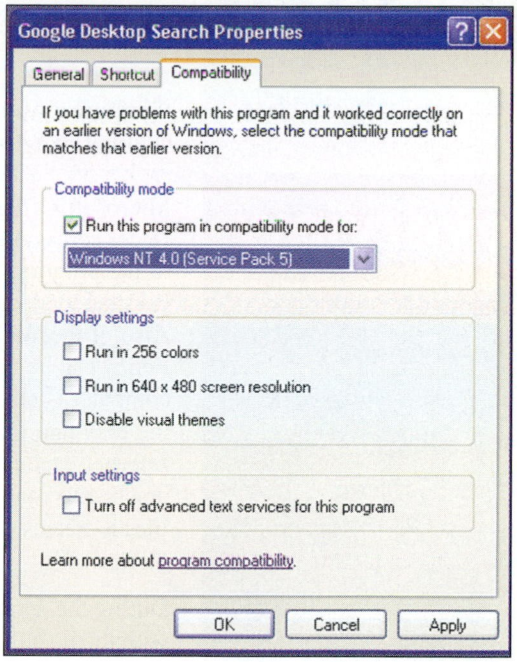

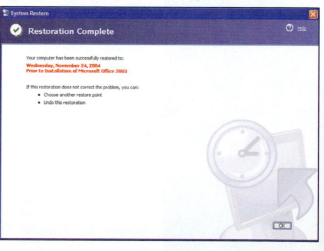

Figure 6-10 **Reverting to the restore point**

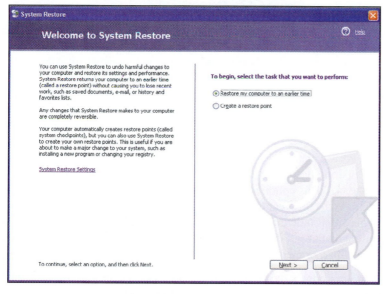

Figure 6-11 **Selecting the restore point**

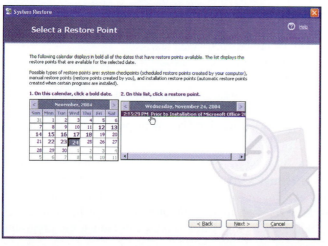

Figure 6-12 **Restoration Complete screen**

skill 3 — *Installing Microsoft Office*

exam objective

Configure and troubleshoot Office applications. Answer end-user questions related to configuring Office applications. Troubleshoot application installation problems.

overview

Microsoft Office 2003 can be installed locally by using a CD or by connecting to a shared folder across the network that contains a compressed CD image, called a **cabinet (CAB) file**, of the program. Although the following example discusses installing Office from a CD, it is possible to create scripts and answer files to further automate and customize the entire process. Also, if the Windows XP computer is a member of a Windows Server 2003 domain, **Group Policy** can be used to further automate and control the deployment process. To make sure the computer is ready for the installation, run Disk Defragmenter to reduce any fragmentation on the disk and Disk Cleanup to if you need to free up some space on the drive by deleting Internet cache and temporary files. After the installation is complete, it is always a good practice to run them again. Although Microsoft Office is designed to remove any temporary files it creates during installation, you should run Disk Cleanup just in case it does not delete them all.

During the actual installation, you will be presented with several different options. One deals with the installation type to perform (**Figure 6-13**). The options include:

- **Typical Install**: This option installs only the most common components for Microsoft Office 2003 Professional.
- **Complete Install**: This option installs all applications and components for Microsoft Office 2003 Professional. This option is a good choice when hard drive space is not an issue and you are a power user of the applications that takes advantage of many of their advanced features. If these features are not installed during the installation process, you will be prompted in the future to insert the CD when you use a feature that is not available.
- **Minimal Install**: This option installs only the minimum components needed to run Microsoft Office 2003 Professional.
- **Custom Install**: This option allows you to install only the specific applications and/or components you want to use. This option is used in the How To exercise that follows this Overview because it allows the most control over the installation process. It allows you to control which programs are installed, their associated components as well as where they will be installed on the computer. For example, if the user works only with Word and Excel and does not use clipart or media files, you can save a lot of disk space.

Another very important prompt comes during the Advanced Customization portion of the installation. This prompt introduces the following options (**Figure 6-14**):

- **Run from My Computer**: This option installs the specific feature you have selected to the hard drive, for example, Microsoft Word 2003.
- **Run all from My Computer**: This option installs the specific feature you have selected and any additional features, for example, Microsoft Word 2003, wizards and templates, add-ins that repair documents with incorrectly displayed text, etc.
- **Installed on First Use**: This option does not copy the files to the computer's hard disk but instead sets up an automatic routine to install the feature later. The routine waits for the component to be requested. Once requested, the component(s) will be copied from the CD or a shared folder on the network.
- **Not Available**: This option will not copy nor will it make any preparation to copy files for a future installation.

Once installation is completed, you will need to activate the product through Microsoft's Activation Wizard (**Figure 6-15**). **Product activation** was introduced by Microsoft as a protection measure against casual copying, a form of software piracy. Product activation ensures the product key has not been used on more computers than that for which it is licensed. For Microsoft Office 2003 Professional Edition, you can launch the programs

Figure 6-13 **Installation type options**

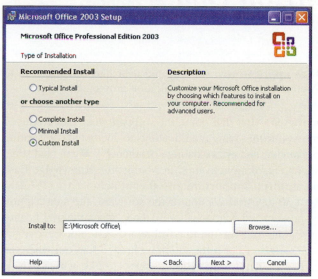

Figure 6-14 **Advanced Customization options**

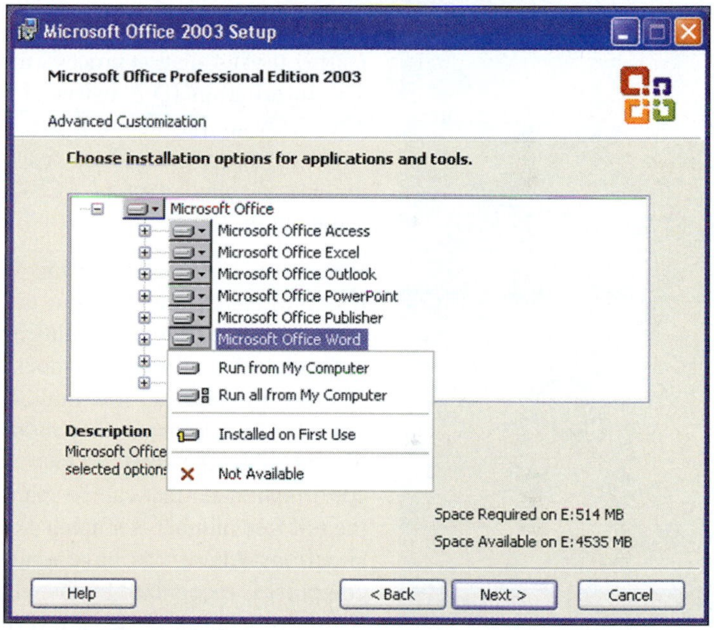

Figure 6-15 **Activation Wizard**

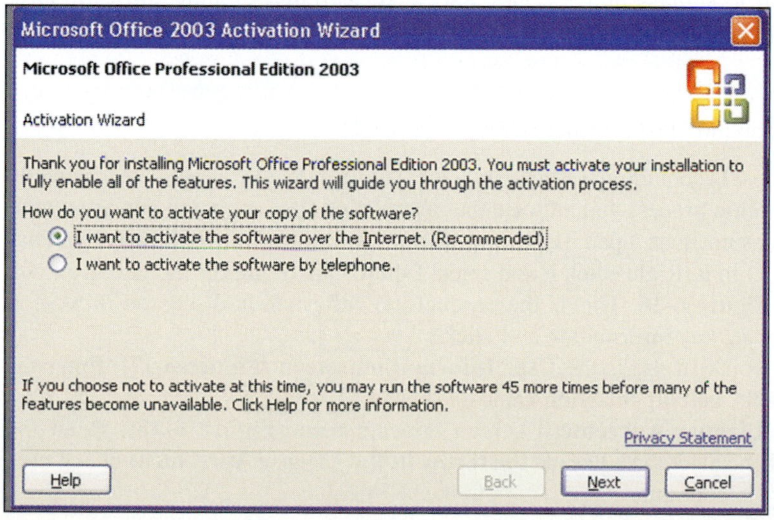

skill 3

Installing Microsoft Office (cont'd)

exam objective

Configure and troubleshoot Office applications. Answer end-user questions related to configuring Office applications. Troubleshoot application installation problems.

overview

a maximum of 50 times without activation. After that point, the software goes into **Reduced Functionality Mode**, which prevents you from saving modifications to documents or creating new documents. You will still be able to view and print existing documents. You can read some of the most frequently asked questions regarding activation in Microsoft's Knowledge Base article 293151, which can be found at: **http://support.microsoft.com/default.aspx?SCID=kb;en-us;293151**. If you are using a 30-day trial version of the software, the subscription period begins when you activate the product and continues for 30 days. When the trial license expires, you will need to either convert the trial version to a full retail version or remove the product and install a new copy of the software. For information on how to find out when the version running expires, read Microsoft's Knowledge Base article 827293, which can be found at: **http://support.microsoft.com/kb/827293#4.** Now that you have a better understanding of the options for activating the product, let's take a closer look at how the activation process works.

During the installation process, the product key is transformed into an installation ID number. The installation ID consists of two components: the product key and a hardware hash. The hardware hash is an 8-byte value that is calculated by running 10 different pieces of hardware through a mathematical formula. Hardware that might be included in the calculation include: display adapters, SCSI adapters, processor serial number, and hard drive volume serial number.

When you run the Activation Wizard with an Internet connection present, it pulls this installation ID number from the computer and sends it to a secure server at Microsoft. Microsoft then provides a confirmation number that is automatically entered and activates the software. If the computer does not have an Internet connection, you can also contact Microsoft over a toll free number (888-652-2342) that will be displayed on the Activation screen. Once connected, you will be prompted for the installation ID that is currently displayed on the screen. Once entered into Microsoft's database, you will be provided a confirmation ID that can be manually entered to complete the activation process. Although the toll free number is a much slower method to use, you may need to take advantage of it in situations where you have made major changes to hardware in your computer and the computer is recognized by the wizard as a different system. For example, each time Windows XP starts, it checks to see if it is running on the same hardware on which it was activated. If it notices that hardware is substantially different, reactivation will be required. This feature was included by Microsoft to address piracy issues associated with disk cloning software. Disk cloning software copies the entire image of a hard disk from one computer to another.

how to

Install Microsoft Office 2003 Professional Edition from a CD.

1. After inserting the CD containing Office 2003, the Auto-run feature should automatically launch the installation process and indicate that installation files are being copied to your computer. If it does not start, open **My Computer** and select the CD-ROM drive that has the installation CD in it. Right-click it and select **Open**. One of the first screens you will see is shown in **Figure 6-16**. This is the product key information discussed in Skill 2. Enter the appropriate key information and click ⬚ Next > ⬚.
2. The next screen you will see is the **User Information** screen (**Figure 6-17**). Enter the user's name, initials, and organization name and select ⬚ Next > ⬚.
3. The **End User License Agreement** screen appears next (**Figure 6-18**). Read the agreement and then select the **I accept the terms in the License Agreement** check box. Click ⬚ Next > ⬚ to continue.

Figure 6-16 Product Key information screen

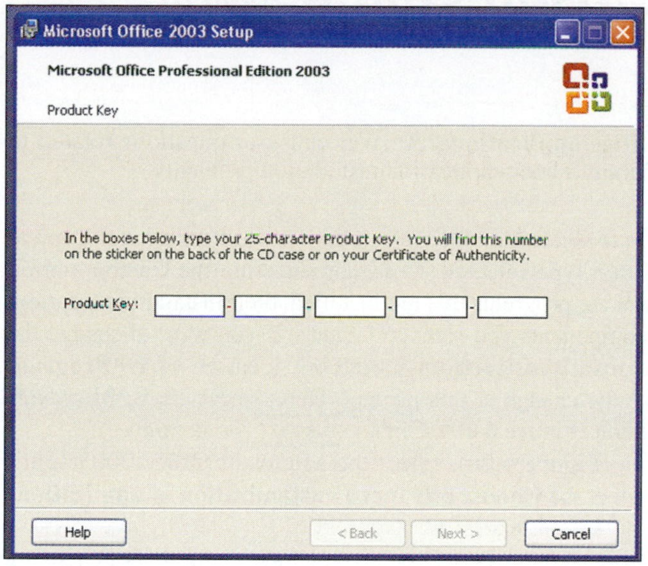

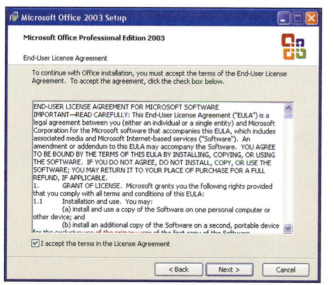

Figure 6-17 User Information screen

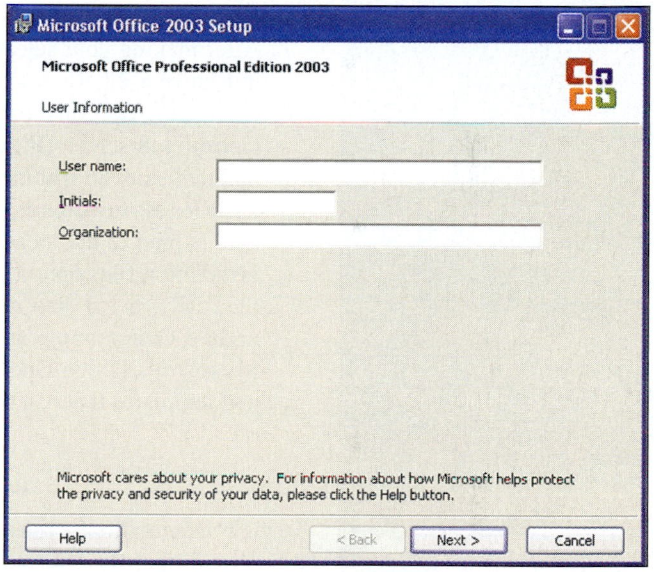

Figure 6-18 End-User License Agreement screen

skill 3   *Installing Microsoft Office (cont'd)*

exam objective

Configure and troubleshoot Office applications. Answer end-user questions related to configuring Office applications. Troubleshoot application installation problems.

how to

4. The next step in the process is to select the type of installation you want to use. **Typical Install** is the default installation type selected. Consider selecting the Custom option because it allows you to control the programs that are installed, their installation location, as well as which additional components you want to include. If you want to change the installation location for Microsoft Office from its default location of **C:\Program Files\Microsoft Office**, make the change at this prompt. Here, select the **E:\Microsoft Office** as the installation location (**Figure 6-19**). Click [Next >] to continue.

5. On the **Custom Setup** screen (**Figure 6-20**), select the Microsoft Office 2003 applications you want to install. Select the **Choose advanced customization of applications** check box and click [Next >] to continue.

6. On the **Advanced Customization** screen (**Figure 6-21**), you have the option of choosing how you want to install each component. Click [Next >] after selecting the desired option.

7. After making your selections, you will be presented with the **Summary** screen as shown in **Figure 6-22**. Review your settings and click [Install] to begin the file copy process.

8. Once the file copy process has completed, you will be presented with the **Setup Completed** screen (**Figure 6-23**). This is a good time to check Microsoft's Web site for updates and additional downloads. Select the **Check the Web for updates and additional downloads** check box. You also have the option of keeping the installation files copied to the local drive during the installation process by not selecting the Delete installation files option. If you keep the files, it will take up more space on the hard drive (272 MB) but it also means that you will not need the Office 2003 installation CD to update Office applications in the future. Click [Finish] and you will be taken to Microsoft's Office Update site to check for updates. You can also find a variety of tools and templates that can be used to get more out of Office 2003.

more

To view a simulation of the activation process for the Windows XP operating system, go to the following link: **http://www.microsoft.com/windowsxp/wmx/wpa100.asx.**

Figure 6-19 Type of Installation screen

Figure 6-20 Custom Setup screen

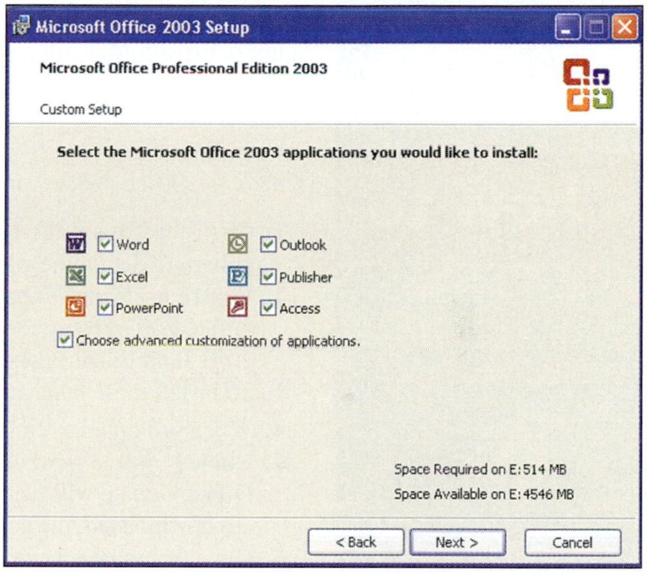

Figure 6-21 Installation options for running programs

Figure 6-22 Summary screen

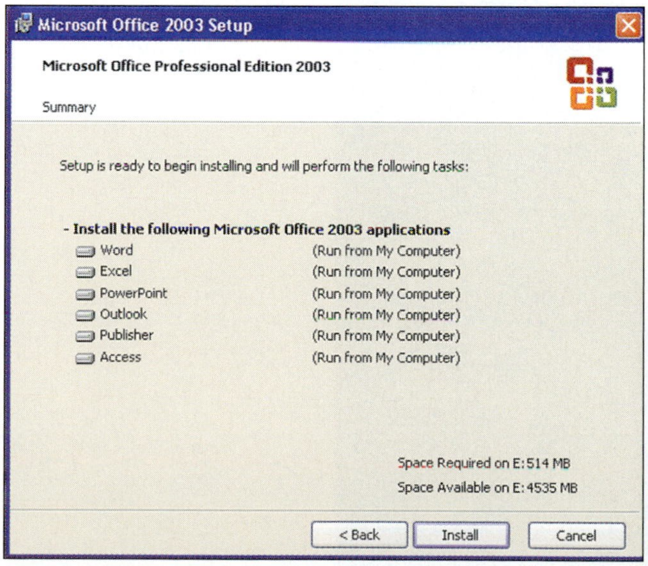

Figure 6-23 Setup Completed screen

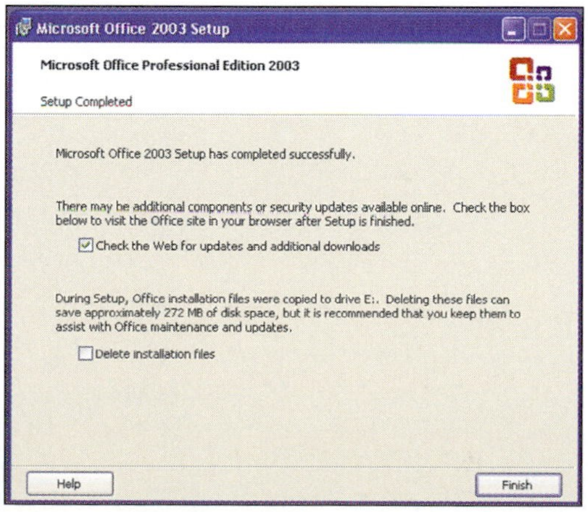

skill 4 *Updating Microsoft Office*

exam objective

Configure and troubleshoot Office applications. Answer end-user questions related to configuring Office applications.

overview

tip
You can download Office updates and install them locally on your computer instead of performing the updates automatically over the Web.

After Office has been installed, it is important that you regularly obtain the latest updates to the software for both security and stability purposes. If you selected the **Check the Web for updates and additional downloads** check box on the **Setup Completed** screen (refer to Figure 6-23), you were taken directly to the updates Web site to begin the update process automatically. If not, you can also manually check for updates. This can be done from within any Office application. For example, to check for updates manually by using Word 2003, click **Help** on the Word menu bar and then select the **Check for Updates** command on the Help menu (**Figure 6-24**). This will automatically open Internet Explorer and take you to the Web address **http://office.microsoft.com/en-us/officeupdate/default.aspx**.

how to

Check for Office updates manually.

1. Click the **Check for Updates** link under **Office Update** to have Microsoft scan your system to determine what, if any, updates are available.
2. **Figure 6-25** shows that two updates have been identified for this version of Microsoft Office 2003 Professional Edition: Office 2003 Service Pack 1 and Update for Outlook 2003 Junk Email Filter (KB873362).
3. To install these updates, click [Agree and Start Installation].
4. When prompted to confirm your selection (**Figure 6-26**), click [Next >].
5. Click [Next >] when prompted to have your CD available.
   Office Update will begin downloading the updates you have selected. Once the updates are downloaded, the actual installation process will begin.
6. Once the updates have been installed, the **Installation Results** screen (**Figure 6-27**) will appear. Click [Finish] after reviewing the information presented.

more

Depending upon the updates being installed, you may have to reboot the computer, provide the Microsoft Office installation CD, and/or close any applications that are currently open. If you want to download updates and install them later, instead of installing them directly over the Web, visit the following link: **http://office.microsoft.com/en-us/officeupdate/CD010200271033.aspx**.

Figure 6-24 Check for Updates within Word

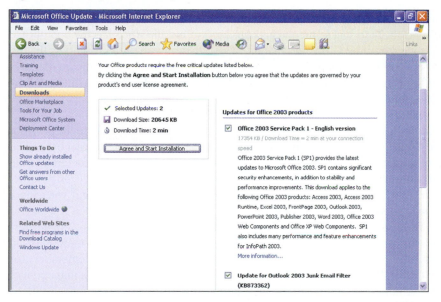

Figure 6-25 Updates required

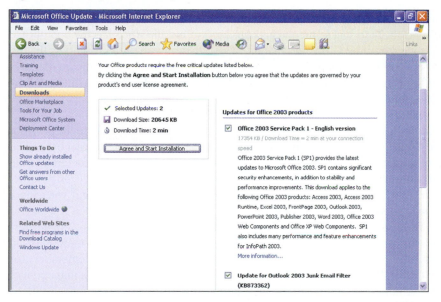

Figure 6-26 Confirm updates selected

Figure 6-27 Installation Result screen

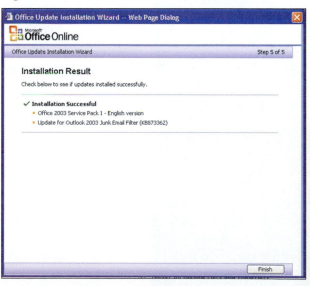

skill 5 — *Troubleshooting Microsoft Office Installations*

exam objective

Configure and troubleshoot Office applications. Troubleshoot application installation problems. Answer end-user questions related to configuring Office applications.

overview

The installation of Microsoft Office should complete without problems if you have thoroughly prepared for the installation in advance, as discussed in Skill 2. Occasionally, you may run into some problems with the installation. Here are just a few that you should be prepared to address:

◆ **Missing or corrupted file errors**: Microsoft allows users to download and install trial versions as well as full versions of software from its Web site at **http://www.microsoft.com/office/trial/default.mspx** and **http://shop.microsoft.com/special/office03/**. If the software has downloaded and the installation error indicates missing or corrupted files, try downloading the software again or requesting a new CD.

◆ **File copy errors**: If you experience errors during the copying phase of the installation, check for the presence of antivirus software. Disable it and see if doing so fixes the problem.

◆ **Permission denied errors**: If the user installing Microsoft Office receives Permission denied errors, check to make sure the account used to install Office has the appropriate privileges to perform the Office installation. If not, then log on with credentials that do have the appropriate permissions to perform the installation. If the company deploys Microsoft Office using Group Policy, check with the person who manages Group Policy to see if there are any software restrictions in place that prevent the installation on the specific user's computer.

◆ **Activation errors**: These types of errors typically occur in situations where the program has already been activated on another computer or when access to the Internet has failed. To address the first issue, you will need to consult product licensing to determine the current limitations on the number of computers running the software. If an Internet connection is not available, remember you can also register over the phone if you cannot wait for the connection to become available.

◆ **Reduced functionality errors**: If a user reports that he or she cannot create new documents or save modified copies of documents, but can print and view existing documents, the problem can be traced back to an activation issue. Remember, for Microsoft Office 2003 Professional Edition, you can launch the programs a maximum of 50 times without activation. After that point, the software goes into Reduced Functionality Mode.

◆ **Typing errors**: When entering product keys and confirmation numbers, make sure you do not replace the letter O with a 0 (zero). This form of a typographical error is very common with the longer product keys used in software applications today.

Microsoft Office 2003 also creates log files that can be used to troubleshoot the setup process. These are shown in **Table 6-3**. These log files are created each time setup is run, therefore, you need to look for the one with the highest number to find the most recent setup log.

more

For more information on the Office 2003 setup logs and how to interpret them, read Knowledge Base article 826511 located at: **http://support.microsoft.com/?scid=kb; en-us;826511&spid=2488&sid=global.**

Table 6-3   Microsoft Office log files*

Log File	Log File Name	Description
Setup.exe	Microsoft Office 2003 Setup (####).txt	This log records information such as reading the setup.ini file to pass information to Windows Installer, verifying the correct operating system and service pack(s) are installed, as well as checking for installed beta version of Office 2003 and versions of certain fonts to be used. It will also tell you if it found enough space to install the local install source files. If the setup log ends with return code 1603, you need to look at the Windows Installer logs for the source of the problem.
Windows Installer (Office Installation)	Microsoft Office 2003 Setup (####)_Task(0001).txt	These logs contain error information that can be used to identify the problem (permission problems, problems removing older version of Office, etc.). Use the Microsoft Knowledge Base to research the specific errors you find.
Windows Installer (System Files Update)	Microsoft Office 2003 Setup (####)_Task(0002).txt	These logs contain error information that can be used to identify the problem (permission problems, problems removing older version of Office, etc.). Use the Microsoft Knowledge Base to research the specific errors you find.

*These files are automatically created in the \Temp folder during the setup of Office 2003. The #### are numbers (0001,0002,0003, etc.). They are incremented each time you run setup.

skill 6   *Customizing Office Applications*

exam objective

Resolve issues related to customizing an Office application. Personalize office features. Answer end-user questions related to customizing Office applications. Customize toolbars.

overview

Once you have installed Microsoft Office, you will most likely need to customize it for the user. **Figure 6-28** shows several toolbars used with Excel that you will need to work with. Similar toolbars can be found in the other applications included with Microsoft Office. The following provides a brief overview of each:

◆ **Standard toolbar**: This toolbar provides shortcuts to create, open, save, and print spreadsheets you are working with in Excel 2003. It also provides shortcuts to perform cut, copy, and paste operations, and use spell checking. Because these are all very common actions performed within Excel, you need to make sure this toolbar is visible and accessible to all of your users.

◆ **Formatting toolbar**: This toolbar provides shortcuts to select fonts, font sizes, formatting options to bold, italicize, and align information. These are also very common actions performed within Excel. Make sure these are available to most users.

◆ **Task pane**: This area contains information that allow new users to easily find information related to Excel through Microsoft's Knowledge Base.

Toolbars can be added, removed, or customized by clicking **View** on the menu bar, pointing to **Toolbars**, and choosing an option on the Toolbars submenu (**Figure 6-29**). Selecting a toolbar either places a check mark beside the toolbar or removes an existing check mark. Checked toolbars are displayed in the application interface. For example, if you have users who prefer not to see the Tasks pane window, you can remove it. Select View on the menu bar and point to Toolbars. Locate the **Task Pane** toolbar and clear the check mark to remove the toolbar from the screen.

To further customize the menu bar and toolbars, you use the **Customize** dialog box (**Figure 6-30**). There are three ways to access this dialog box.

◆ Click **View** on the menu bar, point to **Toolbars** to open the **Toolbars** submenu, and click **Customize**.

◆ Click **Tools** on the menu bar and then click **Customize**.

◆ Right-click the menu or any of the toolbars and select **Customize** from the pop-up box.

The Customize dialog box allows several types of customization.

◆ The **Toolbars** tab allows you to add and remove toolbars.

◆ The **Options** tab provides several general configurations from which to choose. First, you can choose to have both the Standard and Formatting toolbars displayed on the same row by removing the check mark next to **Show Standard and Formatting toolbars on two rows**. You can also enable or disable the personalized menu feature. (**Personalized menus** display only the menu commands that the majority of users use most of the time, while hiding the less used commands from view. As the user begins to use the program, features he or she uses will start to appear higher on the drop-down list.) If the user does not want to use personalized menus, but instead wants to see all options available when selecting the menu item, select **Always show full menus**. The default option, **Show full menus after a short delay**, will result in the user seeing the options used most often. After a few seconds, the full menu will then be shown. If you want to undo any explicit customization, click the **Reset menu and toolbar usage data** button. In the **Other** section on the Options tab, you can increase the size of the icons used on the toolbar if the user is having trouble seeing them clearly. The **List font names in their font** option ensures that the user will see a preview of the font he or she wants to use, which makes choosing a font much easier (**Figure 6-31**). The **Show ScreenTips on toolbars** option provides a pop-up balloon when you place the mouse pointer over objects in the toolbar.

tip

Clicking the Reset menu and toolbar usage data button does not remove any buttons or commands that you have added using the Custom box. It does not add any buttons or commands you have deleted either.

Figure 6-28 Excel toolbars

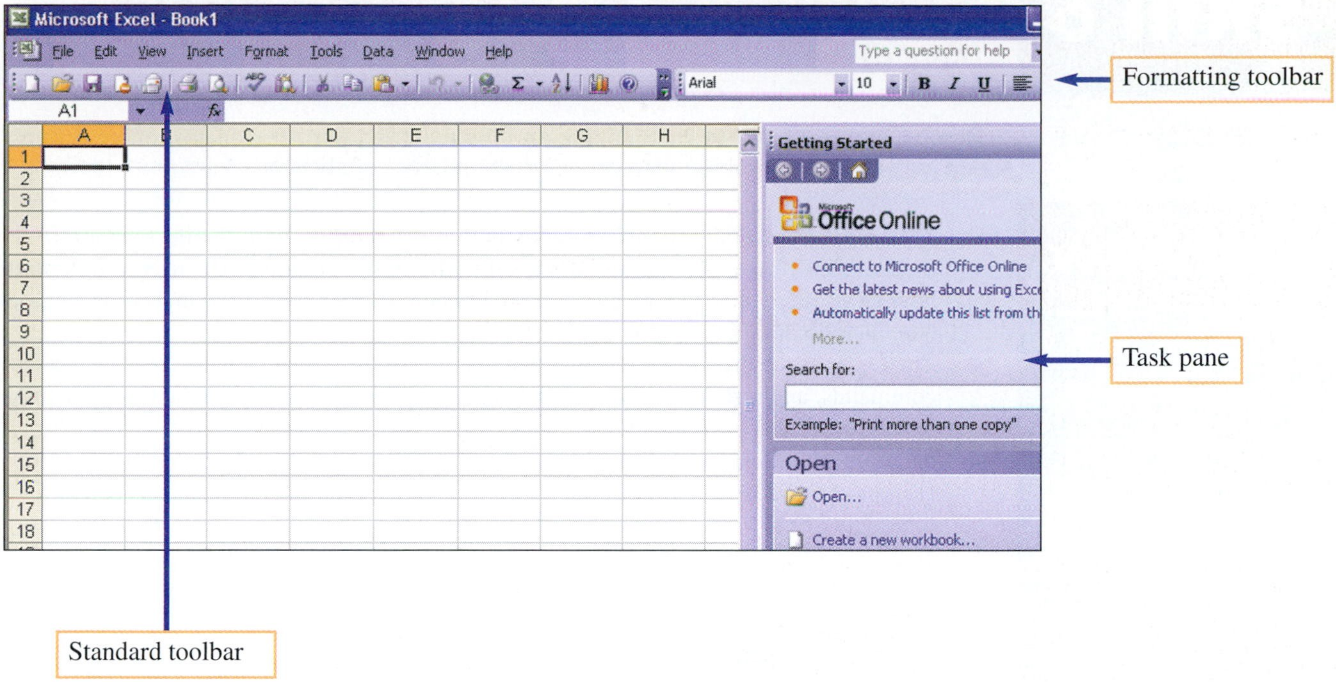

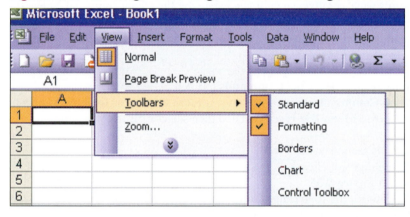

Figure 6-29 Adding, removing, and customizing toolbars

Figure 6-30 Configuration options

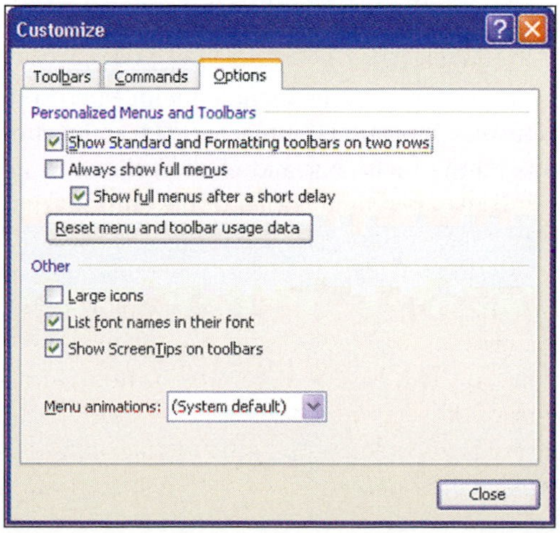

Figure 6-31 Listing font names in their font option

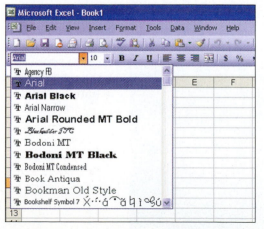

skill 6

Customizing Office Applications
(cont'd)

exam objective

Resolve issues related to customizing an Office application. Personalize office features. Answer end-user questions related to customizing Office applications. Customize toolbars.

overview

This is a very useful option for users who are not familiar with the information in the toolbars. Last but not least, the **Menu animations** option allows the user to determine how he or she would like menus to behave when selected on a drop-down list. Options here include: Random, Unfold, Slide, and Fade.

◆ The **Options** tab provides the ability to add commands to menu and toolbars, rearrange commands, and reset toolbars to their default state. To gain some insight as to how these options work, let's assume the following: A user, who creates pie charts as part of his daily job activities, would like to have access to the feature directly on his main menu. He would also like to rearrange the Edit menu so that the Find command is located first for quicker access. The steps required to perform these actions are set forth in the How To exercise below.

how to

tip

To remove the Pie Chart from the menu, hold down the Alt key while selecting and dragging the button onto the spreadsheet.

Add commands to menu bar.

1. Select **Tools** on the menu bar and click **Customize** to open the **Customize** dialog box.
2. Select the **Commands** tab and highlight **Charting** under **Categories**.
3. In the **Commands** pane, scroll down until you locate the **Pie Chart** command. Select Pie Chart and drag it to the menu bar **Figure 6-32**.
4. **Figure 6-33** shows how the new menu should appear when you are finished.

Rearrange commands.

1. In the **Customize** dialog box, in the **Commands** tab, select [Rearrange Commands...].
2. In the **Rearrange Commands** dialog box, under **Choose a menu or toolbar to rearrange**, make sure **Menu Bar** is selected and then select **Edit** from the drop-down list (**Figure 6-34**).
3. Under the **Controls** section, select **Find**.
4. While **Find** is highlighted, click [Move Up] until **Find** is located at the top of the **Edit** menu, as shown in **Figure 6-35**.
5. Click [Close] to exit the **Rearrange Commands** dialog box. Click [Close] again to leave the **Customize** dialog box.
6. **Find** should now appear at the top of the **Edit** menu as shown in **Figure 6-36**.

more

To reset a toolbar to its default state, select the **Toolbars** tab in the **Customize** dialog box and select the toolbar you want to reset. Click **Reset**.

To prepare yourself for customizing the various applications included with Microsoft Office 2003, spend some time looking at the various configuration options for each application in the suite. To access these options, select **Tools** on the menu bar and click **Options** from within each application. Select the question mark in the upper-right corner of the **Options** dialog box to learn about each configuration provided.

Figure 6-32 Commands pane

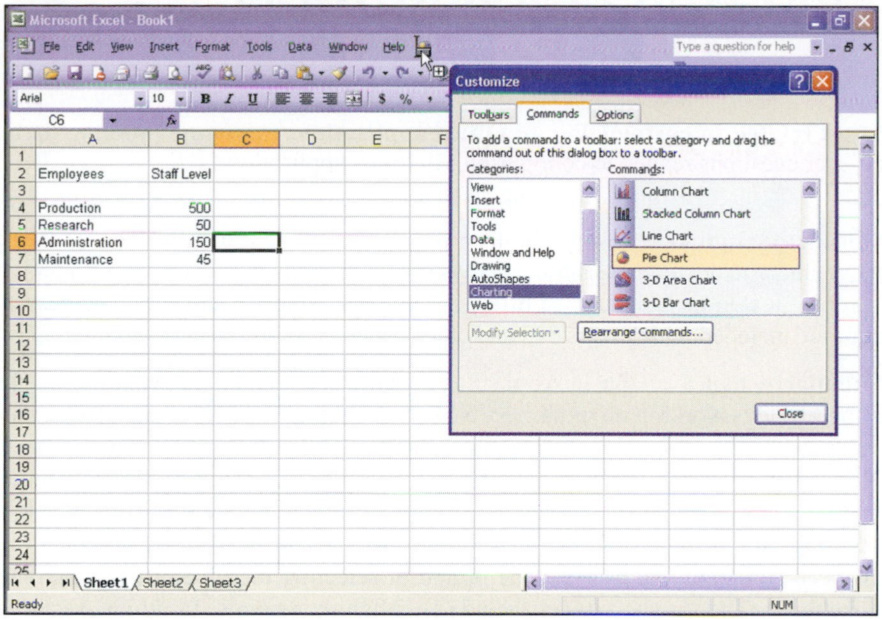

Figure 6-34 Rearrange command

Figure 6-33 New menu after adding Pie Chart command

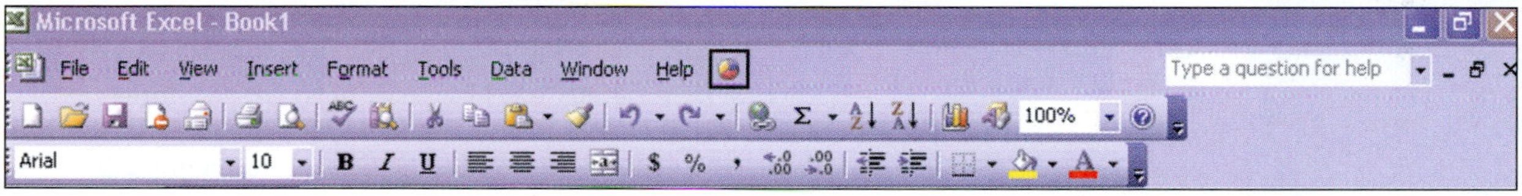

Figure 6-35 Moving the Find command on the Edit menu

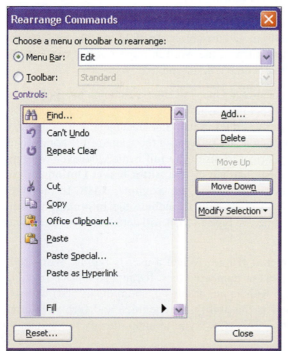

Figure 6-36 The Find command moved to the top of the Edit menu

skill 7 *Working with Proofing Tools*

exam objective

Resolve issues related to customizing an Office application. Configure proofing tools. Answer end-user questions related to configuring Microsoft applications.

overview

Microsoft Office 2003 provides several built-in proofing tools that can be used to check spelling and grammar in documents, automatically correct common typing errors, summarize documents, format text to include bulleted lists, or even format Internet and e-mail addresses. Proofing tools are included with Word 2003 and other applications in the Office Suite.

The **AutoSummarize** tool, available in Word 2003, allows a user to identify the key points in a document he or she is working on or has received from another individual and produce an automatic summary. This is accomplished by having AutoSummarize scan the document for sentences that contain words that are used frequently in the document. The sentences discovered are then given a percentage ranking from high to low. The user can then choose the sentences that are assigned the higher scores to include in her summary. Once the analysis has been complete, the user has the option of selecting the type of summary she wants (**Figure 6-37**). The summary types include Highlight key points; Insert an executive summary or abstract at the top of the document; Create a new document and inserting the summary there; or Hide everything but the summary without leaving the document. You can automatically summarize a document as shown in the How To exercise at the end of this skill.

AutoCorrect is another tool that can make the creation and editing of documents much easier for users. It works by automatically correcting common typos. For example, it will automatically capitalize the first letter of sentences and capitalize the names of days of the week. Other types of corrections are shown in **Figure 6-38**. The Exceptions button allows you to override the AutoCorrect feature if necessary. This is very useful in situations where your company uses certain company names or abbreviations that you do not want the AutoCorrect to capitalize or correct. If you do not use a word frequently enough to create an exception for it, but do not want the word automatically changed to the correct spelling, you can undo the correction of the word by moving your mouse over the word, and clicking the down arrow that appears. The lightning bolt that appears is known as a SmartTag. On the menu that appears, you can choose the correction type you want (**Figure 6-39**).

To correct a misspelled word, you can right-click the misspelled word and select the correct spelling from the pop-up box (**Figure 6-40**) or add the correct spelling for the word into the AutoCorrect list. If you add the correct spelling of the word into the AutoCorrect list, the word will be automatically corrected the next time it is misspelled.

There are a few different ways to use AutoCorrect. One is to enter a common misspelling for a word, such as pasttime, with the correct spelling pastime. You can also use AutoCorrect to avoid retyping the same information numerous times in the same document. For example, if you worked at TriTones Music Store and frequently referenced the name of the company in various documents, you could use AutoCorrect to insert the full name whenever you type "TMS." To do this, select **Tools** on the menu bar and choose **AutoCorrect Options**. In the **Replace** box, enter the word you want to autocorrect, for example, **TMS**. In the **With** column, enter **TriTones Music Store** and click **Add** to include the information in the AutoCorrect list (**Figure 6-41**). The next time you type TMS, it will automatically be replaced with TriTones Music Store.

AutoCorrect also provides the **AutoFormat** feature. When a user is typing, Word 2003 automatically creates the appropriate bullets or numbered lists. It can also replace fractions such as (1/4) with ¼, double hyphens (--) with an em dash (—), and ordinals (1st) with 1st. Another capability of this proofing tool is the ability to recognize and format Internet addresses and network paths as hyperlinks. This allows you to jump directly to the item by clicking the link.

Figure 6-37 AutoSummarize options

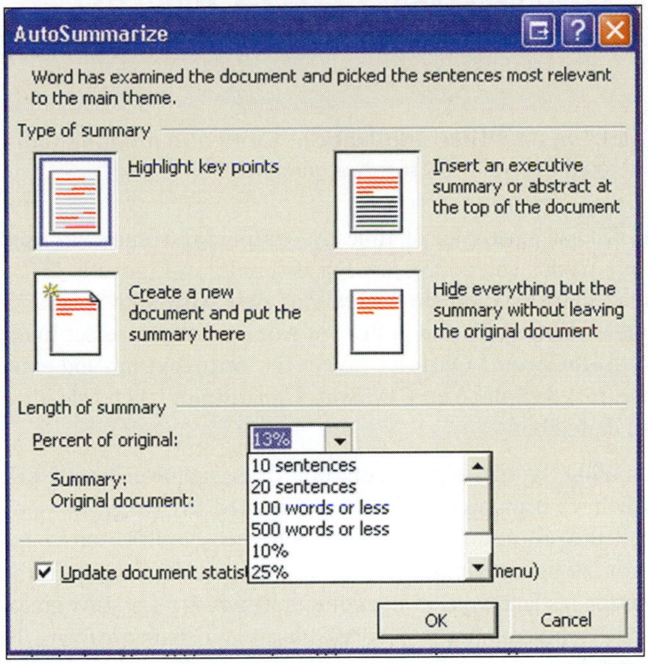

Figure 6-38 AutoCorrect default options

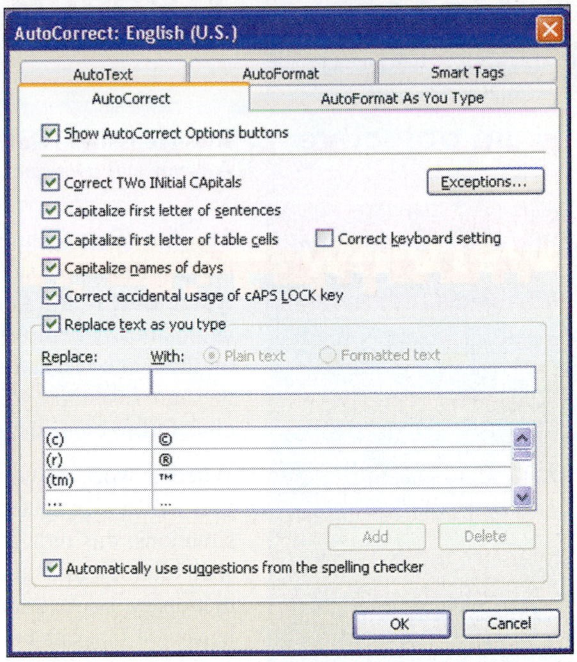

Figure 6-39 Using the SmartTag feature

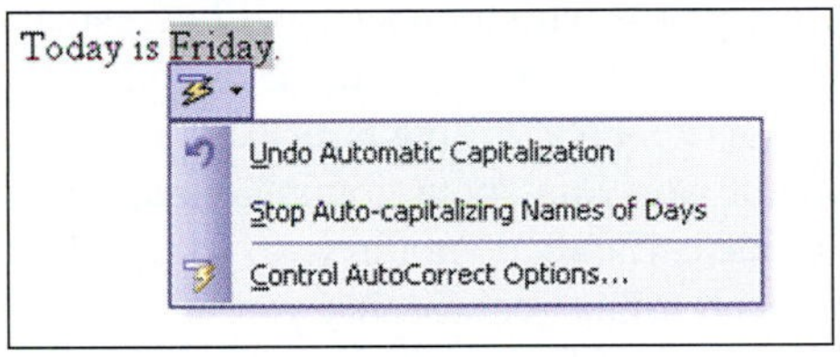

Figure 6-40 Right-click to correct word

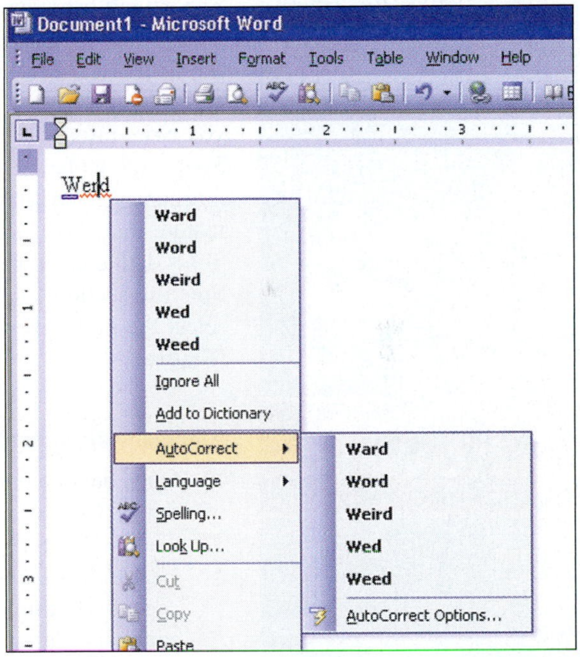

Figure 6-41 Using the AutoCorrect list

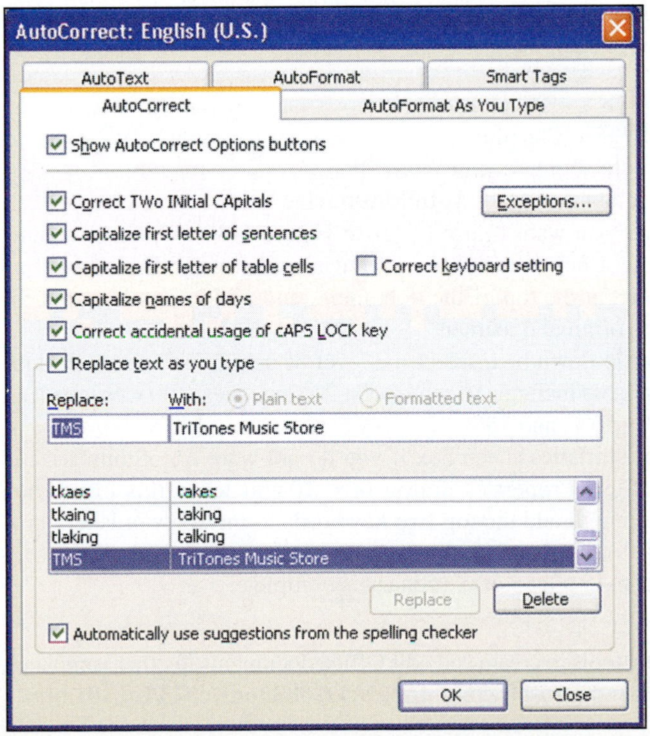

skill 7

Working with Proofing Tools (cont'd)

exam objective

Resolve issues related to customizing an Office application. Configure proofing tools. Answer end user questions related to configuring Microsoft applications.

overview

The **AutoText** feature (**Figure 6-42**) can save a lot of time by completing commonly used words or phrases, such as company names and addresses. For example, in **Figure 6-43**, by typing **Best w**, the AutoText feature offers to complete the entry as **Best wishes**, the phrase is automatically completed if you press [**Enter**]. To add your own AutoText entry, select **Tools** on the menu bar and then choose **AutoCorrect Options**. Select the **AutoText** tab and enter the AutoText entry you want to use, for example: **Mary Wilson, Consultant**, Click Add, then click OK to close the AutoCorrect dialog box.

Whether working within Outlook 2003, Word 2003, Excel 2003 or even PowerPoint 2003, you will notice that certain words have been automatically underlined. Although in many situations, this indicates a misspelled word, it may not always be the case. Office programs will identify and underline words as being misspelled if they cannot find them in the dictionary. For example, vaporware is a slang word in the computer industry for software or hardware that has been advertised for months but isn't available in any shape or form. To avoid having Office programs report the word as being misspelled, the word can be added to the dictionary. The easiest way to train users to do this is to tell them to right-click the word that is underlined and select Add to Dictionary.

The default behavior for the **Spelling & Grammar** options is to check spelling as you type, always suggest corrections, ignore words in uppercase, words with numbers, and Internet and file addresses. For some users, you will need to make modifications to these options. One example might be a user who indicates he likes to free write. Free writing is an exercise where you write information as it comes to your head without worrying about grammar or spelling. Some authors feel it helps them come up with better ideas if they do not have to focus on the mechanics of writing. A user who prefers this approach might request that you turn off the feature that shows spelling and grammatical errors. This can be accomplished by selecting **Tools** on the menu bar and then clicking **Options**. On the Spelling & Grammar tab, under the **Spelling** section, clear the **Check spelling as you type** check box. To hide grammar errors, select the **Hide grammatical errors in this document** check box in the **Grammar** section (**Figure 6-44**).

how to

Automatically summarize a document.

1. Open the document you want to summarize in Word 2003.
2. Select **Tools** on the menu bar and then click **AutoSummarize**.
3. Choose the type of summary you want to use (refer to Figure 6-37). Options include: Highlight key points, Create a new document and put the summary there, Insert an executive summary or abstract at the top of the document, and Hide everything but the summary without leaving the original document.
4. In the **Percent of original** drop-down box, select the level of detail you want to include in the summary. Options available include: 10 sentences, 20 sentences, 100 words or less, 500 words or less, 10%, 25%, 50%, and 75%.
5. Clear the **Update document statistics** check box if you do not want AutoSummarize to update information in the file's Properties dialog box. If you leave this check box selected, then AutoSummarize will add the top five keywords to the Keywords text box, and copy the summary text to the Document contents text box. The file's Properties settings are shown in **Figure 6-45** after AutoSummary is complete.

more

To learn more about using proofing tools to create and edit Office documents in other languages, visit the following link: **http://www.microsoft.com/office/ork/2003/four/ch13/IntA01.htm.**

Figure 6-42 AutoText tab

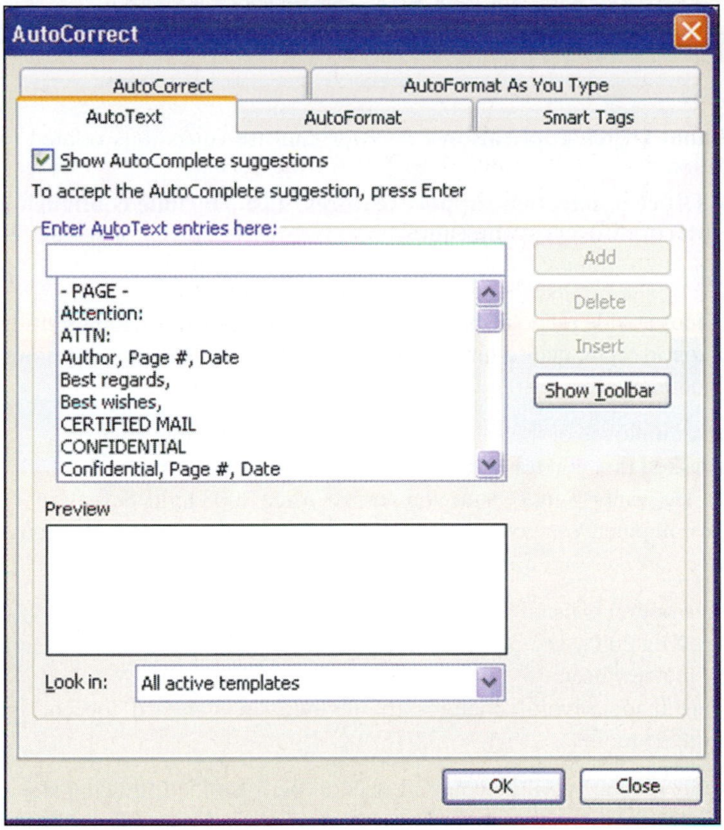

Figure 6-43 Using AutoText

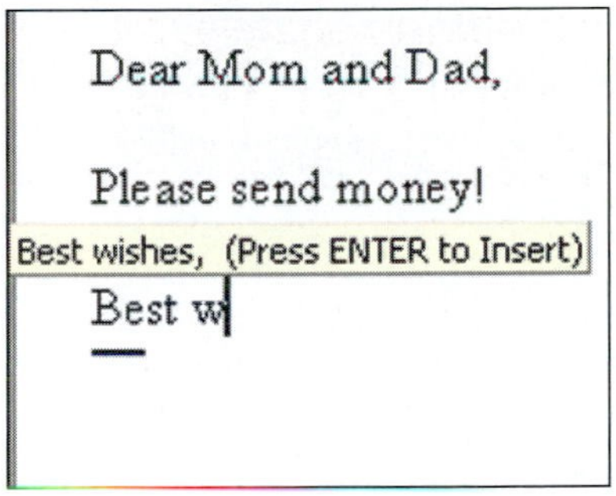

Figure 6-44 Hiding grammar and spelling errors

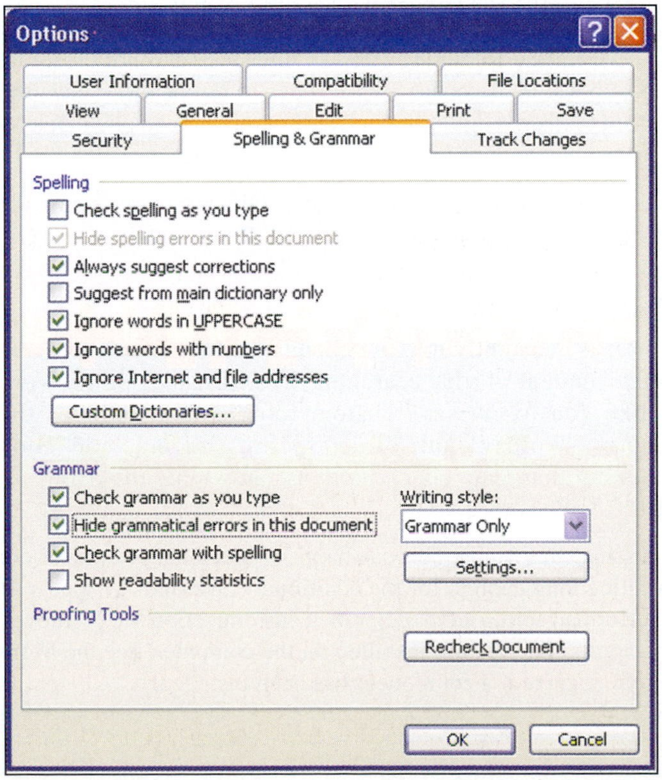

Figure 6-45 Updated document statistics

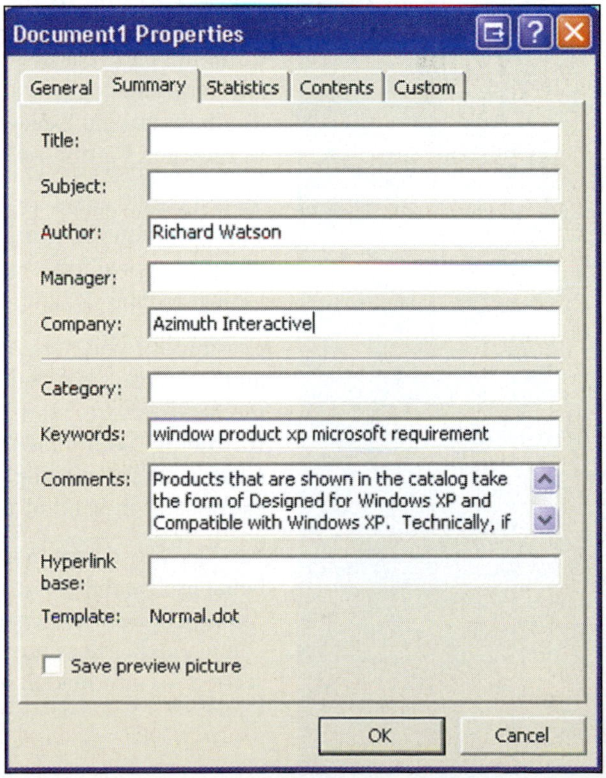

skill 8 — Troubleshooting Word: Common User Issues

exam objective

Configure and troubleshoot Office applications. Answer end-user questions related to configuring Office applications.

Resolve issues related to Office application support features. Tasks include configuring Office applications and interpreting error messages.

overview

tip

Microsoft Office Online Help and Support, the Microsoft Knowledge Base, and TechNet can offer additional troubleshooting assistance.

Microsoft Word 2003 provides a wide range of options that can be modified, each presenting unique challenges to the support technician. This skill focuses on some of the most common user requests you might encounter.

For example, suppose a new employee of the sales department will be starting work on Monday. Her manager has asked that you transfer a computer, recently used by another employee, into her cubicle. He wants to make sure you return Office 2003 to its default settings before she uses the computer. You notice the following changes made by the previous user:

◆ The Save as a Web Page option is listed first under the File menu.
◆ A custom toolbar was created by the previous user that contains several buttons and menus not required by the new user.
◆ The previous user has made several changes to the built-in standard toolbar by rearranging the icons on the toolbar.

To return the File menu to its default settings, you will need to perform the following steps. First open Word 2003. Click **Tools** on the menu bar and then click **Customize**. On the **Commands** tab, in the Customize dialog box, click the **Rearrange Commands** button. In the **Choose a menu or toolbar to rearrange** section, select **Toolbar** and then choose **Menu Bar** in the drop-down box. In the **Controls** section, select the menu to reset (i.e., File) and click the **Reset** button (**Figure 6-46**). In the **Reset changes made to 'Menu Bar' toolbar for** section, make sure Normal.dot is selected and click OK. Click Close to exit the Rearrange Commands dialog box. The Save as a Web Page option should now be moved to its original default location which is six down from the top of the file menu.

To remove the custom toolbar, perform the following (this assumes you did not close the Customize dialog box after Step 4 above; if so, repeat Step 1 above to re-open it). Select the **Toolbars** tab and locate the **Custom** toolbar. Highlight the **Custom** toolbar and click **Delete**, as shown in **Figure 6-47**. When prompted to confirm the deletion, click OK.

To rest the Standard toolbar to its default settings, first select the **Toolbars** tab, make sure the **Standard** toolbar is highlighted (**Figure 6-48**), and then click the **Reset** button. Click OK when prompted to reset changes made to the Standard toolbar. This returns all icons on the toolbar to their default locations.

Or suppose you notice that a user is constantly making changes to her default toolbars and seems to spend an inordinate amount of time searching for commands in the Word menu structure. She would like you to create a custom toolbar that includes the following commands: Thesaurus, Word Count, Hide Spelling Errors, and Hide Grammar Errors. This custom toolbar can be created as shown in the How To exercise at the end of this skill.

Another very common issue is missing commands. This can happen if personalized menus are being used and the user is not waiting long enough for the additional commands to appear. It can also occur when a user has performed some of his or her own customization (i.e., removed commands) or does not have the appropriate feature installed on the computer. See the More section for information on how to recognize if a component has been installed.

Figure 6-46 Resetting the File menu to its default setting

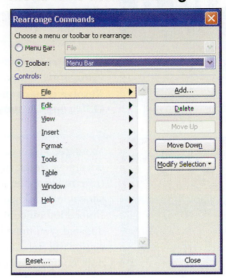

Figure 6-47 Removing a custom toolbar

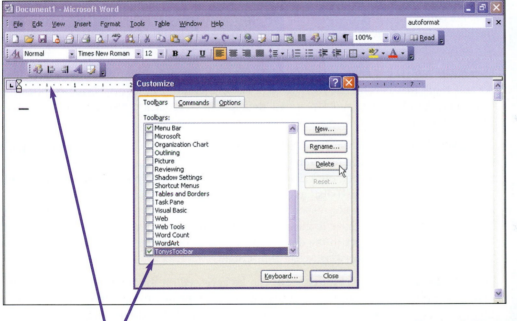

A custom toolbar (in this case, TonysToolbar) can be deleted in the Customize dialog box

Figure 6-48 Resetting the Standard toolbar to its default setting

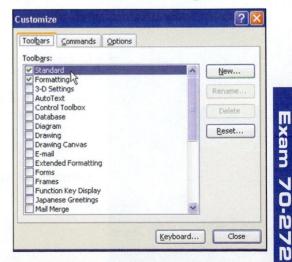

skill 8

Troubleshooting Word: Common User Issues *(cont'd)*

exam objective

Configure and troubleshoot Office applications. Answer end-user questions related to configuring Office applications.

Resolve issues related to Office application support features. Tasks include configuring Office applications and interpreting error messages.

overview

Word 2003 also supports linked and embedded objects. For example, you may create a Word document (referred to as the destination file) that includes a pie chart created in Excel 2003 (referred to as the source file). If you embed the object in the Word document, the information shown in Word becomes static and does not change even if you modify data in the source file. Embedded objects are edited using the source file's program. To ensure the information is updated, you must link it instead. When you link to an object, the information is stored in the source file (i.e., the Excel file that includes the chart). The destination file (i.e., the Word file) only contains information about where the source file is located. A very common problem occurs when the source file (the Excel file that includes the file chart) is moved from its original location. If this occurs and you double-click to edit the pie chart, you will receive a "Cannot edit" error message. Make sure the application (Excel) is running on the computer. If the linked object is not on the local computer, make sure network connectivity is not an issue. Try to ping the other computer and test basic connectivity.

Users will sometimes contact the help desk in a panic if they have lost files. Word offers several tools that can be used to recover. These include: Microsoft Office Application Recovery, AutoRecover, and Open and Repair. These tools are also available in other Microsoft applications.

Microsoft Office Application Recovery (**Figure 6-49**) can be used to exit an application that has stopped responding and report the error to Microsoft if you choose. To access Microsoft Office Application Recovery, click **Start**, point to **All Programs**, point to **Microsoft Office**, point to **Microsoft Office Tools**, and then click **Microsoft Office Application Recovery**. Select the program that is not responding from the list and select **Recover Application** or **End Application**. If you have to choose End Application, any recent changes will be lost. Select **Send Error Report** in the dialog box that appears if you want to make Microsoft aware of the problem. Otherwise, select **Don't Send**.

The **AutoRecover** option (**Figure 6-50**) can be accessed on the **Save** tab of the **Options** dialog box (click **Tools** on the menu bar and select **Options** to open the Options dialog box). It works by periodically saving a temporary copy of the file the user is working on. This occurs every 10 minutes by default. If the user is working with critical documents, consider setting the AutoRecover option to occur more frequently. To see or modify the location where AutoRecover saves the files, look on the File Locations tab (**Figure 6-51**). If this option is enabled, and Word 2003 stops responding, open Microsoft Office Application Recovery and select Recover Application. When the program reopens, you will see the recovered files displayed in the Document Recovery task pane. The data represented reflects the last time AutoRecover saved the files.

The **Open and Repair** option can be used to recover the text from a damaged document. A damaged Word document will typically display incorrect layout and formatting, characters may be unreadable, or cause the computer to stop responding when it is opened. See the How To exercise for instructions on using this feature. For more options on recovering damaged Word 2003 documents, visit the following link: (Microsoft Knowledge Base article number 826864: **http://support.microsoft.com/default.aspx?scid=KB%3BEN-US%3B826864.**

tip

AutoRecover does not replace traditional backups.

Figure 6-49 Microsoft Office Application Recovery

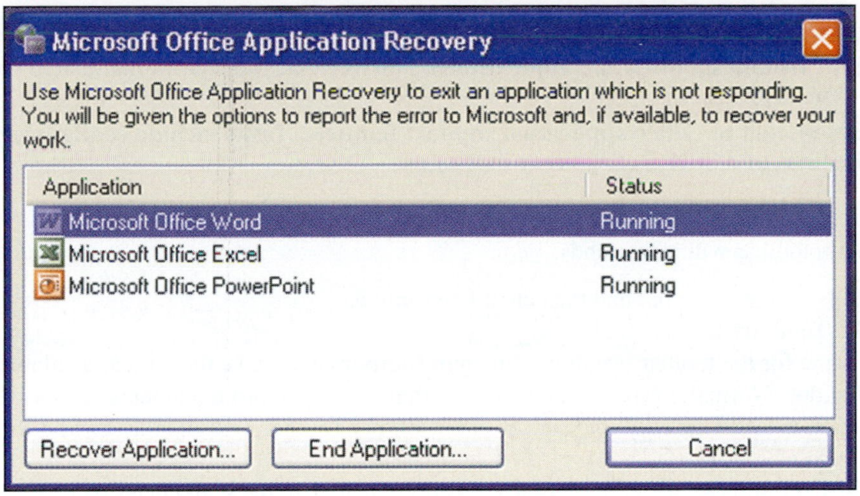

Figure 6-50 AutoRecover

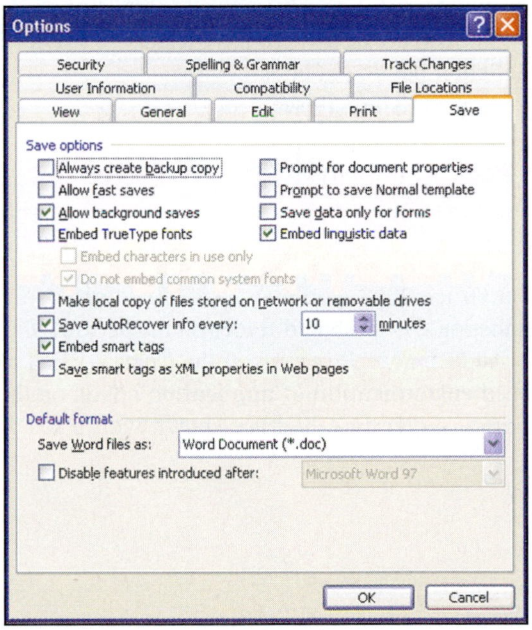

Figure 6-51 AutoRecover file location

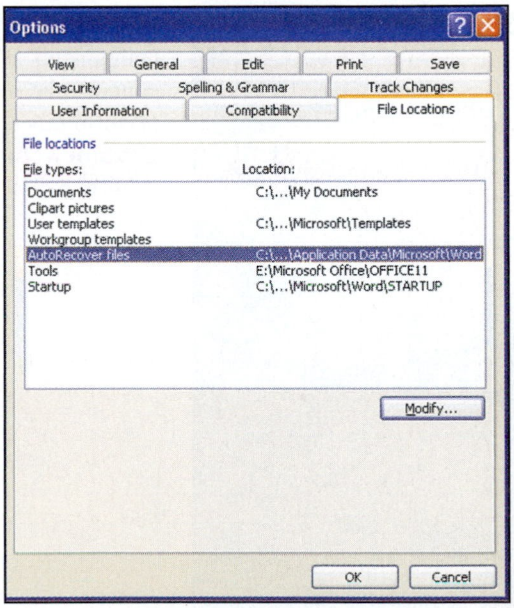

skill 8

Troubleshooting Word: Common User Issues (cont'd)

exam objective

Configure and troubleshoot Office applications. Answer end-user questions related to configuring Office applications.

Resolve issues related to Office application support features. Tasks include configuring Office applications and interpreting error messages.

how to

Create a custom toolbar with commands.

1. Click **Tools** on the menu bar and then click **Customize**.
2. Select the **Toolbars** tab and click [New...].
3. Enter a name for the toolbar (example: **MorganToolbar**) and make the toolbar available to Normal.dot (Normal.dot is the template file that all new Word documents are based on) (**Figure 6-52**). Click [OK]. A small, empty toolbar will display beside the Customize dialog box.
4. Select the **Commands** tab and highlight the **Tools** category in the **Categories** pane.
5. In the **Commands** pane, drag the **Thesaurus**, **Word Count**, **Hide Spelling Errors**, and **Hide Grammar Errors** commands to the toolbar created in Step 3.
6. When all commands have been added to the new toolbar, select [Close] to exit the Customize dialog box.
7. The new toolbar is by default a floating toolbar. That means that it is not attached to one edge of the program window. Drag the toolbar to the program window. This is known as docking the toolbar.

Use the Open and Repair option.

1. Select **File** on the menu bar and click **Open**.
2. Browse to the location of the file you want to retrieve text from by using the **Look in** field. Once the document is located, highlight it but do not click [Open ▾].
3. Instead, look at the right side of [Open ▾] and you will see a down pointing arrow (**Figure 6-53**).
4. Select the arrow and choose **Open and Repair** in the pop-up box.

tip

If you make a mistake while dragging commands to the custom toolbar, just select the command in the toolbar and drag it out to delete it.

more

Depending upon how you installed Microsoft Office 2003, you may need to add or remove components. This requires access to the installation CD or shared folder on the network that contains the installation files. Use Windows Add/Remove Programs in the Control Panel to perform this task. Select the **Choose advanced customization of application** option on the **Custom Setup** screen. Options/features not currently installed are shown with a red X (**Figure 6-54**).

Figure 6-52 **Naming a custom toolbar**

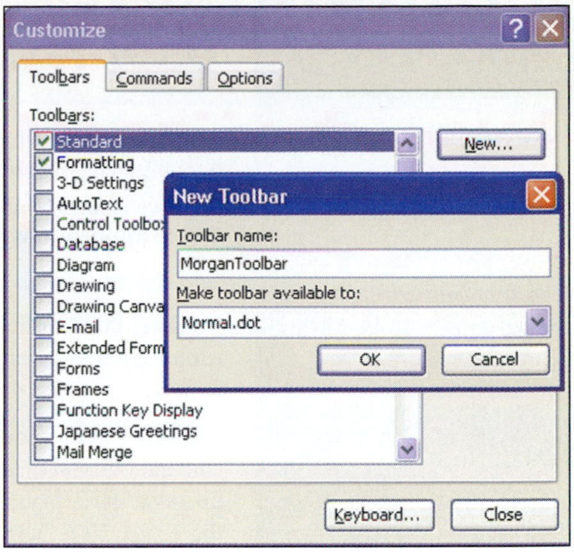

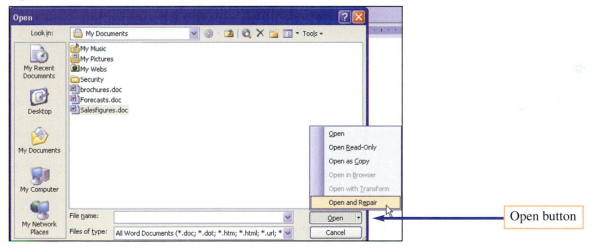

Figure 6-53 **Open and Repair command**

Open button

Figure 6-54 **Options/features not currently installed**

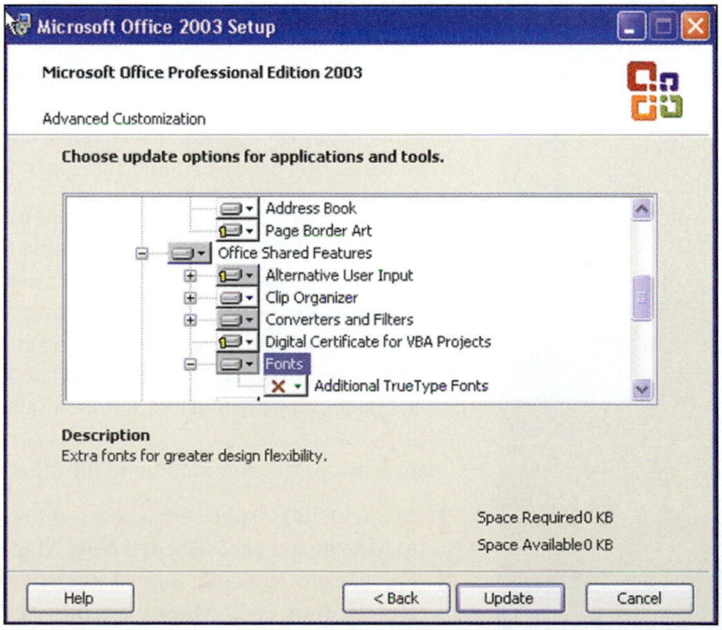

skill 9

Troubleshooting Excel: Common User Issues

exam objective

Configuring and troubleshooting Office applications. Answer end-user questions related to configuring Microsoft applications.

Resolve issues related to Office application support features. Tasks include configuring Office applications and interpreting error messages.

overview

In Excel 2003, users will typically have problems associated with performing calculations, running macros, and recovering lost files. For recovering lost files, Excel uses the same features discussed for Word 2003.

Although many companies have users who are quite comfortable at creating and using calculations and macros in Excel 2003, you should develop some level of comfort supporting users on these matters. Calculations are created by entering formulas in the Formula bar. In the Excel 2003 help file, **formulas** are defined as "equations that perform calculations on values in your worksheet." Formulas always start with an = sign and are shown in the Formula bar of Excel (**Figure 6-55**) .

Users have the option of either creating their own formula or using one of the many provided with Excel. The How To exercise illustrates how to use the built-in AVERAGE formula to determine the average age of a group of students. Although this is a very simple formula, it will provide you with a quick overview of how to use a built-in formula.

To troubleshoot problems users have with formulas, you must understand operators (+, -, /, <, >, ( ), <>) and the order they are processed. For example, if a user has the following formula: =4+2^2, and you calculate from left to right, the answer will be 36 (4+2=6 and 6^2 is 36). However, if your calculation uses the exponentiation first, you will get an entirely different answer. In this case, 8 (2^2=4 + 4). If you had to choose, do you have any idea which is correct? Fortunately, to protect against these types of miscalculations, Excel uses a predefined order to determine which portion of the formula is processed first, second, third and so on. The order is shown in **Table 6-4**. Be prepared to use some of those math skills you have learned in the past to assist users when their calculations do not produce the results they expected! When this occurs, you will need to first understand what the user is trying to accomplish and then determine if the formula being used is correct.

Another common calculation error is the #VALUE! Error, which occurs when Excel is unable to translate a cell's date into the correct format. For example, if a user types in the text **Not In Stock** in cell A4 and the number 50 in cell B4 and then tries to create a formula in cell C4 that adds the two together (A4 + B4), he or she will receive a #VALUE! error in the C4 cell. The value in the B4 cell is seen by Excel as the wrong data type. To troubleshoot this error, click the cell that displays the error (C4), and then click the adjacent button displaying the exclamation mark. This opens a drop-down list of options that allow you to specify how to handle the error (**Figure 6-56**).

Macros are another area that you should understand in order to support users. Although there is a lot of data that is only entered a single time into a worksheet, there are other types of data that are repeated on a regular basis. For users who perform repetitive tasks, macros provide a way to automate the entire process by recording a series of keystrokes and mouse movements that tell Excel what to do. For example, a user who always enters the user name, title, department, and Inventory Record Update Report in every new spreadsheet workbook that he or she creates can use a macro to insert this information automatically.

tip

The correct answer to the problem is 8 because exponents are calculated before addition.

how to

Create a macro to enter automatic information into a new workbook.

1. In Excel 2003, start with a new workbook on Sheet 1, select **Tools** on the menu bar, point to **Macro** and click **Record New Macro**.
2. For the macro name, enter **UserInfo**. For the **Shortcut key**, enter the letter **a**. For the **Description**, enter **Macro to Add User Information** and click [OK] (**Figure 6-57**).

Figure 6-55 Excel Formula bar

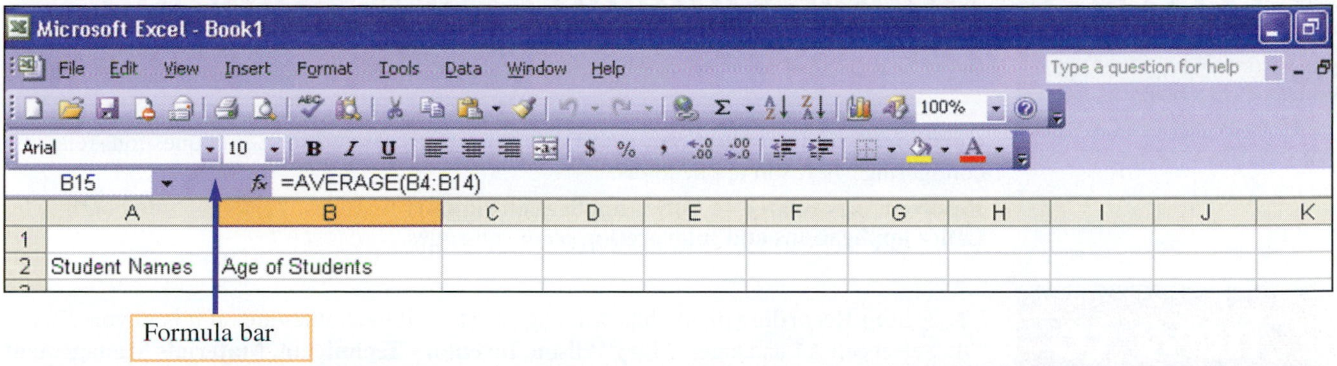

Formula bar

Table 6-4   Order of precedence for operators

Order Processed	Comments
1. Parenthesis	Excel will always perform calculations inside of a parenthesis first. In fact, this is one way you can control the order Excel uses to calculate a formula. Calculations outside the parenthesis are processed according to the order of precedence.
2. Exponents	^
3. Multiply and Divide	*, /
4. Add and Subtract	+,-
5. Equal to, less than, greater than, or comparisons.	=, <, >, <=, >=, <>

Figure 6-56 The #VALUE! error

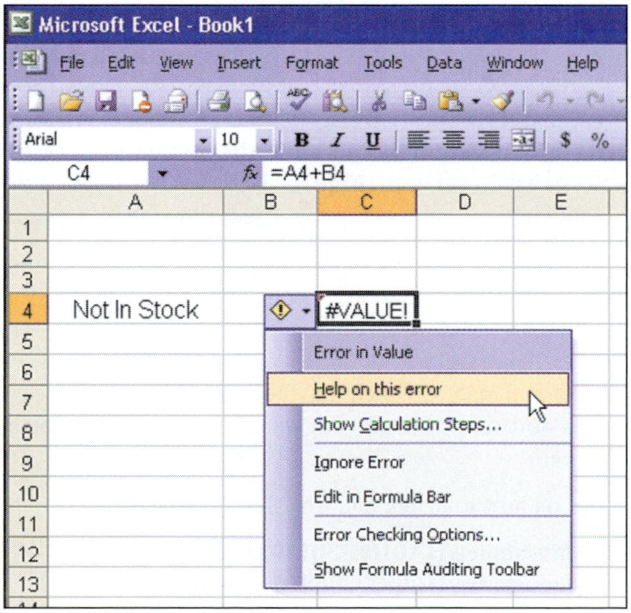

Figure 6-57 Entering a macro name, description, and shortcut key

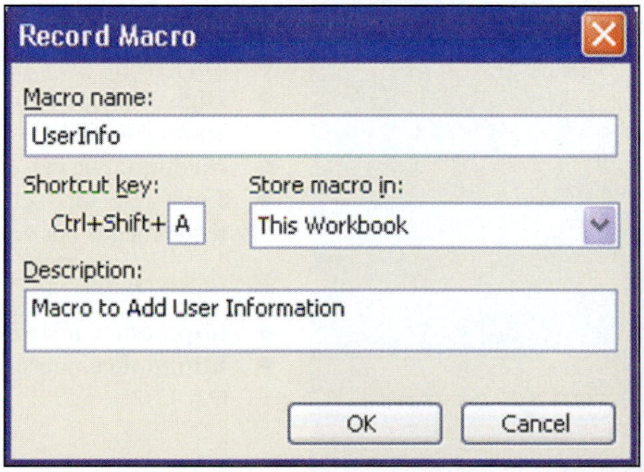

skill 9

Troubleshooting Excel: Common User Issues (cont'd)

exam objective

Configuring and troubleshooting Office applications. Answer end-user questions related to configuring Microsoft applications.

Resolve issues related to Office application support features. Tasks include configuring Office applications and interpreting error messages.

how to

3. A **Stop Recording** dialog box will appear. Move it to another area if it is in your way.
4. Select cell **A1** and enter: **Mary Wilson, Inventory Technician, Materials Management**.
5. Select cell **A2** and enter **Inventory Record Update Report**.
6. Click the small, blue square box inside the **Stop Recording** dialog box to stop the recording process.
7. To run the macro you just created, open **Sheet 2** of the Excel workbook. Click **Tools** on the menu bar, point to **Macro** and click **Macros** to open the Macro dialog box. Select the **UserInfo** macro (**Figure 6-58**) and click [Run]. The information you created in Steps 4 and 5 above should now be entered in the exact same cells (A1 and A2). The macro can also be run by using the shortcut key ([**Ctrl**]+[**a**]).

Create a a custom button for the macro on a custom toolbar.

1. Select **Tools** on the menu bar, click **Customize**, and select the **Toolbars** tab.
2. Click [New...] and enter **Macros** as the toolbar name on the **New Toolbar** dialog box
3. Select the **Commands** tab and highlight the **AutoShapes** category. In the commands pane on the right, select one of the options available. In our example we will select the Chevron command and drag it to our custom toolbar (**Figure 6-59**).
4. Right-click the **Chevron** icon in the custom toolbar and select **Assign Macro** (**Figure 6-60**).
5. In the **Assign Macro** dialog box, select the **UserInfo** macro you created earlier and click [OK]. Click [Close] to exit the Customize dialog box.
6. Dock the Macros toolbar to an empty area of the Excel toolbars. The macro will now run by using the new button on the custom toolbar.

more

Macros are Visual Basic programs that can introduce security risks such as viruses. To address such issues, Excel offers four levels of macro security that can be used. To access these settings, select **Tools** on the menu bar and then click Options. In the **Options** dialog box, select the **Security** tab, and click the **Macro Security** button at the bottom to open the **Security** dialog box. Select the **Security Level** tab (**Figure 6-61**) and configure the appropriate macro security level as dictated by your company's security policy. Options include:

- **Very High**: Only macros installed from trusted locations will be allowed.
- **High**: Unsigned macros are disabled and only signed macros from trusted sources are allowed to run.
- **Medium**: You can choose whether to run macros which may be potentially unsafe.
- **Low**: Use this setting with virus software. Almost any macro can run. Microsoft recommends not selecting this option.

The following links provide several tips on how to debug and troubleshoot macros:

- **http://office.microsoft.com/en-us/assistance/HA010873011033.aspx**
- **http://office.microsoft.com/en-us/assistance/HP052730681033.aspx**

Figure 6-58 **Running a macro**

Figure 6-59 **Creating a custom button to run a macro**

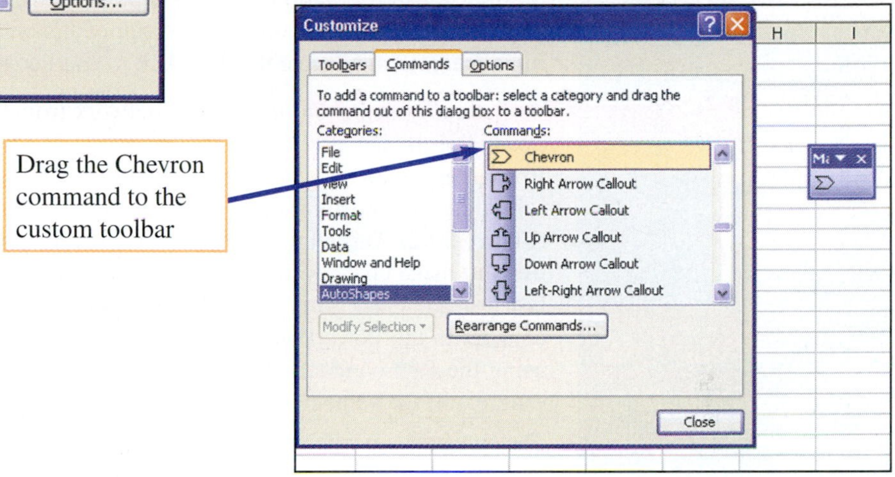

Drag the Chevron command to the custom toolbar

Figure 6-60 **Assigning a macro to a button**

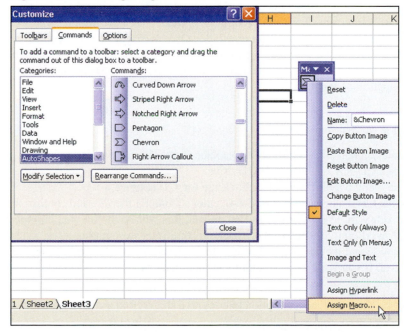

Figure 6-61 **Setting macro security**

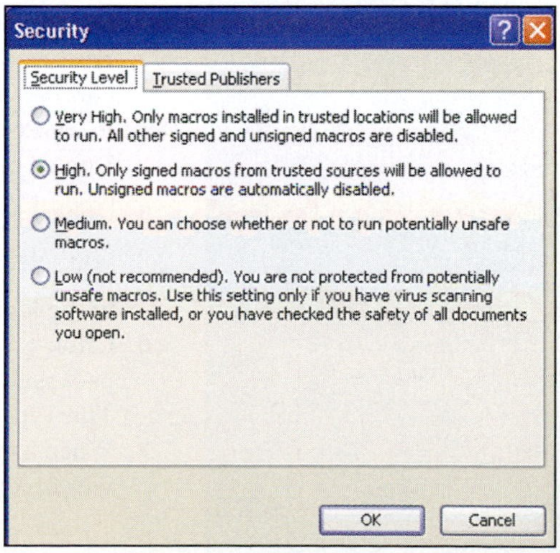

skill 10

Troubleshooting PowerPoint: Common User Issues

exam objective

Configure and troubleshoot Office applications. Answer end-user questions related to configuring Microsoft applications.

Resolve issues related to Office application support features. Tasks include configuring Office applications and interpreting error messages.

overview

Making presentations and their associated support files available to others can sometimes be frustrating to users. The options available for sharing a PowerPoint presentation include: running the presentation on their laptop, sharing the presentation over the network, or packaging the presentation to share with others on a CD, via e-mail, or over the network. To run a presentation, locate the file, click it, and PowerPoint 2003 will automatically start.

To share a presentation file over the network from your computer, first create a folder named **PowerPoints**. Right-click the folder and select **Sharing and Security**. In the **PowerPoints Properties** dialog box, select the **Sharing** tab. In the **Network sharing and security** section, select the **Share this folder on the network** check box and keep the default share name. (**Figure 6-62**). This allows other users the ability to read the file. Note that if you want to allow users to make changes to the file, select the **Allow network users to change my files** check box instead. Click **Apply** to make the changes. Users on the network can now map a drive to connect to the PowerPoints folder, browse for it using Network Neighborhood, or connect using the Run command by entering \\computername\sharename in the Open text box. For example, if the name of the computer is TREX, you would use **\\TREX\powerpoints**.

The only problem with this approach is that the users who want to view the presentation must have either the PowerPoint application installed on their computer or must have the **PowerPoint viewer**. The viewer can be downloaded by visiting **http://www.microsoft.com/ downloads/**. Another option that works much better is the **Package for CD** feature, known as Pack and Go in earlier versions of PowerPoint. This feature allows you to copy one or more presentations along with their support files (graphics, fonts, music) onto a CD or to a folder. Once packaged, it can be copied and e-mailed to other users, shared on the network, or mailed. The packaging process also includes the PowerPoint Viewer, which will allow the presentations on the CD to run even if the user does not have the PowerPoint application installed.

tip

PowerPoint 2003 uses the same options for recovering files as Word 2003 and Excel 2003.

tip

These steps for sharing a presentation assume you are working in a workgroup using Windows XP's Simple File Sharing user interface. For more information on this feature, search the Help and Support Center.

how to

Package a presentation for distribution on a CD.

1. Open the presentation that you would like to package from within PowerPoint 2003.
2. Insert a CD-R or a CD-RW CD into your CD drive.
3. Click **File** on the menu bar and then select **Package for CD** (**Figure 6-63**).
4. In the **Package for CD** dialog box (**Figure 6-64**), enter a name for the CD, and confirm the PowerPoint file you want to copy is shown. By default, this will be the file you currently have open in PowerPoint. If you want to package multiple presentation files, select [Add Files...] to browse and include others. PowerPoint will also include linked files, and the PowerPoint viewer. If you want to make additional modifications to what is included click [Options...].
5. Click [Copy to CD]. (You also have the option to copy to a shared folder on the network. If you select [Copy to Folder...], you will need to assign a name to the folder as well as browse to the location where you want to store the package.
6. Click [Close] once the files have been copied to the CD. Be sure to check your packaged presentation before making it available to others as PowerPoint will not embed TrueType fonts that have copyright restrictions.
7. When a user inserts the CD in their computer, it will automatically launch the PowerPoint viewer and the presentation will begin.

tip

To burn to CD, you must have a drive that supports the feature. If you use a CD-R, you will not be able to add more files after the burning process has completed.

tip

Make sure you remove any comments or annotations before packaging if you do not want others to see them.

Figure 6-62 Sharing a folder for presentations

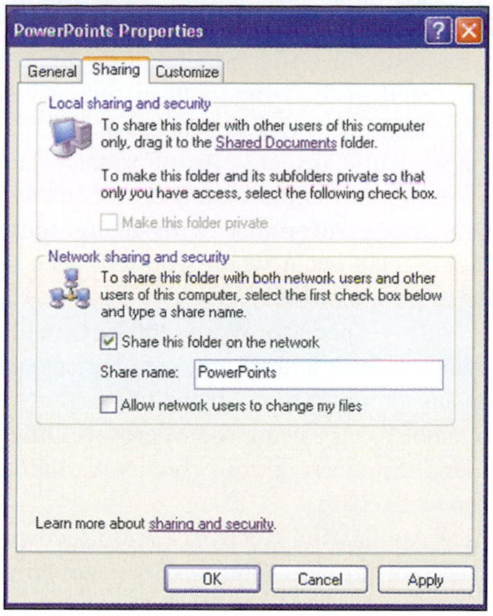

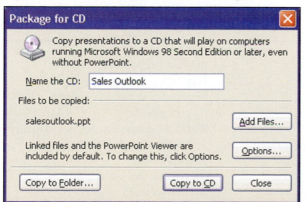

Figure 6-63 File menu's Package for CD command

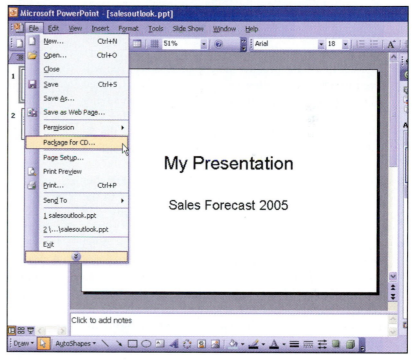

Figure 6-64 Package for CD dialog box

Summary

◆ Microsoft Office 2003 is a software suite that consists of a collection of applications designed to help improve productivity for users in enterprise environments. There are currently six suites that make up the core of the Microsoft Office System (version 11).

◆ As a desktop support technician, you should make sure that the computer on which you are installing Microsoft Office meets the minimum requirements to support the product, is compatible with the operating system on the computer, and that the user or the company has the appropriate licenses and product keys.

◆ Before performing any program installation, create a restore point to enable you to return the computer to a known state if a problem does occur.

◆ Microsoft Office offers the following installation types: Typical, Complete, Minimal, and Custom. Custom allows the most control over the installation process and should be used in most situations.

◆ In order to use the product more than 50 times, you will need to activate it; otherwise, it will go into Reduced Functionality mode, which prevents you from saving modifications to existing documents and creating new documents. Existing documents created before the 50 use limit is reached are not lost however; they can still be read and printed.

◆ Be sure to regularly update Microsoft Office 2003 after completing the installation. The latest updates to the software will provide both additional security and stability.

◆ Although the installation of Microsoft Office 2003 should complete without a problem if you have prepared for installation thoroughly, you may still need to troubleshoot problems related to missing/corrupted files, file copy errors, permission denied errors, and activation problems. Remember, there are logs created during the installation process that can assist you in the troubleshooting process.

◆ Most support requests for Office applications involve adding, removing, and customizing toolbars and menus. Be prepared to perform these types of functions.

◆ AutoSummarize, AutoCorrect, AutoFormat, and AutoText are used to edit and create user documents. Make sure you are comfortable with using these features. Situations may occur where you will need to modify how these features work.

◆ User requests with respect to Word 2003 typically involve modifying toolbars and menus, creating custom toolbars, and using proofing tools. If the user reports a problem you cannot fix, try using the Microsoft Office Online Help and Support option, TechNet, and/or Microsoft's Knowledgebase.

◆ Microsoft Office Application Recovery, AutoRecover, and Open and Repair provide solutions for recovering corrupted files and re-launching applications that have failed to respond. Make sure you are comfortable using these tools.

◆ Excel issues typically revolve around problems with calculations due to incorrect formulas. Make sure you understand how formulas are created in Excel and how Excel uses a predefined order to perform calculations. You may even want to brush up on your math skills!

◆ Make sure you understand how to create macros, launch them from a button and secure them against viruses and other security exploits by configuring the Very High, High, Medium and Low security settings.

◆ Users who work with PowerPoint need to understand how to share their files with others. Be prepared to explain how the Package for CD feature works to both save the support files to a CD or a network folder.

Key Terms

AutoCorrect
AutoFormat
AutoRecover
AutoSummarize
Cabinet (CAB) Files
Document workspaces
Formula
Group Policy
InfoPath 2003
Macros
Microsoft Excel 2003

Microsoft Office Application Recovery
Microsoft Office System
Microsoft Word 2003
Open and Repair
Original Equipment Manufacturer (OEM)
Personalized Menus
PowerPoint viewer
Product activation
Product key

Product license
Program Compatibility Wizard
Reduced Functionality Mode
Restore points
Rights Management Services (RMS)
Smart document
Software suite
System builder license
System Restore
Toolbars
Volume licensing

Test Yourself

1. A user contacts you indicating she is able to view a Word document and print it, but when she tries to modify it she is unable to do so. She cannot create any new Word documents either. What is most likely the problem? (Choose all that apply.)
   a. She has used Word 2003 only 40 times.
   b. She has used Word 2003 only 10 times.
   c. She has used Word 2003 only 50 times.
   d. She has not activated his copy of Word 2003.
   e. None of the above

2. A user is frustrated with the following problem. When he attempts to select a font on the drop-down font list in Word 2003, he cannot see what it will look like before selecting it. He would like to preview the font before including it in the document. What can be done to address the user's concern?
   a. Nothing; this is a feature of Word 2003 that cannot be changed.
   b. Tell the user to go to the Office Update Web site and download the fonts patch.
   c. Select List font names in their font on the Options tab.
   d. Select List font names in their font on the Commands tab.

3. A user has asked you to configure Word 2003 so she can type without seeing any spelling or grammar errors. She will check her document later for errors but finds the current option to be very distracting. Which of the following will address the problem?
   a. Do nothing; the default behavior is to not perform these types of checks.
   b. Select Tools, then click Options and clear the appropriate options on the Edit tab.
   c. Select Tools, then click Options and clear the appropriate options on the Track Changes tab.
   d. Select Tools, then click Options and clear the appropriate options on the Spelling & Grammar tab.

4. You have been asked to move a computer used by a previous employee to another department. Before moving it, you notice that the previous user has made several changes to the Word's built-in Standard toolbar by rearranging the icons. You also notice that the user placed the Save as Web Page first on the File menu. Which options below can be used to remove these changes? (Choose all that apply.)
   a. On the Commands tab in the Customize dialog box, click the Rearrange Commands button. Select Toolbar and choose Menu bar. Select the File menu, and click Reset.

   b. On the Commands tab in the Customize dialog box, click the Reset Commands button. Select Toolbar and choose Menu bar. Select the File menu, and click Reset.
   c. Select the Toolbars tab, make sure the Standard toolbar is highlighted, and click the Reset button.
   d. Select the Toolbars tab, make sure the Standard toolbar is highlighted, and click the Rearrange commands button.

5. Mary, a user in the Human Resources department, is in a panic! She needs to create a document that highlights the main points in a Word 2003 document she received via e-mail regarding a recent employee's dismissal. Which feature can be used to accomplish this?
   a. Configure settings in the AutoCorrect options.
   b. Configure settings in Tools/Options/Track Changes.
   c. Use the AutoSummarize feature.
   d. Word 2003 does not provide this feature.

6. A user has created a presentation in PowerPoint 2003 and would like to share it with others who are both on his local area network and via e-mail with a few users in another company. How would you recommend he do this in the most efficient manner?
   a. Share the folder that contains his presentation on his local hard drive.
   b. Use the Pack and Go feature provided with PowerPoint 2003.
   c. Send them the PowerPoint Viewer.
   d. Use the Package for CD feature provided with PowerPoint 2003.

7. A user is reporting that when she uses Excel, some information is missing from her menus. How can you address the problem? (Choose all that apply.)
   a. Tell the user to wait a moment and the rest of the menu items will appear after shortly.
   b. Remove the feature by selecting Always show full menus under the Options tab in the Customize box.
   c. Tell the user she will need to reinstall Excel to fix the problem.
   d. None of the above.

8. You are troubleshooting several problems that are occurring in PowerPoint 2003, Excel 2003, and Outlook 2003. Which of the following can you use to assist you in finding the problem? (Choose all that apply.)
   a. Microsoft TechNet
   b. Microsoft Knowledgebase
   c. Microsoft Help and Support
   d. Fellow Employees

9. Which of the following represents the correct order Excel 2003 processes calculations?
  a. Exponents, Add and Subtract, Equal to, Multiply and Divide
  b. Add and Subtract, Exponents, Equal to, Multiply and Divide
  c. Exponents, Multiple and Divide, Add and Subtract, Equal to
  d. Exponents, Equal to, Multiply and Divide, Add and Subtract

10. Which of the following are true statements regarding characteristics of the AutoRecover feature? (Choose all that apply.)
  a. It works by periodically saving a temporary copy of the file the user is working on.
  b. The frequency with which the file is saved cannot be configured by the user; by default files are saved every 10 minutes.
  c. Users can control where AutoRecover saves files by going to the File Locations tab which is accessible under Tools, Options.
  d. This is not a feature in Office 2003.

Projects: On Your Own

1. Using Mmsinfo32.exe, determine if your system is capable of supporting Microsoft Office 2003 Professional Edition.
  a. Click **Start**, select **Run**, and enter **msinfo32** in the **Open** text box.
  b. Use the information presented in Table 6-2 in this lesson to determine if your system meets the minimum requirements for the Professional Edition. Make sure **System Summary** is highlighted in the **System Information** dialog box.
  c. For those areas that your system does not meet, research on the Internet how much it would cost you to upgrade your computer.

2. Install a Trial Version of Microsoft Office 2003 Professional Edition and activate it.
  a. Install the trial version into your CD-ROM drive.
  b. Use the step by step information in the How To exercise in Skill 3, "Installing Office 2003 from a CD," as your reference.

Problem Solving Scenarios

1. You receive a call from a small business user who wants to set up Microsoft Office 2003 Professional Edition on her computer. The user is currently running Windows 98 with a Pentium 233 MHz processor and 128 MB RAM. She also has a single hard disk that has a capacity of 60 GB, of which 30 GB of space is free. What recommendations would you make before telling the customer to move to Office 2003?

2. A user reports that the PowerPoint 2003 application has stalled on his computer. When questioned as to the last time he saved the document, he indicates it was an hour ago. What should you suggest he try first?

Supporting Security

Increasing the security of the operating system and applications is one of the key components in Microsoft's new Trustworthy Computing Initiative. Due to the increased risk present in the modern massively networked environment, security is more important than ever. As the speeds of connectivity and processors increase, so does the effectiveness of network hacking tools. Additionally, as the complexity of the operating system and applications increase, so does the potential for security flaws.

To combat these problems, desktop support technicians should have a thorough understanding of system security, including permissions and rights assignments, local policy settings, application security, and best practices. Additionally, desktop support technicians should be aware of how to find and apply updates to Microsoft operating systems to help secure them against commonly known exploits.

This lesson begins with an overview of NTFS permissions and how to secure network resources by assigning permissions to files and folders for every user, whether individually or as a member of a group. You will learn about the types of NTFS permissions and how to apply both standard and special access permissions.

Next you will learn about group membership, how to create and use Windows XP local groups, and how to control security settings in a system's local policy. The lesson also discusses Group Policies, and how they can affect user access to applications and files, as well as determine desktop customization and password policies. You will learn how to investigate Group Policies to determine the source of Group Policy conflicts in your network.

The lesson then discusses how to use Microsoft's Automatic Updates to apply critical updates to the Windows XP operating system and how to install these updates manually. You will also learn how to manage and troubleshoot the security settings in Microsoft Office applications. Finally, you will learn about security-conscious procedures to use while assisting others and how to educate users on important security precautions.

Goals

In this lesson, you will learn how to analyze and configure permissions and rights in Windows XP. Additionally, you will learn how to configure system security settings, apply critical updates, and manage application security.

Lesson 7   Supporting Security

Skill	Exam 70-272 Objective
1. Working with NTFS File and Folder Permissions	**Identify and troubleshoot problems related to security permissions.** Troubleshoot access to local resources. Troubleshoot access to network resources. Troubleshoot insufficient user permissions and rights.
2. Understanding Group Membership	**Identify and troubleshoot problems related to security permissions.** Troubleshoot access to local resources. Troubleshoot access to network resources. Troubleshoot insufficient user permissions and rights.
3. Understanding Group Policy	**Resolve issues related to operating system features. Tasks include operating configuring system features and interpreting error messages.**
4. Configuring and Troubleshooting Local Security Settings	**Resolve issues related to operating system features. Tasks include configuring operating system features and interpreting error messages.**
5. Implementing Critical Updates	**Identify and respond to security incidents.** Apply critical updates.
6. Managing Application Security Settings	**Identify and troubleshoot problems related to security permissions.** Answer end-user questions related to application security settings. **Manage application security settings**
7. Supporting Users in a Security-Conscious Manner	**Identify and respond to security incidents.** Answer end-user questions related to security incidents.

Requirements

To complete this lesson, you will need administrative rights on a Windows XP Professional computer. To complete the How To exercise in Skill 5, Automatic Updates must be installed on the computer.

skill 1 | *Working with NTFS File and Folder Permissions*

Identify and troubleshoot problems related to security permissions. Troubleshoot access to local resources. Troubleshoot access to network resources. Troubleshoot insufficient user permissions and rights.

overview

In addition to shared folder permissions, you can assign **NTFS permissions** to restrict unauthorized access to shared files and folders. NTFS permissions enable you to secure network resources by controlling the level of access to files and folders for each user. For example, you can set up permissions to allow a user only to read the contents of a file or to modify the contents of the file. Additionally, unlike share permissions, NTFS permissions apply to local users as well.

There are two types of NTFS permissions: **NTFS folder permissions** and **NTFS file permissions**. **Table 7-1** describes standard NTFS folder permissions and **Table 7-2** describes standard NTFS file permissions.

Note that when you apply permissions to a drive or folder, you are also applying those permissions to all files and folders underneath it by default. You can change this behavior in the **Advanced Security Settings** dialog box (**Figure 7-1**) for the folder. To do so, right-click the folder in Windows Explorer and click **Sharing and Security** on the pop-up menu to open the folder's **Properties** dialog box. On the Security tab, click the **Advanced** button to open the Advanced Security Settings dialog box. Clear the **Inherit from parent the permission entries that apply to child objects. Include these with entries specifically defined here** check box. Once this is done, a message box will ask you to copy or remove the permissions. If you choose **Copy**, the permissions that are currently being inherited will remain, but the check boxes for these permissions will no longer be grayed out, meaning they can be changed. If you choose **Remove**, all inherited permissions will be immediately removed. Either way, any new permissions set on the folder's parent object will no longer be inherited by the folder or any child objects.

In addition to the standard NTFS permissions, you can assign **special access permissions**. These special NTFS permissions provide a more precise level of control over users' ability to access shared resources. When assigning NTFS permissions, you should refer to the following guidelines:

◆ Create folders to organize your data into categories. For example, you can create application folders, data folders, and a home folder for users to store their files on the file server. This simplifies the task of assigning permissions and of backing up data because all related data will be in one location.

◆ When you are defining the level of permission, always assign users the lowest level of permissions required for them to perform their jobs to protect data from being inadvertently changed or deleted.

◆ Assign the Read and Write permissions to the Users group. The Creator Owner group is assigned the Full Control permission by default. This allows users to change and delete only those files and folders that they create and to read files created by other users.

◆ Avoid assigning the Full Control permission for a folder. Instead, you can assign other permissions, such as Read & Execute or Modify, to ensure that users do not accidentally delete any important data.

◆ Denying permissions should be used sparingly. The Deny condition is useful in cases where you must temporarily lock out particular users. As a general rule, however, you should assign the lowest level of permission that allows users to conduct their work efficiently and avoid using the Deny condition.

◆ Assign permissions to groups rather than to individual user accounts to simplify permission administration.

Table 7-1   Standard NTFS folder permissions

NTFS Folder Permission	Description
Read	Users can open and view the content of files, folders, and subfolders. They can also view the ownership of objects, permissions assigned to objects, and the various folder attributes, such as Read-Only, Hidden, Archive, and System.
Write	Users can create new files and subfolders in a folder. This permission also allows users to view folder ownership, the assigned permissions, and to use the Properties dialog box to change folder attributes.
List Folder Contents	Users can view only the names of subfolders and files in a folder.
Read & Execute	This permission includes the tasks permitted by the Read and List Folder Contents permissions and gives users the ability to navigate through folders for which they do not have permission to get to files and folders for which they do have permissions.
Modify	Users can view, create, delete, and modify the content of folders, as well as change attributes. This permission includes all tasks permitted by the Read, Write, and Read & Execute permissions.
Full Control	Users can change permissions and take ownership of folders. This permission includes all actions that are permitted by all other NTFS permissions and is usually only granted to administrators.

Table 7-2   Standard NTFS file permissions

NTFS File Permission	Description
Read	Users can read the file and view the file attributes, file ownership, and permissions.
Write	Users can change the file, change file attributes, and view file ownerships and permissions.
Read & Execute	Users can view the contents of files and run program applications.
Modify	Users can modify and delete the file, run applications, change attributes, and perform all other actions permitted by the Write and Read & Execute permissions.
Full Control	Users can change permissions, take ownership, and perform all actions permitted by the other NTFS permissions.

Figure 7-1 Advanced Security Settings dialog box

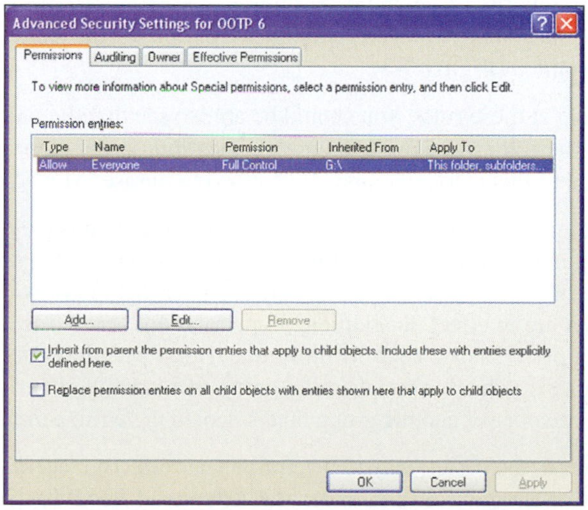

skill 1

Working with NTFS File and Folder Permissions (cont'd)

Identify and troubleshoot problems related to security permissions. Troubleshoot access to local resources. Troubleshoot access to network resources. Troubleshoot insufficient user permissions and rights.

overview

In addition, you must understand the following factors:

◆ **NTFS permissions can be inherited**: Files and folders inherit the permissions assigned to the parent folder by default. However, you can prevent this by setting permissions for individual files and folders that are different from those assigned to the parent folder.

◆ **Assign multiple NTFS permissions**: In addition to assigning permissions to a user account, you can assign permissions to the group to which the user belongs, thus giving them multiple permissions. To determine the permission level for a particular user, you must combine all the permissions assigned. For example, if a user has been assigned the Write permission and belongs to a group having the Read permission, that user will have both the Read and the Write permissions for that file or folder.

◆ **NTFS file permissions override NTFS folder permissions**: If a user does not have access permissions to a folder, but has permissions to access files within that folder, then that user can open those files by typing the full Universal Naming Convention (UNC). The syntax for specifying UNC is \\servername\sharename, where servername is the name of the server and sharename is the name of the shared resource.

◆ **A denied permission overrides an allowed permission**: When you deny a permission to a user, you restrict that permission from the user. For example, if you deny a user the Modify permission for a specific file, this restricts the user from modifying the contents of the file, even if the user is a member of a group that is assigned the Full Control permission for the file.

One other aspect with which you must be familiar is the process by which permissions are inherited when moving or copying files. For instance, if a file or folder is moved from the C: drive to the D: drive, how are permissions affected? There are several rules that determine what happens to the original permissions configured on the file or folder:

◆ If the folder is moved to a FAT partition, all permissions are lost.
◆ If the folder is copied to a FAT partition, permissions on the copy are lost.
◆ If the folder is moved to another NTFS partition, permissions are inherited from the parent folder **(Figure 7-2)**.
◆ If the folder is copied to another NTFS partition, permissions are inherited from the folder above.
◆ If the folder is copied to another location on the same NTFS partition, permissions are inherited from the parent folder.
◆ If the folder is moved to another location on the same NTFS partition, permissions are retained **(Figure 7-3)**.

Looking at these rules, you should be able to see that the only time permissions are retained is when the folder is moved to another location on the same NTFS partition. An easy way to remember this is to remember the following phrase: Moved to same, permissions remain.

The most common indicator of a permissions problem is the Access denied error message when attempting to access a file or folder. When you receive this error, your first task is to determine the permissions applied to the file. Remember that not only the permissions applied directly to the user are in effect. In addition, all permissions applied to any group the user is a member of also apply. Finally, keep in mind that Deny permissions override allow permissions. For example, if you are a member of a group that has full control permission for a file, but you are also a member of another group that is denied the write permission, you cannot write to the file.

In general, the easiest way to determine your **effective permissions** to a resource is to view the Effective Permissions tab under the **Advanced Security Settings** dialog box **(Figure 7-4)**.

Figure 7-2 Inherited NTFS permissions

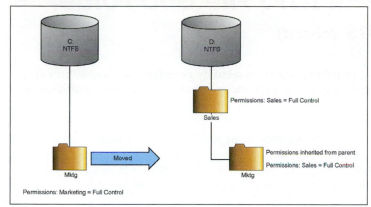

Figure 7-3 Retained NTFS permissions

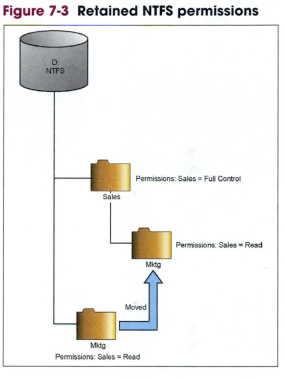

Figure 7-4 Advanced Security Settings dialog box

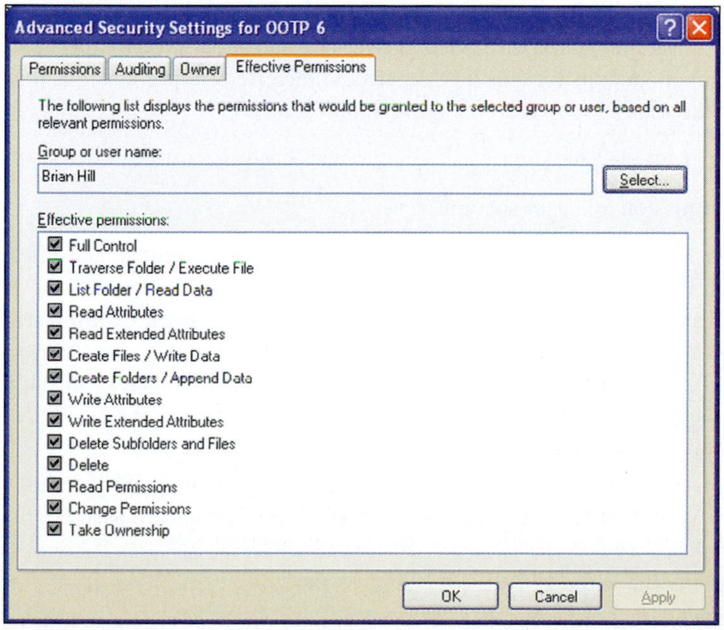

skill 1   *Working with NTFS File and Folder Permissions (cont'd)*

exam objective

Identify and troubleshoot problems related to security permissions. Troubleshoot access to local resources. Troubleshoot access to network resources. Troubleshoot insufficient user permissions and rights.

overview

To access this tab, simply open the **Properties** dialog box for the file or folder, then select the **Security** tab (**Figure 7-5**). Click the **Advanced** button at the bottom to open the **Advanced Security Settings** dialog box (**Figure 7-6**). Finally, select the **Effective Permissions** tab, click the **Select** button, and type the name of the user you want to examine (**Figure 7-7**).

Finally, when troubleshooting permissions, consider the following points:

◆ Verify that permissions have been assigned to the user account and check to see if any permission denials have been entered that are overriding the assigned permissions. You must also check for denials assigned to the groups to which the user is a member.
◆ Sometimes, permissions will change when files and folders are transferred across volumes because they inherit permissions from the folder to which they have been moved or copied. Therefore, you must also verify the permissions assigned to the user for that file or the folder.
◆ If a resource is local, shared permissions are immaterial, and only NTFS permissions must be checked. However, if the resource is remote rather than local, you can apply both shared folder and NTFS permissions, so you must check both the share-level and the NTFS permissions for the file or folder. In such cases, the most restrictive permissions apply to the resource. One effective way to handle this is to create shared folders and set the share permissions to Full Control for the Everyone group. Then use NTFS permissions to secure the resources. Because the most restrictive permission applies, as long as you have fine-tuned your NTFS permissions so that groups have the appropriate level of access, your resources will be secure. Additionally, because NTFS permissions operate locally, you can be confident that security for files and folders on the computers on which they are stored is effective, even when more than one user accesses the computer.
◆ Sometimes, a user will not be able to access a file or folder after you have added the user to a group. This problem can occur because the access token has not been updated. An access token stores data about the groups of which a user is a member, and it is created each time he or she logs on. For the access token to be updated, have the user log off and log back on again.
◆ One new tool in Windows Server 2003 and Windows XP that is extremely helpful in troubleshooting NTFS permissions issues is the Effective Permissions tab in the Advanced Security Settings dialog box, discussed above. This tab allows you to query the file system and group memberships for a user to determine the effective permissions that user has, taking all of the user's group memberships into account.

how to

Assign the Write NTFS permission to a user account.

1. Right-click any folder located on an NTFS partition in **Windows Explorer** and click **Properties** to open the **Properties** dialog box for the folder.
2. Click the **Security** tab and then click [Add...] to open the **Select Users, Computers, or Groups** dialog box.
3. Type the name of the Administrator account in the Select Users, Computers, or Groups dialog box and click [Add].
4. Click [OK] to close the Select Users, Computers, or Groups dialog box.
5. Select the **Allow** check box for the **Write** permission (**Figure 7-8**). Note that by default, the Read & Execute, List Folder Contents, and Read NTFS permissions are assigned to the user account.
6. Click [OK] to assign the Write permission to the account.
7. Close Windows Explorer.

Figure 7-5 **Security tab**

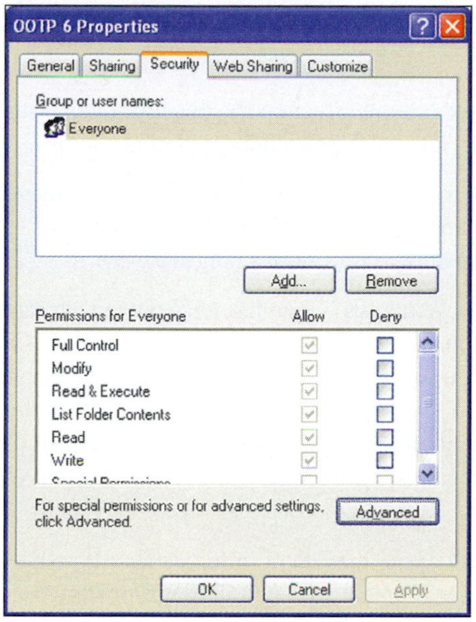

Figure 7-6 **Advanced Security Settings dialog box**

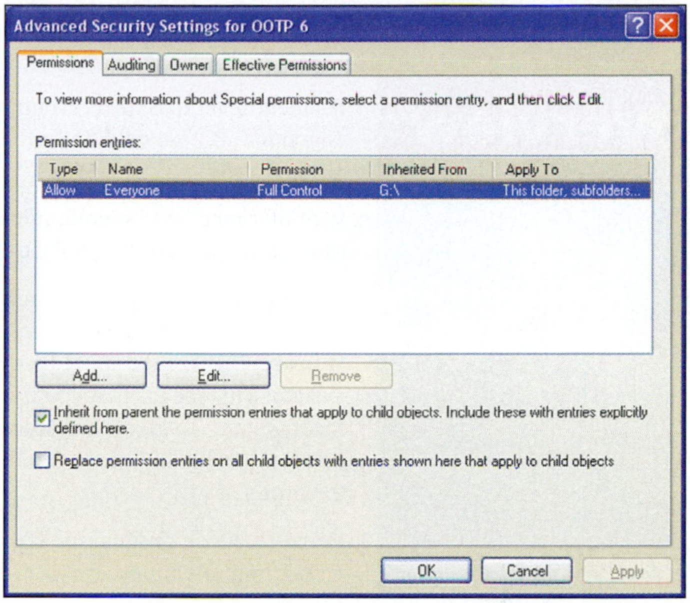

Figure 7-7 **Effective Permissions tab**

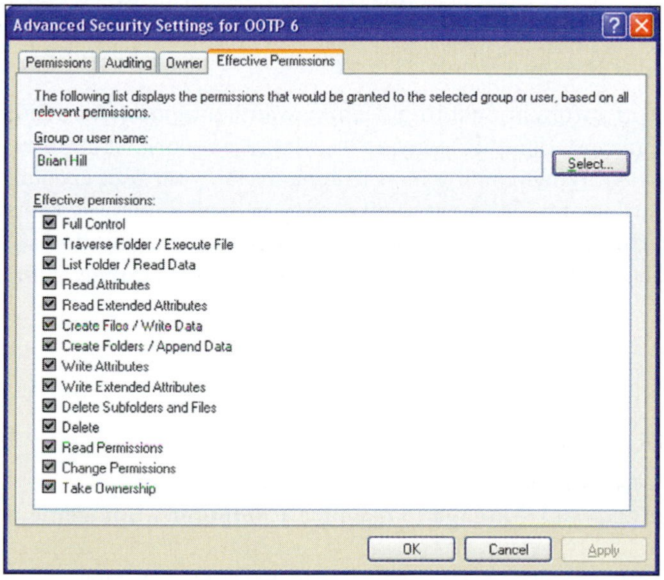

Figure 7-8 **Allowing the Write permission**

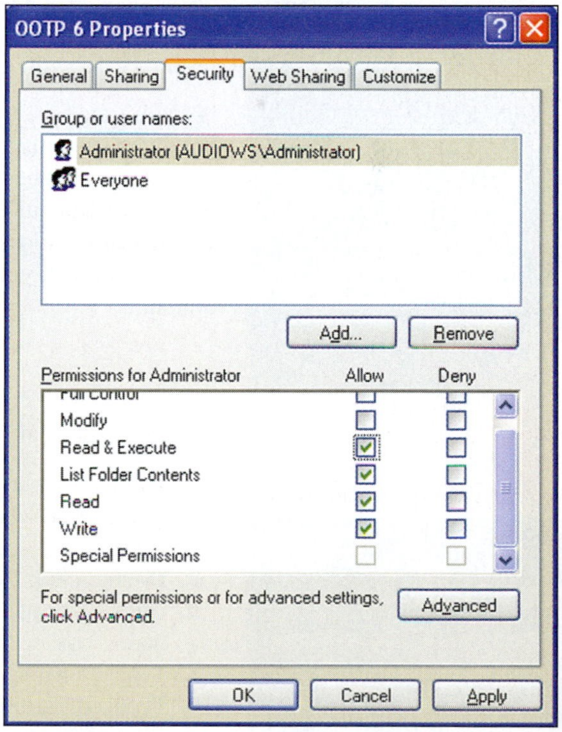

skill 2 *Understanding Group Membership*

Identify and troubleshoot problems related to security permissions. Troubleshoot access to local resources. Troubleshoot access to network resources. Troubleshoot insufficient user permissions and rights.

overview

As mentioned in Skill 1, group membership can have a large effect on the permissions a user is granted. Before delving further into this, however, let's examine what a group is.

A **group** is an object used to apply permissions to many users at once. By organizing users with the same access requirements into groups and applying permissions to the group instead of to each user, you can reduce the effort required to apply permissions (**Figure 7-9**).

Local groups are the only available group type on a Windows XP computer. You can access, create, and modify local groups through the Computer Management snap-in in Windows XP (**Figure 7-10**). Like local user accounts, local group accounts are valid only on the local system. This means that you use local groups to give users access to resources located on the local system. To give users access to resources located on a remote system, you would need to create a local group on the remote system and add local user accounts on the remote system to the group.

Because local groups are only locally significant, you may encounter difficulty when attempting to gain access to a remote resource. For example, examine the diagram shown in **Figure 7-11**. If Bob logs on to PC 1, he can access resources on PC1 for which either he or Group 1 has permissions. However, when he attempts to access PC2, his access will fail because PC2 does not have a local user account named Bob. To allow seamless access to PC2, you must create a local user account on PC2 named Bob that uses the same password as the Bob account on PC1. You can then add the Bob account on PC2 to Group 1 on PC2 to give the account access to the remote resource. Then, when Bob on PC1 attempts to access the resource on PC2, he will automatically be logged in as Bob on PC2. Because the Bob account on PC2 is a member of Group 1 on PC2, and this group has been given permissions to the resource, Bob will now be able to access the resource.

As you can see, there is a lot of effort in enabling seamless authentication to occur between systems using local groups. For this reason, in a large network, it is often considerably easier to use a domain. When you log in as a domain user, your user account is now valid on all systems in the domain. This means you can log in to all domain systems without any additional effort. This also means that your user account (and any domain groups to which you are a member) can be given access to resources on any systems in the domain.

tip
For more information on domains and domain groups, please see the Prentice Hall Certification Series Exam 70-290 textbook.

how to

Create a new local group on your Windows XP system.

1. Log on to your system as an **Administrator**.
2. Right-click **My Computer** and click **Manage** to open the **Computer Management** console.
3. Double-click **Local Users and Groups** to view the subfolders in the Details pane.
4. Click **Groups**, open the **Action** menu, and click **New Group** to open the **New Group** dialog box.
5. Type the name of the new group, **Managers**, in the **Group name** text box.
6. Type a description for the group, **Mid-level managers**, in the **Description** text box.
7. Click [Add...] to open the **Select Users or Groups** dialog box.
8. Type **Administrator** in the **Enter the Object Names to Select** prompt (**Figure 7-12**).

caution
Local group names cannot contain the following characters / \ [ ] : ; | = , + * ? < >.

Figure 7-9 Using groups to reduce the administrative effort of applying permissions

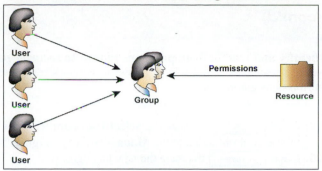

Figure 7-10 Computer Management snap-in

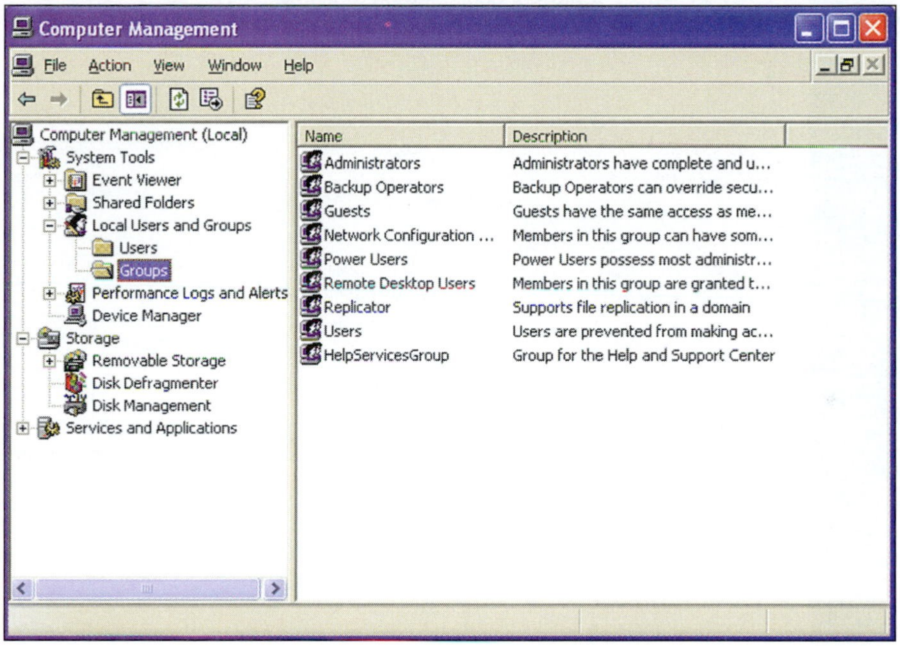

Figure 7-11 Permissions example

Figure 7-12 Selecting the Administrator account

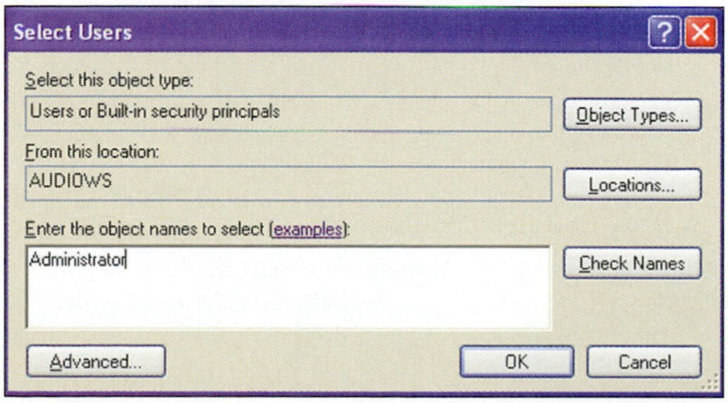

skill 2

Understanding Group Membership
(cont'd)

exam objective

Identify and troubleshoot problems related to security permissions. Troubleshoot access to local resources. Troubleshoot access to network resources. Troubleshoot insufficient user permissions and rights.

how to

9. Click [OK] to close the **Select Users and Groups** dialog box. The **Administrator** user account is added to the **Managers** group **(Figure 7-13)**.
10. Click [Create] to create the new local group.
11. Click [Close] to close the New Group dialog box. The new local group appears in the Groups folder in the Computer Management console **(Figure 7-14)**.
12. Close the Computer Management console.

**Figure 7-13 Adding the Administrator account
to the Managers group**

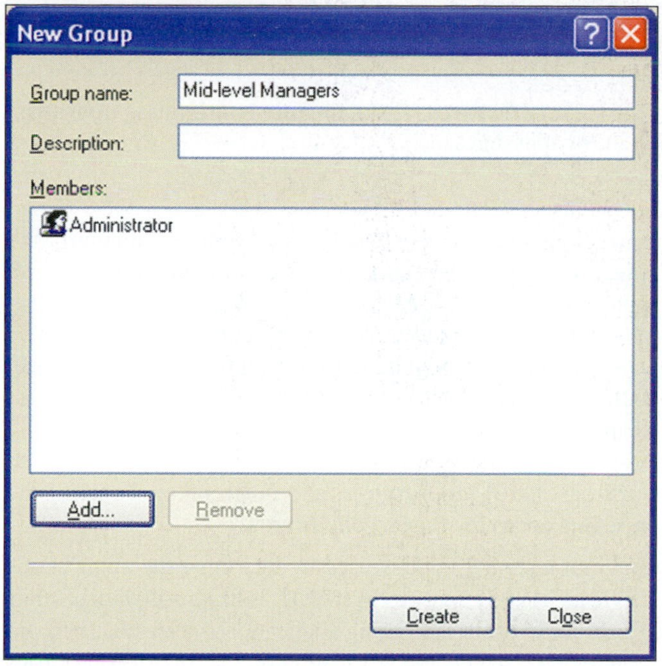

Figure 7-14 The new local group

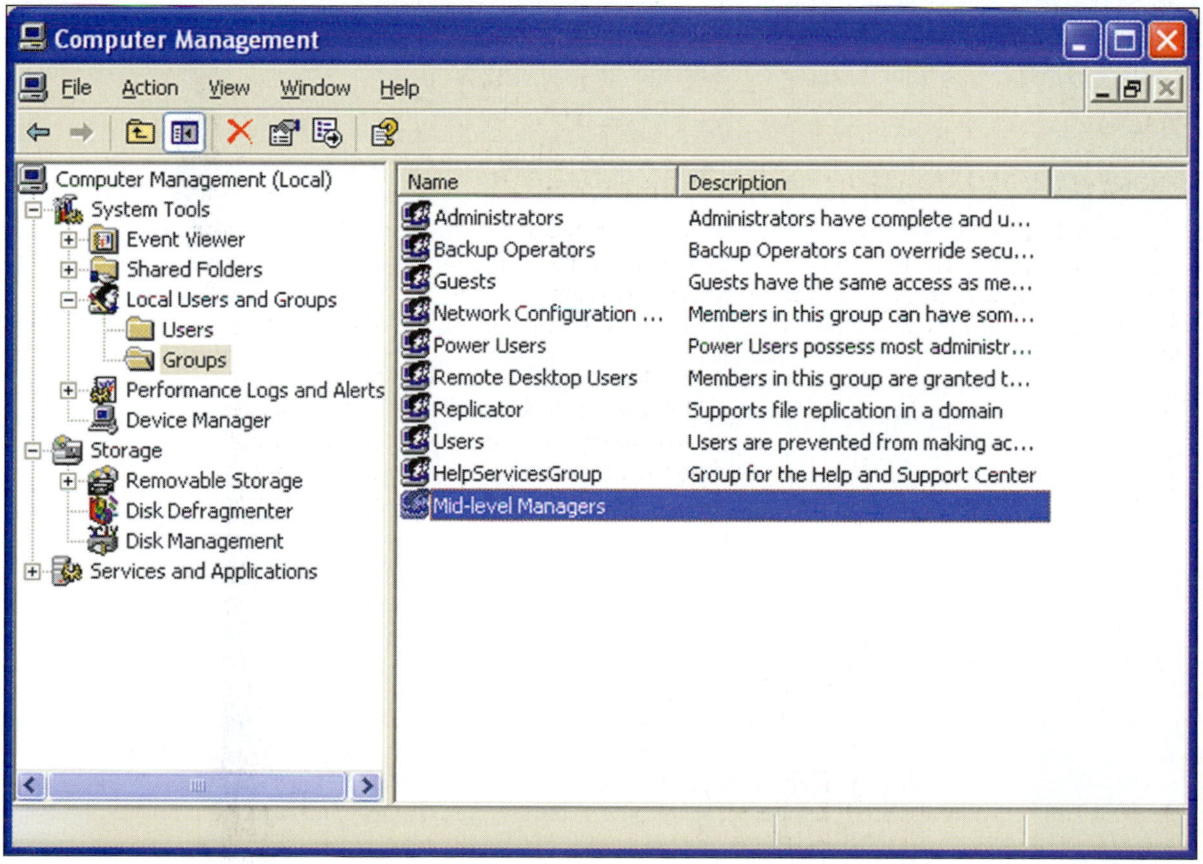

skill 3

Understanding Group Policy

exam objective

Resolve issues related to operating system features. Tasks include configuring operating system features and interpreting error messages.

overview

Group Policies are used to enhance and secure the work environment for users. Most Group Policy settings are associated with the Registry. You can create Group Policies to control the installation of applications on the user's computer. You can also use Group Policies to automate tasks when a user logs on to a computer. In an Active Directory environment, there are different types of Group Policies categorized according to the different network components and Active Directory objects they influence. Group Policies are located in the Group Policy snap-in. You can use the Group Policy snap-in to modify the default settings for Group Policies according to your requirements. The Group Policy snap-in is divided into a Computer Configuration node and a User Configuration node. Group Policy settings that affect the computer environment implement changes in the operating system settings, hardware, services, and much more. Some of the different **Computer Configuration** setting nodes for Group Policies are:

◆ **Software Settings**: This configuration setting node is used to determine the applications that will be distributed to users via a Group Policy object (GPO). You use software settings to either assign or publish applications to users. Assigning applications means that they are set to install automatically when the user selects the application on the Start menu or tries to open a document created in the program. Publishing applications means that a list of applications that the user can install using the Add/Remove Programs utility will display in Active Directory.

◆ **Windows Settings**: This node contains two divisions for computers: Scripts and Security Settings (**Figure 7-15**). **Scripts** are used to assign scripts and batch files that are configured to run at specific times, such as during system startup or shutdown. You can use scripts to automate repetitive tasks such as logon and logoff for users and system startup and shutdown for computers. **Security Settings** are used to configure computers on your network to use IP security and to specify settings for everything from user rights to system services. Account lockout policy, password policy, user rights, audit policy, public key access, Registry and Event Log access, and system service operation are all controlled in the Security Settings node (**Figure 7-16**).

◆ **Administrative Templates**: This node is used to regulate Registry settings that control the behavior and appearance of the desktop and other Windows 2003 Server components and applications. There are four folders under Administrative Templates: **Windows Components**, **System**, **Network**, and **Printers**. The Windows Components folder contains subfolders for NetMeeting, Internet Explorer, Task Scheduler, and Windows Installer. In the NetMeeting folder, you can set a Group Policy that disables remote desktop sharing, or you can disable the ability to run tasks on an individual computer in the Task Scheduler folder. In the System folder, there are subfolders for Logon, Disk Quotas, DNS Client, Group Policy, and Windows File Protection. In the Logon subfolder, you can have the operating system notify users when a slow network link is detected. You can set policies to control the use of Offline Folders in the Network folder. There are literally hundreds of Group Policy settings you can configure in this node.

Group Policy settings that affect the user environment include shortcuts, color schemes, access to Control Panel utilities, and other desktop settings. As with the Computer Configuration node, there are three main **User Configuration** settings nodes: Software Settings, Windows Settings, and Administrative Templates. Within the **Windows Setting** node, there are five folders: Internet Explorer Maintenance, Scripts, Security Settings, Remote Installation Services, and Folder Redirection. Remote Installation Services Group Policies are used to control the RIS installation options available to the user when the Client Installation Wizard is initiated. Folder Redirection Group Policies are used to relocate special folders, such as My Documents, Start Menu, or Desktop. You can redirect these folders from their default locations in a user profile to alternate locations. They can be managed from a central location, accessed when the user is roaming, or made available in an offline folder when the user is not connected to the network.

Figure 7-15 **Windows settings node**

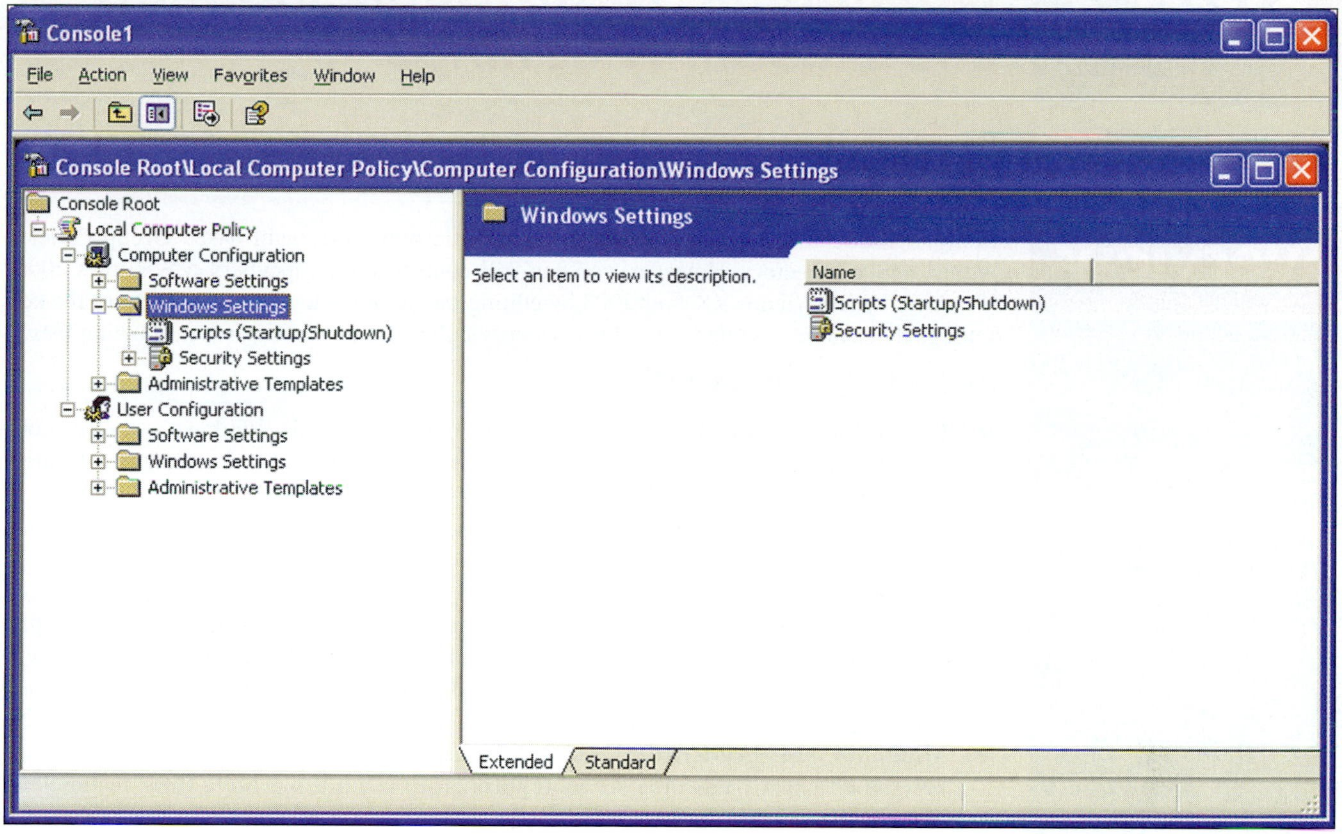

Figure 7-16 **Security Settings node**

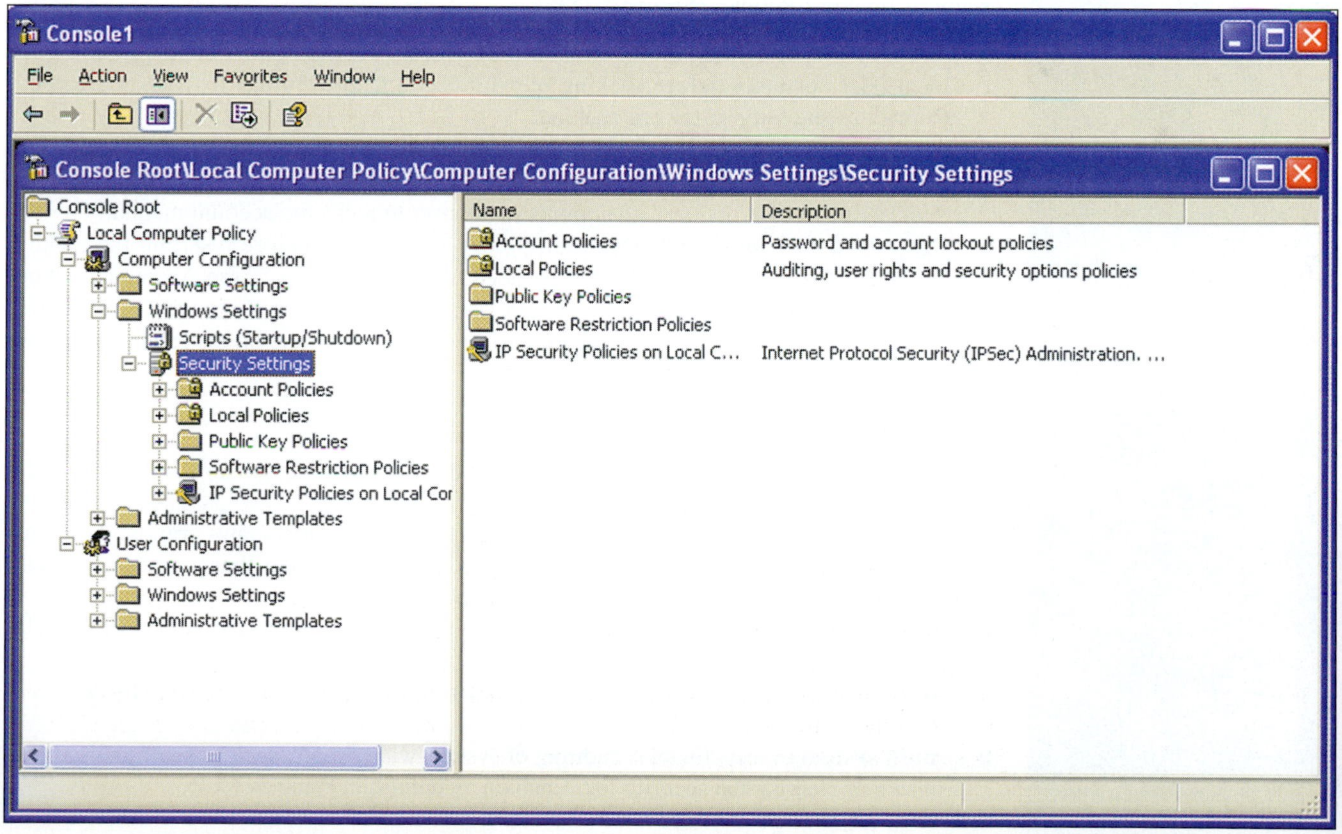

skill 4

Configuring and Troubleshooting Local Security Settings

exam objective

Resolve issues related to operating system features. Tasks include configuring operating system features and interpreting error messages.

overview

Many of the features of Group Policy are available only in domain-based Group Policies within Active Directory. However, you can still control many aspects of a Windows 2000, Windows XP, or Windows Server 2003 by editing the system's local policy. Some of the key settings that can be modified in the local security policy are discussed in the following lists.

Password Policies (Figure 7-17):

- **Enforce password history**: Determines how many passwords Windows will remember for local user accounts. Forces users to create new passwords each time they change their password, instead of using the same password over and over.
- **Maximum password age**: Determines how many days can elapse before you are required to change your password for local user accounts. Forces users to change passwords at regular intervals.
- **Minimum password age**: Determines the minimum number of days that must elapse before you are allowed to change your password for local user accounts. Prevents users from circumventing the Enforce Password History policy by changing the password several times in rapid succession.
- **Minimum password length**: Defines the minimum length of passwords for local user accounts. Longer passwords are more difficult to crack using brute force techniques. The maximum value for this setting is 14.
- **Password must meet complexity requirements**: If enabled, this setting forces the user to utilize three of the following four character types in each password: Uppercase letters (R), lowercase letters (r), numbers (9), and symbols (@). This setting greatly decreases the likelihood of brute force techniques cracking a password.

Account Lockout Policies (Figure 7-18):

- **Account lockout threshold**: Determines how many failed logon attempts to allow for local user accounts before locking out the account, preventing it from being used. Combats brute force password hacking.
- **Account lockout duration**: Determines how long (in minutes) an account is locked out for after the Account Lockout Threshold has been eclipsed. Configuring this setting to 0 locks the account out until an administrative user unlocks the account manually.
- **Reset lockout count after**: Determines how long to wait before resetting the lockout counter if the user does not lock their account. For example, if the Account Lockout Threshold is set to 3, the Reset Lockout Counter After is set to 5 minutes, and the user mistypes the password twice, if the user waits for 5 minutes, he or she can try two more times without locking out the account.

Audit Policies (Figure 7-19):

- **Audit logon events**: Enables auditing whenever a user logs on to the local system. Enabled by default in Windows XP.
- **Audit object access**: Enables auditing of access to files, folders, and printers. You must also manually configure auditing on each file, folder, or printer that you want to audit. File and folder auditing is supported only on NTFS partitions.
- **Audit policy change**: Enables auditing of modifications to the Local Policy. Enabled by default in Windows XP.
- **Audit privilege use**: Enables auditing of use of rights or privileges. Enabled by default in Windows XP.
- **Audit system events**: Enables auditing of system-wide events, such as shutting down the system or clearing the security log. Enabled by default in Windows XP.

tip

Windows 2000 and greater can support up to 127-character passwords.

Figure 7-17 Password Policy

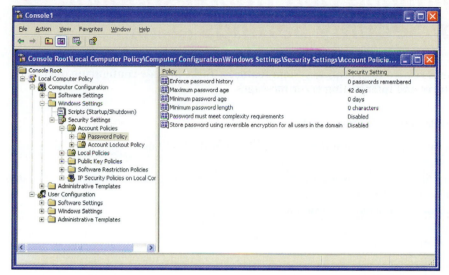

Figure 7-18 Account Lockout Policy

Figure 7-19 Audit Policy

skill 4

Configuring and Troubleshooting Local Security Settings (cont'd)

exam objective

Resolve issues related to operating system features. Tasks include configuring operating system features and interpreting error messages.

overview

User Rights Assignment (Figure 7-20):

◆ **Access this computer from the network**: Enables the listed users and groups to access the computer remotely.

◆ **Back up files and directories**: Enables the listed users and groups to back up any file on the system, regardless of permissions settings.

◆ **Log on locally**: Enables the listed users and groups to access the computer by locally logging on.

◆ **Manage auditing and security log**: Allows the listed users and groups to read and clear events from the security log, as well as change the configuration of the security log.

◆ **Restore files and directories**: Allows the listed users and groups to restore any file or directory to the system, regardless of permissions settings.

◆ **Shut down the system**: Allows the listed users and groups to shut down or restart the system.

◆ **Take ownership of files and other objects**: Allows the listed users and groups to take ownership of any object, regardless of permissions.

Security Options (Figure 7-21):

◆ **Accounts: Administrator account status**: Determines the account status (enabled or disabled) of the Administrator account.

◆ **Accounts: Guest account status**: Determines the account status (enabled or disabled) of the Guest account.

◆ **Accounts: Limit local use of blank passwords to console logons only**: Determines if blank passwords are allowed when logging on to a console session from a remote system (for instance, when using Remote Desktop). This does not affect the use of blank passwords when logging on locally.

◆ **Accounts: Rename administrator account**: Renames the Administrator account to the entered name.

◆ **Accounts: Rename guest account**: Renames the Guest account to the entered name.

◆ **Devices: Unsigned driver installation behavior**: Determines whether the user is blocked, allowed, or the user is warned but allowed to continue when installing unsigned drivers.

◆ **Interactive Logon: Do not display last user name**: Clears the name of the last user to log on from the Logon dialog box. This setting only functions in Windows XP when the system is using the classic style logon.

◆ **Interactive Logon: Do not require CTRL+ALT+DEL**: Disables the requirement of pressing [Ctrl]+[Alt]+[Del] when logging on. This setting functions only in Windows XP when the system is using the classic style logon.

◆ **Shutdown: Allow system to be shut down without having to log on**: Allows the system to be shut down without requiring the user to log on.

As you can see, there are a number of Group Policy settings that can greatly affect the operation of the system. In fact, Windows XP supports over 700 individual policy settings, though some of these settings can be configured only when in an Active Directory domain.

Perhaps the best way of examining the vast array of Group Policy options is to examine the policy settings. Windows XP includes excellent Group Policy help which explains each Group Policy setting in easy to understand language. To do this, you must first open the local policy by opening a new Microsoft Management Console (MMC) and adding the Group Policy snap-in. (See the How To exercise following this Overview.) Next, select the policy setting on which you want more information and examine the details pane (**Figure 7-22**). As

Figure 7-20 User Rights Assignment

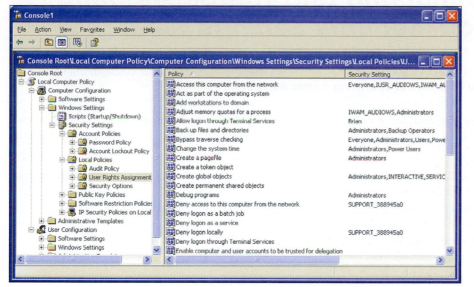

Figure 7-21 Security Options

Figure 7-22 information display

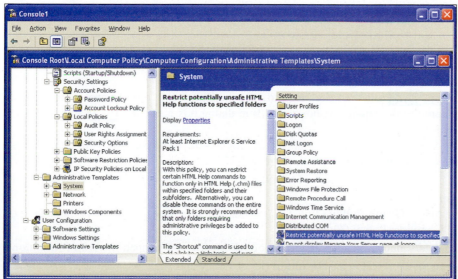

skill 4

Configuring and Troubleshooting Local Security Settings *(cont'd)*

exam objective

Resolve issues related to operating system features. Tasks include configuring operating system features and interpreting error messages.

overview

you can see, Microsoft provides ample information about each policy setting. Alternately, you can view the same help text by double-clicking the policy setting and selecting the **Explain** tab (**Figure 7-23**).

Knowing how to find the description of each Group Policy setting will go a long way toward helping you resolve problems related to Group Policy. However, in some cases, the problem the user is experiencing may be set by a Group Policy configured in Active Directory, which will not be shown in the Local Policy console. To determine if this is the case, you will need to use a few other tools: Gpresult.exe, Resultant Set of Policy (RSoP), and Group Policy Management Console (GPMC).

Gpresult.exe is the simplest of these tools, and simply displays which policies are applied to the computer and user account. Gpresult.exe can be useful when you already know which settings are configured in each policy, and simply want to see which ones are being applied, but because it does not show each individual policy setting, it is much less useful than the other tools. To access Gpresult.exe, simply type **gpresult** in a Command Prompt window (**Figure 7-24**).

A useful new MMC console in Windows 2003 is **RSoP**, which enables you to visually examine the application of Group Policy. To use RSoP, you must open a MMC and create a new console. You then query Active Directory for the Group Policies applying to a specific level of the hierarchy or, alternately, a specific object. RSoP then returns a list of all Group Policy settings, shows you the configuration for that setting, and tells you the Group Policy that configured that particular setting. RSoP is an extremely useful tool in troubleshooting Group Policy application, allowing you to quickly and easily determine the source of the GPO conflicts in your network. RSoP is installed by default in Windows XP, and can be added through the Add Standalone Snap-in dialog box in MMC (**Figure 7-25**).

The final tool for troubleshooting Group Policy, **GPMC**, is primarily used by administrators in a domain environment. GPMC performs many of the same functions as RSoP. However, GPMC does so in a more user-friendly environment and also adds Group Policy linking, creation, deletion, import/export, and modification functionality. GPMC does not come installed in any operating system, and must be downloaded from the following address: **http://www.microsoft.com/windowsserver2003/gpmc/gpmcintro.mspx**.

how to

Add the Group Policy and RSoP snap-ins to a custom console.

1. Boot the system and log on as a local administrator.
2. Click **start** and then click **Run** to open the **Run** dialog box (**Figure 7-26**).
3. Type **mmc** in the **Open** text box in the Run dialog box and click **OK** to open a new MMC console.
4. Click **File** on the menu bar and then click **Add/Remove Snap-in** to open the **Add/Remove Snap-in** dialog box (**Figure 7-27**).
5. Click **Add...** to open the **Add Standalone Snap-in** dialog box (**Figure 7-28**). Locate **Group Policy** and click **Add**.
6. In the **Select Group Policy Object** dialog box, click **Finish** to accept the default of Local Computer Policy (**Figure 7-29**).
7. In the Add/Remove Snap-in dialog box, click **Add...** to open the **Add Standalone Snap-in** dialog box. Locate **Resultant Set of Policy** and click **Add**.

Figure 7-23 Explain tab

Figure 7-24 Gpresult

Figure 7-25 Adding the RsoP snap-in

Figure 7-26 Run dialog box

Figure 7-28 Add Standalone Snap-in dialog box

Figure 7-27 Add/Remove Snap-in dialog box

Figure 7-29 Accepting the default Local Computer Policy

skill 4

Configuring and Troubleshooting Local Security Settings (cont'd)

exam objective

Resolve issues related to operating system features. Tasks include configuring operating system features and interpreting error messages.

how to

8. Click [OK] to close the Add/Remove Snap-in dialog box.

9. Expand the Local Computer Policy snap-in and explore the settings, but be very careful that you do not accidentally change any settings. Use the built-in help to learn about the effects of the different settings.

10. Right-click **Resultant Set of Policy** and select **Generate RSoP Data** to open the **Resultant Set of Policy Wizard (Figure 7-30)**.

11. Click [Next >] through each screen of the wizard to accept the default settings. Click [Finish] when complete.

12. Expand the user name or computer name in the left pane of the console and then expand the **Computer** section **(Figure 7-31)**. This is where you will see policy settings applied to the computer account. If no domain-based Group Policies are effecting your computer, however, each policy setting will be listed as Not Configured.

13. When finished, close MMC. Click [No] when prompted to save console settings.

14. Close all open dialog boxes and log off of the system.

Figure 7-30 The RSoP Wizard

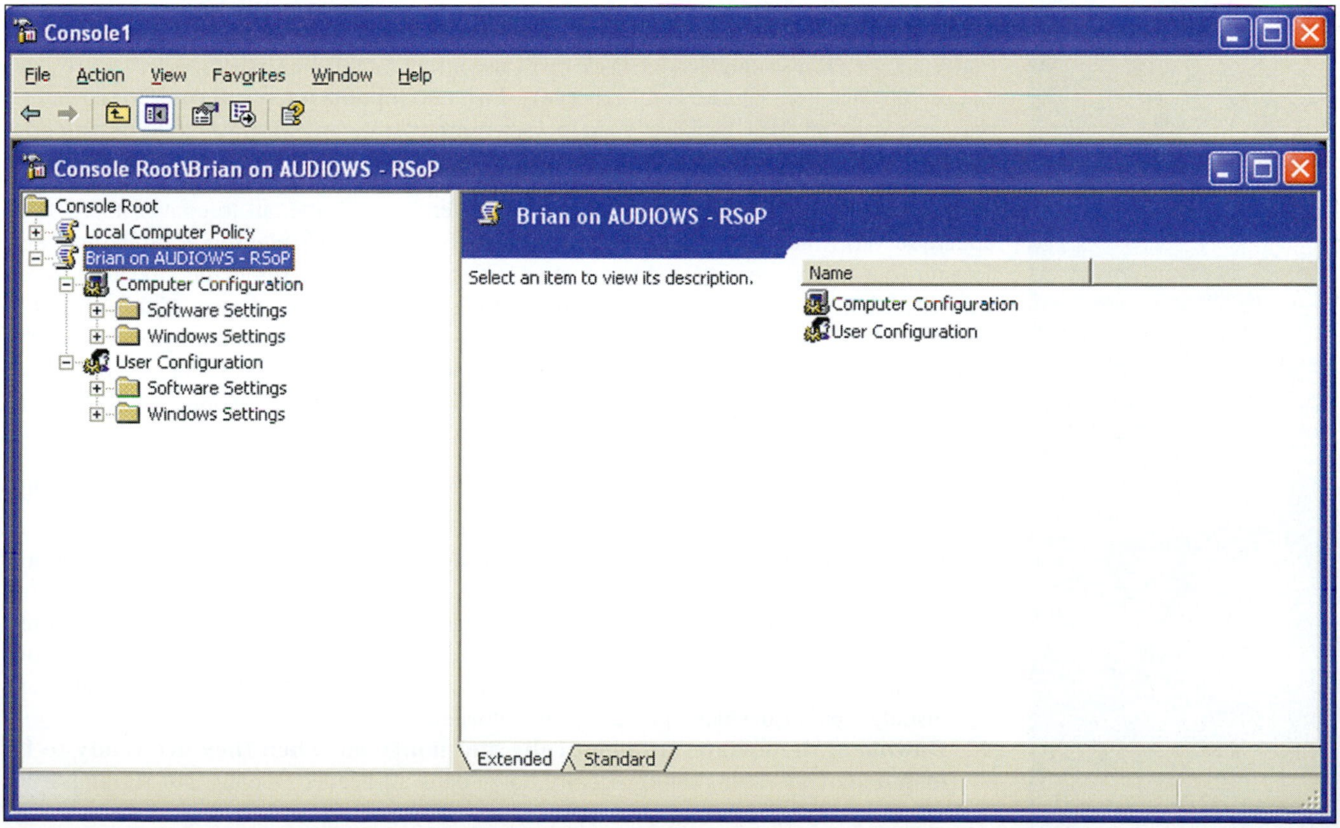

Figure 7-31 Expanding RSoP

skill 5

Implementing Critical Updates

exam objective

Identify and respond to security incidents. Apply critical updates.

overview

Critical updates are an important part of any security strategy. Microsoft defines a critical security concern as a problem that could lead to the propagation of a virus or worm without proper intervention. Although not all security updates are critical, all updates are applied in the same manner as critical updates.

For most operating systems, the easiest way to apply a critical update manually is to visit the Windows Update Web site at **http://windowsupdate.Microsoft.com** **(Figure 7-32)**. Choosing Custom Install on this page allows you to install optional updates as well, including hardware driver updates.

Instead of manually downloading and applying updates, in most Microsoft operating systems, you can configure the system to automatically download and apply updates. To allow the system to be updated manually, you can utilize the **Automatic Updates** service. The Automatic Updates service is not included with any operating system except Windows 2003 Server, but it is available as a free download for the following operating systems:

◆ Windows 2000 Professional (SP2)
◆ Windows 2000 Server (SP2)
◆ Windows 2000 Advanced Server (SP2)
◆ Windows XP Home
◆ Windows XP Professional

If your environment contains legacy operating systems, such as Windows 98 or Windows NT, these computers will not be able to take advantage of Automatic Updates. A third-party or add-on product (such as Microsoft Systems Management Server) is required to gain this functionality.

To install Automatic Updates on a Windows 2000 client or server, you install Service Pack 3. For Windows XP, installing Service Pack 1 will also install Automatic Updates. Alternatively, you can use the Windows Update Web site at **http://windowsupdate.microsoft.com/**, or download the service as an MSI package at **http://www.microsoft.com/windows2000/downloads/ recommended/susclient/default.asp.**

Once you have installed Automatic Updates, the service will attempt to contact the default update server, which will normally be the Microsoft Windows Update server on the Internet. Twenty-four hours after establishing contact with the server, the Automatic Updates service will display a wizard to the local administrator to configure the service. If this period is unacceptable, a local administrator can configure the computer by manually accessing the Automatic Updates service. In Windows XP or Windows 2003 Server, Automatic Updates are accessed through **System Properties** dialog box **(Figure 7-33)**; in Windows 2000, they are accessed through the Automatic Updates applet in Control Panel **(Figure 7-34)**.

From the client side, there are only a few manual configuration options, each of which are detailed below:

◆ **Keep my computer up to date**: This setting determines whether or not Automatic Updates are enabled.
◆ **Notify me before downloading any updates**: This setting allows you to be notified before Automatic Updates attempts to download any updates, and also before they are installed. This method allows you precise control over not only which updates are installed, but also which updates are downloaded.
◆ **Download the updates automatically and notify me when they are ready to be installed**: This setting automatically downloads all needed updates but refrains from installing any updates until you approve them. This is the default setting.

caution

If you choose either of the notification options, you must be logged on to the computer as a local administrator to receive the update notification.

Figure 7-32 The Windows Update Web site

Figure 7-33 Automatic Updates in Windows XP

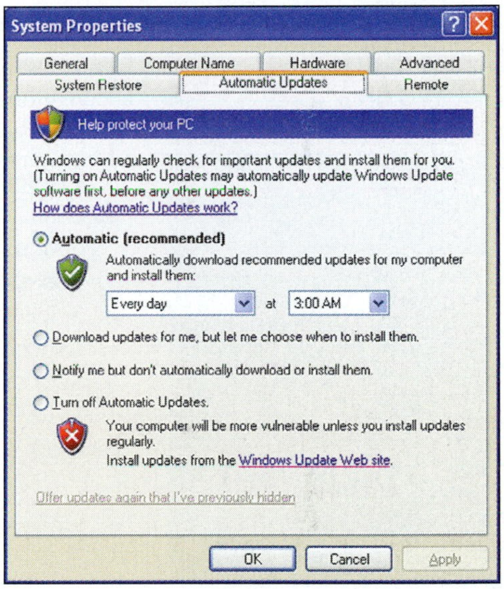

Figure 7-34 Automatic Updates in Windows 2000

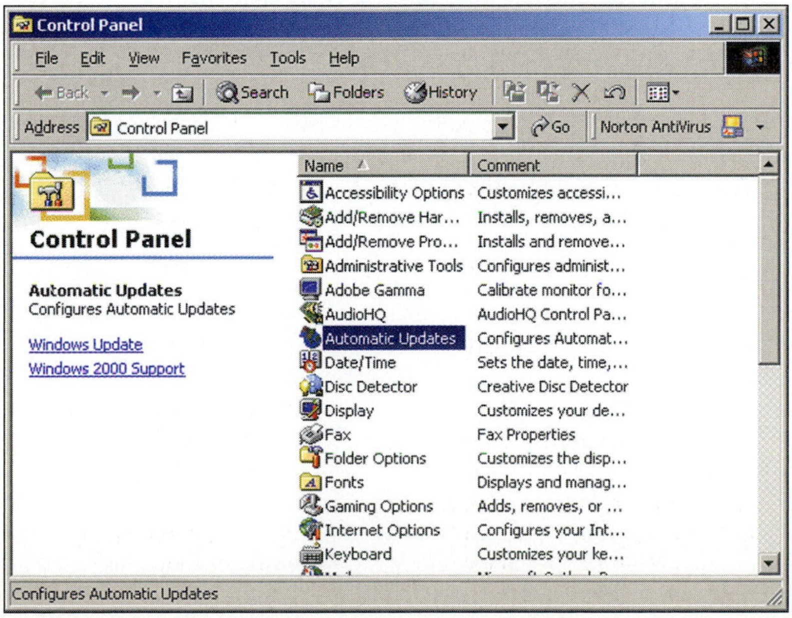

skill 5   *Implementing Critical Updates (cont'd)*

exam objective

Identify and respond to security incidents. Apply critical updates.

overview

◆ **Automatically download the updates and install them on the schedule that I specify**: This setting automatically downloads any needed updates, and then installs them on the day of the week and at the specific time you specify. If necessary, this option will even restart the computer automatically.

If you choose to be notified, a small reminder balloon will appear on the taskbar when updates are ready to be downloaded (if you chose to notify before downloading), or when they are ready to be installed (if you chose to download them automatically). Once you install the updates, your system may require a restart. Automatic Updates will prompt you to restart your system, but you can defer this for up to three days by choosing the **Remind me later** button. If you schedule the installation of updates, the system will automatically restart after applying the updates, if necessary.

how to

Configure Automatic Updates on a Windows XP computer. To perform this exercise, you will need Automatic Updates installed.

1. Click **start**, right-click **My Computer**, and choose **Properties** to open the **System Properties** dialog box.
2. Click the **Automatic Updates** tab to display the Automatic Updates configuration options (refer to Figure 7-33).
3. Make sure that the **Keep my computer up to date** check box is selected.
4. Select the **Automatically download the updates and install them on the schedule that I specify** option button to enable scheduling of update installations.
5. Set the schedule using the drop-down boxes to install your updates every Sunday at 1 A.M. **(Figure 7-35)**.
6. Click   OK   to accept the changes and close the Properties dialog box.

Figure 7-35 **Setting the Automatic Updates schedule**

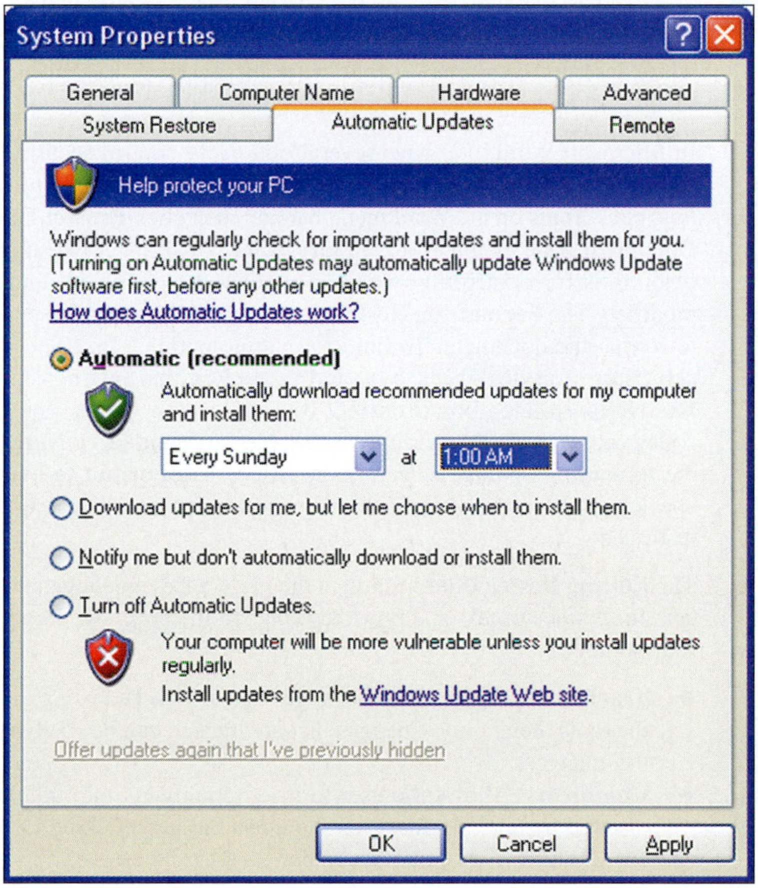

skill 6

Managing Application Security Settings

exam objective

Identify and troubleshoot problems related to security permissions. Answer end-user questions related to application security settings.
Manage application security settings

overview

Application security is a less thought-about but no less significant concern in business environments. Macro viruses, improper modification of documents, and privacy concerns are all important security considerations.

While nearly all applications have some application security settings, a Microsoft Certified Desktop Support Technician should be well versed in configuring Microsoft Office security settings. The security settings you should understand include settings within Word, Excel, PowerPoint, Outlook, and Internet Explorer. Settings for Outlook were covered in Lesson 5, while Internet Explorer settings were discussed in Lesson 3. This skill concentrates on security settings for Word, Excel, and PowerPoint.

In Microsoft Word, you have several options to control security. First, you can restrict who can modify the document and how those users are permitted to modify the document. To do this, click **Tools** on the Word menu bar and then click **Protect Document** to open the **Protect Document** pane within Word (**Figure 7-36**). The Protect Document pane gives you a number of options for controlling who can modify the document and how the document can be modified. The **Formatting Restrictions** section allows you to define which styles can be used to format the document. To limit formatting options, first select the **Limit formatting to a selection of styles** check box, and then click the **Settings** link to open the **Formatting Restrictions** dialog box (**Figure 7-37**). In this dialog box, you can either manual select the styles you wish to allow, or use the **All**, **Recommended**, or **None** buttons to automatically set the formatting options. Selecting the **Allow AutoFormat to override formatting decisions** check box allows the AutoFormat function to function properly even if the styles it uses are restricted.

The **Editing Restrictions** section in the Protect Document pane is used to define who can edit certain sections of text and how they can edit the text. The drop-down box in this section has four options:

- **Tracked Changes**: Allows changes that are tracked using the track changes option under the tools menu only. Changes that are tracked can be easily reversed by right-clicking on the change.
- **Comments**: Allows the user to insert comments into the document (comments can be inserted by clicking Insert on the menu bar and clicking Comment), but does not allow any modifications to the document.
- **Filling in Forms**: Allows the user to fill form fields as normal, but does not allow any other changes.
- **No Changes (Read Only)**: Does not allow any changes to the document.

After choosing the level of protection you wish to enable, you can selectively choose which users have full modification rights to the document under the **Exceptions** sub-section. To access more users and groups, click the **More Users** link to open the Add Users dialog box (**Figure 7-38**). Finally, click the **Yes, start enforcing protection** button to enable protection on the document.

In addition to configuring document protection, you can also configure a number of security options through the security tab of the options dialog (**Figure 7-39**). Entering a password in the **Password to open** text box encrypts the document with the password, preventing users who do not have the password from opening the document. By clicking on the **Advanced** button, you can open the **Encryption Type** dialog box where you can choose the type and level of encryption for the document. It is recommended that you do not modify these settings unless

tip

The settings discussed in this lesson apply to Office 2003 applications. Previous versions of MS Office may not include some of these settings.

tip

By default, the Editing Restrictions selected apply to the entire document. You can selectively apply editing restrictions by selecting a block of text and applying restrictions specifically to the selection.

Figure 7-36 Protect Document pane

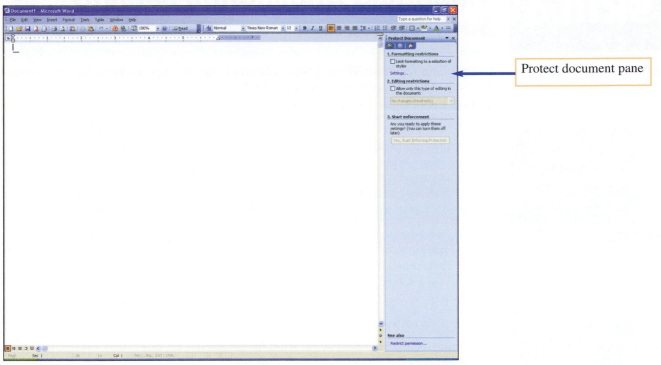

Protect document pane

Figure 7-38 Add Users dialog box

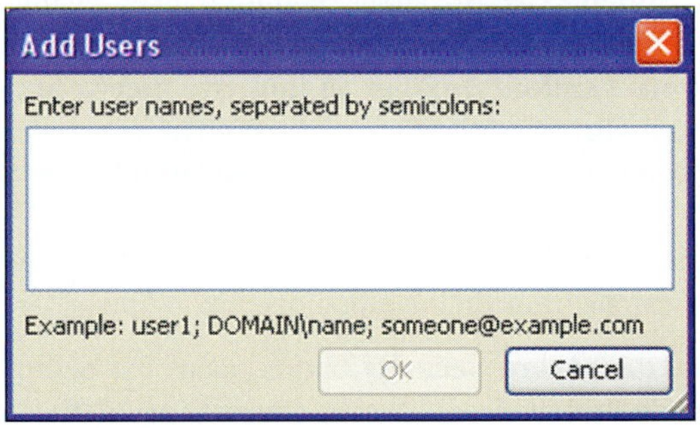

Figure 7-39 Security tab of the Options dialog box in Word

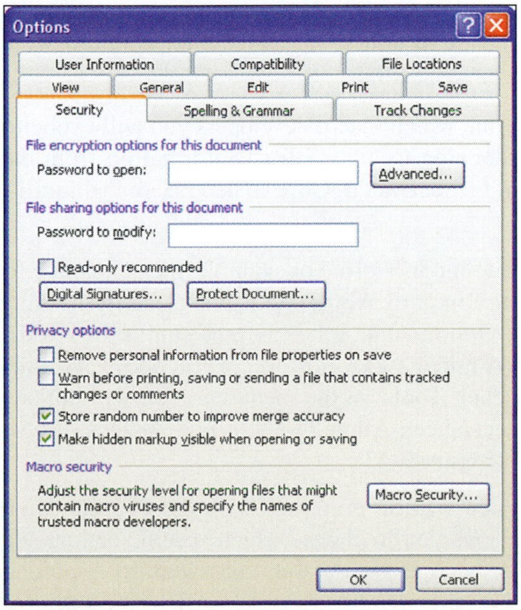

Figure 7-37 Formatting Restrictions dialog box

skill 6

Managing Application Security Settings (cont'd)

exam objective

Identify and troubleshoot problems related to security permissions. Answer end-user questions related to application security settings.
Manage application security settings

overview

you are directed to do so by the network security team, as higher levels of encryption may cause problems when trying to open the document on other systems. Under the File sharing options section, you can define a password that is required to modify the document, or simply suggest read-only access, which will open a dialog requesting that the user open the document in read only mode, but still allows modifications if the user declines read-only access.

Clicking the **Digital Signatures** button opens the **Digital Signature** dialog box, where you can add one or more digital signatures to the document. This proves that you personally created or modified the document, but does not prevent access to the document in any way. Clicking the **Protect document** button simply opens the Protect Document pane discussed previously.

In the Privacy section, you have four options:

◆ **Remove personal information from file properties on save:** Removes the names and other personally identifiable information from the file when it is saved, ensuring privacy.
◆ **Warn before printing, saving, or sending a file that contains tracked changes or comments:** Warns about sending tracked changes in a document, which allows you to ensure private comments and changes are not sent accidentally.
◆ **Store random number to improve merge accuracy:** Removes any random numbers used for file merge operations. These numbers are hidden, but could be used to demonstrate a relationship between documents. Disabling this option may cause a reduction in the ability to merge documents.
◆ **Make hidden markup visible when opening or saving:** Displays comments and other revisions immediately upon opening a file.

Finally, the **Macro Security** button opens the **Security** dialog box **(Figure 7-40)**, which is used to control the level of macro security and define trusted and untrusted macro sources. On the Security Level tab, you can define the level of security to use with macros. The Medium level is the lowest level suggested for any user, and is only suggested for advanced users. Using the Medium level, any unsigned and untrusted macros in a document will bring up a dialog box asking the user if they wish to run the macro. At the High level, on the other hand, all unsigned or untrusted macros are automatically disabled. The Very high level disables all macros not specifically defined in the trusted publishers tab.

The **Trusted Publishers** tab allows you to define which macro developers you will explicitly trust. Publishers are added to this tab by choosing to always trust information from this publisher when a macro from the publisher is first activated. Only signed macros will utilize the settings in this tab.

Excel uses many of the same security features found in Word. For example, the dialog box for macro security is exactly the same as the one found in Word, and it is located in the same place. Similarly, the Security tab of Excel's Options dialog box is very similar to Word's, containing most of the same security options **(Figure 7-41)**. However, Excel does have a few security options that are unique. When you click **Tools** on the menu bar, you will notice a **Protection** submenu with four options: Protect Sheet, Allow Users to Edit Ranges, Protect Workbook, and Protect and Share Workbook **(Figure 7-42)**.

If you select the **Protect Sheet** command, you will be presented with the **Protect Sheet** dialog box **(Figure 7-43)**. This dialog box allows you to choose which specific actions you will or will not let users perform in the worksheet, as well as set a password to disable all protection.

Figure 7-40 Security dialog box

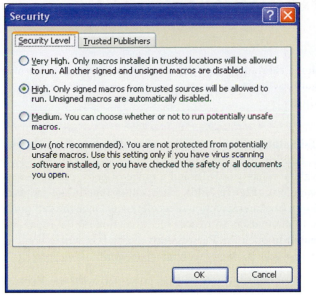

Figure 7-41 Security tab of the Options dialog box in Excel

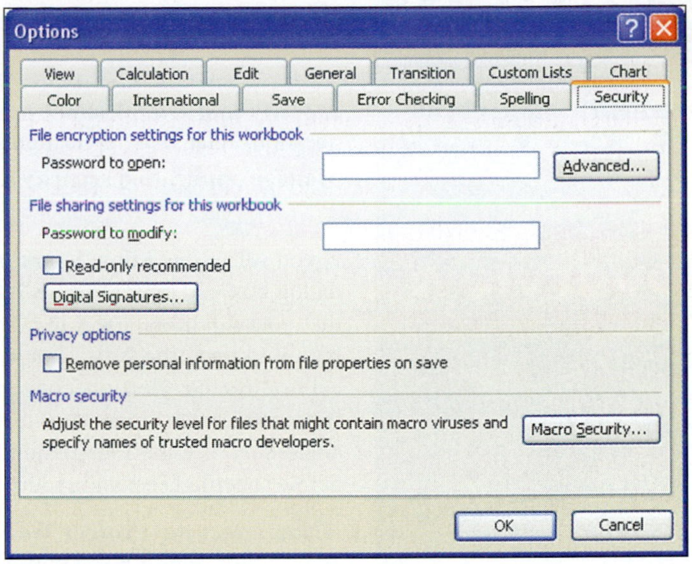

Figure 7-42 Protection submenu in Excel

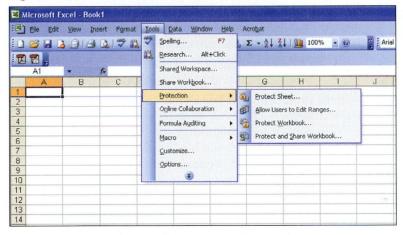

Figure 7-43 Protect Sheet dialog box box

skill 6 — *Managing Application Security Settings (cont'd)*

exam objective

Identify and troubleshoot problems related to security permissions. Answer end-user questions related to application security settings.
Manage application security settings

overview

If you select the **Allow Users to Edit Ranges** command, the **Allow Users to Edit Ranges** dialog box will open (**Figure 7-44**). In this dialog box, you can define specific ranges of cells that you will allow users to edit without a password. To add a range of cells, click the new button to open the **New Range** dialog box (**Figure 7-45**). Here, either type in the range of cells or use the selection icon to allow a freehand selection of a cell range. Once the cell range is entered, enter a password to use to allow users to bypass the protection on the range, or, alternately, use the **Permissions** button to open the **Permissions** dialog box where you can define specific users and groups that can edit the range without a password.

If you select the **Protect Workbook** command, you will be presented with the **Protect Workbook** dialog box (**Figure 7-46**). In this dialog box, you can choose to protect the structure of the workbook (disabling the ability to add, delete, move, hide, or otherwise modify worksheets within the workbook), and/or protect the windows within the workbook (ensuring that the windows are always the same size and in the same position and cannot be moved or modified). Optionally, you can define a password that can be used to prevent users from removing this protection. If a password is not defined, any user will be able to remove the protection you configure here by deselecting these options.

Finally, if you choose the **Protect and Share Workbook** command, you will be presented with the **Protect Shared Workbook** dialog box (**Figure 7-47**). Selecting the **Sharing with track changes** check box allows the workbook to be simultaneously viewed and modified by multiple users. It also enables change tracking and does not allow users to change this setting. However, if you do not supply a password in this dialog box, any user will be able to disable the sharing and change tracking on the workbook.

Finally, PowerPoint also utilizes most of the standard security options available in Word. Macro security is controlled through the same mechanisms, and uses the same dialog boxes and menu items to do so. Similarly, the Security tab in the Options dialog box for PowerPoint is nearly identical to the same tab in Excel (**Figure 7-48**).

how to

Configure the security options in Microsoft Word to prompt for a password when opening the document, suggest read-only mode, and remove personally identifiable information on save.

1. Log on to the computer as an Administrator.
2. To open Word, click **start**, point to **All Programs**, point to **Microsoft Office**, and click **Microsoft Office Word 2003**.
3. Click **Tools** on the Word menu bar and click **Options** to open the **Options** dialog box.
4. Select the **Security** tab and configure the tab as shown in **Figure 7-49**. Enter **password1** as the password required when opening the document.
5. Click **OK** to close the Options dialog box.
6. Click **File** on the menu bar and then click **Save As** to open the **Save As** dialog box. Select **My Documents** in the left-hand pane of the dialog box to select a location for saving the document and type **Doc1.doc** as the file name. Click **Save** to save the document.
7. Exit Word.
8. Click **start**, point to **My Recent Documents**, and click **Doc1.doc** to reopen the document. Confirm that you are required to supply a password and that Word requests that you open the document in read-only mode.
9. Close all applications and log off of the system.

Figure 7-44 Allow Users to Edit Ranges dialog box

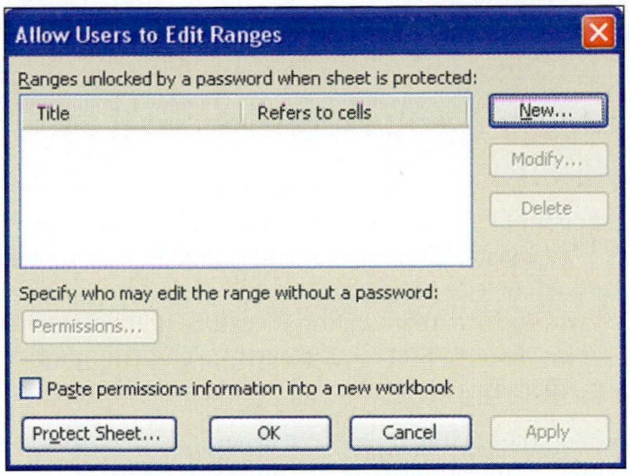

Figure 7-45 New Range dialog box

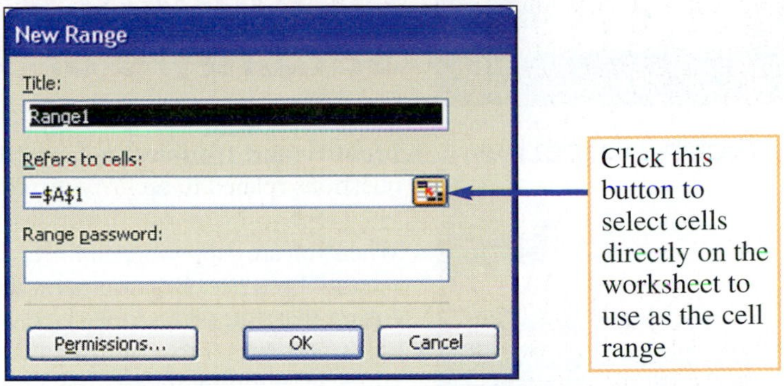

Click this button to select cells directly on the worksheet to use as the cell range

Figure 7-46 Protect Workbook dialog box

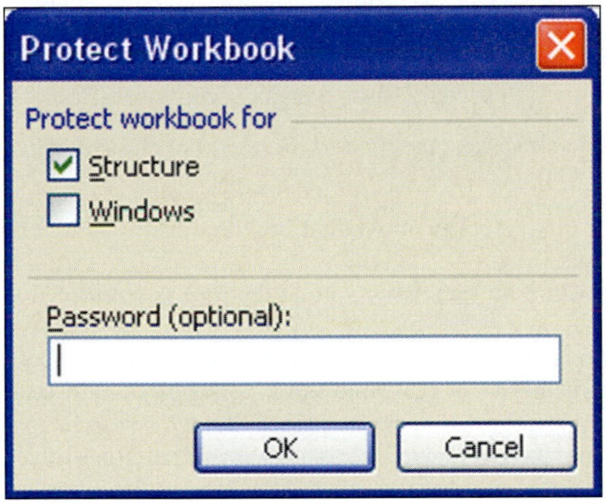

Figure 7-47 Protect Shared Workbook dialog box

Figure 7-48 Security tab of the Options dialog box in PowerPoint

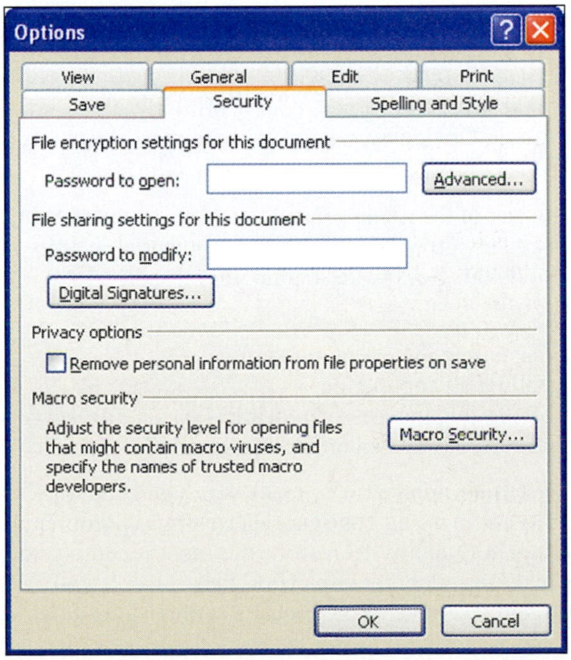

Figure 7-49 Configuring the Security tab in Word

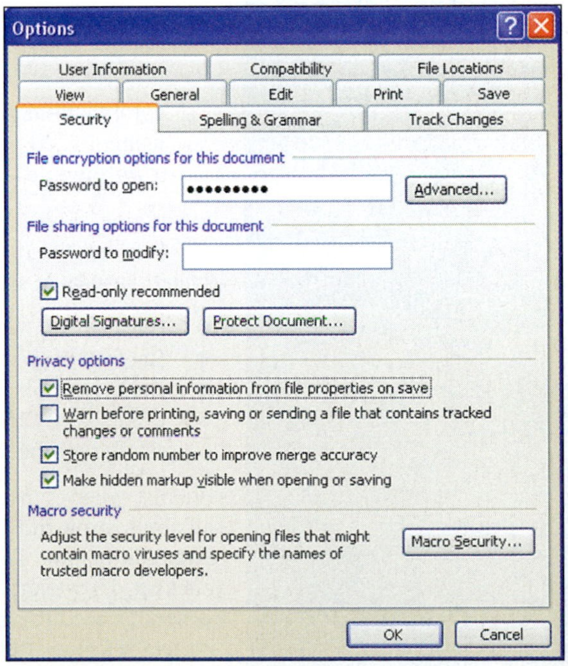

skill 7
Supporting Users in a Security-Conscious Manner

exam objective

Identify and troubleshoot problems related to security permissions. Answer end-user questions related to security incidents.

overview

When you are supporting end-users, ample opportunity exists to permit or assist in the creation of security breaches. Because users are largely uneducated in proper security practices, you must ensure that you take proper precautions and attempt to maintain security while resolving the user's problems. First, you should ensure that proper authentication measures are maintained when attempting to resolve problems. This means that you should take a number of precautions when operating a user's system, including:

◆ Always log on to the system with a non-administrative account when possible, and use the **Run As** service **(Figure 7-50)** to open applications with administrative powers.

◆ Never ask users for their passwords. If you must perform actions under their user account, have the user log in and then perform the activities.

◆ Do not take ownership of the user's resources unless absolutely necessary, and even then, ensure that you transfer ownership back when complete.

◆ Do not leave the system logged on with your user account. Because you likely have higher permissions and rights levels than the user, this would cause a major security breach.

Next, educate the user as much as possible about best practices with regard to authentication security. These include:

◆ Using complex passwords of eight characters or more that include uppercase letters, lowercase letters, numbers, and symbols.

◆ Using passwords that are easy for the user to remember so that the user is not forced to write the password down.

◆ Using passwords that are not directly related to the user. The use of Social Security numbers, birthdays, names of friends, family members, or pets, and other personally identifiable information is a bad practice because this information can be gained through research.

◆ Changing the password frequently. Any password can be broken with a brute force attack if the attacker has unlimited time. Modern brute-force password hacking applications can cycle through over 1200 passwords per second. To put this into perspective, you must examine the number of possible combinations for any given password scenario. If the user is using a 4–character password consisting of only lowercase characters, for instance, then there are only 456,976 possible combinations **(Figure 7-51)**, which would most likely mean that the hacker would have the password cracked within 3–6 minutes. On the other hand, an 8-character password, consisting of numbers, letters (upper and lowercase), and symbols provides for over 72,000,000,000,000,000 possible combinations **(Figure 7-52)**. This would take, on average, over 1 billion years to crack using a 1200 password-per-second cracker. Obviously, using long, complex passwords is a worthwhile improvement.

In addition to insuring that the user is cognizant of the issues related to password security, you must also ensure that the user's data is adequately protected, and that any potential security or system problems are adequately logged. To do this, follow these guidelines:

◆ Back up all event logs, especially security logs, before clearing them.
◆ Back up important user data before reinstalling the operating system.
◆ Back up application data before reinstalling an application.
◆ Make sure that the user is aware of the advantages of storing data on file servers (including the advantage of regular backups of the data on the file server).

Finally, when reinstalling the operating system or applications, make sure you keep track of all application and operating system security settings and configure the settings appropriately after the install. The easiest way to do this is typically to restore the most recent system backup. However, many users fail to make regular backups. For these users, you will generally need to examine all applications and take note of the security settings to restore the correct settings after reinstallation.

Figure 7-50 Run As service

Figure 7-51 A small number of combinations with small, simple passwords

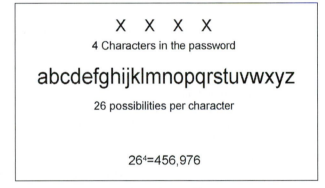

X   X   X   X

4 Characters in the password

abcdefghijklmnopqrstuvwxyz

26 possibilities per character

$26^4 = 456,976$

Figure 7-52 A large number of combinations with a large, complex password

X   X   X   X   X   X   X   X

8 Characters in the password

SPACE!"#$%&'()*+,-./0123456789:;<=>?@
ABCDEFGHIJKLMNOPQRSTUVWXYZ[\]^
_`abcdefghijklmnopqrstuvwxyz{|}~
DELETE

128 possibilities per character

$128^8 = 72,057,594,037,927,936$

Summary

- NTFS permissions enable you to secure network resources by controlling the level of access to files and folder for each user.
- Unlike share permissions, NTFS permissions apply to local users as well.
- Note that when you apply permissions to a drive or folder, you are also applying those permissions to all files and folders underneath it, by default.
- In addition to the standard NTFS permissions, you can assign special access permissions.
- Create folders to organize your data into categories.
- When you are defining the level of permission, always assign users the lowest level of permissions required for them to perform their jobs to protect data from being inadvertently changed or deleted.
- Assign the Read permission and the Write permission to the Users group.
- Avoid assigning the Full Control permission for a folder.
- The Deny condition is useful in cases where you must temporarily lock out particular users.
- Assign permissions to groups rather than to individual user accounts to simplify permission administration.
- Files and folders inherit the permissions assigned to the parent folder by default.
- To determine the permission level for a particular user, you must combine all the permissions assigned.
- When you deny a permission to a user, you restrict that permission from the user.
- Remember the following phrase: Moved to same, permissions remain.
- The most common indicator of a permissions problem is the access denied error message when attempting to access a file or folder.
- In general, the easiest way to determine your effective permissions to a resource is to use the effective permissions tab under the advanced security dialog box.· If a resource is local, shared permissions are immaterial and only NTFS permissions must be checked.
- If the resource is remote rather than local, you can apply both shared folder and NTFS permissions, so you must check both the share-level and the NTFS permissions for the file or folder. In such cases, the most restrictive permissions will apply to the resource.

- By organizing users with the same access requirements into groups and applying permissions to the group instead of to each user, you can reduce the effort required to apply permissions.
- Like local user accounts, local group accounts are valid only on the local system.
- You can control many aspects of a Windows 2000, Windows XP, or Windows Server 2003 system by editing the system's local policy.
- Perhaps the best way of examining the vast array of Group Policy options is to examine the policy settings.
- Knowing how to find the description of each Group Policy setting will go a long way toward helping you resolve problems related to Group Policy.
- For most operating systems, the easiest way to apply a critical update manually is to visit the Windows update Web site.
- If your environment contains legacy operating systems, such as Windows 98 or Windows NT, these computers will not be able to take advantage of Automatic Updates.
- Always log on to the system with a non-administrative account when possible.
- If you must perform actions under their user context, have the user log in and then perform the activities.
- Do not take ownership of the user's resources unless absolutely necessary, and even then, ensure that you transfer ownership back when complete.
- Do not leave the system logged on with your user account.
- Teach users to use complex passwords of eight characters or more that are not directly related to the user.
- Changing the password frequently is a good security practice.
- Back up all event logs, especially security logs, before clearing them.
- Back up important user data before reinstalling the operating system.
- Back up application data before reinstalling an application.
- Make sure that the user is aware of the advantages of storing data on file servers (including the advantage of regular backups of the data on the file server).

Key Terms

Automatic Updates
Gpresult.exe
Group
Group Policies
Group Policy Management Console
  (GPMC)

Local groups
NTFS file permissions
NTFS folder permissions
NTFS permissions

Resultant Set of Policy (RSoP)
Scripts
Security Settings
Special access permissions

Test Yourself

1. Which of the following would you use to configure user rights?
   a. Windows Explorer
   b. The Users applet in Control Panel
   c. Group Policy
   d. The Sharing tab in the Folder Properties dialog box

2. Which of the following is considered a best practice in regard to security? (Choose all that apply.)
   a. Use passwords of eight characters or less.
   b. Use complex passwords.
   c. Write down your passwords.
   d. Use passwords related to the user.
   e. Do not give your password to other users.

3. You are attempting to help a user with a problem related to permissions settings. The user is receiving an access denied error message when she attempts to write to a document. The user is a member of the Sales and Marketing groups, as well as the Users group. The permissions on the resource are as follows:

   > User account: Full Control
   > Sales group: Read and Write
   > Marketing group: Read
   > Users group: Deny Write
   > Administrators group: Full control

   Which permissions setting is the likely cause of the user's problem?

   a. User account
   b. Sales group
   c. Marketing group
   d. Users group

4. You are attempting to determine why a user is receiving an error each time they try to change their password. The password they are attempting to use is bob232. Which of the following Group Policy settings could be preventing them from using this password? (Choose all that apply.)
   a. Minimum password length
   b. Minimum password age
   c. Maximum password age
   d. Password complexity requirements

5. Which of the following would you use to download and install updates on a Windows XP system without any user intervention?
   a. Windows update Web site
   b. Gpresult.exe
   c. Automatic Updates
   d. GPMC

6. You have a user that is using Windows XP with the classic logon. The user is highly concerned about security, and wants to ensure that the user name of the last user to use the system is not displayed in the logon dialog box each time a user attempts to log on. Which tool would you use to meet his request?

   a. System Properties dialog box
   b. Users applet in Control Panel
   c. Group Policy console
   d. Gpresult.exe
   e. Network Properties dialog box

7. Which of the following is true regarding multiple NTFS permissions applying to a single user account? (Choose all that apply.)
   a. The most restrictive permissions apply.
   b. All permissions are added up.
   c. Deny permissions are ignored.
   d. Deny permissions apply only when accessing the resource remotely.
   e. Deny permissions override allow permissions.

8. You are attempting to help a user with a problem related to permissions settings. The user is receiving an "Access is denied" error message when they attempt to read to a document. The user is a member of the Accounting group, as well as the Users group. The permissions on the resource are as follows:

   > Legal group: Read and Write
   > Managers group: Deny Write
   > Administrators group: Full control

   Which permissions setting is the likely cause of the user's problem?

   a. Managers group
   b. Legal group
   c. Administrators group
   d. None of the above

9. You are attempting to educate a user named Bob about secure password choices. He is complaining that his current password is sufficient, and that he does not need to increase its security. His current password is bobandmindy9282002. Which of the following points would you make regarding the security of this password (choose all that apply)?
   a. The password should not be related to the user in any way.
   b. The password be complex.
   c. The password should be longer.
   d. The password should not contain the user's name.

10. Which of the following are valid reasons for using Windows update to keep a system up to date (choose all that apply)?
    a. Added protection from new viruses by keeping the virus definitions up to date.
    b. Protection from security flaws.
    c. Ensuring that critical updates are applied properly.
    d. Ensuring that the user conforms to organization security requirements.

Projects: On Your Own

1. Configure the permissions on an NTFS file to deny access to the guests group.
   a. Log on to the system as a local administrator.
   b. Open **Windows Explorer**.
   c. Open the **Properties** dialog box for an NTFS file or folder.
   d. Select the **Security** tab.
   e. Click **Add** and type **guests** to add the Guests group.
   f. Select the **Deny** permission for **Full Control** for the **Guests** group.
   g. Click **OK**.
   h. Close all open dialog boxes and log off of the system.

2. Log on as a non-administrative user and use the Run As service to open the computer management console with administrative privileges.
   a. Log on to the system as a normal user
   b. Open a command prompt.

   c. In the command prompt, type the following command:
   runas /user:administrator "mmc.exe compmgmt.msc"
   Ensure that you type the command exactly as entered (including quotes) and press **[Enter]**. When you receive the password prompt, type in the administrator password and hit enter.
   d. If you receive any errors, ensure that you have typed the command exactly as shown.
   e. Examine the Computer Management console. The console is now running with administrative privileges.
   f. Close all open applications and dialog boxes and log off of the system.

Problem Solving Scenarios

1. You have recently been promoted within your company and are now the senior technician in charge of user education regarding security. You need to establish a policy for security of user systems. Define the settings you will suggest, as well as the training you will suggest for both desktop support technicians and users.

2. You are examining a user's system when you notice that several group-policy enabled security options are not functioning properly. You need to determine why these options are not functioning as they should. All other systems are functioning properly. Describe the steps you would take to diagnose this problem.

Identifying and Responding to Security Incidents

Security breaches can be one of the most serious threats to any business. Small breaches in system security can lead to major exploitations and loss of data, consumer confidence, or future business. Although most companies do not operate in an environment that requires extreme security measures, all organizations need to protect confidentiality of data and intellectual property. Failure to protect these key corporate assets can increase the damage caused by unauthorized users.

Because of these risks, business leaders are likely to be fearful of security breaches and expect desktop technicians to be able to spot and resolve security breaches as quickly as possible. Additionally, for some organizations, such as government contractors, serious consequences can arise from substandard security practices, up to and including criminal prosecution. Although the desktop support technician's role in network security may seem to be a minor one, it can have a profound effect on overall network security.

You will find that the best way to support security is to prevent breaches in the first place. As the saying goes, an ounce of prevention is worth a pound of cure, and it holds true with regard to security as well. By ensuring that your systems are free of viruses and spyware, you can significantly reduce the likelihood of system breaches. Similarly, by ensuring that security updates are applied regularly and thoroughly, you can significantly reduce the number of operating system vulnerabilities available for exploitation.

As you will find throughout this lesson, user education is often the best safeguard against security breaches. Although technical measures for enforcing and auditing security are extremely helpful, none of these measures will ensure security in an environment where poor user practices are commonplace. System security begins with the user, and should be supported and enforced by the technical staff.

Goals

In this lesson, you will learn how to identify and recover from the most common types of security breaches. Additionally, you will learn how to protect systems against many different types of breaches and educate the user base about best practices in regard to system security.

Lesson 8 *Identifying and Responding to Security Incidents*	
Skill	**Exam 70-272 Objective**
1. Introducing Viruses	**Identify and respond to security incidents.** Identify a virus attack.
2. Protecting Systems Against Viruses	**Identify and respond to security incidents.** Identify a virus attack.
3. Recognizing and Responding to Virus Attacks	**Identify and respond to security incidents.** Identify a virus attack.
4. Examining Spyware	**Identify and respond to security incidents.** Identify a virus attack.
5. Identifying and Responding to Other Security Incidents	**Identify and respond to security incidents.** Identify a virus attack.

Requirements

To complete this lesson, you will need administrative rights on a Windows XP Professional computer with SP2 and Norton or Symantec AntiVirus and Microsoft Baseline Security Analyzer (MBSA) installed.

skill 1 *Introducing Viruses*

exam objective

Identify and respond to security incidents. Identify a virus attack.

overview

Viruses are a major security problem and are probably the most well publicized type of security problem. A **virus** is any application that has the ability to replicate itself and spread. There are several definitions of what actually constitutes a virus, but in general, the basic definition given above fits the most common usage of the term. By this definition, many applications can be labeled viruses, including special types of malicious applications, such as Trojan horses and worms. Although there are more strict definitions of the term, most information technology (IT) professionals consider any self-replicating malicious application a virus.

Viruses come in many forms, the more common of which are listed below and in **Table 8-1**. Viruses can be carried in a variety of ways (**Table 8-2**), but the most common transmission method for any type of virus is as an executable disseminated through e-mail. In many cases, the executable may seem to perform some non-damaging function (such as ejecting a CD) as part of a joke, but in the background, the application is installing the virus into your system.

◆ **Backdoor viruses**: Backdoor viruses provide a secret entry point, called a backdoor, into the operating system, bypassing the system's security measures. They are typically distributed as part of an executable attached to e-mail. They can also be found in software, whether programmed by the original developers or attached later during the software's distribution by hackers.

◆ **Boot-sector viruses**: Boot-sector viruses overwrite the hard-disk's boot sector, effectively executing each time the system boots. These types of viruses normally come in the form of a bootable floppy. Once a floppy is infected with the virus, booting from that floppy will execute the code in the virus and cause the virus to copy itself onto the hard disk's boot sector.

◆ **Macro viruses**: Macro viruses are written using an application's built-in macro language. These viruses are typically distributed as part of an e-mailed document, such as a Word (.doc) or Excel (.xls) document. They execute when opening the document, and typically embed themselves in the template documents for the application, thus ensuring that they are replicated to all documents the user opens in the future.

◆ **Scripts**: Viruses can also be written in a scripting language, such as VBScript or JScript. These viruses are normally sent as e-mail attachments and are typically disguised by having dual extensions (such as I Love You.txt.vbs). Opening the attachment executes the script, which infects the host operating system. They may also be a part of a Web page, such as an ActiveX control or Java application.

◆ **Trojan horses**: Trojan horses (also referred to as Trojans) masquerade as a benign function or application while actually performing a hidden, malignant function in the background. They are typically distributed as part of an executable attached to e-mail.

◆ **Worms**: Worms are viruses that perform no malicious function other than replicating themselves infinitely to completely saturate the resources of their host system or network. Worms are typically distributed as part of an executable attached to e-mail.

more

In addition to all of the above viruses, there are also the common virus hoaxes that are sent by e-mail. These are typically intended to drum up anxiety about fictional viruses and tend to spread like chain letters.

If you receive an e-mail message regarding a virus, even if it appears to be from a trusted source, you should research the virus at one of the major antivirus Web sites, such as Symantec.com or McAfee.com. All major antivirus companies keep a running list of current Internet hoaxes, and generally are aware of actual virus threats in a matter of hours. If you find that the alert is a hoax, be sure to inform your users so that they will not propagate the hoax by spreading the e-mail.

Table 8-1   Virus descriptions

Category	Description	Typical Distribution	Example
Backdoor	Virus programmed to bypass a system's security measures	E-mail executable; software	Back Orifice was programmed to exploit holes in Microsoft software. It gives remote access to an infected computer and can be used to capture keystrokes or set up File Transfer Protocol (FTP), Hypertext Transfer Protocol (HTTP), or Telnet servers.
Boot sector	Overwrites hard disk's boot sector	Bootable floppy	The Ripper virus randomly corrupts small segments of data as they are written to disk. The corruption is so negligible at first that it typically doesn't produce any noticeable change in the system for several weeks, at which point the corruption has spread to many files and has made important data unrecoverable.
Macro virus	Written using an application's built-in scripting language	E-mailed document	The Word macro Appder tries to delete key system files that will prevent Windows from booting.
Script	Written in a scripting language such as VBScript	E-mail executable	Melissa, a Visual Basic virus, was distributed in a Word document. Melissa sent e-mail copies of itself to addresses found in Microsoft Outlook.
Trojan horse	Appears to be benign functions or applications	E-mail executable; software	One famous Trojan, AOLgold, was seemingly an application update but in truth deleted the contents of critical directories on the user's C: drive.
Worm	Replicates itself throughout a system or network	E-mail executable	The MyDoom worm propagated itself through e-mail and peer-to-peer networks and launched Denial of Service (DoS) attacks against a single Web site.

Table 8-2   Sources of viruses

Source	Notes
Floppy disk	Even blank disks, once formatted, can carry a virus. On rare occasions, viruses have been found on manufacturer's software distribution disks.
E-mail	An attachment, even if it is not executed, can infect a system with a virus if the attachment is downloaded and saved to disk.
Internet download	Viruses can be embedded in pirated software. Shareware can also be infected, not necessarily by the original programmers.

skill 2 | *Protecting Systems Against Viruses*

exam objective | **Identify and respond to security incidents.** Identify a virus attack.

overview

Your best defense against virus attacks is education. If users are educated about the risks of virus attacks and the distribution methods of virus attacks, they will be less likely to open questionable applications. Some of the precautions each user should take include:

◆ Never open executables attached to e-mail unless you are certain of the application's validity and you have scanned the application with an up-to-date virus scanner.
◆ Pay close attention to any error messages or warnings you receive from Internet Explorer or your e-mail application.
◆ Scan all floppy disks with a virus scanning application before using them.
◆ Ensure that write protection is enabled before using a floppy disk in an untrusted system.
◆ Never open an e-mail attachment with a .vbs, .js, or .wsh extension.
◆ Pay close attention to any prompts to run macros when opening any document. Only allow macros to run if you are sure they are required and are safe.

As a second line of defense, you should ensure that the security settings for your applications, especially Internet Explorer and your e-mail application, are properly configured to disable unsafe content. For instance, in Internet Explorer, you can disable the activation of unsigned ActiveX controls and limit the execution of JavaScript.

Finally, you should ensure that you have an antivirus application installed, that the virus signatures for the application are up-to-date, and that real-time scanning is enabled.

In general, **antivirus applications** are utilities designed to search for, eliminate, and protect against the installation of malicious applications. This skill examines the detection and protection aspects of the antivirus software. Eliminating viruses is discussed in Skill 3.

To detect viruses, antivirus applications generally use two types of scanning, signature scanning and heuristics scanning. **Signature scanning** is the more mature and accurate of these two methods. Signature scanning relies on an up-to-date database of virus definitions, or signatures, that are used to identify, or fingerprint, a virus. Because signature scanning relies on a fingerprint match of the virus, it is very accurate, relatively quick, and generates few false positives. However, this same fingerprinting mechanism relies on up-to-date definitions of all known viruses and their variants. If the definition database is out of date, signature scanning will be ineffective at finding current viruses. Nearly all antivirus applications use signature scanning as part of their defense mechanism and include applications (usually integrated) to update the virus definitions (**Figure 8-1**).

Heuristics scanning, on the other hand, is a mechanism for identifying viruses that are new or are polymorphic. **Polymorphic viruses** are viruses that have the ability to mutate or change their code to avoid virus detection algorithms. To combat these viruses, heuristics scanning uses several techniques, including examination of the application's code structure and activity. Because heuristics scanning is a complicated and relatively new process, it is not as accurate as signature scanning (its accuracy is claimed to be as high as 80 percent, however). Because of the reduced accuracy, heuristics scanning is known to generate far more false positives than signature scanning. Additionally, due to the increased complexity of heuristics scanning, the scanning process is slower than signature scanning. Due to the nature of heuristics scanning, up-to-date signatures are not required.

Many modern antivirus applications make use of both scanning mechanisms, although heuristics scanning is typically optional. Additionally, almost all antivirus applications have the option of utilizing both on-demand scanning and on-access scanning.

On-demand scanning is what most people associate with antivirus applications. It involves either manually initiating a virus scan (**Figure 8-2**) or scheduling a system scan during off-peak hours, such as at night. Either way, the scan is activated by the user.

Figure 8-1 Updating virus definitions in Symantec AntiVirus

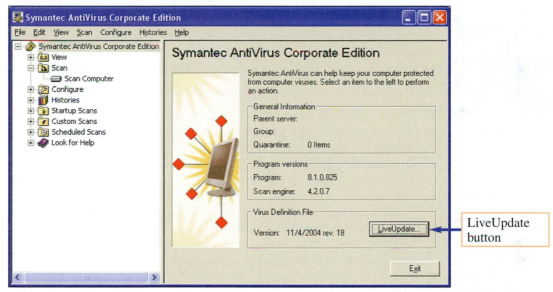

skill 2

Protecting Systems Against Viruses
(cont'd)

exam objective

Identify and respond to security incidents. Identify a virus attack.

overview

On-access scanning, on the other hand, occurs without user intervention. On-access scanning enables the antivirus application to automatically scan files before they are executed or opened to catch virus attacks before the offending files are executed. Some antivirus applications call this type of scanning "real-time protection" **(Figure 8-3)**. This is the primary method antivirus applications use to protect against infection. Unfortunately, on-access scanning decreases the performance of the operating system due to the nature of the process. For this reason, on-access scanning can typically be disabled.

In addition to antivirus measures, an additional layer of protection is available from the **Microsoft Baseline Security Analyzer (MBSA)**, which can be downloaded from the Microsoft Web site. Although not specifically meant to help protect against viruses, MBSA dynamically evaluates your system security and warns you of potential vulnerabilities. Additionally, MBSA can also check for missing security updates for the operating system and application software **(Figure 8-4)**.

Every time that you perform a scan with MBSA, a security report is generated for each scanned computer and saved on the computer on which MBSA is running **(Figure 8-5)**. The location of these reports is listed at the top of the screen, and each report is saved in XML format.

The following is a summary of the various checks performed by MBSA:

◆ **System configuration checks**: MBSA scans for security issues in the Windows operating system, such as Guest account status, file system type, available file shares, members of the Administrators group, and so on.

◆ **Internet Information Server (IIS)**: This group of checks scans for security issues in IIS 4.0, 5.0, and 6.0, such as sample applications and certain virtual directories present on the computer. The tool also checks if the IIS Lockdown tool has been run on the computer, which can help administrators configure and secure their IIS servers.

◆ **Microsoft SQL Server**: This group of checks scans for security issues in SQL Server 7.0 and SQL Server 2000, such as the type of authentication mode, SQL account password status, and SQL service account memberships.

◆ **Desktop application checks**: This group of checks scans Internet Explorer 5.01+ zone settings for each local user account and macro settings for Office 2000, Office XP, and Office System 2003.

◆ **Security updates**: MBSA can determine which critical security updates are applied to a system by referring to an Extensible Markup Language (XML) file, mssecure.xml, that is continuously updated and released by Microsoft. The XML file contains information about which security updates are available for particular Microsoft products.

◆ **Administrators group membership**: This check identifies and lists the individual user accounts that belong to the Local Administrators group. If more than two individual Administrative accounts are detected, the tool will list the account names and flag the check as a potential vulnerability.

◆ **Auditing**: This check determines whether auditing is enabled on the scanned computer. Windows has an auditing feature that tracks and logs specific events on your system, such as successful and failed logon attempts. By monitoring your system's Event Log, you can help identify potential security issues and malicious activity.

◆ **Auto Logon**: This check determines whether the Auto Logon feature is enabled on the scanned computer, and if the logon password is encrypted in the Registry or stored in plain text. If Auto Logon is enabled and the logon password is stored as plain text, the security report reflects this as a high-level vulnerability. If Auto Logon is enabled and the

Figure 8-2 Manually initiating a virus scan

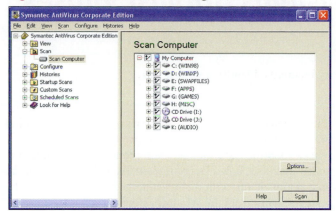

Figure 8-3 Enabling on-access scanning

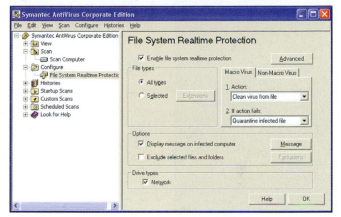

Figure 8-4 Microsoft Baseline Security Analyzer

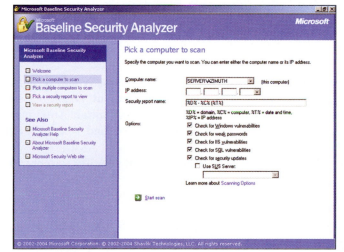

Figure 8-5 MBSA security reports

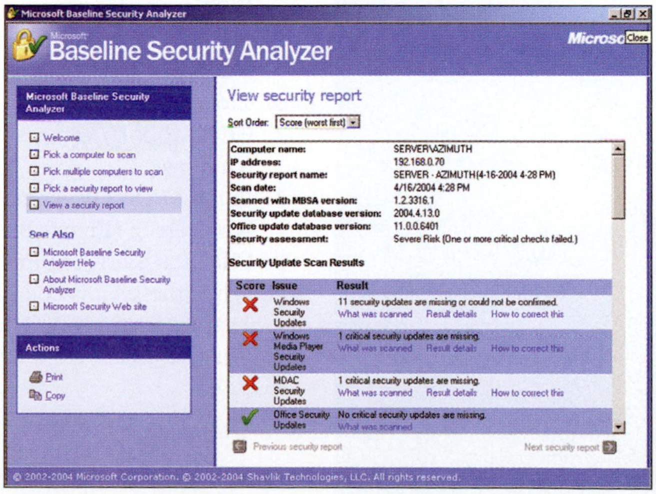

skill 2

Protecting Systems Against Viruses
(cont'd)

exam objective

Identify and respond to security incidents. Identify a virus attack.

overview

password is encrypted in the Registry, the security report flags this as a potential vulnerability.

◆ **Automatic Updates**: This check identifies whether the Automatic Updates feature is enabled on the scanned computer and if so, how it is configured. Automatic Updates can keep your computer up-to-date automatically with the latest updates from Microsoft by delivering them directly to your computer from the Windows Update site.

◆ **Check for unnecessary services**: This check determines whether any network services are enabled on the scanned computer, such as HTTP, FTP, SMTP, and Telnet services. A service is a program that runs in the background whenever the computer is running the operating system. Any unneeded services should be disabled to prevent attackers from accessing these service ports.

There are several other checks performed by MBSA on the system configuration of a server, such as domain controller status, insecure passwords, file system shares and so on. Finally, MBSA can be used to scan a range of systems by IP address and report vulnerabilities on all systems in the network. This last option makes it a very powerful tool for ensuring ongoing system security in a large environment. You can install MBSA via a free download from **http://www.microsoft.com/technet/security/tools/mbsahome.mspx**.

how to

Scan the system using Norton or Symantec Antivirus. You will need a registered copy of Norton or Symantec AntiVirus installed on the system. Then, scan the local system with MBSA. You will need to have MBSA installed on the system.

1. Log on to the system as an Administrator.
2. Click **start**, point to **All Programs**, point to **Norton SystemWorks/Symantec**, point to **Norton/ Symantec AntiVirus**, and click **Norton/Symantec AntiVirus** to start Norton/Symantec AntiVirus (**Figure 8-6**). (If the **Norton/Symantec AntiVirus** application does not start, right-click the icon on the taskbar and select **Open Norton/Symantec AntiVirus**.)
3. In the Norton/Symantec Antivirus window, expand **Scan** in the left pane and select **Scan Computer** (**Figure 8-7**).
4. In the right pane, ensure that the box beside **My Computer** is checked and click **Scan**.
5. Wait for the scan to complete, and then analyze the results. The scan may take an extended period of time. If a virus is found, follow the recommended action to dispose of the virus.
6. Close all dialog boxes.
7. Click **start**, point to **All Programs** and click **Microsoft Baseline Security Analyzer**.
8. In the MBSA Welcome screen, click **Scan a computer** to open the **Pick a computer to scan** screen (**Figure 8-8**).
9. Click the Start scan link to begin the scan.
10. When the scan is complete, examine the results and follow the directions to resolve any security issues MBSA has found.
11. When finished, close all dialog boxes and log off the system.

Figure 8-6 Selecting Scan Computer in
Symantec AntiVirus

Figure 8-7 Selecting the volume to scan

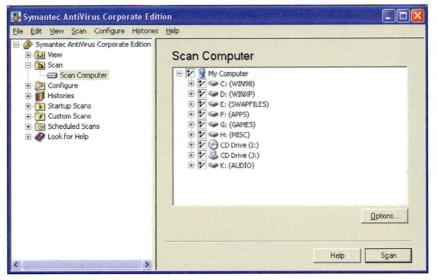

Figure 8-8 Scanning a computer with MBSA

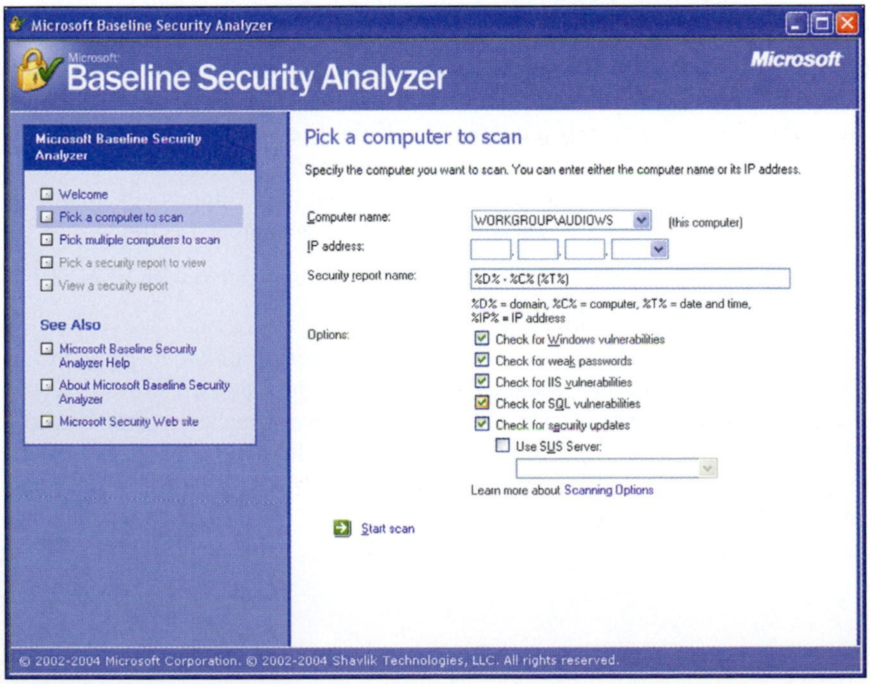

skill 3

Recognizing and Responding to Virus Attacks

exam objective

Identify and respond to security incidents. Identify a virus attack.

overview

Virus attacks vary in intensity and complexity of detection. Some are very easy to spot (such as most boot sector viruses), whereas others may display no outward signs of infection until they are activated by a specific keystroke or date. The best way of detecting a virus attack is to scan the system with a modern antivirus application that has up-to-date signatures. In some cases, it may be necessary to scan the system from a bootable recovery CD or Safe Mode (**Figure 8-9**), because some viruses will integrate themselves into the operating system and can effectively hide while the system is booted normally. Still, most viruses will display some outward signs of infection. Some of the more common symptoms of virus infection are listed in **Table 8-3**.

If you have any of these symptoms, you should thoroughly examine the system with one or more antivirus utilities before attempting to troubleshoot the problem using other methods.

When a virus attack occurs, you need to inspect the system using antivirus software with up-to-date virus definitions. This software informs you if a virus is found and gives you some options for repairing infected files. In general, antivirus applications use three methods for cleaning an infection:

◆ **Repairing infected files**: This method attempts to remove the virus from the infected files while leaving the core functionality of the infected application intact. This method rarely works.

◆ **Deleting infected files**: This method attempts to remove the file and all references to the file from the operating system. This removes the virus, but it may also render a loss of functionality.

◆ **Quarantining infected files**: Sometimes the antivirus application cannot determine if the file is a required component of a legitimate software application. In this case, the antivirus software may recommend that you quarantine the file to see if legitimate applications are affected. If they are, you can restore the file from quarantine. In general, this is a way to allow you to use the information on the file provided by the antivirus software to make a determination if whether or not the file is a false positive without permanently deleting it or risking further infection.

Once you scan the system, examine the scan report to see if any files are infected. If the system has a virus, you should generally follow the antivirus software's recommendation on how to deal with the virus. However, if a quarantine of the file is suggested, you should immediately research the affected file and virus information provided by the antivirus report to determine if the detection is a false positive. When in doubt, it is often better to simply delete the file and reinstall any affected applications rather than quarantine the file.

In addition to using an antivirus application, you can further protect your system by enabling the Internet Connection Firewall (**Figure 8-10**).

Once you enable the firewall, you will be prompted whenever an unknown application attempts to access the network. Thus, when a Trojan or backdoor attempts to utilize the network, you will be alerted to its presence. Additionally, whenever a malicious user attempts to connect to a backdoor on your system, you will be prompted. In either case, you can deny access, thus preventing your system from being hijacked by the virus. For more information on Internet Connection Firewall, see Lesson 9.

Figure 8-9 System Configuration Utility

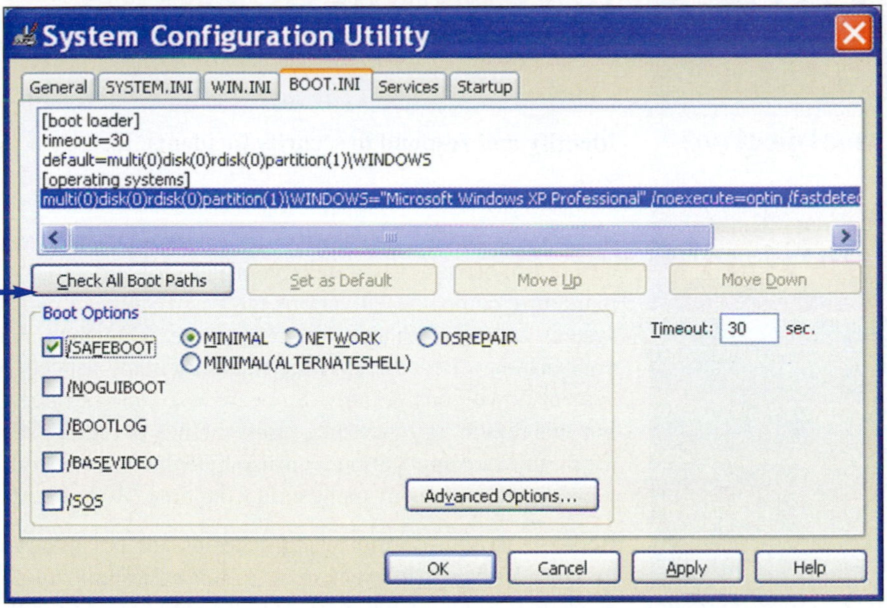

To boot in Safe Mode, enter **msconfig** in the Run dialog box to open up the System Configuration Utility and select /Safeboot on the Boot.ini tab

Table 8-3 Symptoms of virus infection

- Files copying themselves
- Spontaneous formatting of a hard disk
- Unexplainable changes in security settings
- Applications opening by themselves
- Random, strange message boxes
- Strange sounds or graphics appear randomly
- Unexplainable network activity
- Disk utilities do not function correctly

- Loss of data
- E-mails being automatically sent without your knowledge
- Sudden degradation of system performance
- Your antivirus program is disabled and cannot be enabled
- Attachments automatically added to all outbound e-mail
- The system will not boot
- Out of Memory error messages for no apparent reason

Figure 8-10 Enabling Internet Connection Firewall

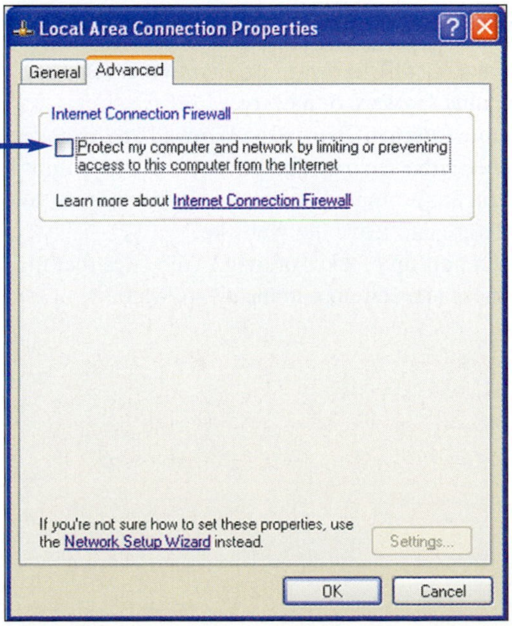

Select this check box on the Advanced tab of the Local Area Connection Properties dialog box to enable Internet Connection Firewall

skill 4   *Examining Spyware*

exam objective

Identify and respond to security incidents. Identify a virus attack.

overview

Spyware is a common culprit when a computer is behaving erratically or slowly. Spyware is a type of software that tracks your activity and sends this information to advertising and marketing companies at various intervals. Spyware can also add links and shortcuts to your system, as well as change your home page, add you to mailing lists, and launch pop-up ads in your browser. Because spyware tracks so many aspects of your system, it tends to slow the system down considerably. Spyware also tends to be very difficult to locate and remove. For this reason, spyware, like viruses, tends to require special software to locate and remove. Many spyware applications can also hide themselves from known scanners, so you should run your spyware removal application from Safe Mode to safely remove these applications.

Because spyware removal applications are not as mature as antivirus applications, you may need several different spyware removal applications to ensure that your system is well protected. Some of the more popular applications for this purpose include Ad-aware, Pest Patrol, and Spy Sweeper. Most spyware removal applications utilize signature scanning, like antivirus applications, to locate spyware. However, a few also make use of heuristics scanning.

Like antivirus software, you must scan the system for spyware and choose how and what to remove **(Figure 8-11)**. Be aware that some applications, particularly free or shareware applications, have integrated spyware to provide a revenue stream to the developer. For this reason, removing some spyware may make these applications inoperable.

If you are concerned about the possibility of spyware being present on your system, your first step should be to use a good spyware removal application to scan the system. Most systems of spyware infection mirror virus infection. Some of the more common symptoms include:

◆ Increased Internet traffic
◆ Your home page changes without your knowledge
◆ Pop-up advertisements increase in frequency or occur when you are not connected to the Internet
◆ System performance decreases
◆ Your Search toolbar in Internet Explorer changes

Additionally, there are a few things you can do to help protect your system against spyware:

◆ Do not install freeware or shareware software without researching to determine if it contains spyware or adware.
◆ Enable Internet Connection Firewall and examine all outgoing and incoming alerts.
◆ Increase the security and privacy settings within Internet Explorer.
◆ If you are prompted to install software before you can visit a Web page, do not install the software and leave the Web site.
◆ Use a pop-up blocker or avoid Web sites that utilize large numbers of pop-up ads. Many of these sites attempt to install spyware.

Figure 8-11 Scanning for spyware with Pest Patrol

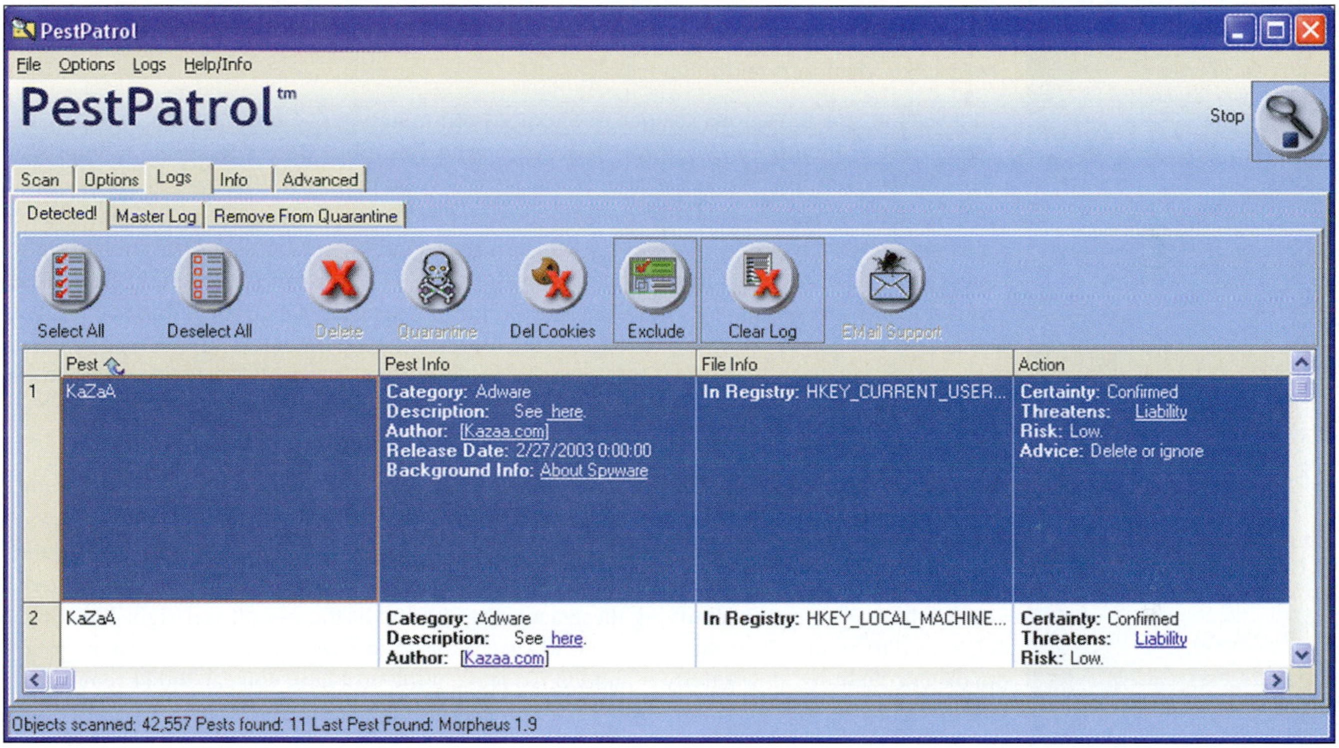

skill 5

Identifying and Responding to Other Security Incidents

Identify and respond to security incidents. Identify a virus attack.

overview

When responding to a security breach, as with any other troubleshooting scenario, you need to determine the source of the problem. This means getting as much information regarding the nature of the breach as possible. Once you have determined the source of the problem, you can work to protect the system against further breaches.

Although there are numerous types of security breaches, they tend to fall into a few general categories (**Figure 8-12**):

◆ Improper access to resources
◆ Misuse of user rights
◆ Denial of Service (DoS) attacks

The methods used to initiate these attacks will differ greatly, but each type of attack has its own set of identifiers and solutions.

Improper access to resources is one of the more common types of breaches, but it is perhaps the easiest to identify and control. This type of breach relies on exploitation of improper permissions settings, hacked accounts, or system vulnerabilities. To identify this type of attack, audit system resources (such as files and folders). Once auditing is enabled, by viewing the Security log, you can see which user accounts are accessing (or attempting to access) the resources, and modify permissions settings as necessary. Although this technique works well for direct attacks via improper permissions settings, for hacked accounts, you must also change the password for all affected user accounts. For attacks of this type centered on system vulnerabilities, first and foremost ensure that all critical security updates are applied to the system. Then, ensure that all unnecessary services are disabled. These two actions should eliminate most of these attacks.

Misuse of user rights is a more difficult problem to identify and control. Misuse of user rights occurs when a user utilizes rights that he or she rightfully requires to perform some malicious action. One example of this type of attack would be an administrative user taking ownership of a file to change the permissions on it and give himself inappropriate access to it. In most cases, the only way of identifying these activities is to audit the use of user rights. You may also need to audit policy change as well to ensure that if the user modifies the system policy to disable auditing, this activity is audited. To prevent the problem, you can either remove the user's rights (in the case of improper rights allocation) or discipline the user.

Finally, **Denial of Service (DoS) attacks** are perhaps the simplest attacks to detect, but they can be extremely difficult to control. A DoS attack is an attack that has no purpose other than to render the system or a service on the system unusable by authorized users. For instance, flooding a Web server with traffic to cause legitimate users to time out is an example of a DoS attack. In most cases, your best defense against DoS attacks are the combination of a strong firewall and regular security updates. Many DoS attacks make use of known security vulnerabilities, either in the network service or operating system itself. Security updates are designed to eliminate these vulnerabilities, rendering the DoS attack useless. Other DoS attacks rely on malformed packets or false addressing to confuse the attacked system. By installing a strong firewall, many of these types of packets will be dropped before they ever reach the system.

Figure 8-12 Different types of system attacks

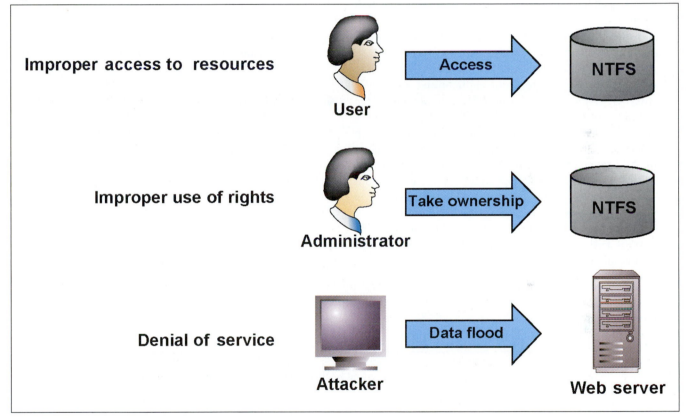

Improper access to resources

User   Access → NTFS

Improper use of rights

Administrator   Take ownership → NTFS

Denial of service

Attacker   Data flood → Web server

Summary

- The most common transmission method for any type of virus is through e-mail.
- Your best defense against virus attacks is education.
- Never open executables attached to e-mail unless you are certain of the application's validity and you have scanned the application with an up-to-date virus scanner.
- Pay close attention to any error messages or warnings you receive from Internet Explorer or your e-mail application.
- Scan all floppy disks with a virus scanning application before using them.
- Make sure that write protection is enabled before using a floppy disk in an untrusted system.
- Never open an e-mail attachment with a .vbs, .js, or .wsh extension.
- Pay close attention to any prompts to run macros when opening any document.
- As a second line of defense, you should make sure that the security settings for your applications, especially Internet Explorer and your e-mail application, are properly configured to disable unsafe content.
- You should ensure that you have an antivirus application installed, that the virus signatures for the application are up-to-date, and that real-time scanning is enabled.
- Many modern antivirus applications make use of both scanning mechanisms, though heuristics scanning is typically optional.
- The best way of detecting a virus attack is to scan the system with a modern antivirus application that has up-to-date signatures.
- If the system has a virus, you should generally follow the antivirus software's recommendation on how to deal with the virus.
- In addition to using an antivirus application, you can further protect your system by enabling the Internet Connection Firewall and data execution protection.
- Many spyware applications can also hide themselves from known scanners, so you are advised to run your spyware removal application from safe mode to safely remove these applications.
- Most spyware removal applications utilize signature scanning, like antivirus applications, to locate spyware.
- If you are concerned about the possibility of spyware being present on your system, your first step should be to utilize a good spyware removal application to scan the system.
- Do not install freeware or shareware software without researching to determine if it contains spyware or adware.
- Enable Internet Connection Firewall and examine all outgoing and incoming alerts.
- If you are prompted to install software before you can visit a Web page, do not install the software and leave the Web site.
- In most cases, your best defense against DoS attacks are the combination of a strong firewall and regular security updates.

Key Terms

Antivirus application
Backdoor virus
Boot-sector virus
Denial of Service (DoS) attacks
Heuristics scanning
Macro virus

Microsoft Baseline Security Analyzer (MBSA)
On-access scanning
On-demand scanning
Polymorphic virus
Script

Signature scanning
Spyware
Trojan Horse
Virus
Worm

Test Yourself

1. You have recently found out that a user's system is infected with a Trojan horse. Which of the following is most likely responsible for the installation of this type of virus?
   a. Boot sector of a commonly used floppy disk
   b. E-mail attachment with the .vbs extension
   c. E-mail attachment with the .exe extension
   d. Application update downloaded from the vendor's Web site

2. Which of the following should be the first step in preventing virus transmission?
   a. Antivirus software
   b. Spyware removal software
   c. User education
   d. Firewall software

3. A user calls you to ask your advice on a warning message she has received. When visiting an untrusted Web site, she was presented with a dialog box that claims that she must install a application called Gator.exe to continue. What should you advise the user to do?
   a. Cancel the installation and attempt to revisit the Web site.
   b. Cancel the installation and leave the Web site.
   c. Continue with the installation.
   d. Disconnect from the network.

4. You are informed by another technician that a user is complaining that some of his files are being changed without his knowledge. The technician wants to know if there are any built-in tools in Windows XP that will allow him to track who is modifying the files. Which of the following features should you advise the technician about?
   a. Auditing
   b. Logging
   c. Virus scanning
   d. Spyware scanning

5. Which of the following attacks would be most correctly described as denial of service (DoS) attacks? (Choose all that apply.)
   a. Changing of permissions on files by unauthorized users
   b. Hacking a user account
   c. Flooding a Web server with bogus data
   d. Access of files by unauthorized users
   e. Exploiting a security vulnerability to crash a system.

6. You are concerned about increased network activity from one user's system. This network activity occurs even when the user is not browsing the Internet. You run Network Monitor to examine traffic from the user's system, and find a large quantity of traffic destined for the following address: Adserver.spammarketers.com. Which of the following is the most likely cause of this traffic?
   a. Trojan horse
   b. Backdoor virus
   c. Boot sector virus
   d. Spyware
   e. Script virus

7. Which of the following are common symptoms of a virus? (Choose all that apply.)
   a. Unexplainable loss of data
   b. Degradation of system performance
   c. System will not boot
   d. Disk utilities displaying incorrect information
   e. Out-of-memory errors for no apparent reason

8. Which of the following most correctly describes the process of quarantining a virus?
   a. The viral code is removed from the offending file.
   b. The offending file is deleted.
   c. The offending file is moved to a special storage location that is inaccessible.

9. Which of the following are checked when you run an MBSA scan on a system? (Choose all that apply.)
   a. IIS security
   b. Security Updates
   c. File system type
   d. Trojan horses
   e. Auditing
   f. Spyware

10. Which of the following actions should you perform first when a user e-mails you a message from an unreliable source concerning a new virus threat?
    a. Immediately scan all systems for the virus.
    b. Follow the directions in the e-mail to scan for and remove the virus from all systems.
    c. Forward the e-mail to your boss.
    d. Research the virus on your antivirus software manufacturer's Web site.
    e. Forward the e-mail to all users.

Projects: On Your Own

1. Utilize Pest Patrol's free Web-based system scanner to inspect your system for spyware. You will need Internet access to complete this exercise.
   a. Log on to the system as a local Administrator.
   b. Open **Internet Explorer**.
   c. Type **http://www.pestscan.com/** in your browser's address bar and press **[Enter]**.
   d. Click the **Start Your Free Scan Now** button to begin the scan.
   e. Follow the directions to enable the ActiveX control and begin the system scan.
   f. Examine the list of applications, cookies, and other settings that are returned. You cannot clean the system with this utility, but it should give you an idea of how badly the system is infected.
   g. Close all open dialog boxes and log off of the system.

2. Use McAfee's free Web based system scan to scan your system for viruses. You will need Internet access to complete this exercise.
   a. Log on to the system as a local Administrator.
   b. Open **Internet Explorer**.
   c. Type **http://us.mcafee.com/** in your browser's address bar and press [Enter].
   d. Click the **FreeScan** link under **Free Tools** in the bottom left corner of the page.
   e. Enter your information to register for the free system scan.
   f. Follow the directions to enable the ActiveX control and begin the system scan.
   g. Examine the virus report that is returned. You cannot clean the system with this utility, but it should give you an idea of how badly the system is infected.
   h. Close all open dialog boxes and log off of the system.

Problem Solving Scenarios

1. You are working for Dothis, Inc., a sign company. Your company is in the process of bidding for government contracts, and as a result, is increasingly concerned about system security. You have been asked to determine what measures should be taken to ensure system security. Prepare a document listing all of the processes, Windows features, and applications you will suggest to management.

2. You are a new Desktop Support Technician for Whoa!, an automotive braking systems manufacturer. As part of your duties, you are required to educate users on how to respond to virus and spyware threats, including hoaxes. List the items you feel need to be covered in your discussion.

Troubleshooting Application Connectivity

Troubleshooting application connectivity actually consists of troubleshooting most components in the system. To troubleshoot any network connectivity problem, you must troubleshoot all aspects of network connectivity, including name resolution, network adapter configuration, and permissions. Because any of these issues could potentially cause an application connectivity error, troubleshooting network connectivity issues largely revolves around eliminating potential sources of errors to arrive at the cause of the error.

In addition, you may be presented with error conditions that do not relate to network connectivity, but rather, are based on lack of connectivity to local resources. For these errors, you must examine the hardware components of the system very carefully to determine if hardware or software is the cause of the error.

This lesson begins with a discussion of the types of network names used in Microsoft operating systems and how name resolution problems cause network connectivity problems. You will learn how to troubleshoot name resolution problems and use utilities such as Ping and Ipconfig to examine connectivity issues.

Next, you will learn how to identify and fix problems with network adapters, from cabling problems to incorrect IP configuration, and how to determine whether a connectivity problem is due to network configuration or a client system configuration. You will learn about firewalls and how firewall configuration can cause specific types of connectivity problems.

The lesson continues with a discussion of how insufficient user permissions and rights can cause problems with installing and running applications locally and in accessing network resources. Lastly, you will learn how to troubleshoot problems in accessing local resources, such as hard drives, and locally connected devices, such as printers.

Goals

In this lesson, you will learn how to troubleshoot application connectivity problems.

Requirements

To complete this lesson, you will need administrative rights on a Window XP Professional computer with Service Pack 1 installed. You will also need to have access to the Internet.

skill 1

Troubleshooting Name Resolution Problems

exam objective

Identify and troubleshoot name resolution problems. Indications of such problems include application errors.

overview

Name resolution problems are possibly the most common type of network connectivity problem, and they are also completely overlooked by inexperienced technicians in many cases. Luckily, in most cases, name resolution problems are very easy to resolve. First, however, you must understand how and why name resolution problems can cause other network connectivity errors.

Name resolution is the process of resolving a friendly name, such as **www.microsoft.com**, into a protocol address, such as 207.46.244.188. Because the computer makes contact with the remote computer using the protocol (in this case, IP) address, the computer requires the protocol address, not the name, to communicate. However, people have a notoriously difficult time remembering numbers, so we use names to associate with these resources. Name resolution, in short, converts people-friendly names into computer-friendly numbers.

The process for resolving the name differs depending on the type of name. In Microsoft operating systems, two types of names can be used: **Network Basic Input/Output System (NetBIOS) names** (also known as computer names) and **Fully Qualified Domain Names (FQDNs**, also known as host names). Let's take a closer look at each type of name. NetBIOS names are single word, 15-character names. This means that the number of NetBIOS names is severely limited as opposed to FQDNs, but the simplicity of NetBIOS is also its greatest strength. Where the FQDN for a system might be PC1.support.corp.com, the NetBIOS name could be as simple as PC1.

NetBIOS names can be resolved in several manners:

1. **NetBIOS name cache**: Anytime you resolve a NetBIOS name, the resolution entry for that name is stored in the NetBIOS name cache. This is done so that future requests for that name do not require resolution. The NetBIOS name cache is stored in system RAM.
2. **Windows Internet Naming Service (WINS) server**: A WINS server is a server that maintains a dynamic database of NetBIOS names. When a WINS client needs to resolve a NetBIOS name, it sends a query to the WINS server, which looks up the name and sends the client the IP address associated with the name.
3. **Broadcast**: The client tries a basic network broadcast to query all hosts on a subnet. When the destination host receives the broadcast, it sends its IP address to the client. These broadcasts do not cross routers; therefore, this method is not suitable for large networks with many subnets.
4. **LMHOSTS file**: An LMHOSTS file is a text file that is stored on the local computer. The LMHOSTS file contains a list of mappings of NetBIOS names to IP addresses for the network (**Figure 9-1**). If an entry for the destination NetBIOS resource exists, the NetBIOS name is resolved. The LMHOSTS file can be edited with a text editor, such as Notepad. The LMHOSTS file is stored in the *%systemroot %*\system32\drivers\etc folder. This file is not installed by default, but a sample version of an LMHOSTS file called lmhosts.sam can be used to create the file. To create an LMHOSTS file, edit **lmhosts.sam** as required, and then save it as **lmhosts** with no file extension.

FQDNs (host names), on the other hand, are a bit more complex. FQDNs are hierarchical, which means that the names follow a pattern of increasing specificity, which flows from right to left, with the most specific part of the name located on the left. For example, examine **Figure 9-2**. In this example, the least specific part of the name is the dot (".") on the far right, which represents the root. The root is the beginning of the namespace. Next, you have the top level domain, com. Obviously, there are multiple millions of "dot coms" on the Internet, so that is not very specific, but it is more specific than the root, which contains all .coms, .nets, .orgs, etc.

Figure 9-1 LMHOSTS file

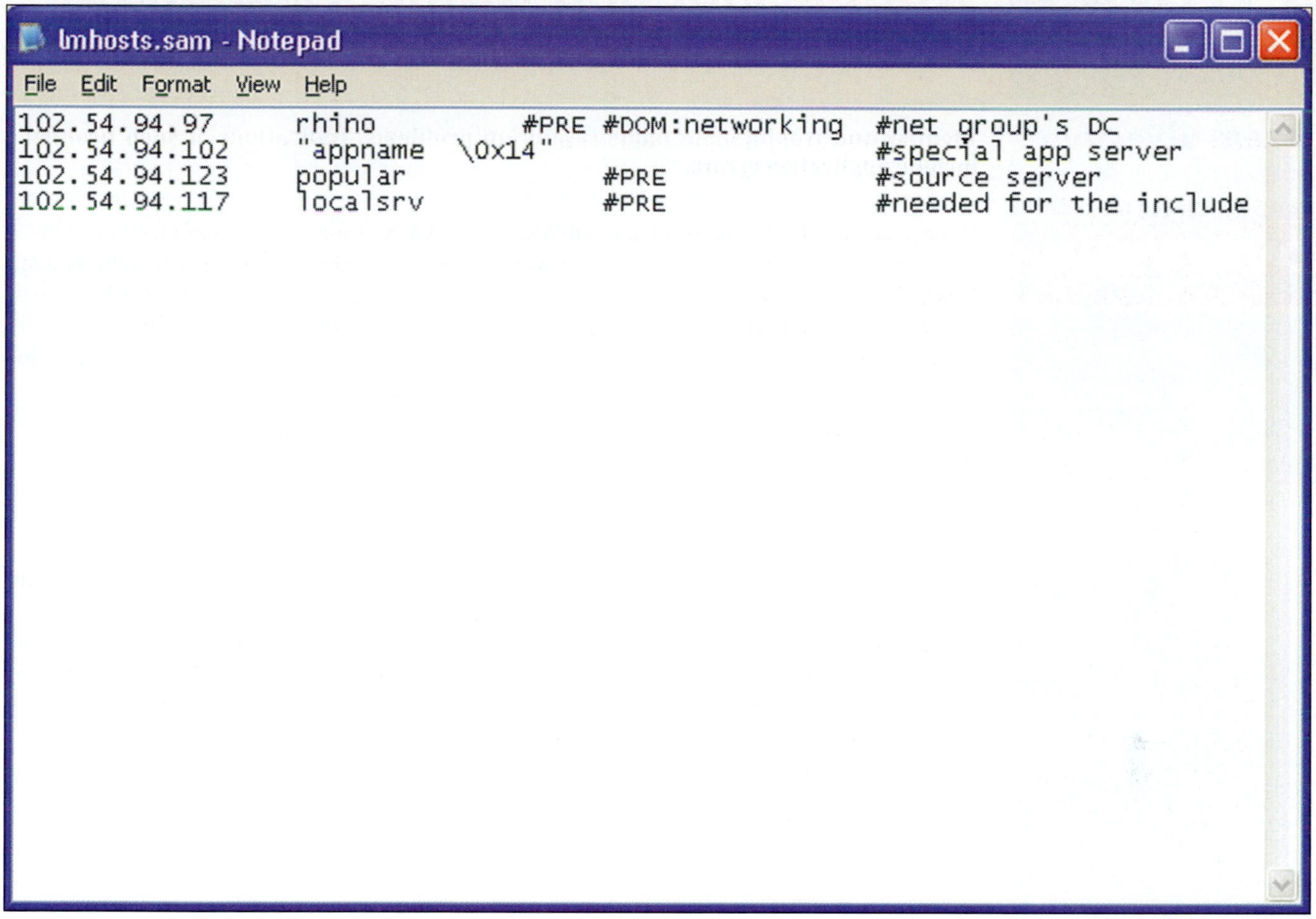

lmhosts.sam - Notepad
File Edit Format View Help
102.54.94.97 rhino #PRE #DOM:networking #net group's DC
102.54.94.102 "appname \0x14" #special app server
102.54.94.123 popular #PRE #source server
102.54.94.117 localsrv #PRE #needed for the include

Figure 9-2 Examining the DNS namespace

WWW . SUPPORT . MICROSOFT . COM .
Host
Subdomain
Second-Level Domain
Root
Top-Level Domain

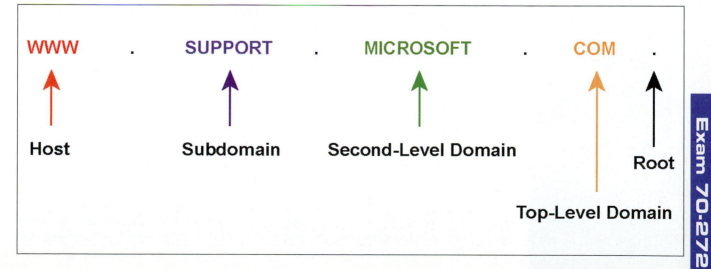

skill 1

Troubleshooting Name Resolution Problems (cont'd)

exam objective

Identify and troubleshoot name resolution problems. Indications of such problems include application errors.

overview

Next, you have the second level domain, Microsoft, which is one specific organization. This is obviously more specific than .com, but it is still a long way from identifying a specific system. Next, you have support, which is a specific subset (like a department) of the Microsoft organization. Support is more specific than Microsoft but still does not identify a specific system. Finally, you have the most specific section, the name www, which identifies a specific host.

As with NetBIOS names, there are many different methods of resolving host names:

1. **Domain Name System (DNS) cache**: The DNS cache, like the NetBIOS cache, stores names that have previously been resolved by the client. Also like the NetBIOS name cache, the DNS cache is stored in system RAM.
2. **DNS servers**: DNS servers are servers that resolve DNS names using the hierarchical DNS database. Name resolution via DNS servers will be explained later in the skill.
3. **HOSTS file**: The HOSTS file is a simple text file equating FQDNs with IP addresses. Like the LMHOSTS file, it is stored in the *%systemroot %*\system32\drivers\etc folder. Unlike the LMHOSTS file, the HOSTS file is enabled by default but is configured only with a single entry **(Figure 9-3)**.

Resolving names using a DNS server is a bit of a complex process due to the requirement that DNS be a hierarchical database. This requirement exists because there are simply too many names to use a single DNS database. Because of this, the DNS database is distributed among thousands of DNS servers, with each server responsible for maintaining information only regarding its own small portion of the total DNS namespace. To resolve an FQDN, referrals are utilized to send the query to the specific DNS server responsible for that portion of the DNS namespace.

For example, suppose that you want to resolve the name **www.corp.com (Figure 9-4)**. First, your system will check its DNS cache. If the entry is not found, it sends a query to the primary DNS server configured in its IP Properties dialog box. This DNS server will look in its local database to see if it "owns" that portion of the DNS namespace. Finding that it does not, it will send a query to the root servers, which are the top level of the DNS hierarchy. The root servers will not know the IP address of **www.corp.com**, but they will know how to reach the servers responsible for the .com portion of the namespace and will refer the DNS server to them. The com servers will also not have direct knowledge of **www.corp.com**, but they will know where the server responsible for the corp domain is and will refer the DNS server to it. The DNS server will then ask the corp.com DNS server about **www.corp.com**, and because this DNS server does have direct knowledge of the name, it will respond back to your DNS server with the IP address, and your DNS server will forward that information to your system.

Now that you have a basic understanding of how each type of name is resolved, let's explore how to troubleshoot name resolution problems. First, you need to understand how to recognize name resolution problems. The primary key to this process is to understand that any network error that occurs while using a friendly name can potentially be a name resolution error. With this in mind, the key to troubleshooting name resolution is to pinpoint name resolution as the cause of the problem.

The primary method used to pinpoint name resolution as the problem is to ping the resource by name and then ping the resource by IP. If you can reach the resource by IP, but not by name, then name resolution is the most likely culprit. If this is the case, you should check the entries for DNS and WINS servers in the system's IP configuration by running the command **ipconfig /all (Figure 9-5)**. Ensure that the servers listed are correct. If not, manually configure the server addresses in the TCP/IP (Transmission Control Protocol/Internet Protocol) Properties dialog box.

Figure 9-3 Hosts file

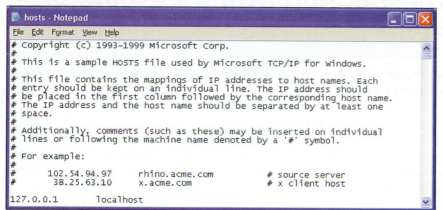

```
# Copyright (c) 1993-1999 Microsoft Corp.
#
# This is a sample HOSTS file used by Microsoft TCP/IP for Windows.
#
# This file contains the mappings of IP addresses to host names. Each
# entry should be kept on an individual line. The IP address should
# be placed in the first column followed by the corresponding host name.
# The IP address and the host name should be separated by at least one
# space.
#
# Additionally, comments (such as these) may be inserted on individual
# lines or following the machine name denoted by a '#' symbol.
#
# For example:
#
#      102.54.94.97     rhino.acme.com          # source server
#       38.25.63.10     x.acme.com              # x client host

127.0.0.1       localhost
```

Figure 9-4 DNS name resolution

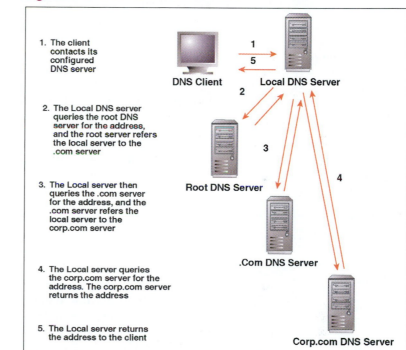

1. The client contacts its configured DNS server

2. The Local DNS server queries the root DNS server for the address, and the root server refers the local server to the .com server

3. The Local server then queries the .com server for the address, and the .com server refers the local server to the corp.com server

4. The Local server queries the corp.com server for the address. The corp.com server returns the address

5. The Local server returns the address to the client

Figure 9-5 Output from the ipconfig /all command

```
D:\Documents and Settings\Brian>ipconfig /all

Windows IP Configuration

        Host Name . . . . . . . . . . . . : audious
        Primary Dns Suffix  . . . . . . . :
        Node Type . . . . . . . . . . . . : Unknown
        IP Routing Enabled. . . . . . . . : No
        WINS Proxy Enabled. . . . . . . . : No
        DNS Suffix Search List. . . . . . : launchmoden.com

Ethernet adapter Local Area Connection 2:

        Connection-specific DNS Suffix  . : launchmoden.com
        Description . . . . . . . . . . . : 3Com 3C920B-EMB Integrated Fast Ethernet Controller
        Physical Address. . . . . . . . . : 00-0E-A6-10-3D-85
        Dhcp Enabled. . . . . . . . . . . : Yes
        Autoconfiguration Enabled . . . . : Yes
        IP Address. . . . . . . . . . . . : 192.168.1.96
        Subnet Mask . . . . . . . . . . . : 255.255.255.0
        Default Gateway . . . . . . . . . : 192.168.1.254
        DHCP Server . . . . . . . . . . . : 192.168.1.254
        DNS Servers . . . . . . . . . . . : 192.168.1.254
                                            192.168.1.254
        Lease Obtained. . . . . . . . . . : Tuesday, October 19, 2004 9:47:09 AM
        Lease Expires . . . . . . . . . . : Wednesday, October 20, 2004 9:47:09 AM

Ethernet adapter Local Area Connection:

        Media State . . . . . . . . . . . : Media disconnected
        Description . . . . . . . . . . . : NVIDIA nForce MCP Networking Adapter
        Physical Address. . . . . . . . . : 00-0E-A6-24-09-B9
```

skill 1 Troubleshooting Name Resolution Problems (cont'd)

exam objective

Identify and troubleshoot name resolution problems. Indications of such problems include application errors.

overview

Although entering the correct WINS server address generally solves most NetBIOS name resolution problems, DNS can be slightly more complicated. If the correct DNS server is entered in the configuration, but you still cannot reach the resource, you may have a **negative response** that has been cached. A negative response is an answer to your query that basically says "I can't find the resource." This type of response is most commonly issued when there is a configuration error on the server. If the DNS server sends your client such a response, your client will, by default, cache this response. Because the response is cached, even when the server is reconfigured and can resolve the resource, you may still not be able to reach the resource. To resolve this problem, you need to clear the DNS cache. To clear all entries from the DNS cache, simply use the command **ipconfig /flushdns** on a Windows 2000 or higher system. If you are using Windows NT or 9x, rebooting the system will clear the cache.

how to

Use Ipconfig to examine your IP configuration and to clear the DNS resolver cache on a Windows XP system.

1. Boot the system and log on as a local administrator.
2. Click **start**, point to **All Programs**, point to **Accessories**, and click **Command Prompt** to open a Windows command prompt (**Figure 9-6**).
3. In the command prompt window, type **ipconfig /all** and press **[Enter]** to view your IP configuration (Refer to **Figure 9-5**). Take note of the IP address, subnet mask, default gateway, DNS and WINS server settings.
4. Type **ipconfig /displaydns** to view the DNS resolver cache on your system (**Figure 9-7**). This displays the addresses DNS has resolved and entered into the cache. Take note of the number of entries in the cache.
5. Type **ipconfig /flushdns** (**Figure 9-8**). This will clear the DNS resolver cache.
6. Type **ipconfig /displaydns** to view the now empty DNS resolver cache.
7. Type **exit** and press **[Enter]** to close the command prompt.
8. Close all open dialog boxes and log off of the system.

Figure 9-6 Opening the command prompt

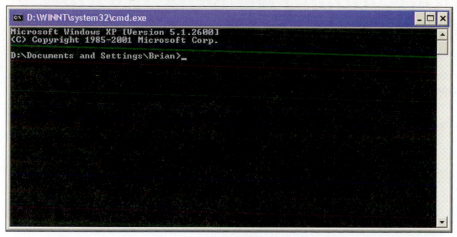

Figure 9-7 Viewing the DNS cache

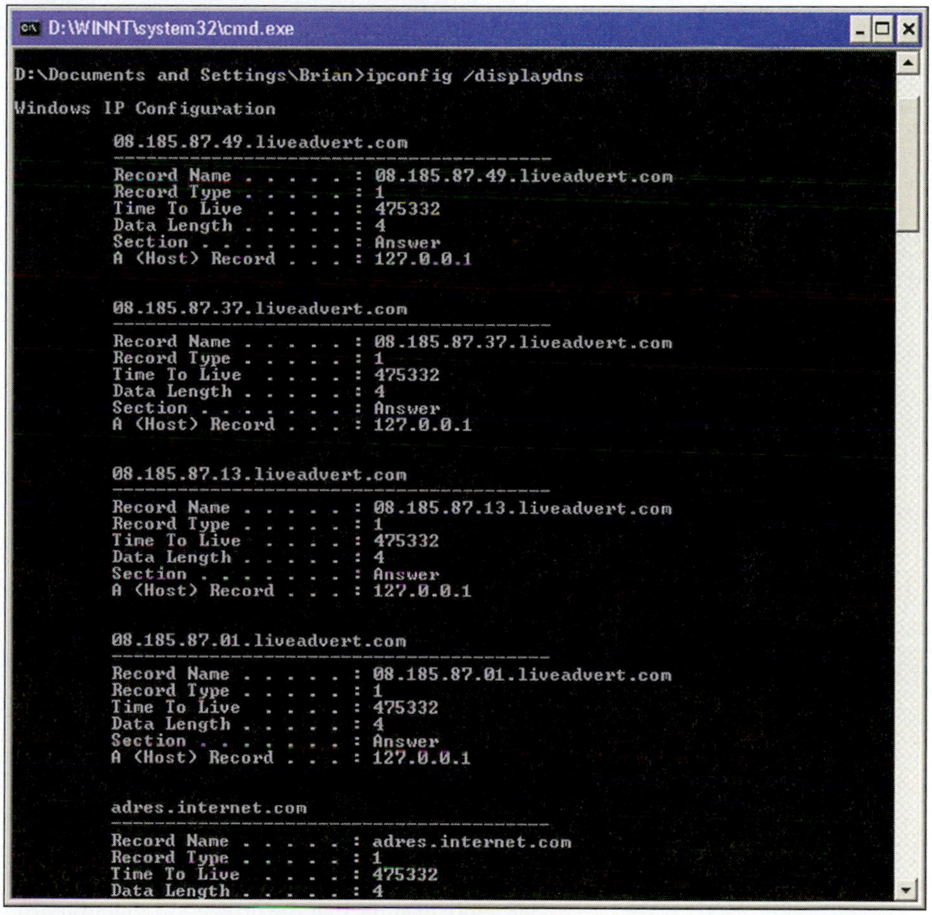

Figure 9-8 Clearing the DNS cache

skill 2

Troubleshooting Network Adapter Configuration Problems

exam objective

Identify and troubleshoot network adapter configuration problems. Indications of such problems include application errors.

overview

Unlike name resolution problems, problems with network adapters, in most cases, tend to be relatively simple to diagnose and repair. Some of the more common network adapter problems follow, in the general order that you should use to troubleshoot the adapter.

◆ **Cabling problems**: Cabling problems are perhaps the simplest of all problems and should be the first area you examine with any networking problem. In Windows 2000 and above, the operating system will notify you of a cable being disconnected by displaying a notification icon on your taskbar **(Figure 9-9)**. Additionally, if you open up the properties for Network Connections (Windows 2000) or My Network Places (Windows XP), you can also easily see that the adapter is disconnected **(Figure 9-10)**. However, in some cases, you may get the network disconnected notification even when the cable is properly connected. In these cases, examine the link light on the adapter to see if a link is present. If a link is not present, you may have the wrong cable type (crossover versus straight), or you may have a faulty cable.

◆ **Disabled adapter**: Assuming that you have no cabling problems, the next thing you should check is whether the adapter is disabled. This is generally easy to determine by simply examining the icon for the adapter in Network Connections (Windows 2000) or My Network Places (Windows XP). If the adapter is disabled, it will be grayed out, as is shown in **Figure 9-11**. You can also check to see if the adapter is disabled by opening Device Manager and examining the adapter. A disabled adapter will have a red X over the icon **(Figure 9-12)**.

◆ **Resource conflicts**: If the adapter is not disabled, examine the adapter's Properties dialog box from within the Device Manager for resource conflicts. In general, this is typically only a common problem with ISA adapters. PCI adapters are always Plug and Play, and due to the bus-mastering nature of PCI, resource conflicts are rare. If you have a resource conflict, the icon of the adapter in the Device Manager will be overlaid with a yellow circle containing a black exclamation point **(Figure 9-13)**. Additionally, in the adapter's Properties dialog box, you will be able to see which devices the adapter is conflicting with. For an ISA adapter, changing the resource settings from within Windows is not typically the best option, as many ISA adapters use hardware jumpers to change the resource settings. Typically, the best solution to the problem is to enter the Plug and Play configuration section of the system BIOS and reserve the resources for the ISA adapter. By reserving the resources, you are instructing the system to exclude those resources from the list of resources assigned to PCI devices by Plug and Play.

◆ **Incorrect or faulty driver**: If your problem is still not resolved, you should examine the driver to ensure that it is the latest signed driver for the hardware. Signed drivers are verified to work with the operating system by Windows Hardware Quality Labs, which basically ensures that the driver will function properly. You can check to see if the driver is signed by examining the Drivers tab in the Properties dialog of the adapter from within Device Manager. Sometimes, however, even signed drivers can become corrupted. In this case, the solution is to remove the driver and reinstall it.

◆ **Incorrect transceiver setting**: An incorrect transceiver setting is a rare problem with modern adapters, but it can occur with older adapters. A transceiver is short for transmitter/receiver, and is, essentially, the port you plug into on the network interface card (NIC). In some NICs, there may be more than one transceiver, enabling the adapter to support multiple network cabling types. For instance, a 10 MB Ethernet adapter might contain transcieivers for Attachment Unit Interface (AUI), Registered Jack 45 (RJ-45),

Figure 9-9 Notification icon on the taskbar

Notification of disconnection

Figure 9-10 Disconnected cable on an adapter

Figure 9-11 Disabled adapter

Figure 9-12 Disabled adapter in Device Manager

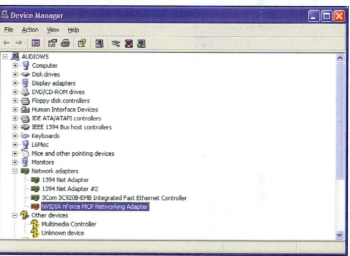

Figure 9-13 Resource conflict

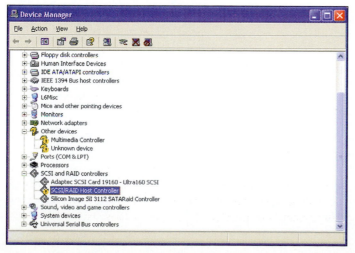

skill 2

Troubleshooting Network Adapter Configuration Problems (cont'd)

exam objective

Identify and troubleshoot network adapter configuration problems. Indications of such problems include application errors.

overview

and Bayonet-Neill-Concelman (BNC) connections **(Figure 9-14)**. These adapters are commonly called combo cards. Although most modern combo cards will auto detect which transceiver to use, many older combo cards relied on a jumper or DIPswitch (DIP stands for Dual Inline Package) setting to configure the transceiver. On these adapters, you must ensure that the correct transceiver is selected.

◆ **Incorrect speed/duplex settings**: You should ensure that the speed and duplex settings are correctly configured on Ethernet adapters. Most modern adapters allow you to modify this setting through the adapter properties **(Figure 9-15)**, but some may require a special configuration utility or may rely on jumpers to configure these settings. Additionally, most modern adapters support auto detection of these settings, but by allowing the adapter to auto detect these settings, you run the risk of the adapter selecting the wrong settings. If you are having difficulty communicating and all of the other issues discussed are not causing the problem, try manually configuring the adapter to the correct speed and duplex setting.

◆ **Incorrect IP configuration**: As a final step in troubleshooting a problematic adapter, check the IP configuration settings for the system. The easiest way to do this is typically to run **ipconfig /all**. The most important aspects of the IP configuration are the IP address and subnet mask. If these sections contain incorrect information, then the computer will likely not be able to communicate at all. Next, check the default gateway setting. If the default gateway address is incorrect, the computer will not be able to reach other networks (including the Internet). Finally, as discussed in Skill 1, examine the DNS and WINS server settings.

Figure 9-14 Combo card

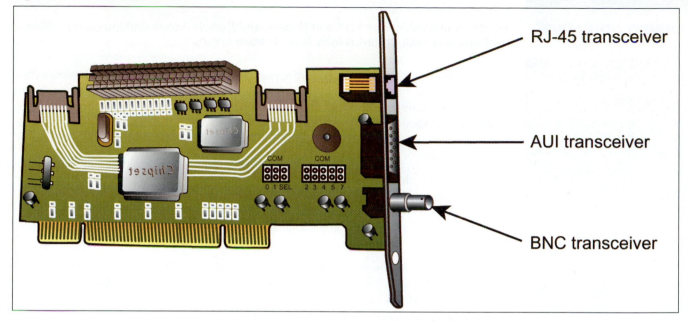

RJ-45 transceiver

AUI transceiver

BNC transceiver

Figure 9-15 Modifying the link speed on the adapter

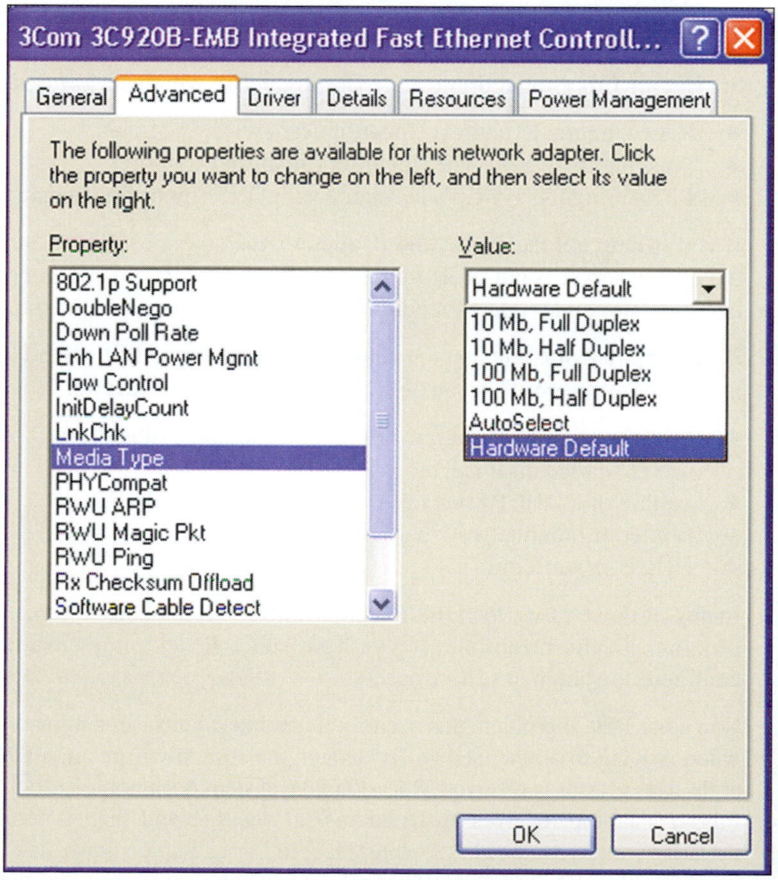

skill 3

Troubleshooting LAN/Routing/Remote Access Configuration Problems

exam objective

Identify and troubleshoot LAN and Routing and Remote Access configuration problems. Indications of such problems include application errors.

overview

As a desktop support technician, you are expected to be able to determine if a problem with a client's network connectivity is related to the client's configuration or the network configuration. Additionally, if you can provide specific information regarding the error to the IT department, they can resolve network problems much faster. For this reason, it is important that you understand the basics of troubleshooting network problems that are not caused by misconfiguration of client systems.

Local area network (LAN) problems can come in many forms, from simple configuration problems to complex routing issues. Some of the problems you will be expected to recognize include Dynamic Host Configuration Protocol (DHCP) configuration and routing problems, in addition to the basic client configuration and name resolution problems discussed earlier in the lesson.

DHCP problems are perhaps the easiest problems to recognize. When a client on a Windows 98, Me, 2000, or XP system fails to obtain a DHCP IP address, it will generate an **Automatic Private IP Addressing (APIPA)** address. This address allows the client to reach all other computers on the local subnet in the event that the DHCP server is down, but it will not allow any connectivity to remote networks. You can determine if a client has an APIPA address by using Ipconfig and examining the client's IP address. An APIPA address will always start with 169.254, meaning that APIPA addresses will be in the range from 169.254.0.1 to 169.254.255.254.

If the client has an APIPA IP address, your first step should be to determine if the problem is unique to that client. If the problem is unique to that client, then the first step to resolving the client's problem should be to run **ipconfig /renew**. Alternately, on Windows XP, you can use the **Repair this connection** feature (**Figure 9-16**), which performs several actions, including:

◆ Renewing the IP address (**ipconfig /renew**)
◆ Flushing the DNS cache (**ipconfig /flushdns**)
◆ Registering the system's hostname with DNS (**ipconfig /registerdns**)

If you still do not receive a valid IP address, then the most likely cause of the problem is that the DHCP server is out of IP addresses to lease. At this point, you need to contact the DHCP administrator and request for additional addresses to be added to the server.

If the majority of clients on the network are receiving APIPA IP addresses, then the problem is a bit more severe. This can be caused by a number of factors, including:

◆ DHCP server configuration errors (no valid range of addresses, too few addresses, DHCP server service disabled, etc.)
◆ Failure of a DHCP relay agent
◆ Router or other network hardware failure
◆ DHCP server failure

In any of these cases, the DHCP administrator will need to be contacted and informed of the problem. In the meantime, if you have static IP addresses available, you can statically configure the client to restore access.

One other DHCP problem that occurs with mobile clients is retention of a DHCP IP address even when moving to a new facility. By default, the system will retain a DHCP IP address for up to eight days after it is received. Rebooting the system does not release the IP address. Because of this, if a laptop receives an IP address at one site and then is transported to another site, the address may be invalid. For instance, in the example shown in **Figure 9-17**, if the laptop receives the IP address 192.168.1.100 when connected to the network at building 1, then is powered down and moved to building 2, it will not have a valid IP address for building

tip

Microsoft Knowledge Base article 289256 details each step performed when the Repair this connection feature is used.

tip

The Repair this connection feature is only available in Windows XP.

Figure 9-16 **Repair this connection feature**

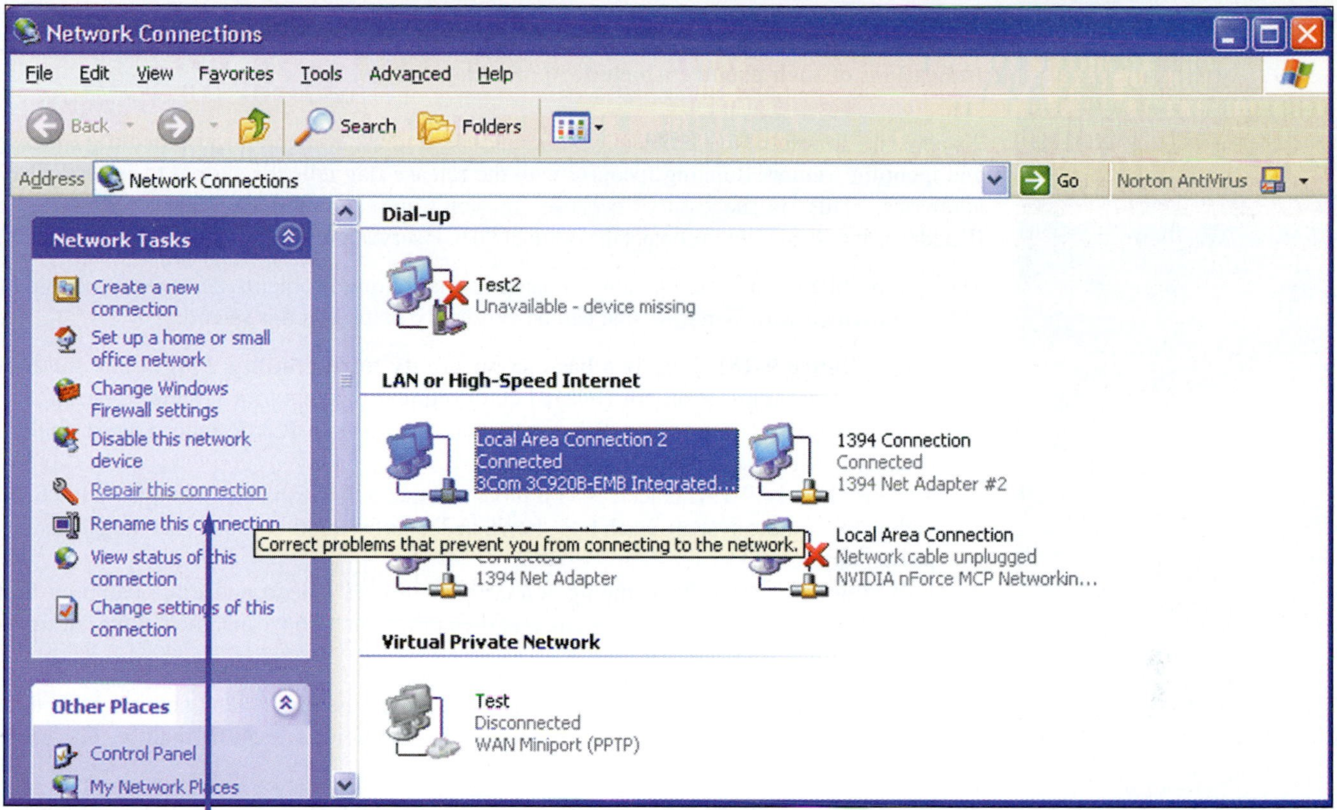

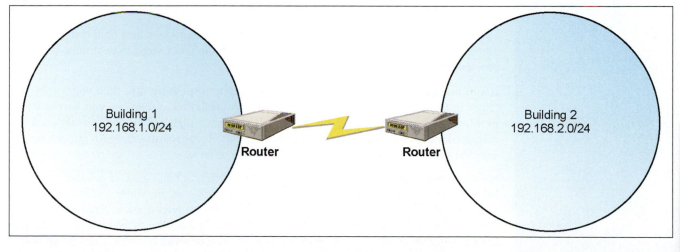

Use the Repair this connection link to renew the IP address, flush the DNS cache, and register the system's hostname with DNS

Figure 9-17 **Example network**

skill 3

Troubleshooting LAN/Routing/Remote Access Configuration Problems (cont'd)

exam objective

Identify and troubleshoot LAN and Routing and Remote Access configuration problems. Indications of such problems include application errors.

overview

2's network. To resolve this problem, you actually need to use two commands: **ipconfig /release** and **ipconfig /renew**. Running Ipconfig with the release flag tells the system to release all IP addresses. This is necessary because if you just tell the system to renew the IP address, it will attempt to contact the original DHCP server and simply extend its current lease.

The next problem you should be able to recognize is routing problems. There are a couple of utilities provided with Windows that can be extremely helpful in this regard:

◆ **Ping (Figure 9-18)**: Ping is a basic connectivity testing utility. Ping sends Internet Control Messaging Protocol (ICMP) echo request packets to a system to see if that system is up and responsive. When a system receives an ICMP echo request packet, it sends ICMP echo reply in response.

◆ **Tracert (Figure 9-19)**: Tracert is a bit more advanced than Ping and attempts to trace the path to the remote system. Each hop shown in Tracert is another router that the packet has passed through.

◆ **Pathping (Figure 9-20)**: Pathping is a combination of Tracert and Ping. Pathping first traces the route to the remote system, and then pings each hop a specific number of times and tracks statistics on each ping.

For basic troubleshooting, the Ping command is extremely helpful. Using nothing more than Ping, you can determine whether the source of the problem is local or remote. The basic troubleshooting method using Ping is as follows:

◆ **Run ipconfig /all**. This ensures that the client has a valid IP configuration. Examine all of the information provided to ensure that it is correct.

◆ **Ping the client's IP address**. This ensures that TCP/IP is bound properly and that the default routes are listed in the client's routing table.

◆ **Ping a local host (name and IP)**. This ensures that connectivity to the local network exists. By pinging by both name (ping PC1.corp.com) and IP address (ping 192.168.1.100), you determine if name resolution is functioning.

◆ **Ping the default gateway**. By pinging the default gateway shown in the client's IP configuration, you ensure that the client can reach the local router and that the router is responding to packets.

◆ **Ping a remote host (name and IP)**. By pinging a remote host, you ensure that network connectivity between the client and the remote system exists.

The simple method of performing these steps is to ping the remote host first. If this succeeds, all other steps will succeed. If it fails, then you use the other steps to determine where the problem is occurring.

If you do not see correct IP information after running **ipconfig /all**, then your problem is either in the client's configuration (for statically configured clients) or you have a DHCP problem. If you cannot ping the client's IP address, then either the TCP/IP stack has malfunctioned, or someone has manually edited the local routing table. In either case, the simplest solution is usually to renew the client's IP address.

If you cannot ping a local host, then try to ping a different local host. If you can ping some local hosts but not others, you may have a cabling or network hardware problem segmenting the network, or you may have an incorrect subnet mask entered on the client. If you cannot ping any local hosts, then your IP configuration may be invalid, or you may have a major network hardware problem (such as one or more hubs/switches being down).

Figure 9-18 Ping

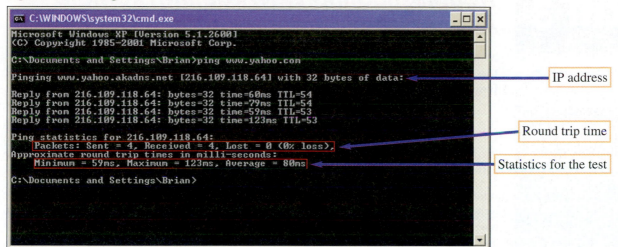

```
C:\WINDOWS\system32\cmd.exe                                    _ □ ×

Microsoft Windows XP [Version 5.1.2600]
(C) Copyright 1985-2001 Microsoft Corp.

C:\Documents and Settings\Brian>ping www.yahoo.com

Pinging www.yahoo.akadns.net [216.109.118.64] with 32 bytes of data:

Reply from 216.109.118.64: bytes=32 time=60ms TTL=54
Reply from 216.109.118.64: bytes=32 time=79ms TTL=54
Reply from 216.109.118.64: bytes=32 time=59ms TTL=53
Reply from 216.109.118.64: bytes=32 time=123ms TTL=53

Ping statistics for 216.109.118.64:
    Packets: Sent = 4, Received = 4, Lost = 0 (0% loss),
Approximate round trip times in milli-seconds:
    Minimum = 59ms, Maximum = 123ms, Average = 80ms

C:\Documents and Settings\Brian>
```

IP address

Round trip time

Statistics for the test

Figure 9-19 Tracert

```
C:\WINDOWS\system32\cmd.exe                                    _ □ ×

(C) Copyright 1985-2001 Microsoft Corp.

C:\Documents and Settings\Brian>tracert www.yahoo.com

Tracing route to www.yahoo.akadns.net [216.109.118.72]
over a maximum of 30 hops:

  1     1 ms    <1 ms    <1 ms  launchmodem [192.168.1.254]
  2    16 ms    40 ms    53 ms  68.208.254.6
  3    41 ms    45 ms    50 ms  68.208.254.53
  4    15 ms    15 ms    15 ms  205.152.174.29
  5    30 ms    31 ms    31 ms  axr00asm-7-2-0-1.bellsouth.net [65.83.237.62]
  6    59 ms    31 ms    31 ms  axr01asm-0-2-0.bellsouth.net [65.83.236.9]
  7    47 ms    47 ms    47 ms  AXR00AEP-0-1-0.bellsouth.net [65.83.236.50]
  8    58 ms   105 ms    57 ms  65.83.236.66
  9    62 ms    58 ms    58 ms  65.83.237.254
 10    61 ms    59 ms    59 ms  UNKNOWN-216-115-96-183.yahoo.com [216.115.96.183
]
 11    58 ms    58 ms    58 ms  UNKNOWN-216-109-120-202.yahoo.com [216.109.120.2
02]
 12    90 ms    61 ms   109 ms  p9.www.dcn.yahoo.com [216.109.118.72]

Trace complete.

C:\Documents and Settings\Brian>_
```

Figure 9-20 Pathping

```
C:\WINDOWS\system32\cmd.exe                                    _ □ ×
C:\Documents and Settings\Brian>pathping www.yahoo.com

Tracing route to www.yahoo.akadns.net [216.109.118.64]
over a maximum of 30 hops:
  0  audiows.launchmodem.com [192.168.1.97]
  1  launchmodem [192.168.1.254]
  2  68.208.254.6
  3  68.208.254.53
  4  205.152.174.29
  5  axr00asm-7-2-0-1.bellsouth.net [65.83.237.62]
  6  axr01asm-1-2-0.bellsouth.net [65.83.236.11]
  7  AXR00AEP-0-1-1.bellsouth.net [65.83.236.52]
  8  65.83.236.66
  9  65.83.237.254
 10  vlan201-msri.dcn.yahoo.com [216.115.96.163]
 11  UNKNOWN-216-109-120-205.yahoo.com [216.109.120.205]
 12  p1.www.dcn.yahoo.com [216.109.118.64]

Computing statistics for 300 seconds...
            Source to Here   This Node/Link
Hop  RTT    Lost/Sent = Pct  Lost/Sent = Pct  Address
  0                                            audiows.launchmodem.com [192.168.1.97]
                                0/ 100 =  0%   |
  1   0ms    0/ 100 =  0%      0/ 100 =  0%   launchmodem [192.168.1.254]
                                0/ 100 =  0%   |
  2  22ms    0/ 100 =  0%      0/ 100 =  0%   68.208.254.6
                                0/ 100 =  0%   |
  3  28ms    0/ 100 =  0%      0/ 100 =  0%   68.208.254.53
                                0/ 100 =  0%   |
  4  25ms    0/ 100 =  0%      0/ 100 =  0%   205.152.174.29
                                0/ 100 =  0%   |
  5  45ms    0/ 100 =  0%      0/ 100 =  0%   axr00asm-7-2-0-1.bellsouth.net [65.83.237.62]
                                0/ 100 =  0%   |
  6  42ms    0/ 100 =  0%      0/ 100 =  0%   axr01asm-1-2-0.bellsouth.net [65.83.236.11]
                                0/ 100 =  0%   |
  7  58ms    1/ 100 =  1%      1/ 100 =  1%   AXR00AEP-0-1-1.bellsouth.net [65.83.236.52]
                                0/ 100 =  0%   |
  8  72ms    0/ 100 =  0%      0/ 100 =  0%   65.83.236.66
                                0/ 100 =  0%   |
  9  ----   100/ 100 =100%    100/ 100 =100%  65.83.237.254
                                0/ 100 =  0%   |
 10  69ms    0/ 100 =  0%      0/ 100 =  0%   vlan201-msri.dcn.yahoo.com [216.115.96.163]
                                0/ 100 =  0%   |
 11  65ms    0/ 100 =  0%      0/ 100 =  0%   UNKNOWN-216-109-120-205.yahoo.com [216.109.120.205]
                                2/ 100 =  2%   |
 12  69ms    2/ 100 =  2%      0/ 100 =  0%   p1.www.dcn.yahoo.com [216.109.118.64]

Trace complete.
C:\Documents and Settings\Brian>_
```

skill 3

Troubleshooting LAN/Routing/Remote Access Configuration Problems (cont'd)

exam objective

Identify and troubleshoot LAN and Routing and Remote Access configuration problems. Indications of such problems include application errors.

overview

If you cannot ping the default gateway, then the default gateway may be down. However, some networks may use packet filtering or otherwise disable the router's ability to respond to ICMP echo packets for security reasons. Your best advice in either case is to contact the network administrators about the issue.

If you cannot ping a remote host, then first determine if you simply cannot connect to a single remote host, a single IP range, or all remote hosts. For instance, if you fail in your efforts to ping 192.168.2.100, try to ping other IP addresses beginning with 192.168.2. If you fail to connect to any addresses on the 192.168.2.0 subnet, then try to ping clients on other subnets (such as 192.168.3.0). If you cannot ping any remote clients, then the problem is occurring on your default gateway. If you can ping some subnets but not others, then use Tracert to determine what the path difference is between the different subnets. For example, in **Figure 9-21**, the problem is with the router for the 192.168.2.0 network, because the tracert is successful for all other paths.

However, in some cases, you may get inconsistent errors when connecting or transferring data to a network. This is where Pathping can become very useful. Whereas Tracert simply verifies that the path is functioning, Pathping tracks performance statistics along the path. Using these statistics, we can see where a single router might be causing problems along the path. For example, in **Figure 9-22**, each router from hop 9 on has a very high round trip time, which could be an indication that the router at hop 9 is overloaded.

These steps will go a long way toward helping you diagnose any TCP/IP problem. However, in the case of a remote access connection, there are a few more aspects to take into account.

First, remote access connections come in two forms, dial-up and virtual private network (VPN). A dial-up connection uses a regular telephone line and number to connect a client with a RRAS server. A VPN connection takes place by first connecting to the Internet, and then connecting to the VPN server via name or IP address.

Despite the difference in the types of connections, both use the same authentication protocols, and both must successfully authenticate to establish the connection. For this reason, let's examine the authentication options for remote access connections before we delve into the options available for each type of connection.

On the Security tab in the connection's Properties dialog box (**Figure 9-23**), you can see that you have two major options, Typical and Advanced. Typical simply configures the connection from a list of easy to understand options. First, you choose how to validate your identity, either unsecured password (clear text), secured password (encrypted), or smart card. In general, you want to avoid using an unsecured password for security reasons, but you may find it helpful to use an unsecured password when troubleshooting authentication problems. Underneath the **Validate my identity as follows** combo box are two check boxes, **Automatically use my Windows login name and password** and **Require data encryption**. If you are connecting to a RRAS server in a Windows domain that you are a member of, you will generally want to select the **Automatically use my Windows login name and password** check box so that your domain preference is transmitted at logon. Otherwise, you will be assumed to be a member of the same domain as the RRAS server, and if not, you will not be able to connect. When using a VPN connection, it is recommended that you also select the check box to require data encryption, as otherwise, information might be sent across the Internet as clear text.

tip

The unsecured password option is available only for dial-up connections.

Figure 9-21 Troubleshooting with tracert

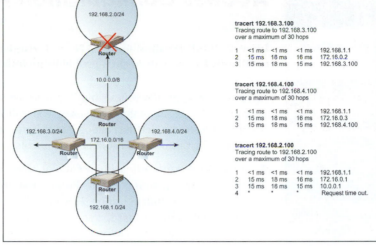

Figure 9-22 Troubleshooting with pathping

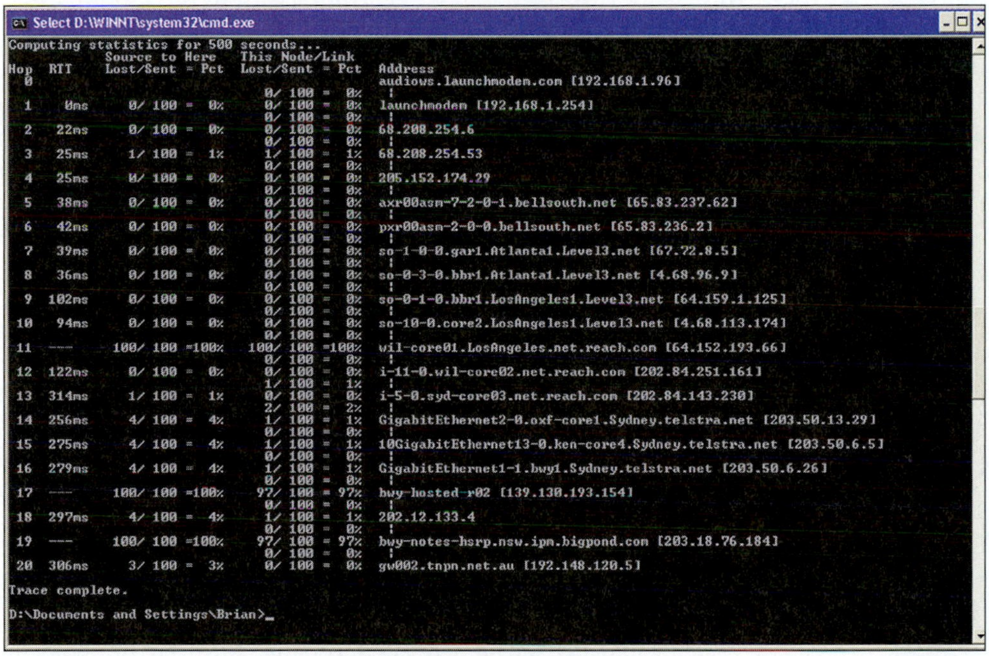

Figure 9-23 Security tab

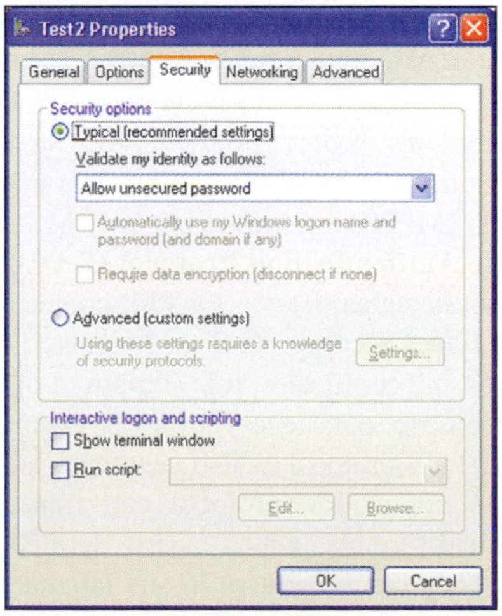

skill 3
Troubleshooting LAN/Routing/Remote Access Configuration Problems *(cont'd)*

exam objective

Identify and troubleshoot LAN and Routing and Remote Access configuration problems. Indications of such problems include application errors.

overview

Although the **Typical** settings simplify the process of configuring a connection for end users, to properly troubleshoot the connection, you will generally want to choose **Advanced**. In the **Advanced Security Settings** dialog box **(Figure 9-24)**, you can specifically choose the list of authentication protocols to use. These protocols are:

◆ **Password Authentication Protocol (PAP)**: PAP is the least secure authentication protocol used with Point-to-Point Protocol (PPP) connections. It uses plain text passwords for authentication. However, PAP is used when a more secure authentication method cannot be used, and this protocol may be necessary for creating dial-up connections with non-Windows networks that do not encrypt passwords. Finally, you may choose to use PAP when attempting to troubleshoot connection problems, and PAP is the most compatible of all authentication protocols.

◆ **Shiva Password Authentication Protocol (SPAP)**: SPAP is an authentication protocol that is used if you are connecting to a Shiva server. This protocol is more secure than PAP but less secure than CHAP or MS-CHAP. Data encryption is not supported with SPAP.

◆ **Challenge Handshake Authentication Protocol (CHAP)**: CHAP is a protocol that provides authentication on the basis of a one-way hash created by seeding the Message Digest 5 (MD5) encryption algorithm with the password. Essentially, the client sends its username to the RAS server in plain text form but does not send the password. The server then creates a challenge message and sends this challenge to the client. The client computer then uses the MD-5 algorithm, seeded with the user's password, to encrypt the challenge. When the client sends this challenge to the server, it compares the client's hash to the hash it expected to receive (based on the password it has listed for the client). If the values match, the client is allowed to connect, and if not, the client is dropped. It is important to note that for CHAP to function properly, the password that CHAP uses must be in plain text. On Windows Server 2003, this requires that you store domain passwords in a reversibly encrypted format. This means that the password's encryption can be quickly and easily reversed, which is a major security consideration. For this reason, the use of CHAP is not generally recommended.

◆ **Microsoft CHAP (MS-CHAP)**: MS-CHAP is Microsoft's version of CHAP. The challenge message is specifically designed for Windows operating systems, and one-way encryption is used. MS-CHAP is used with Windows 9x and NT, and only the client is authenticated. In the extended version, MS-CHAP2, both the client and the server are authenticated. Windows 9x clients can now be modernized so that they are compatible with MS-CHAP2 by downloading the patch for Dial-Up Networking that upgrades it to version 1.3. Windows NT clients can download and install SP4 or higher to gain MS-CHAP2 authentication. MS-CHAP2 also uses a different encryption key for transmitting data and for receiving data. MS-CHAP v1 CPW and MS-CHAP v2 CPW are updated versions of these protocols in which the user can change an expired password. Both versions of MS-CHAP support data encryption using the Microsoft Point-to-Point Encryption (MPPE) algorithm, but only MS-CHAP 2 supports mutual authentication.

◆ **Extensible Authentication Protocol (EAP)**: EAP is used to customize your method of remote access authentication for PPP connections. It supports authentication using either Transport Layer Security (TLS) or Message Digest 5-CHAP (MD5-CHAP). TLS supports smart cards and certificates. It is composed of two layers: the TLS Record protocol, which uses symmetric data encryption to ensure that connections are private, and the TLS Handshake protocol, which negotiates an encryption algorithm and cryptographic key before the application protocol can transmit or receive any data. Algorithms are mathematical formulas with a clearly defined endpoint that are used to solve a particular problem. They can be written in any language from English to programming languages.

Figure 9-24 Advanced Security Settings dialog box

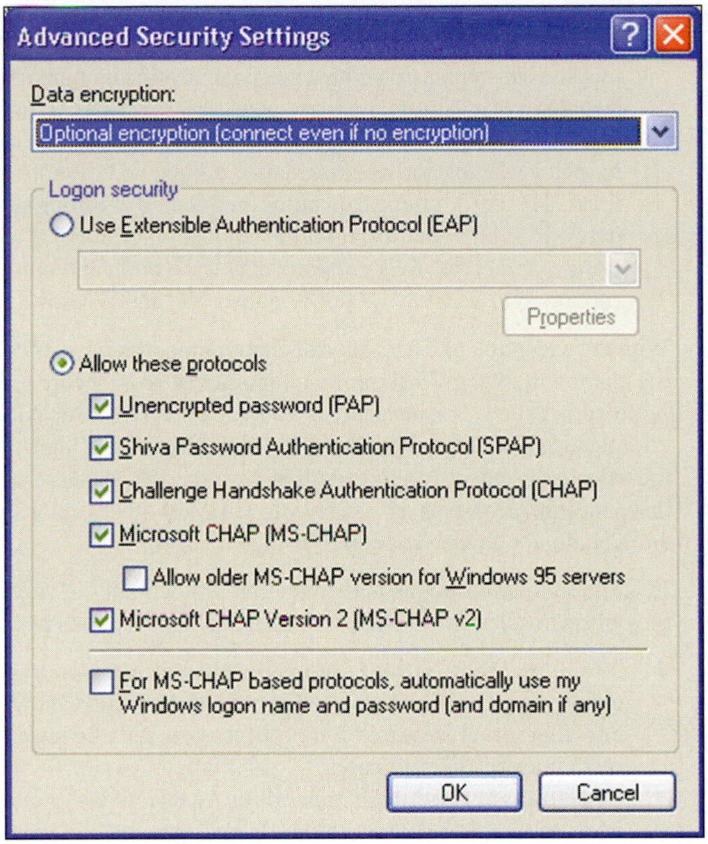

skill 3

Troubleshooting LAN/Routing/Remote Access Configuration Problems (cont'd)

exam objective

Identify and troubleshoot LAN and Routing and Remote Access configuration problems. Indications of such problems include application errors.

overview

Smart cards store user certificates and public/private keys that are used for authentication purposes in conjunction with a personal identification number (PIN). Certificates are digital signatures that validate users and networks. MD5-CHAP uses an MD5 algorithm to encrypt user names and passwords. MD5 is a hashing algorithm. Hashing algorithms transform data in such a way that the resulting data is unique and cannot be converted back to its original form. Hence, a client can be authenticated without sending the password over the network. EAP is the strongest authentication protocol available, but it is used only when using smart cards. EAP supports data encryption and mutual authentication. EAP is only supported in Windows 2000, Windows XP, and Windows Server 2003.

With the exception of EAP, you can choose more than one of the authentication protocols, and the client will attempt each protocol in order of most secure to least secure until a compatible protocol is found. For instance, if you chose PAP, CHAP, MS-CHAP, and MS-CHAP2, the client would attempt MS-CHAP2, then MS-CHAP, then CHAP, then PAP. If none of the selected protocols are compatible with the RRAS server settings, then the client will be disconnected. However, if you choose EAP, all other options are grayed out (**Figure 9-25**), and you do not have the option of using other protocols.

In addition to choosing an authentication protocol, at the very top of the dialog box, you see the option to select encryption requirements. Your options here are:

◆ **No encryption**: If this option is selected, data encryption will be disabled on the connection (password encryption will still function, however). If you select this option and the server requires encryption, you will be disconnected. This setting is not recommended in most cases.

◆ **Optional encryption**: If this option is selected, the client will try all supported data encryption protocols in order from strongest to weakest until a protocol that is compatible with the server is found. If none of the encryption protocols are compatible, the client will connect unencrypted. This is the most compatible setting and is recommended when you do not know what the server settings are.

◆ **Require encryption**: If this option is selected, the client will try all supported data encryption protocols in order from strongest to weakest until a protocol that is compatible with the server is found. If none of the encryption protocols are compatible, the client will disconnect. If you select this option, you must use EAP, MS-CHAP, or MS-CHAP2 as the authentication protocol.

◆ **Maximum strength encryption**: If this option is selected, the client will try its strongest encryption only, and will disconnect if the server does not support that level of encryption. If you select this option, you must use EAP, MS-CHAP, or MS-CHAP2 as the authentication protocol. Finally, at the bottom of the dialog box, you have the option of using your Windows authentication credentials automatically.

Now let's examine the options specific to each type of connection.

For dial-up connections, you have a number of unique options. On the **Options** tab (**Figure 9-26**), you can choose to display connection progress, prompt for user credentials, prompt for Windows domain information, and even prompt for the phone number on each connection attempt. Under **Redialing options**, you can choose how many times the system redials the connection (in case of busy signals or failed connections), how long to wait between redial attempts, how long to leave an idle connection up before disconnecting, and whether or not to redial the connection if it is dropped. The **X.25** button is used to configure connections to X.25 networks, which is a very specialized process that is beyond the scope of this material.

Figure 9-25 Selecting EAP

Figure 9-26 Options tab in the dial-up connection Properties dialog box

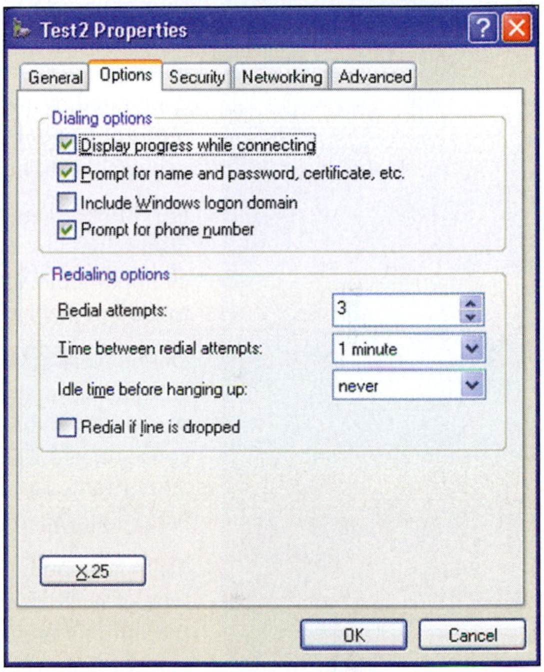

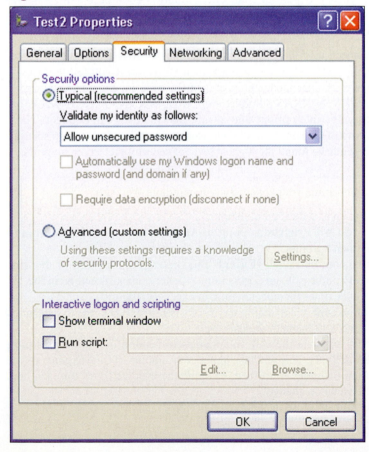

Figure 9-27 Security tab

skill 3

Troubleshooting LAN/Routing/Remote Access Configuration Problems (cont'd)

exam objective

Identify and troubleshoot LAN and Routing and Remote Access configuration problems. Indications of such problems include application errors.

overview

On the **Security** tab (**Figure 9-27**), you are given two additional options for dial-up connections: Show terminal window and Run script. These settings are typically used only when connecting to Unix Serial Line Internet Protocol (SLIP) remote access servers, as SLIP requires a terminal-based logon process.

The **Networking** tab (**Figure 9-28**) is broken up into two sections. In the top section, you can choose whether to use PPP or SLIP to connect to the RRAS server. Anytime you are connecting to a Windows RRAS server, and nearly any time you connect to an ISP, you should choose PPP. SLIP is typically only used by very old Unix systems. In the bottom section, you can choose the protocols and services to bind to the dial-up connection. You can also configure protocol settings (such as IP address) in this dialog box, though if the server is configured to disallow static configuration, your settings will be overridden. In general, it is best to leave **File and Print Sharing for Microsoft Networks** disabled for RRAS connections to help ensure the security of the local system.

For VPN connections, you have many of the same options, but a few tabs require further discussion. On the **General** tab, you can choose to dial a specific dial-up connection before attempting the VPN connection (**Figure 9-29**). This is useful because you must be connected to the Internet before you can establish a VPN connection.

On the **Networking** tab (**Figure 9-30**), you have the option to choose the type of VPN, either Automatic, Layer 2 Tunneling Protocol (L2TP), or Point-to-Point Tunneling Protocol (PPTP). Automatic is the most compatible of these settings and will try L2TP and then PPTP upon connecting. L2TP is used when you want to connect to Windows 2000 or Windows Server 2003 RRAS servers and is the most secure option. PPTP is used when connecting to Windows NT, 2000, and 2003 RRAS servers, as well as most other vendor's RRAS servers.

Troubleshooting RRAS connections follows the same principles as troubleshooting any other type of network connection once you have been connected. However, if you fail to connect, the options mentioned above are the most likely culprit. In general, the quickest way to resolve the problem is to ask your RRAS administrators what settings to use. If that is not possible, select the most compatible options and ensure that the user can connect. Then, gradually increase the security of the connection by increasing the authentication and security options one at a time until you have found the highest level of security the server supports.

how to

Use Tracert and Pathping to examine your connectivity to a remote Web site.

1. Boot the system and log on as a local administrator.
2. Click ![start], point to **All Programs**, point to **Accessories**, and click **Command Prompt** to open a command prompt.
3. Type **ping www.yahoo.com** and click [**Enter**]. Take note of the amount of the time listing for each packet. For a broadband connection, excellent times should be in the 15-30 ms range, whereas poor times include any time in excess of 100 ms.
4. Type **tracert www.yahoo.com** and examine the results (**Figure 9-31**). Try to determine where the largest bottleneck in the path seems to be.
5. Use Pathping to further examine the path in a statistical fashion by typing **pathping www.yahoo.com** (**Figure 9-31**). This will take a moderate amount of time to generate the required statistics. When Pathping is finished, examine the average times for each hop. Did the apparent bottleneck hop change?
6. Type **exit** and press [**Enter**] to close the command prompt.
7. Close all open dialog boxes and log off of the system.

Figure 9-28 The Networking tab in the dial-up connection Properties dialog box

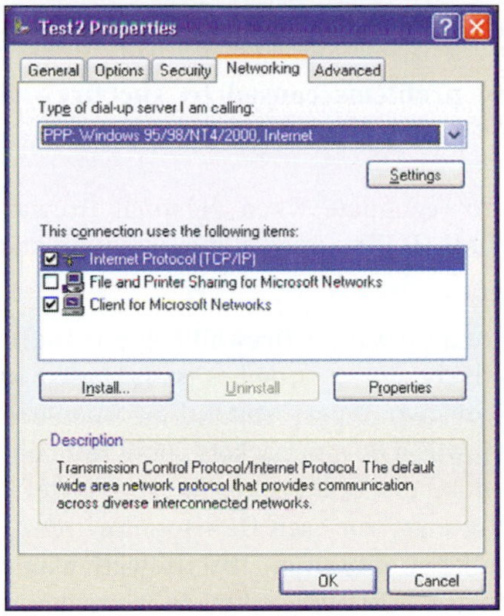
Test2 Properties
General
Options
Security
Networking
Advanced
Type of dial-up server I am calling:
PPP: Windows 95/98/NT4/2000, Internet
Settings
This connection uses the following items:
Internet Protocol (TCP/IP)
File and Printer Sharing for Microsoft Networks
Client for Microsoft Networks
Install...
Uninstall
Properties
Description
Transmission Control Protocol/Internet Protocol. The default wide area network protocol that provides communication across diverse interconnected networks.
OK
Cancel

Figure 9-29 General tab in the VPN connection Properties dialog box

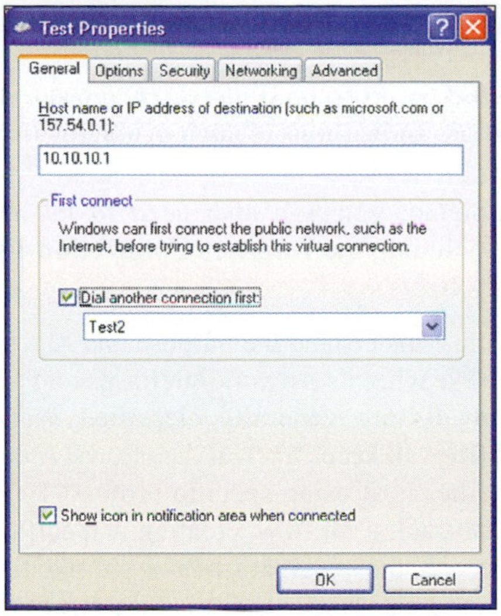
Test Properties
General
Options
Security
Networking
Advanced
Host name or IP address of destination (such as microsoft.com or 157.54.0.1):
10.10.10.1
First connect
Windows can first connect the public network, such as the Internet, before trying to establish this virtual connection.
Dial another connection first:
Test2
Show icon in notification area when connected
OK
Cancel

Figure 9-30 Networking tab in the VPN connection Properties dialog box

Test Properties
General
Options
Security
Networking
Advanced
Type of VPN:
Automatic
Settings
This connection uses the following items:
Internet Protocol (TCP/IP)
File and Printer Sharing for Microsoft Networks
Client for Microsoft Networks
Install...
Uninstall
Properties
Description
Transmission Control Protocol/Internet Protocol. The default wide area network protocol that provides communication across diverse interconnected networks.
OK
Cancel

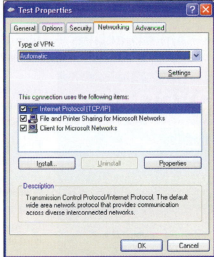

Figure 9-31 Running a tracert to yahoo.com

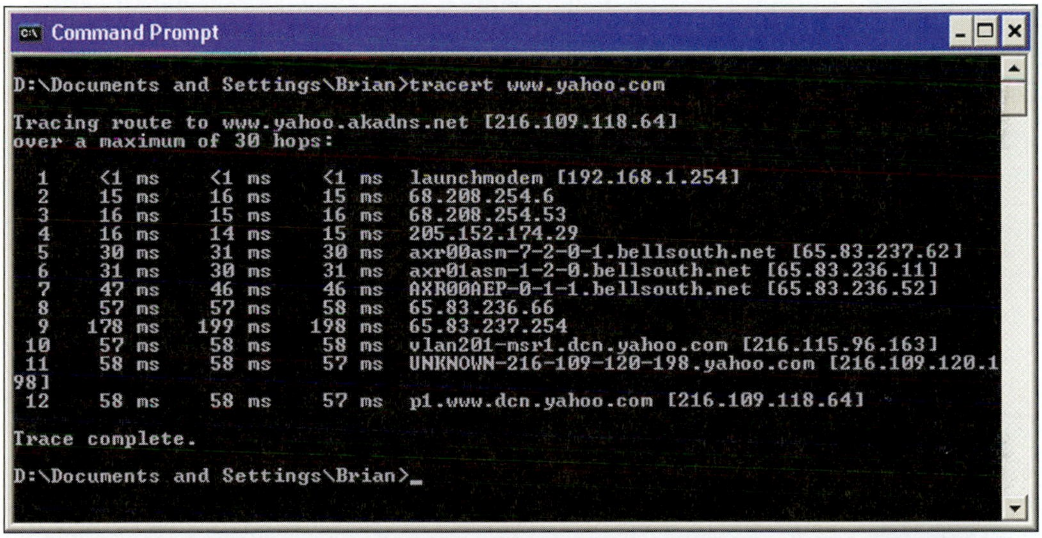
Command Prompt
D:\Documents and Settings\Brian>tracert www.yahoo.com
Tracing route to www.yahoo.akadns.net [216.109.118.64]
over a maximum of 30 hops:
1 <1 ms <1 ms <1 ms launchmodem [192.168.1.254]
2 15 ms 16 ms 15 ms 68.208.254.6
3 16 ms 15 ms 16 ms 68.208.254.53
4 16 ms 14 ms 15 ms 205.152.174.29
5 30 ms 31 ms 30 ms axr00asm-7-2-0-1.bellsouth.net [65.83.237.62]
6 31 ms 30 ms 31 ms axr01asm-1-2-0.bellsouth.net [65.83.236.11]
7 47 ms 46 ms 46 ms AXR00AEP-0-1-1.bellsouth.net [65.83.236.52]
8 57 ms 57 ms 58 ms 65.83.236.66
9 178 ms 199 ms 198 ms 65.83.237.254
10 57 ms 58 ms 58 ms vlan201-msr1.dcn.yahoo.com [216.115.96.163]
11 58 ms 58 ms 57 ms UNKNOWN-216-109-120-198.yahoo.com [216.109.120.198]
12 58 ms 58 ms 57 ms p1.www.dcn.yahoo.com [216.109.118.64]
Trace complete.
D:\Documents and Settings\Brian>_

Figure 9-32 Running a pathping to yahoo.com

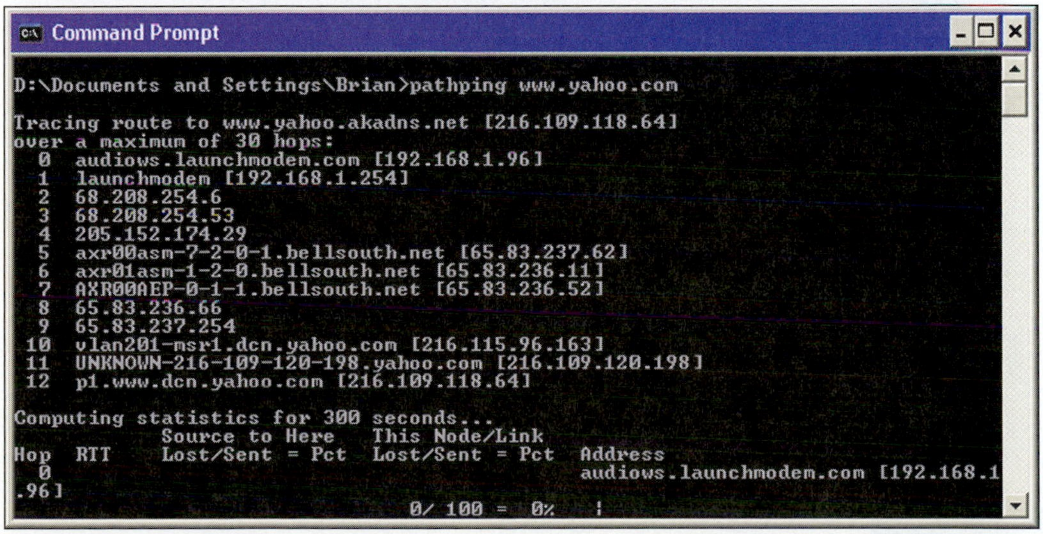
Command Prompt
D:\Documents and Settings\Brian>pathping www.yahoo.com
Tracing route to www.yahoo.akadns.net [216.109.118.64]
over a maximum of 30 hops:
0 audiows.launchmodem.com [192.168.1.96]
1 launchmodem [192.168.1.254]
2 68.208.254.6
3 68.208.254.53
4 205.152.174.29
5 axr00asm-7-2-0-1.bellsouth.net [65.83.237.62]
6 axr01asm-1-2-0.bellsouth.net [65.83.236.11]
7 AXR00AEP-0-1-1.bellsouth.net [65.83.236.52]
8 65.83.236.66
9 65.83.237.254
10 vlan201-msr1.dcn.yahoo.com [216.115.96.163]
11 UNKNOWN-216-109-120-198.yahoo.com [216.109.120.198]
12 p1.www.dcn.yahoo.com [216.109.118.64]
Computing statistics for 300 seconds...
Source to Here This Node/Link
Hop RTT Lost/Sent = Pct Lost/Sent = Pct Address
0 audiows.launchmodem.com [192.168.1.96]
0/ 100 = 0% |

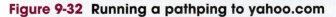

skill 4 *Troubleshooting Firewall Problems*

exam objective

Identify and troubleshoot network connectivity problems caused by the firewall configuration. Indications of such problems include application errors.

overview

As a technician, you will also need to be able to recognize when personal firewall products, including the **Internet Connection Firewall (ICF)**, is causing application and connectivity errors.

First, you must understand the purpose and function of a firewall. A **firewall** inspects traffic entering and leaving its network interfaces and selectively allows or denies traffic based on rules. Firewalls are generally classified as one of two types: stateful or stateless. A **stateful firewall** keeps track of data flows. A data flow is a flow of packets going from one host to another host using specific protocols, port numbers, and packet flags. A stateful firewall will track each flow, creating a specific filter entry for each flow to allow return traffic to reach the originator. In a simple firewall configuration, the firewall would automatically create rule entries to allow return traffic for a flow created by an internal host to enter the private network, while denying all other traffic **(Figure 9-33)**. Additionally, because a stateful firewall tracks each flow, if will recognize a FIN bit in a TCP header, which is a message to the remote system to end the communications session. Because it recognizes the FIN bit, it will automatically remove the rule associated with that data flow once it is ended, effectively closing holes when they are no longer needed. Most modern firewalls, including ICF, are stateful.

Stateless firewalls, on the other hand, do not monitor traffic flows. While most have the ability to dynamically create rules, these rules are simply controlled by a time limit. In other words, once a dynamic entry is created, it will remain active for a particular amount of time, regardless of the state of the session. This functionality means that a stateless firewall may leave return holes open for long after clients have ended the session. This means that stateless firewalls, in general, are significantly less secure than stateful firewalls. However, due to lower processing needs, stateless firewalls can be slightly higher performing than stateful firewalls.

Because most of the firewalls you are likely to use are stateful, we will concentrate our efforts on stateful systems. As was mentioned previously, most firewalls are configured by default to allow all outgoing traffic, but only to allow incoming traffic if it is part of a flow that was originated internally. This configuration means that internal resources that external clients need to be able to establish a connection to will be inaccessible **(Figure 9-34)**. To allow external clients to establish connections to internal resources, you must therefore create a specific rule to allow that access. For this, you will need to be aware of the port numbers associated with the application. Some common TCP port numbers are shown in **Table 9-1**.

Additionally, you may want to configure custom rules to deny traffic for certain types of applications even if the traffic originates from internal clients. For instance, you may want to reduce bandwidth usage by restricting the use of peer-to-peer file sharing applications, such as Kazaa or BitTorrent. To do this, you would create a custom rule to deny those ports **(Figure 9-35)**.

As you may have noticed from the figures, there are a number of important aspects to a filter rule. These are:

◆ **Interface**: The NIC to which the rule applies.
◆ **Direction**: Either incoming or outgoing. Defines the direction of the traffic flow to which the rule applies.
◆ **Source address**: The IP address in the source IP address field of the packet.

Figure 9-33 Dynamic firewall entry

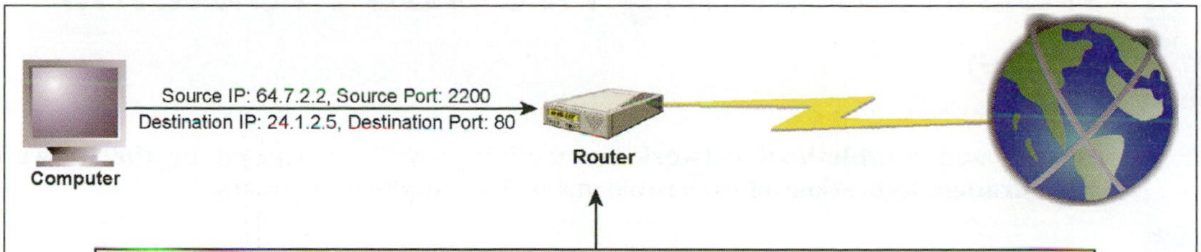

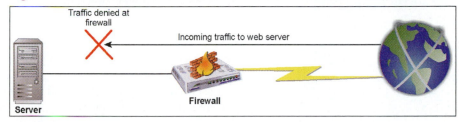

Source IP: 64.7.2.2, Source Port: 2200
Destination IP: 24.1.2.5, Destination Port: 80

Computer

Router

Dynamic Packet Filter

Interface	Protocol	Source IP	Source Port	Destination IP	Destination Port	Direction	Action
External	TCP	24.1.2.5	80	64.7.2.2	2200	Incoming	Allow

Figure 9-34 External clients cannot reach internal resources

Traffic denied at firewall

Incoming traffic to web server

Server

Firewall

Table 9-1   Common ports

Application	Protocol	Port
FTP	TCP	20, 21
Telnet	TCP	23
SMTP	TCP	25
HTTP	TCP	80
POP3	TCP	110
NNTP	TCP	119
HTTPS	TCP	443
RDP	TCP	3389

Figure 9-35 Creating a custom rule to deny peer-to-peer file-sharing traffic

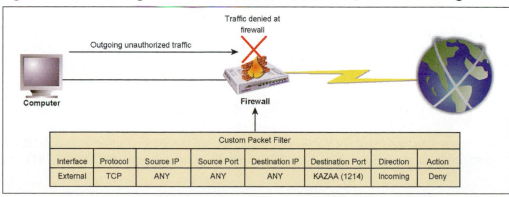

Traffic denied at firewall

Outgoing unauthorized traffic

Computer

Firewall

Custom Packet Filter

Interface	Protocol	Source IP	Source Port	Destination IP	Destination Port	Direction	Action
External	TCP	ANY	ANY	ANY	KAZAA (1214)	Incoming	Deny

skill 4 — *Troubleshooting Firewall Problems*
(cont'd)

Identify and troubleshoot network connectivity problems caused by the firewall configuration. Indications of such problems include application errors.

overview

- ◆ **Destination address**: The IP address in the destination IP address field of the packet.
- ◆ **Protocol**: The protocol to which the filter applies. In general, this will either be TCP/UDP.
- ◆ **Source port**: The TCP or UDP port number in the source port field of the packet.
- ◆ **Destination port**: The TCP or UDP port number in the destination port field of the packet.

First, let's tackle the directional nature of each rule. The terms incoming and outgoing tend to confuse many people, but they are really very simple. In **Figure 9-36**, you can see that the direction simply defines the direction of the flow of traffic.

As a best practice, you should create filters of incoming traffic only on a given interface. This is because an outgoing filter applies only to the traffic after it has already been processed (routed) by the firewall. By applying an outgoing filter, you are essentially telling the system to process a packet and then drop it, instead of just dropping the packet before processing it. So, if you were trying to control internal traffic destined for the Internet, you would apply an incoming filter on the internal interface of the firewall, instead of an outgoing filter on the external interface (**Figure 9-37**). Similarly, to control traffic coming into the network from the Internet, you would apply an incoming filter to the external interface instead of an outgoing filter on the internal interface (**Figure 9-38**).

Also important are the source and destination IP address and port fields in relation to the direction. For example, suppose you wanted to allow external clients to establish connections to your internal Web server behind a firewall (**Figure 9-39**). To support this, you must create a custom filter. First, decide on the interface and direction. Because the traffic is coming from the Internet to the internal network, you can either create an incoming filter on the external interface, or an outgoing filter on the internal interface. Again, it is always best to use an incoming filter when possible, so choose an incoming filter on the external interface. Now you need to think about how the packet appears when it enters the external interface (**Figure 9-40**). The source address will define the system that is sending the packet, and the source port will define the network service that is establishing the connection. Because you want all external clients to be able to reach the Web server, simply choose "any" for the source IP address. Similarly, because clients use random source port numbers to connect to resources as a general practice, do not be concerned with the source port either. For this reason, set the source port to also be any.

The destination IP address in the packet will be where the packet is going, which in this case, will be the Web server. Set the destination address in the filter to be the same as the Web server's IP address. If you did not set this field to correspond to a single IP address (if you selected **Any**, for instance), then external clients would be able to access more systems on your internal network than the Web server, which is a security hole. Similar to the destination IP address, the destination port defines the server service for which the packet is destined. In this case, you want the external clients to be able to access Hypertext Transfer Protocol (HTTP), and only HTTP, so set this field to equal 80, the port number for HTTP. Because HTTP uses TCP, set the protocol field to use TCP.

Now that you understand how packet filters work, let's examine configuration of the Internet Connection Firewall.

ICF is a stand-alone feature of Windows XP that supports stateful inspection of packets. ICF is designed to function as either a system-wide firewall for a small network (**Figure 9-41**), or a

tip

When you are using a basic personal firewall such as ICF, you may sometimes be required to configure an outgoing filter, but in general, you should avoid outgoing filters if at all possible.

Figure 9-36 **Examining direction**

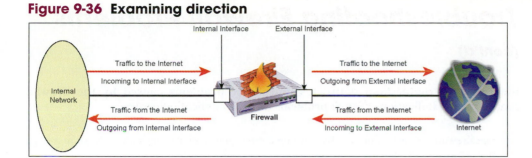

Figure 9-37 **Applying an incoming filter to an internal interface**

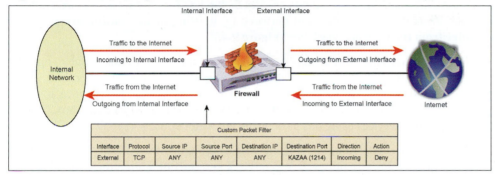

Custom Packet Filter							
Interface	Protocol	Source IP	Source Port	Destination IP	Destination Port	Direction	Action
External	TCP	ANY	ANY	ANY	KAZAA (1214)	Incoming	Deny

Figure 9-38 **Applying an incoming filter to an external interface**

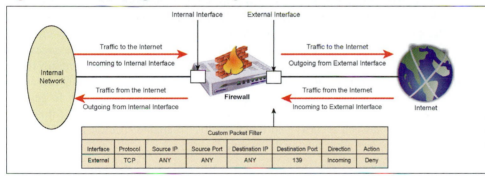

Custom Packet Filter							
Interface	Protocol	Source IP	Source Port	Destination IP	Destination Port	Direction	Action
External	TCP	ANY	ANY	ANY	139	Incoming	Deny

Figure 9-39 **Custom filter for external client access**

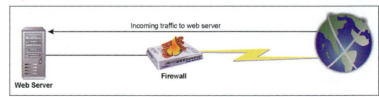

Figure 9-40 **Creating the custom filter**

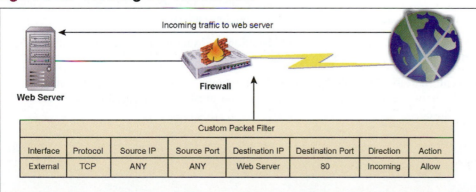

Custom Packet Filter							
Interface	Protocol	Source IP	Source Port	Destination IP	Destination Port	Direction	Action
External	TCP	ANY	ANY	Web Server	80	Incoming	Allow

skill 4

Troubleshooting Firewall Problems
(cont'd)

exam objective

Identify and troubleshoot network connectivity problems caused by the firewall configuration. Indications of such problems include application errors.

overview

personal firewall for each computer backing up a more powerful system-wide firewall in a large network (**Figure 9-42**). In either case, the same configuration principles apply.

The first step in this process is to enable ICF. ICF is disabled by default on all network connections. To enable ICF, open the Properties dialog box for your Internet connection and select the **Protect my computer and network by limiting or preventing access to this computer from the Internet** check box (**Figure 9-43**).

Once ICF is enabled, click the **Settings** button at the bottom of the **Advanced** tab to open the **Settings** dialog box for ICF (**Figure 9-44**). The first tab in this dialog box, **Services**, allows you to enable incoming traffic based on the network service it is using. For instance, to enable incoming HTTP traffic, you would select the box **Web Server (HTTP)** check box. You can also add your own services using this page, using the **Add** button.

The second tab, **Security Logging (Figure 9-45)**, configures the ICF log file. By default, ICF will write to a log file pfirewall.log in the **%systemroot%** directory. Here, you can choose what ICF logs and how large the log file is allowed to grow.

The final tab, **ICMP (Figure 9-46)**, allows you to define how incoming Internet Control Messaging Protocol traffic is handled by ICF. ICMP is primarily a diagnostic protocol, used to troubleshoot connectivity. For instance, the Ping, Tracert, and Pathping tools rely on ICMP packets (Ping uses ICMP echo messages, Tracert uses ICMP time exceeded messages, and Pathping uses both types of messages). By default, ICF will discard all incoming ICMP traffic. There is some risk associated with allowing ICMP traffic, as some Denial of Service attacks are based on ICMP, but for the most part, the risk is relatively minor. In general, allowing most types of ICMP messages to allow for connection troubleshooting is a worthwhile tradeoff between security and functionality. To enable specific ICMP message types, select the check box associated with the specified type.

While ICF is a useful new feature in Windows XP, especially for home networks or SOHO networks, it is not a substitute for a dedicated firewall. However, every layer of additional protection can increase security and potentially help avert disaster. For this reason, you are advised to use ICF whenever possible.

Now that we have examined firewall configuration, let's take a look at the major problems that can be caused by firewall configuration errors. Firewall problems really only come in two varieties:

◆ Access is allowed when it should be denied
◆ Access is denied when it should be allowed

If access is being allowed when it should be denied, first, ensure that the ICF is enabled. Next, ensure that the application or port does not have an exception configured.

If access is being denied when it should be allowed, examine the exceptions list and ensure that the application is correctly configured on the list.

This is all there is to troubleshooting ICF on a single system. However, remember that all firewalls between the source and the destination must be configured properly for access to be allowed.

tip

In ICF, exceptions always allow access.

Figure 9-41 Using ICF to provide a system-wide firewall

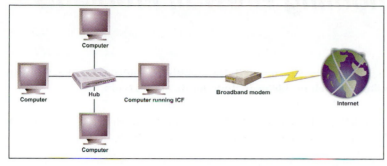

Figure 9-42 Using ICF as a personal firewall

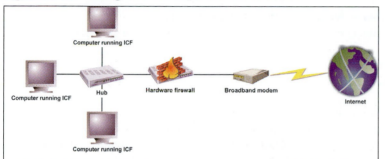

Figure 9-43 The Advanced tab of the adapter's Properties dialog box

Local Area Connection Properties

General | Authentication | Advanced

Internet Connection Firewall

☑ Protect my computer and network by limiting or preventing access to this computer from the Internet

Learn more about Internet Connection Firewall.

If you're not sure how to set these properties, use the Network Setup Wizard instead.   Settings...

OK   Cancel

Figure 9-44 Advanced Settings dialog box

Advanced Settings

Services | Security Logging | ICMP

Select the services running on your network that Internet users can access.

Services

☐ FTP Server
☐ Internet Mail Access Protocol Version 3 (IMAP3)
☐ Internet Mail Access Protocol Version 4 (IMAP4)
☐ Internet Mail Server (SMTP)
☐ Post-Office Protocol Version 3 (POP3)
☐ Remote Desktop
☐ Secure Web Server (HTTPS)
☐ Telnet Server
☐ Web Server (HTTP)

Add...   Edit...   Delete

OK   Cancel

Figure 9-45 Security Logging tab

Advanced Settings

Services | Security Logging | ICMP

Logging Options:

☐ Log dropped packets
☐ Log successful connections

Log file options:

Name:

C:\WINDOWS\pfirewall.log

Browse...

Size limit: 4096 KB

Restore Defaults

OK   Cancel

Figure 9-46 ICMP tab

Advanced Settings

Services | Security Logging | ICMP

Internet Control Message Protocol (ICMP) allows the computers on a network to share error and status information. Select the requests for information from the Internet that this computer will respond to:

☐ Allow incoming echo request
☐ Allow incoming timestamp request
☐ Allow incoming mask request
☐ Allow incoming router request
☐ Allow outgoing destination unreachable
☐ Allow outgoing source quench
☐ Allow outgoing parameter problem
☐ Allow outgoing time exceeded
☐ Allow redirect

Description:

Messages sent to this computer will be repeated back to the sender. This is commonly used for troubleshooting, for example, to ping a machine.

OK   Cancel

skill 4

Troubleshooting Firewall Problems
(cont'd)

exam objective

Identify and troubleshoot network connectivity problems caused by the firewall configuration. Indications of such problems include application errors.

how to

Enable ICF and configure ICF to allow incoming HTTP traffic. You will need a system with Windows XP SP2 installed to perform this exercise.

1. Boot the system and log on as a local administrator.
2. Click ⊞ *start* and click on **Network Connections** to open the Network Connections dialog box.
3. Right-click on your external network adapter (the adapter connected to the external network) and select **Properties** to open the adapter's **Properties** dialog box (**Figure 9-47**).
4. Click on the **Advanced** tab and select the **Protect my computer and network by limiting or preventing access to this computer from the Internet** check box to enable ICF.
5. Select [Settings...] to open the ICF settings dialog box (refer to Figure 9-44).
6. On the **Services** tab, click **Add Port** to open the **Add Port** dialog box.
7. In the **Add Port** dialog box, type **Custom Application** in the Name field, **8088** in the Port number field, and select the **TCP** option button (**Figure 9-48**). Click [OK] to close the **Add Port** dialog box.
8. Click [OK] to close the ICF dialog box.
9. Click [OK] to close the adapter's Properties dialog box.
10. Close all open dialog boxes and log off of the system.

Figure 9-47 Adapter Properties dialog box

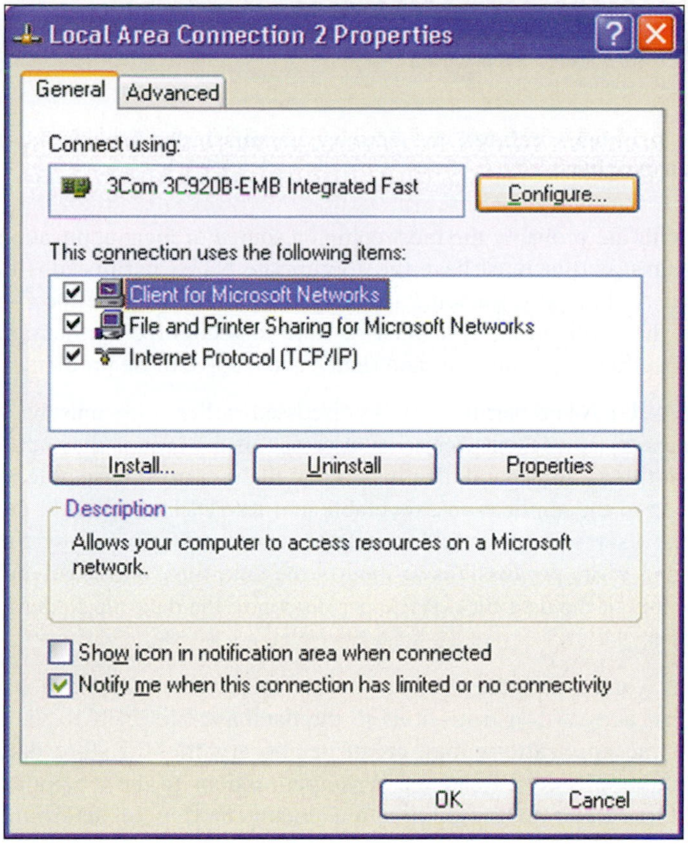

Figure 9-48 Add a Port dialog box

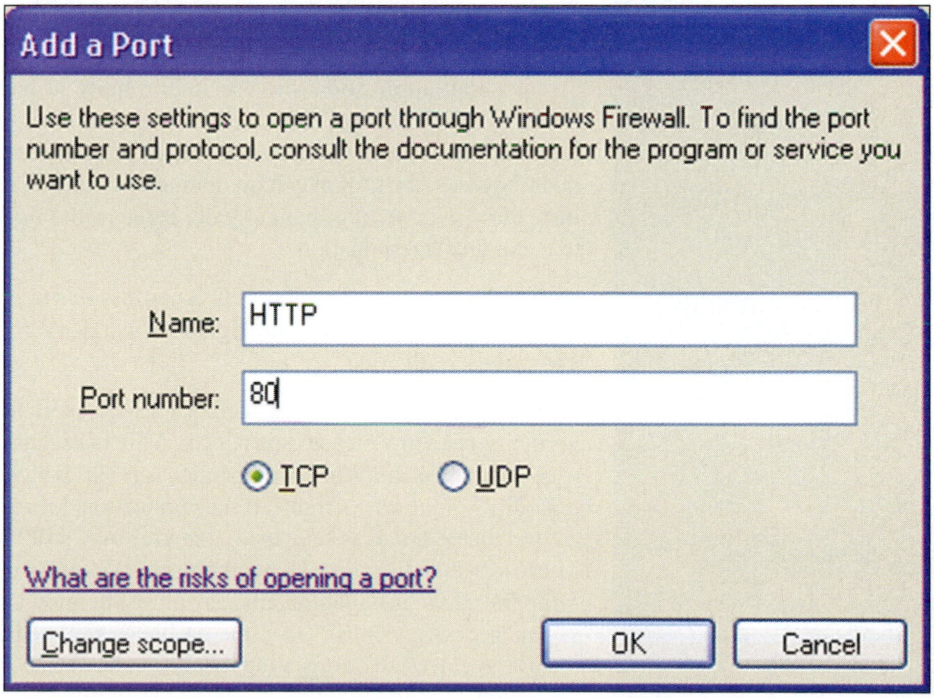

skill 5
Troubleshooting Insufficient User Permissions and Rights

exam objective

Identify and troubleshoot problems related to security permissions. Troubleshoot insufficient user permissions and rights.

overview

Insufficient permissions or rights are probably the most common source of local application access and installation problems. A user must have the appropriate NTFS permissions to access or install an application. Additionally, for some applications, a user must have specific user rights to run or install the application. You must be able to recognize application problems that are caused by insufficient permissions and rights, and resolve those problems.

First, let's tackle problems related to NTFS permissions. As discussed earlier, users must have appropriate permissions granted to either their user account or one of the groups they are a member of to access NTFS partitions. In general, this means that the user must have at least Read and Execute permissions to the application executable and any DLLs related to the application. Additionally, the user will need at least Read permissions to access the application data files, Read and Write permissions to modify the data files, and Read and Modify permissions to delete any of the data files. Write permission to the data file folder is required to create new data files.

However, some applications may use a database to store information. For these applications, the user will likely need Read and Write permissions to the database file itself to view and modify data. Finally, some applications may create temporary files to store data temporarily. In this case, the user will need Read and Write permissions to the temporary folder used by the application. Refer to the application documentation to determine where temporary files are stored.

When troubleshooting Access Denied errors, be sure to examine all groups of which the user is a member. If a Deny permission is configured for any of these groups, it will override the allow permissions applied to the other groups. For example, if the user is a member of Group A which grants him Read permissions, Group B which grants Write permissions, and Group C which denies Write permissions, the user will have only Read permissions (**Figure 9-49**).

To install an application, the user will require at least Read and Write permissions to the folder to which the application will be installed. To apply a patch or update to the application, the user will need Read and Write permissions in nearly all cases. Additionally, in a few cases, the user may require modify permissions, as the patch may actually delete files instead of overwriting them. Again, refer to the documentation included with the update to make this determination.

Although users always require NTFS permissions to install or run an application, users do not normally require any special rights to install or run an application. However, there are exceptions to this rule.

To install an application that includes a Microsoft Installer (MSI) file, the user should not normally need any elevated privileges. This is because MSI files automatically run under the user context of the Windows Installer service, which allows the application to be installed regardless of the user's rights. If the application does not include an MSI file, and instead uses an executable (such as setup.exe), the user may still be able to install the application through Microsoft Installer. First, have the user attempt to install the application by executing the setup file. If the installation fails, pay close attention to the errors the user receives. If the error states "access is denied," then the problem is related to permissions, not rights. However, if the user receives an error stating that he or she does not have appropriate privileges to perform the action, then the problem is related to rights.

tip

Remember that the only difference between the Write and Modify NTFS permissions is that Modify grants the user the ability to delete the file.

Figure 9-49 Effective permissions determination

Group	Permission
Group A	Read
Group B	Write
Group C	Deny Write

Final Permissions
Read+Write – Write = Read

skill 5

Troubleshooting Insufficient User Permissions and Rights (cont'd)

exam objective

Identify and troubleshoot problems related to security permissions. Troubleshoot insufficient user permissions and rights.

overview

Next, tell the user to try installing the application by launching the setup executable through Add or Remove Programs in the Control Panel. To perform this process, launch the **Add or Remove Programs** applet, select add a new program from the options on the left, and click the **CD or Floppy** button **(Figure 9-50)**. This process attempts to install the application using the Windows Installer service, which may allow the user to install the application using Windows Installer's privileges instead of their own.

If both of these steps fail, you may need to install the application for the user by using the Runas service, or temporarily add the user account to the local administrators group to give them sufficient rights. However, these steps should only be taken as a last resort.

Similarly, users should not normally require elevated rights to run an application. However, some older Windows NT applications expect the rights associated with the Users group on Windows NT to be present. Since Windows 2000 and Windows XP reduce the rights associated with the Users group, some of these applications may fail to function properly. For these applications, the simplest solution is often to add the user account to the Power Users group, which has rights similar to the Windows NT Users group.

Figure 9-50 **Adding a program through the Add or Remove Programs applet**

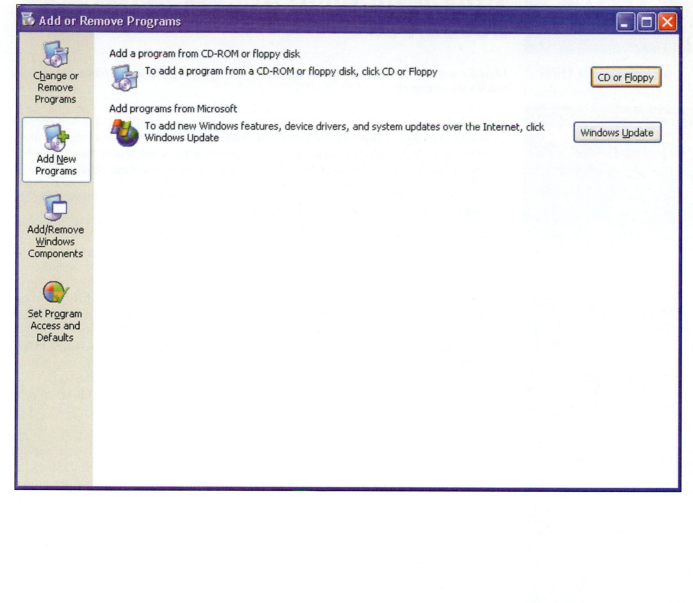

skill 6

Troubleshooting Access to Network Resources

exam objective

Identify and troubleshoot problems related to security permissions. Troubleshoot access to network resources.

overview

Troubleshooting access to network resources is a common activity for desktop support personnel. Although a large part of troubleshooting access to network resources involves troubleshooting network connectivity as was discussed earlier in the lesson, there are a few specific errors that can occur even when network connectivity can be established.

First and foremost, try different methods of connecting to the resource. You can connect to a network resource in many different ways including:

- **From a Run prompt**: Type *server**share* in the Run dialog box to connect to the resource, where *server* is the name (or IP address) of the system you want to connect to, and *share* is the shared folder on that system (**Figure 9-51(a)**). This type of address is known as a **Universal Naming Convention (UNC)** pathname.
- **From a command line**: Type net use *x: \\server\share,* where *x:* is the drive letter you want to map to the resource, *server* is the name (or IP address) of the system you want to connect to, and *share* is the shared folder on that system (**Figure 9-51(b)**).
- **From the Map Network Drive option**: You can right-click either **My Network Places** or **My Computer** and click **Map Network Drive** on the pop-up menu to map a drive letter to a network resource using the resource's UNC pathname (**Figure 9-51(c)**).
- **Browsing**: Using **My Network Places** or Windows Explorer, you can browse for the resource (**Figure 9-51(d)**).

Typically, browsing is where you tend to encounter the most problems, and this does not necessarily indicate an error condition. Browsing relies on the network browser service building a browse list, which is a list of network resources. Unfortunately, the network browser service is a bit notorious for taking very long periods of time to rebuild the browse list. For this reason, there may be resources available that do not appear on the browse list. For this reason, it is suggested that you use another method to connect to the resource before assuming that there is a network problem.

If you still can't access the resource, examine the error message you receive. In most cases, the error message will go a long way toward telling you why the connection failed. For instance, you may get an "access is denied" message even though you are sure that the user account has the appropriate NTFS permissions. In this case, the most likely cause is that the share permissions do not allow access. Remember that a user must have both share and NTFS permissions to the resource to access the resource remotely. Another common problem occurs when you try to connect to another computer in a workgroup but do not have an account with an identical username and password on the remote system. Because a workgroup is a peer-to-peer infrastructure, each computer contains its own accounts database. To connect to another computer, you must have a valid user account on that system. Additionally, if the user account on the remote system does not have the same username and password as the account on your system, you will need to login when connecting to the remote resource.

Figure 9-51 **Ways of connecting to network resources**

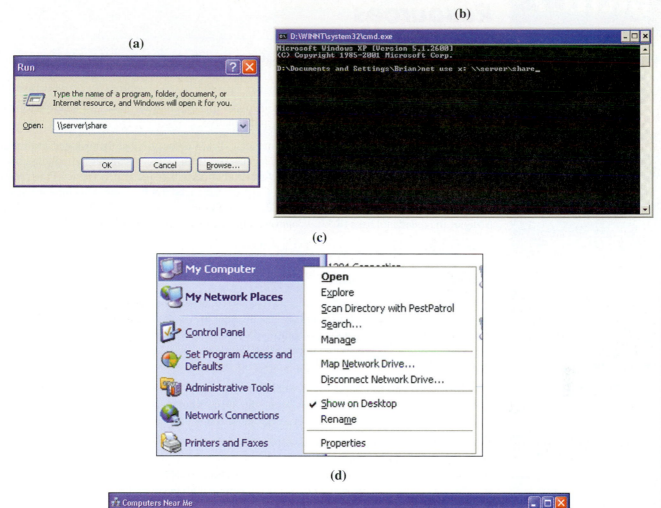

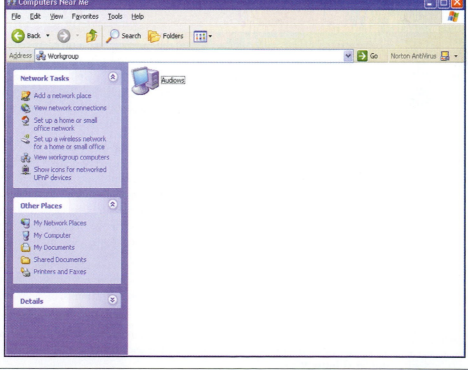

skill 7

Troubleshooting Access to Local Resources

exam objective

Identify and troubleshoot problems related to security permissions. Troubleshoot access to local resources.

overview

Troubleshooting access to local resources involves troubleshooting access to local disks and printers. Let's examine each type of device individually.

When a user is having difficulty accessing the local disk, first ensure that the disk and controller are visible from a hardware level. Both can be checked from Device Manager by looking under disk drives for the physical disks **(Figure 9-52)** and under either Integrated Device Electronics (IDE) Advanced Technology Attachment (ATA) / Advanced Technology Attachment Packet Interface (ATAPI) controllers or Small Computer Systems Interface (SCSI) and Redundant Array of Independent Disks (RAID) controllers for the disk controllers **(Figure 9-53)**.

If the devices are not recognized in Device Manager, check to see if the devices are recognized, but listed as an unknown device. If not, you likely have a hardware problem that must be resolved before you can continue.

Once you have ensured that the devices are recognized, ensure that the correct drivers are loaded for each device. If the correct drivers are installed but are outdated, updating the drivers at this point may result in resolving the problem, especially if the drivers were originally written for a different operating system (for example, using Windows 2000 drivers in Windows XP). At this point, it is also important to ensure that you do not have any resource conflicts as well.

Once you have ensured that the physical and driver configuration are correct, examine the partitions or volumes on the disks from the Disk Management snap-in **(Figure 9-54)**. At this point, your most likely cause of the problem is one of the following:

◆ Incorrect NTFS permissions
◆ No partitions or volumes on the disk
◆ The disk is dynamic and is not viewable from Windows NT
◆ The disk is using a file system that is incompatible with the operating system
◆ The disk has been compressed with Drivespace
◆ The disk is unformatted

For access problems with printers, again, the most common problems are physical. Ensure that the printer cabling is connected properly and that power is properly applied. Once this is done, examine the printer port (Line Printing Terminal (LPT), Universal Serial Bus (USB), etc.) and make sure that it is detected by Windows and that the drivers are properly installed and configured from within Device Manager. Again, updating to the most current drivers is suggested.

One other common set of problems are spooling problems. Spooling errors can manifest in several different ways, but the most common error is a hung queue. When a document is sent to the printer, it is actually queued by the Print Spooler service in a special storage area on the hard disk. This is done to allow the source application to transition back to a productive state more quickly. This process also allows several documents to be printed in rapid succession, even though the printer is still busy printing the first document. You can view the documents currently in the queue by double-clicking on the printer from within the Printers folder in Control Panel **(Figure 9-55)**.

If a document is in the queue but is not printing (even though the status of the document may be listed as "printing"), you may need to clear the document out of the queue to allow the queue to process the rest of the documents. If the queue repeatedly hangs, then you should stop and restart the print spooler service from within the Services console **(Figure 9-56)**.

If none of these resolve the issue, then the issue is likely caused by the user not having proper access permissions to the printer. To print, the user must have at least print permissions on the printer **(Figure 9-57)**.

tip

Microsoft recommends that the drivers you use are digitally signed. In reality, signed drivers are sometimes more compatible, but unsigned drivers are not always buggy or incompatible.

Figure 9-52 **Examining physical disks in Device Manager**

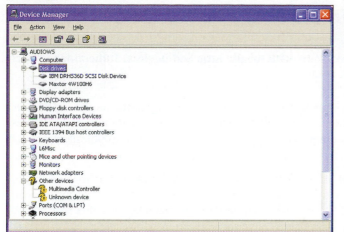

Figure 9-53 **Examining controllers in Device Manager**

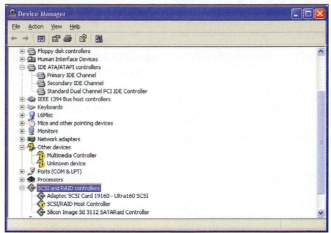

Figure 9-54 **Disk Management console**

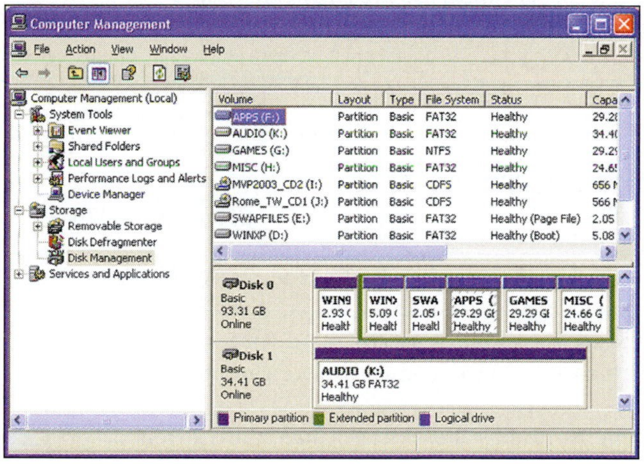

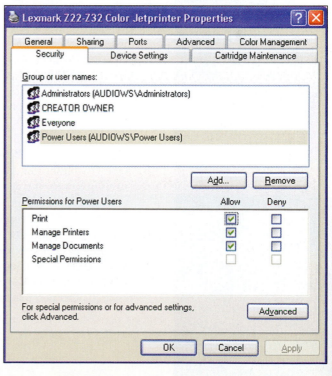

Figure 9-55 **Viewing the print queue**

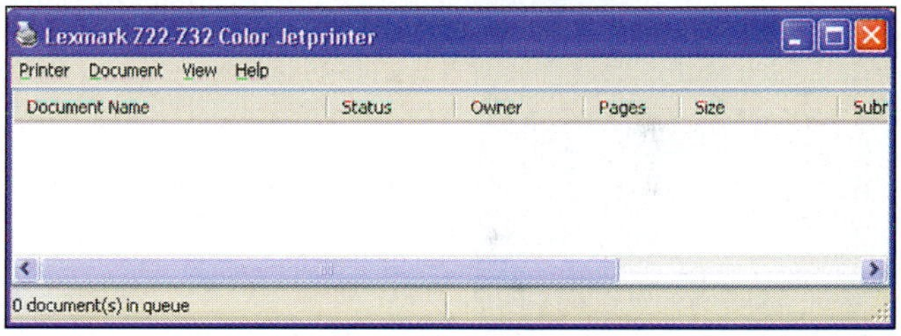

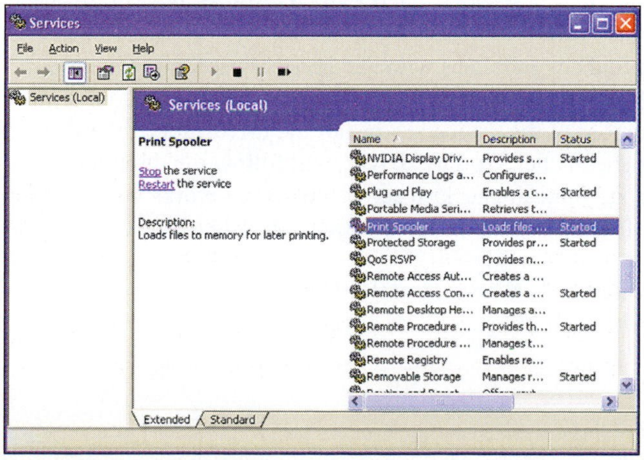

Figure 9-57 **Examine printing permissions**

Figure 9-56 **Services console**

skill 8

Troubleshooting Problems with Locally Connected Devices

exam objective

Identify and troubleshoot problems with locally attached devices. Indications of such problems include application errors.

overview

"Locally connected devices" is a broad category that includes many different types of devices, from serial devices such as modems, to FireWire-connected cameras and multimedia devices. Although all of these devices present different challenges, the process of troubleshooting each is essentially the same.

First, as with any other device, ensure that physical connectivity is established and that all physical needs (such as power to peripherals) are met. A large number of problems with locally attached peripherals lies in the physical needs of the devices. For this reason, it is especially important that you ensure that all physical connections are secure.

Next, make sure that the devices are detected properly by Windows. If not, examine the controllers for the device (USB root hub, Firewire ports, serial ports, etc.) are properly installed, configured and enabled using Device Manager (**Figure 9-58**).

Finally, examine the drivers and software configuration for the device. Again, if possible, update the drivers to the latest versions, using signed drivers where possible.

how to

Troubleshoot a local device.

1. Ensure that all cables and connectors are in place and properly seated.
2. Use Device Manager to examine the device status. Click ⊞ start , right-click **My Computer**, and select **Properties**.
3. Select the **Hardware** tab and click [Device Manager] to open Device Manager.
4. Click the plus sign next to the device type for the device in question.
5. If a red X is shown beside the device (**Figure 9-59**), the device has been disabled. To enable the device, right-click on the device icon and select **Enable** from the pop-up menu.
6. If a yellow exclamation point is beside the device, then the device or devices configuration has a problem. To view the operating system's explanation of the problem, open up the device's **Properties** dialog box by right-clicking the device icon and selecting **Properties**. In the **Properties** dialog box, check the device's status on the **General** tab (**Figure 9-60**). The message here will explain a likely cause and solution for the problem.
7. If there is no indication of a problem in Device Manager, use the Troubleshooter utility. Open up the device's **Properties** sheet by right-clicking the device icon, selecting **Properties**, and then clicking [Troubleshoot...] on the **General** tab. Follow the directions in the Troubleshooter.
8. If the Troubleshooter does not find any problems with the device, make sure you have the latest drivers for the device. Go to the manufacturer's Web site and download the most recent driver for the model number of the device. To install the driver, select the **Driver** tab of the device's **Properties** sheet, click **Update driver**, and follow the directions.
9. If the device is still not working, you can check to see if the device works with another computer system, if possible. If it does, then assess the differences between the systems to determine the problem.
10. You can also visit the manufacturer's Web site and other technical support sites to research other possible causes of the problem you are experiencing.

Figure 9-58 **Device Manager**

Figure 9-59 **Disabled device in Device Manager**

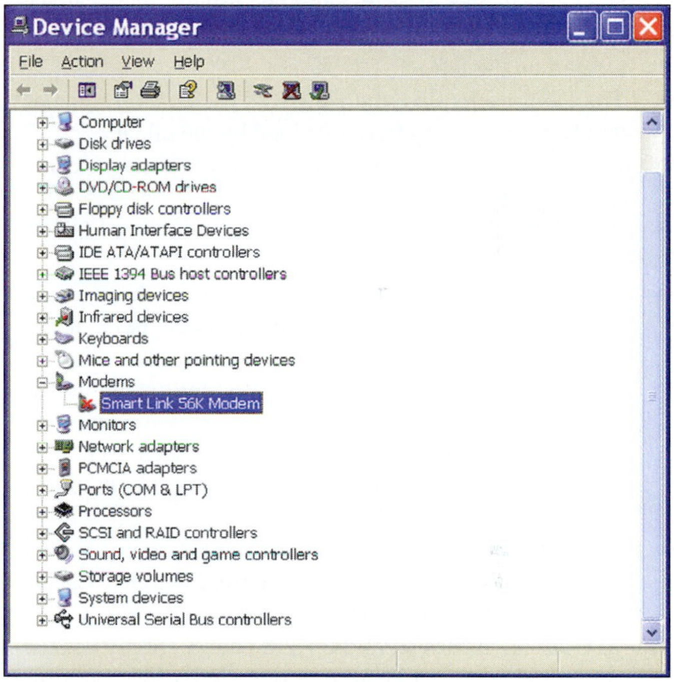

Figure 9-60 **Checking the device's status on the General tab**

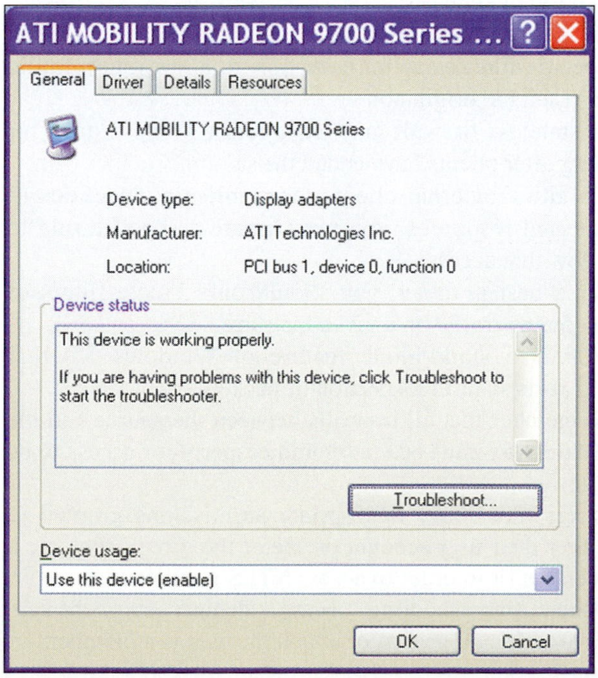

Summary

◆ The process for resolving a friendly name differs depending on the type of name. In Microsoft operating systems, two types of names can be used: NetBIOS names (also known as computer names) and Fully Qualified Domain Names (FQDNs, also known as host names).

◆ Anytime you resolve a NetBIOS name, the resolution entry for that name is stored in the NetBIOS name cache.

◆ When a WINS client wants to resolve a NetBIOS name, it sends a query to the WINS server, which looks up the name and sends the client the IP address associated with the name.

◆ The LMHOSTS file contains a list of mappings of NetBIOS names to IP addresses for the network.

◆ FQDNs are hierarchical, which means that the names follow a pattern of increasing specificity, which flows from right to left, with the most specific part of the name located on the left.

◆ The DNS cache, like the NetBIOS cache, stores names that have previously been resolved by the client.

◆ DNS servers are servers that resolve DNS names using the hierarchical DNS database.

◆ The HOSTS file is a simple text file equating FQDNs with IP addresses.

◆ Understand that any network error that occurs while using a friendly name can potentially be a name resolution error.

◆ The primary method used to pinpoint name resolution as the problem is to ping the resource by name and then ping the resource by IP. If you can reach the resource by IP, but not by name, then name resolution is the most likely culprit.

◆ If the correct DNS server is entered in the configuration, but you still cannot reach the resource, you may have a negative response that has been cached.

◆ To clear all entries from the DNS cache, simply use the command ipconfig /flushdns on a Windows 2000 or higher system.

◆ Cabling problems are perhaps the simplest of all problems, and should be the first area you examine with any networking problem.

◆ If you have a resource conflict, the icon of the adapter in Device Manager will be overlaid with a yellow circle containing a black exclamation point.

◆ Signed drivers are verified to work with the operating system by Windows Hardware Quality Labs, which basically ensures that the driver will function properly.

◆ In some NICs, there may be more than one transceiver, enabling the adapter to support multiple network cabling types.

◆ The most important aspects of the IP configuration are the IP address and subnet mask.

◆ When a client on a Windows 98, ME, 2000, or XP system fails to obtain a DHCP IP address, it will generate an Automatic Private IP Addressing (APIPA) address.

◆ In general, you want to avoid using an unsecured password for security reasons, but you may find it helpful to use an unsecured password when troubleshooting authentication problems.

◆ PAP is the least secure authentication protocol used with PPP connections. It uses plain text passwords for authentication.

◆ SPAP is an authentication protocol that is used if you are connecting to a Shiva server.

◆ CHAP is a protocol that provides authentication on the basis of a one-way hash created by seeding the Message Digest 5 (MD5) encryption algorithm with the password.

◆ Both versions of MS-CHAP support data encryption using the Microsoft Point-to-Point Encryption (MPPE) algorithm, but only MS-CHAP 2 supports mutual authentication.

◆ EAP is the strongest authentication protocol available, but it is only used when using Smart Cards.

◆ With the exception of EAP, you can choose more than one of the authentication protocols, and the client will attempt each protocol in order of most secure to least secure until a compatible protocol is found.

◆ Any time you are connecting to a Windows RRAS server, and nearly any time you connect to an ISP, you should choose PPP.

◆ L2TP is used when you want to connect to Windows 2000 or 2003 RRAS servers and is the most secure option.

◆ PPTP is used when connecting to Windows NT, 2000, and 2003 RRAS servers, as well as most other vendor's RRAS servers.

◆ Firewalls are generally classified as one of two types: stateful or stateless.

◆ A stateful firewall tracks each data flow, creating a specific filter entry for each flow to allow return traffic to reach the originator.

◆ A stateless firewall may leave return "holes" open for long after clients have ended the session.

◆ To allow external clients to establish connections to internal resources, you must create a specific rule to allow that access.

◆ As a best practice, you should only create filters of incoming traffic on a given interface.

◆ ICF is a stand-alone feature of Windows XP that supports stateful inspection of packets.

◆ Remember that all firewalls between the source and the destination must be configured properly for access to be allowed.

◆ Users must have appropriate permissions granted to either their user account or one of the groups they are a member of in order to access NTFS partitions.

◆ When troubleshooting "access is denied" errors, be sure to examine all groups of which the user is a member.

◆ To install an application that includes a MSI file, the user should not normally need any elevated privileges.

◆ Some older Windows NT applications expect the rights associated with the Users group on Windows NT to be present.

◆ The network browser service is a bit notorious for taking very long periods of time to rebuild the browse list.

◆ To connect to another computer in a workgroup, you must have a valid user account on that system.

◆ Spooling errors can manifest in several different ways, but the most common error is a hung queue.

Key Terms

Automatic Private IP Addressing (APIPA) addresses
Broadcast
Challenge Handshake Authentication Protocol (CHAP)
Data flows
Extensible Authentication Protocol (EAP)
Firewall
Fully Qualified Domain Name (FQDN)

Internet Connection Firewall (ICF)
LMHOSTS file
Microsoft CHAP (MS-CHAP)
Name resolution
Negative responses
NetBIOS name cache
NetBIOS names
Password Authentication Protocol (PAP)
Pathping
Ping

Shiva Password Authentication Protocol (SPAP)
Stateful firewalls
Stateless firewalls
Tracert
Universal Naming Convention (UNC)
Virtual private networks (VPNs)
Windows Internet Naming Service (WINS) server

Test Yourself

1. Which of the following best describes the Internet Connection Firewall?
   a. A low-security stateless firewall
   b. A medium-security stateful firewall
   c. A virus protection application
   d. A high-security stateless firewall

2. You are attempting to resolve a problem on your small office network. A user is unable to access remote resources by either name or IP. Place the steps you would take to diagnose this problem in the correct order.
   a. Ping the client's IP address
   b. Ping the default gateway
   c. Ping a local system
   d. Ping a remote system
   e. Run ipconfig /all

3. You work for a small company that sells golf supplies through the Internet. The company has a small network that consists of Windows Server 2003 computers and Windows XP desktops. A user named Bob has just been hired as a new sales associate for your company. Sales associates use a custom order entry application to perform their daily duties. However, each time Bob attempts to launch the application, he receives an "access is denied" error. What is the most likely cause of this problem?

   a. The application is not compatible with Windows XP.
   b. Bob does not have the Log on interactively right on his local system.
   c. Bob does not have Read and Execute permissions for the application executable.
   d. Bob does not have the Act as part of the operating system right on his local system.

4. You are attempting to diagnose an application connectivity problem on a client's system. The application is network-based, and utilizes files that are stored on a shared folder. Each time the user attempts to execute the application, an error appears stating that the network destination cannot be found. You examine the client's Ethernet card and notice that link lights are not present. What should you do to resolve this problem? (Choose all that apply.)
   a. Check to see if the driver is loaded in Device Manager.
   b. Use the repair network connection feature.
   c. Replace the network cable with a known good cable.
   d. Ensure that the adapter's transceiver setting is correct.
   e. Run ipconfig /renew.

5. You are attempting to reach a distant server on the Internet with a network application, but the application is repeatedly timing out. After several tries, you manage to connect, but the speed is unacceptably slow. You are concerned that the problem is caused by an overloaded router in you network. Which utility would you use to verify the path to the remote resource and diagnose latency problems?
   a. Ping
   b. Ipconfig
   c. Pathping
   d. Routepath

6. You are attempting to connect to a server in your network with a custom network application. Each time you attempt to connect, you receive the error *Could not find host server1.corp.com.*

   You attempt to ping the system by IP address and are successful. After contacting your DNS administrator, the administrator verifies the problem on the DNS server and reconfigures the DNS server. He instructs you to try the application again. However, you continue to receive the error. What should you do next to attempt to resolve the problem?
   a. Reboot the system.
   b. Replace the network card with a known good network card.
   c. Update the drivers for the network card.
   d. Run the ipconfig /flushdns command.
   e. Ensure that the network cabling is correctly connected.

7. Select the answers from the list below that most closely describe NetBIOS naming. (Choose all that apply.)
   a. 15-character names
   b. Hierarchical naming
   c. Highly scalable
   d. Can be resolved with an LMHosts file
   e. Can be resolved via broadcasts

8. You need to configure your firewall to allow external clients to reach a custom application server on your internal network. The application utilizes TCP port 2112 for communications. Which of the following should you do to configure the firewall?
   a. Create a packet filter on the internal interface of the firewall that allows outgoing traffic destined for port 2112.
   b. Disable the firewall.
   c. Create a packet filter on the internal interface of the firewall that allows incoming traffic destined for port 2112.
   d. Create a packet filter on the external interface of the firewall that allows outgoing traffic destined for port 2112.
   e. Create a packet filter on the external interface of the firewall that allows incoming traffic destined for port 2112.

9. You are troubleshooting an error with connectivity on a user's system. The user complains that he cannot connect to any resources. The user is connected to a 10baseT Ethernet network. Which of the following troubleshooting steps should you do first when attempting to diagnose this problem?
   a. Replace the network cable with a known good cable.
   b. Use the Repair Network Connection feature.
   c. Examine the link light on the adapter.
   d. Change the resource assignments for the adapter.
   e. Renew the IP address.

10. You are responding to a user who is having difficulty accessing remote resources. You have checked local connectivity, and it is functioning properly. You suspect that the error is caused by some improper TCP/IP settings. Which of the following tools will allow you to verify that the user's IP configuration is correct?
    a. Ping
    b. Ipconfig
    c. Pathping
    d. Tracert

Projects: On Your Own

1. Enable the Internet Connection Firewall on your interface to the local network. Then, disable all ICMP traffic on the interface and test to ensure that pings no longer function.
   a. Log on to the system as a local administrator.
   b. From the **Start** menu, open the **Network Connections** dialog box.
   c. Open the **Properties** dialog box for your network connection to the local network.
   d. Select the **Advanced** tab and enable the **Internet Connection Firewall**.
   e. Click the **Settings** button to open the **Advanced Settings** dialog box and select the ICMP tab.
   f. Clear all check boxes in the ICMP settings dialog box, then click OK on each dialog box to close all dialog boxes and apply the settings.
   g. **Ping** your system from another system on the network.
   h. Return to your system.
   i. Open the **Properties** dialog box for your network connection to the local network.
   j. Select the **Advanced** tab and disable the Internet Connection Firewall.
   k. Close all open dialog boxes and log off of the system.

2. Use Google and pathping to locate and examine connectivity to websites around the world.
   a. Log on to the system as a local administrator.
   b. Open a browser window and navigate to www.google.com.
   c. In the search text box, type .au to bring up a list of websites with the .au designation (such as news.com.au). The .au designation is a country code reserved for websites in or about Australia.
   d. Open a command prompt and use the pathping utility to generate statistics to the remote site.
   e. Use Google to locate other remote sites in the United Kingdom, the Netherlands, and Japan. The country codes for these sites are .uk, .nl, and .jp, respectively.
   f. Use Pathping to trace statistics to these sites. Compare your results. To which countries do you have the best and worst connectivity?
   g. When finished, close all open dialog boxes and log off of the system.

Problem Solving Scenarios

1. You have recently been promoted into a new position within your company. As the company's first network support technician, you are required to create guidelines for all desktop support technicians to utilize when troubleshooting network connectivity problems. The document or documents must detail the exact procedures for determining the cause of all common network connectivity errors, from physical errors to inability to browse for resources. Create these documents, ensuring that you pay special attention to the exact steps required when troubleshooting each type of problem.

2. Your company has recently decided to upgrade the hard disks on all computers. However, management is concerned about errors that may occur as part of this process. All data will be backed up before hand, so data loss is not a concern. You have been given the responsibility for writing a document detailing the steps technicians need to take when diagnosing hard disk related problems during and after the upgrade. Make an ordered list of the steps that desktop support technicians should take in troubleshooting hard disk problems.

Troubleshooting Access Problems on Multiuser and Multiboot Computers

Multiuser and multiboot systems bring a special set of requirements and have their own unique troubleshooting challenges. This is mostly due to the additional complexity inherent in these systems. To enable you to fully understand the unique challenges these systems pose, this lesson examines each type of system in detail.

A single-user system is a system that is primarily used by one user. Although other users may log into the system occasionally, they do so only for short periods and do not require significant access to local applications. This is the simplest system type.

A multiuser system is a system upon which multiple users regularly log in for extended periods. This essentially results in a system that is shared by several users, all of whom need access to specific applications and data. A home computer shared among all family members would be an example of such a system.

A multiboot system is a system with more than one operating system installed. The user chooses which operating system to load through a boot loader, such as the one provided by Windows XP, at startup. To switch operating systems, the user must restart the system and choose the appropriate operating system from the boot loader menu. These systems are perhaps the most complex of the three system types and can significantly complicate the troubleshooting process.

With these definitions in mind, let's take a closer look at the troubleshooting process for multiuser and multiboot systems.

Goals

In this lesson, you will learn how to troubleshoot application access on multiuser and multiboot systems. Additionally, you will learn how to resolve file access problems on multiuser systems.

Lesson 10   Troubleshooting Access Problems on Multiuser and Multiboot Computers

Skill	Exam 70-272 Objective
1. Managing File System Access and File Permission Problems on Multiuser Computers	**Identify and troubleshoot problems related to security permissions.** Troubleshoot access to local resources. Troubleshoot access to network resources. Troubleshoot insufficient user permissions and rights.
2. Troubleshooting Application Access on Multiuser Computers	**Configure the operating system to support applications.** Answer end-user questions related to configuring the operating system to support an application. Configure access to applications on multiuser computers. Configure and troubleshoot application access on a multiple user client computer
3. Configuring Access to Applications on Multiboot Computers	**Configure the operating system to support applications.** Answer end-user questions related to configuring the operating system to support an application. Configure and troubleshoot file system access and file permission problems on multiboot computers.

Requirements

To complete this lesson, you will need administrative rights on a Windows XP Professional computer. This system should have at least one NTFS partition or volume, and simple file sharing should be enabled (the default setting). You will need two user accounts. Additionally, both accounts need to log in at least once to create their profiles. One user account should be a member of the local Administrators group.

skill 1

Managing File System Access and File Permission Problems on Multiuser Computers

exam objective

Identify and troubleshoot problems related to security permissions. Troubleshoot access to local resources. Troubleshoot access to network resources. Troubleshoot insufficient user permissions and rights.

overview

When multiple users utilize the same system, an additional layer of complexity is added to the troubleshooting process. Because each user account has its own permissions and rights, the access granted to one user may be very different from the access granted to another. Additionally, many users forget to log off of the system after using it, which can result in another user getting inappropriate permissions.

When troubleshooting access to resources, such as files and folders, you should first determine the user account under which the user is logged on. The process for determining which user account is currently logged on is fairly simple, but it differs slightly depending on operating system. The simplest way is usually to press **[Ctrl]+[Alt]+[Del]** to bring up the Windows Security dialog box. On some Windows XP systems, pressing **[Ctrl]+[Alt]+[Del]** may bring up Task Manager instead. From Task Manager, select Shutdown on the menu bar and then select **Log off <username>** (**Figure 10-1**). The listed user name is the currently logged on user. Additionally, if the current policy allows **Log Off** to be displayed on the **Start** menu, you can simply click **Start** and select the **Log Off** option (**Figure 10-2**).

Once you have determined which user is logged into the system, you should examine the permissions settings for the resource he or she is trying to access. You can do this on all operating systems from within the Properties dialog box for the file or folder. On Windows NT and Windows 2000 systems, the Properties dialog box has a Security tab where you can click to view the security settings configured on the file or folder. On Windows XP systems, however, the Security dialog box may be missing, even on NTFS resources. This is because when simple file sharing is enabled, only minimal security options are available to the end user. In this case, to see the permissions assigned to the user, you will first need to disable simple file sharing from the folder options dialog box under the tools menu. Once this is done, the Security tab will be available .

Once you open the Security tab, analyze the permissions assigned to the user to determine if the user is being denied access to the resource due to the groups of which he or she is a member.

tip

All users have the same level of access to local FAT partitions.

tip

Windows 9x systems do not support NTFS and therefore do not include a Security tab.

tip

Resources stored on FAT partitions will not have a Security tab.

how to

Disable simple file sharing.

1. Boot the system and log on as a local administrator.
2. Click **start** and select **My Computer** to open the **My Computer** window (**Figure 10-3**).
3. Right-click on the drive letter for an NTFS partition and select **Properties** to open the drive **Properties** dialog box (**Figure 10-4**).
4. Click on the **Sharing** tab to examine the simple file sharing options (**Figure 10-5**).
4. Click [Cancel] to close the drive's **Properties** dialog box without making changes.
5. In the **My Computer** window, click the **Tools** on the menu bar (**Figure 10-6**) and click **Folder Options** to open the **Folder Options** dialog box.

Figure 10-1 Logging off through Task Manager

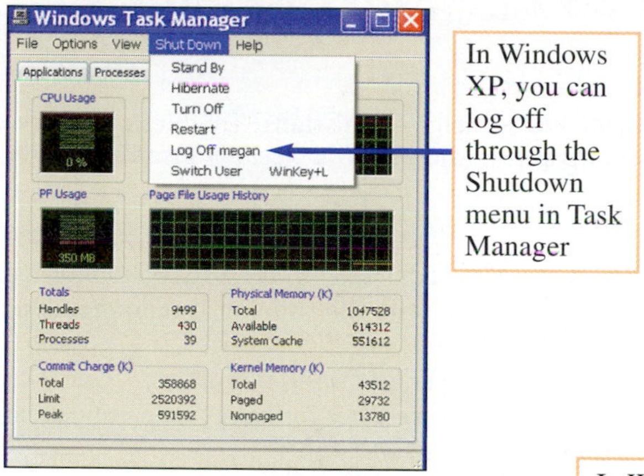

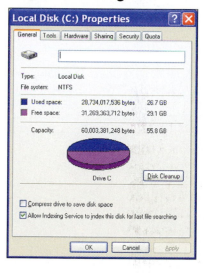

In Windows XP, you can log off through the Shutdown menu in Task Manager

Figure 10-2 Logging off through the Start menu

In Windows XP, you can also log off through the Start menu

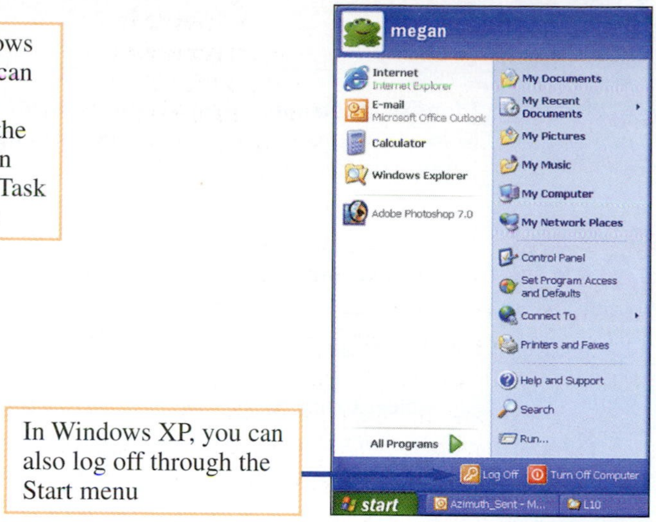

Figure 10-4 Local Disk Properties dialog box

Figure 10-3 My Computer

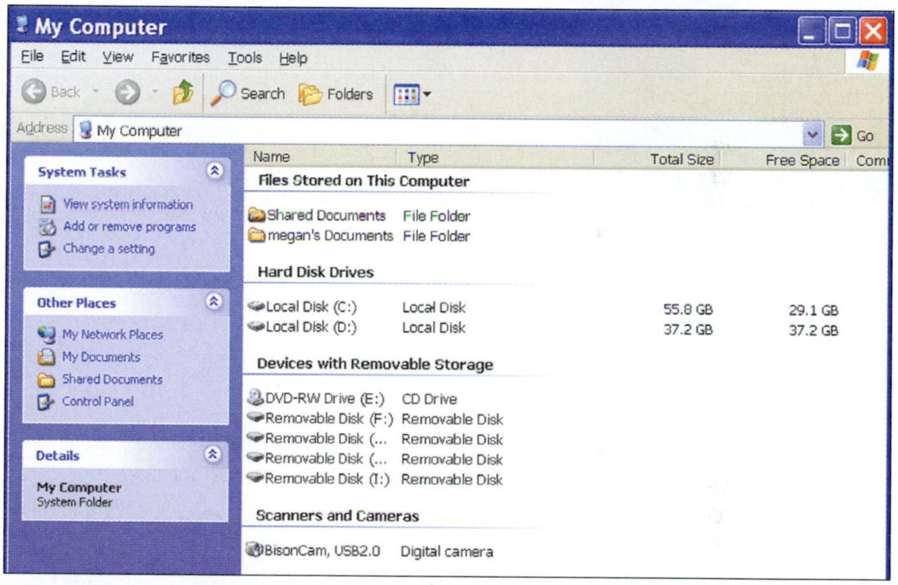

Figure 10-5 Sharing tab

Figure 10-6 The Tools menu in the My Computer window

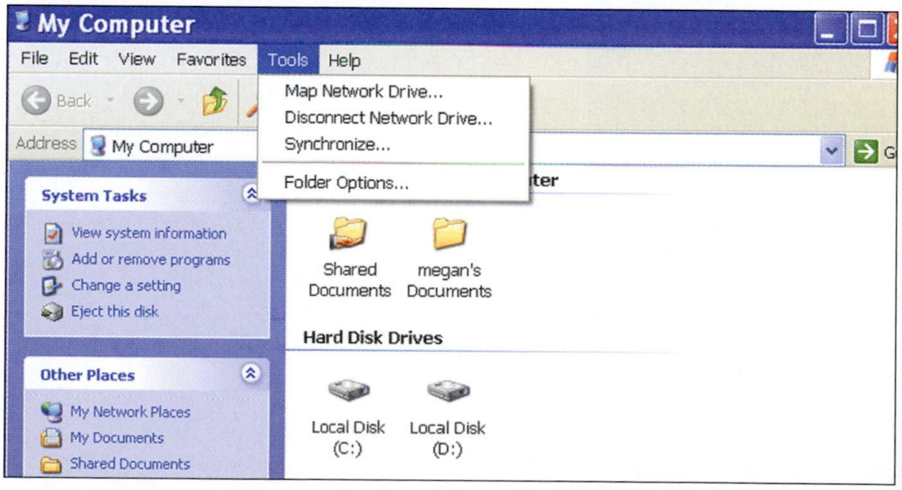

skill 1

Managing File System Access and File Permission Problems on Multiuser Computers
(cont'd)

exam objective

Identify and troubleshoot problems related to security permissions. Troubleshoot access to local resources. Troubleshoot access to network resources. Troubleshoot insufficient user permissions and rights.

how to

6. In the **Folder Options** dialog box, click the **View** tab, scroll to the very bottom of the **Advanced Settings** list box, and clear the **Use simple file sharing (recommended)** check box (**Figure 10-7**).
7. Click [OK] to close the Folder Options dialog box.
8. In the **My Computer** window, right-click on the drive letter for an NTFS partition and select **Properties** to open the drive **Properties** dialog box.
9. Confirm that the **Security** tab is now available (**Figure 10-8**).
10. Close all open dialog boxes and log off of the system.

Figure 10-7 Disabling simple file sharing

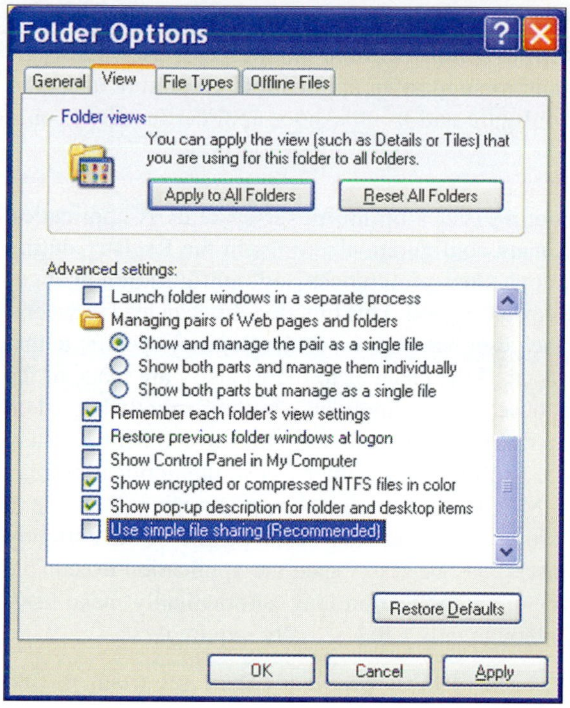

Figure 10-8 Security tab

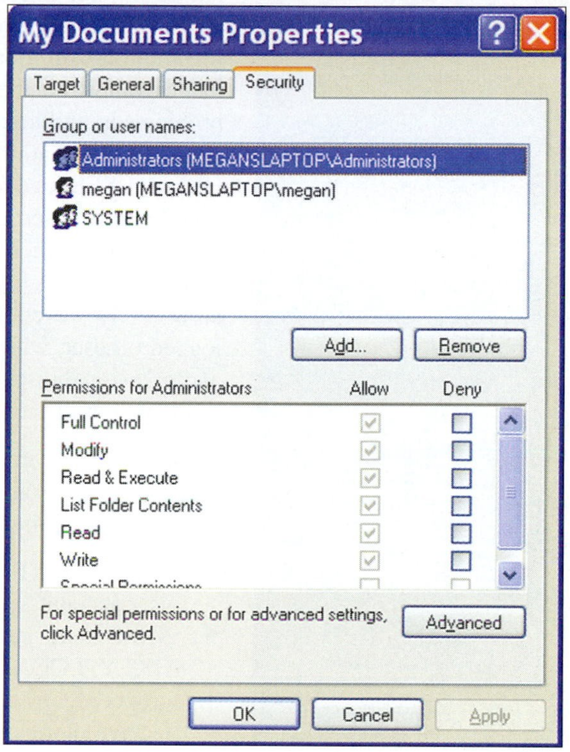

skill 2

Troubleshooting Application Access on Multiuser Computers

Configure the operating system to support applications. Answer end-user questions related to configuring the operating system to support an application. Configure access to applications on multiuser computers. Configure and troubleshoot application access on a multiple user client computer

overview

An additional concern when troubleshooting issues on multiuser systems is application access. Most modern applications place many configuration settings in the Registry during installation. Additionally, many applications store preferences and configuration changes made from within the application in the Registry as well. This functionality can lead to several problems in multiuser systems, because each user has a subset of the Registry specific to that user stored in that user's profile. For instance, if the changes to the Registry are made to the HKEY_USER hive for that specific user, those changes apply only to the currently logged on user. So, if the user installed an application that wrote all changes to this hive, other users may receive errors when attempting to run the application. In other cases, the application may make the changes to the HKEY_LOCAL_MACHINE hive, which would make it available to all users. However, the application may create a shortcut only in the profile of the currently logged on user, which means that other users may need to locate the application executable and create a shortcut manually. Even worse, an application may automatically make itself available for all users on the system, even though only a few actually require it.

Although there are various solutions to each of these problems, it is important to first understand the various installation behaviors that applications can exhibit. In general, applications will install in one of the four following manners (**Figure 10-9**):

◆ **Single-user**: The application writes the Registry changes only to the profile of a single-user account, specifically, the user account that installed the application.
◆ **Multiuser, missing shortcut**: The application writes Registry changes to HKEY_LOCAL_MACHINE, making the application available to all users, but fails to properly copy the shortcut to all profiles. Only the user who installed the application will receive shortcuts to the application.
◆ **Multiuser**: The application writes Registry changes to HKEY_LOCAL_MACHINE, making the application available to all users, and automatically copies the shortcut to all profiles.
◆ **User choice**: The user is given the option to make the application available to all users or just his or her user account during the installation.

Which application installation method is best for you depends upon your goals. If you want to install the application for all users, then either Multiuser or User choice is preferred. However, if you want to make the application available only to specific users, then the Single user or User choice methods are best. However, application support for these methods is not guaranteed, and you must know how to resolve various problems arising from an application being installed using a less preferred method.

One of the more common issues you will need to know how to resolve involves an application that was installed to a single user's profile when that application is required by all users. In this case, you have several options, depending on the application's installation method. If the application installation allows user choice, then simply reinstall the application and choose to install the application for all users. If the application is multiuser but does not create a shortcut, then you can simply copy the shortcut or shortcuts from the installing user's profile into each other user's profile. In both of these cases, the solution was quite simple; however, for single-user applications, the solution is considerably more complex.

One solution, and the best in most cases, is to deploy the application to the computer account with Group Policy. By deploying the application to the computer account, you ensure that all

Figure 10-9 Application support for multiuser systems

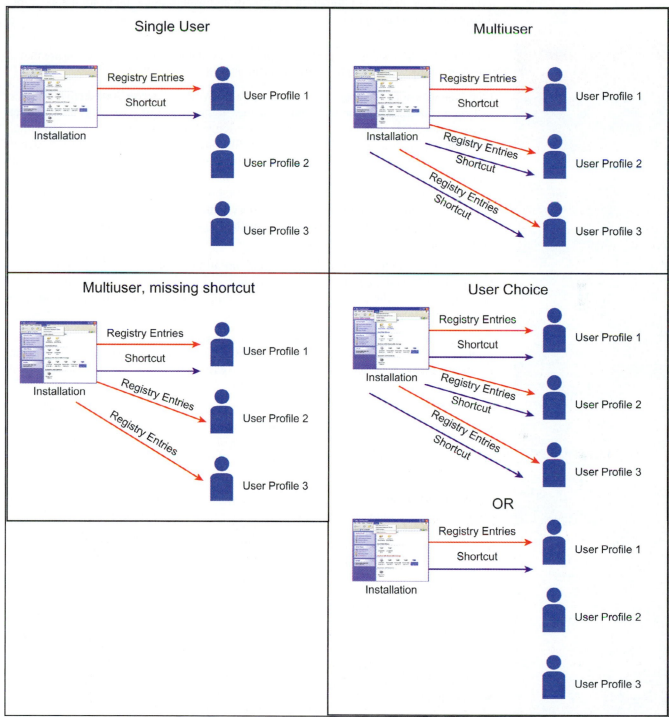

skill 2

Troubleshooting Application Access on Multiuser Computers (cont'd)

exam objective

Configure the operating system to support applications. Answer end-user questions related to configuring the operating system to support an application. Configure access to applications on multiuser computers. Configure and troubleshoot application access on a multiple user client computer

overview

users who use the system will have the application available. In addition, you ensure that all new users of the system will have that application available as well.

If the system is not a member of a Windows 2000 or Windows Server 2003 Active Directory domain, however, this option will be unavailable. In this case, if the system is a new system (i.e., no users other than the administrator have logged on to the system), you can simply install the application to the administrator's profile, and then copy that profile to the default user profile. Because each user's local profile is built by copying the default user profile, this ensures that each user of the system will receive the application (**Figure 10-10**). However, since the default user profile is only copied the first time a user logs into the system, this is only plausible for a new system. In addition, since roaming profiles are copied from a server, and not from the default user profile, this method does not work for users with roaming profiles.

Another solution to the problem is to manually install the application for each user account that logs into the system. Although this may be your only option in some cases, you should do this only if one of the previously discussed methods does not work, because it involves considerable administrative overhead.

One other problem you may run into involves a restricted application that automatically installs for all user accounts. In this case, a serious security violation could occur by allowing unauthorized users to access the application. Again, this problem has several possible solutions.

First, some applications have vendor-defined flags than can be set, either by running the installation through the command line or by changing a Registry or initialization file setting, which allow the application to install only for a single user. If your application supports changing the installation mode in this manner, you can do this and then install the application manually for the users who require it.

A second, and usually preferred, method is to deploy the application to user accounts with Group Policy. By applying an application deployment Group Policy object (GPO) to a specific organization unit (OU) that contains only the user accounts that require the application, you can ensure that only those users receive the application. However, to do this, the system must be a member of a Windows 2000 or 2003 Active Directory domain, and the users must have accounts in that domain.

One final method, typically used in addition to the other two methods, is to use NTFS permissions to define which users can access the application directory and data files. in general, denying the Read and Execute permissions for unauthorized users on the application executables keeps unauthorized users from executing the application (**Figure 10-11**). Similarly, denying all permissions for unauthorized users on the application data files ensures that unauthorized users do not gain access to the data files with another application (**Figure 10-12**).

Another problem that can occur with multiuser applications is that the application tracks preferences globally (for all users) in a single Registry location. When this occurs, each user does not get their own preferences for the application. Instead, each change made by any user applies to all users on the system. This problem is not easily remedied and generally requires an update from the application vendor.

Figure 10-10 Copying the Default User profile

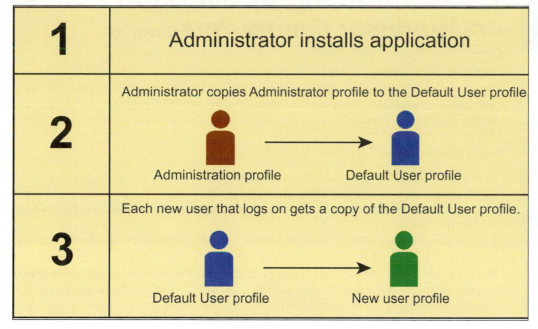

1	Administrator installs application
2	Administrator copies Administrator profile to the Default User profile. Administration profile → Default User profile
3	Each new user that logs on gets a copy of the Default User profile. Default User profile → New user profile

Figure 10-11 Preventing the Guests group from accessing an application

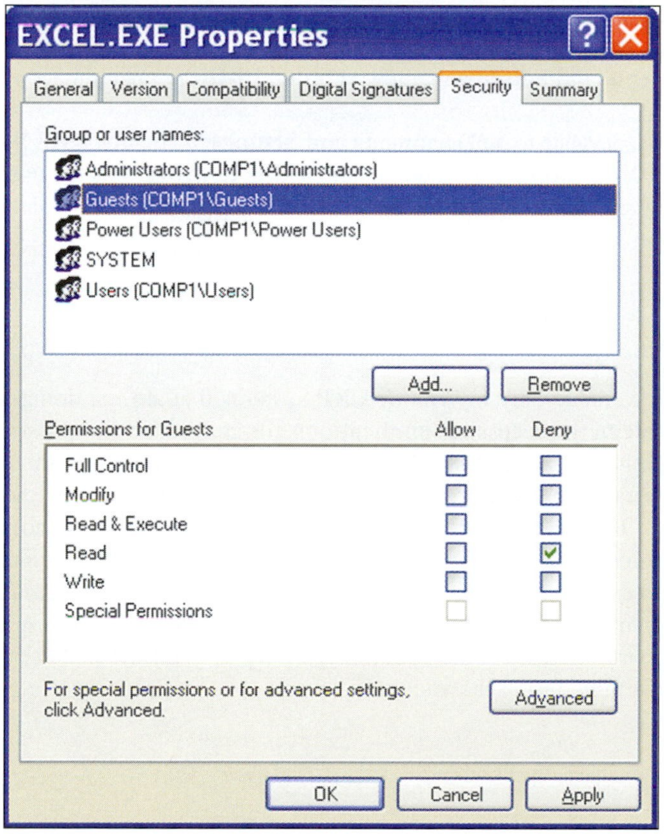

EXCEL.EXE Properties

General | Version | Compatibility | Digital Signatures | Security | Summary

Group or user names:

- Administrators (COMP1\Administrators)
- Guests (COMP1\Guests)
- Power Users (COMP1\Power Users)
- SYSTEM
- Users (COMP1\Users)

Add...   Remove

Permissions for Guests	Allow	Deny
Full Control	☐	☐
Modify	☐	☐
Read & Execute	☐	☐
Read	☐	☑
Write	☐	☐
Special Permissions	☐	☐

For special permissions or for advanced settings, click Advanced.   Advanced

OK   Cancel   Apply

Figure 10-12 Preventing the Guests group from accessing application data files

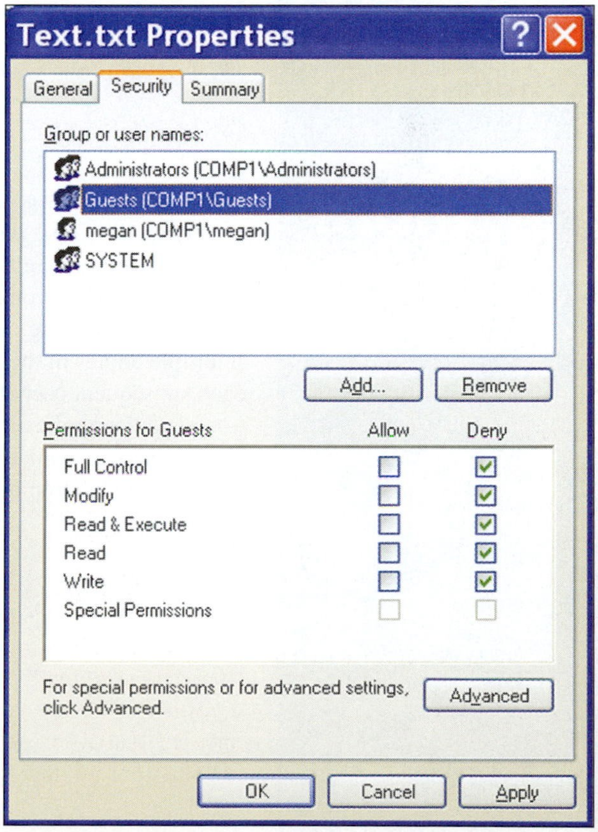

Text.txt Properties

General | Security | Summary

Group or user names:

- Administrators (COMP1\Administrators)
- Guests (COMP1\Guests)
- megan (COMP1\megan)
- SYSTEM

Add...   Remove

Permissions for Guests	Allow	Deny
Full Control	☐	☑
Modify	☐	☑
Read & Execute	☐	☑
Read	☐	☑
Write	☐	☑
Special Permissions	☐	☐

For special permissions or for advanced settings, click Advanced.   Advanced

OK   Cancel   Apply

skill 2

Troubleshooting Application Access on Multiuser Computers (cont'd)

exam objective

Configure the operating system to support applications. Answer end-user questions related to configuring the operating system to support an application. Configure access to applications on multiuser computers. Configure and troubleshoot application access on a multiple user client computer

how to

Copy a shortcut to a user's profile.

1. Log onto the system as an administrative user.
2. To create a shortcut on the desktop, right-click a blank area on the desktop, point to **New** on the shortcut menu, and click **Shortcut**. This will open the **Create Shortcut** wizard (**Figure 10-13**).
3. In the **Type the location of the item** text box, type **%systemroot%\system32\mmc.exe** and click [Next >] .
4. On the **Select a Title for the Program** screen, type **Microsoft Management Console** (**Figure 10-14**) as the name for the shortcut, and click [Finish] . This creates a shortcut to the chosen application on the desktop.
5. To copy the shortcut, first navigate to the current user profile. To do this, open **My Computer** and in the **Address** bar, type **X:\Documents and Settings**, where **X:** is the drive letter containing your profile folder, which is C: by default (**Figure 10-15**). This opens the **Documents and Settings** folder.
6. Next, double-click the folder that corresponds with the user name you are currently logged in as, then double-click the **Desktop** folder to open the list of files in that folder.
7. Select the **Microsoft Management Console** shortcut and click the **Copy this file** link in the left pane of the **Documents and Settings** window (**Figure 10-16**) to open the Copy Items dialog box
8. In the **Copy Items** dialog box, navigate to **X:\Documents and Settings\%USERNAME%\ Desktop**, where **X:** is the disk the profile is located on and **%USERNAME%** is the user for whom you want to copy the shortcut (**Figure 10-17**). Click [OK] to complete the copy.
9. Log off of the system.

more

Fast user switching, a feature available only to Windows XP systems that are not domain members, can also cause problems in accessing applications for multiuser computers. Fast user switching allows a user to switch accounts and reload a new user's settings without logging off. When you switch users using fast user switching, all applications for the previous user are left running. Because of this, if the application does not support multiple instances (multiple copies of the application running at the same time), then you may get an error when each subsequent user attempts to execute the application. The best solution to this problem is to update the application to support fast user switching. However, if the application does not have an update available to support this feature, then your only option is to ensure that users close the application before performing fast user switching.

tip

Fast user switching is available only on Windows XP systems that are members of a workgroup.

Figure 10-13 Create Shortcut wizard

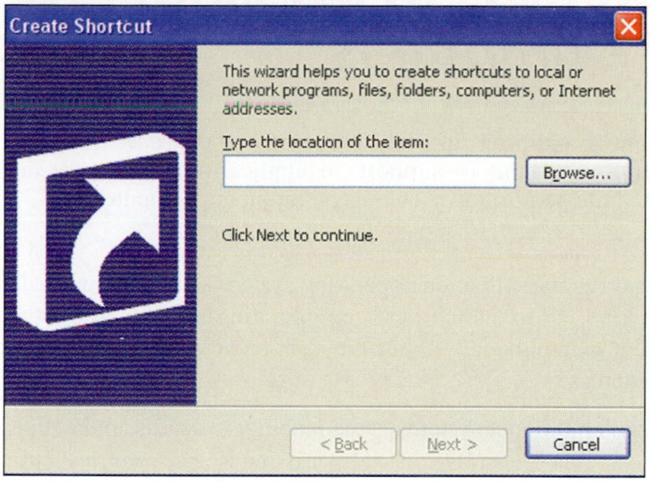

Create Shortcut
This wizard helps you to create shortcuts to local or network programs, files, folders, computers, or Internet addresses.
Type the location of the item:
Browse...
Click Next to continue.
< Back
Next >
Cancel

Figure 10-14 Naming the shortcut

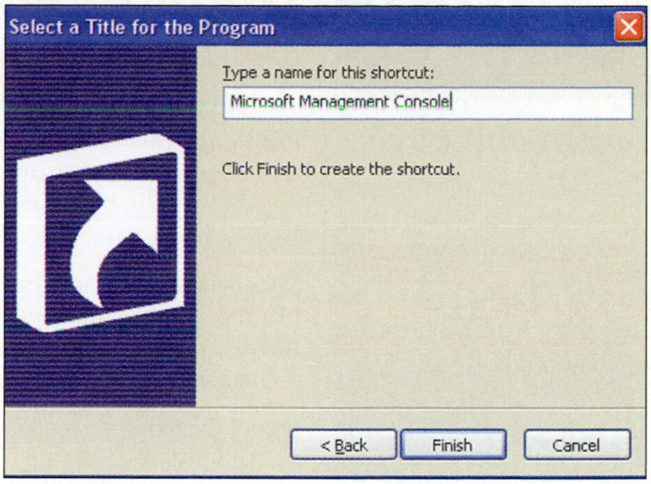

Select a Title for the Program
Type a name for this shortcut:
Microsoft Management Console
Click Finish to create the shortcut.
< Back
Finish
Cancel

On this computer, system, files, including the Documents and Settings folder, are located on the D drive

Figure 10-15 Locating the current user profile

Documents and Settings
D:\Documents and Settings
File and Folder Tasks
Other Places
Details
Administrator.AUDIOWS
All Users
All Users.WINNT
Beth
Brian
Default User
Default User.WINNT
LocalService
NetworkService

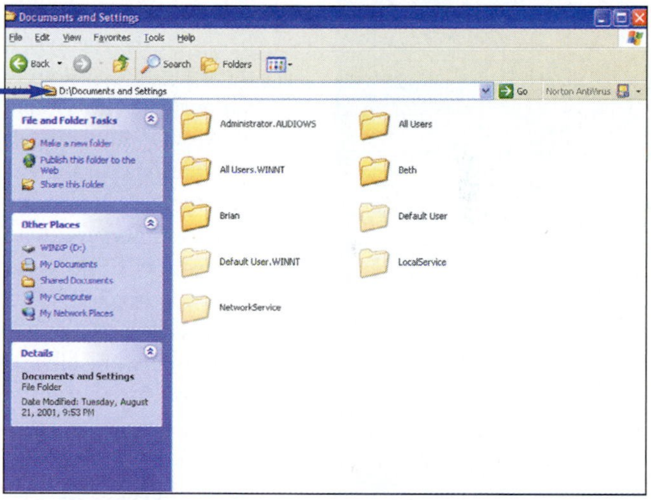

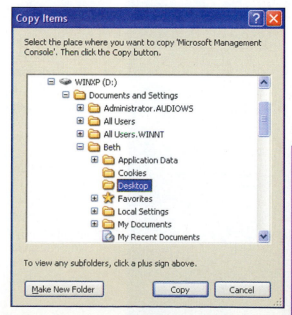

Figure 10-16 Copying the shortcut

Desktop
File Edit View Favorites Tools Help
Back
Search
Folders
Address D:\Documents and Settings\Brian\Desktop
Go
Norton AntiVirus
File and Folder Tasks
Rename this file
Move this file
Copy this file
Publish this file to the Web
E-mail this file
Delete this file
Microsoft Management Console Shortcut
2 KB
Microsoft XML 4.0 Parser SDK
Shortcut
2 KB
MYIE2
Shortcut
1 KB

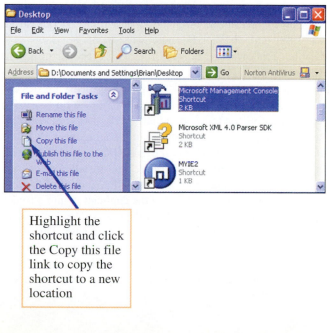

Highlight the shortcut and click the Copy this file link to copy the shortcut to a new location

Figure 10-17 Placing the shortcut in its new location

Copy Items
Select the place where you want to copy 'Microsoft Management Console'. Then click the Copy button.
WINXP (D:)
Documents and Settings
Administrator.AUDIOWS
All Users
All Users.WINNT
Beth
Application Data
Cookies
Desktop
Favorites
Local Settings
My Documents
My Recent Documents
To view any subfolders, click a plus sign above.
Make New Folder
Copy
Cancel

skill 3 | Configuring Access to Applications on Multiboot Computers

exam objective

Configure the operating system to support applications. Answer end-user questions related to configuring the operating system to support an application. Configure and troubleshoot file system access and file permission problems on multiboot computers.

overview

Multiboot systems are systems that run more than one operating system, using a boot loader like the one provided with Windows XP to switch between operating systems at startup. Because of the complexity inherent in multiboot systems, they can prove even more difficult to troubleshoot than multiuser systems.

One of the most common issues with multiboot systems is the inability to access applications from all installed operating systems. This is usually caused by missing Registry entries, but it can also be caused by file system incompatibility or improper NTFS security settings. Let's examine each possible problem in turn (**Figure 10-18**).

◆ **File system incompatibility**: First, you need to ensure that each operating system will be able to support the file system on each drive it needs to access. For quick reference, a listing of the file systems each operating system supports is provided in **Table 10-1**. For the operating system to access the data and/or applications on a given partition, it must support the file system used on that partition. Also, be aware that Windows 2000 and above will automatically convert any NTFS 4 partitions on the system to NTFS 5 during installation. For this reason, you should make sure that SP 4 or greater is installed on any multiboot system using Windows NT before installing Windows 2000, Windows XP, or Windows Server 2003.

◆ **Improper NTFS security settings**: Once you have ensured that the file system on each drive is compatible with the chosen operating systems, you should examine the NTFS permissions on each NTFS drive to make sure that all users using any operating system on the network have permissions to access the files. Additionally, examine the files in question for encryption. Encrypted files will be inaccessible from Windows NT. They will also be inaccessible from the Encrypting File System (EFS)-compatible operating systems on the same system by default, unless roaming profiles are used. This problem occurs because EFS uses a certificate to decrypt each file, and the certificate is stored in the user's profile. By default, if you are using local profiles, each user will have a different local profile for each installed operating system. To resolve this issue, you can ensure that the user's profile for each operating system is stored in the same location (by changing the profile path). But be aware that this solution works only for EFS-compatible operating systems (Windows 2000 and above). For any version of Windows NT, encrypted files will be unavailable. Windows 9x/Me cannot access NTFS partitions, so they can also never access encrypted files.

◆ **Registry entries missing**: Next, you need to ensure that the proper Registry entries for the applications are written to all operating systems. The easiest way to do this is to install the application from each operating system individually. You should also install the applications to a central application partition. In addition to reducing the disk space used, this will also ease application management tasks (**Figure 10-19**). For instance, you might create an E: partition specifically for application storage, and install applications directly to this partition. If you were using a dual-boot system with Windows 2000 and Windows XP, you would boot into Windows 2000 and install the application into a folder on the E: partition, such as E:\Word. Then, you would reboot the system, load Windows XP, and install the same application, picking E:\Word as the installation path. This loads the appropriate entries into the Registry of both operating systems but only results in a single installation of the application files. Additionally, using this method, patches will usually only need to be applied once, unless the patch modifies Registry entries (this is usually detailed in the patch's documentation).

Figure 10-18 **Possible causes of application problems on multiboot systems**

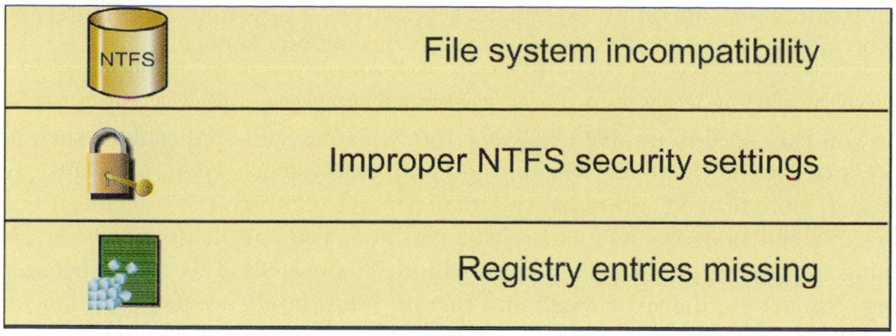

NTFS	File system incompatibility
🔒	Improper NTFS security settings
	Registry entries missing

Figure 10-19 **Installing applications to a central application partition**

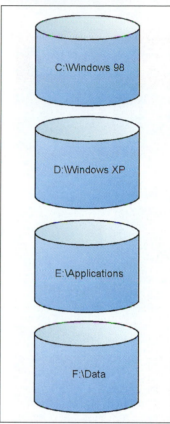

C:\Windows 98

D:\Windows XP

E:\Applications

F:\Data

Table 10-1   File system support by operating system

OPeRATiNG SYSTEM Version	FAT16	FAT32	NTFS 4	NTFS 5
Windows 95 (Original Release)	Yes	No	No	No
Windows 95 (OSR 2)	Yes	Yes	No	No
Windows 98	Yes	Yes	No	No
Windows Me	Yes	Yes	No	No
Windows NT 3.5/3.51	Yes	No	Yes	No
Windows NT 4 (pre-SP 4)	Yes	No	Yes	No
Windows NT 4 (SP 4 or above)	Yes	No	Yes	Yes
Windows 2000	Yes	Yes	Yes*	Yes
Windows XP	Yes	Yes	Yes*	Yes
Windows Server 2003	Yes	Yes	Yes*	Yes

*Windows 2000 and above will automatically convert any NTFS 4 partitions on the system to NTFS 5 during installation.

skill 3

Configuring Access to Applications on Multiboot Computers *(cont'd)*

exam objective

Configure the operating system to support applications. Answer end-user questions related to configuring the operating system to support an application. Configure and troubleshoot file system access and file permission problems on multiboot computers.

overview

Another issue you may need to resolve involves errors with standard applications, such as Outlook Express or Internet Explorer, when using multiboot systems. These problems can occur if you install more than one operating system to a single partition. For instance, if you install Windows 98 and Windows XP on the same partition, you will likely receive errors when attempting to start these applications from within Windows 98. This occurs because both operating systems use the same location, Program Files, on the system partition for storage of these applications. Because different versions of IE exist for each operating system, when you install Windows XP, it overwrites the Windows 98-specific version of these programs with the Windows XP version, which will cause errors in the application from Windows 98. To resolve this problem, reinstall the operating systems on different partitions.

Finally, you should be aware that Windows 2000, Windows NT, Windows XP, and Windows Server 2003 are not compatible with **Drivespace** file compression available in Windows 9x. For this reason, you should not use Drivespace file compression on partitions that need to be accessed by these operating systems.

Note that although Microsoft does not officially support installing multiple operating systems on the same computer, it is important to understand these concepts.

how to

Change the profile path for a user account.

1. To perform this exercise, first copy the **Administrator** folder structure from the **Documents and Settings** folder to a folder called **Profiles** on your **C:** partition.
2. Log onto the system as a user account that is a member of the Administrators group but is not the default Administrator account.
3. Click **Start**, right-click the **My Computer** icon, and click **Manage** on the shortcut menu to open the **Computer Management** console.
4. In the left pane of the **Computer Management** console, expand the **System Tools** node by clicking the plus sign beside it. Similarly expand the **Local Users and Groups** node and then select the **Users** folder (**Figure 10-20**). The listing of user accounts displays in the right pane of the **Computer Management** console.
5. Double-click on the **Administrator** account to open the **Administrator Properties** dialog box and select the **Profile** tab.
6. In the **Profile Path** text box, type **C:\Profiles\%USERNAME%** (**Figure 10-21**), and click **OK**.
7. Close all open windows and dialog boxes, and log off of the system.

Figure 10-20 Selecting the Users folder

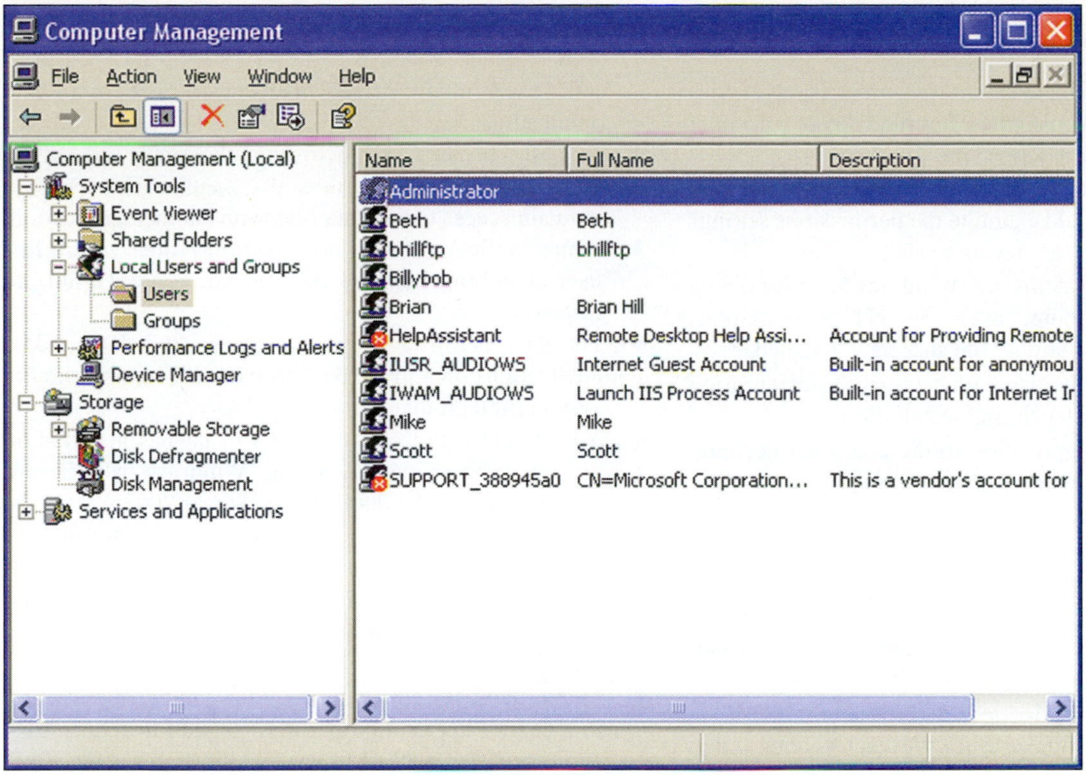

Figure 10-21 Typing the profile path

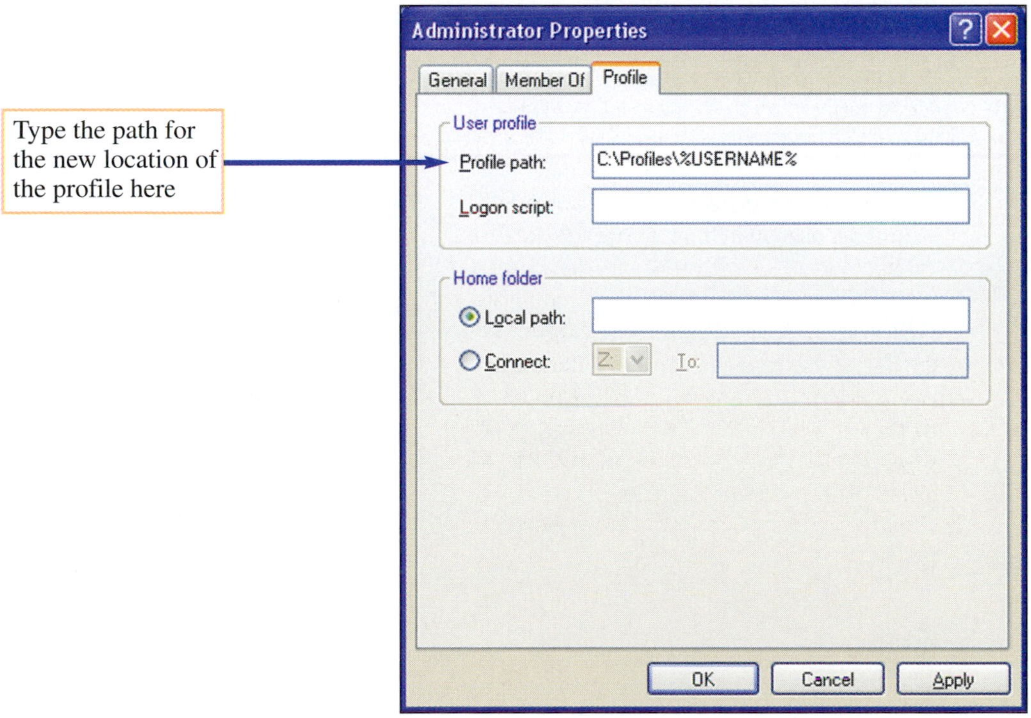

Type the path for
the new location of
the profile here

Summary

- When troubleshooting access to resources (such as files and folders), you should first determine the user account with which the user is logged on.
- Once you have determined which user is logged on to the system, you should examine the permissions settings for the resource they are trying to access.
- On Windows XP systems, the Windows Security dialog box may be missing, even on NTFS resources. This occurs because simple file sharing is enabled.
- Most modern applications place many configuration settings in the Registry during installation.
- By deploying the application to the computer account, you ensure that all users who use the system will have the application available.
- Some applications have vendor-defined flags than can be set, either by running the installation through the command line or by changing a Registry or initialization file setting, which allow the application to only install for a single user.
- By applying an application deployment GPO to a specific OU that contains only the user accounts that require the application, you can ensure that only those users receive the application.
- Generally, denying the Read and Execute permissions for unauthorized users on the application executables will keep unauthorized users from executing the application.
- Denying all permissions for unauthorized users on the application data files ensures that unauthorized users do not gain access to the data files with another application.
- Some applications will not function properly with fast user switching because they do not support multiple instances.
- For the operating system to access the data and/or applications on a given partition, it must support the file system used on that partition.
- You should make sure that SP 4 or later is installed on any multiboot system using Windows NT before installing Windows 2000, XP, or Server 2003.
- Windows 2000 and above will automatically format any FAT partition of 2 GB or greater as FAT32.
- Encrypted files will be inaccessible from Windows NT. Windows 9x/Me cannot access NTFS partitions, so they can also never access encrypted files.
- In multiboot systems, you should install the applications to a central application partition as well to reduce disk space used, as well as to ease application management tasks.
- Windows 2000, NT, XP, and Server 2003 are not compatible with Drivespace file compression available in Windows 9x.

Key Terms

Single-user system
Multiuser system

Multiboot system
Fast user switching

Drivespace

Test Yourself

1. Which of the following is a common cause of application access problems on multiuser systems? (Choose all that apply.)
   a. Registry entries for the application are missing.
   b. User permissions deny access.
   c. A shortcut to the application does not exist in the user's profile.
   d. The application was installed to C:\Program Files.

2. Which of the following file systems does Windows 95 OSR2 support? (Choose all that apply?)
   a. NTFS4
   b. NTFS5
   c. HPFS
   d. FAT16
   e. FAT32

3. A user named Bob is working on a system that dual boots between Windows XP and Windows NT. The application Bob needs to use functions only under Windows NT. Another user, John, has created a Microsoft Word document from within Windows XP that Bob needs to open from within Windows NT. This document is stored on an NTFS 5 disk. Bob cannot open the document. The error message he receives states that access is denied. You verify that Bob can open other Word documents without any problems. You check the permissions on the file and see that Bob's user account has explicit permission to read and write to the file. Which of the following is the most likely cause of Bob's problem?
   a. The file is compressed using Drivespace.
   b. The file is compressed using NTFS compression.
   c. The file is encrypted.
   d. Bob's user account needs to be given ownership of the file.

4. You have recently installed a system for your outside sales people to use when in the office. This system will be shared by three different sales departments. Each department has its own order entry application. The application for the corporate sales department will only function from Windows 98. The other applications only function from Windows XP. For this reason, the system is configured to dual-boot between Windows 98 and Windows XP. You configure the system, and verify that all order entry applications function properly. However, a few days later one of the sales associates from the corporate sales department informs you that he gets the following error whenever he starts Internet Explorer: *Iexplore caused an Invalid Page Fault.*

   You need to resolve this problem in the most efficient manner possible, and Internet Explorer needs to be available from both Windows 98 and Windows XP. What should you do?

   a. Reinstall Internet Explorer.
   b. Reinstall Windows 98, overwriting old files.
   c. Delete all files from the system. Perform a fresh install of Windows 98 to the C:\Windows folder. Perform a fresh install of Windows XP to the C:\WinNT folder. Reinstall all order entry applications.
   d. Delete all files from the system. Perform a fresh install of Windows 98 to the C:\Windows folder. Perform a fresh install of Windows XP to the D:\Windows folder. Reinstall all order entry applications.
   e. Reinstall Windows XP, overwriting old files.

5. You have an application that must be made available to six users of a system. To meet this goal in the most efficient manner possible, you decide to deploy the application with Group Policy. Which of the following must be true in order for this solution to work? (Choose all that apply.)
   a. The system must be using Windows 2000, Windows XP, or Windows Server 2003.
   b. The system must be using Windows NT, Windows 2000, Windows XP, or Windows Server 2003.
   c. The system must be a member of a workgroup.
   d. The system must be a member of an Active Directory domain.

6. You need to make an application available to all users of a Windows XP system. The system is a member of the Corp.com Active Directory domain. The application installs only for the specific user who ran the installation. The application makes many changes to this user's profile. You want to make this application available to all users of the system, and you want it to be immediately available to new users of the system. Which of the following solutions performs these tasks with the least amount of administrative effort?
   a. Install the application to each user individually. Manually install the application for each new user.
   b. Create a shortcut to the application executable and place it in the default user folder.
   c. Create a shortcut to the application executable and place it in the all users folder.
   d. Deploy the application to the computer account using Group Policy.
   e. Deploy the application to the user accounts using Group Policy.

7. A user named Mark calls you to inform you that he cannot access resources in his documents folder. Mark uses two user accounts on this system. You verify that Mark's primary user account has permissions to the files. What is the next question you should ask Mark?
   a. Ask Mark if he has a backup of the files.
   b. Ask Mark which user account he is currently logged in as.

c. Ask Mark when he last modified the files.

d. Ask Mark if he has rebooted recently.

8. You are configuring a new Windows XP system for a new employee. You have just ensured that the drives are all NTFS and are attempting to configure the NTFS permissions. However, when you go into the properties for NTFS folders, you cannot locate the security tab. How could you resolve this problem?

a. Convert the drive to NTFS.

b. Reinstall Windows XP

c. Install the latest service pack

d. Log on as an Administrator

e. Disable simple file sharing

9. A custom application has recently been deployed to systems in your network. This application should only be used by specific users. However, the application automatically installs to all user accounts, and there doesn't appear to be any way to change this functionality. Without reinstalling the application, how can you ensure that only authorized users can use the application?

a. Redeploy the application to the OU that contains the authorized users using Group Policy.

b. Redeploy the application to the OU that contains the computers that the authorized users will use to run the application.

c. Configure NTFS permissions on the application executable to deny the read and execute permissions to unauthorized users. Configure NTFS permissions on the application data files to deny the read and write permissions to unauthorized users.

d. Remove the shortcut to the application and only tell authorized users where the application is located.

10. You create a new FAT partition in Windows XP. The partition is 2,500 MB in size. Which file type will the new partition be?

a. FAT12

b. NTFS4

c. NTFS5

d. FAT32

e. FAT16

Projects: On Your Own

1. Configure NTFS permissions for an application on your local system to prevent Guest access.

a. Log on to the system with an administrative account.

b. Open **Windows Explorer** and navigate to the directory for the application you want to modify.

c. Open the **Properties** dialog box for the application executable and select the **Security** tab. If the **Security** tab is unavailable, ensure that the application resides on an NTFS partition and that simple file sharing is disabled.

d. Add the **Guests** group to the permissions list and deny the Read and Execute permissions.

e. Close all open dialog boxes and log off of the system.

2. Examine effective NTFS permissions on the Windows folder on your system.

a. Log on to the system with an administrative account.

b. Open **Windows Explorer** and navigate to the Windows folder.

c. Open the **Properties** dialog box for the application executable and select the **Security** tab. If the **Security** tab is unavailable, ensure that the application resides on an NTFS partition and that simple file sharing is disabled.

d. Click the Advanced button to open the **Advanced Security Settings** dialog box.

e. Click the **Effective Permissions tab**, and click the **Select User** button to select a user account to examine permissions for.

f. Examine the permissions that are returned.

g. Close all open dialog boxes and log off of the system.

Problem Solving Scenarios

1. You have recently been hired as a senior technician for NegativeKarma Oil, Inc. Your first task is to teach a short course on troubleshooting to the company's junior technicians. Create an outline of the topics and key points to cover.

2. You are working for NosesUp!, a leading high-fashion boutique chain, as a support technician. Each location has a single computer system that is used by all employees of that location for various tasks. All applications must be available to all users of the system. The corporate policy states that all systems should use Windows XP whenever possible. However, there is a single order entry application for a specific vendor that functions only on Windows 98. The vendor has no plans to update the application, and you must determine how to support access from multiple users as well as support this application while maintaining compliance with corporate policy as much as possible. Create a document defining the system configuration you would specify to meet these goals.

Appendix: Windows XP Service Pack 2

In August 2004, in response to a long series of security flaws and exploitable gaps in the operating system that had been surfacing with regularity, Microsoft released Service Pack 2 (SP2) for Windows XP. Industry experts believe that the arrival of the Slammer worm, and the havoc it caused in 2003, convinced Microsoft management to go beyond the simple combination of updates and fixes (including all of those in SP1) that had originally been planned for SP2. Instead, they diverted resources from the development of Longhorn—the planned next major release of Windows—to add those security enhancements in SP2. The new, rethought service pack was delayed nearly a year beyond the pre-Slammer release date to meet this new goal. Although the emphasis of SP2 is clearly on enhancing security, a number of other features such as a pop-up blocker for Internet Explorer, a simpler and better wireless configuration, and general improvements to the operating system and infrastructure, were also developed.

As a desktop support technician, you will be asked to support SP2 as well as applications and programs affected by SP2, and you need to be familiar with the changes that SP2 makes. You will also be asked to assist in deploying SP2 and troubleshooting problems following new deployments. In addition, it can be expected that Microsoft will eventually update the MCDST examinations following the release of SP2; hence, you will need to be able to answer any questions that are based on the changes SP2 brings with it.

This appendix examines key features and changes to Windows XP that SP2 brings to the system when it is installed. It also discusses the steps necessary to prepare for and execute a deployment of SP2. Finally, it reviews problems and issues that may arise when SP2 exists on a system. Although not every detail can be covered in a short appendix such as this, the essentials that are covered here will be important to you in your role as a desktop support technician.

Key features and changes in Windows XP SP2: As with all Windows service packs, Windows XP SP2 includes all of the critical updates released for Windows XP to date. In addition, SP2 includes a large number of new enhancements to Windows XP—enhancements aimed at increasing the default level of security for the operating system.

Security Center: The first difference that you will probably notice is the new Windows **Security Center (Figure A-1)**. An addition to Control Panel and running as a background process, Security Center is designed as a single, centralized point for users to access the security features of Windows XP, such as the firewall. It also provides links to security resources (such as programs, Help files, and documentation) both on the local computer and at the Microsoft Web site. In addition to the Control Panel icon, you can access Security Center through **All Programs**,

Accessories, **System Tools**. You can also double-click the **Security Center** icon that appears in the notification area of the Windows taskbar to open the main Security Center window. When Security Center detects a security condition (such as missing or improperly configured settings), it displays a balloon in the same area (**Figure A-2**). You can turn off reminder balloons by clicking **Change the way Security Center alerts me** under **Resources** to open the **Alert Settings** dialog box and then clearing the **Firewall**, **Automatic Updates**, and/or **Virus Protection** check boxes. As you will read about later in this appendix, in some instances, such as when a third-party firewall or an antivirus program you are using is not detected, you will want to turn off the reminders.

When opened, the Security Center window offers users the following information:

- Links to places where you can find out more about security-related issues.
- The state of Windows Firewall (enabled or disabled). If the firewall is disabled, the user is informed and given options to activate it.
- The state of the Automatic Updates feature. If the user has turned it off or not used the recommended settings,

Figure A-1 The Windows Security Center

Figure A-2 Reminder balloon

he or she is given the recommendations and the opportunity to amend the situation and a link to change the settings.

◆ An assessment of antivirus software: whether it is present, whether it is up to date, and if scanning is turned on. Security Center tells you how to correct the problem and offers a set of options to correct the security flaw.

◆ Additional shortcuts for opening the Internet Options and System dialog boxes.

You should note that if your computer is part of a domain, the security settings are typically managed by a network administrator. In this case, Security Center does not display the security status or send alerts.

Windows Firewall: In both the original release of the operating system and in SP1, Windows XP came with an optional component called Internet Connection Firewall (ICF). In SP2, ICF has been replaced with the renamed and much more powerful, stateful, and host-based Windows Firewall which, unlike ICF, is enabled by default after you install SP2. As you learned earlier in the text, a firewall is a piece of software or hardware designed to protect a system from attack and unwanted penetrations (usually malicious) that originate outside the network or computer, primarily from the Internet. Firewalls work by blocking incoming network traffic except through ports that you specifically configure it to allow. As you should know, some protocols always use the same "friendly ports." For example, HTTP traffic ordinarily uses port 80, FTP uses port 21, SMTP uses port 110, and POP3 uses port 25. These ports are normally allowed. However, there are thousands of ports that, if left open, can become a means for entry into your system. Consequently, security experts and Microsoft currently recommend that any computer connected directly to the Internet either as a stand-alone connection or a system providing Internet Connection Sharing (ICS) services for other computers on a network should have a firewall enabled.

Windows Firewall not only replaces ICF but a number of features have been added. For instance, the interface has been improved to be less confusing and more helpful. Previously, ICF was enabled by selecting a check box on the Advanced tab of the Properties dialog box for a specific connection. To configure services, logging and Internet Control Message Protocol (ICMP) settings required clicking a Settings button to access a different dialog box. SP2 replaces this with a Settings button that launches the new Windows Firewall Control Panel applets, allowing the configuration of all firewall settings, logging, and ICMP settings in a unified interface. The Windows Firewall now applies to all network settings. This includes local area network (LAN) (wired and wireless), dial-up, and virtual private network (VPN) connections that existed when Windows XP SP2 was installed. If you create a new network connection after installing SP2, Windows Firewall is enabled by default. Another valuable feature in Windows

Firewall is the option to configure global options. With ICF, firewall settings had to be configured individually for each connection. Windows Firewall allows you to set global configurations that apply to all of the connections of the computer. What this means is that if you change a global Windows Firewall setting, the change is applied to all of the connections on which Windows Firewall is enabled. Of course, you can still apply configurations to individual connections, as necessary.

Another key point to bear in mind is that because it is stateful, Windows Firewall behaves differently than ICF with regard to when it becomes active. ICF begins to protect a connection when either the ICF or ICS service is successfully started. In other words, there is a potentially exploitable delay between the time a computer becomes active on a network and the time protections inherent in the firewall kick in. SP2 contains a policy that forces stateful packet filtering at startup. Hence the computer is protected from the moment it begins to perform such basic system tasks as contacting a Dynamic Host Configuration Protocol (DHCP) server for an IP address and other settings and/or the Domain Name System (DNS) server to resolve fully qualified domain names and still be protected.

The real power of Windows Firewall comes in the way it manages ports and incoming traffic. All incoming traffic that isn't either solicited or excepted is denied entry through the firewall. Solicited traffic is that which is sent in response to a request by the system, for example, a Web page you have instructed the browser to pass through the HTTP protocol. Excepted traffic is inbound traffic that you have configured the firewall to allow to pass through.

Let's take a quick run through the various setting of Windows Firewall. To open it, click **Start**, click **Control Panel** (in Classic View), and then double-click the **Windows Firewall** applet.

There are three tabs in the **Windows Firewall Properties** dialog box: General, Exceptions, and Advanced. On the **General** tab, you can turn the firewall on (recommended) or off (not recommended). If set to **on**, you have the option to allow exceptions. Windows Firewall settings can only be altered by users with the credentials of the local Administrators group.

To enable or disable Windows Firewall for a specific network connection:

1. Click **Start**, and then click **Control Panel**.
2. In the **Control Panel** window, double-click **Windows Firewall**.
3. On the **General** tab of the **Windows Firewall** dialog box, shown in **Figure A-3**, select the **On (recommended)** option to enable the firewall for all connections. Select **Off (not recommended)** to disable the firewall for all connections.
4. Click **OK**.

Figure A-3 The Windows Firewall dialog box

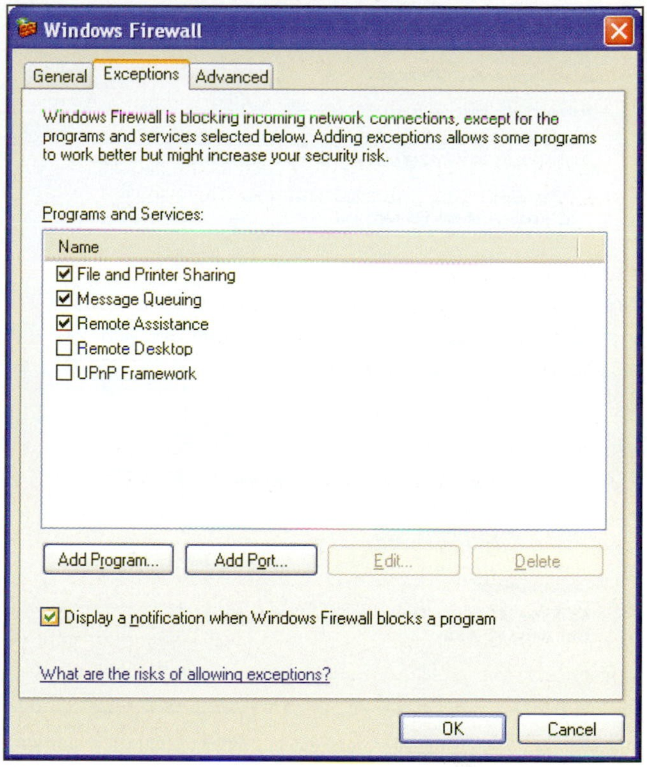

Figure A-4 The Exceptions tab

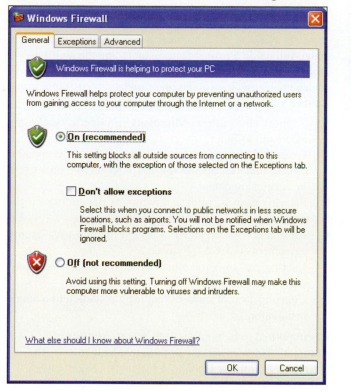

To enable or disable Windows Firewall for a specific connection, follow steps 1 and 2 in the preceding list. Then, after the Windows Firewall dialog box opens:

1. Select the **Advanced** tab.
2. To enable Windows Firewall for a connection, select the check box for that connection. To disable Windows Firewall for a connection, clear the check box for that connection.
3. Click **OK** to close the Windows Firewall dialog box.

The **Exceptions** tab **(Figure A-4)** raises the question of which exceptions, if any, to allow. Each time that you allow an exception for a program to communicate through Windows Firewall, your computer is made more vulnerable. However, typically some exceptions are going to have to be allowed. You may, for example, want to allow Remote Desktop or a custom program on the network that your company needs. Although there are no hard and fast rules to exceptions, you should try to adhere to the following guidelines to reduce any security risk:

◆ Allow an exception only when doing so is essential.
◆ Do not allow an exception for a program that you do not recognize.
◆ Remove an exception once it is not needed.

The Exceptions tab provides a list of programs and services that have existing exceptions as a result of blocking incoming network connections. There are five built-in items: File and Printer Sharing, Message Queuing, Remote Assistance, Remote Desktop, and UPnP Framework. You can create an exception to these by selecting the check box to the left of each item. Buttons near the bottom of the Exceptions tab

allow you to edit or delete existing exceptions. You can also add a program or port to the exceptions list. Typically, for ease of administration, it is better to create an exception using an application file name rather than a specific port. When the application runs, Windows Firewall monitors the ports on which the application listens and automatically adds them to the list of allowed incoming traffic. You can also configure Windows Firewall so that excepted traffic is restricted by IP address (or IP address range), allowing only traffic from computers with pre-approved IP addresses through the firewall. You also have the option to allow Windows Firewall to notify you when it blocks a program.

To create a global exception for an application:

1. Click **Start**, and then click **Control Panel**.
2. In the **Control Panel** window, double-click **Windows Firewall**.
3. Select the **Exceptions** tab.
4. Select the **Remote Desktop** check box. You could also click **Add Program** to specify the executable file for a particular program installed on your computer. Windows Firewall then monitors the program and configures the proper Transmission Control Protocol (TCP) or User Datagram Protocol (UDP) port information for you. Alternatively, you could click **Add Port** to create an exception based on a TCP or UDP port number. To configure this, you must know the proper port number used by an application.
5. Click **OK** to close the Windows Firewall dialog box and activate the exception.

Figure A-5 The Advanced tab

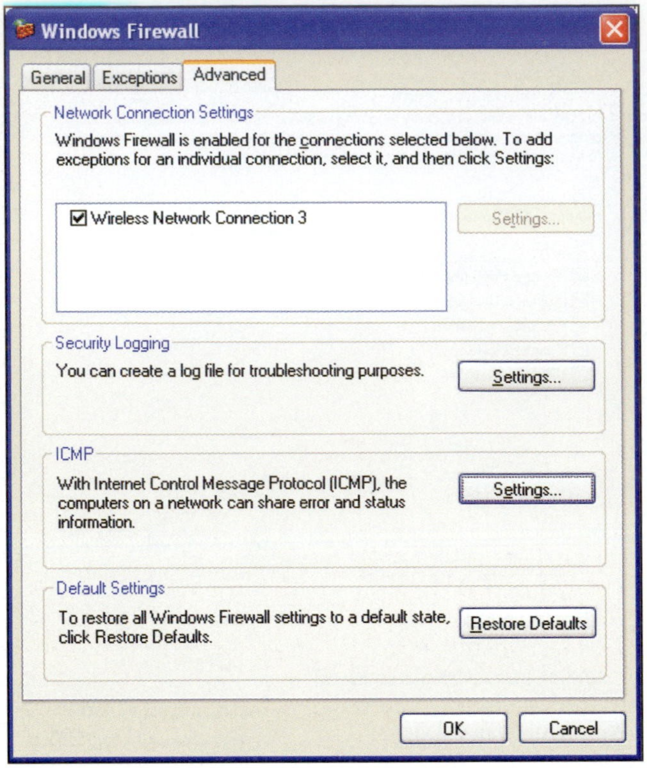

The **Advanced** tab (**Figure A-5**) contains a number of additional options allowing you to configure exceptions for individual connections, set up security logging, activate ICMP, and restore Windows Firewall to its default state. Desktop technicians and network administrators use ICMP requests to troubleshoot network connectivity. Normally, you should only enable ICMP options when you need them, and then disable them as soon as you have finished them. Note that ICMP settings cannot be made globally, but an exception for a particular network connection must be created.

As you can see, the procedure for configuring Windows Firewall is very simple and intuitive. One known problem is that Windows Firewall does not work with third-party firewalls, such as the popular ZoneAlarm. To use a third-party firewall in Windows XP SP2, you must disable Windows Firewall. To do so, open Security Center, and click **Windows Firewall** under the **Manage security settings for** section to open the **Windows Firewall** dialog box. On the **General** tab, select the **Off (not recommended)** check box. This tell the system that the firewall setting will be manually, rather than automatically, controlled. When you return to the Security Center, you will notice that the setting for Windows Firewall now reads **Unknown**.

Automatic Updates: Microsoft introduced **Automatic Updates** to allow users to obtain critical updates and patches directly from the Microsoft Web site as they were released. Automatic Updates connects periodically to Windows Update on the Internet (or to a Windows Update Services server on a corporate network). When Automatic

Updates discovers new updates that apply to the computer, it can be configured to install all updates automatically (the recommended method) or to alert the system's user that an update is available. SP2 provides a number of enhancements to the Automatic Updates feature, including the ability to download more categories of updates, better bandwidth management, and consolidation of updates so that less user input is required. Specifically these changes include:

◆ Support for other Microsoft products, including Microsoft Office
◆ Expanded automatic downloading of security updates, critical updates, update roll-ups, and service packs (not just critical updates)
◆ Prioritization of update downloads depending on the importance and size of the updates
◆ Elimination of the need to accept the end user license agreements (EULAs) by users
◆ User control over the reboot process for updates requiring a system restart
◆ Consolidation of updates requiring restarts into a single installation

It is important to be familiar with how to configure Automatic Updates and the options available to you. To access the Automatic Updates setting, click **Start**, click **Control Panel**, and double-click **Security Center**. Click **Automatic Updates** at the bottom of the window to open the **Automatic Updates** dialog box (**Figure A-6**). (If you are using Category View in Control Panel, click **Start**, click **Control Panel**, click **Performance and Maintenance**, click **System**, and then click the **Automatic Updates** tab.)

Figure A-6 The Automatic Updates dialog box

The Automatic Updates dialog box has four different settings:

◆ **Automatic (recommended)**: Automatically downloads Microsoft-recommended updates for the user's system and installs them. You should make it a practice to recommend that users select this setting unless instructed otherwise by system administrators who may be employing third-party patch management software. When enabled, you can configure Automatic Updates as to the frequency and time of day that updates are downloaded and installed. Ordinarily, users with high-bandwidth, dedicated connections (such as a cable modem) should be configured to check daily at a time the user is not normally using the computer. If users have a low-bandwidth connection, Automatic Updates should be set to check less frequently. If the computer is off during a scheduled update, the updates are installed the next time the computer starts.

◆ **Download updates for me, but let me choose when to install them**: Allows user to have the updates downloaded to the system but no installation takes place until the user chooses to install them.

◆ **Notify me but don't automatically download or install them**: Configures Automatic Updates to simply advise the user that a recommended update is available. The user determines when and if to install the update.

◆ **Turn off Automatic Updates**: Disables the feature. The user will not receive any communications from Automatic Updates unless he or she enables the Automatic Updates feature.

An alternative option for users who do not wish to use Automatic Updates is to download the latest updates from the Windows Update Web site at **http://v5.windowsupdate.microsoft.com/v5consumer/default.aspx?ln=en-us**. Users employing this option should be educated to routinely and frequently visit the Windows Update site. Once there, they should perform an **Express Install** that will scan for, download, and install critical and security updates.

Virus protection: Microsoft doesn't have its own antivirus software, but Security Center includes a virus-protection component that does an adequate job. If it detects a problem, it reports it and makes recommendations that you can review by clicking the **Recommendations** button in the main Security Center window. However, Security Center does not detect all antivirus programs. If your preferred antivirus software is not detected, you have the option to turn off Security Center's monitoring by selecting the check box next to **I have an antivirus program that I'll monitor myself (Figure A-7)**.

Internet Explorer security improvements: With the growth of malware (malicious software), viruses, Trojans, worms, spyware, adware, pop-ups, security risks, and other potential dangers on the Internet, something had to be done to protect computers. At the same time, as Internet Explorer took more of the browser market, it was also targeted by a larger number of hackers seeking and rapidly exploiting its

Figure A-7 Viewing recommendations

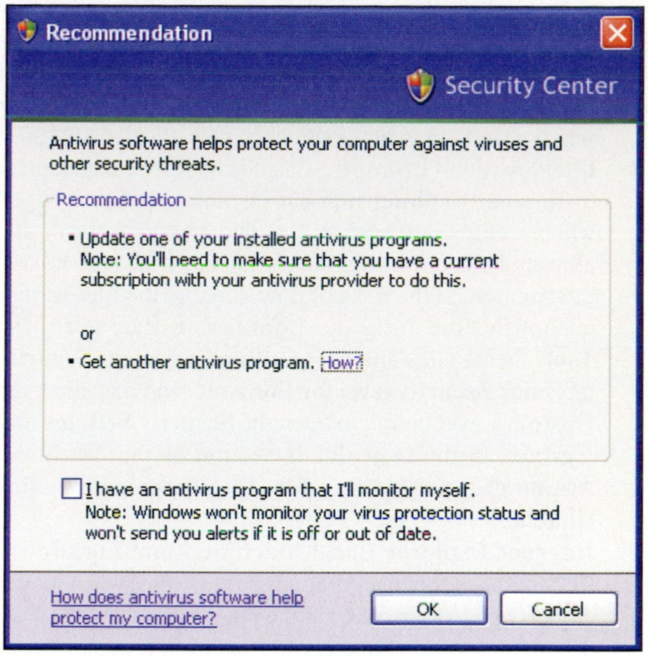

vulnerabilities. SP2 makes three major changes to Internet Explorer with the addition of an information bar, a pop-up blocker, and an add-on manager.

◆ **Information Bar**: SP2 adds the Information Bar to Internet Explorer as a replacement for a large number of the common dialog boxes. The new bar also provides a common area for displaying notifications such as blocked ActiveX installations, blocked pop-up windows, and downloads. The Information Bar appears below the toolbars and above the main browsing window, but only when it has a message to send. When a notification is presented, you can click or right-click the **Information Bar** to open a shortcut menu that relates to the notification. If users prefer not to use the Information Bar or notifications, they can disable it but have to do so for each type of message, thus returning to using separate dialog boxes.

◆ **Pop-up Blocker**: SP2 introduces the first pop-up blocker in Internet Explorer history. The Pop-up Blocker, as the name implies, blocks pop-up windows that show up on some Web sites. Most of these are merely annoying but a growing number can harbor a wide range of security threats and social engineering attacks designed to spoof a user into providing a means of breaching computer or network security. They can also contribute to instability of Internet Explorer. When a pop-up is blocked, the Information Bar displays a notification. Right-clicking the notification bar gives you the option to show the blocked pop-up or allow all pop-ups on the current site, as well as configure other settings. You can configure the Pop-up Blocker in **Internet Explorer** by selecting the **Tools** menu, clicking **Internet Options**, and then selecting the **Privacy** tab. In the **Pop-Up Blocker** section, select the **Block pop-ups** check box. Click **OK** to close the Internet Options dialog box (**Figure A-8**). To turn off Information Bar messages regarding pop-ups, click the **Settings** button in the same section to open the **Pop-up Blocker Settings** dialog box (**Figure A-9**) and clear the **Show Information Bar when a pop-up is blocked** check box.

◆ **File download prompt**: SP2 adds another enhancement to Internet Explorer that causes a dialog box to open when a user downloads a file. The new dialog box displays publisher information for the file (if available) and information on the risks of downloading the file. To turn on notification from the Information Bar, select the **Tools** menu, click **Internet Options**, select the **Security** tab, click **Security level for this zone**, and then click the **Custom Level** button to open the **Security Settings** dialog box. In the **Downloads** section of the list, under **Automatic prompting for file downloads**, click **Enable**.

◆ **Internet Explorer Local Machine Zone Lockdown**: SP2 includes this background process that, when a Web page is opened, limits what the page can do based on the assigned security zone for the page. SP2 adds restrictions to the Local Machine security zone that prevents its exploitation by hackers—who previously took advantage of the fact that this zone had the least restrictions—to breach security. Any time-restricted content attempts to run, a notification appears on the Internet Explorer Information Bar, giving you the option to click and remove the restriction, and allow access to the content.

◆ **Add-on Manager**: The SP2 enhanced Internet Explorer allows you to view and control what add-ons can be loaded, thus improving system security and stability. This is important because an unintentionally installed

Figure A-9 The Pop-up Blocker Settings dialog box

add-on could covertly record your Web usage and report it to a central server. In the past, identifying and removing these add-ons required a high degree of technical skills and specialized software. The Add-on Manager simplifies this task and provides an interface for you to select which add-ons you want turned on or turned off. To access the **Add-on Manager**, open **Internet Explorer** and select the **Tools** menu. Click **Manage Add-ons** to open the **Manage Add-ons** dialog box (**Figure A-10**). In the **Show** drop-down list, you can select one of the following options:

Figure A-8 The Privacy tab

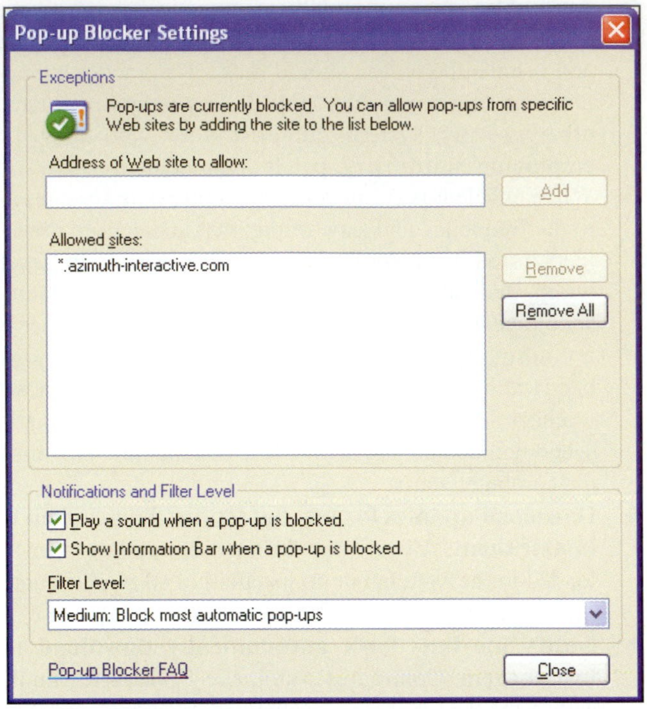

Figure A-10 The Manage Add-ons dialog box

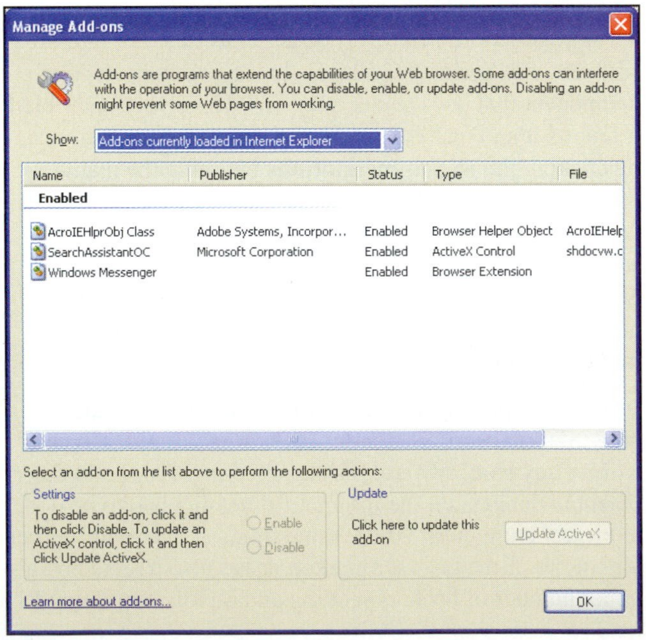

❖ **Add-ons currently loaded in Internet Explorer**: This option lists the add-ons that have been loaded into memory within the current Internet Explorer process and those that have been blocked from loading. This includes ActiveX controls that were used by Web pages that were previously viewed within the current process.

❖ **Add-ons that have been used by Internet Explorer**: This option lists all add-ons that have been referenced by Internet Explorer and are still installed.

In the central window, you can select any add-on from the list by clicking it once. This activates the options in the **Settings** area. Clicking **Enable** re-enables a previously disabled add-on, whereas selecting the **Disable** option disables an add-on.

In the **Update** area, when you click the **Update ActiveX** button, the browser searches for an update at the location where the original control was found. If a newer one is available, Internet Explorer downloads and installs it. Keeping ActiveX controls at the current version can help prevent system and security issues.

Note that the crashes (accidental or intentional) caused by add-ons are identified and recorded, and you are presented with the information. You can then disable the add-on to prevent future problems.

To turn off notification from the Information Bar, select the **Tools** menu, select **Internet Options,** select the **Security** tab, and then click the **Custom Level** button to open the **Security Settings** dialog box. In the **ActiveX controls and plug-ins** section of the **Settings** list, under **Automatic prompting for ActiveX controls**, click **Enable**.

Outlook Express enhancements: The basic e-mail program that comes packaged with Internet Explorer and Windows XP, Outlook Express, is used by a number of home users and small businesses as their primary e-mail program. Outlook Express has been a point of attack by hackers and malware exploitation, and has received a greatly needed security upgrade, including some features that debuted in Outlook 2003.

◆ **E-mail attachment prompt**: When a message with an attachment arrives and you attempt to open or save it, you are now prompted about the dangers. As a further security measure, executable files are checked for a publisher. If the executable file does not include a publisher signature, has an invalid publisher, or has a publisher who has been previously blocked, the file is not allowed to run.

◆ **Plain text mode**: SP2 adds an option to allow users to display all incoming e-mail messages in plain text instead of HTML, avoiding common security problems presented by HTML messages. This is a growing issue as security specialists point to the growth of messages with malware code written in the HTML of an otherwise seemingly innocuous advertisement or message. Users also do not have to endure delays waiting for the content to download. You can enable plain text mode by opening **Outlook Express**, selecting the **Tools** menu, and then selecting **Options** to open the **Options** dialog box. Select the **Read** tab and select the **Read all messages in plain text** check box (**Figure A-11**). Clear the check box to disable plain text mode.

◆ **Block external HTML content**: Many messages arriving in HTML format contain content or graphics that have to be downloaded from an external server. Unfortunately, this kind of content is being used increasingly by senders of spam and malware to include references to images that reside on their Web servers (sometimes messages that are only a single pixel in size). In the past, when a user opened such a message or viewed it in the preview pane, Outlook Express automatically downloaded and displayed the images, verifying to the sender that you have an active e-mail address. SP2 turns off the downloading of external content by default. One advantage of blocking external content includes the need to reconnect to the Internet to view the full message if

Figure A-11 The Read tab

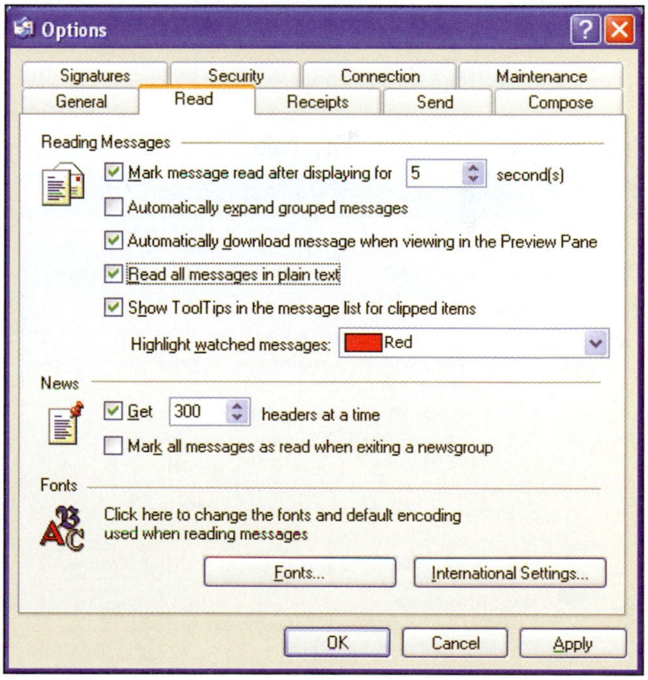

the user uses a dial-up Internet connection. You can confirm or change the setting for this option by opening **Outlook Express**, selecting the **Tools** menu, and then clicking **Options**. In the **Options** dialog box, select the **Security** tab and select the **Block images and other external content in HTML e-mail** check box to turn it on or clear it to disable the function (**Figure A-12**).

Other features: SP2 includes a number of other new features and enhancements to Windows XP. These include, but are not limited to:

◆ Addition of more than 600 new Group Policy object (GPO) settings applicable only to computers running Windows XP SP2. The new GPOs control all of the SP2 features and others as well. For a complete list see: **http://www.microsoft.com/downloads/details.aspx?FamilyID=ef3a35c0-19b9-4acc-b5be-9b7dab13108e&displaylang=en**

◆ Alerter service and Messenger service are turned off by default.

◆ Improved Bluetooth support.

◆ Improved wireless support.

◆ Addition of Data Execution Prevention (DEP) to prevent code from running in memory areas where it shouldn't be present. This requires additional hardware support, but newer computers come equipped with it. You can access these setting by opening **Control Panel**, double-clicking **System** (or clicking **Performance and Maintenance** and then **System** if you are using Category View), and then selecting the **Advanced** tab. In the **Performance** area, click the **Settings** button to open the **Performance Options** dialog box. Select the **Data Execution Prevention** tab to review and change the settings (**Figure A-13**).

Figure A-13 **The Data Execution Prevention tab**

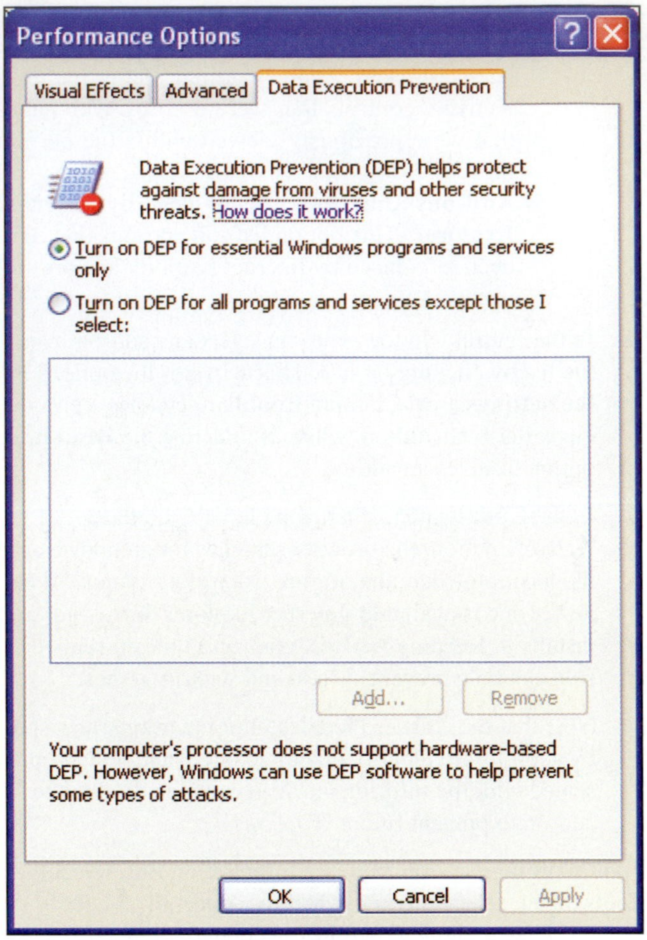

◆ Added support for Internet Protocol version 6 (the current implementation).

◆ Improved Remote Procedure Call (RPC) protection.

◆ In Internet Explorer, prevention of scripts to reposition or resize windows to obscure or hide their true identity or obscure the status bar.

◆ Addition of Windows Media Player 9.0.

◆ Addition of DirectX 9.0b.

Deploying SP2: Before deploying SP2 (or any service pack), you need make sure that the target systems meet the hardware requirements. In addition, given the ramifications of SP2, network administrators should thoroughly test SP2 to assure that it works on their network and that applications are compatible with it. An Application Compatibility Guide is available at: **http://www.microsoft.com/downloads/details.aspx?FamilyID=9300becf-2dee-4772-add9-ad0eaf89c4a7&display-lang=en**

You can use any of the usual Windows XP installation methods to place SP2 on target systems, such as slipstreaming SP2 into a Windows XP installation or from Windows Update as a critical update, to name a few. Also, if Automatic Updates is enabled on a system, it will download

Figure A-12 **The Security tab**

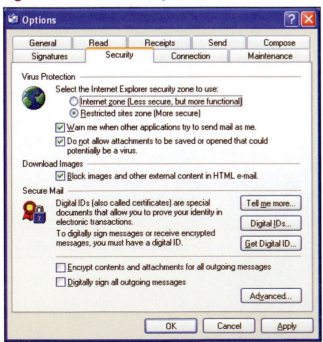

and install SP2 automatically (if the user is logged on as the local Administrator). Note that installation via Automatic Updates requires user interaction.

Troubleshooting SP2: Most user concerns and problems surrounding SP2 come from enabling or disabling features associated with the new enhancements. For example, users may complain about the frequency of notifications in Internet Explorer, reminders and alerts about their security settings from Security Center, or the seeming loss of ability to download external HTML content. As with all troubleshooting, you should assure that you have properly identified the problem before attempting a solution. Given the fairly limited avenues that SP2 problems are likely to follow, you should also thoroughly familiarize yourself with the features discussed previously and how to turn them on and off. You should also be very careful when adjusting security settings.

Some issues and problems you will most likely have to address are:

◆ Client/server communications don't work for some programs. Check the Windows Firewall settings and try adding the application to the excepted list under the **Exceptions** tab. This may also apply to some multimedia streaming programs.

◆ Remote Desktop no longer functions. This is by design. You need to activate it on the **Exceptions** tab of Windows Firewall.

◆ Third-party firewalls don't work with Security Center. This is by design. The only workable solution is to turn off Windows Firewall and set Security Center's **Firewall** setting to **Unknown**.

◆ Can't download an executable file in an attachment via Outlook Express. This is by design, and means that Outlook Express has detected a problem with the file. If necessary, you can disable the security setting.

This is, of course, a short list of the issues and problems you could face with SP2, but with the information you have obtained in this book, and the skills you have developed throughout this course, the problems presented by a SP2 deployment should not present any serious challenges!

Glossary

Address bar A specialized toolbar in Internet Explorer that displays the URL or Web address of the Web page or item being contacted.

Address book In e-mail software, a list of saved e-mail addresses and contact information.

Attachment A file that is not part of the e-mail message but is sent with the e-mail.

AutoArchive The act of automatically creating an archive backup of old items in your personal folders based on date.

AutoComplete A feature that saves the information a user enters in Web-based forms, and uses it to complete information being entered in subsequent forms.

AutoFormat Feature in Office applications that allows you to quickly apply headings, bulleted and numbered lists, borders, numbers, etc.

Automated System Recovery (ASR) A utility that is used to create an Automated System Recovery Backup. The ASR Backup is used to restore the System state and all files stored on the system volume.

Automatic Private IP Addressing (APIPA) addresses Addresses autogenerated by Windows 98 and later systems that allow the system to use a temporary, locally significant address to reach local systems in the event of a DHCP failure.

Automatic Updates A mechanism included with Windows 2000 and Windows XP that allows the operating system to automatically download and install system updates.

AutoRecover Feature in Office applications that automatically saves copies of all open files at a user-definable interval (10 minutes by default).

Backdoor viruses Viruses that provide a secret entry point, or back door, into the operating system, bypassing the system's security measures.

Baseline information System configuration and performance data taken at various times to mark hardware and software changes. You compare current performance parameters to the baseline information to determine the effects of recent changes on system performance.

Basic Input/Output System (BIOS) Built-in computer software that determines what a computer can do without accessing any programs from a disk. The BIOS on a PC contains all of the code required to control the keyboard, display screen, disk drives, serial communications, and other miscellaneous functions.

Boot-sector viruses Viruses that overwrite a hard disk's boot sector, effectively executing each time the system boots.

Business card (vCard) In e-mail, the contact information for a user that is formatted in the vCard standard for exchanging digital contact information with other users.

Cabinet (CAB) files A set of related files that are contained in a folder. They save space and time during the installation of the product.

Certificate A digitally signed document that functions as a component of PKI. Digital certificates verify the identity of a user, computer, service, or the security of a Web site, and are issued by a Certificate Authority

Chkdsk Utility used to check for hard disk errors as well as provide information regarding the file system type that is in use (FAT/NTFS).

Clear text Text that is viewable in its original form without any special processing requirements.

Cluster The smallest unit that a file system is able to recognize. You can only store a single file in a cluster. A file can spread across multiple clusters.

Compact policy A condensed computer-readable privacy statement used in communication between machines to certify that data will not be misused.

Compact To minimize the disk space used by files or folders.

Content Advisor A configurable component of Internet Explorer, that helps you control the types of content that a computer can access on the Internet. It is disabled by default.

Cookies Text files that store information on your computer, such as your preferences when visiting a site. Cookies may also store personally identifiable information, such as your name or e-mail address.

Critical update Critical updates update the operating system with fixes and files critical to maintaining system security.

Custom application An application that is created for a specific industry or organization.

Data execution protection (DEP) A new feature of Windows XP SP2 that allows the OS or system processor to protect segments of memory in order to prevent malicious applications from inserting damaging functions into running code.

Data flows Flows of packets going from one host to another host using specific protocols, port numbers, and packet flags.

DBX file An Outlook Express mail folder; these database files have a .dbx extension.

Denial of Service (DoS) attacks A type of security breach that has no purpose other than to render the system or a service on the system unusable by authorized users.

Desktop support technician A technican whose role is typically to provide the first line of support for clients having problems with operating system and desktop applications.

Detect model A six-step troubleshooting model developed by Microsoft for addressing operating system problems.

Device Manager A utility used to view and change device properties, update device drivers, configure device settings, and uninstall devices.

Dial-up connection A modem-based means of establishing contact with an Internet Service Provider

Disk Cleanup tool (Cleanmgr.exe) A built-in Windows XP utility designed to clear unnecessary files from your computer's hard disk.

Disk Defragmenter A utility that analyzes volumes and locates and consolidates fragmented files and folders.

Document workspaces Windows Sharepoint Services sites. Each is centered around one or more documents that can be worked on by a group of users.

Drivespace A compression technique for FAT partitions that compresses all files on the drive into a single database file. Drivespace is only compatible with Windows 9x.

E-mail Digital mail messages exchanged over the Internet through the use of mail servers.

E-mail filtering The act of removing e-mail based on certain criteria.

Encoding In e-mail, configuring the message text and headers to support a specific language and character set.

Encryption algorithm A mathematical formula used to translate text into a format readable only by others that have the valid encryption key.

Error message A method of reporting system status either directly to the user, or internally to processes within a system.

Event Viewer Console that contains the Application, Security, and System logs. These logs may contain information that can be helpful for determining the cause of a problem.

Expert user A computer user with a great deal of knowledge and/or skills with a specific computer application or operating system. It is worth noting, that this individual may not be highly skilled in other aspects.

Extensible Firmware Interface (EFI) Firmware is known as the Basic Input/Output System (BIOS) on x86-based computers and internal adapters, and as EFI on Itanium-based computers. EFI is an updated BIOS model, developed by Intel for Itanium-based computers. The EFI interface is designed to be independent of any specific operating system platform so that it can concentrate on support for feature functionality rather than operating system compatibility.

Fast user switching Allows a user to switch accounts and reload a new user's settings without logging off. When you switch users using fast user switching, all applications for the previous user are left running.

File association Web service Assists users in locating and/or finding a program that will open a file with a specific extension.

File Signature Verification A utility that is part of the Windows File Protection file-checking process. It can be run to identify and view information about unsigned files on a computer.

Firewalls Software that inspects traffic entering and leaving its network interfaces and selectively allows or denies traffic based on rules.

Firmware Programming instructions, or code, contained in the motherboard. Firmware contains operating system independent code necessary for the operating system to perform low-level functions such as startup self-tests and the initialization of the devices required to start Windows XP. Firmware is also known as the Basic Input/Output System (BIOS) on x86-based computers and internal adapters, and as Extensible Firmware Interface (EFI) on Itanium-based computers.

First-party cookie A cookie sent to your computer from the Web site you are currently viewing. These cookies are commonly used to store information, such as your preferences when visiting that site.

Formula An equation that performs calculations on values in your Excel worksheet.

Fully Qualified Domain Names (FQDNs) Hierarchical namespaces that follow a pattern of increasing specificity from right to left, with the most specific part of the name located on the left.

gpresult.exe A utility available in Windows 2000 and XP that allows you to see which group policies are applying to the system and user, as well as the order in which they are applying.

Group Policies A collection of Registry changes and other settings designed to configure and control the user environment.

Group Policy Provides directory-based configuration of desktop configuration management.

Group Policy Management Console (GPMC) An MMC snap-in that allows you to see which policy settings are configured and the group policies those settings are inherited from. The GPMC snap-in does not come installed by default, and must be downloaded and installed from Microsoft.

Group An object used to apply permissions to many users at once.

Groupware An application that enhances the communication of clients within a network. While many applications fit this general and rather broad description, normally only e-mail and other communication applications are considered groupware.

Help desk A function within an organization dedicated to assisting users with general computer problems.

Heuristics scanning A type of system scanning that uses several techniques, including examination of the application's code structure and activity. Because heuristics scanning is such a complicated and relatively new process, it is not as accurate as signature scanning (accuracy is claimed to be as high as 80%, however). Because of the reduced accuracy, heuristics scanning is known to generate far more false positives than signature scanning. Additionally, due to the increased complexity of heuristics scanning, the scanning process is slower and more involved than signature scanning.

History A browser's list of links to all the Web sites and pages visited in previous days and weeks.

Home page The Web page configured to be the default Web page opened by a Web browser upon start up.

Hot fixes These types of security updates consist of a package of one or more files (packaged in an executable/self installing format) that are designed to fix specific software problems.

Hypertext Markup Language (HTML) A method of formatting text so that it is readable by Web browsers.

InfoPath 2003 Available with the Professional Enterprise Edition only, can be used to help teams gather information by creating dynamic forms. These forms can then provide a mechanism to input status reports, expense reports, or even loan information that connects directly to the company's databases and servers. This information can then be reused by others in the company.

Intermediate user A computer user with some knowledge and/or skills with a specific computer application or operating system.

Internet Connection Firewall (ICF) A software security configuration that prevents computers outside your network from having access to resources on your home or small office network.

Internet Connection Sharing (ICS) A software configuration that allows you to share a single Internet connection among multiple computers. This method is typically used in homes and small businesses.

Internet Mail Application Protocol (IMAP) An Internet protocol for receiving e-mail.

Java applet A small Internet-based program written in Java. Usually applets can also run in HTML.

Junk e-mail E-mail that is sent to your e-mail account but that you do not wish to read. Most junk e-mail is termed as "spam" or Unsolicited Commercial E-mail (UCE) and may include links to remote systems, images, pop-up ads, or other techniques in an attempt to advertise or sell a product or service.

Last Known Good Configuration A startup option that is used to start a computer using the information that was saved in the Registry after the last successful log on.

Log files Files saved by the operating system or an application typically in a text format. You can use Notepad or an equivalent text editor to view the contents of a text log file to determine whether it contains information useful for troubleshooting a problem.

Macro viruses Viruses written using an application's built-in macro language.

Macros A set of keystrokes and mouse movements that are recorded, saved, and assigned a shortcut key or button. When the shortcut key or button is clicked, the instructions recorded are executed.

Mail Application Program Interface (MAPI) The Microsoft standard for e-mail transmission and reception.

Mail-user agent (MUA) User software, such as the e-mail application Outlook Express, used to send and retrieve e-mail to or from a Message Transfer Agent, also referred to as mail client.

Master File Table (MFT) Identifies the cluster or clusters in which a file is stored.

Message transfer agent (MTA) Software that is used to deliver and receive e-mail messages, also referred to as a mail server.

Microsoft Exchange The Microsoft server platform for e-mail, contacts, calendar, and other groupware-related services. Exchange provides a highly scalable, extensible, configurable, and reliable platform for business communications.

Microsoft Office Application Recovery Used to exit an application that has stopped responding and report the error to Microsoft.

Microsoft Office System A family of integrated applications, servers, and services that allows users to connect people and organizations to information, business processes, and each other.

Msinfo32 Provides information regarding a system's hardware resources, components, software environment, and Internet settings.

Multi-boot system A system with more than one operating system installed. The user will choose which operating system to load through a boot loader, such as the one provided by Windows XP, at startup. To switch operating systems, the user must restart the system and choose the appropriate OS from the boot loader menu.

Multilingual User Interface Pack A set of language-specific resource files that can be added to the English version of Windows that allows you to change the user interface language to one of 33 supported languages.

Multi-user system A system where multiple users regularly log in for extended periods. This essentially results in a system that is shared by several users, all of whom need access to specific applications and data.

Name resolution The process of resolving a friendly name into a protocol address.

NetBIOS names Single word, 15-character names.

Network News Transfer Protocol (NNTP) Internet protocol used for exchanging messages in the newsgroup format.

Newsgroup A message center for Internet messages, typically focusing on a specific topic of common interest, that are addressed to the group as a whole.

Notification area Provides information on programs that are running in the background.

Novice user A computer user that may not have a great deal of knowledge and/or skills with a specific computer application or operating system. It is worth noting, that this individual may be highly skilled in other aspects.

NTFS Permissions Permissions applied to files and folders stored on NTFS partitions that apply to both local and remote users.

Offline storage file (ost) A file, similar to a personal storage file, used to hold cached copies of Exchange mailboxes for use when the system is offline.

On-access scanning A type of scanning that enables the antivirus application to automatically scan files before they are executed or opened in order to catch virus attacks before the offending files are executed. Also known as real-time protection.

On-demand scanning A type of scanning that involves either manually initiating a virus scan or scheduling a system scan during off-peak hours.

Open and Repair Feature used to recover text from a damaged document.

Operating system A specialized piece of software designed to allow the user to interface with a computer's hardware.

Original Equipment Manufacturer (OEM) A company that acquires a product and incorporates it into another product that is sold under its brand name.

Outlook rule A custom set of rules and criteria used to perform specialized actions on e-mail or other items.

Performance console A Microsoft Management Console (MMC) snap-in that includes the System Monitor and the Performance Logs and Alerts tool. The System Monitor is used to view a graphical presentation of the performance of the resources on a computer system and the Performance Logs and Alerts toll is used to record the performance of resources in logs and to configure alerts to tell you when certain thresholds have been passed.

Peripheral firmware Peripheral firmware includes small computer system interface (SCSI) adapters, CD and DVD-ROM drives, hard disks, video cards, and audio devices, which contain device-specific instructions that enable a device to perform specific functions, but are independent of the operating system.

Persistent cookie A cookie stored as a file on your computer that remains after you close Internet Explorer. This type of cookie can be read by the Web site that created it when you visit that site again.

Personal storage file (.pst) A file used to store information associated with non-exchange accounts. All items in your personal folders are stored in your .pst file.

Personalized menus Used to simplify the user interface by hiding items the user has not recently used, while keeping those they do visible.

PHO (physical, hardware, operating system) The initial troubleshooting hierarchy: physical, hardware, operating system. Check all the physical issues first, the hardware issues second, and the operating system issues last. This strategy follows the most generic to the most complex troubleshooting strategy recommended by most professionals in the information technology field.

Plain text Unformatted ASCII text.

Plug and Play A standard, developed by Microsoft, which enables the operating system to automatically recognize a device when it is attached to a computer.

Polymorphic viruses Viruses that can mutate or change their code to avoid virus detection algorithms.

Port A logical (as opposed to physical) communications channel, typically allocated to specific types of communication protocols, such as HTTP.

Post Office Protocol (POP) A protocol for receiving e-mail.

PowerPoint viewer A program, available from Microsoft, which allows users who are not running the PowerPoint application on their computers to view PowerPoint presentations.

Product activation A protection measure against casual copying, a form of software piracy.

Product key An alphanumeric string unique to an individual software product that is entered by the user during installation of some programs.

Program Compatibility Wizard Windows XP Wizard that helps you test compatibility settings for older programs that experience problems running in Windows XP.

Proxy server A server in place between the Web browser, and an external Web server. The proxy server intercepts all requests to the Web server. If it can fulfill the requests itself it does so, if not it forwards the request. Proxy servers are usually used to filter traffic going to and from the Internet.

Public Key Infrastructure (PKI) A public key infrastructure is a framework for issuing, validating, and revoking certificates. It will include one or more certificate authorities (CAs), servers which are responsible for issuing and revoking certificates.

Quick Launch Allows you to bypass the Start menu to find and launch your most frequently used programs.

Read receipt A message you receive back when the remote party opens and reads your e-mail.

Receipts A message sent back to the sender by the recipient of an e-mail message to signify that the message has been received.

Reduced Functionality Mode A mode that is reached for Microsoft Office 2003 if you do not activate the software after 50 times. The user will be able to read his or her documents and print them but not be able to create a new document or modify existing ones.

Regional Options Options that allow you to change the format Windows uses to display times, currency, dates, numbers, etc.

Remote-control software Software that allows a designated remote user to access a system over a network or the Internet, and take control of the system as if they were sitting in front of it.

Restore points A representation of a stored state on your computer that is created by System Restore at specific intervals.

Resultant Set of Policy (RSoP) An MMC snap-in that allows you to see which policy settings are configured and the group policies from which those settings are inherited.

Rights Management Services (RMS) A service that runs on Windows Server 2003 that is based on public key cryptography. It uses digital certificates to identify users and computers and determine their rights. When used in combination with the Office 2003 Information Rights Management component, user can control who can view their documents, what they can do with them, and how long they are available for viewing.

Root domain A section of an e-mail or Web address that signifies the type of institution owning the address, such as COM for commercial institutions.

Root-cause analysis The practice of searching for the source of problems to prevent them from recurring.

Scripts Text files used to execute commands or functions in a specific order. Typically used to map drives, copy files, or otherwise configure a system at log on. Viruses can also be scripts.

Sectors Physical units of storage on a hard drive. During the logical formatting process, sectors are grouped together into clusters.

Secure password authentication (SPA) An authentication mechanism that utilizes encryption to secure password transmission to e-mail servers.

Security settings A section of group policy containing settings controlling account lockout policy, password policy, user rights, audit policy, public key access, Registry and Event Log access, and system service operation.

Security updates These types of updates are designed to fix security-related vulnerabilities and are rated (Critical, Important, Moderate, or Low).

Security Zone A group of four security areas used and configured within Internet Explorer that supports different security settings. These zones are Internet, Local Intranet, Trusted Sites, and Restricted Sites.

Service pack A tested, cumulative set of all hot fixes, security updates, critical updates, and updates that have been issued over a period of time for an operating system. Service packs can also contain additional fixes for problems discovered by the manufacturer since the product release and design changes requested by customer.

SFC /scannow This command initiates the Windows File Protection service to scan protected files and verify integrity.

Signature scanning A type of system scanning that relies on an up-to-date database of virus definitions, or signatures, that are used to identify, or fingerprint, a virus. Because signature scanning relies on a fingerprint match of the virus, it is very accurate, relatively quick, and generates few false positives.

Signature Standard closing lines or graphics that a user can define and choose to insert at the end of his or her e-mail messages.

Simple Mail Transfer Protocol (SMTP) The Internet protocol by which e-mails are sent.

Single-user system A system that is primarily used by one user. Although other users may log in to the system occasionally, they do so only for short periods and do not require significant access to local applications.

Software suite A set of applications that are bundled together and sold as a group.

Spyware A type of software that tracks your activity and sends this information to advertising and marketing companies at various intervals.

Start menu Provides access to other programs on the computer, documents that have been recently opened, support tools, as well as many other items.

Stateful firewalls Firewalls that keep track of data flows, creating a specific filter entry for each flow to allow return traffic to reach the originator.

Stateless firewalls Firewalls that do not monitor traffic flows. While most have the ability to dynamically create rules, these rules are simply controlled by a time limit.

Stationery Files that contain predetermined formatting and style that can be used to give e-mail messages a standard look and feel.

Style sheet A type of template for specifying how different styles should appear throughout a Web page or site.

System Configuration Utility Utility that can be used for a number of tasks, including stopping services. It is used to temporarily disable startup programs to alter how Windows XP Professional starts up. In order to use the System Configuration utility, you must be logged on as an Administrator or a member of the Administrators group.

System File Checker (SFC) Utility introduced back in the days of Windows 98. It allows you to restore missing, modified, or corrupt operating system files.

System Information (msinfo32.exe) Console that stores information about a computer, such as what devices are installed and loaded and the history of the drivers that have been installed on the machine. You can look here to find out whether a new driver has recently been installed. You can also access other troubleshooting tools in the System Information console.

System Restore A tool used to save or restore system states. The System Restore tool can be used to roll back operating system changes that may have made a system unstable, including Registry changes. It works by creating backup copies of configuration information before the change has occurred. These backup copies are made based on predefined trigger events (system restore points), which include activities such as installing an unsigned driver, installing applications, and auto-update installations.

System restore point A saved snapshot of the data on a computer and the system state at a particular point in time. System restore points are created by default every 24 hours if the computer is left on, and if it is shut down, a new restore point is created if the previous restore point is more than 24 hours old. If an unsigned driver is installed, a restore point will also be created.

System State data A collection of system-specific data maintained by the operating system that must be backed up as a unit. The System State data includes the Registry, COM+ Class Registration database, system files, boot files, and files under Windows File Protection.

Taskbar Provides information regarding the programs and files that are currently running on the computer and provides a method to quickly move between them.

Temporary (or session) cookie A cookie that is stored only for the current browsing session and is deleted when you close Internet Explorer. Temporary cookies typically enable a site to determine the client browser, language, and screen resolution that the user is using.

Temporary Internet Files Web pages and files (such as graphics) that are stored on your computer as you view them over the Internet. This speeds up the display of pages you frequently visit or have already seen, because Internet Explorer can open them from your hard disk instead of from the Web.

Third-party cookie A cookie that is sent to your computer from a Web site different from the one you are currently viewing. Normally these come from advertisers on the site being visited and track Web-page use for advertising or other marketing purposes. Third-party cookies can either be persistent or temporary.

Tier 1 Provides front-line support for client operating systems, applications, and hardware by using a predesigned script. Tier 1 support technicians typically have less than six months' experience.

Tiered support A support framework in which calls are initially answered by a help desk support technician with more general troubleshooting skills and expertise, and more complex problems are escalated to more specialized individuals.

Timeout An interval of time between a request for a response and the actual response.

Toolbars Collections of commands displayed graphically or as text on a vertical or horizontal bar in an application's interface.

Trojan Horses Viruses that appear to perform a benign function while actually performing a hidden, malignant function in the background.

Troubleshooting The process of isolating the source of a problem and fixing it.

Troubleshooting wizards Designed to help you diagnose and resolve problems that are occurring on your computer. When a wizard is started, you are asked to answer a series of questions that deal with the problem you are currently experiencing.

Unsatisfactory cookie A cookie that might allow access to personally identifiable information that could be used for a secondary purpose without your consent.

Virtual Private Networks (VPNs) Remote access connections that utilize a tunneled connection to create a private connection across a public network.

Virus A small program written to alter the way a computer operates, without the permission or knowledge of the user. It executes and replicates itself by copying itself to an executable file.

Volume licensing A licensing option used when multiple copies of a program are needed. It can provide substantial savings over other licensing models.

WAB file An Outlook Express Address Book file.

Windows Backup A utility that is used to prevent the accidental loss of data to hardware or software failure or user error. It is used to backup system and data files for disaster recovery purposes. It can also be used to schedule system and data backups at regular intervals

Windows File Association Web page Web page provide by Microsoft to identify programs that can open specific file extensions.

Windows Update An operating system feature that works in conjunction with Microsoft's Web site (http://windowsupdate.microsoft.com) and is used to scan, recommend, and install operating system updates.

Worms Viruses that perform no malicious functions other than replicating themselves infinitely in order to completely saturate the resources of their host system or network.

Index

The Prentice Hall Certification Series features a building-block approach that organizes the material into a series of skills that students master one at a time. We adopted a two-page spread featuring a highly graphical approach with hundreds of screenshots that shows students how and why Windows Server 2003/Windows 2000/Windows XP works, rather than forcing them to memorize rote software procedures.

Windows Server 2003 Core Exam Texts

Exam 70-290: Microsoft Windows Server 2003: Managing and Maintaining

Text: 0-13-144743-2
Project Lab Manual: 0-13-144974-5
Interactive Solution CD-ROM: 0-13-144974-5

Exam 70-291: Microsoft Windows Server 2003: Network Infrastructure: Implementing, Managing and Maintaining

Text: 0-13-145600-8
Project Lab Manual: 0-13-145603-2
Interactive Solution CD-ROM: 0-13-145604-0

Exam 70-293: Microsoft Windows Server 2003: Network Infrastructure: Planning and Maintaining

Text: 0-13-189306-8
Project Lab Manual: 0-13-189307-6
Interactive Solution CD-ROM: 0-13-189308-4

Exam 70-294: Microsoft Windows Server 2003: Active Directory Infrastructure: Planning, Implementing, and Maintaining

Text: 0-13-189312-2
Project Lab Manual: 0-13-189314-9
Interactive Solution CD-ROM: ISBN TBD

Value Pack Options Available

Exam 70-297: Designing a Microsoft Windows Server 2003 Active Directory and Network Infrastructure

Text: 0-13-189316-5
Project Lab Manual: 0-13-189320-3
Interactive Solution CD-ROM: ISBN TBD

Exam 70-298: Designing Security for a Microsoft Windows Server 2003 Network

Text: 0-13-117670-6
Project Lab Manual: 0-13-146684-4
Interactive Solution CD-ROM: ISBN TBD

Series Features

The ONLY academic series developed by instructors for instructors that correlates to the MCSE and MCSA exam objectives.

4-color, 2-page layout
- Improves student retention through clear, easy-to-follow, step-by-step instructions.

Skills-Based Systematic Approach
- Uses integrated components: Main text, Project Lab Manual, Interactive Solution CD-ROM, and Web site with online quizzes.

Hands-on projects and problem-solving projects at the end of each lesson
- Help students better understand the material being taught.

Learning Aids
- Include Test Your Skills, On Your Own Projects, and Problem-Solving Cases at the end of each lesson.

Instructor's Resource CD
- PowerPoint slides containing all text graphics and lecture bullet points.
- Instructor's Manual that includes sample syllabus, teaching objectives, answers to exercises, and review questions.
- Test Bank with 40+ questions per lesson based on the text. Not generic MCSE questions.

Windows Server 2003 Enterprise 180 day evaluation software included in every text.

Project Lab Manuals

The Project Lab Manuals are designed as an additional tool that allow students to implement the concepts and practice the skills they have read about in the textbooks and CD-ROMs. With more hands-on projects and concept review, the Project Lab Manuals enable students to learn more about Windows 2003/2000/XP in real-world settings, practice the skills needed to prepare for the MCSE/MCSA exams, and prepare for a career as a network administrator.

The Project Lab Manual features:
- An overview of the task to be completed tied directly to the MCSA/MCSE Exam Objectives.
- 4-6 projects per lesson directly associated with the MCSA/MCSA Exam Objectives.
- Specific hardware requirements necessary to complete each lab.
- Step-by-step, hands-on instruction—it's like having an MCSE right by your side.
- Tips and Cautions elements designed to ease the learning process.
- Suggested completion times for each lab.

Interactive Solutions CD-ROMs

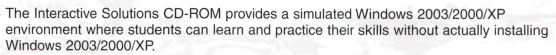

The Interactive Solutions CD-ROM was designed to directly support the Prentice Hall Certification Series texts by giving students a number of ways to enhance their studies.

The Interactive Solutions CD-ROM provides a simulated Windows 2003/2000/XP environment where students can learn and practice their skills without actually installing Windows 2003/2000/XP.

The learning modules are organized according to Microsoft knowledge domains and objectives. Conceptual overview sessions provide concise, animated descriptions of key networking concepts. Three types of interactive sessions (Play, Practice, and Assessment) provide students with hands-on experience with Windows Server 2003 and a realistic, challenging assessment environment.

Prentice Hall Certification Series for Windows 2000/Windows XP

Exam 70-210: Microsoft Windows 2000 Professional: Installing, Configuring, and Administering; Text: 0-13-142209-X; Lab Manual: 0-13-142257-X; Interactive Solutions CD-ROM: 0-13-142260-X

Exam 70-215: Microsoft Windows 2000 Server: Installing, Configuring, and Administering; Text: 0-13-142211-1; Lab Manual: 0-13-142281-2; Interactive Solutions CD-ROM: 0-13-142284-7

Exam 70-216: Microsoft Windows 2000 Network Infrastructure: Implementing and Administering; Text: 0-13-142210-3; Lab Manual: 0-13-142278-2; Interactive Solutions CD-ROM: 0-13-142277-4

Exam 70-217: Microsoft Windows 2000 Active Directory: Implementing and Administering; Text: 0-13-142208-1; Lab Manual: 0-13-142252-9; Interactive Solutions CD-ROM: 0-13-142254-5

Exam 70-218: Managing Microsoft Windows 2000 Network Environment; Text: 0-13-144744-0; Lab Manual: 0-13-144813-7; Interactive Solutions CD-ROM: 0-13-144812-9

Exam 70-270: Microsoft Windows XP Professional; Text: 0-13-144132-9; Lab Manual: 0-13-144450-6; Interactive Solutions CD-ROM: 0-13-144449-2

Test with Pearson VUE and Save 50%!

Get Certified Through the Microsoft Authorized Academic Testing Center (AATC) Program:

You invested in your future with the purchase of this textbook from Prentice Hall. Now, take the opportunity to get the recognition your skills deserve. Certification increases your credibility in the marketplace and is tangible evidence that you have what it takes to provide top-notch support to your employer.

Save 50% On Microsoft Exams!

Take advantage of this money-saving offer now. The cost of taking the exam is $60.00 with this offer.

COUPON

Offer Good for 50% Off Select MCP Exams

To register for this discount, visit
http://www.pearsonvue.com/aatc/ph

PEARSON VUE

Microsoft CERTIFIED
Exam Provider

Select Microsoft® exams, including the full suite of MCDST and MCSA exams, are available at the discounted price to students and instructors who attend, or are employed by, academic institutions. Students and instructors can take advantage of this offer via the URL below.

MCDST on Microsoft® Windows® XP Operating System Requirements for Students

Core Exams: Windows XP

70-271   Supporting Users and Troubleshooting a Microsoft Windows XP Operating System

70-272   Supporting Users and Troubleshooting Desktop Applications on a Microsoft Windows XP Operating System

MCSA on Microsoft Windows Server 2003 Certification Requirements for Students

Core Exams: Networking System (2 Exams Required)

70-290   Managing and Maintaining a Microsoft Windows Server 2003 Environment

70-291   Implementing, Managing, and Maintaining a Microsoft Windows Server 2003 Network Infrastructure

Core Exams: Client Operating System (1 Exam Required)

70-270   Installing, Configuring, and Administering Microsoft Windows XP Professional

70-210   Installing, Configuring, and Administering Microsoft Windows 2000 Professional

Elective Exams (1 Exam Required)

70-086   Implementing and Supporting Microsoft Systems Management Server 2.0

70-227   Installing, Configuring, and Administering Microsoft Internet Security and Acceleration (ISA) Server 2000, Enterprise Edition

70-228   Installing, Configuring, and Administering Microsoft SQL Server™ 2000 Enterprise Edition

70-284   Implementing and Managing Microsoft Exchange Server 2003

70-299   Implementing and Administering Security in a Microsoft Windows Server 2003 Network

Upgrade Exam for an MCSA on Windows 2000

An MCSA on Windows 2000 has the option to take Exam 70-292 instead of the two core network exams. No additional core or elective exams are required for an MCSA on Windows 2000 who passes Exam 70-292.

Upgrade Exam for an MCSA on Windows 2000 (1 Exam Required)

70-292   Managing and Maintaining a Microsoft Windows Server 2003 Environment for an MCSA Certified on Windows 2000

Offer also good on selected Windows 2000 exams.

For more information on Prentice Hall textbooks for MCSA and MCAD,
visit www.prenhall.com/certification

Take advantage of this great offer!
Go to www.pearsonvue.com/aatc/ph
for complete details and to schedule a
discounted exam at an AATC near you!

ESM   Spring 2005   All trademarks and registered trademarks are copyrighted and protected by their respective manufacturers.